PHILIP'S

C000230378

STREET ATLAS
Cambridgeshire

First published in 2001 by

Philip's, a division of
Octopus Publishing Group Ltd
2–4 Heron Quays, London E14 4JP

First edition 2001
Fourth impression with revisions 2004

ISBN 0-540-08096-9 (hardback)
ISBN 0-540-08097-7 (spiral)

© Philip's 2004

Ordnance Survey®

This product includes mapping data licensed
from Ordnance Survey® with the permission of
the Controller of Her Majesty's Stationery Office.
© Crown copyright 2004. All rights reserved.
Licence number 100011710.

Printed and bound in Spain
by Cayfosa-Quebecor

Contents

III	**Key to map symbols**
IV	**Key to map pages**
VI	**Route planning**
VIII	**Administrative and Postcode boundaries**
1	**Street maps** at 3½ inches to 1 mile
208	**Street maps** at 1¾ inches to 1 mile
239	**Street maps** at 3½ inches to 1 mile
246	**Street map of Cambridge city centre** at 7 inches to 1 mile
247	**Town maps** of King's Lynn and Saffron Walden
248	**Index** of towns and villages
250	**Index** of streets, hospitals, industrial estates, railway stations, schools, shopping centres, universities and places of interest

Digital Data

The exceptionally high-quality mapping found in this atlas is available as digital data in TIFF format, which is easily convertible to other bitmapped (raster) image formats.

The index is also available in digital form as a standard database table. It contains all the details found in the printed index together with the National Grid reference for the map square in which each entry is named.

For further information and to discuss your requirements, please contact Philip's on 020 7644 6932 or james.mann@philips-maps.co.uk

22a	**Motorway** with junction number
	Primary route – dual/single carriageway
	A road – dual/single carriageway
	B road – dual/single carriageway
	Minor road – dual/single carriageway
	Other minor road – dual/single carriageway
	Road under construction
	Pedestrianised area
DY7	Postcode boundaries
	County and unitary authority boundaries
	Railway
	Railway under construction
	Tramway, miniature railway
	Rural track, private road or narrow road in urban area
	Gate or obstruction to traffic (restrictions may not apply at all times or to all vehicles)
	Path, bridleway, byway open to all traffic, road used as a public path

The representation in this atlas of a road, track or is no evidence of the existence of a of a right of way

231	**Adjoining page indicators** (The colour of the arrow indicates the scale of the adjoining page - see scales below)
84	
173 / 165	**Adjoining page indicator** showing the pages adjoining the top and bottom halves of the current page
246	
203	**The map areas within the pink/blue bands are shown at a larger scale on the page, indicated by the red/blue blocks and arrows**

Abbr	Full	Abbr	Full
Allot Gdns	**Allotments**	Meml	**Memorial**
Acad	**Academy**	Mon	**Monument**
Cemy	**Cemetery**	Mus	**Museum**
C Ctr	**Civic Centre**	Obsy	**Observatory**
CH	**Club House**	Pal	**Royal Palace**
Coll	**College**	PH	**Public House**
Crem	**Crematorium**	Recn Gd	**Recreation Ground**
Ent	**Enterprise**	Resr	**Reservoir**
Ex H	**Exhibition Hall**	Ret Pk	**Retail Park**
Ind Est	**Industrial Estate**	Sch	**School**
Inst	**Institute**	Sh Ctr	**Shopping Centre**
Ct	**Law Court**	TH	**Town Hall/House**
L Ctr	**Leisure Centre**	Trad Est	**Trading Estate**
LC	**Level Crossing**	Univ	**University**
Liby	**Library**	Wks	**Works**
Mkt	**Market**	YH	**Youth Hostel**

Walsall	**Railway station**
	Private railway station
	Bus, coach station
	Ambulance station
	Coastguard station
	Fire station
	Police station
+	**Accident and Emergency entrance to hospital**
H	**Hospital**
+	**Place of worship**
i	**Information Centre** (open all year)
P	**Parking**
P&R	**Park and Ride**
PO	**Post Office**
X	**Camping site**
	Caravan site
	Golf course
X	**Picnic site**
Prim Sch	**Important buildings, schools, colleges, universities and hospitals**
River Medway	**Water name**
	River, stream
	Lock, weir
	Water
	Tidal water
	Woods
	Houses
Church	**Non-Roman antiquity**
ROMAN FORT	**Roman antiquity**

■ The small numbers around the edges of the maps identify the 1 kilometre National Grid lines ■ The dark grey border on the inside edge of some pages indicates that the mapping does not continue onto the adjacent page

The scale of the maps is 5.52 cm to 1 km 3¹/₂ inches to 1 mile 1: 18103	0 ¹/₄ ¹/₂ ³/₄ 1 mile 0 250m 500m 750m 1 kilometre
The scale of the maps on pages numbered in green is 2.76 cm to 1 km 1³/₄ inches to 1 mile 1: 36206	0 ¹/₄ ¹/₂ ³/₄ 1 mile 0 250m 500m 750m 1 kilometre
The scale of the maps on pages numbered in red is 11.04 cm to 1 km 7 inches to 1 mile 1: 9051.4	0 220 yards 440 yards 660 yards ¹/₂ mile 0 125m 250m 375m ¹/₂ kilometre

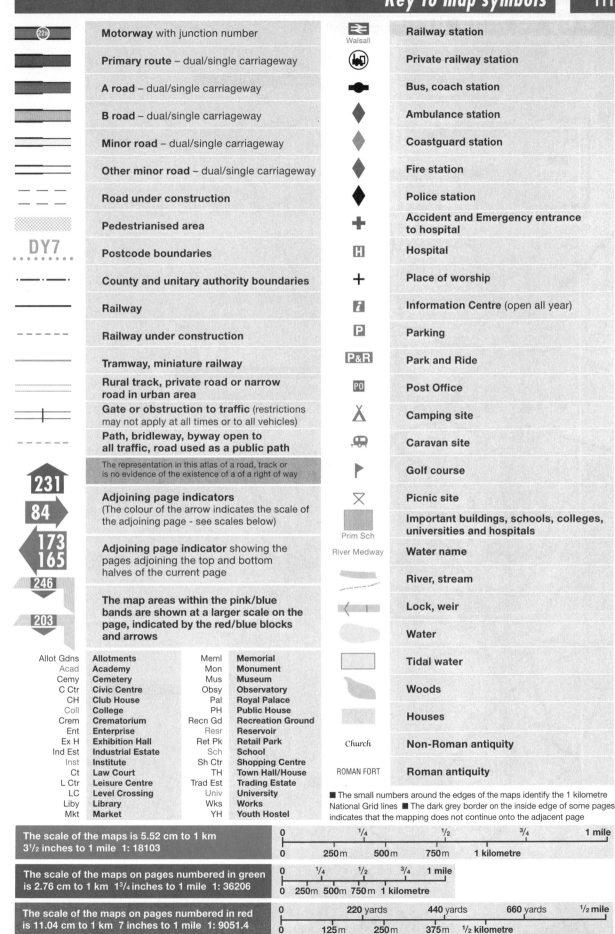

IV

Key to map pages

246	Map pages at 7 inches to 1 mile
244	Map pages at 3½ inches to 1 mile
226	Map pages at 1¾ inches to 1 mile

Scale

0 — 5 — 10 — 15 km
0 — 5 — 10 miles

Bourne
Spalding
Crowland

Leicestershire STREET ATLAS

Market Deeping
Tallington
Etton
206 207
Newborough

244
230 231
Stamford
Barnack
203 204 205
Werrington
Eye

Thornhaugh
192 193 194 195 196 197 198 199
Wansford
Ailsworth
Peterborough

183 184 185 186 187 188

178 179 180 181 182
Warmington
Yaxley

Stilton
174 175 176 177
Denton
Glatton
A1(M)

166 167 168 169 170
Sawtry

Clopton
Woodwalton
156 157 158 159 160 161 162
Hamerton
Upton
Wennington

Buckworth
145 146 147 148 149 150 151 152
Molesworth
Leighton
Bromswold
Little Stukeley

Catworth
Huntingdon
135 136 137 138 139 140 141
Covington
Easton
Brampton

Grafham
113 114 115 116 117 118
Kimbolton
West Perry
Buckden

Dillington
93 94 95 96 97
Hail Weston
Great Paxton

St Neots
74 75 76

Bedfordshire STREET ATLAS

56 57
Waresley

40 41
Everton

Uppingham

Market Harborough

Corby

Kettering

Thrapston

Raunds

Rushden

Wellingborough

Northampton

Towcester

Buckinghamshire STREET ATLAS

Newport Pagnell

Bedford
Kempston

Northamptonshire STREET ATLAS

Bletchley

Baldock
Letchworth

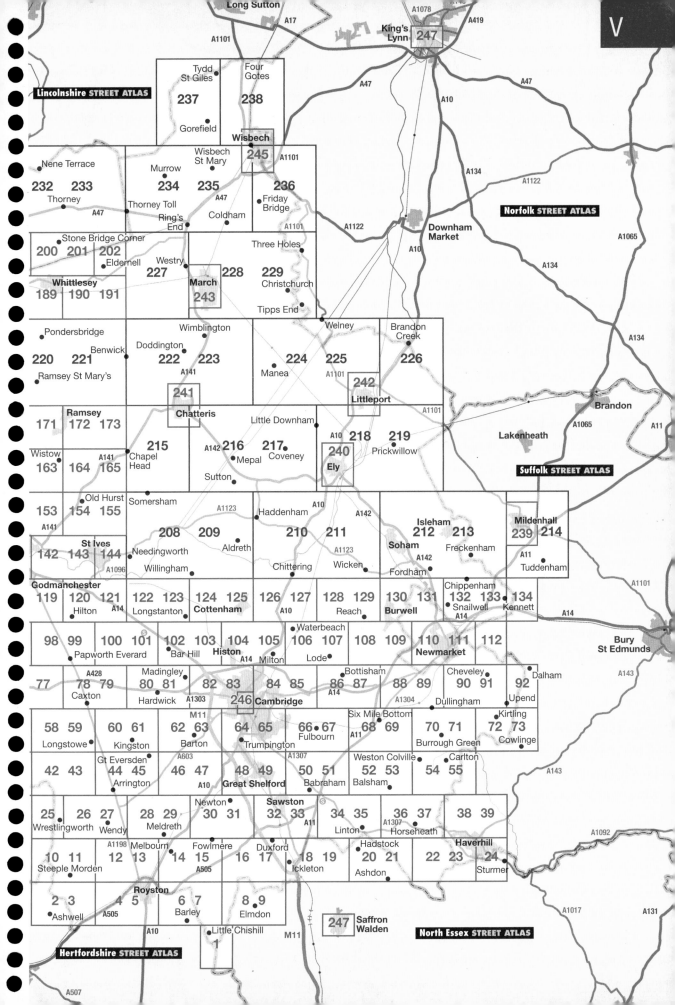

Long Sutton

A1078

A419

King's Lynn **247**

A17

A1101

A47

A47

A10

Lincolnshire STREET ATLAS

Tydd St Giles **237**

Four Gotes **238**

Gorefield

A1101

A134

A1122

Nene Terrace

Murrow

Wisbech St Mary

Wisbech **245**

A1101

Norfolk STREET ATLAS

232 **233**

234 **235**

236

A1065

Thorney

Thorney Toll

A47

Coldham

Friday Bridge

Downham Market

Ring's End

A47

A1101

A134

Stone Bridge Corner

200 **201** **202**

Eldernell

Westry

Three Holes

229

A1122

A10

Whittlesey

227

March

228

Christchurch

A1065

189 **190** **191**

243

Tipps End

Pondersbridge

Wimblington

Welney

Brandon Creek

Brandon

220 **221**

Benwick

Doddington

222 **223**

224 **225**

226

A1065

Ramsey St Mary's

A141

Manea

A1101

242

Littleport

A1101

A11

Ramsey

241

Chatteris

Little Downham

A10 **218** **219**

Lakenheath

171 **172** **173**

215

A142 **216**

Mepal

217

Coveney

240

Prickwillow

Suffolk STREET ATLAS

Wistow

163 **164** **165**

A141

Chapel Head

Sutton

Ely

Old Hurst

Somersham

A1123

Haddenham

A10

A142

Isleham

Mildenhall

153 **154** **155**

208 **209**

210 **211**

212 **213**

239 **214**

A141

Needingworth

Aldreth

A1123

Soham

Freckenham

A11

St Ives

Willingham

Chittering

Wicken

A142

Fordham

Tuddenham

142 **143** **144**

A1096

Chippenham

A1101

Godmanchester

119 **120** **121**

122 **123**

124 **125**

126 **127**

128 **129**

130 **131**

132 **133** **134**

Bury St Edmunds

Hilton

A14

Longstanton

Cottenham

A10

Reach

Burwell

Snailwell

Kennett

A14

Waterbeach

98 **99**

100 **101**

102 **103**

104 **105**

106 **107**

108 **109**

110 **111** **112**

Papworth Everard

Bar Hill

Histon

Milton

Lode

Newmarket

A428

Madingley

A14

Bottisham

Cheveley

Dalham

77

78 **79**

80 **81**

82 **83**

84 **85**

86 **87**

88 **89**

90 **91**

92

A143

Caxton

Hardwick

A1303

246

Cambridge

A14

A1304

Dullingham

Upend

M11

Six Mile Bottom

Kirtling

58 **59**

60 **61**

62 **63**

64 **65**

66 **67**

68 **69**

70 **71**

72 **73**

Longstowe

Kingston

Barton

Trumpington

Fulbourn

A11

Burrough Green

Cowlinge

Gt Eversden

A603

Weston Colville

Carlton

42 **43**

44 **45**

46 **47**

48 **49**

50 **51**

52 **53**

54 **55**

A143

Arrington

A10

Great Shelford

Babraham

Balsham

Newton

Sawston

25 **26** **27**

28 **29**

30 **31**

32 **33**

34 **35**

36 **37**

38 **39**

A1092

Wrestlingworth

Wendy

Meldreth

A11

Linton

A1307

Horseheath

Haverhill

A1198

Melbourn

Fowlmere

Duxford

Hadstock

10 **11**

12 **13**

14 **15**

16 **17**

18 **19**

20 **21**

22 **23**

24

Steeple Morden

A505

Ickleton

Ashdon

Sturmer

A1017

A131

Royston

2 **3**

4 **5**

6 **7**

8 **9**

247

Saffron Walden

Ashwell

A505

Barley

Elmdon

North Essex STREET ATLAS

A10

Little Chishill

M11

Hertfordshire STREET ATLAS

A507

Route planning

Scale

0 5 10 15 km

0 5 10 miles

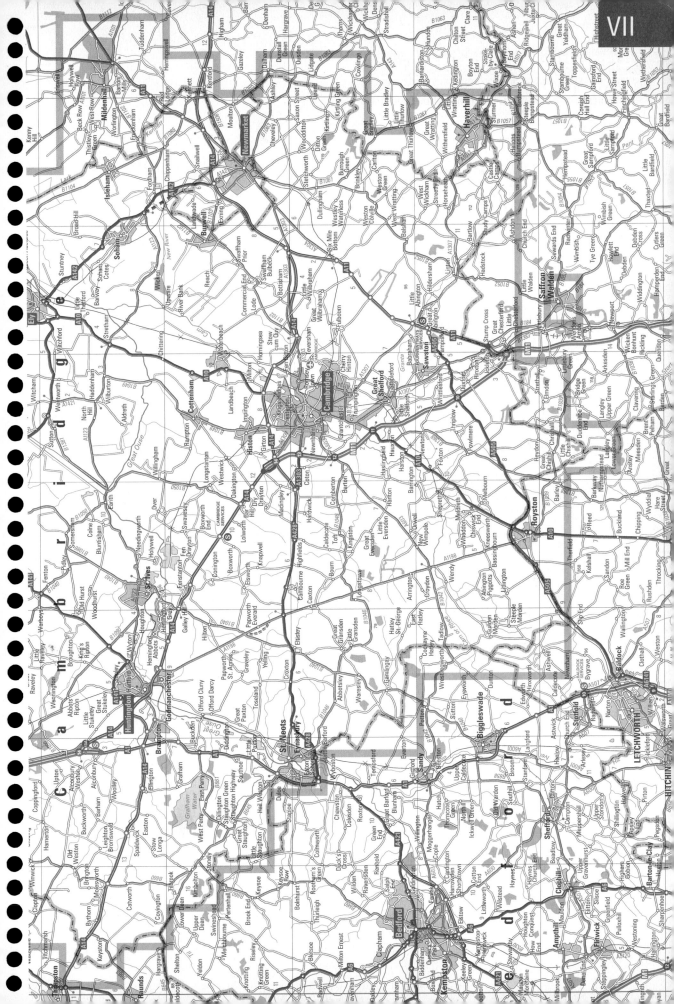

Administrative and Postcode boundaries

	County and unitary authority boundaries
	District boundaries
	Postcode boundaries
	Area covered by this atlas

Scale

0 5 10 15 20 25 30 km
0 5 10 15 20 miles

Lincolnshire

Rutland

Norfolk

PE12
Newton
PE14
PE13
Wisbech
PE12
Parson Drove
Elm
Stamford
PE9
Deeping St James
Pilsgate
City of Peterborough
PE6
PE4
Eye
Thorney
Coldham
Ring's End
PE14
Upwell
PE8
PE1
PE6
PE8
Wansford
PE5
PE3
Peterborough
PE2
Whittlesey
March
Fenland
Tipsend
PE8
PE7
PE7
Yaxley
PE15
Elton
Doddington
PE38
Brandon Creek
Stilton
CB6
Northants
PE26
Littleport
CB7
Ramsey
Chatteris
Pymoor
Sawtry
PE16
Prickwillow
Clopton
Church End
Warboys
Mepal
Ely
NN14
Huntingdonshire
PE28
Pidley
Sutton
CB6
Molesworth
Abbotts Ripton
Cambridgeshire
East Cambridgeshire
CB7
Woolley
Stretham
Isleham
Mildenhall
Catworth
Brampton
Huntingdon
St Ives
Willingham
Soham
IP28
NN9
Covington
PE27
Wicken
Fordham
Kimbolton
East Perry
PE29
Cottenham
Burwell
Southoe
CB4
Newmarket
Suffolk
PE19
Boxworth
Histon
CB5
Cheveley
MK44
St Neots
Yelling
CB3
CB8
Dullingham
Caxton
Toft
Barton
Cambridge
Six Mile Bottom
Waresley
SG19
South
Cambridge
CB1
Gamlingay
Cambridgeshire
CB2
Balsham
Great Shelford
Wendy
Sawston
Linton
CB9
Bedfordshire
Tadlow
SG8
Melbourn
Hadstock
Haverhill
Kneesworth
Stump Cross
Ashwell
Royston
Barley
SG7
Essex
SP TL
Hertfordshire

TF
TL

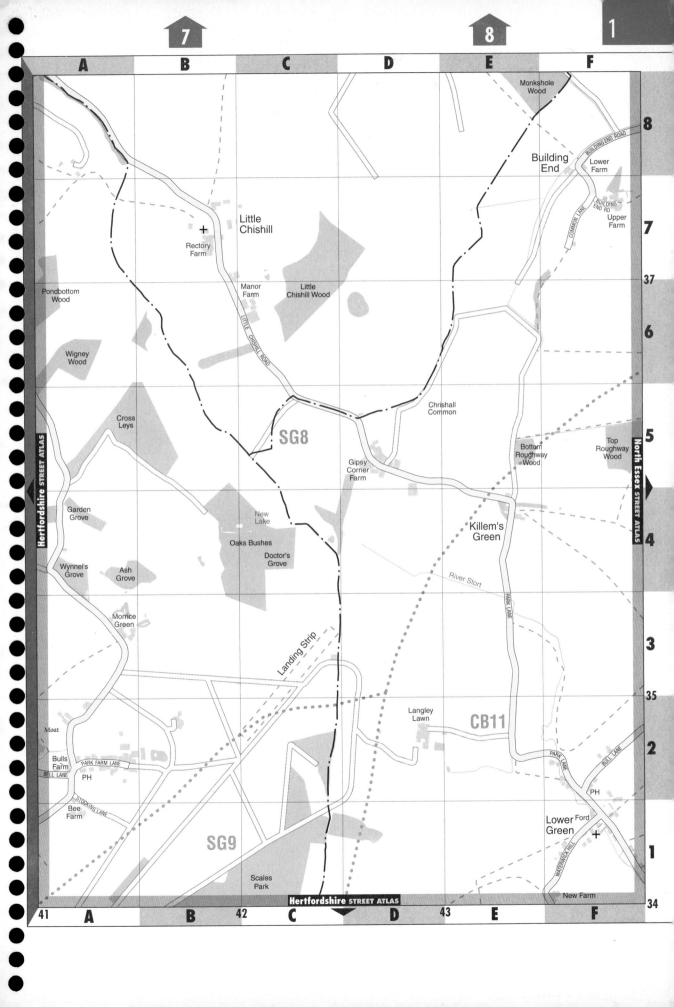

A B C D E F

8

Monkshole
Wood

Building
End

BUILDING END ROAD

Lower
Farm

COMMON LANE

BUILDING END RD

Upper
Farm

7

Little
Chishill

+

Rectory
Farm

37

Pondbottom
Wood

Manor
Farm

Little
Chishill Wood

6

Wigney
Wood

LITTLE CHISHILL ROAD

Chrishall
Common

5

Cross
Leys

SG8

Gipsy
Corner
Farm

Bottom
Roughway
Wood

Top
Roughway
Wood

Garden
Grove

New
Lake

Killem's
Green

4

Wynnel's
Grove

Ash
Grove

Oaks Bushes

Doctor's
Grove

River Stort

PARK LANE

Morrice
Green

Landing Strip

3

35

Langley
Lawn

CB11

PARK LANE

BULL LANE

2

Moat

Bulls
Farm

PARK FARM LANE

BELL LANE

PH

PH

STOCKING LANE

Bee
Farm

Lower Ford
Green

+

SG9

1

WATERWICK HILL

Scales
Park

New Farm

34

Hertfordshire STREET ATLAS

North Essex STREET ATLAS

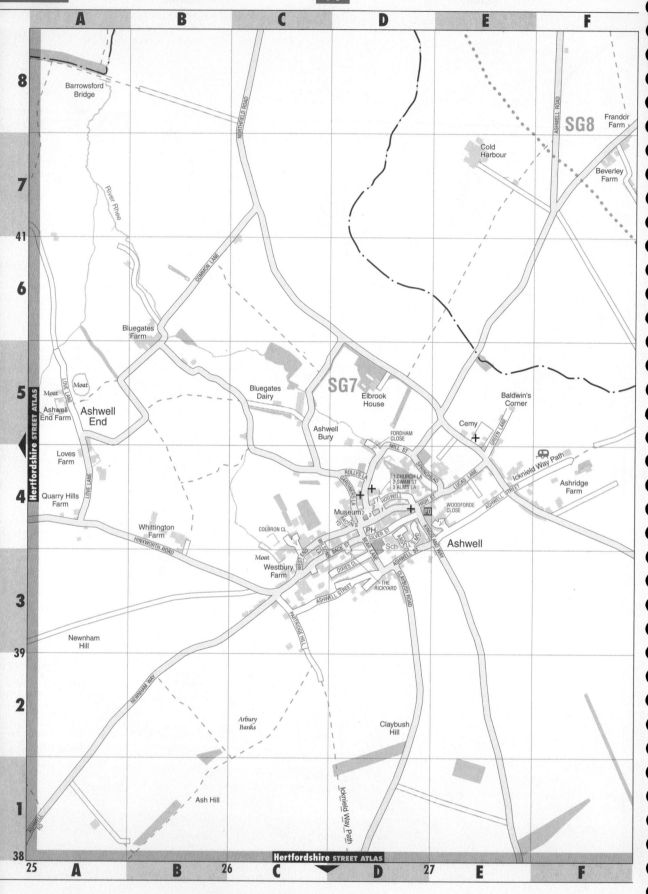

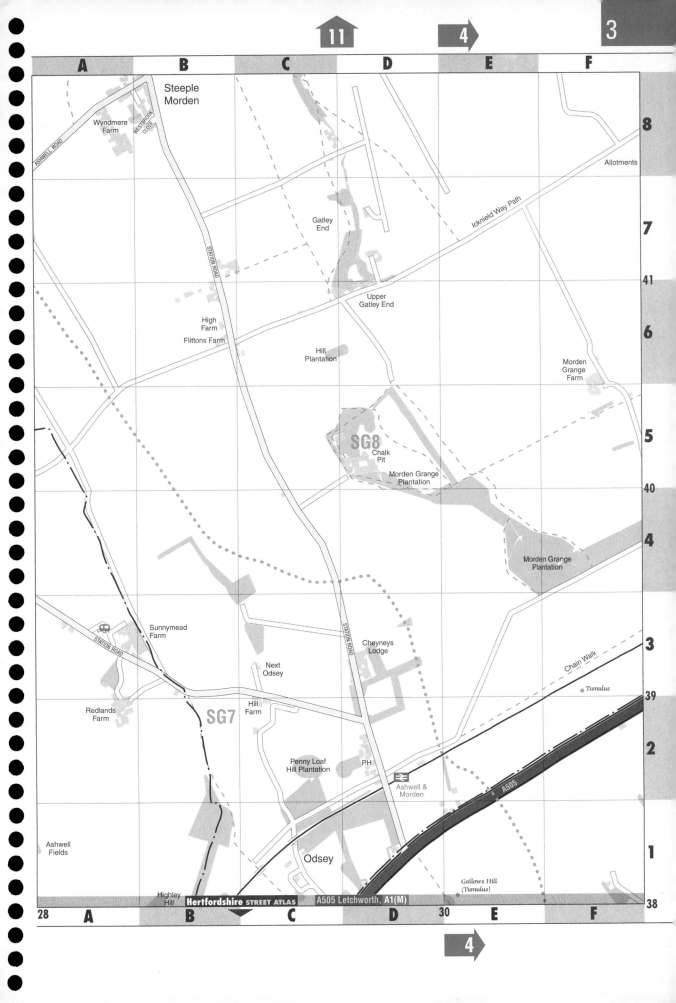

3

12

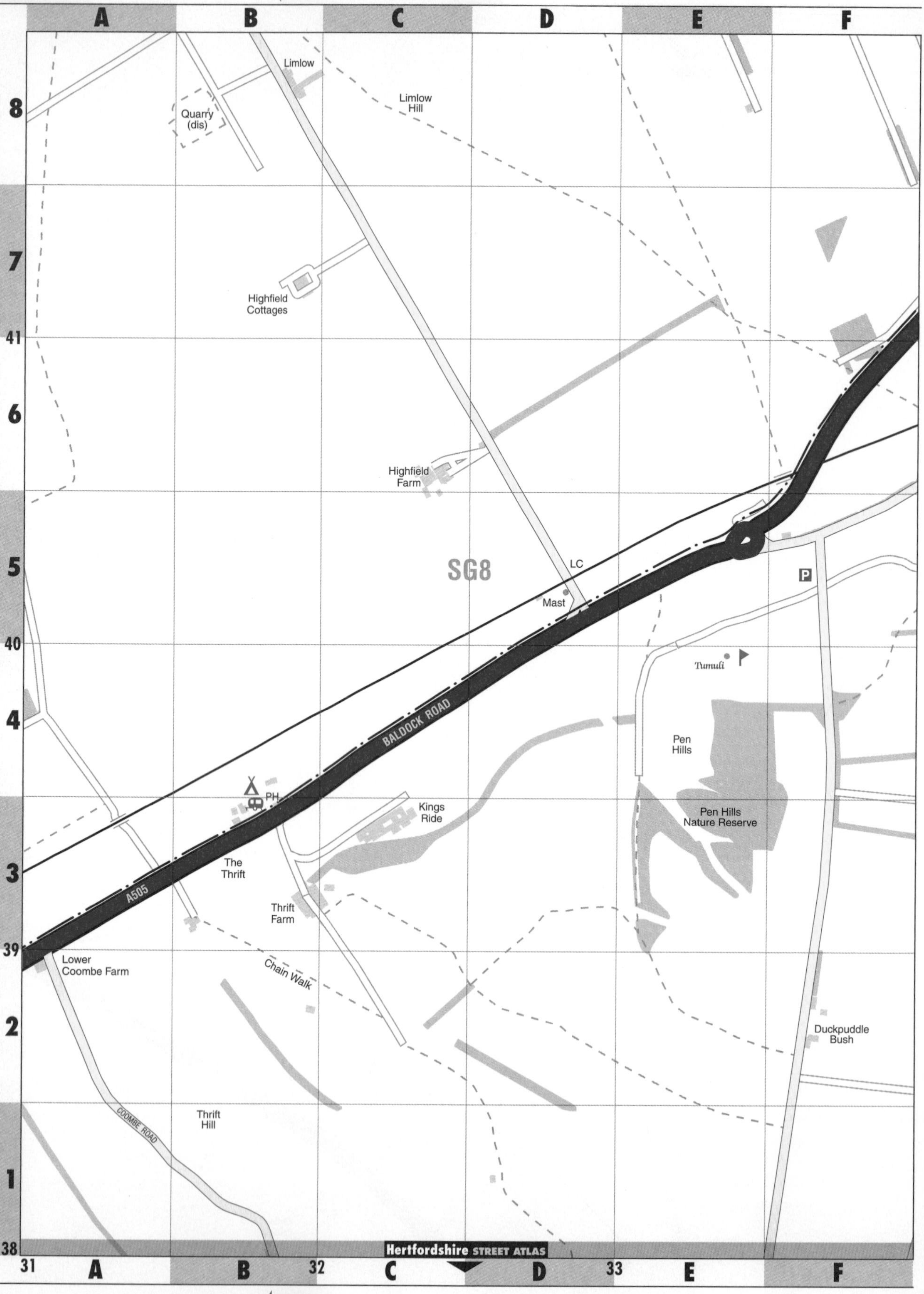
A
B
C
D
E
F
8
7
41
6
5
40
4
3
39
2
1
38
31
32
33
Limlow
Limlow Hill
Quarry (dis)
Highfield Cottages
Highfield Farm
SG8
LC
Mast
BALDOCK ROAD
A505
PH
Kings Ride
The Thrift
Thrift Farm
Lower Coombe Farm
Chain Walk
COOMBE ROAD
Thrift Hill
Tumuli
Pen Hills
Pen Hills Nature Reserve
Duckpuddle Bush
P
Hertfordshire STREET ATLAS

3

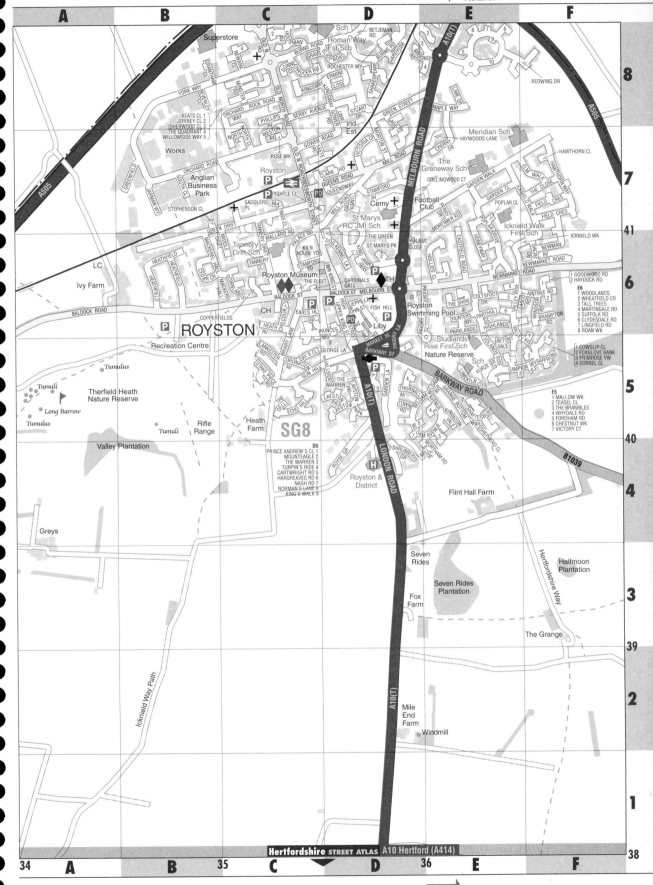

13

6

5

E8
1 KIPLING RD
2 ACKROYD RD
3 COOMBELANDS RD
4 BYRON RD
5 CORMAS CL
6 CURLEW CR

7 KESTREL WY
8 OWALL WK
9 SKYLARK PL
10 FIELDFARE WY

Superstore

Roman Way Fst Sch

Betjeman RD

Meridian Sch
HAYWOODS LANE

The Greneway Sch

Anglian Business Park

Royston

Ind Est

Works

Football Club

Icknield Walk First Sch

ICKNIELD WK

St Marys RC JMI Sch

Tannery Drift Sch

Royston Museum

The Green St Marys PK

Royston Swimming Pool

Studlands Rise First Sch

Ivy Farm

E6
1 GOODWOOD RD
2 HAYDOCK RD

E6
1 WOODLANDS
2 WHEATFIELD CR
3 TALL TREES
4 MARTINGALE RD
5 SUFFOLK RD
6 CLYDESDALE RD
7 LINGFIELD RD
8 ROAN WK

1 COWSLIP CL
2 FOXGLOVE BANK
3 PRIMROSE VW
4 SORREL CL

ROYSTON

Recreation Centre

CH

Studlands Rise Nature Reserve

E5
1 MALLOW WK
2 TEASEL CL
3 THE BRAMBLES
4 WHYDALE RD
5 FORDHAM RD
6 CHESTNUT WK
7 VICTORY CT

Tumulus

Therfield Heath Nature Reserve

Long Barrow

Tumuli

Rifle Range

Heath Farm

SG8

D5
1 PRINCE ANDREW'S CL
2 MOUNTEAGLE
3 THE WARREN
4 TURPIN'S RIDE
5 CARTWRIGHT RD
6 HARGREAVES RD
7 NASH DR
8 NORMAN'S LANE
9 KING'S WALK

Valley Plantation

Tumuli

Royston & District

B1039

Greys

Flint Hall Farm

Halfmoon Plantation

Seven Rides

Hertfordshire Way

Seven Rides Plantation

Fox Farm

The Grange

Icknield Way Path

Mile End Farm

Windmill

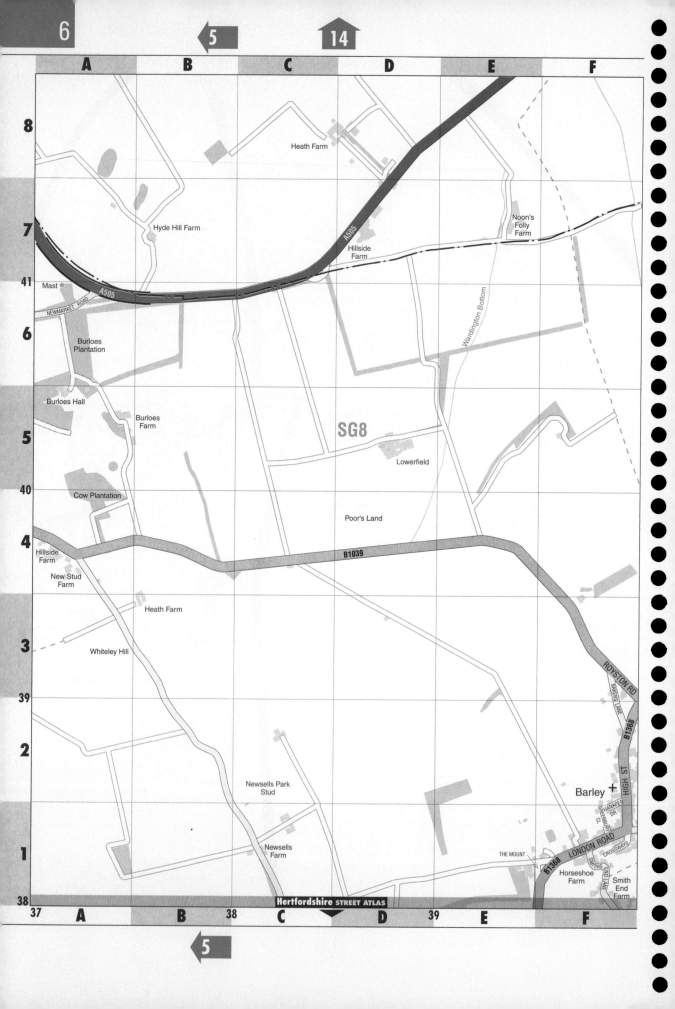

8

Heath Farm

7

Hyde Hill Farm

Noon's
Folly
Farm

Hillside
Farm

41

Mast

A505

NEWMARKET ROAD

Wardington Bottom

6

Burloes
Plantation

Burloes Hall

Burloes
Farm

SG8

5

Lowerfield

40

Cow Plantation

Poor's Land

4

Hillside
Farm

B1039

New Stud
Farm

Heath Farm

3

Whiteley Hill

39

ROYSTON RD

BAKERS LANE

B1368

2

HIGH ST

Newsells Park
Stud

BARLEY +

GREENBURY
DR

CHANAPER
CL

1

Newsells
Farm

THE MOUNT

LONDON ROAD

CROSSWAYS

B1368

SMITHS

END LANE

Horseshoe
Farm

Smith
End
Farm

38

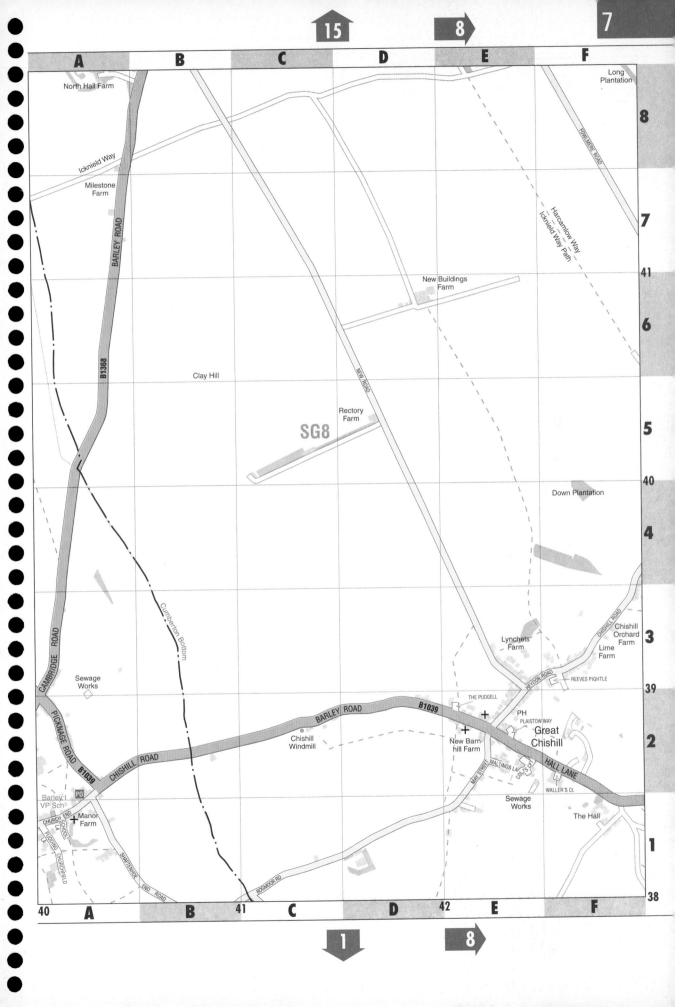

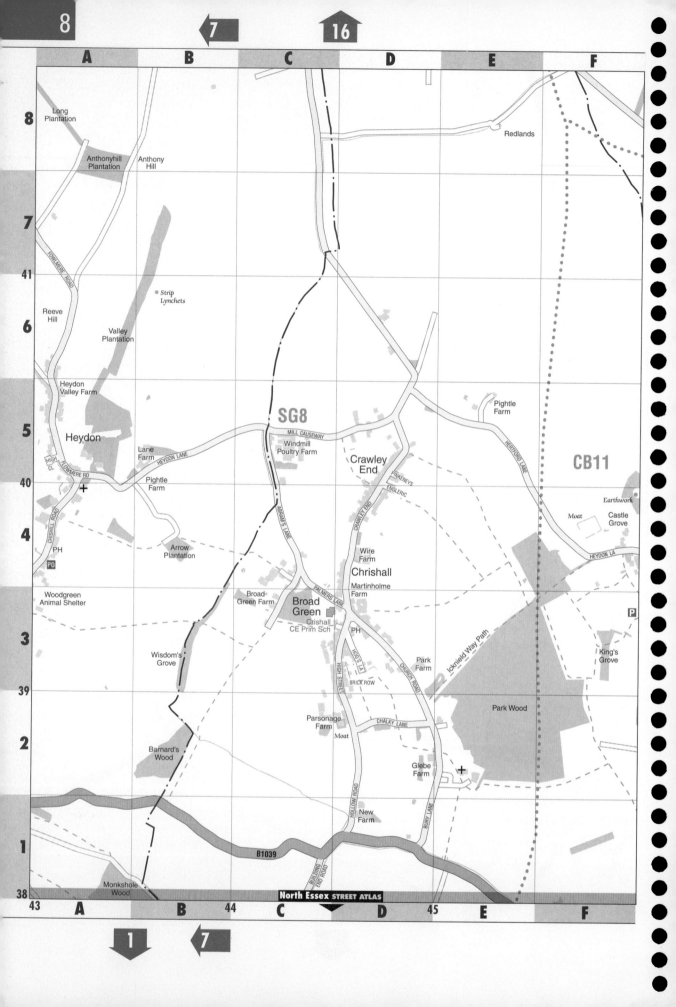

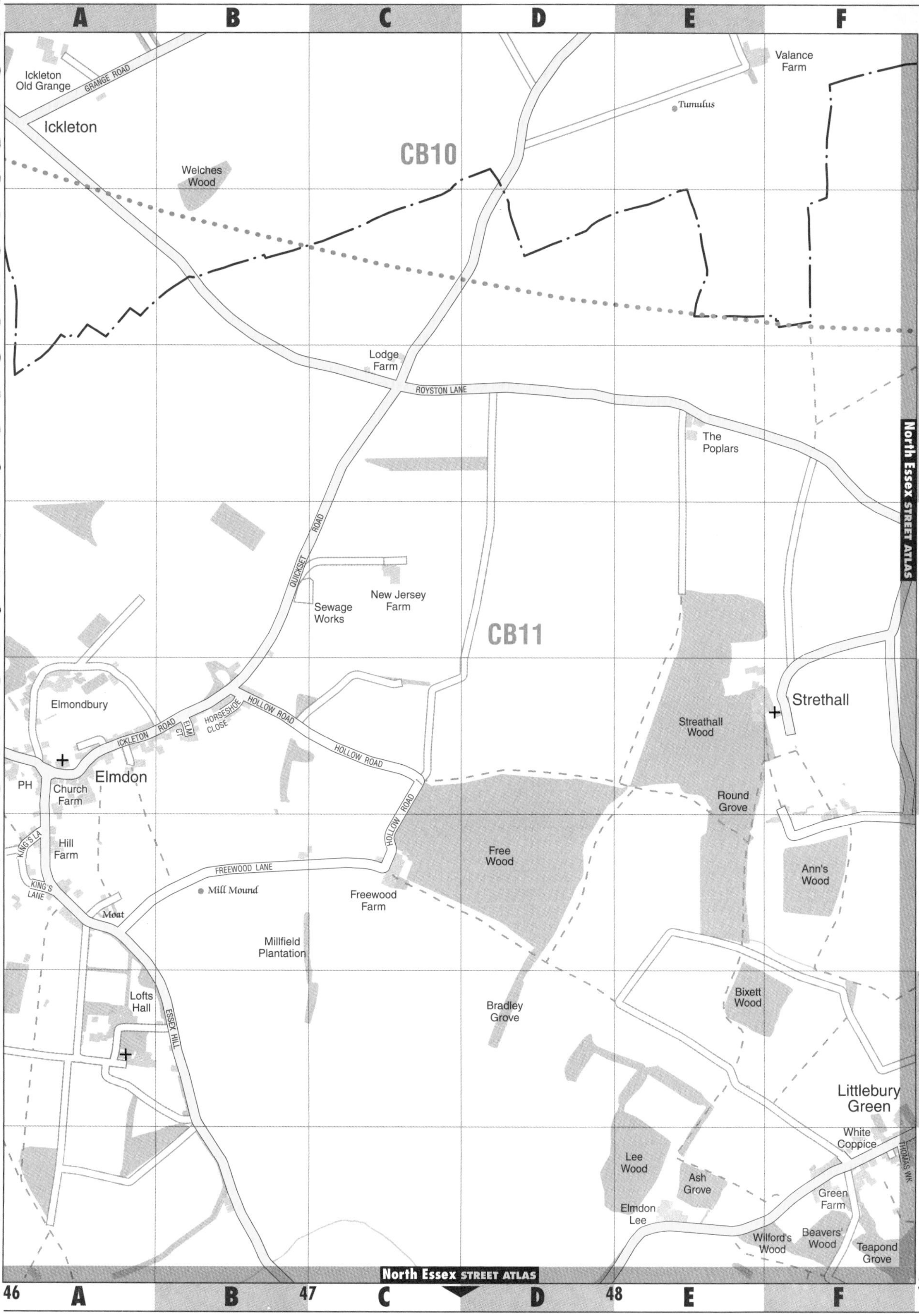

A B C D E F

Ickleton
Old Grange
GRANGE ROAD

Valance
Farm

Ickleton

CB10

Tumulus

Welches
Wood

8

Lodge
Farm

7

41

ROYSTON LANE

The
Poplars

6

North Essex STREET ATLAS

QUICKSET ROAD

Sewage
Works

New Jersey
Farm

CB11

5

40

Elmondbury

ICKLETON ROAD

HORSESHOE CLOSE

ELM C

HOLLOW ROAD

HOLLOW ROAD

Strethall

Streathall
Wood

Strethall

4

Church
Farm

PH

Elmdon

Round
Grove

Ann's
Wood

KING'S LA

Hill
Farm

FREEWOOD LANE

HOLLOW ROAD

Free
Wood

KING'S
LANE

Mill Mound

Freewood
Farm

3

Moat

Millfield
Plantation

Bixett
Wood

39

Lofts
Hall

ESSEX HILL

Bradley
Grove

2

Littlebury
Green

White
Coppice

THOMAS WK

Lee
Wood

Ash
Grove

Green
Farm

Elmdon
Lee

Beavers'
Wood

1

Wilford's
Wood

Teapond
Grove

46 A B 47 C D 48 E F 38

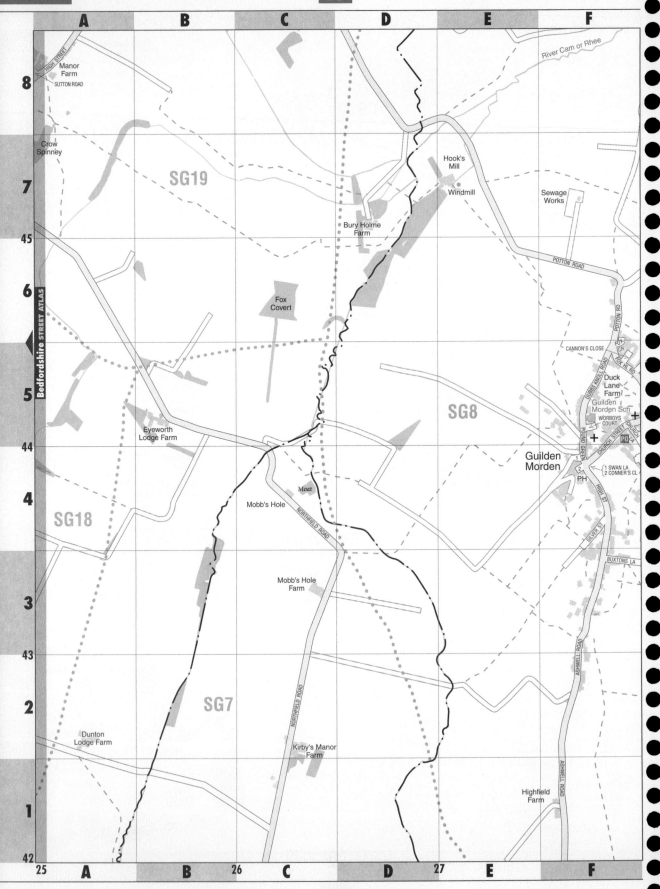

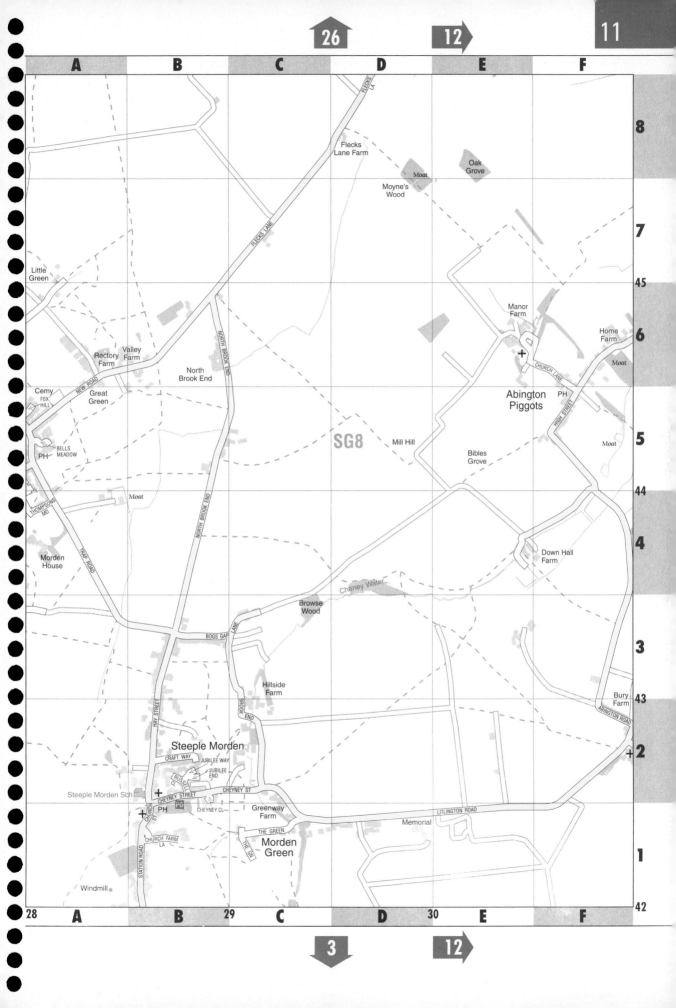

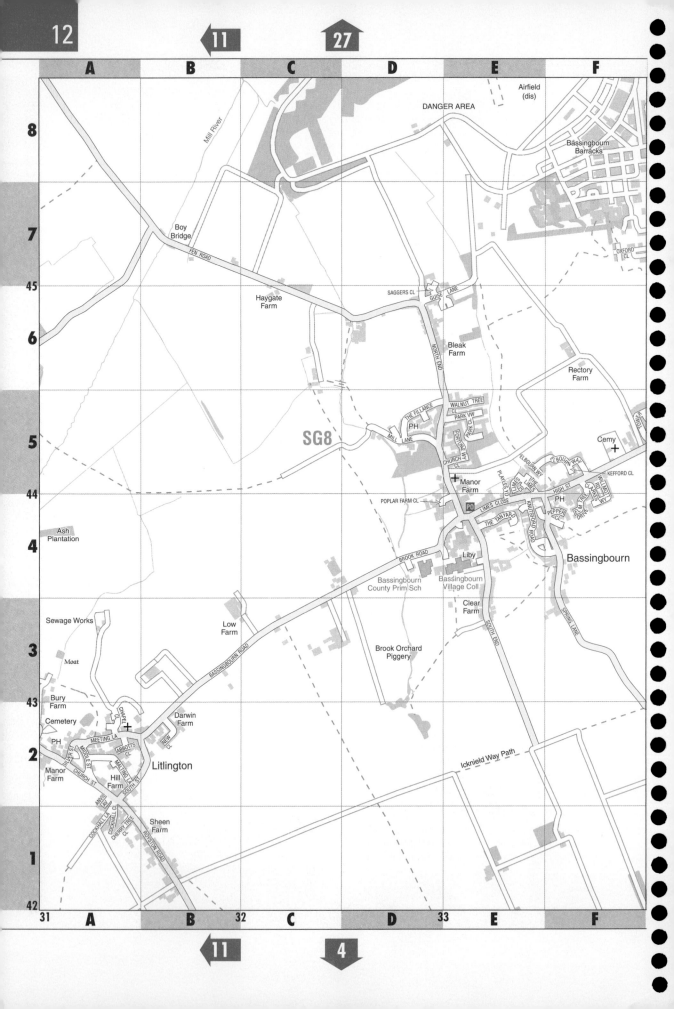

A B C D E F

8

Mill River

Airfield (dis)

DANGER AREA

Bassingbourn Barracks

7
Boy Bridge

FEN ROAD

OXFORD CL

45
SAGGERS CL
GUISE LANE
Haygate Farm

6
NORTH END
Bleak Farm

Rectory Farm

THE FILLANCE
WALNUT TREE CL
PARK VW
PARK CL

5
SG8
MILL LANE
PH
CHURCH CL
FORTUNE WY
Cemy

FELBOURN WY
C'BOURN WAY
THE LIMES
KEFFORD CL

Manor Farm
PLATTES YD
WILLMOTT ROAD
CLARKES WY
HIGH ST
WHITTLE CL

44
POPLAR FARM CL
PO
LIMES CLOSE
KNUTSFORD ROAD
PH
PEPPER CL
CLARKES DRIVE

THE TANYARD

Ash Plantation

4
BROOK ROAD
Liby
Bassingbourn
Bassingbourn County Prim Sch
Bassingbourn Village Coll

Clear Farm

Sewage Works
SOUTH END
SPRING LANE

3
Moat
Low Farm
BASSINGBOURN ROAD
Brook Orchard Piggery

43
Bury Farm
Cemetery
CHAPEL CL
Darwin Farm
Icknield Way Path

PH
MEETING LA
NEW CL
ABBOTTS CL

2
SILVER ST
MIDDLE ST
MALTING LA
Litlington

Manor Farm
CHURCH ST
Hill Farm
SOUTH ST

ANVIL LA
COCKHALL LA
CHERRY TREE CL
Sheen Farm
ROYSTON ROAD

1

42
31 A B 32 C D 33 E F

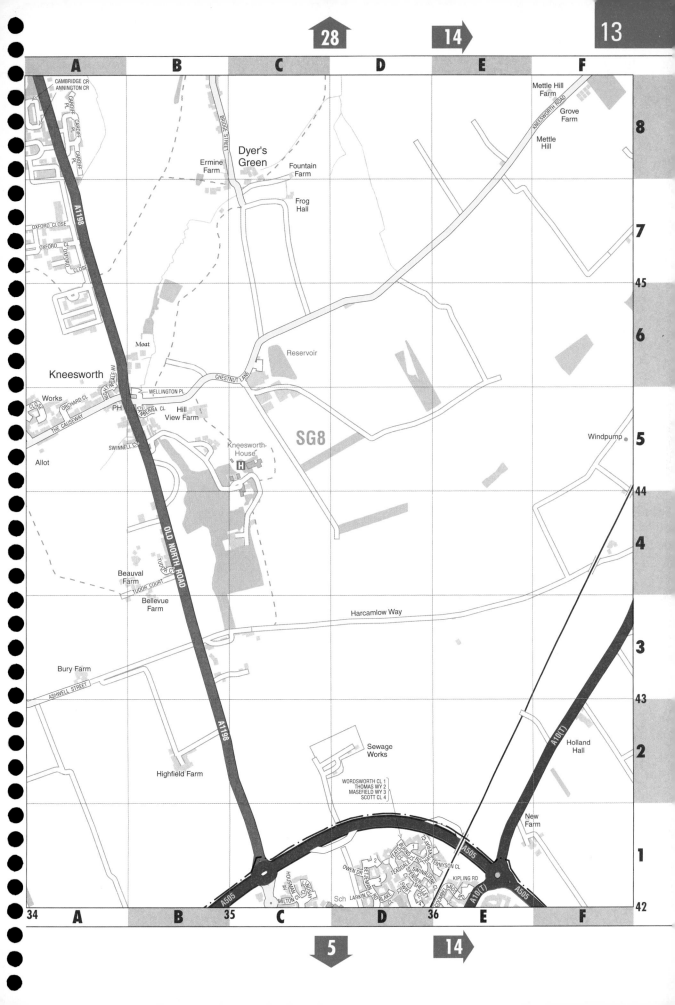

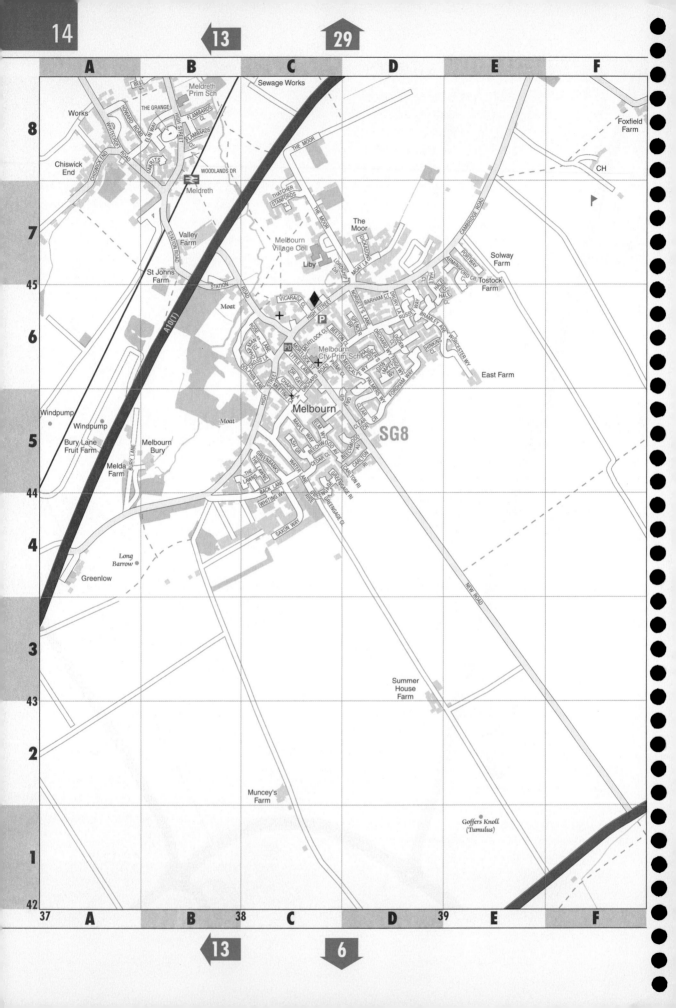

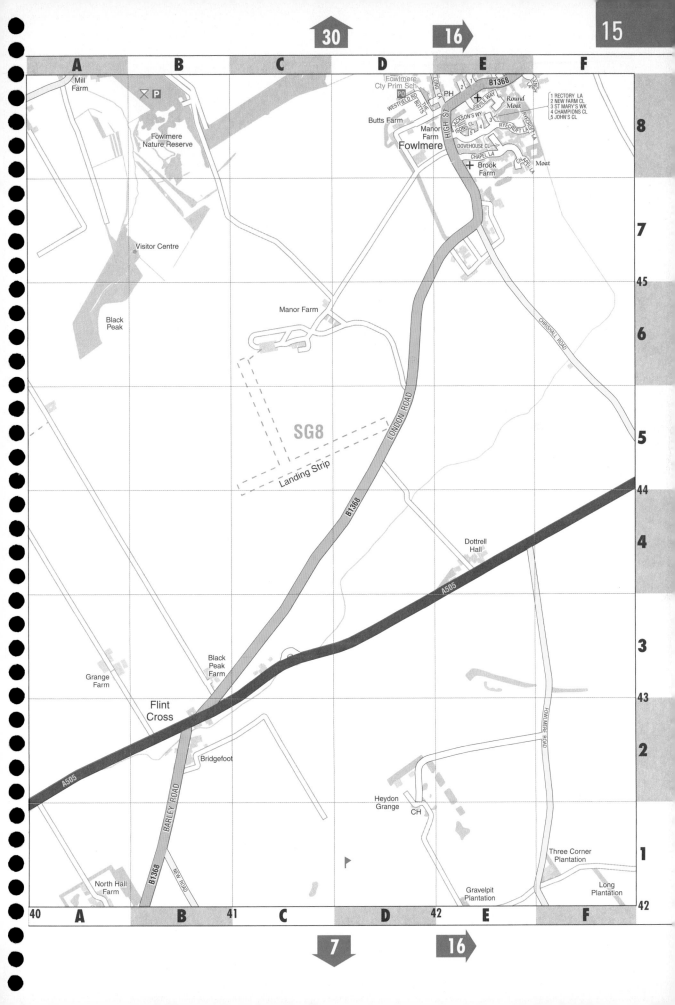

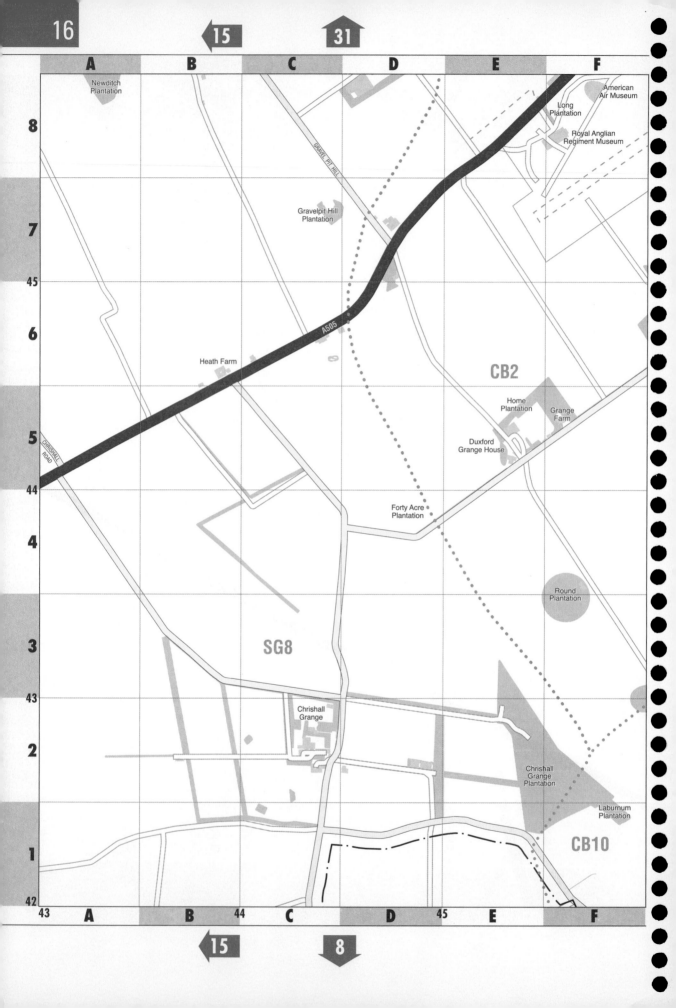

A B C D E F

8
45
7
6
CB2
5
44
4
SG8
3
43
2
1
42

Newditch
Plantation

Gravelpit Hill
Plantation

Long
Plantation

American
Air Museum

Royal Anglian
Regiment Museum

Heath Farm

A505

Home
Plantation

Grange
Farm

Duxford
Grange House

Forty Acre
Plantation

Round
Plantation

Chrishall
Grange

Chrishall
Grange
Plantation

Laburnum
Plantation

CB10

CHRISHALL ROAD

GRAVEL PIT HILL

43 A B 44 C D 45 E F

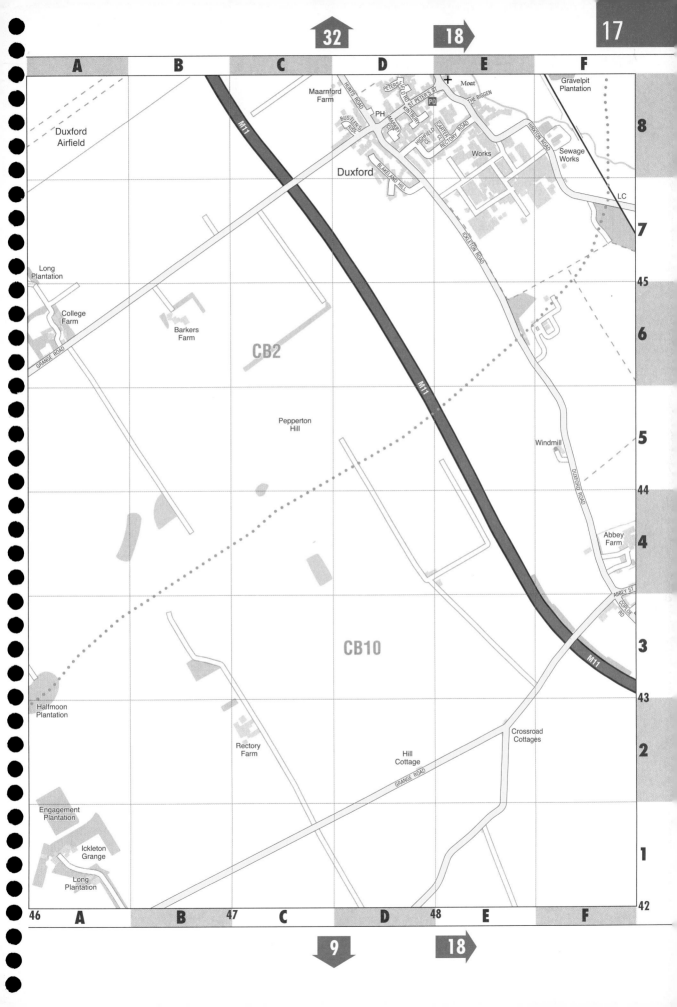

A B C D E F

Gravelpit
Plantation

Maarnford
Farm

Duxford
Airfield

Duxford

8

Works

Sewage
Works

LC

7

45

Long
Plantation

College
Farm

Barkers
Farm

6

CB2

Pepperton
Hill

Windmill

5

44

Abbey
Farm

4

CB10

3

Halfmoon
Plantation

43

Crossroad
Cottages

Rectory
Farm

Hill
Cottage

2

Engagement
Plantation

Ickleton
Grange

Long
Plantation

1

42

46 A B 47 C D 48 E F

GRANGE ROAD

GRANGE ROAD

M11

HUNTS ROAD

PETERSFIELD RD

ST PETER'S ST

KINTBURY

HIGHFIELD CL

CARTER CL

RECTORY ROAD

ICKLETON ROAD

HINXTON ROAD

DUXFORD ROAD

BLAKELAND HILL

BUSTER'S RISE

THE BIGGEN

ABBEY ST

COPLOE RD

PH

PO

Moat

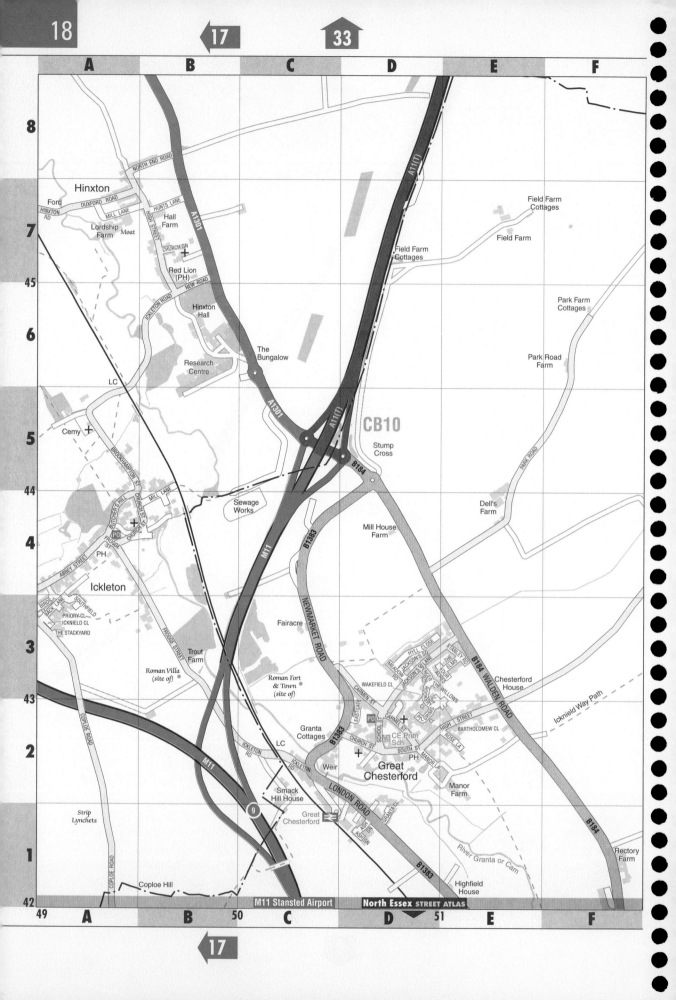

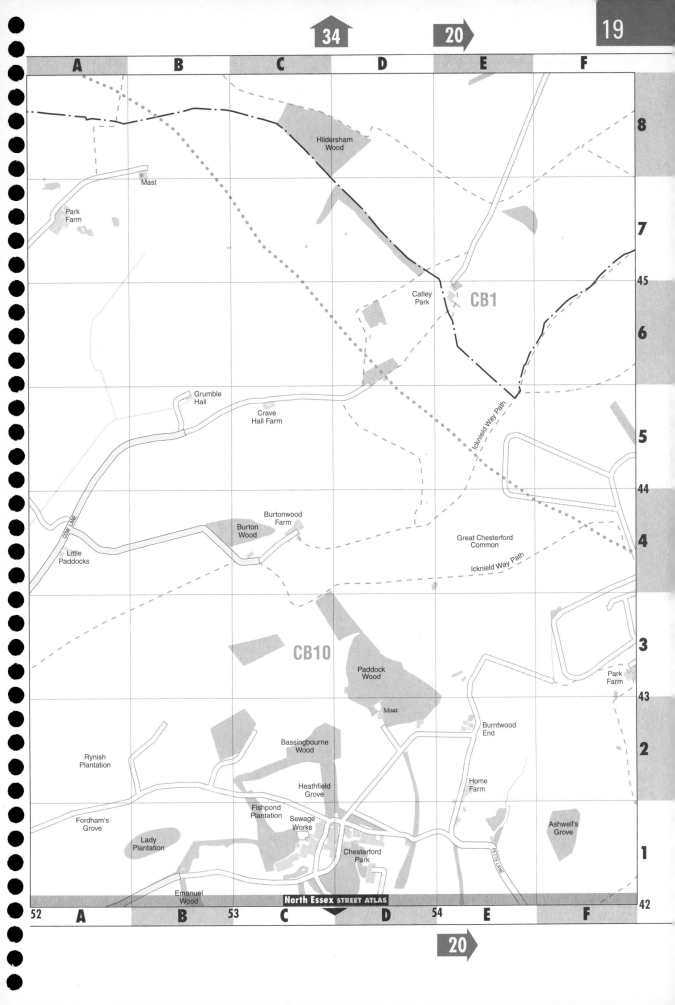

A B C D E F

8

7
45
6

5
44
4

3
43
2

1
42

Hildersham
Wood

Mast

Park
Farm

Catley
Park

CB1

Grumble
Hall

Crave
Hall Farm

Icknield Way Path

Burtonwood
Farm

Burton
Wood

COW LANE

Little
Paddocks

Great Chesterford
Common

Icknield Way Path

CB10

Paddock
Wood

Park
Farm

Moat

Burntwood
End

Rynish
Plantation

Bassingbourne
Wood

Home
Farm

Heathfield
Grove

Fishpond
Plantation

Sewage
Works

Fordham's
Grove

Ashwell's
Grove

Lady
Plantation

Chesterford
Park

PETTS LANE

Emanuel
Wood

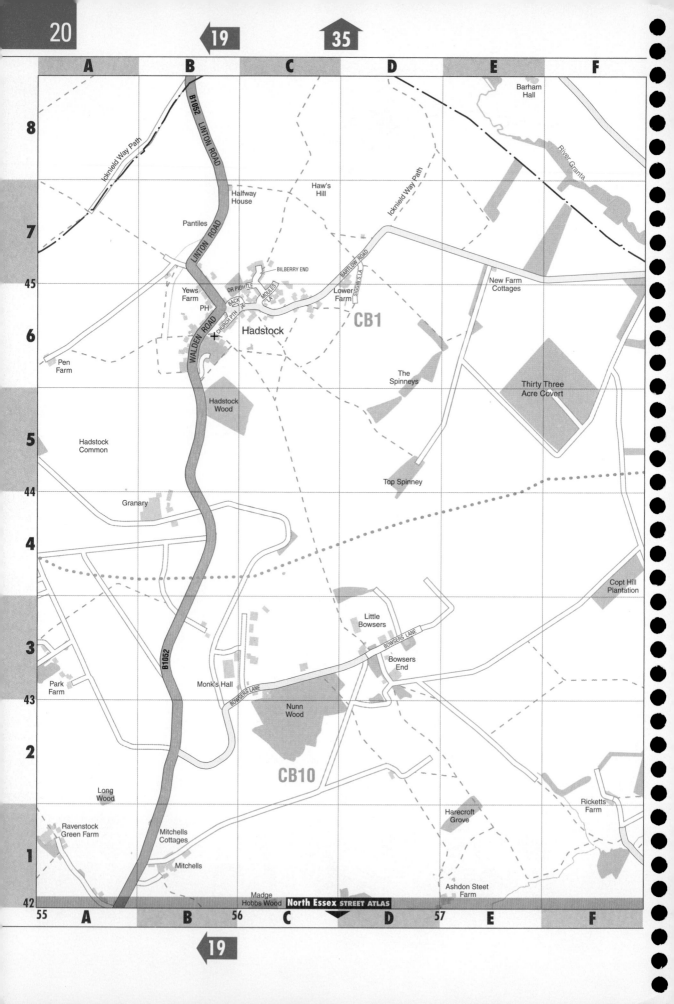

A B C D E F

8

7

45

Barham
Hall

River Granta

Icknield Way Path

B1052

LINTON ROAD

Halfway
House

Haw's
Hill

Pantiles

Icknield Way Path

BILBERRY END

DR PIGHTLE

Yews
Farm

PH

BACK

MOULES LA

CHURCH PTH

SEGEN'S LA

BARTLOW ROAD

Lower
Farm

New Farm
Cottages

WALDEN ROAD

Hadstock

CB1

6

Pen
Farm

The
Spinneys

Thirty Three
Acre Covert

Hadstock
Wood

5

Hadstock
Common

44

Granary

Top Spinney

4

Copt Hill
Plantation

Little
Bowsers

BOWSERS LANE

Bowsers
End

3

Park
Farm

B1052

Monk's Hall

BOWSERS LANE

Nunn
Wood

43

2

CB10

Long
Wood

Harecroft
Grove

Ricketts
Farm

Ravenstock
Green Farm

Mitchells
Cottages

1

Mitchells

Ashdon Steet
Farm

Madge
Hobbs Wood

42

North Essex STREET ATLAS

55 A B 56 C D 57 E F

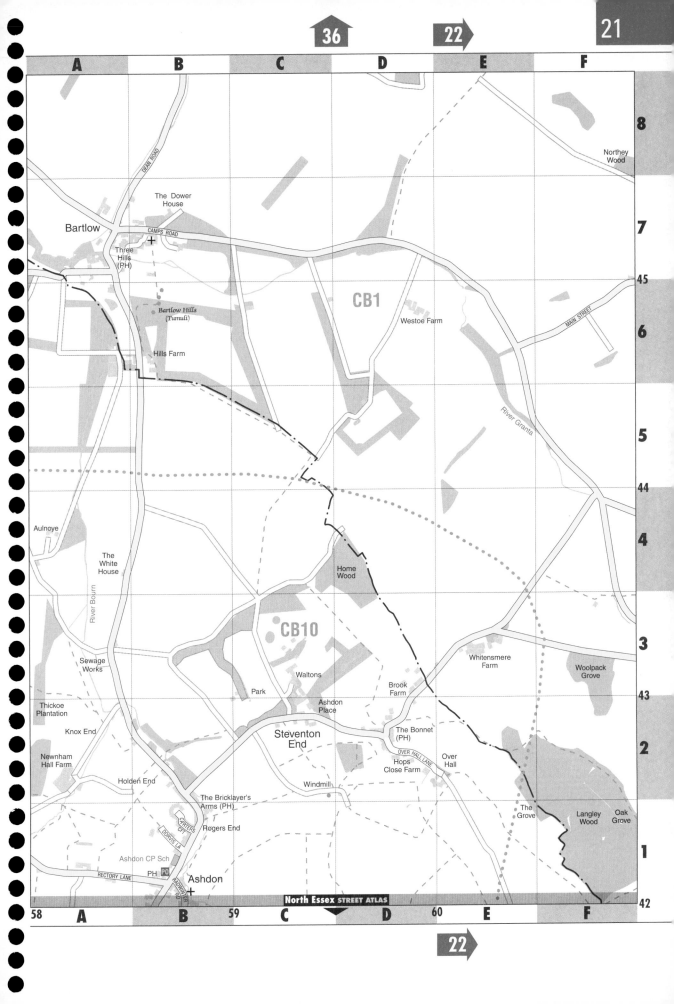

A B C D E F

Northey
Wood

The Dower
House

DEAN ROAD

Bartlow

CAMPS ROAD

Three
Hills
(PH)

CB1

Westoe Farm

MAIN STREET

Bartlow Hills
(Tumuli)

Hills Farm

River Granta

Aulnoye

The
White
House

Home
Wood

River Bourn

CB10

Whitensmere
Farm

Woolpack
Grove

Sewage
Works

Waltons

Brook
Farm

Thickoe
Plantation

Park

Ashdon
Place

Knox End

Steventon
End

The Bonnet
(PH)

OVER HALL LANE

Over
Hall

Newnham
Hall Farm

Hops
Close Farm

Holden End

Windmill

The Bricklayer's
Arms (PH)

The
Grove

Langley
Wood

Oak
Grove

CARTERS CFT

DORVIS LA

Rogers End

RADWINTER RD

Ashdon CP Sch

PH PO

RECTORY LANE

Ashdon

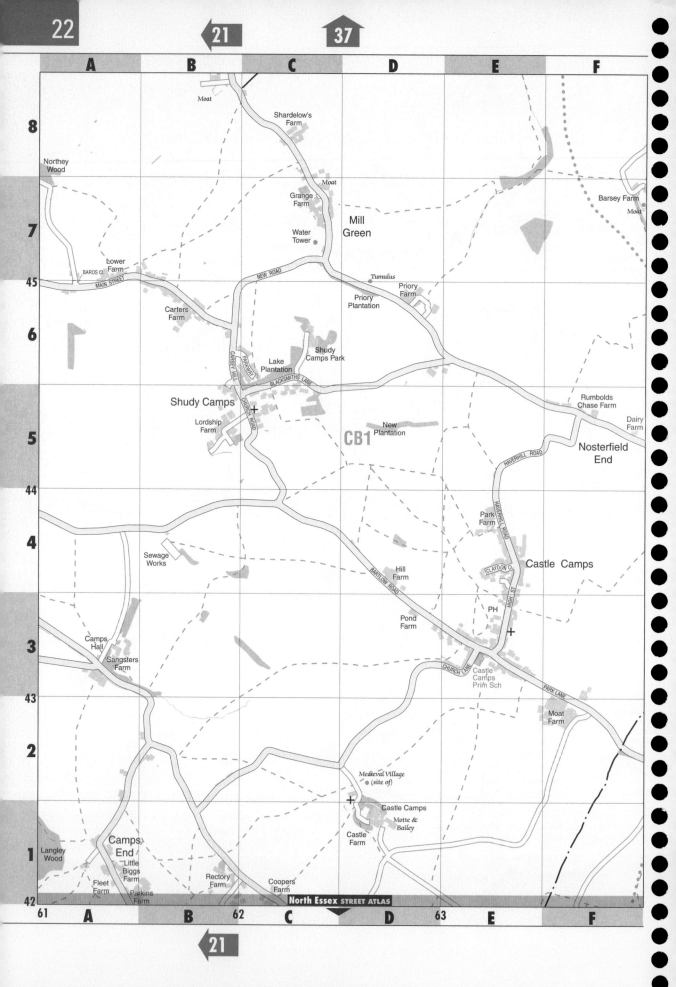

North Essex STREET ATLAS

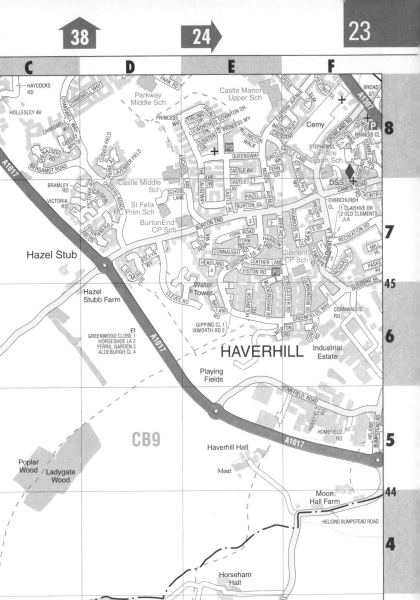

A B C D E F

Hanchet Hall

HAYCOCKS RD
HOLLESLEY AV

CHIMSWELL WAY
CHIMSWELL WAY

CASTLE WHITE

GRENADIER

BERGAMOT ROAD

BRAMLEY RD

VICTORIA RD

Barsey Groves

Duncey Plantation

Parkway Middle Sch

PARK RD

PRINCESS WY
STIRLING DR

LULWORTH DR

DUNSTER DR

CLOVER FIELD

LAVENDER FIELD

CHIVERS ROAD

CRISPIN

STRAWBERRY FIELDS

VICTORIA RD

PRINCESS WY

DOWNTON DR

PRINCESS WY

Castle Manor Upper Sch

Cemy

BROAD ST

A1307

Chestnut CL

ELM

GROVE

EASTERN AVENUE

BROADCROFT

Castle Middle Sch

St Felix RC Prim Sch

BurtonEnd CP Sch

Hazel Stub

Hazel Stubb Farm

SEYMOUR DR

BULLEN

QUEENSWAY

SCHOOL LANE

THE CAUSEWAY

SCHOOL LANE

THE

THE CW

CASTLE AV

CASTLE

AV

NORTH WK

FERN GR

CASTLE LANE

HAZEL CL

BURTON CL

ALLINGTON WALK

CASTLE LANE

ST BOTOLPH'S

PRIORY AV

HAZEL AVENUE

LAYER RD

CLEM

HL

PHS DR

Cemy

GRONLAND RD
DOWNS CR

Cemy

HL

DOWNS CRES

FRANCIS CL

DOWNS

STEPHEN CL

Stephen's Place
Farm Sch

DSS

CAMPS ROAD

DUDDERY RD

PUNTRY

OVERCHURCH CL

1 CLAYHIVE DR
2 OLD CLEMENTS LA

Clements CP Sch

RECREATION RD

MILL RD

ORCHARD CT

PASKE AV

CLARENDON RD

CLEMENTS LA

Burton End

YORK ROAD

CONNAUGHT RD

HARROW

WY

HEADLAND

4

LEATHER LANE

ELSTON RD

PO

2

GLOUCESTER RD

GREENFIELDS WAY

GREENFIELDS WAY

CORNWALLIS RD

GIPPING CL 1
IXWORTH RD 2

NORTON RD

45

7

6

Water Tower

ROPE WK

YORK WY

CLEVES RD

BUCKINGHAM RD

MAY RD

HOLBROOK

RD

HAVERHILL

Industrial Estate

E7
GREENWOOD CLOSE 1
HORSESHOE LA 2
YERRIL GARDEN 3
ALDEBURGH CL 4

A1017

A1017

Playing Fields

Haverhill Hall

Moat

HOMEFIELD ROAD

HOMEFIELD RD

HOMEFIELD RD

A1017

HELIONS BUMPSTEAD RD

5

44

4

CB9

Poplar Wood

Ladygate Wood

Moon Hall Farm

HELIONS BUMPSTEAD ROAD

Nosterfield Farm

Goodwards Farm

CB1

Horseham Hall

CAPS HILL

COPY HILL

Copy Farm

3

43

2

Board Barn Farm

Draper's Farm

DRAPERS LANE

Lancelots Farm

CAMPS ROAD

Wiggens Green

Whites Farm

Haven Farm

Wiggins Farm

Jacobs Farm

Pale Green

1

42

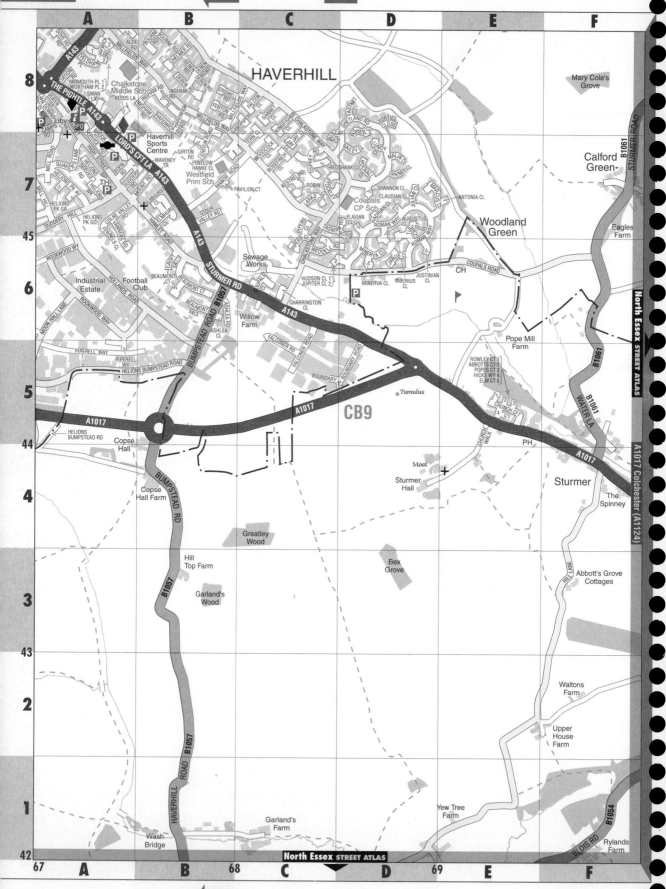

HAVERHILL

Mary Cole's Grove

Calford Green

Woodland Green

Eagles Farm

Pope Mill Farm

CB9

Sturmer

The Spinney

Copse Hall

Copse Hall Farm

Greatley Wood

Hill Top Farm

Garland's Wood

Bex Grove

Abbott's Grove Cottages

Waltons Farm

Upper House Farm

Yew Tree Farm

Wash Bridge

Garland's Farm

Rylands Farm

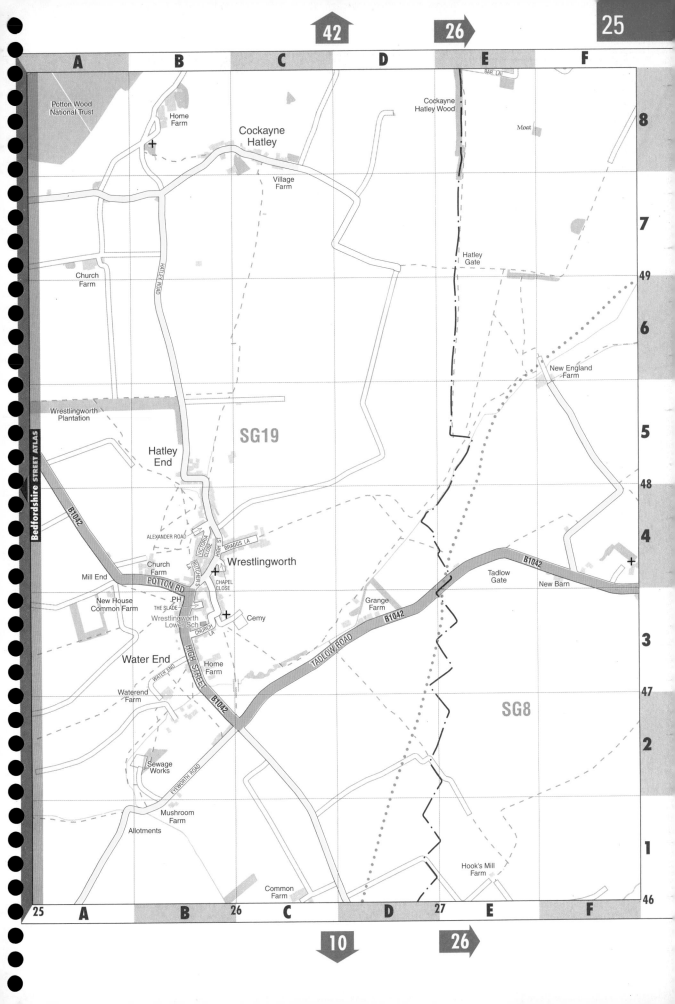

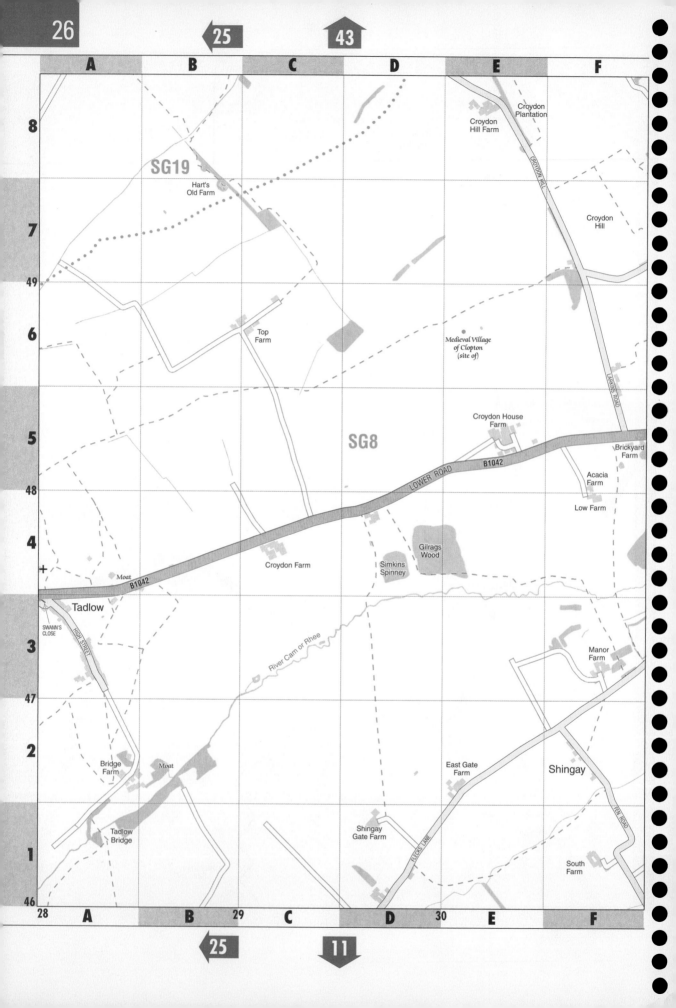

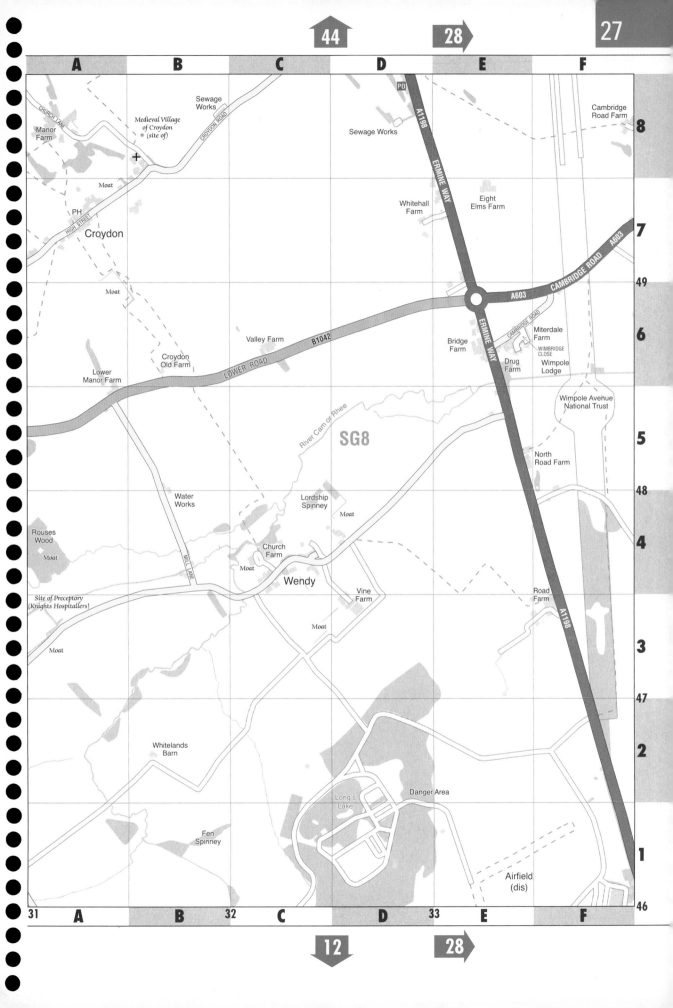

A B C D E F

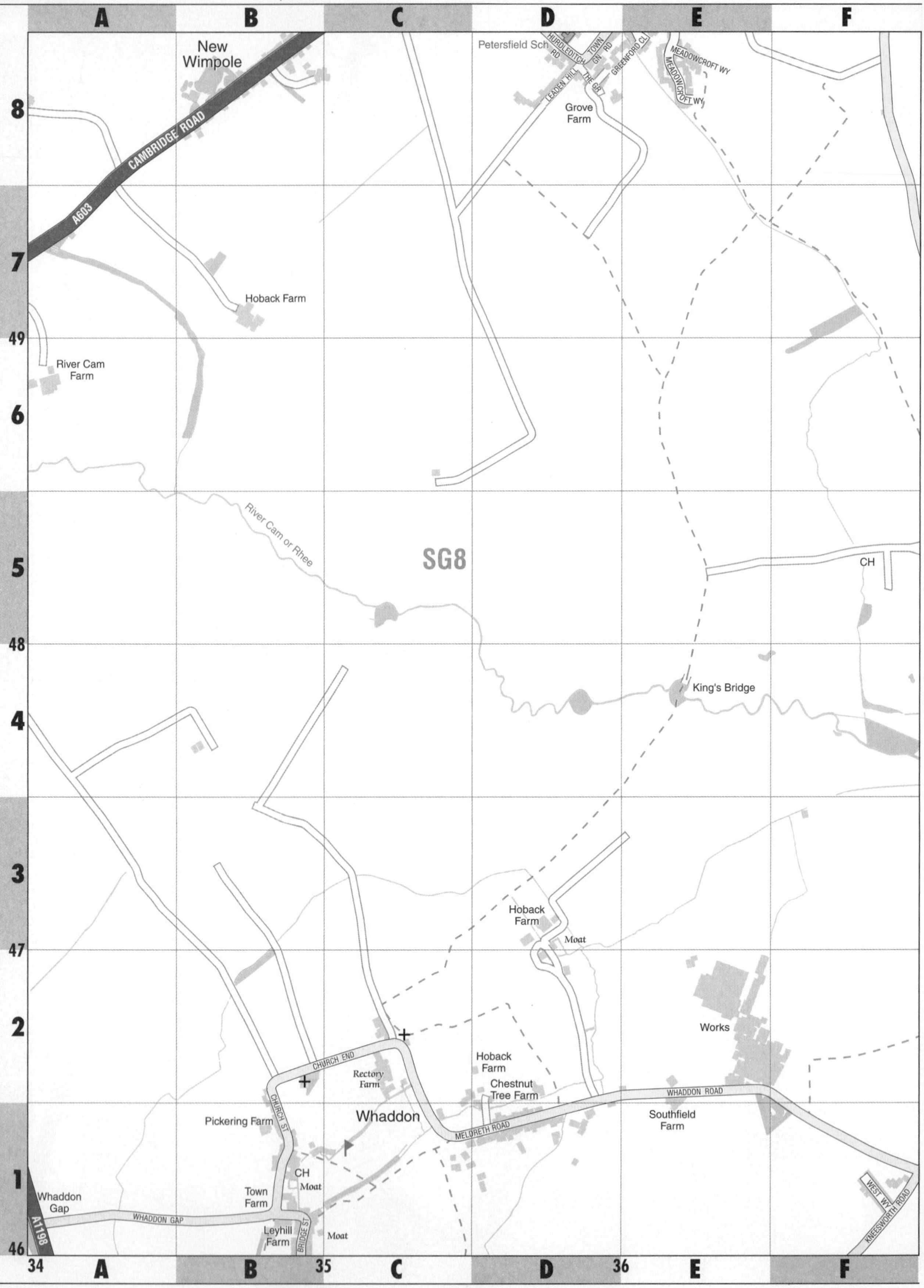

New Wimpole

Petersfield Sch

Grove Farm

MEADOWCROFT WY

MEADOWCROFT WY

GREENFORD CL

LEADEN HILL

THE GR

TOWN GN RD

AURALEDITCH

CAMBRIDGE ROAD

A603

8

Hoback Farm

7

49

River Cam Farm

6

River Cam or Rhee

SG8

CH

5

48

King's Bridge

4

3

Hoback Farm

Moat

47

Works

2

Hoback Farm

Church End

Rectory Farm

Chestnut Tree Farm

WHADDON ROAD

Whaddon

MELDRETH ROAD

Southfield Farm

Pickering Farm

CHURCH ST

CH

Moat

Town Farm

BRIDGE ST

Leyhill Farm

Moat

WEST WY

KNEESWORTH ROAD

1

Whaddon Gap

A1198

WHADDON GAP

46

34 | A | B | 35 | C | D | 36 | E | F

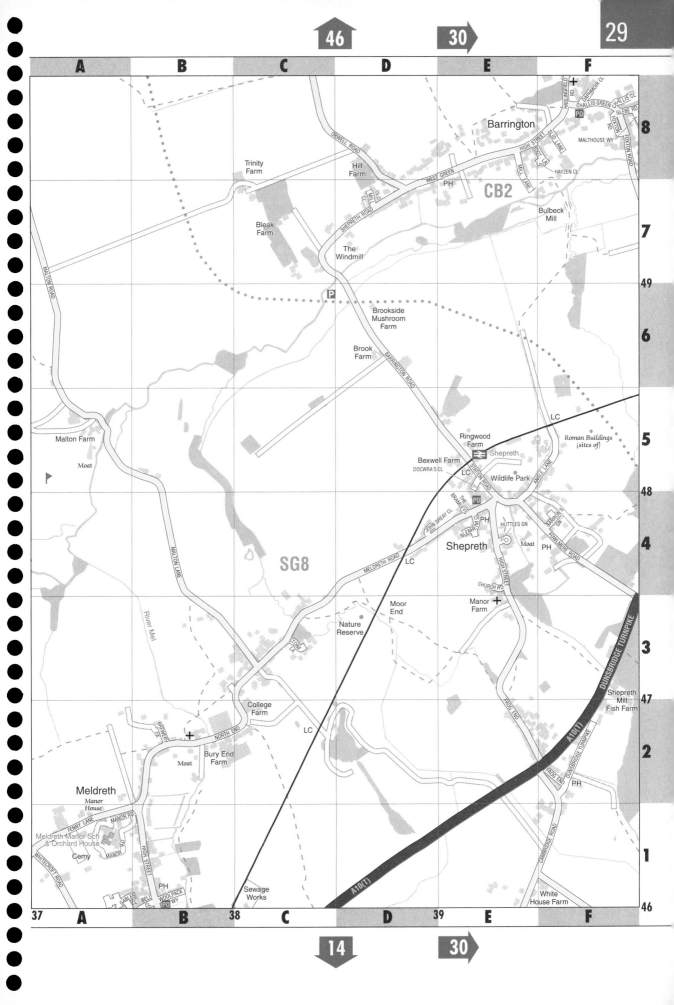

29
47

A B C D E F

8

7

49

6

CB2

5

Foxton

48

4

3

47

SG8

2

1

46

40 A B 41 C D 42 E F

29
15

BENDYSHE WY
GLEBE ROAD
MALTHOUSE WY
FOXTON ROAD
LC
Sewage Plant & Works
College Farm
BARRINGTON ROAD
River Cam or Rhee
Hoffers Brook Farm
ROYSTON RD
Hoffer Bridge
Manor Farm
Strip Lynchets
Rowley's Hill
CAMBRIDGE ROAD
BARRINGTON RD
LC
Foxton
A10(T)
HALL CL
STATION ROAD
Bury Farm
Moat
Mortimer's Farm
Foxton Prim Sch
BARONS LA
MORTIMERS LA
PH
Windmill
HIGH STREET
PO
ST LAURENCE RD
Foxton
Hoffer Brook
ROYSTON ROAD
Beech Tree Farm
MALTING LANE
ROWLANDS CL
ILLINGWORTH WY
HILLFIELD
Hill Farm
SHEPRETH ROAD
THE GN
WEST FIELD RD
Stocks Farm
CAXTON LANE
West Hill
FOWLMERE ROAD
Rushmoor Plantation
SHEPRETH ROAD
Field Farm
CAMBRIDGE ROAD
B1368
Cemy
North Farm
The Cottage
Lower Farm
LONG LANE
Lower Farm
Works
RAYNER'S CL
RECTORY LA
Home Farm
THRIPLOW ROAD
Fowlmere

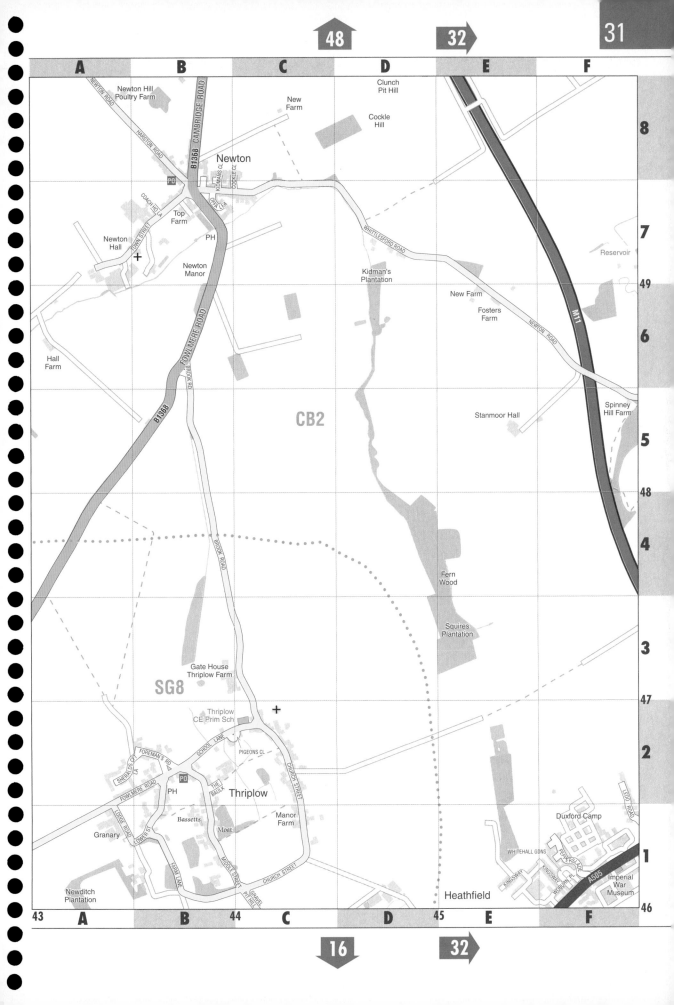

31
49

A B C D E F

8

WHITTLESFORD ROAD

Mill Farm

LC

A1301

Cemy

Sawston Village Coll

Liby

WOODLAND RD

WINDMILL CL

QUEENSWAY

EDINBURGH

DEAL GR

BABRAHAM ROAD

ASHLEY

CHURCHFIELD AVENUE

HOLME WY

THE LIMES

HILLSIDE

RIDE CL

DALE END

FIELD WY

WHITE FIELD WY

BELBIN WAY

ELDER CL

NEW ROAD

LUFFEN WAY

EVANS WAY

MARTINDALE

WEST MOOR AV

EVANS WY

MILNER CL

John Paxton Jun Sch

John Falkner Inf Sch

THE BAULKS PH

SELSINGEN WY

P

HAYFIELD AV

VICARAGE AVE

THE STAKINGS

MILL LANE

CHESTNUT CL

TOWN CL

RUBRYS RD

ORCHARD CL

CHURCH LA

BUTLERS WY

PO

PORTOBELLO LA

7

Wells Farm

Common Lane Farm

COMMON LANE

COMMON LANE

Sawston Hall

HIGH STREET

KINGFISHER CL

SHINGAY

PRINCE WILLIAM WY

49

Park Wood

Rayner's Grove

PH

Rayners Farm

SHELFORD ROAD

NEWTON RD

MIDDLEMOOR ROAD

NORTH ROAD

DSS

The Spike

MEADOWFIELD

GRANTA RD

SPRINGFIELD ROAD

BROOKFIELD RD

NORTH TP

NORTH FIELD CL

SOUTH TR

GLOVER CL

TANNERY RD

SILVER ST

RIDE

ROMAN

HAWTHORN AV

PARK RD

CHAMOIS CL

MAPLE

LONDON RD

PH

6

CHURCH CL

CHURCH CL

CHURCH LA

RADEGUNDS

Moat

LETTICE MARTIN CFT

William Westley CE Prim Sch

THE LAWN

MILL LANE

Whittlesford

MAYNARDS

MAYNARDS

HIGH ST

PO

CB2

Tannery

5

Middle Moor

WHIPPLETREE ROAD

MAYNARDS

VICARAGE LA

SCOTTS CO

FARM RI

ORCHARD TR

FARM LA

ASHMAN

Markings Farm

Moor Plantation

WEST END

WREN PK

Orchard Farm

Millfield Farm

DUXFORD ROAD

River Cam or Granta

A1301

Mill Farm

48

Stud Farm

4

M11

Hill Farm

HILL FARM ROAD

Station Rd West

STATION ROAD E

PH

P

Chapel

Whittlesford

MOORFIELD RD

MOORFIELD RD

Heritage Centre

Whittlesford Bridge Plantation

3

ROYSTON ROAD

A505

47

A505

2

10

BURMA RD

LEVEL

A505

Reservoir

M11

THE FIRS

LACEY'S WY

LACEY'S WY

LACEY'S WY

GREENACRES

GREEN STREET

CHAPEL LA

Moat

MILL LANE

TEMPLE

1

Imperial War Museum

Duxford Airfield

Duxford

THE RUSTONS

ELMS CL

ST JOHN'S STREET

College Farm

Duxford CE Com Prim Sch

MARGETS LA

Gravelpit Plantation

46

46 A B 47 C D 48 E F

A · B · C · D · E · F

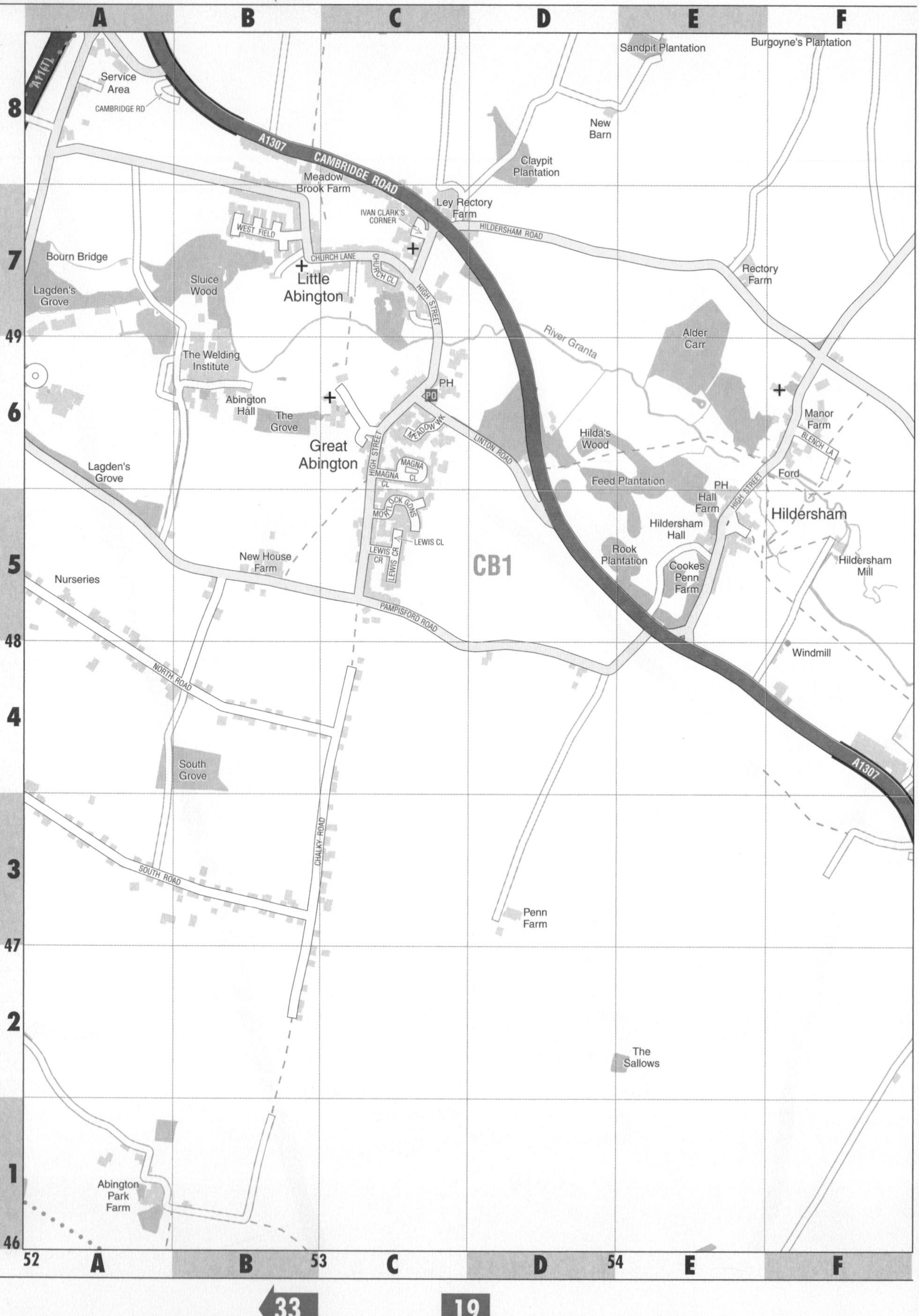

8

Service Area
CAMBRIDGE RD
A1307 CAMBRIDGE ROAD

Sandpit Plantation
Burgoyne's Plantation
New Barn
Claypit Plantation

Meadow Brook Farm
WEST FIELD
Ivan Clark's Corner
Ley Rectory Farm
HILDERSHAM ROAD

7

Bourn Bridge
Sluice Wood
CHURCH LANE
CH CL
Little Abington
HIGH STREET

Rectory Farm

49

Lagden's Grove
The Welding Institute
River Granta
Alder Carr

6

Abington Hall
The Grove
PH
PO
Great Abington
HIGH STREET
MEADOW WK
LINTON ROAD
Hilda's Wood

Manor Farm
BLENCH LA

Lagden's Grove
MAGNA CL
MAGNA CL
MATLOCK GDNS
MO
LEWIS CL
Feed Plantation
PH
Hall Farm
Ford
HIGH STREET
Hildersham

5

Nurseries
New House Farm
LEWIS CR
LEWIS CL
CB1
Rook Plantation
Hildersham Hall
Cookes Penn Farm
Hildersham Mill

PAMPISFORD ROAD

48

NORTH ROAD
Windmill

4

South Grove

3

CHALKY ROAD
SOUTH ROAD
Penn Farm

47

2

The Sallows

1

Abington Park Farm

46

52 · A · B · 53 · C · D · 54 · E · F

A1307

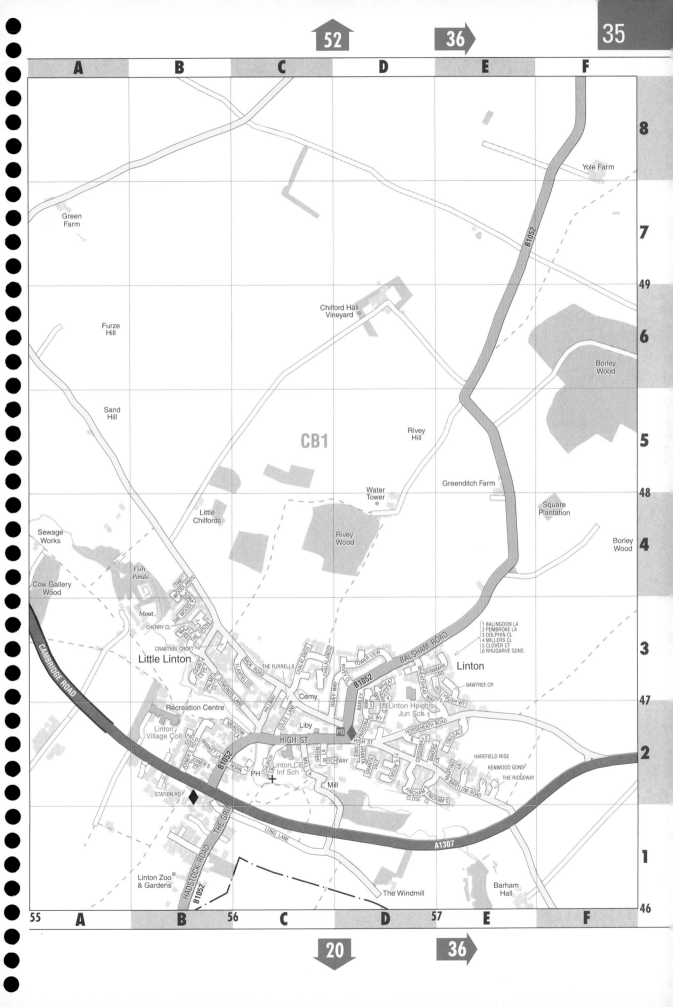

A B C D E F

8

Water Tower

Balsham Wood

MILL ROAD

Bottle Hall

7

Icknield Way Path

49

Chalk Pit (dis)

6

Borley Wood

Sewage Works

WEBB'S ROAD

5

CB1

Mark's Grave

Ford

Streetly Hall

48

4

Borley Wood

Horseheath Lodge

Heath Farm

3

A1307

LINTON RD

PH

A1307

47

2

A1307

Crofts Wood

Point to Point Racecourse

1

46

58 A B 59 C D 60 E F

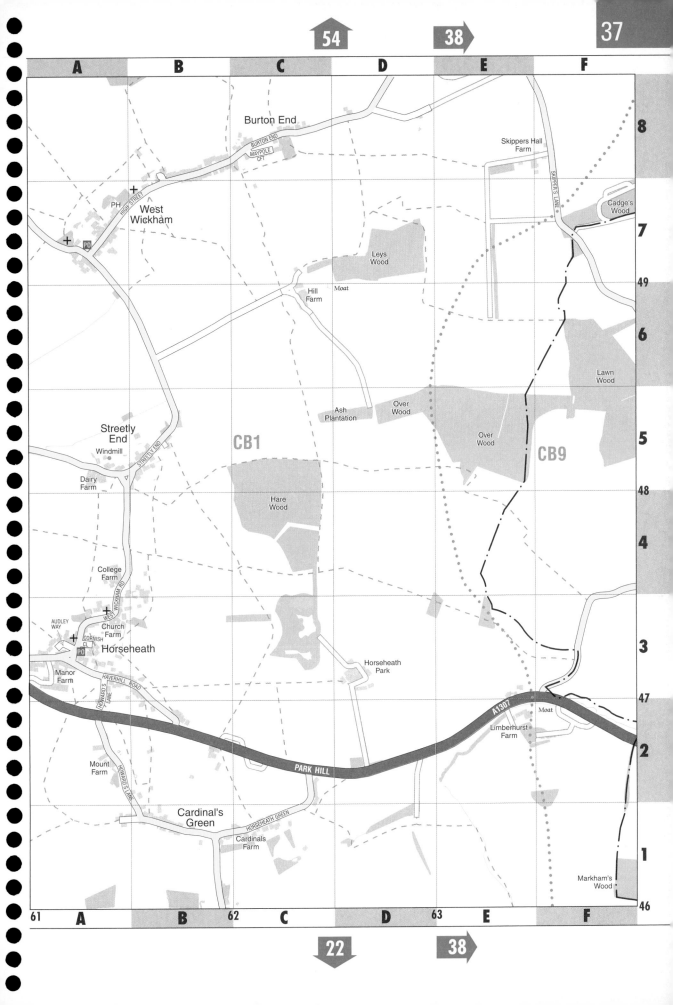

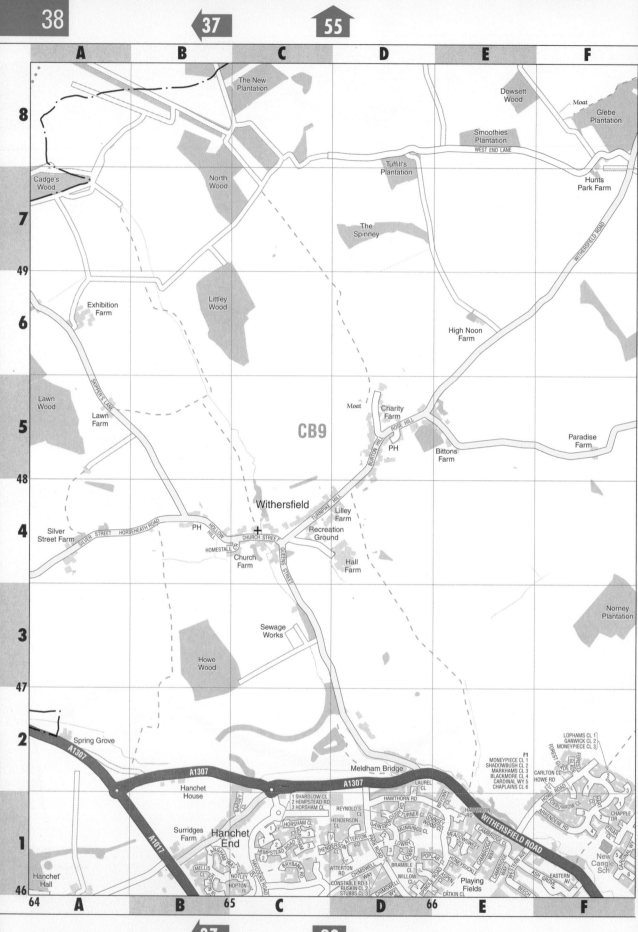

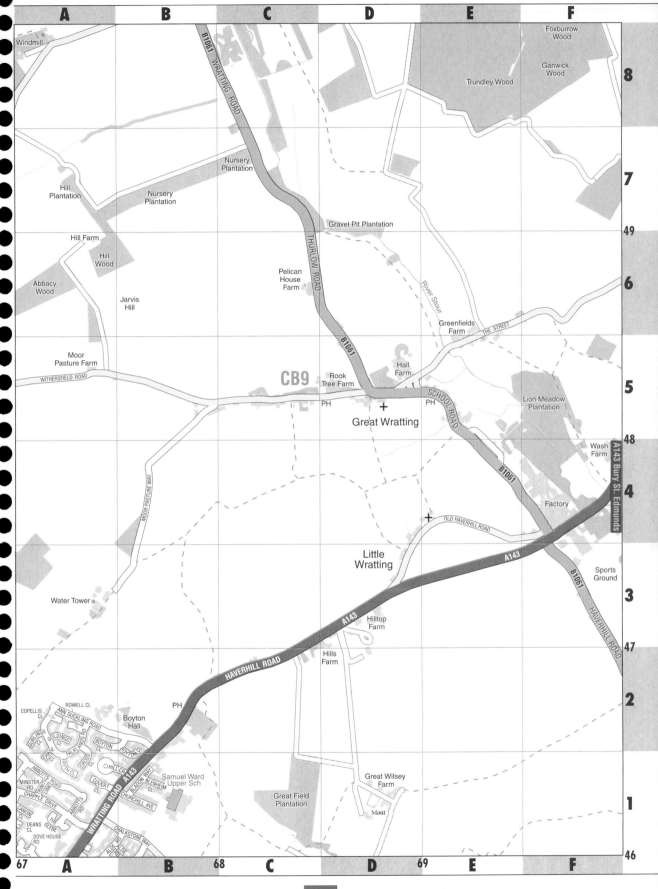

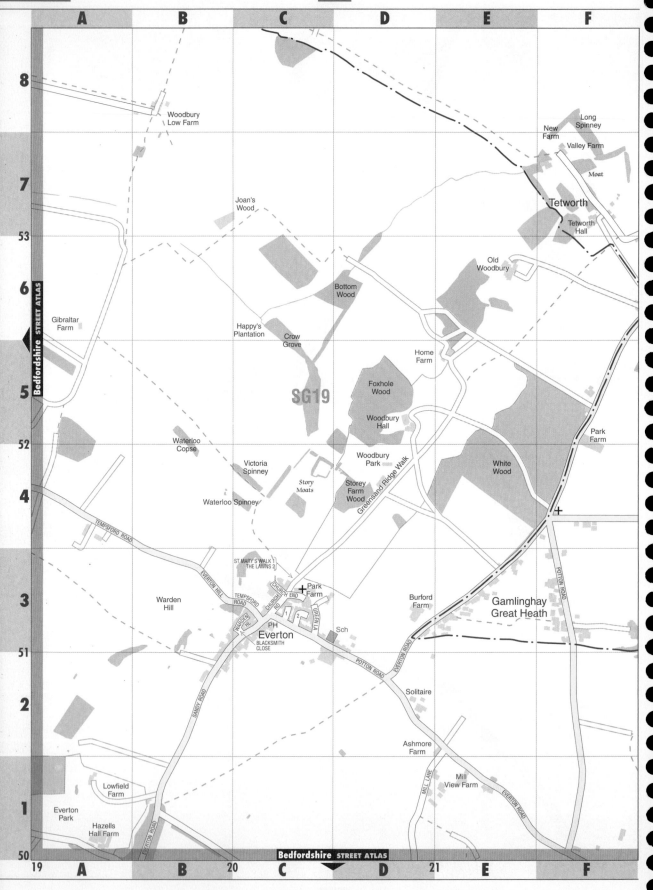

A B C D E F

8

Woodbury
Low Farm

New
Farm

Long
Spinney

Valley Farm

Moat

7

Joan's
Wood

Tetworth

53

Tetworth
Hall

Old
Woodbury

6

Gibraltar
Farm

Bottom
Wood

Happy's
Plantation

Crow
Grove

Home
Farm

5

SG19

Foxhole
Wood

Woodbury
Hall

52

Waterloo
Copse

Victoria
Spinney

Woodbury
Park

Park
Farm

White
Wood

Storey
Moats

Storey
Farm
Wood

Greensand Ridge Walk

4

TEMPSFORD ROAD

Waterloo Spinney

ST MARY'S WALK 1
THE LAWNS 2

Park
Farm

Burford
Farm

Gamlinghay
Great Heath

3

Warden
Hill

EVERTON HILL

TEMPSFORD ROAD

CHURCH RD

CHURCH END

GREEN LA

1 2

Sch

WARDEN HIL

PH

Everton

BLACKSMITH
CLOSE

EVERTON ROAD

POTTON ROAD

51

Solitaire

2

SANDY ROAD

Ashmore
Farm

MILL LANE

Mill
View Farm

EVERTON ROAD

POTTON ROAD

1

Lowfield
Farm

Everton
Park

EVERTON ROAD

Hazells
Hall Farm

50

19 A B 20 C D 21 E F

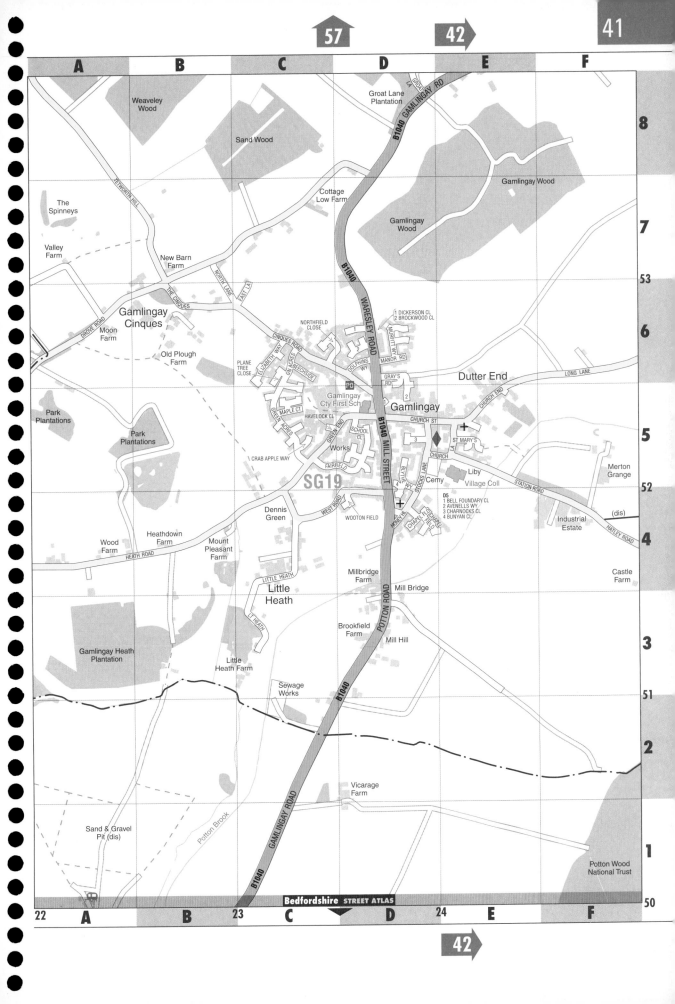

A B C D E F

8

7

53

6

5

52

4

3

51

2

1

50

Weaveley
Wood

Sand Wood

Groat Lane
Plantation

B1040 GAMLINGAY RD

GROAT LA

Gamlingay Wood

Gamlingay
Wood

TETWORTH HILL

Cottage
Low Farm

The
Spinneys

Valley
Farm

New Barn
Farm

THE CINQUES

NORTH LANE

EAST LA

B1040

WARESLEY ROAD

1 DICKERSON CL
2 BROCKWOOD CL

Gamlingay
Cinques

DROVE ROAD

Moon
Farm

Old Plough
Farm

NORTHFIELD
CLOSE

CINQUES ROAD

ELIZABETH WAY

GN ACRES

BEECHSIDE

DOLPHINS WY

MURRITT WY

MANOR RD

Dutter End

LONG LANE

PLANE
TREE
CLOSE

GRAY'S
RD

CHURCH END

Gamlingay
Cty First Sch

PO

Park
Plantations

GREEN END

MAPLE CT

HAVELOCK CL

GREEN ACRES

SCHOOL
CL

B1040 MILL STREET

Gamlingay

CHURCH ST

3

ST MARY'S
CHURCH

Merton
Grange

Park
Plantations

CRAB APPLE WAY

Works

FAIRFIELD

BLYTHE WY

STOCKS LANE

Cemy

Liby
Village Coll

STATION ROAD

52

SG19

Dennis
Green

WEST ROAD

WOOTON FIELD

CHAPEL FLD

CHURCH FLD

D5
1 BELL FOUNDARY CL
2 AVENELLS WY
3 CHARNOCKS CL
4 BUNYAN CL

(dis)

HATLEY ROAD

Industrial
Estate

Wood
Farm

Heathdown
Farm

Mount
Pleasant
Farm

HEATH ROAD

MOLE HL

4

Castle
Farm

Little
Heath

LITTLE HEATH

Millbridge
Farm

Mill Bridge

POTTON ROAD

LT HEATH

Brookfield
Farm

Mill Hill

Gamlingay Heath
Plantation

Little
Heath Farm

Sewage
Works

B1040

Vicarage
Farm

Potton Wood
National Trust

Sand & Gravel
Pit (dis)

Potton Brook

GAMLINGAY ROAD

B1040

A B C D E F

8

7

53

6

Long Lane

Allotments

5

SG19

52

4

Hatley Road

Castle Farm

Newlands Buildings

Fuller's Hill Farm

Crooked Billet Farm

Model Farm

Church Farm

BALK LANE

3

51

Dower House

BAR LANE

Hatley Park

2

Wood Farm

Cockayne Hatley Wood

BAR LANE

1

Potton Wood National Trust

50

BUFF LANE

25 A B 26 C D 27 E F

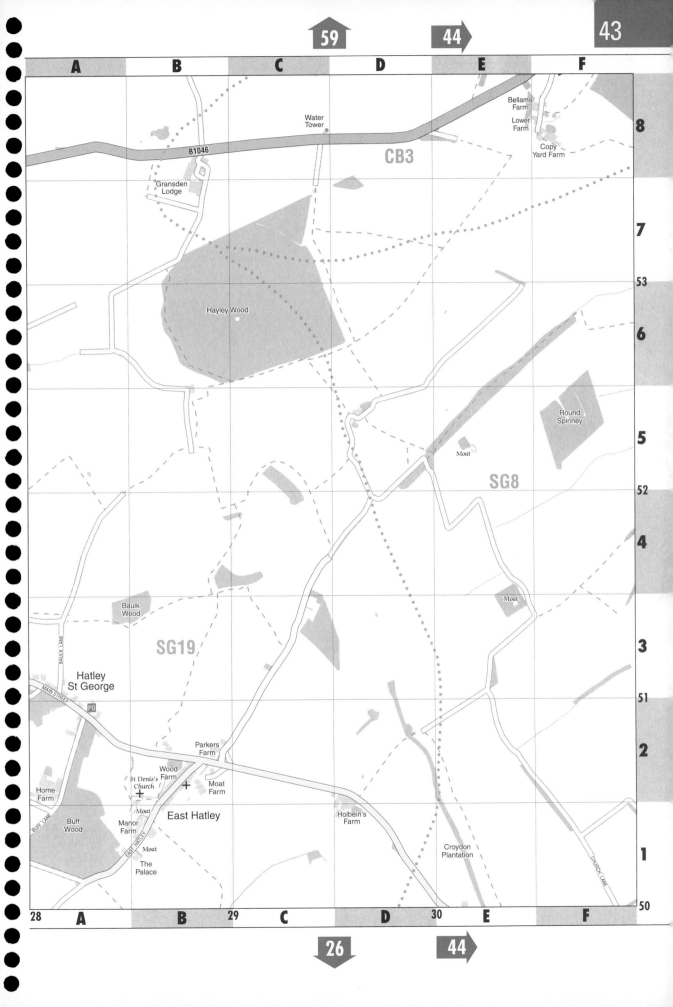

A   B   C   D   E   F

8
7
53
6
5
52
4
3
51
2
1
50

Water
Tower

Bellams
Farm

Lower
Farm

B1046

Copy
Yard Farm

CB3

Gransden
Lodge

Hayley Wood

Round
Spinney

Moat

SG8

Baulk
Wood

Moat

SG19

BAULK LANE

Hatley
St George

MAIN STREET

PO

Parkers
Farm

Wood
Farm

St Denis's
Church

Moat
Farm

Home
Farm

BUFF LANE

Buff
Wood

Manor
Farm

Moat

EAST HATLEY

East Hatley

Moat

Holbein's
Farm

Croydon
Plantation

CHURCH LANE

The
Palace

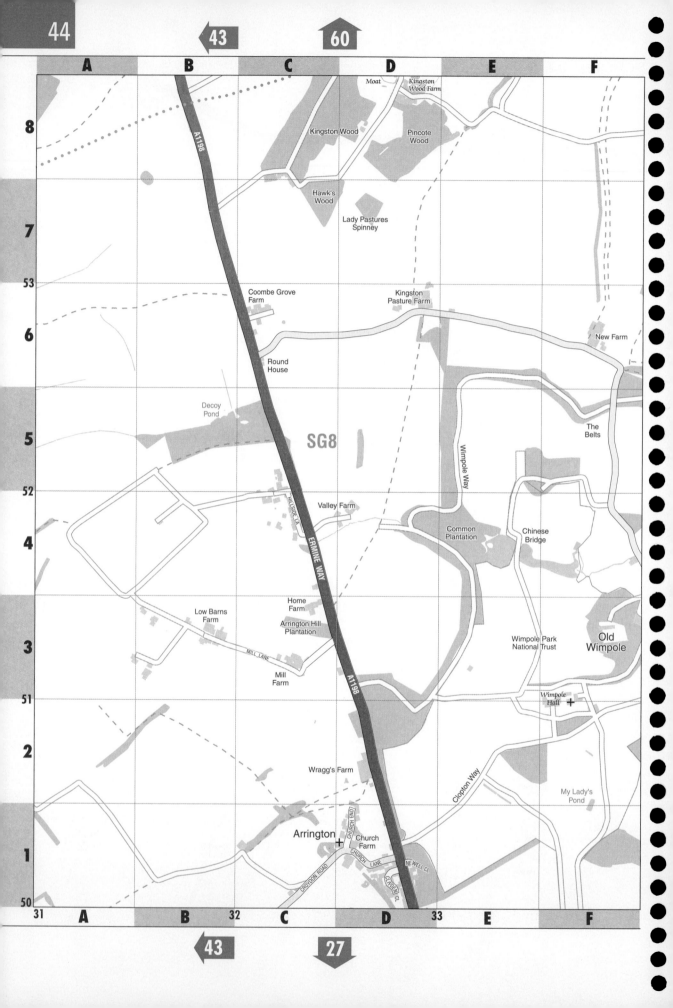

A B C D E F

8

53

7

6

52

5

4

52

3

51

2

1

50

31 A B 32 C D 33 E F

Moat

Kingston
Wood Farm

Kingston Wood

Pincote
Wood

Hawk's
Wood

Lady Pastures
Spinney

Coombe Grove
Farm

Kingston
Pasture Farm

New Farm

Round
House

The
Belts

Decoy
Pond

SG8

Wimpole Way

Valley Farm

Common
Plantation

Chinese
Bridge

Old
Wimpole

Low Barns
Farm

Home
Farm

Arrington Hill
Plantation

Wimpole Park
National Trust

MILL LANE

Mill
Farm

Wimpole
Hall

Wragg's Farm

Clopton Way

My Lady's
Pond

Arrington

Church
Farm

CROYDON ROAD

CHURCH END

CHURCH LANE

NEWELL CL.

A1198

ERMINE WAY

HILLSIDE LA.

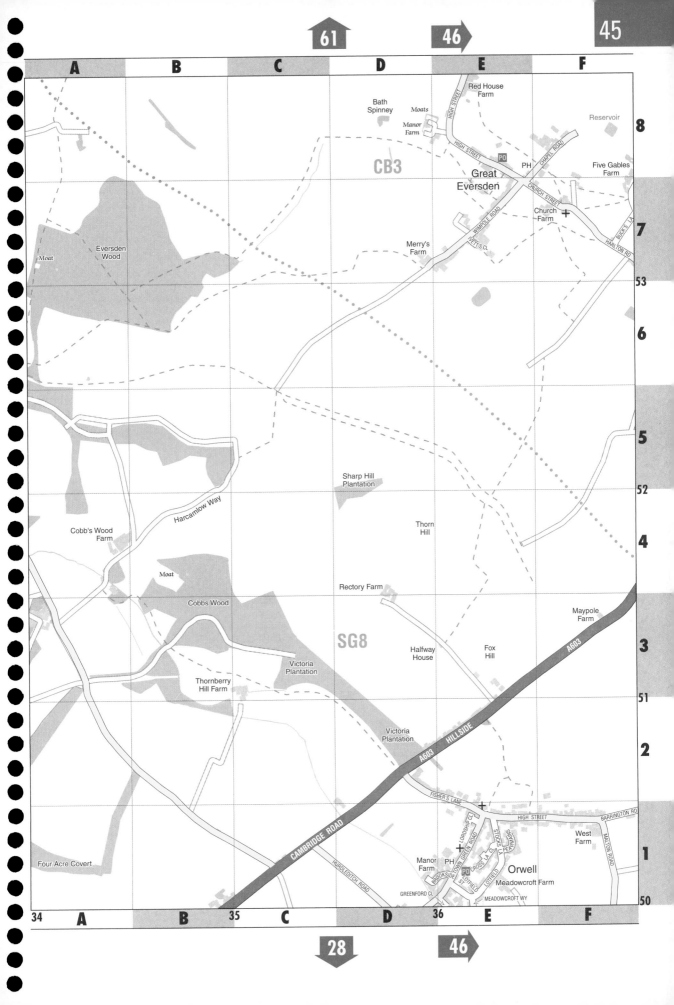

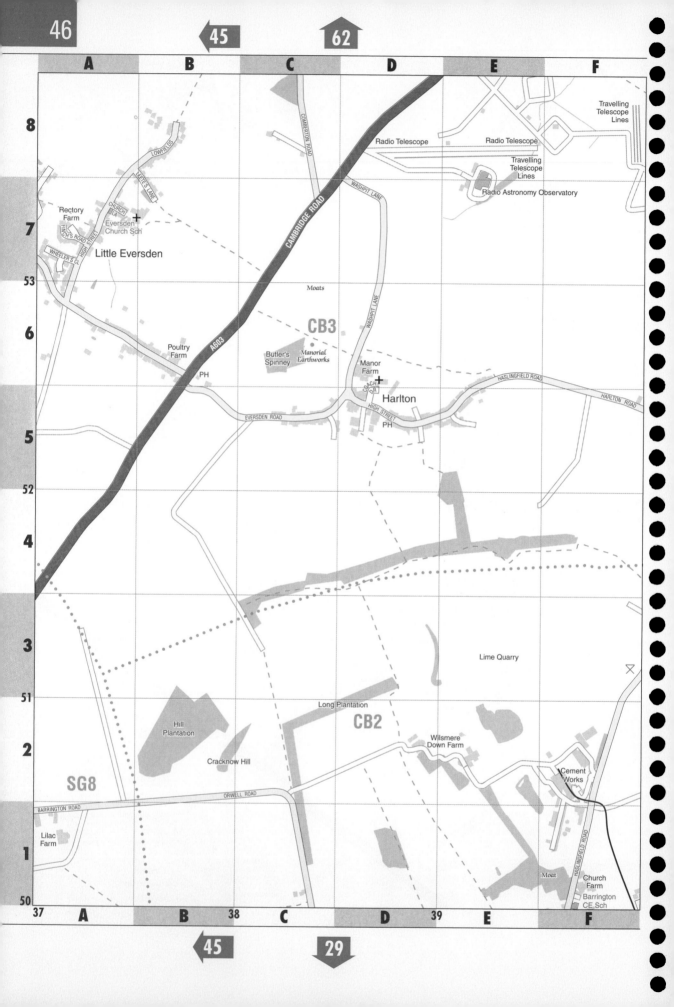

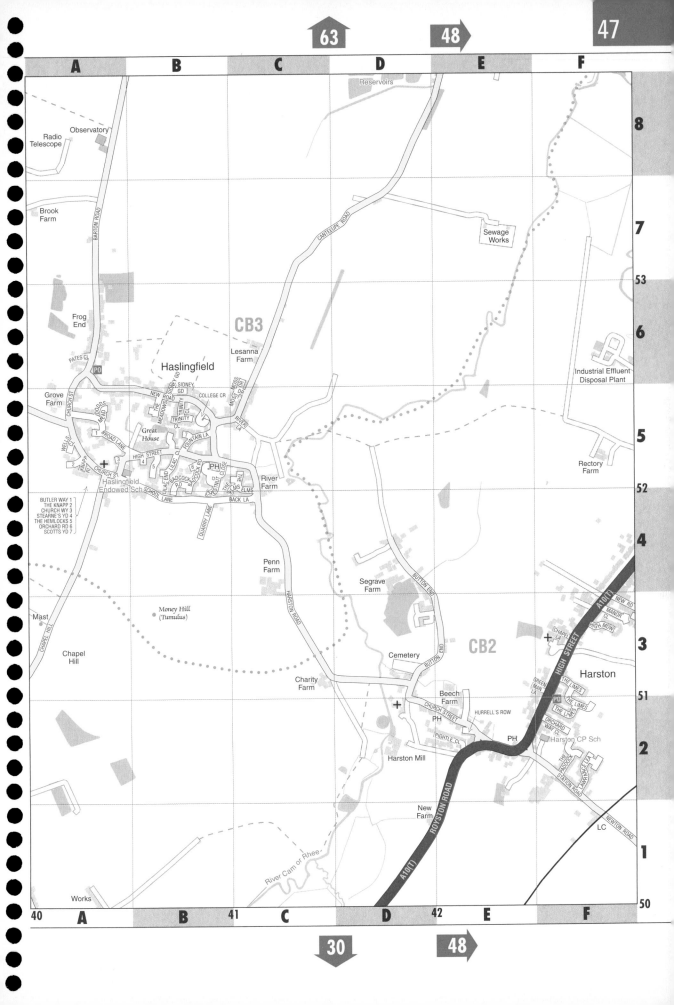

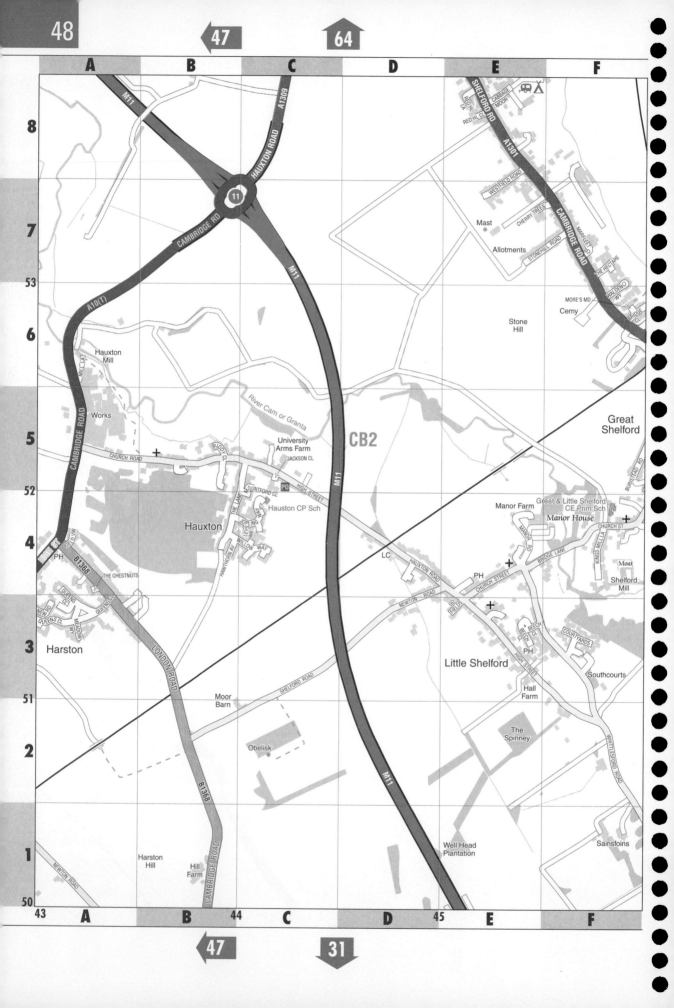

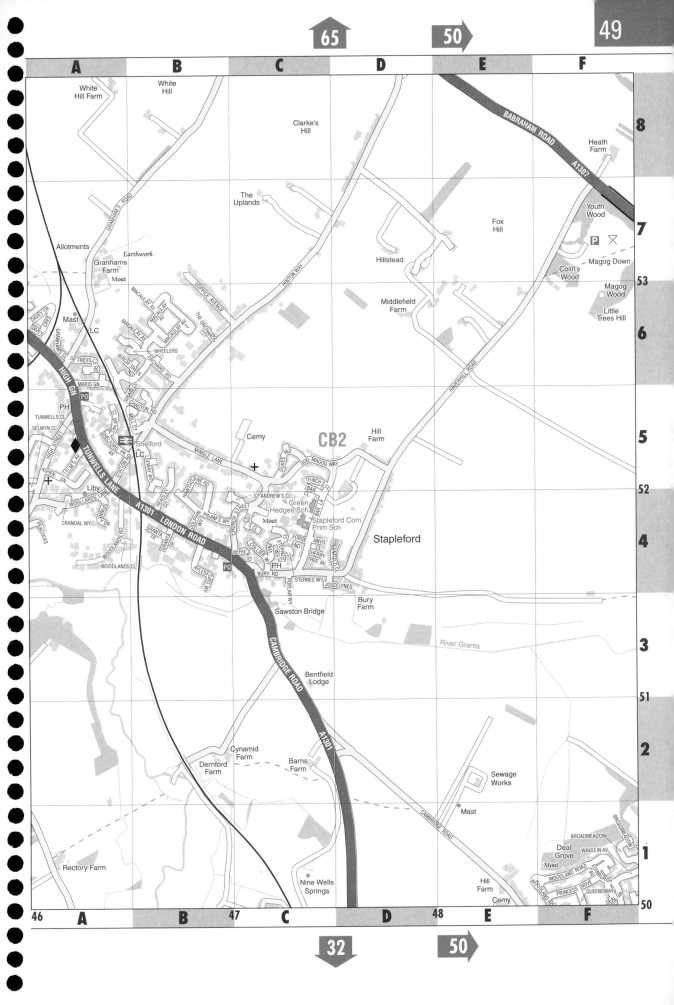

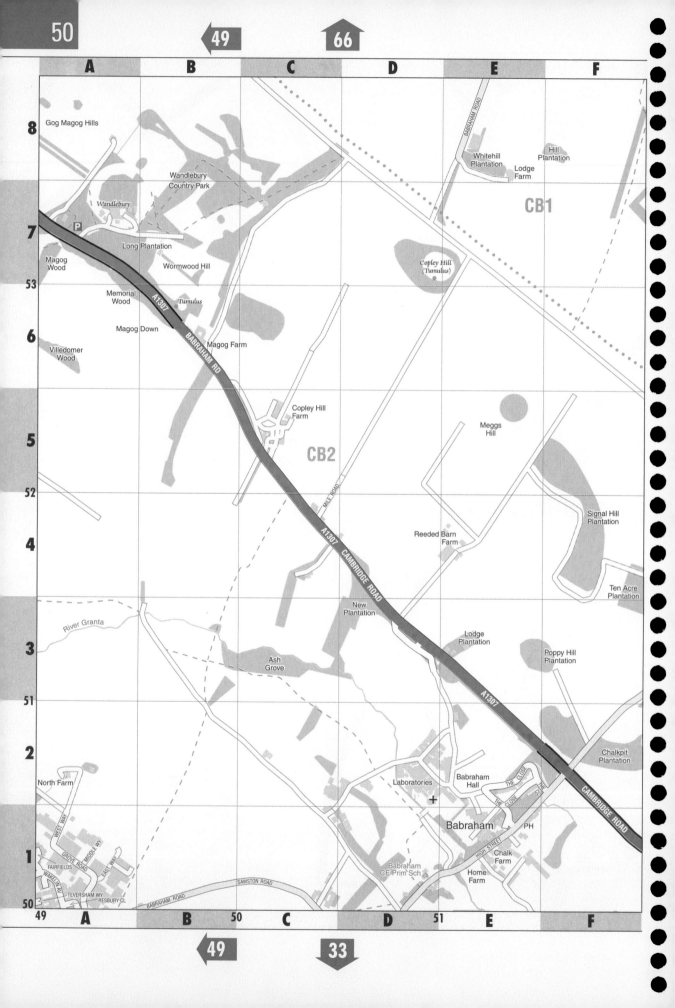

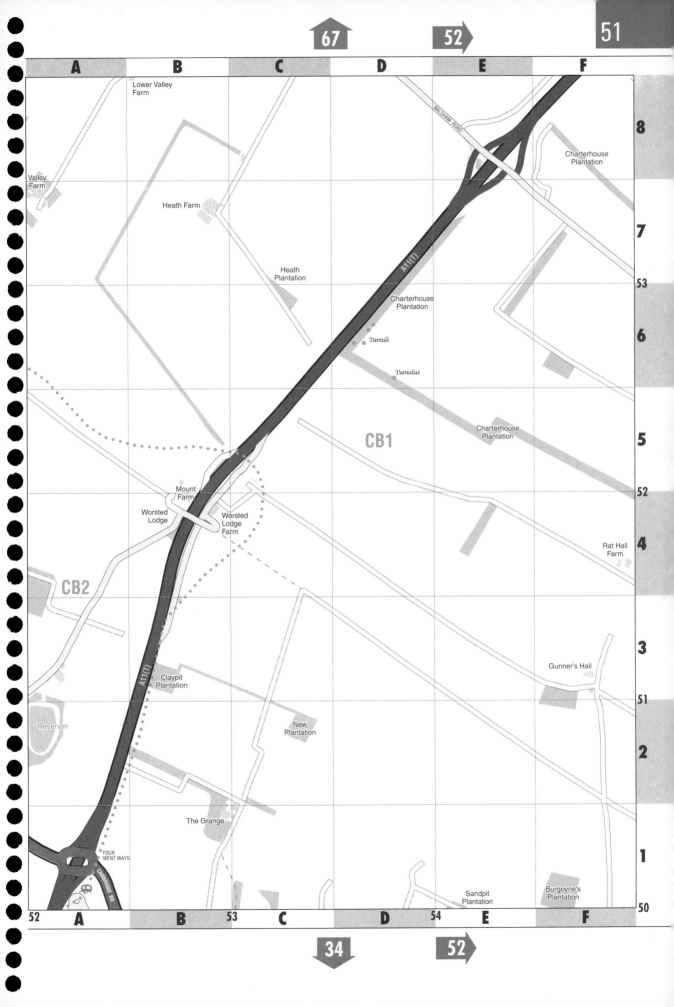

A B C D E F

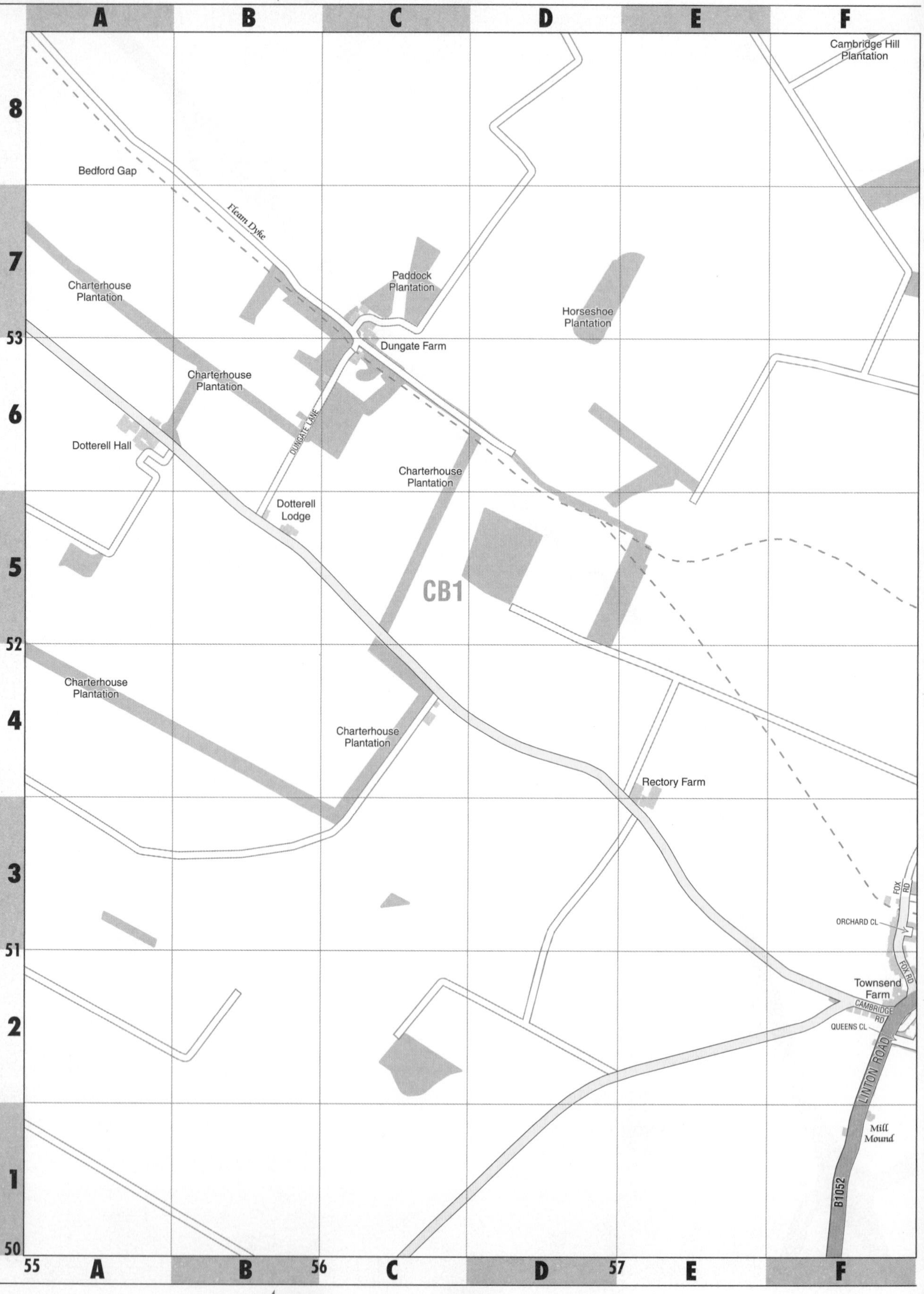

8

Cambridge Hill
Plantation

Bedford Gap

Fleam Dyke

7

Charterhouse
Plantation

Paddock
Plantation

Horseshoe
Plantation

53

Dungate Farm

Charterhouse
Plantation

6

Dotterell Hall

DUNGATE LANE

Charterhouse
Plantation

Dotterell
Lodge

5

CB1

52

Charterhouse
Plantation

4

Charterhouse
Plantation

Rectory Farm

3

FOX RD

ORCHARD CL

51

Townsend
Farm

CAMBRIDGE RD

2

QUEENS CL

FOX RD

LINTON ROAD

Mill
Mound

1

B1052

50

55 A B 56 C D 57 E F

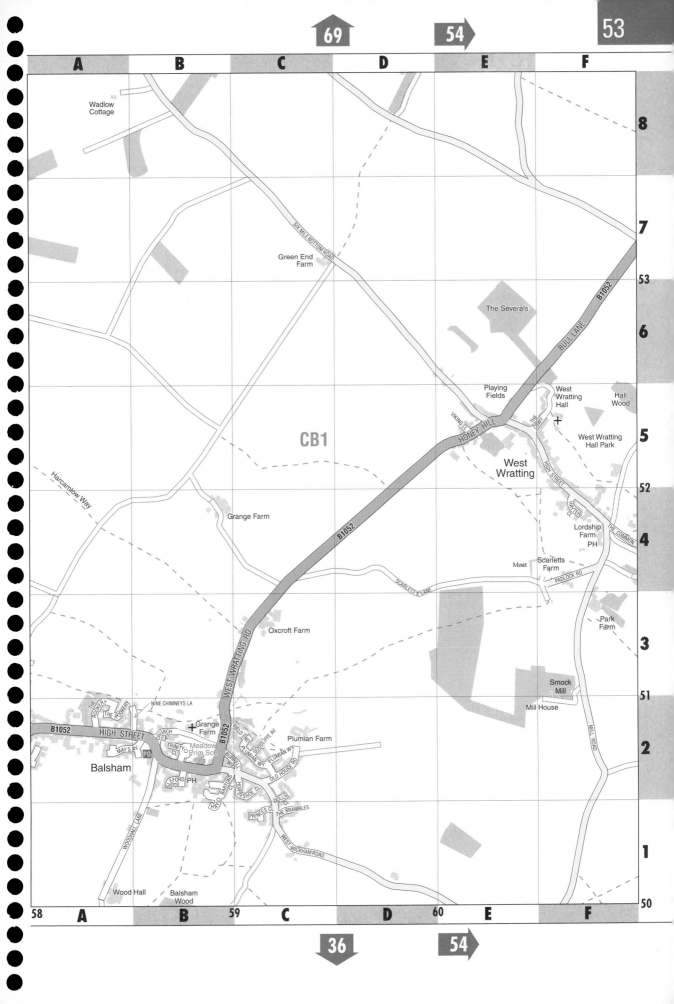

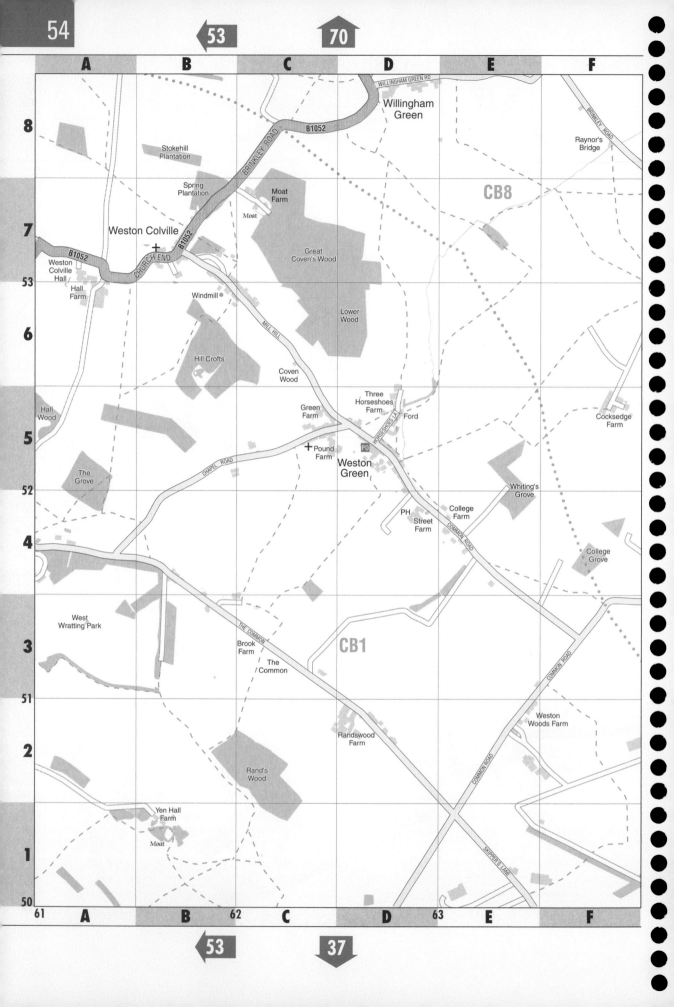

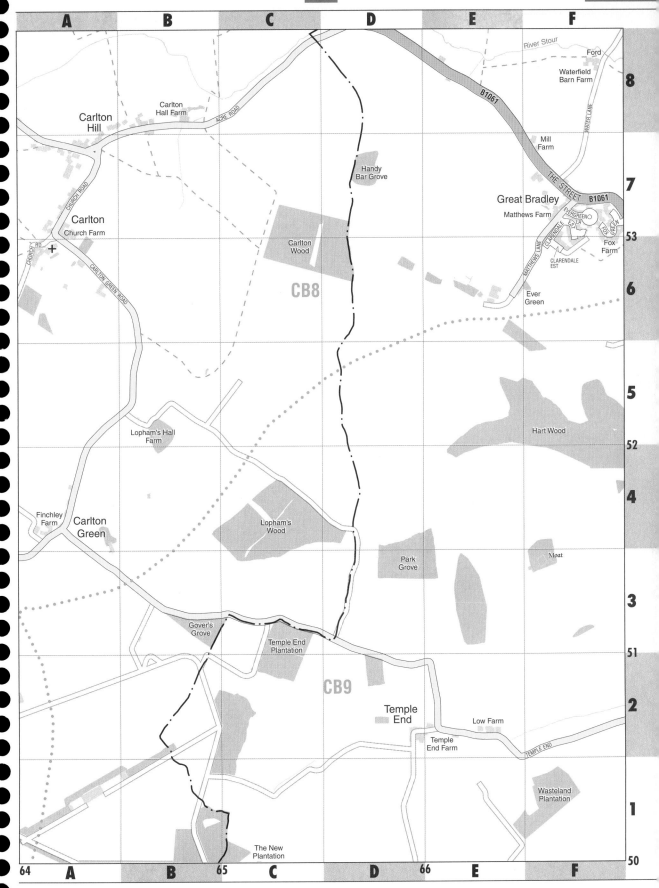

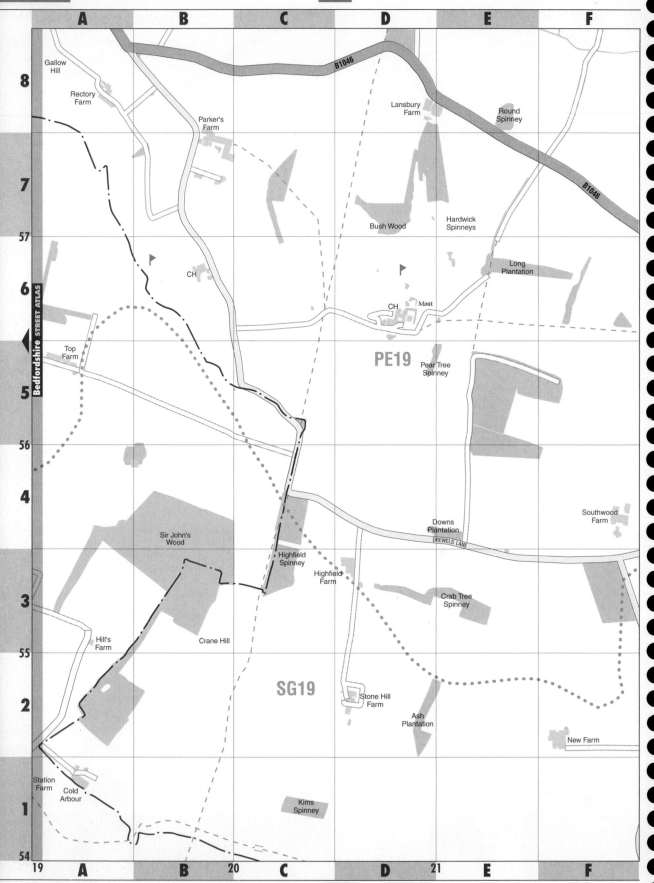

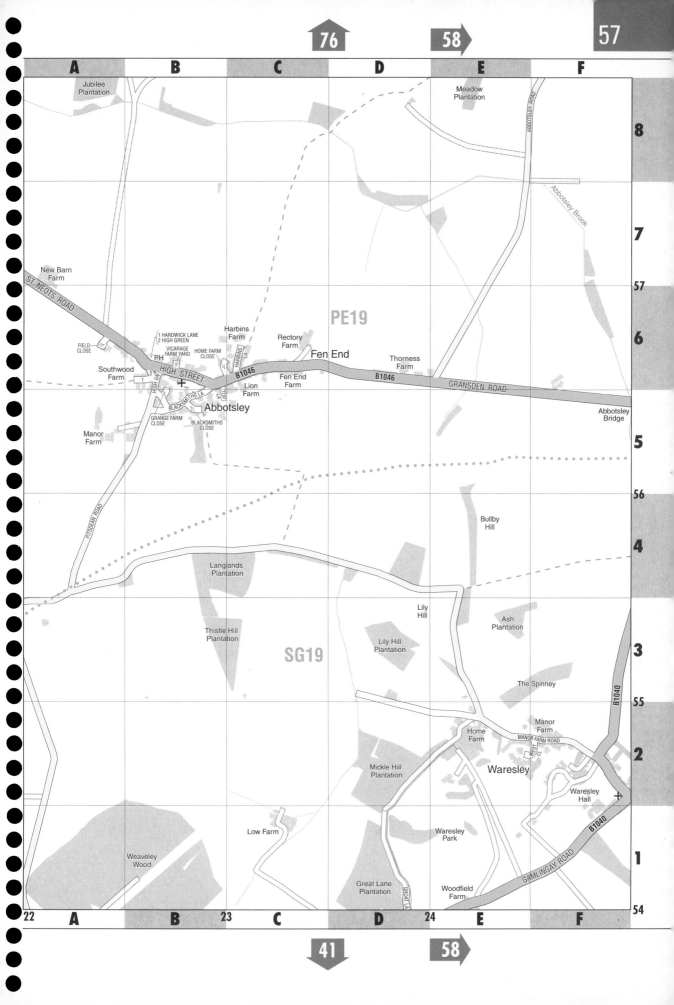

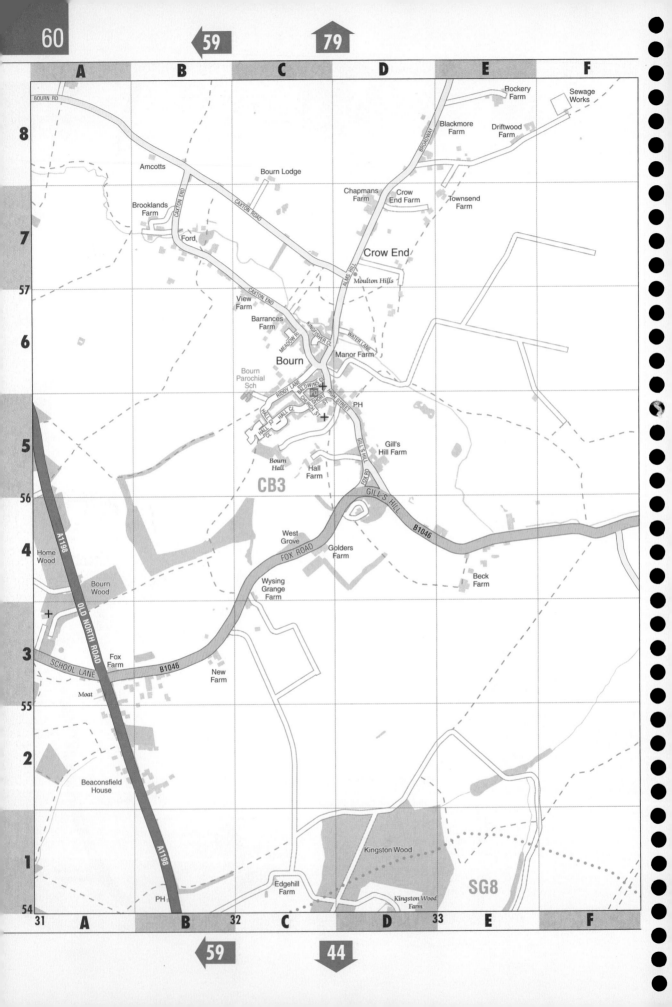

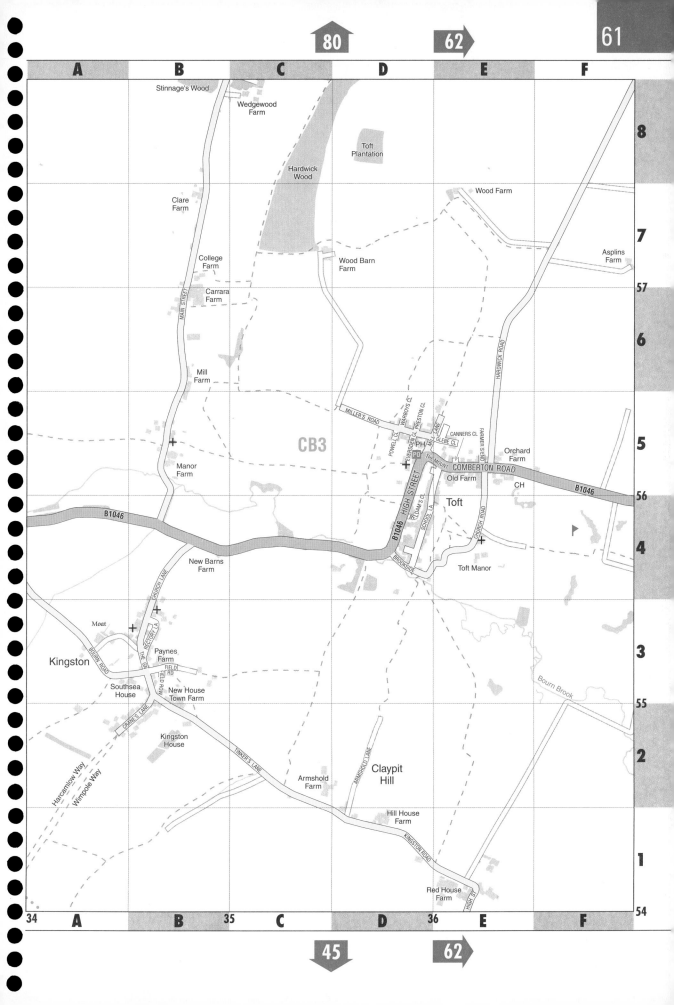

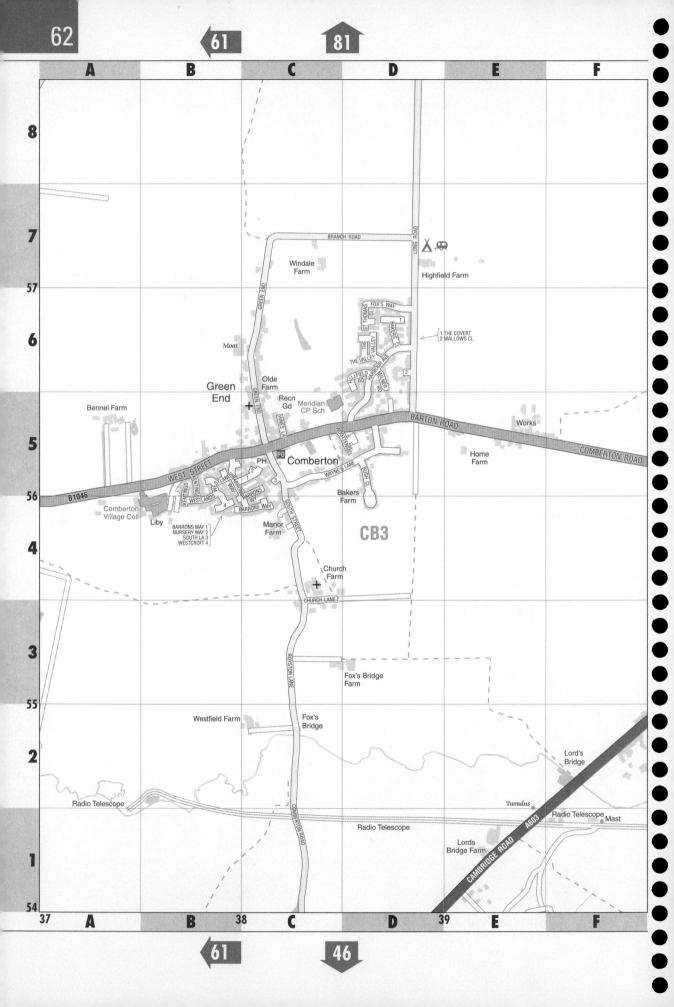

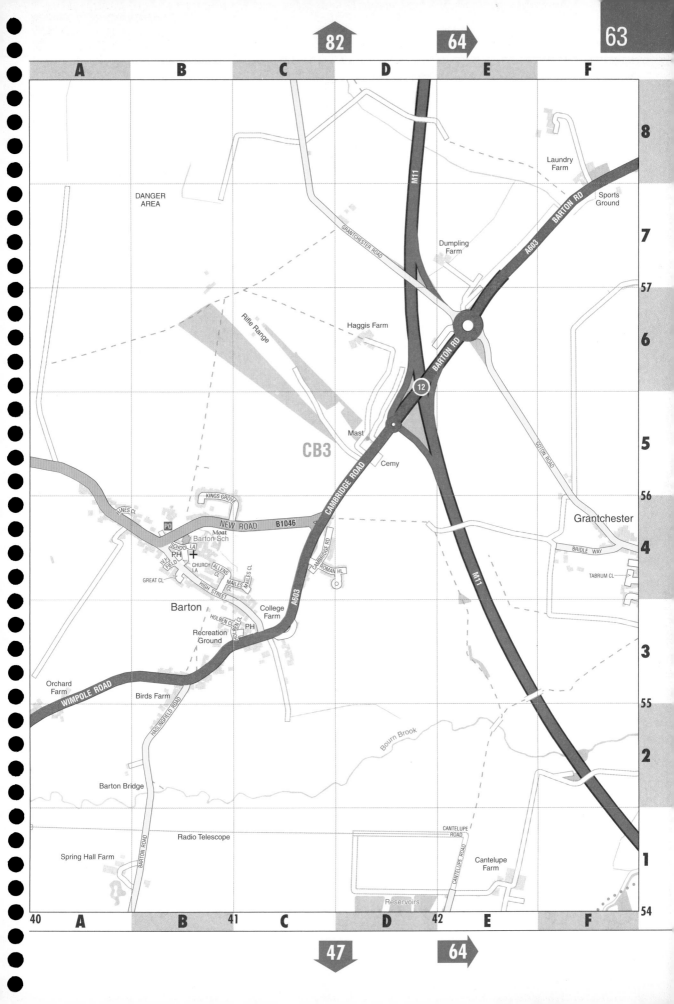

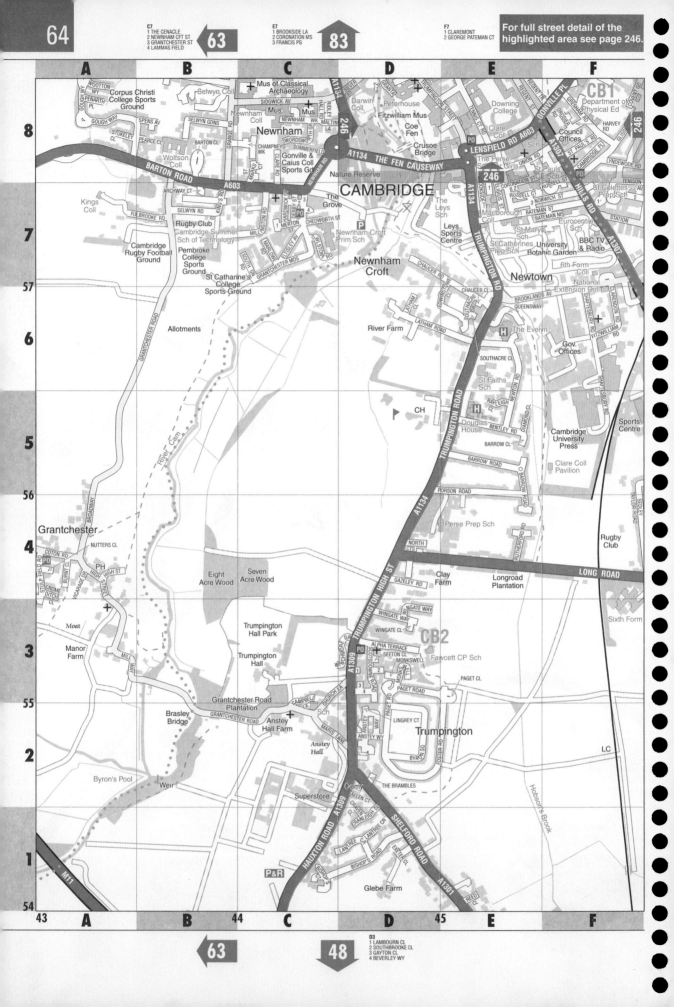

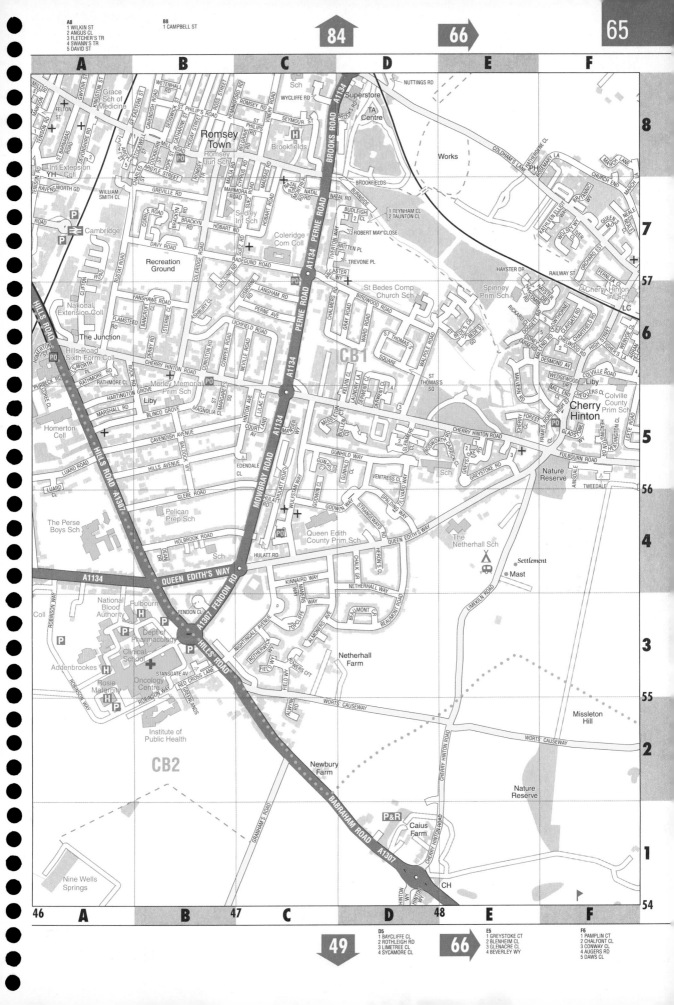

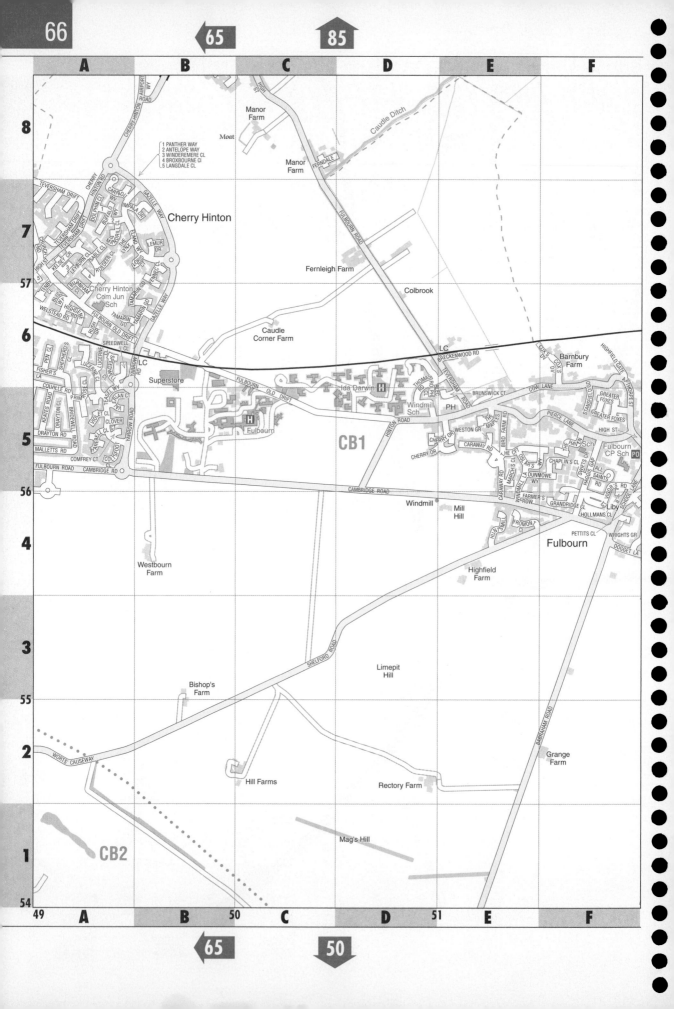

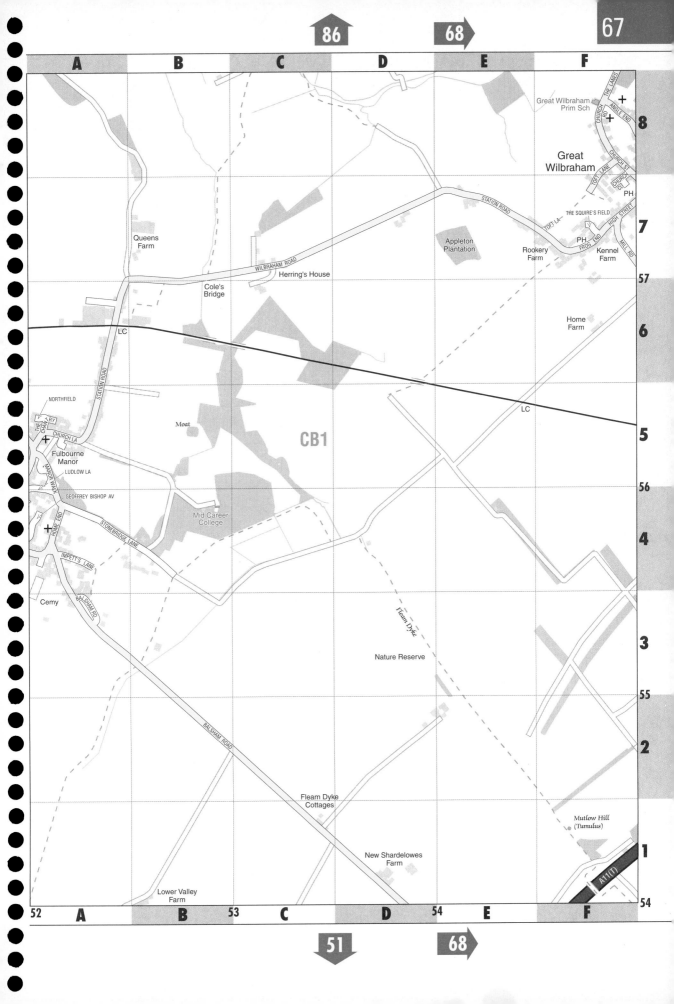

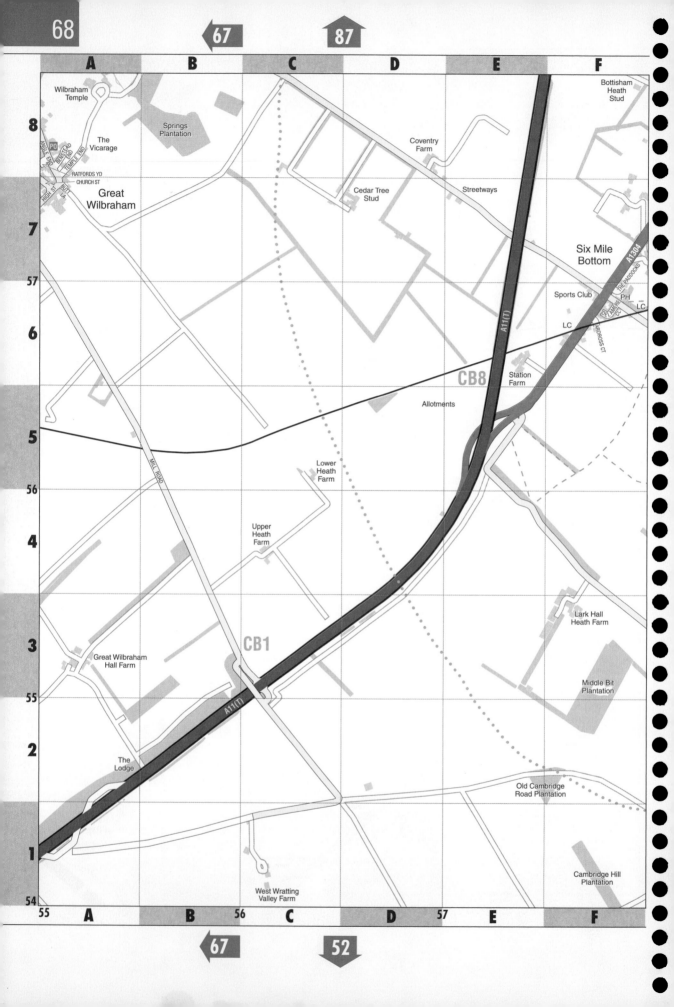

A B C D E F

8

Wilbraham
Temple

Springs
Plantation

The
Vicarage

Coventry
Farm

Bottisham
Heath
Stud

Cedar Tree
Stud

Streetways

ANGLE END
BENNELL END
TEMPLE END
RATFORDS YD
CHURCH ST
HIGH ST
BELL
PO

Great
Wilbraham

7

57

Six Mile
Bottom

A1304

Sports Club

PH

DEVANBRE CT
THE PADDOCKS
CT
LC

6

LC

ARDROSS CT

CB8

A11(T)

Station
Farm

Allotments

5

MILL ROAD

Lower
Heath
Farm

56

Upper
Heath
Farm

4

Lark Hall
Heath Farm

3

CB1

Great Wilbraham
Hall Farm

Middle Bit
Plantation

55

A11(T)

2

The
Lodge

Old Cambridge
Road Plantation

1

Cambridge Hill
Plantation

54

West Wratting
Valley Farm

55 A B 56 C D 57 E F

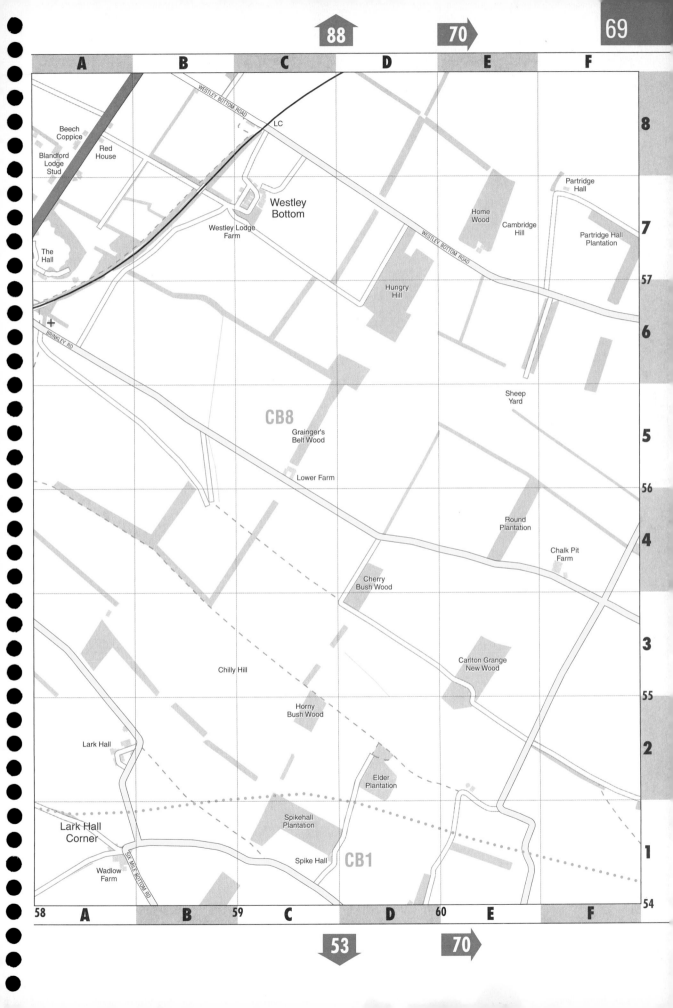

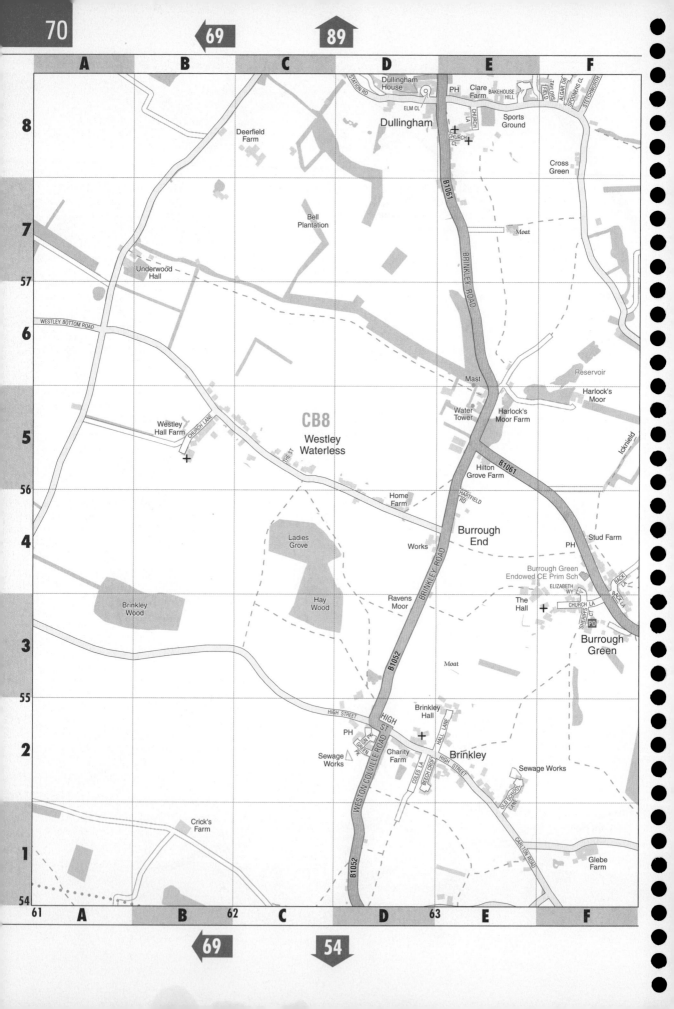

8

7

57

6

56

5

56

4

55

3

55

2

1

54

Deerfield
Farm

Bell
Plantation

Underwood
Hall

WESTLEY BOTTOM ROAD

Westley
Hall Farm

CHURCH LANE

THE ST

CB8

Westley
Waterless

Ladies
Grove

Brinkley
Wood

Hay
Wood

Home
Farm

Works

Ravens
Moor

HIGH STREET

HIGH ST

WESTON COLVILLE ROAD

Crick's
Farm

Sewage
Works

PH

Charity
Farm

COLES LA

BEECH CROFT

GREEN PK

PH

Brinkley
Hall

HALL LANE

HIGH STREET

Brinkley

Sewage Works

OLD SCHOOL LANE

CARLTON ROAD

Glebe
Farm

B1052

B1052

Dullingham
House

STATION RD

ELM CL

Dullingham

PH

CHURCH LA

CHURCH
CL

Clare
Farm

BAKEHOUSE
HILL

Sports
Ground

TAYLORS FIELD

ALGAR DR

SPOONERS CL

STETCHWORTH

Cross
Green

Moat

Mast

Water
Tower

Harlock's
Moor Farm

Harlock's
Moor

Reservoir

Icknield

BRINKLEY ROAD

B1061

B1061

Hilton
Grove Farm

HARTFIELD
RD

Burrough
End

PH

Stud Farm

BRINKLEY ROAD

Burrough Green
Endowed CE Prim Sch

ELIZABETH
WY

The
Hall

CHURCH LA

SHERIFFS CT

BACK LA

BACK LA

PO

Burrough
Green

Moat

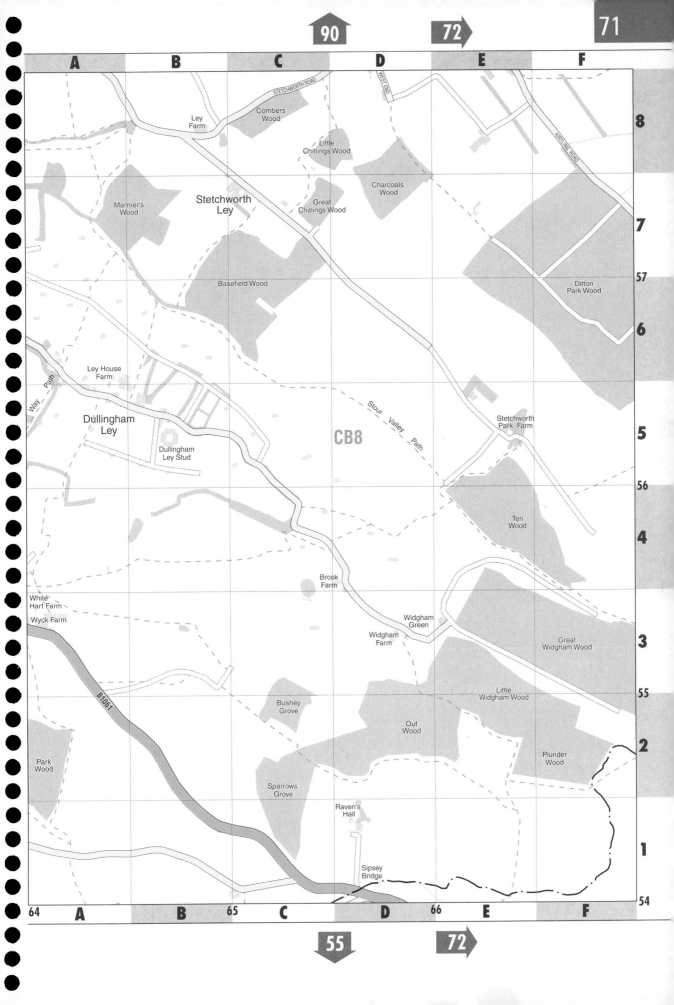

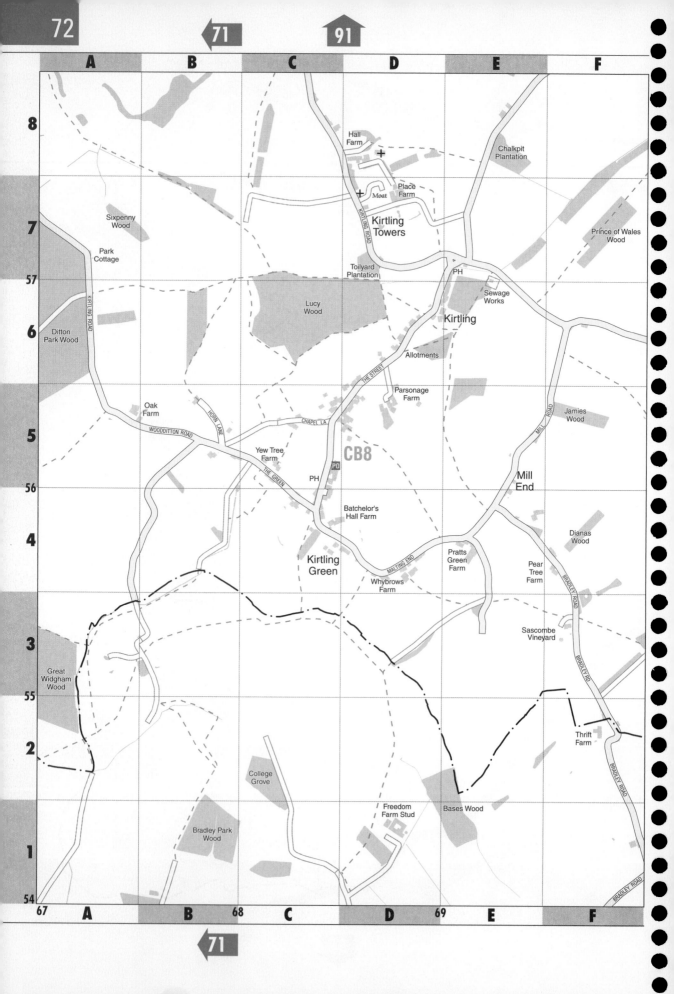

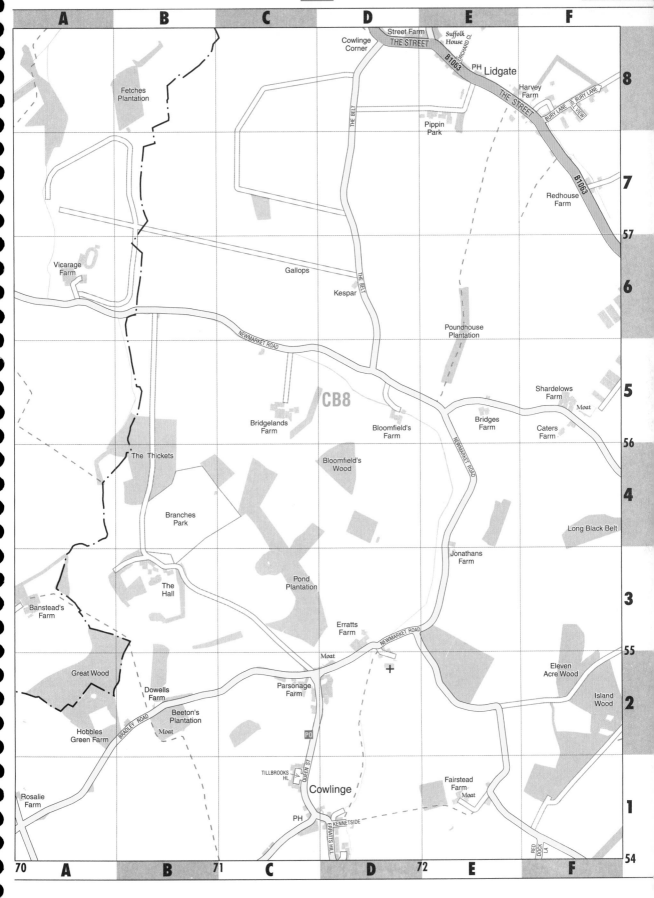

A B C D E F

8
7
57
6
5
56
4
55
2
1
54

Fetches Plantation

Cowlinge Corner
Street Farm
THE STREET
Suffolk House
ORCHARD CL
B1063
PH Lidgate
Harvey Farm
BURY LANE
HILL VIEW
BURY LANE
THE STREET
B1063
Pippin Park
Redhouse Farm

THE BELT

Vicarage Farm
Gallops
Kespar
THE BELT

NEWMARKET ROAD

Poundhouse Plantation

CB8

Shardelows Farm
Moat
Bridgelands Farm
Bloomfield's Farm
Bridges Farm
Caters Farm

The Thickets
Bloomfield's Wood

NEWMARKET ROAD

Branches Park
Long Black Belt

Jonathans Farm

The Hall
Pond Plantation

Banstead's Farm
Erratts Farm

Moat

NEWMARKET ROAD

Eleven Acre Wood

Great Wood
Parsonage Farm
Island Wood

Dowells Farm
Beeton's Plantation
Moat
BRADLEY ROAD
PO

Hobbles Green Farm

QUEEN ST

Fairstead Farm
Moat

Rosalie Farm
TILLBROOKS HL.
Cowlinge
PH
KENNETSIDE
ERRATTS HILL
RED DOCK LA

70 A B 71 C D 72 E F 54

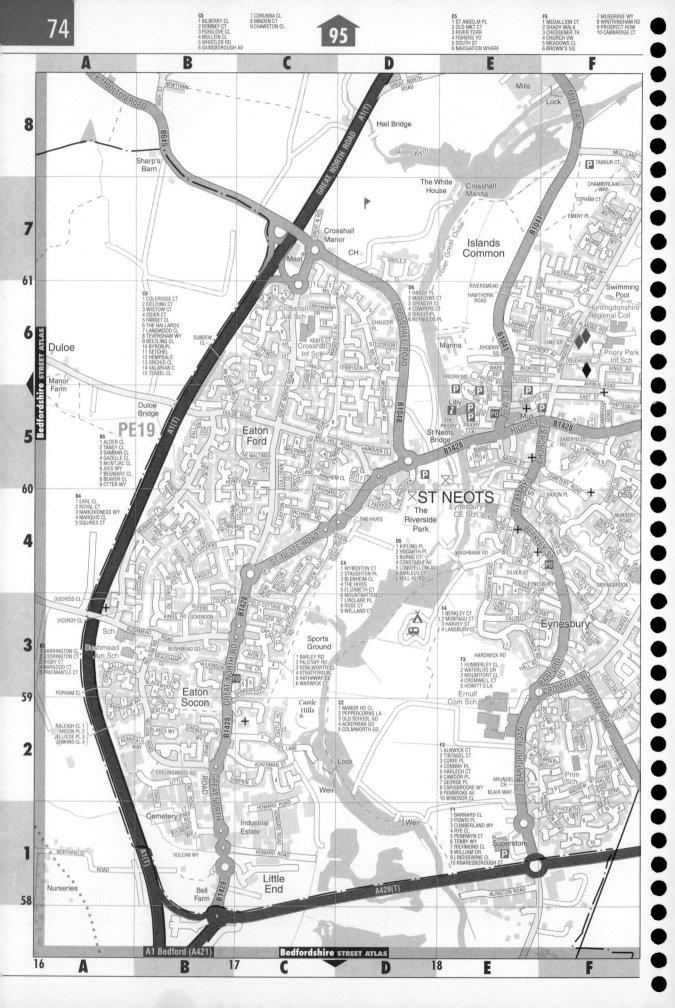

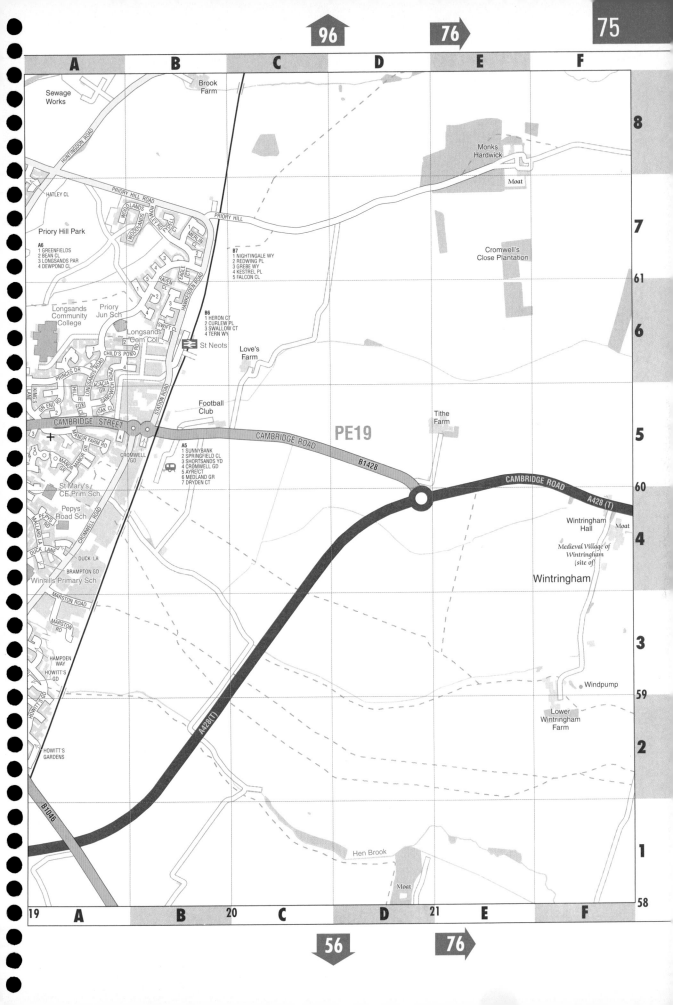

A   B   C   D   E   F

8

7

61

6

5

60

4

3

59

2

1

58

Sewage Works

Brook Farm

Monks Hardwick

Moat

HATLEY CL

PRIORY HILL ROAD

PRIORY HILL

Priory Hill Park

Cromwell's Close Plantation

WOODLANDS

RONKEY RD

MERLIN CL

A6
1 GREENFIELDS
2 BEAN CL
3 LONGSANDS PAR
4 DEWPOND CL

B7
1 NIGHTINGALE WY
2 REDWING PL
3 GREBE WY
4 KESTREL PL
5 FALCON CL

Longsands Community College

Priory Jun Sch

RAVEN CL

EAGLE CT

SWIFT CL

HAWKESDEN ROAD

B6
1 HERON CT
2 CURLEW PL
3 SWALLOW CT
4 TERN WY

Longsands Com Coll

CHILD'S POND

St Neots

Love's Farm

PRINCES DR

ACACIA GR

SANDPIT

FOX

OAK CL

Football Club

STATION ROAD

Tithe Farm

KING'S LANE

GN ENO RD

HILL RI

CAMBRIDGE STREET

CAMBRIDGE ROAD

PE19

CROMWELL GD

A5
1 SUNNYBANK
2 SPRINGFIELD CL
3 SHORTSANDS YD
4 CROMWELL GD
5 AYRE CT
6 MEDLAND GR
7 DRYDEN CT

B1428

CAMBRIDGE ROAD

A428 (T)

Wintringham Hall

Moat

MANOR FARM RD

MANOR GR

St Mary's CE.Prim Sch

Medieval Village of Wintringham (site of)

PEPYS RD

Pepys Road Sch

CROMWELL ROAD

Wintringham

MALLARD LA

DUCK LANE

DUCK LA

BRAMPTON GD

Winhills Primary Sch

MARSTON ROAD

MARSTON RD

Windpump

HAMPDEN WAY

HOWITT'S GD

Lower Wintringham Farm

A428(T)

HOWITT'S GD

HOWITT'S GARDENS

B1046

Hen Brook

Moat

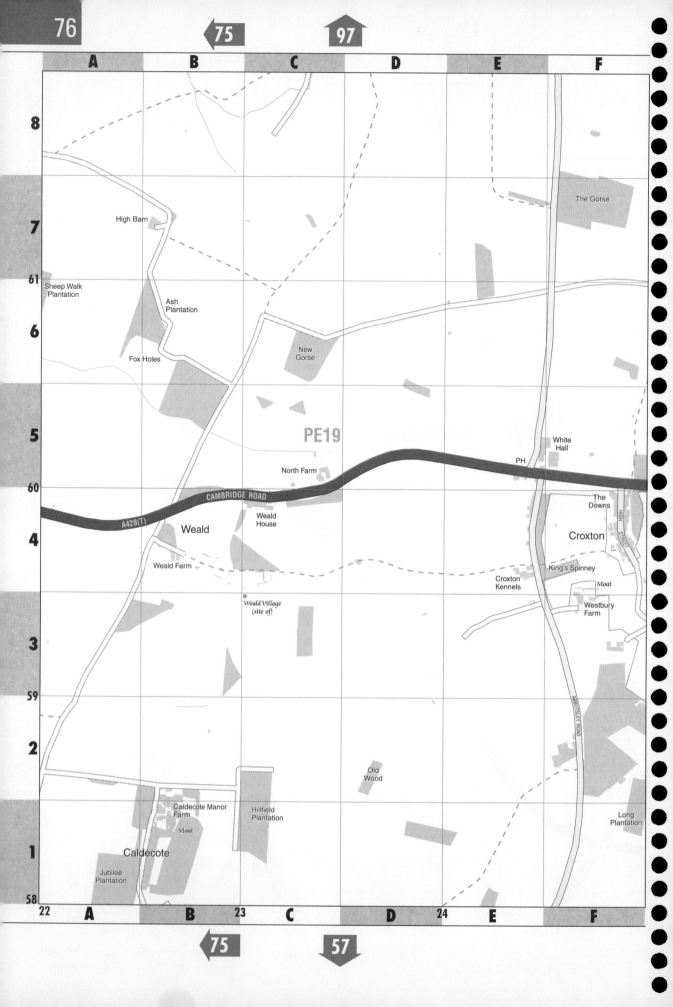

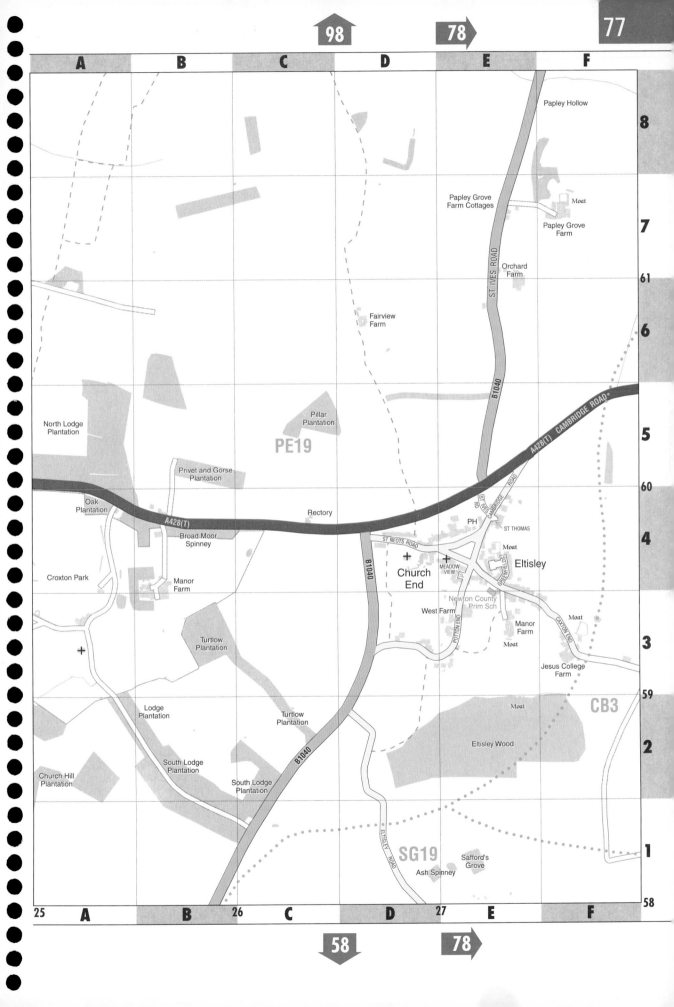

A B C D E F

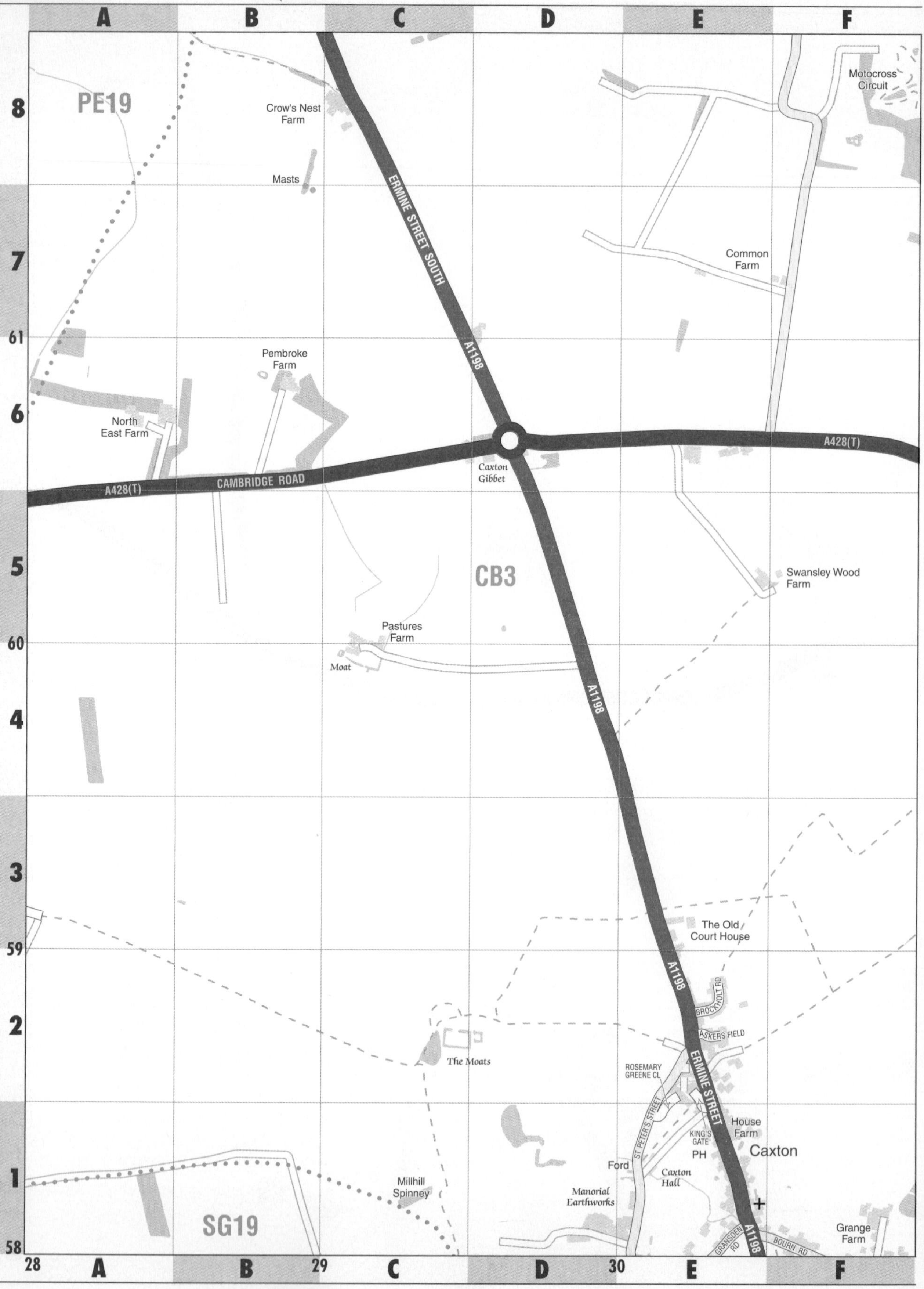

8

PE19

Crow's Nest Farm

Masts

ERMINE STREET SOUTH

7

61

Pembroke Farm

A1198

6

North East Farm

CAMBRIDGE ROAD

A428(T)

A428(T)

Caxton Gibbet

Motocross Circuit

Common Farm

Swansley Wood Farm

5

CB3

Pastures Farm

Moat

A1198

60

4

3

The Old Court House

A1198

BROCKHOLT RD

59

2

The Moats

ASKERS FIELD

ROSEMARY GREENE CL

ERMINE STREET

House Farm

Caxton

KING'S GATE

PH

ST PETER'S STREET

1

Millhill Spinney

Ford

Caxton Hall

Manorial Earthworks

Grange Farm

SG19

GRANSDEN RD

A1198

BOURN RD

58

28 A B 29 C D 30 E F

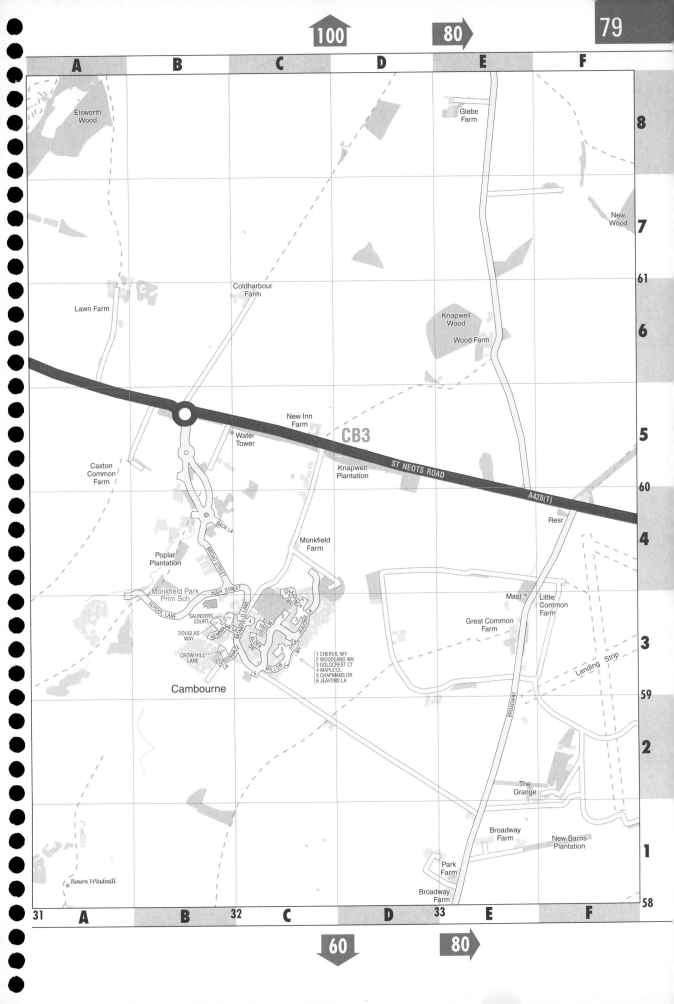

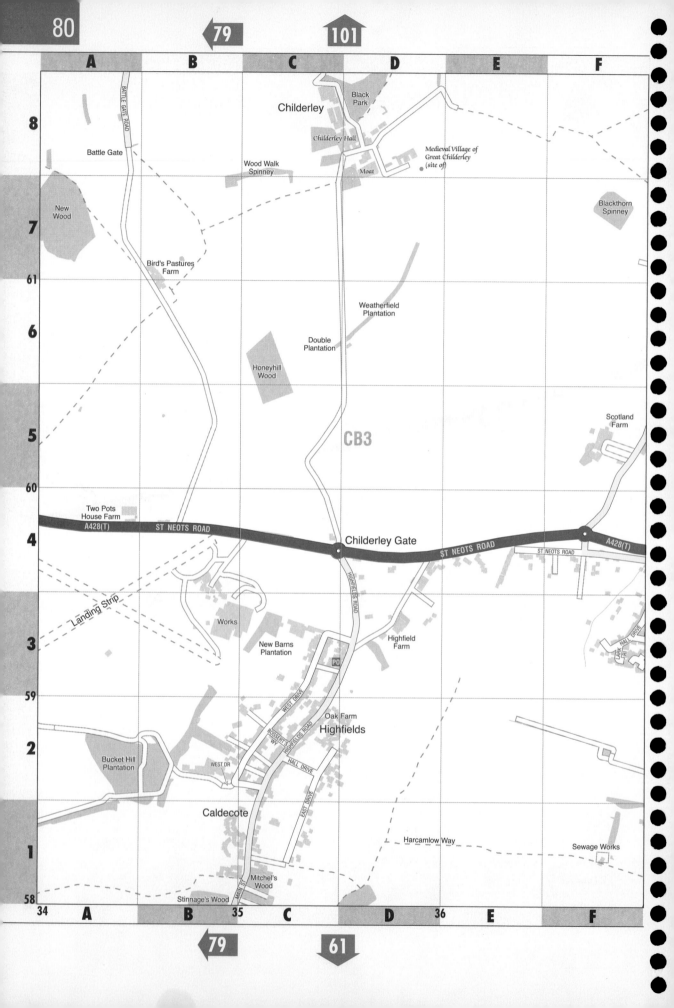

79
101

A   B   C   D   E   F

8

Childerley

Black
Park

BATTLE GATE ROAD

Battle Gate

Childerley Hall

Wood Walk
Spinney

Moat

Medieval Village of
Great Childerley
(site of)

New
Wood

7

Blackthorn
Spinney

Bird's Pastures
Farm

61

Weatherfield
Plantation

6

Double
Plantation

Honeyhill
Wood

5

CB3

Scotland
Farm

60

Two Pots
House Farm

A428(T)   ST NEOTS ROAD

4

Childerley Gate   ST NEOTS ROAD   ST NEOTS ROAD   A428(T)

HIGHFIELDS ROAD

Landing Strip

Works

LARK HALL DRIVE

3

New Barns
Plantation

Highfield
Farm

PO

59

WEST DRIVE

Oak Farm

Highfields

BOSSERY WY

HIGHFIELDS ROAD

2

Bucket Hill
Plantation

WEST DR

HALL DRIVE

EAST DRIVE

Caldecote

MAIN ST

Harcamlow Way

Sewage Works

1

Mitchel's
Wood

Stinnage's Wood

58

34   A   B   35   C   D   36   E   F

79
61

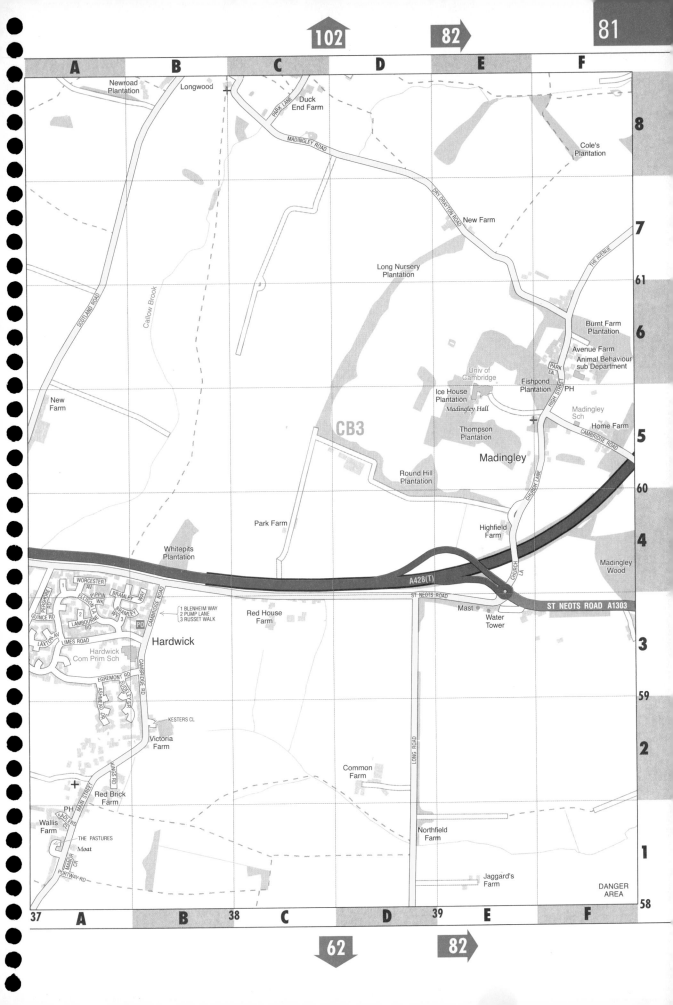

A B C D E F

8

Beck Brook Farm

THE AVENUE

Hanchard Plantation

WASHPIT ROAD

LAWRENCE CL

Orchard Farm

DUCK END

CHURCH LANE

HICKS LANE

CHERRY HINTON RD

GIFFORD'S CL

STERNDALE CL

REDGATE

CAMBRIDGE ROAD

MAYFIELD RD

ST VINCENT'S CL

Allot

ST VINCENT'S CLOSE

PEPYS WAY

WEAVER'S FIELD

Girton

7

A14(T)

A1307

61

14

Biotechnology Centre

GRANGE DRIVE

HUNTINGDON ROAD

M11

ORCHARD DRIVE

ORCHARD DRIVE

WELLBROOK WY.

GIRTON ROAD

THORNTON ROAD

WILDERSON CL

Cambridge University Farm

Girton Coll

ST MARGARET'S ROAD

BARTON RD

THORNTON ROAD

A1307

6

A428(T)

Ladybush Close

Trinity Farm

5

Wrangling Corner

60

Pheasant Plantation

4

CAMBRIDGE ROAD

Madingley Wood

Cambridge American Cemetery

Mill Windmill Farm

Moor Barns Farm

Trinity Conduit Head

P&R

A1303

ST NEOTS ROAD

MADINGLEY ROAD

13

LANSDOWNE ROAD

CONDUIT HEAD RD

A1303

3

CAMBRIDGE ROAD

PO

Rectory Farm

Dept of Engineering

Dept of Clinical Veterinary Medicine

Merton Hall Farm

59

CB3

Coton C of E Com Prim Sch

HIGH ST

ST CATHARINES HALL

PH

High Cross

M11

Coton

SADLER'S CL

CHURCH END

THE FOOTPATH

WHITWELL WAY

ST PETER'S ROAD

BENN'S WAY

SILL FRIME

ST JOHN'S ROAD

SILVERDALE CL

BROOKFIELD RD

Manor Farm

BROOK LANE

Rec Gnd

Harcamlow Way

2

Spring

Whitwell Farm

GRANTCHESTER ROAD

1

DANGER AREA

Bin Brook

58

40 A 41 B C 42 D E F

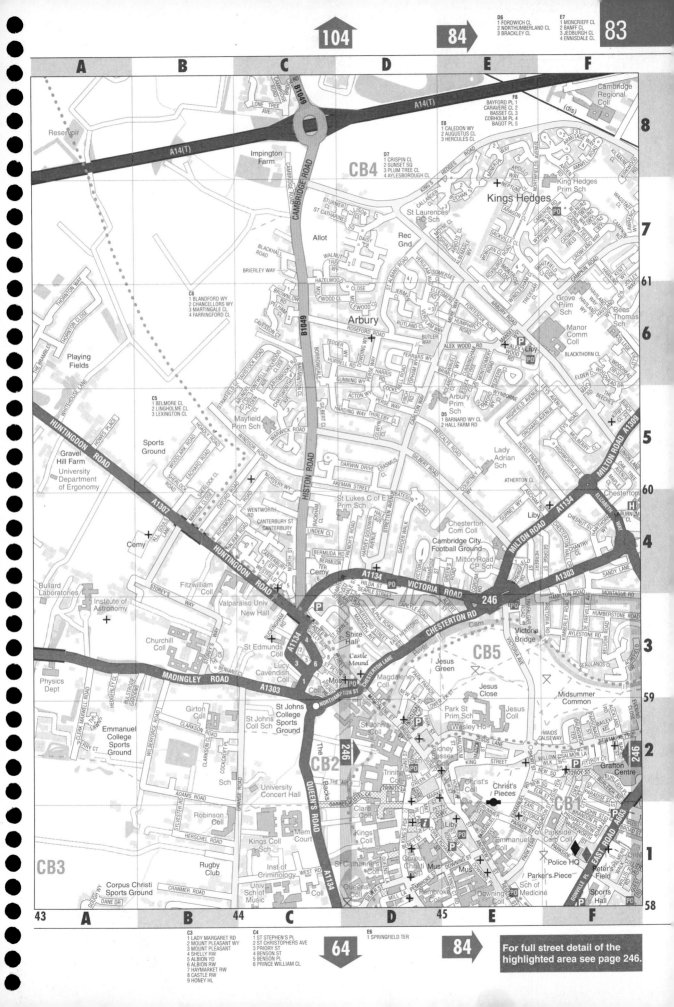

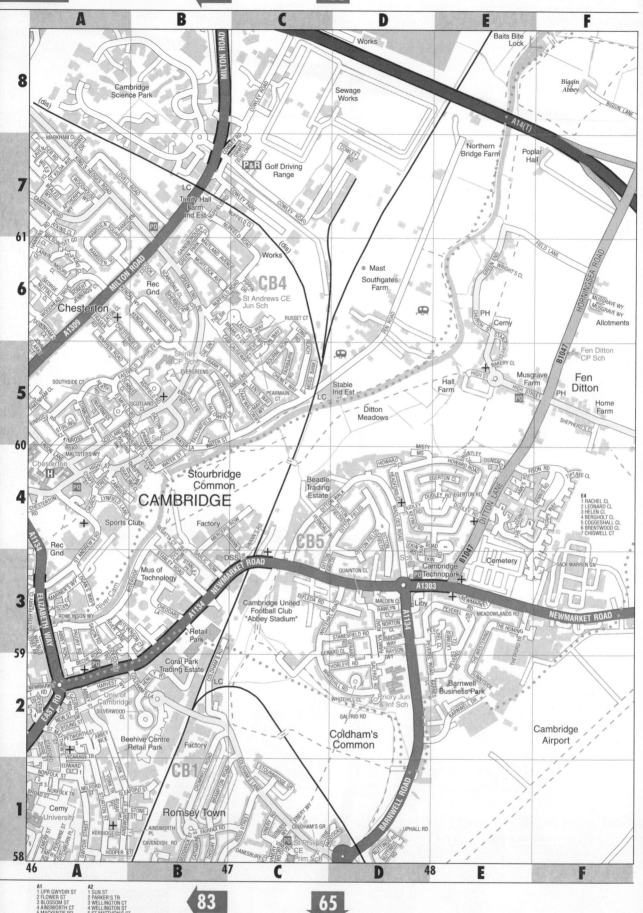

A B C D E F

8

7

61

6

5

60

4

3

59

2

1

58

(dis)

Cambridge
Science Park

MILTON ROAD

Works

Sewage
Works

Baits Bite
Lock

Biggin
Abbey

BIGGIN LANE

A14(T)

Northern
Bridge Farm

Poplar
Hall

COWLEY ROAD

P&R

Golf Driving
Range

LC

Trinity Hall
Farm
Ind Est

COWLEY ROAD

COWLEY PARK

NUFFIELD RD

ORWELL RD

COWLEY RD

MARKHAM CL

(dis)

Works

CB4

St Andrews CE
Jun Sch

Mast

Southgates
Farm

FEN ROAD

Wright's CL

GREEN END

FIELD LANE

HORNINGSEA ROAD

Musgrave WY

MUSGRAVE WY

Allotments

Chesterton

MILTON ROAD

A1309

Rec
Gnd

RUSSET CT

LONG REACH

MOSS BANK

CAXTON WAY

Shirley
CP Sch

EVERGREENS

FRANK'S LA

CHEYNE WAY

FAIRBAIRN

PEARMAIN
CT

LC

Stable
Ind Est

Ditton
Meadows

Hall
Farm

PH

Cemy

HIGH ST

BAKERY CL

Musgrave
Farm

PO

HIGH STREET

B1047

Fen Ditton
CP Sch

Fen
Ditton

PH

Home
Farm

SHEPHERD S CL

CHESTERTON

A1134

Chesterton

H

PO

Stourbridge
Common

CAMBRIDGE

Sports Club

Rec
Gnd

Factory

Mus of
Technology

RIVERSIDE

River Cam

CHEDDARS
LA

A1134

Retail
Park

Coral Park
Trading Estate

LC

NEWMARKET ROAD

DSS

CB5

DITTON WALK

DITTON FIELDS

Beadle
Trading
Estate

DITTON WALK

HOWARD ROAD

Howard
MS

MISTY
MS

FISON RD

E4
1 RACHEL CL
2 LEONARD CL
3 HELEN CL
4 BERGHOLT CL
5 COGGESHALL CL
6 BRENTWOOD CL
7 CHIGWELL CT

EGERTON CL

DUDLEY RD

EGERTON RD

Cambridge
Technopark

B1047

Cemetery

JACK WARREN GN

THORPE WY

DITTON LANE

EKIN ROAD

Cambridge United
Football Club
"Abbey Stadium"

ELFLEDA RD

QUAINTON CL

PO

A1303

A1134

Liby

NEWMARKET

MEADOWLANDS RD

NEWMARKET ROAD

THE HOMING

STANESFIELD RD

MALDEN CL

RAWLYN
CL

NORTON
CL

RAYSON
RD

PEVEREL RD

MEADOWLANDS RD

THE WESTERING

THE TREFOID

SUNNYSIDE

GERARD CL

HORLEYE RD

WHITEHILL RD

GALFRID RD

Priory Jun
& Inf Sch

Barnwell
Business Park

BARNWELL DR

ELIZABETH WAY

EAST RD

NEWMARKET
RD

Univ of
Cambridge

SILVERWOOD
CL

Beehive Centre
Retail Park

Factory

CB1

Romsey Town

Coldham's
Common

BARNWELL ROAD

Cambridge
Airport

Cemy

University

AINSWORTH
PL

CAVENDISH RD

DANESBURY CT

COLDHAM'S GR

St Philips
CE
Prim Sch

UPHALL RD

A1
1 UPR GWYDIR ST
2 FLOWER ST
3 BLOSSOM ST
4 AINSWORTH CT
5 MACKENZIE RD

A2
1 SUN ST
2 PARKER'S TR
3 WELLINGTON CT
4 WELLINGTON ST
5 ST MATTHEW'S CT

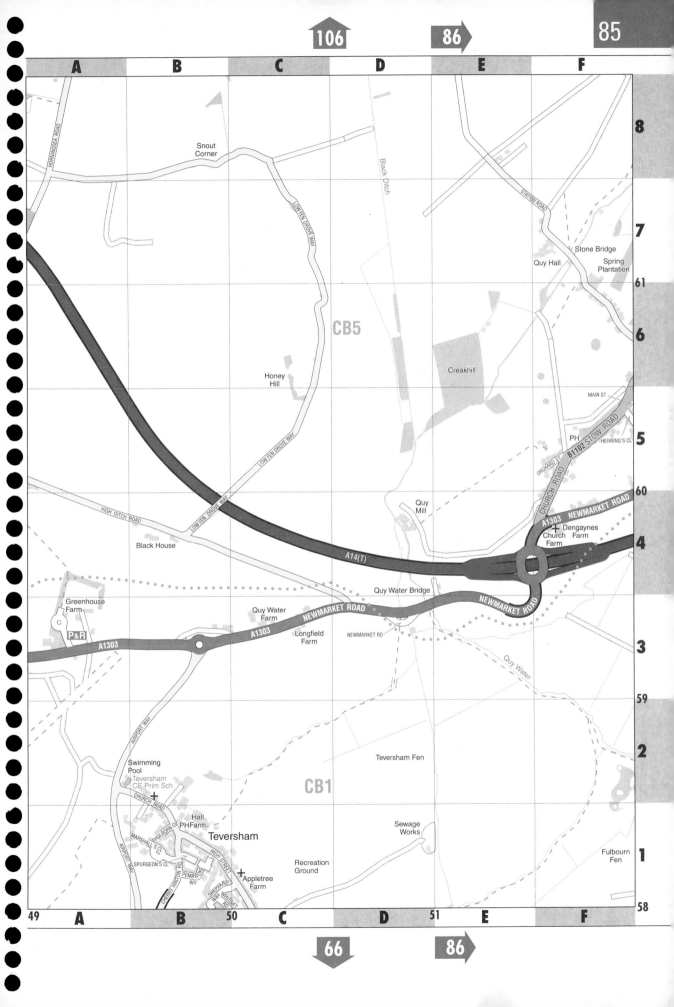

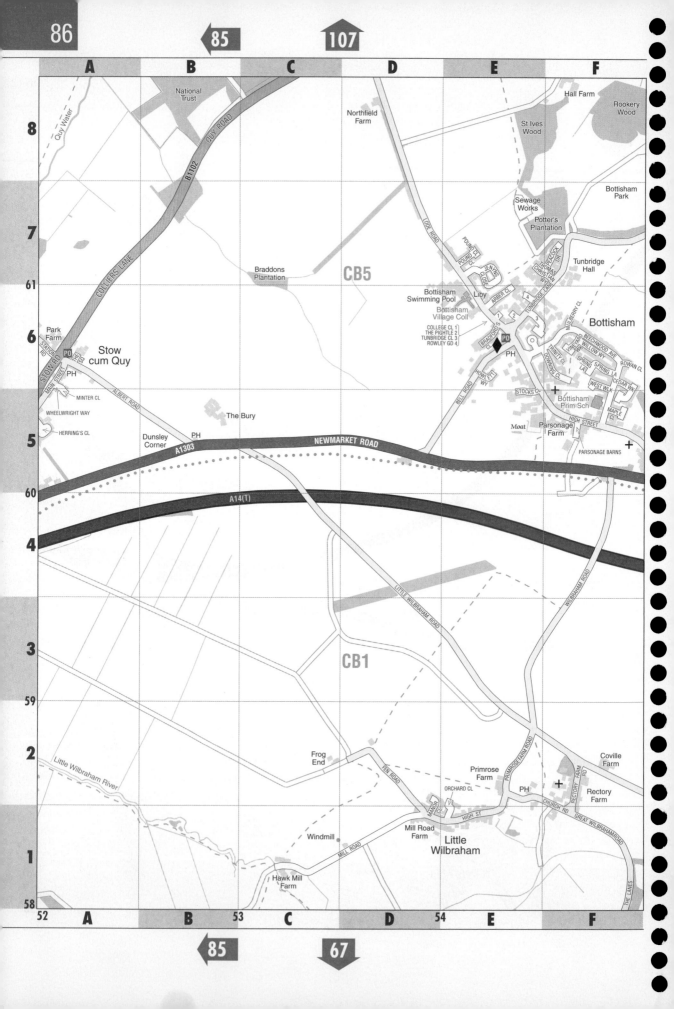

A B C D E F

8

Quy Water

National Trust

Northfield Farm

Hall Farm

Rookery Wood

St Ives Wood

Bottisham Park

QUY ROAD

B1102

7

Sewage Works

Potter's Plantation

LODE ROAD

Tunbridge Hall

COLLIERS LANE

Braddons Plantation

CB5

POUND CL

POUND CL

THOMAS CHRISTIAN WY

PEACOCK DR

JENYNS CLOSE

61

Bottisham Swimming Pool

Liby

ARBER CL

TUNBRIDGE LANE

Bottisham

6

Park Farm

STATION RD

PO

Stow cum Quy

Bottisham Village Coll

COLLEGE CL 1
THE PIGHTLE 2
TUNBRIDGE CL 3
ROWLEY GD 4

BRADFORD'S CL

PO

PH

TRINITY CL

WILBERRY CL

BEECHWOOD AVE

VINEYARD

WILLOW WY

ROWAN CL

SPRING LA

SPRING LA

CEDAR WK

MAIN STREET

PH

MINTER CL

ALBERT ROAD

HOWL CL

BELL ROAD

DOWNING CL

WEST WLK

WHEELWRIGHT WAY

The Bury

STOCKS CL

Bottisham Prim Sch

MAPLE CL

5

HERRING'S CL

Dunsley Corner

PH

NEWMARKET ROAD

Moat

Parsonage Farm

HIGH STREET

A1303

PARSONAGE BARNS

60

A14(T)

4

LITTLE WILBRAHAM ROAD

WILBRAHAM ROAD

3

CB1

59

2

Frog End

FEN ROAD

Primrose Farm

PRIMROSE FARM ROAD

PH

Coville Farm

RECTORY FARM RD

Rectory Farm

ORCHARD CL

Windmill

MANOR CL

HIGH ST

CHURCH RD

GREAT WILBRAHAM ROAD

Mill Road Farm

MILL ROAD

Little Wilbraham

Little Wilbraham River

1

Hawk Mill Farm

THE LANES

58

52 A 53 B C 54 D E F

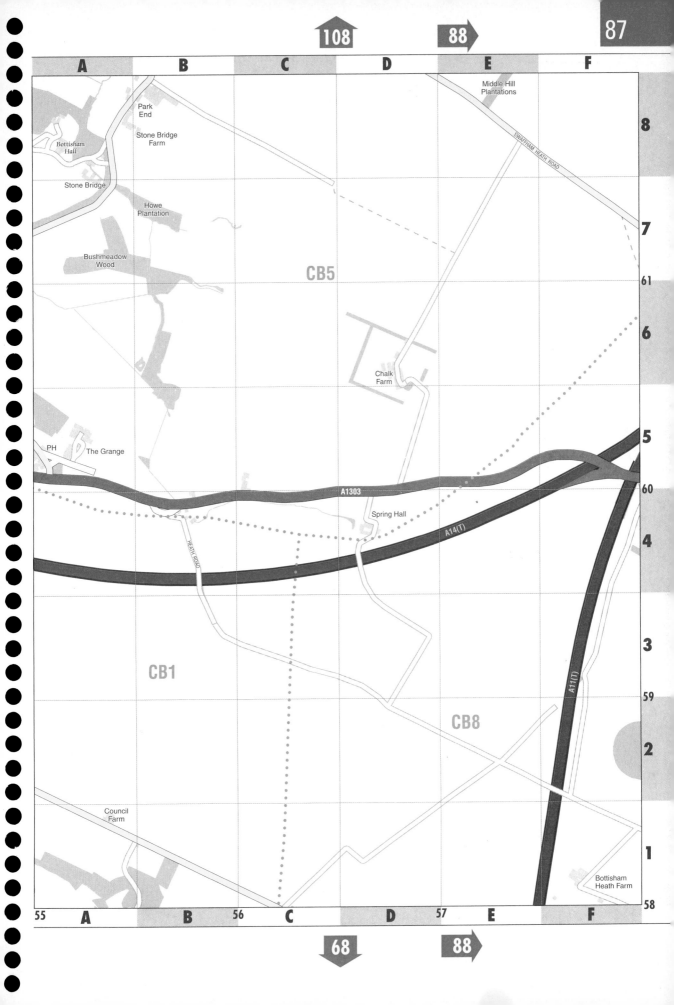

A B C D E F

8

Middle Hill
Plantations

Park
End

SWAFFHAM HEATH ROAD

Stone Bridge
Farm

7

Bottisham
Hall

Stone Bridge

Howe
Plantation

61

CB5

Bushmeadow
Wood

6

Chalk
Farm

5

PH The Grange

A1303

60

Spring Hall

A14(T)

4

HEATH ROAD

CB1

3

A11(T)

59

CB8

2

Council
Farm

1

Bottisham
Heath Farm

58

55 A B 56 C D 57 E F

87
109

A B C D E F

8

CB5

Beacon (Cesarewitch)

Memorial

The
National
Stud

Round Course

Round Course

Egerton
Stud

7

New England
Farm

A14(T)

Egerton
House

61

New England
Stud

SWAFFHAM HEATH ROAD

6

A1303

5

CB8

Lordship
Stud

Four Mile
Stable Farm

A1304

60

Mast

Tumulus

4

Lower Hare
Park Farm

Gran's
Plantation

3

Hare Park
Stud

Hare
Park

White
Wood

Hut Plantation

59

Allington
Hill Farm

2

Tumulus

Lower Hare
Park Farm

Lower
Farm

Bungalow
Farm

A1304

1

Windmill

WESTLEY BOTTOM RD

Bungalow
Hill

58

58 A 59 B C 60 D E F

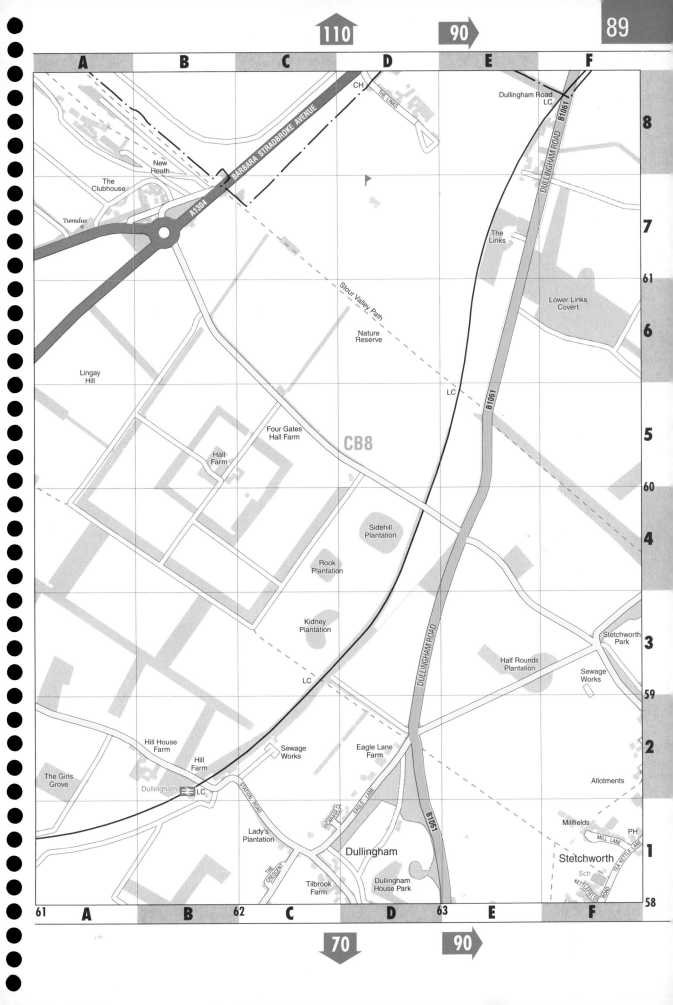

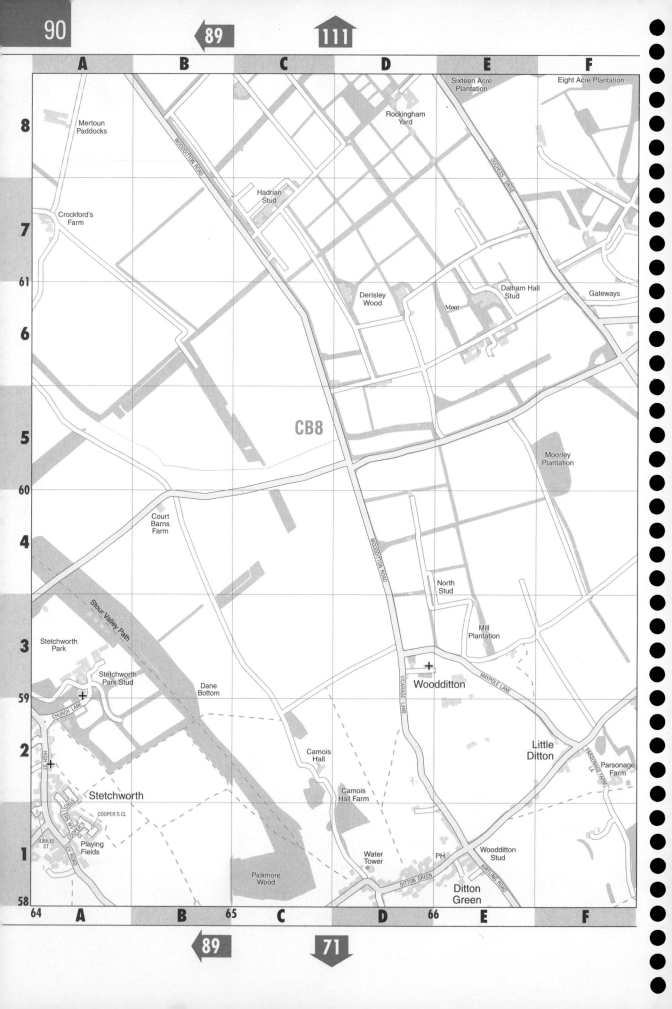

A B C D E F

8

Mertoun
Paddocks

Rockingham
Yard

Sixteen Acre
Plantation

Eight Acre Plantation

WOODDITTON ROAD

DUCHESS' DRIVE

7

Crockford's
Farm

Hadrian
Stud

61

Derisley
Wood

Moat

Dalham Hall
Stud

Gateways

6

CB8

Moorley
Plantation

5

60

Court
Barns
Farm

WOODDITTON ROAD

4

Stour Valley Path

North
Stud

Mill
Plantation

3

Stetchworth
Park

Stetchworth
Park Stud

Dane
Bottom

VICARAGE LANE

MAYPOLE LANE

Woodditton

59

CHURCH LANE

Little
Ditton

PARSONAGE FARM LA

2

HIGH ST

Camois
Hall

Parsonage
Farm

Stetchworth

COOPER'S CL

Camois
Hall Farm

JOHN'S
COOPER'S
SELLERS WAY CL
LEY ROAD

Water
Tower

PH

Woodditton
Stud

1

JUBILEE
CT

Playing
Fields

KIRTLING ROAD

Pickmore
Wood

DITTON GREEN

Ditton
Green

58

64 A B 65 C D 66 E F

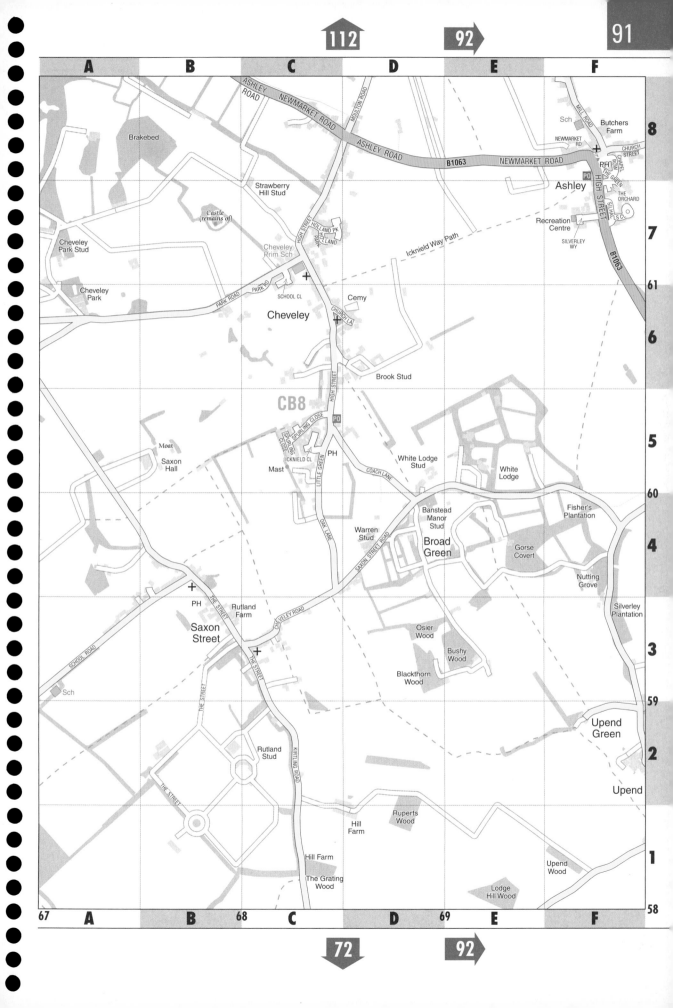

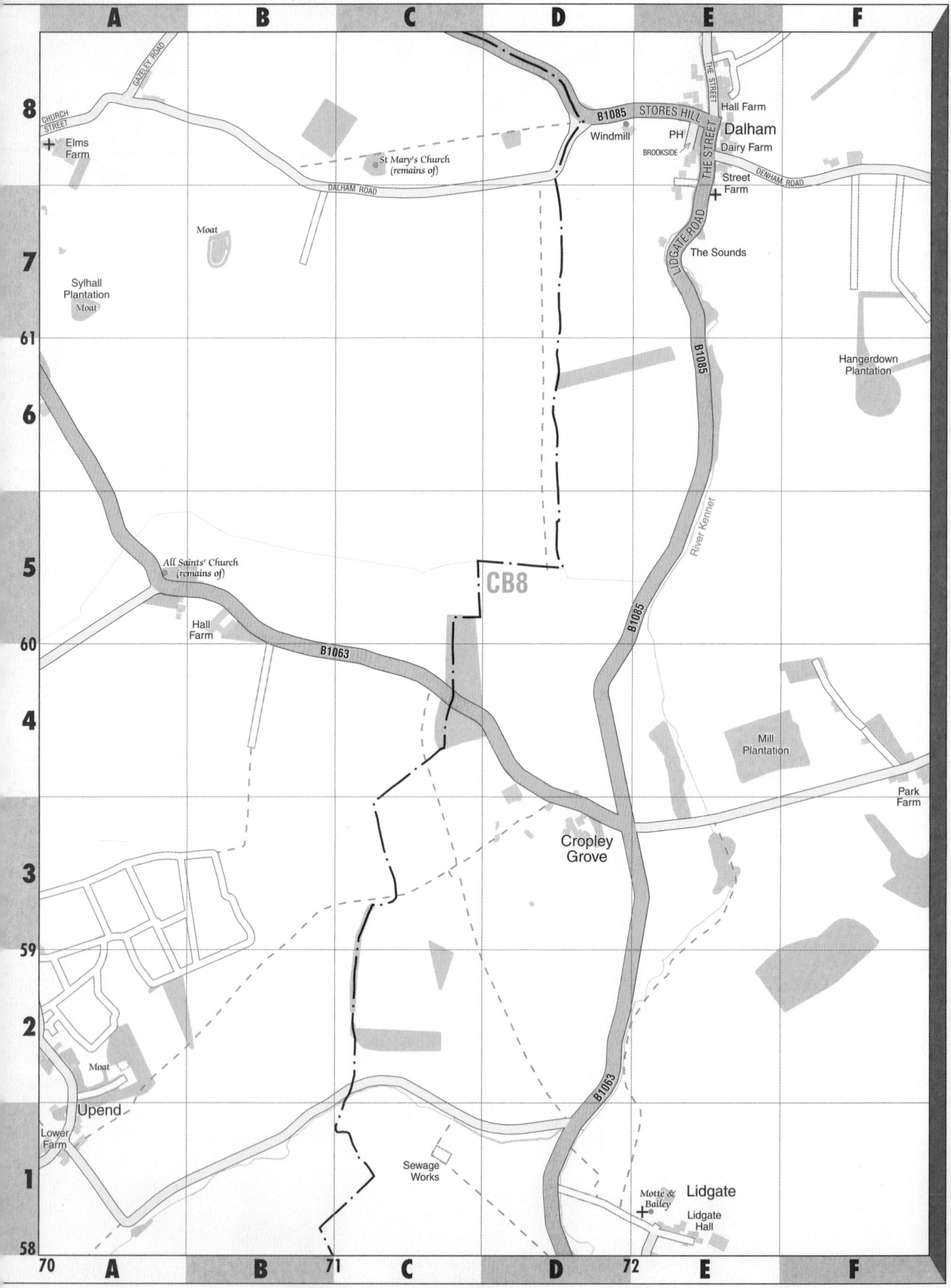

A B C D E F

8

Church Street

Gazeley Road

Elms Farm

St Mary's Church (remains of)

Dalham Road

Moat

B1085 STORES HILL

Windmill

Hall Farm

The Street

PH

BROOKSIDE

Dalham

Dairy Farm

Street Farm

DENHAM ROAD

7

Sylhall Plantation Moat

Lidgate Road

B1085

The Sounds

Hangerdown Plantation

61

6

All Saints' Church (remains of)

River Kennet

5

CB8

60

Hall Farm

B1063

B1085

4

Mill Plantation

Park Farm

3

Cropley Grove

59

2

Moat

Upend

B1063

Lower Farm

1

Sewage Works

Motte & Bailey

Lidgate

Lidgate Hall

58

70 A B 71 C D 72 E F

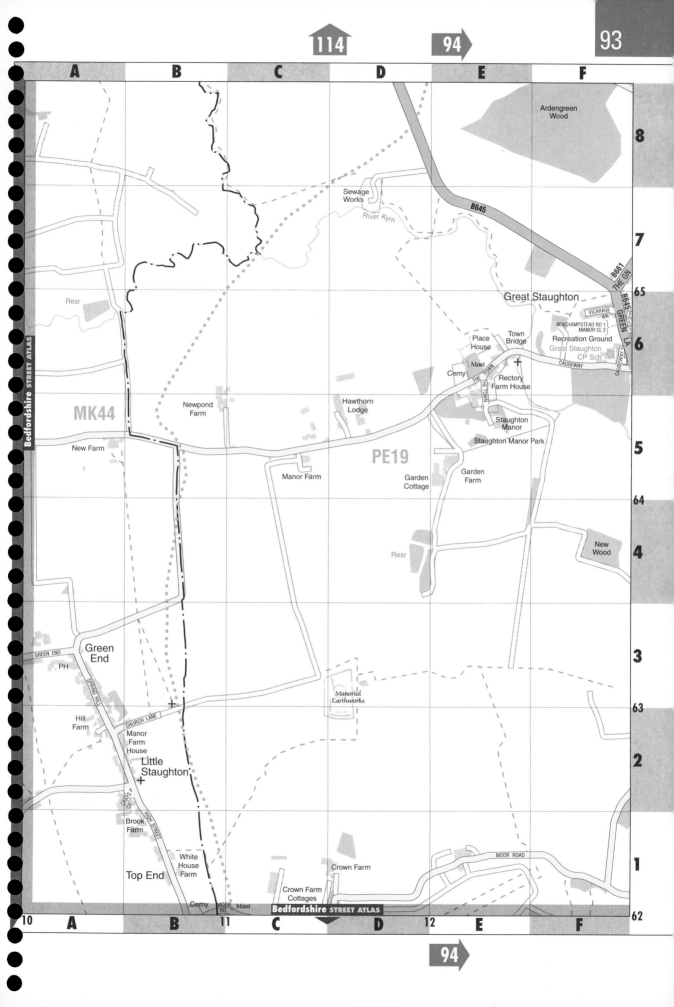

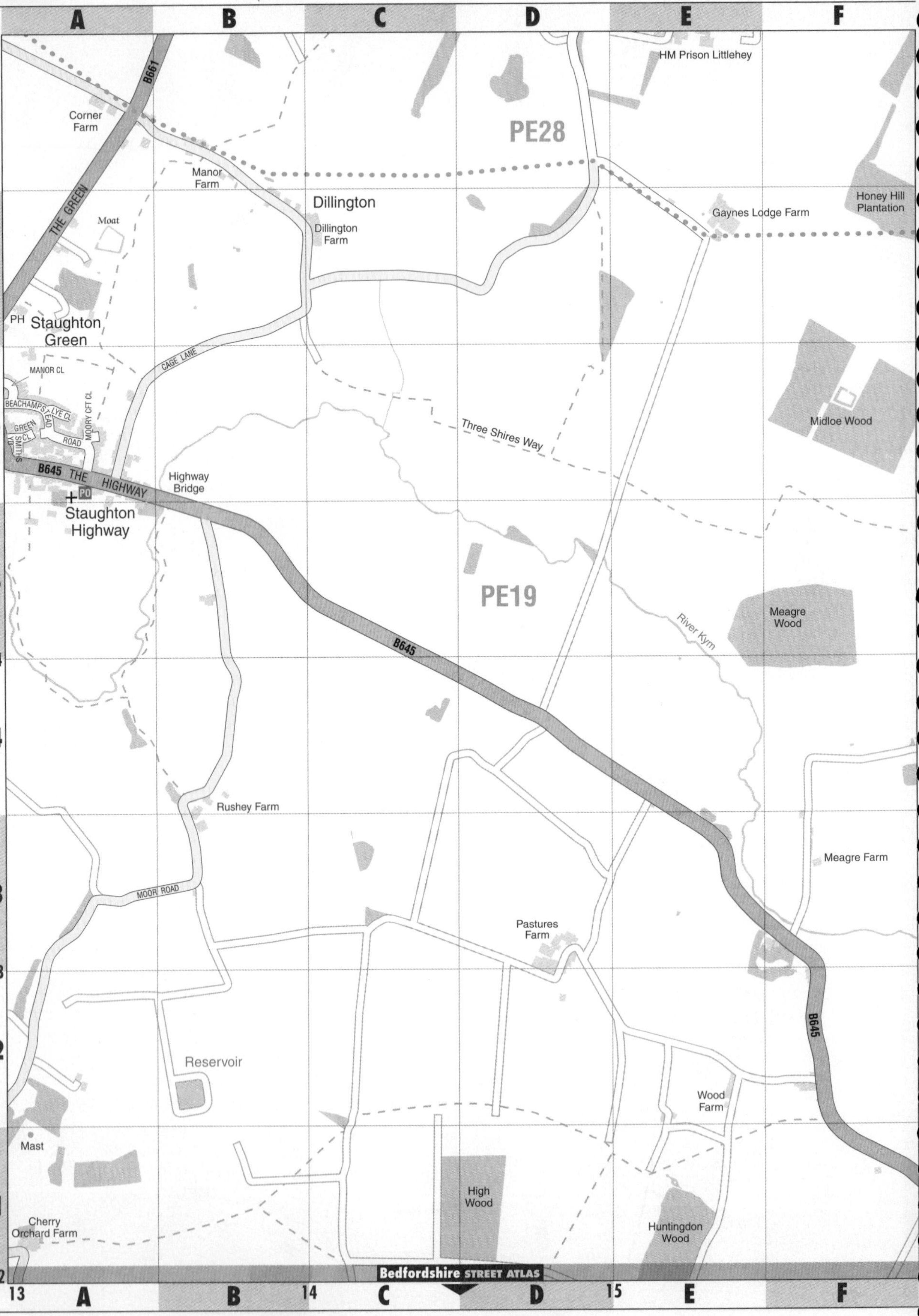

A **B** **C** **D** **E** **F**

8

B661

Corner
Farm

HM Prison Littlehey

PE28

Manor
Farm

Dillington

Honey Hill
Plantation

THE GREEN

Moat

Dillington
Farm

Gaynes Lodge Farm

7

PH

Staughton
Green

65

CAGE LANE

MANOR CL

Three Shires Way

Midloe Wood

6

BEACHAMPS
LYE CL

MOORY CFT CL

GREEN
SMITHS YD
SNC CL

LYE CL

ROAD

B645 THE HIGHWAY

Highway
Bridge

PO
Staughton
Highway

River Kym

5

PE19

Meagre
Wood

B645

64

4

Meagre Farm

Rushey Farm

3

MOOR ROAD

Pastures
Farm

63

Wood
Farm

2

Reservoir

B645

Mast

High
Wood

1

Cherry
Orchard Farm

Huntingdon
Wood

62

13 **A** **B** 14 **C** **D** 15 **E** **F**

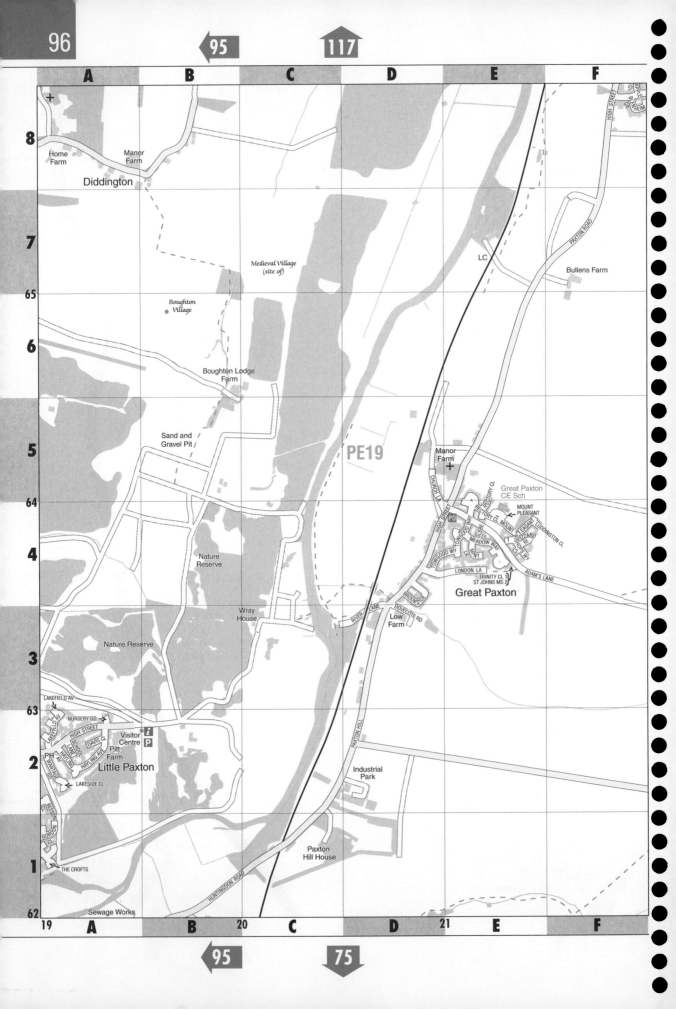

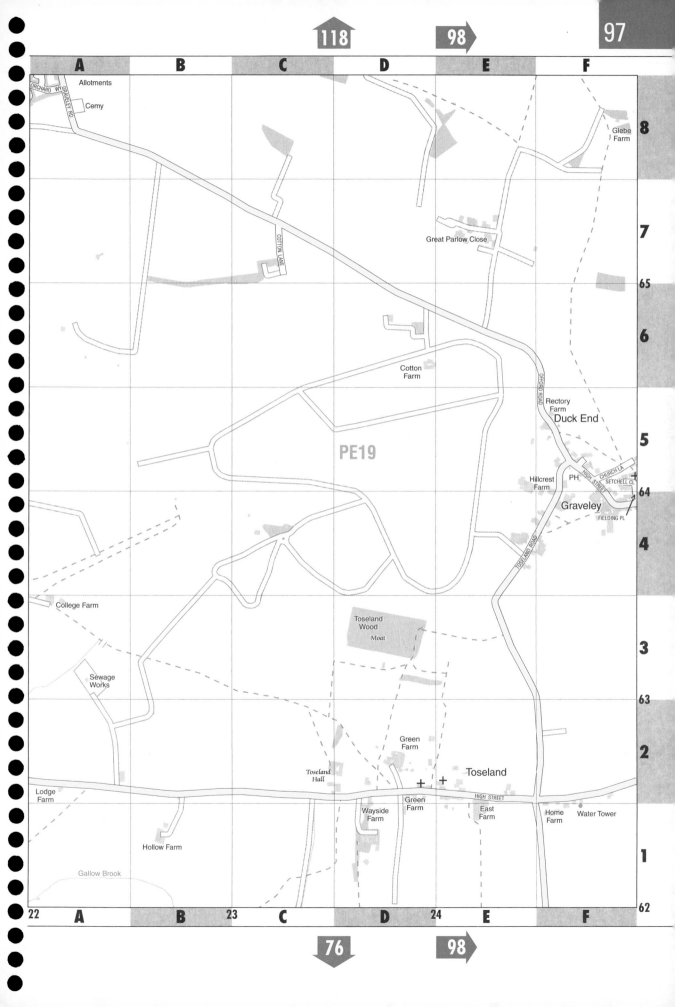

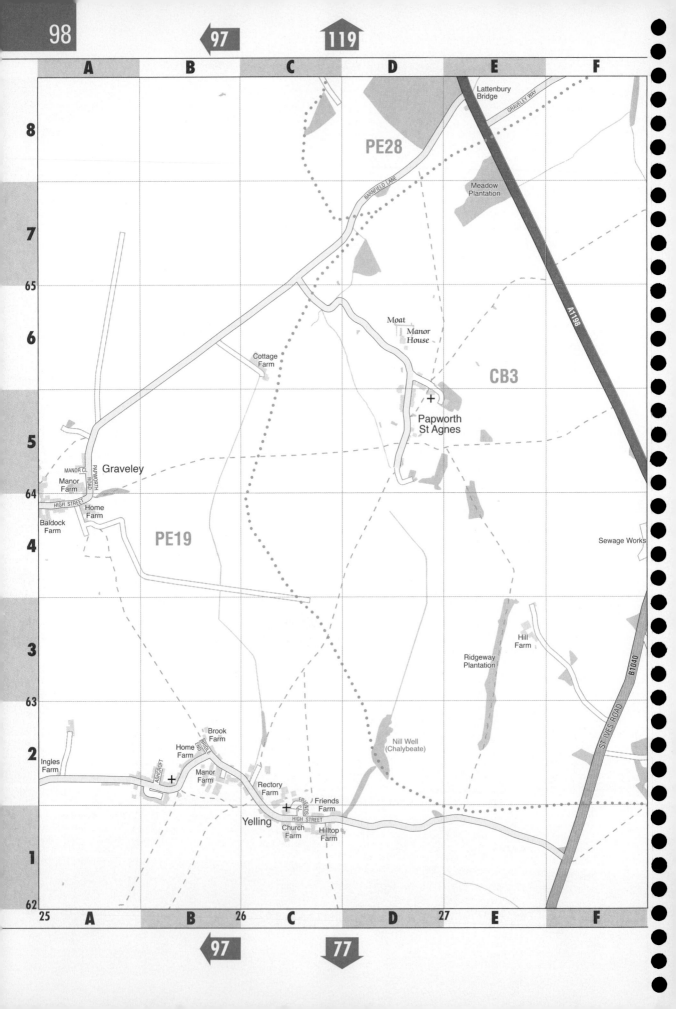

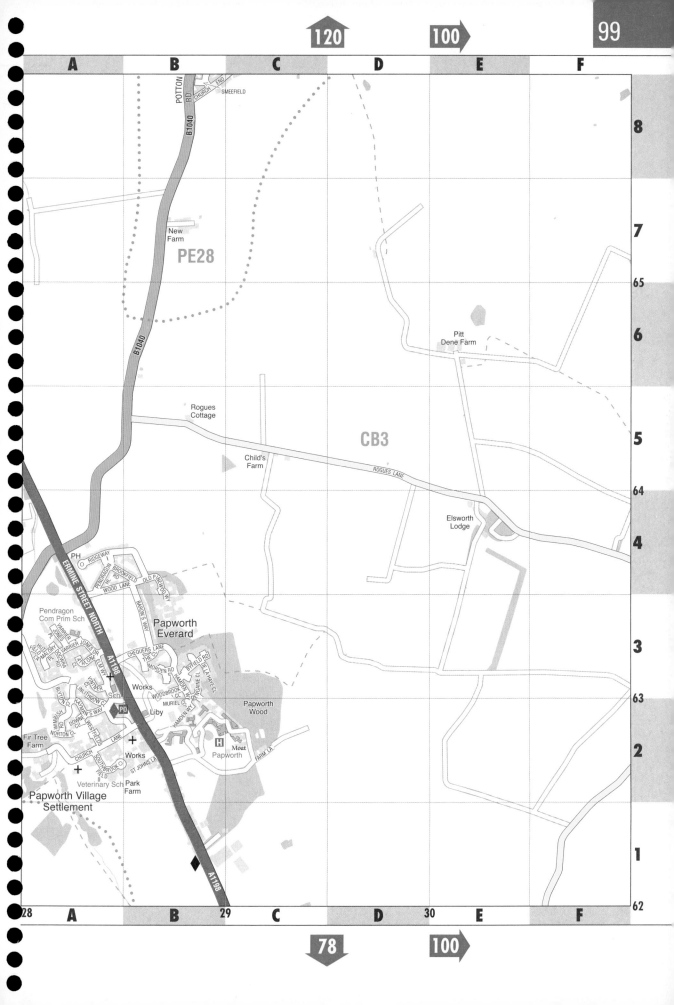

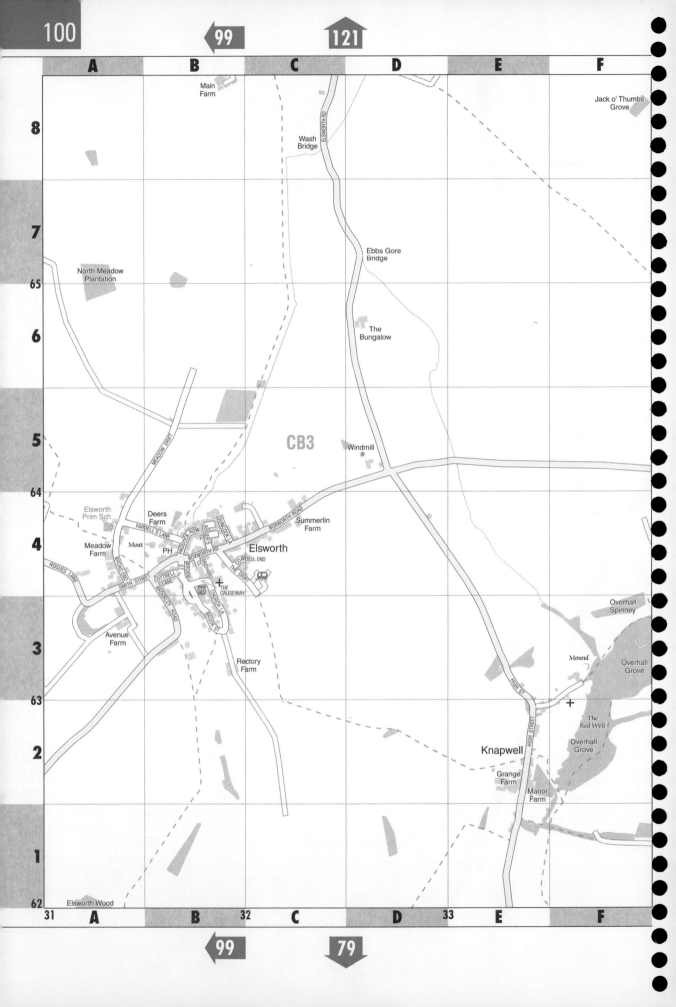

99
121

A B C D E F

8

Main Farm

Jack o' Thumbs Grove

Wash Bridge

ELSWORTH RD

7

Ebbs Gore Bridge

North Meadow Plantation

65

6

The Bungalow

CB3

5

Windmill

MEADOW DRIFT

64

Elsworth Prim Sch

Deers Farm

Summerlin Farm

BOXWORTH ROAD

4

Meadow Farm

Moat

PH

Elsworth

FARDELL'S LANE

PADDOCK ROW

ROGER'S

DUNNOCK LA.

COWDELL END

BROOK

ORCHARD CL.

THE DRIFT

ROGUES LANE

BROAD END STREET

SMITH STREET

COTTRELL'S LANE

BROCKLEY ROAD

CHURCH LA.

THE CAUSEWAY

PO

BROOK ST.

Overhall Spinney

3

Avenue Farm

Rectory Farm

Mound

Overhall Grove

63

The Red Well

Overhall Grove

2

Knapwell

HIGH STREET

Grange Farm

Manor Farm

1

62

Elsworth Wood

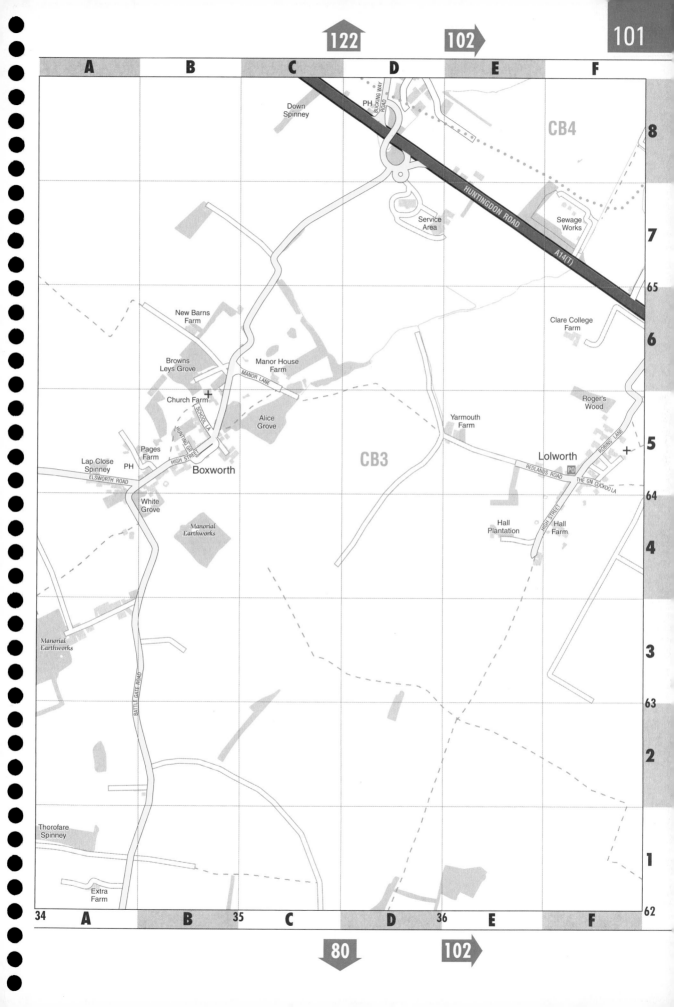

A   B   C   D   E   F

8

Bar Farm

7

Hill Farm

65

CB4

6

A14(T)

Noon
Folly Farm

New Close
Farm

HUNTINGDON ROAD

Mast

HATTON'S ROAD

B1050

5

The Grange

Moat

64

TRAFALGAR WK
TRAFALGAR WY
TRAFALGAR WY
NORMAN PK
NORMAN WAY
B1050

4

Works
PO

County
Prim Sch

Liby

Inf Sch

VIKING WY
VIKING WAY
VIKING WAY

SAXON WAY
OTTER CL
PARTRIDGE CL
HANTLEY
GLADSIDE

OATLANDS AVE

SAXON WAY

ROBIN CL
ALMOND GR
ACORN AV
ACORN AV

Hotel
CH

FOX HOLLOW
FOX HOLLOW

HOLLYTREES

CRAFTS WAY

Slate
Hall
Farm

3

PHEASANT RISE

STONE FIELD
LITTLE MEADOW
FIELD VW
FIELD VW
FIELD VW
SAXON WAY
THE SPINNEY

APPLETREES
APPLETREES

WATERMEAD
BROOKSIDE

HILLCREST

CRAFTS WAY

CRYSTAL RI
THRUPLE

THE BRAMBLES
THE GABLES

THE FAIRWAY

HUNTINGDON ROAD

Bar Hill

63

CB3

Craft's Hill

A14(T)

Hackers
Fruit Farm

2

OAKINGTON ROAD

Cambridge City
Crematorium

PETTIT'S CL
PETTIT'S CL
PETTIT'S
PETTIT'S LANE

HIGH ST

PARK WAY

1

Rectory Farm

Sheepclose
Spinney

SEARLES MD
OLD RECTORY DR
SCOTLAND RD
COTTON'S FIELD
COTTON'S FIELD

Dry
Drayton

Dry Drayton
Prim Sch

PH

MARK ST
PARK ST
PARK ST
PARK LA

62

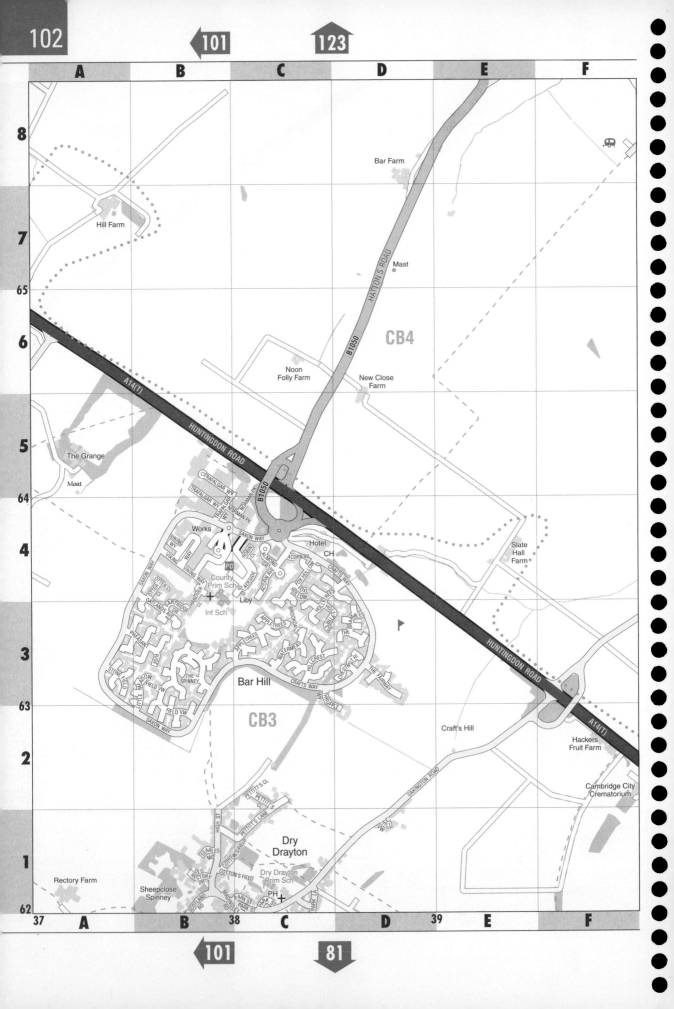

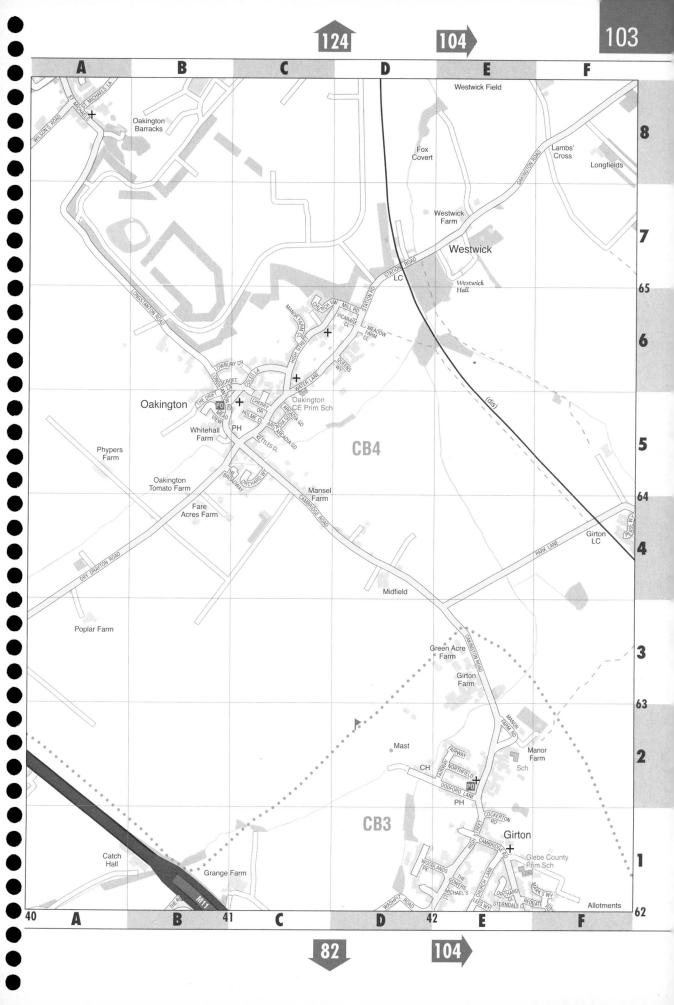

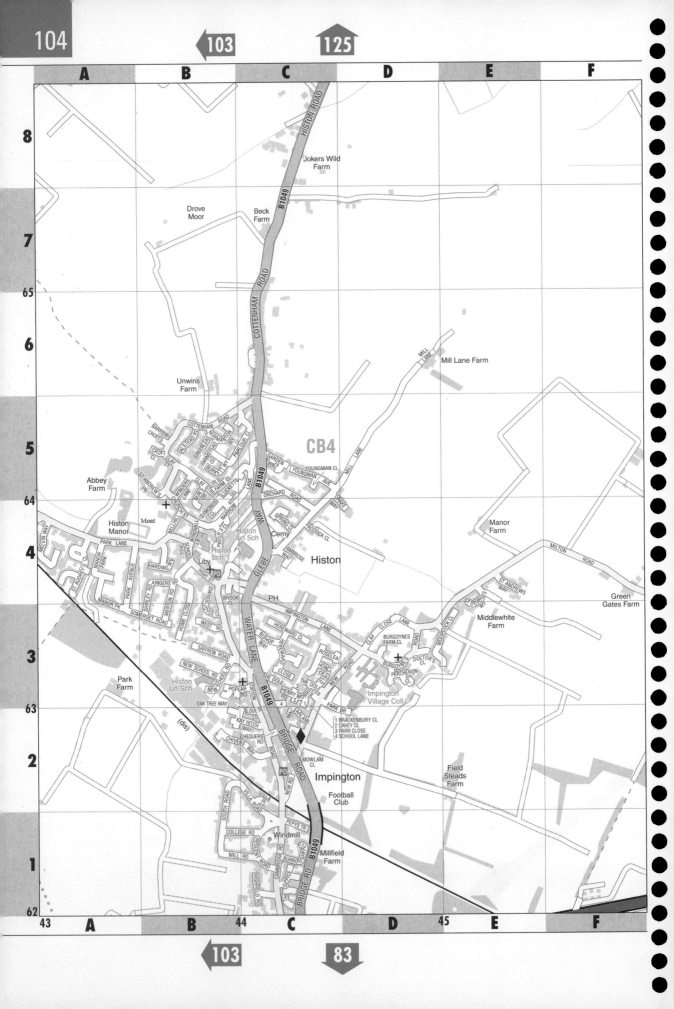

103
125

8

7

65

6

5

64

4

3

63

2

1

62

43 A B 44 C D 45 E F

103
83

HISTON ROAD
B1049
Jokers Wild Farm
Drove Moor
Beck Farm
COTTENHAM ROAD
MILL LANE
Mill Lane Farm
Unwins Farm
CB4
BARROW CROFTS
COTTENHAM ROAD
ALSTEAD RD
GREATLEAS
CRIMMINGTON
PARLOUR CL
CROFT CL
CLAY CL ST
FARMSTEAD CL
BURKEFT WY
OLD FARM CL
WINDERS
WIN'S ST
PAPWORTHS
CLAY ST
SYMONDS CL
MARROW LANE
LICKETTS
GARDEN WK
YOUNGMAN CL
YOUNGMAN AVE
TINKET WAY
B1049
ORCHARD ROAD
Abbey Farm
St ANDREW'S PK
SPRING CL
PADDOCK CL
Manor Farm
Histon Manor
BELLHILL CL
CHURCH ST
WINDMILL
HISTON SCH
Histon Jun Sch
Cemy
AMBROSE WAY
MILTON ROAD
Moat
PARK LANE
Histon Sch
GLEBE WAY
Histon
St ANDREWS WAY
MEVIN WAY
St ANDREY'S CL
MANOR PARK
HARDING WY
Liby
HIGH ST
PO
St GEORGE'S WY
Green Gates Farm
PARK AVENUE
SHIRLEY RD
MERTON RD
AINGERS RD
BROOK CL
PH
IMPINGTON LANE
CLAY CLOSE LANE
WOODCOCK CL
Middlewhite Farm
MANOR PK
HOME CLOSE
WEST RD
BISHOP
HEREWARD CL
ROSELEA
BURGOYNES FARM CL
SOMERSET ROAD
SAFFRON ROAD
HEREWARD CLOSE
HOME
NEW ROAD
DOCTOR'S CL
BURGOYNES
Park Farm
NEW SCHOOL RD
SCHOOLS RD
THE DOLE
3
THE DOLE
PERCHERON CL
Histon Jun Sch
POPLAR RD
NEW RD
HENRY MORRIS
1
Impington Village Coll
OAK TREE WAY
STATION ROAD
B1049
MACFARLANE LANE
PARK DR
LOVE'S WAY
KAY HITCH WAY
1 BRACKENBURY CL
2 DAVEY CL
3 PARR CLOSE
4 SCHOOL LANE
(dis)
CHEQUERS RD
CHIVERS WAY
BRIDGE ROAD
MOWLAM CL
Field Steads Farm
PO
Impington
NEW RD
SOUTH ROAD
VILLA ROAD
VILLA PL
Football Club
PEPYS TR
College RD
CAMBRIDGE RD
Windmill
BURROUGH CL
B1049
Millfield Farm
MILL RD
HIGHFIELD RD
THE COPPICE
BRIDGE RD

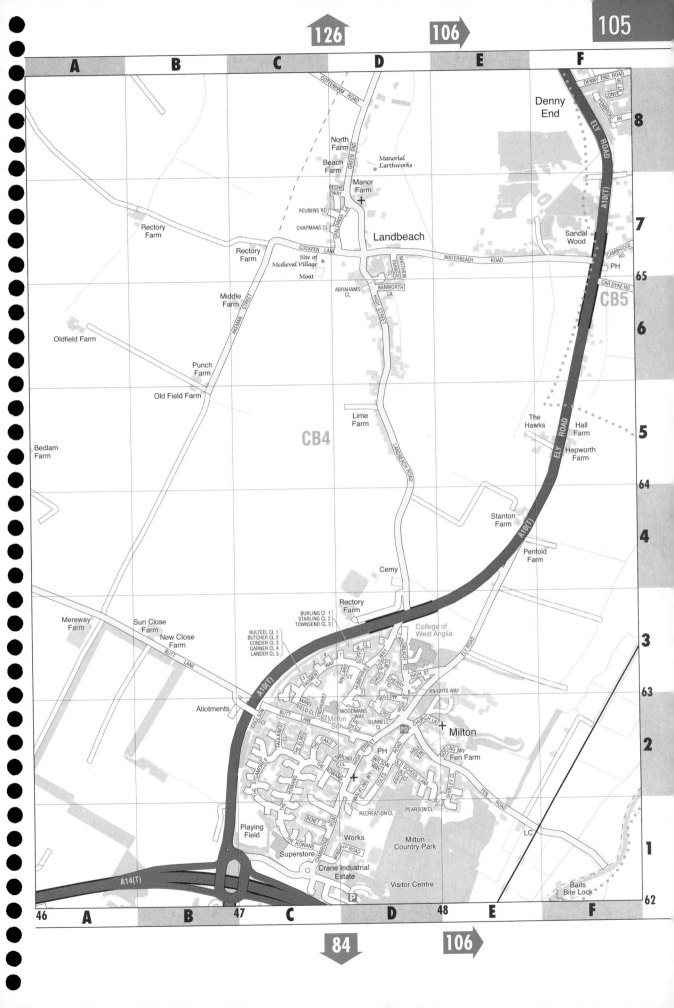

126
106

A   B   C   D   E   F

Denny End

8

North Farm

COTTENHAM ROAD

Beach Farm

Manorial Earthworks

GREEN END

BECHE WAY

Manor Farm

7

REUBENS RD

SPALDINGS LA

Landbeach

Sandal Wood

CHAPMANS CL

Rectory Farm

COCKFEN LANE

Rectory Farm

MATHEW PARKER CL

WATERBEACH ROAD

PH

CAMBRIDGE RD

65

Site of Medieval Village

Moat

ABRAHAMS CL

BANWORTH LA

CAR DYKE RD

CB5

Middle Farm

AKEMAN STREET

HIGH STREET

6

Oldfield Farm

Punch Farm

Old Field Farm

Lime Farm

CB4

The Hawks

ELY ROAD

Hall Farm

5

Hepworth Farm

Bedlam Farm

LANDBEACH ROAD

64

Stanton Farm

A10(T)

4

Penfold Farm

Cemy

Rectory Farm

BURLING CI 1
STARLING CL 2
TOWNSEND CL 3

College of West Anglia

3

Mereway Farm

Sun Close Farm

New Close Farm

BUTT LANE

BULTEEL CL 1
BUTCHER CL 2
CONDER CL 3
GARNER CL 4
LANDER CL 5

A10(T)

CL

LANDBEACH RD

ELY RD

Allotments

COULSON

BUTT LANE

MANS-FIELD CL

LYNDHURST

FROMENT WAY

BALLARD

HUMPHRIES

SUTTY

DAVID CL

WAY

CHERRY

WILLOW CRES

HIGH ST

HIGH ST

KNIGHTS WAY

63

Milton Sch

FALLANER CL

THE ELMS

THE OAKS

EDMUND CL

HIGH STREET

WOODMANS WAY

GUNNELL CL

PH

WILSON WAY

COLES RD

HALL END

CHURCH LA

PO

Milton

GOODING WY

Fen Farm

2

THE SYCAMORES

THE ROWANS

WALKLING WY

PRIORY CL

OLD SCHOOL LANE

SHIRLEY CL

FEN ROAD

Playing Field

THE ROWANS

BENET CL

CAMBRIDGE RD

WINSHIP ROAD

Works

Milton Country Park

RECREATION CL

PEARSON CL

LC

1

Superstore

Crane Industrial Estate

A14(T)

Visitor Centre

Baits Bite Lock

62

46   A   B   47   C   D   48   E   F

84
106

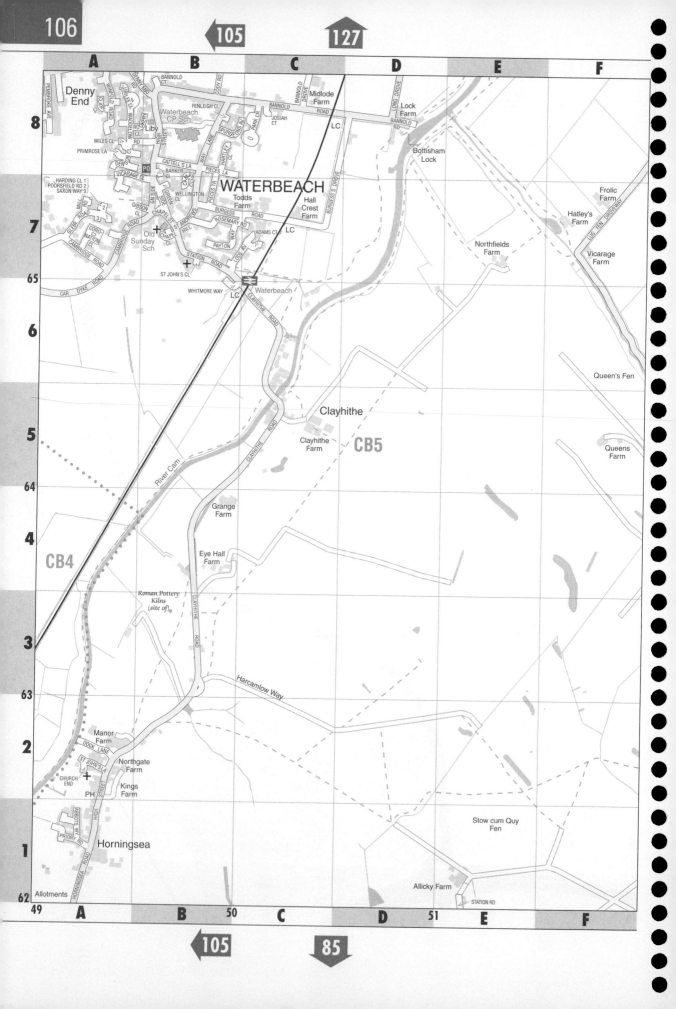

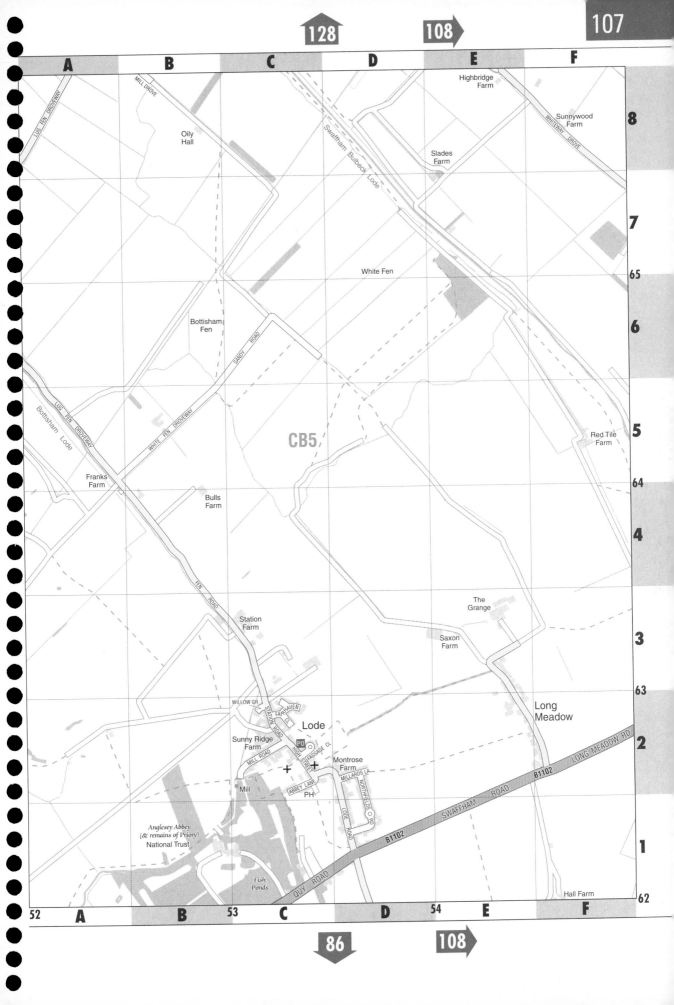

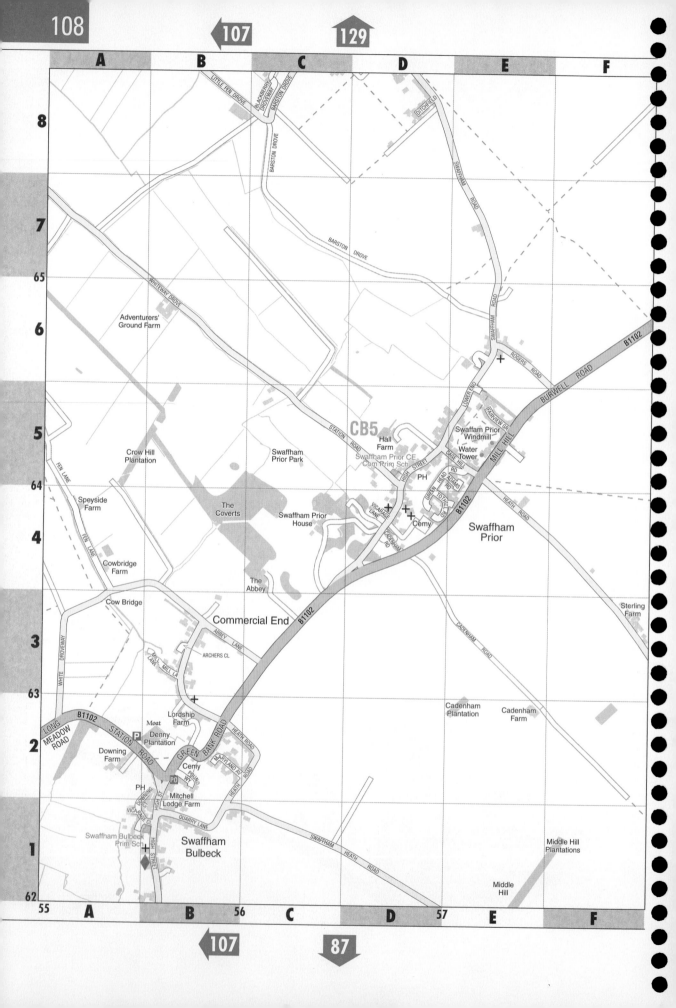

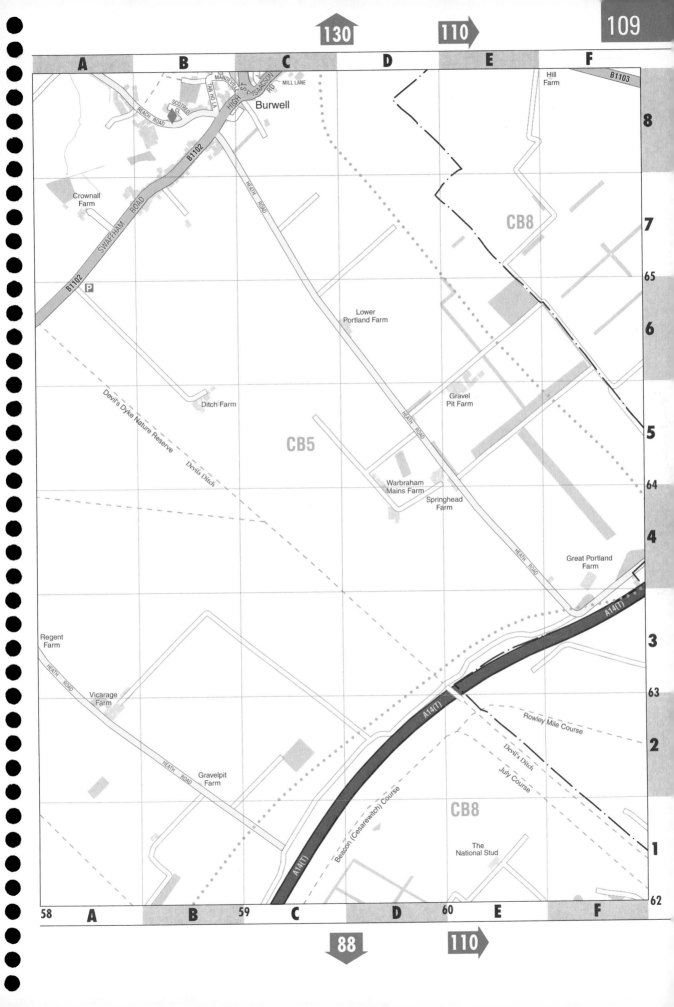

A   B   C   D   E   F

8

B1103 BURWELL ROAD
THE DRIFT
Orchard Farm
NEW RD
NEW RD
MILL LA.
ANNE'S CL
Park
GEORGE GIBSON CLOSE
Windmill Hill
THE HIGHLANDS
A142 FORDHAM RD
Studlands Park
NIMBUS WAY
AUREOLE WK
QUEENS VIEW
CECIL KING GEORGE AV
KING GEORGESWAY QUEENSWAY
OXFORD ST
SWAN LA
CHURCH WOOD CL
COTTON END RD
B1103
SAXON CL
ROYAL PALACE CLOSE
WATER
HYPERION
PINZA CL
PERSIMMON
TUVAL WALK
PARKERS WALK
PARKERS WALK
AUREOLE WALK
NIMBUS WAY
HYPERION WAY
A142
Exning
Exning CP Sch
PO
SWAN GR
CHURCH CL
Exeter Stud
Cemy
BRICKFIELDS AV
GOLDEN MILLER CLOSE
PRETIGO
HETHERSETT CLOSE
STUDLANDS
PARK
AVENUE
OAKS DRIVE
Works
Studlands Park

7

Harraton Stud
WENDRED'S WAY
ST WENDRED'S STREET
HIGMORE
LACEY'S LANE
DUCKS LANE
ST MARY'S CL
Allotments
Brickfield Stud
Sports Club
VICTORIA WAY
Studlands Park Business Centre
STUDLANDS PARK
Studlands Park Ind Estate
WILLIE SMITH ROAD
Works
Playing Fields
St Felix CE VC Middle Sch

65

HEATH ROAD
A14(T)
EXNING ROAD
B1103
HAMMOND CL
AUREATE SCHOOL RD
LAUREATE PADDOCKS
LAUREATE GDNS
DOUG SMITH CL 1
GORDON RICHARDS CL 2
LESTER PIGGOTT WAY 3
MATT DAWSON CL 4

6

Industrial Estate
HAMILTON ROAD
Laureate CP Sch
Factory
CPORT ROAD
GUINEA'S CL
DEPOT ROAD
CRAVEN WY
CORSICAN PINE CL
GREVILLE
STARKEY AV 1
TOM JENNINGS CL 2
GEORGE LAMBTON AVENUE
MESTON WY
HURLESS

5

Seven Springs
CB8
Hamilton Stud
E5
ANDREW RD 1
BARTONS PL 2
COLLINGS PL 3
DURHAM WAY 5
FEILDEN WAY
ROSEBERY WAY
CHURCHILL AVENUE
ELIZABETH AVENUE
FARNHAM WAY
HALIFAX WAY
NORFOLK AVE
DERBY WY
RIVERTON
Scaltback Middle Sch
EVERSON
KING EDWARD VII RD
Philips CL
ST FABIANS CL
B1103
PO
FIELD TR RD
LINTON CL
HESMAN CL
H

64

SEFTON WAY
LANSING
PRINCE AV
ROCHFORT
LEADER'S WAY
SUFFOLK RD
PRIMROSE
DSS
Sports Ctr
HAMILTON ROAD
Pool
Paddocks CR Sch
STIRLING GR
SOMERSET
TANNERSFIELD WAY
MILL BANK
FRESHFIELDS
EXNING ROAD

4

Southfield Farm
A14(T)
Equine Pool
PHILLIPS
DRINKWATER CL
EDINBURGH WAY
MANDERSTON RD
WINDSOR RD
Playing Field
Newmarket Upper Sch
1 BAHAM CL
2 SOUTHFIELDS CL
COASTAL CLOSE
ASTRAL CLOSE
KINGSWAY
Playing Field
ROWLEY DR
LOWTHER ST
BLACK BEAR LANE

3

PRINCESS PORTLAND RD
CHARLES CL
HILL CL
VALLEY WAY
PO
1
Holdsworth Valley CP Sch
HAMILTON ROAD
ROWLEY ROWS
THE ROWS
FALMOUTH AV
LISLE CL
CECIL CL
Newmarket Swimming Pool

63

Newmarket Heath
THE HAMILTONS
Government Offices
Cooper Memorial Fountain
Cemetery
HIGH ST
FAIRLAWNS RD 1
HALLWYCK GDNS 2
B1061

2

Rowley Mile Course
The Millennium Grandstand
BARBARA STRADBROKE AVENUE
DULLINGHAM ROAD

1

Racecourses
Cambridge Hill
A1304
Wyck Hall Stud
B1061

62

Devil's Ditch

61   A   62   B   C   63   D   E   F

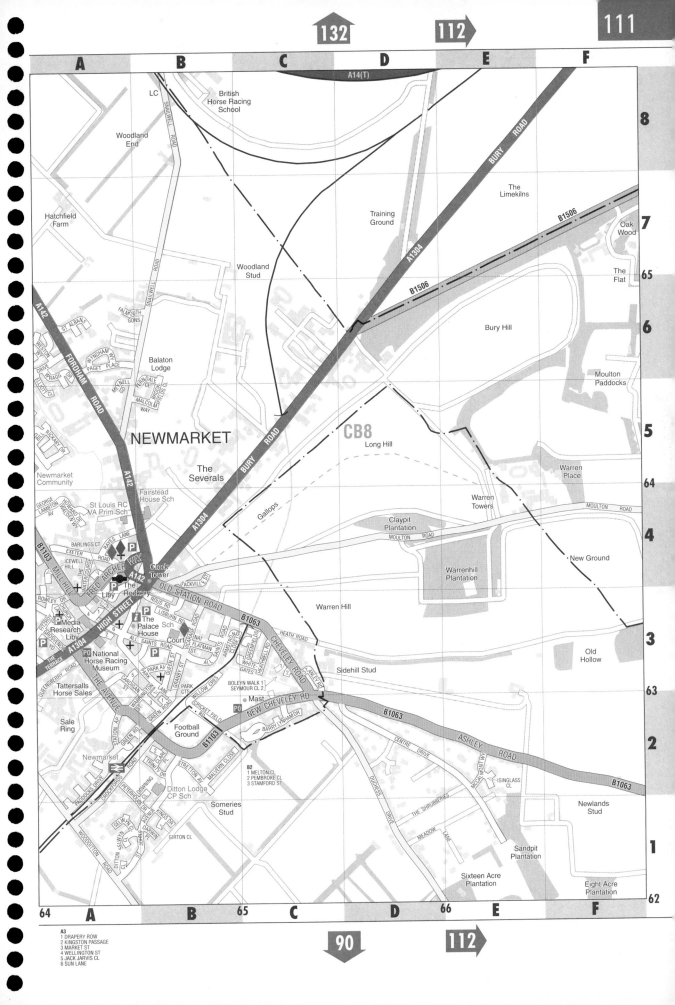

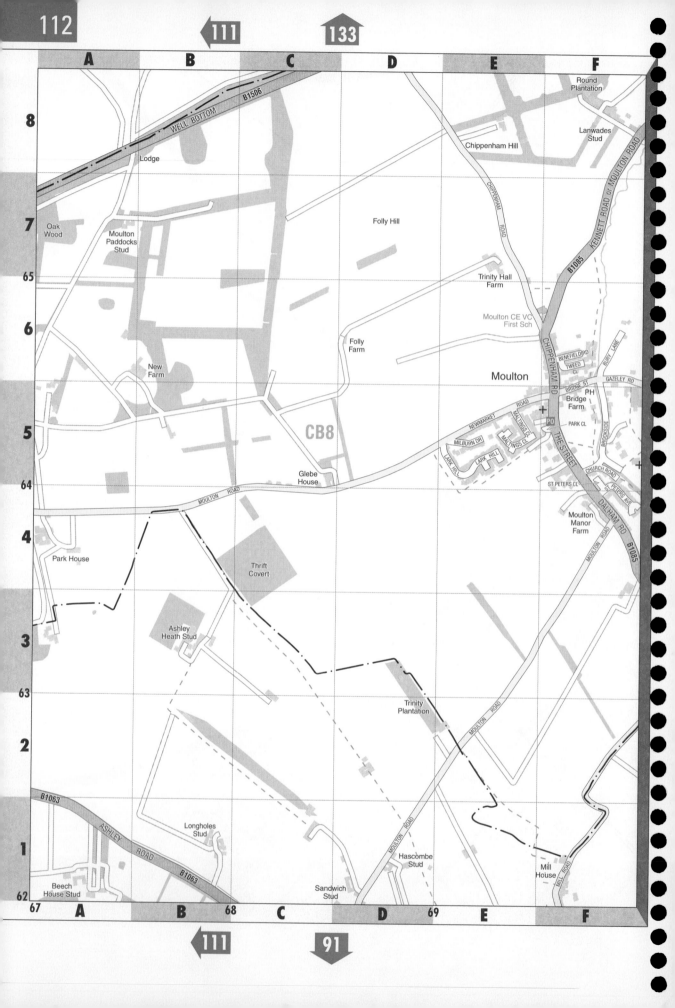

A B C D E F

8

Round
Plantation

Well Bottom B1506

Chippenham Hill

Lanwades
Stud

Lodge

7

Oak
Wood

Folly Hill

Moulton
Paddocks
Stud

Chippenham Road

Kennett Road or Moulton Road

65

Trinity Hall
Farm

B1085

6

Folly
Farm

Moulton CE VC
First Sch

New
Farm

Benefield Rd

Bury Lane

TWEED
CL

Moulton

Chippenham Rd

Gazeley Rd

5

CB8

Newmarket
Road

Maltings Cl

PH
Bridge
Farm

Brookside

Milburn Dr

PO

Park Cl

The Street

Lark Hill

Maltings Cl

Lark Hill

Glebe
House

64

Moulton Road

St Peters Cl

Church Road

St Peters Ave

4

Moulton
Manor
Farm

Dalham Rd

Park House

Thrift
Covert

Moulton Road

B1085

3

Ashley
Heath Stud

63

Trinity
Plantation

Moulton Road

2

B1063

Longholes
Stud

Ashley Road

Moulton Road

1

B1063

Hascombe
Stud

Mill
House

Mill Road

62

Beech
House Stud

Sandwich
Stud

67 A B 68 C D 69 E F

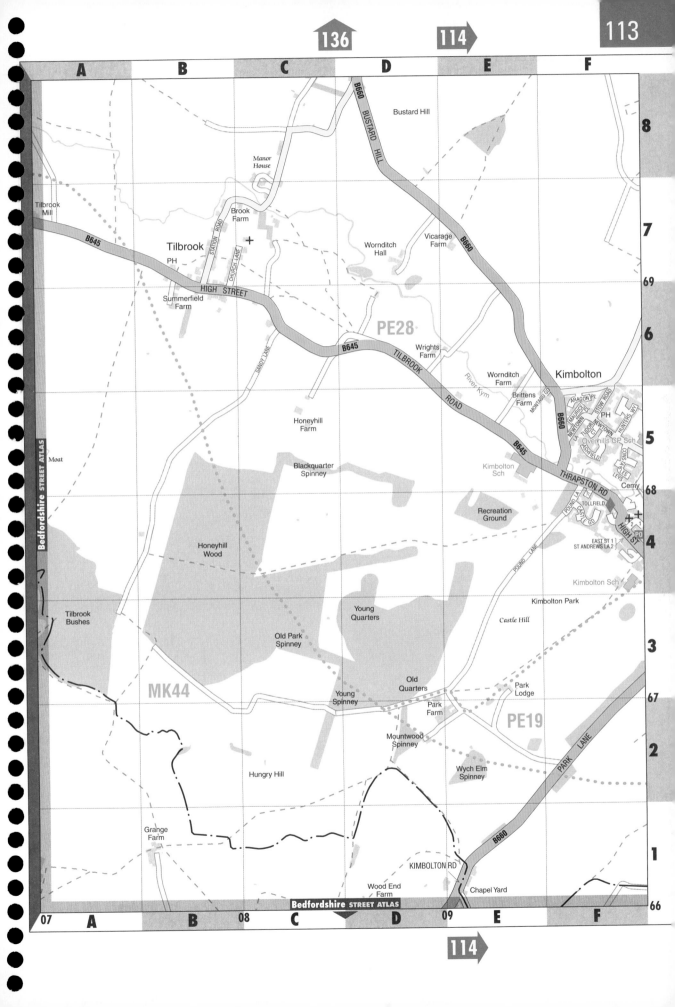

113
137

A
B
C
D
E
F
8
7
69
6
5
68
4
3
67
2
1
66
10
11
12
Airfield
(disused)
Airfield
(disused)
GROVEMERE CT
NENE RD
KIM RD
OUSE RD
RIVER RD
BROOK RD
Bicton
Industrial
Estate
Mast
Mast
STOCKING LANE
Magpie
Farm
PE28
High
Park Farm
BIGRAM'S LANE
Bigram's
Farm
Lowen
Wood
Warren
Hill
Newtown
Overhills
CP Sch
Warren
Spinney
NEWTOWN
Cemy
EASTON ROAD
Priory
Farm
PE19
Dudney
Wood
Three Shires Way
Kimbolton
EAST ST
LONDON RD
Sch
Kimbolton
Castle
Moat
Kimbolton
Park
B660
PARK LANE
Stonely
EASTON ROAD
Lady
Grove
Stonely
Grange
HATCHET LA
HATCHET LA
OLD FORD LANE
B645
Stonely
Hill Farm
Claylands
Farm
Agden Hill
Farm
College
Farm
Gimbers End
River Kym
MK44
Agdengreen
Spinney
Lower
Park Farm

113
93

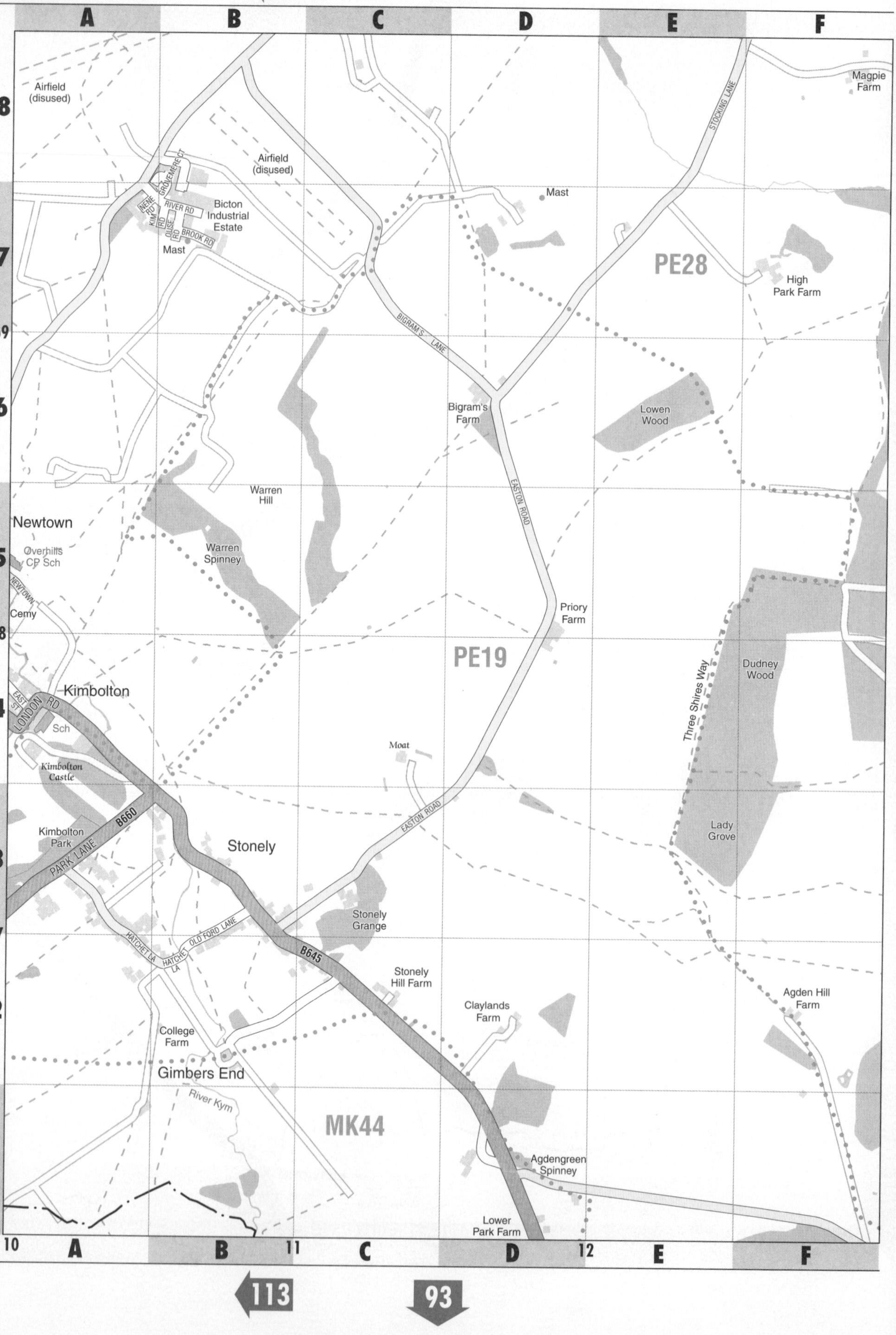

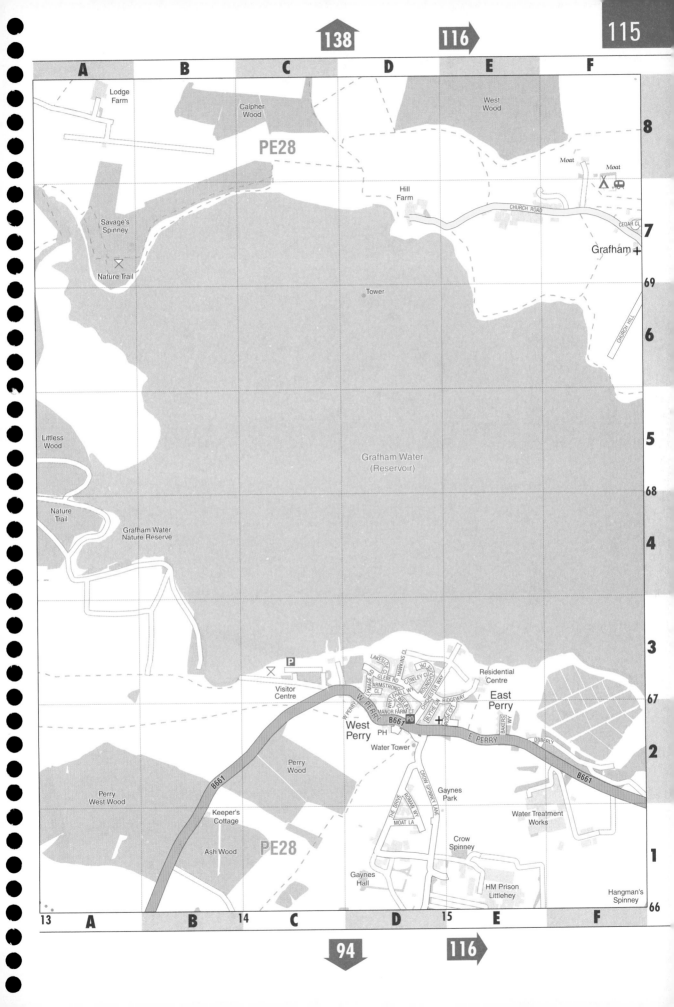

115
139

	A	B	C	D	E	F

8

Sparrow's Spinney

Brampton Wood Nature Reserve

P

7

MEADOW END

BREACH ROAD

CEDAR CL

ALSYKE CL

VAN DIEMANS WY

HARTCRAFT CL

CLEARANCE FIELD CL

Playing Fields

BRAMPTON RD

Moat

HARTHAM CL

INHAMS WY

CHURCH RD

THE PIGHTLE

Grafham

69

CHURCH HILL

CHESTNUT CL

HOME CL

Water Tower

BUCKDEN ROAD

Thistle Hill

6

Moat

PE28

5

PE19

P

Hardonian Farm

TAYLORS LANE

68

Grafham Water Exhibition Centre

Paddock Farm

Model Farm

4

Buckden Wood

Wood Farm

PERRY ROAD **B661**

3

Grafham Water (Reservoir)

Westfield Farm

Tower

B661

Moat

Shooter's Hollow

67

GREAT NORTH ROAD

2

Diddington Wood

Diddington Brook

P

Coronation Wood

1

Highfield Farm

Diddington Wood

Jubilee Copse

A1(T)

66

Lodge Farm

Paxton Road Farm

16	A	B	17	C	D	18	E	F

115
95

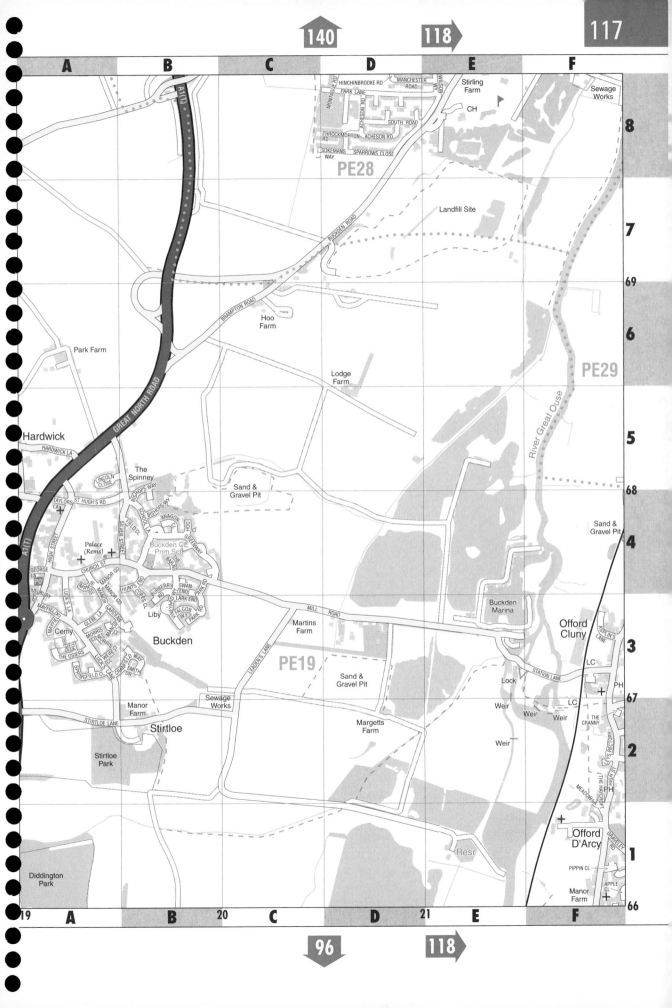

117
141

A B C D E F

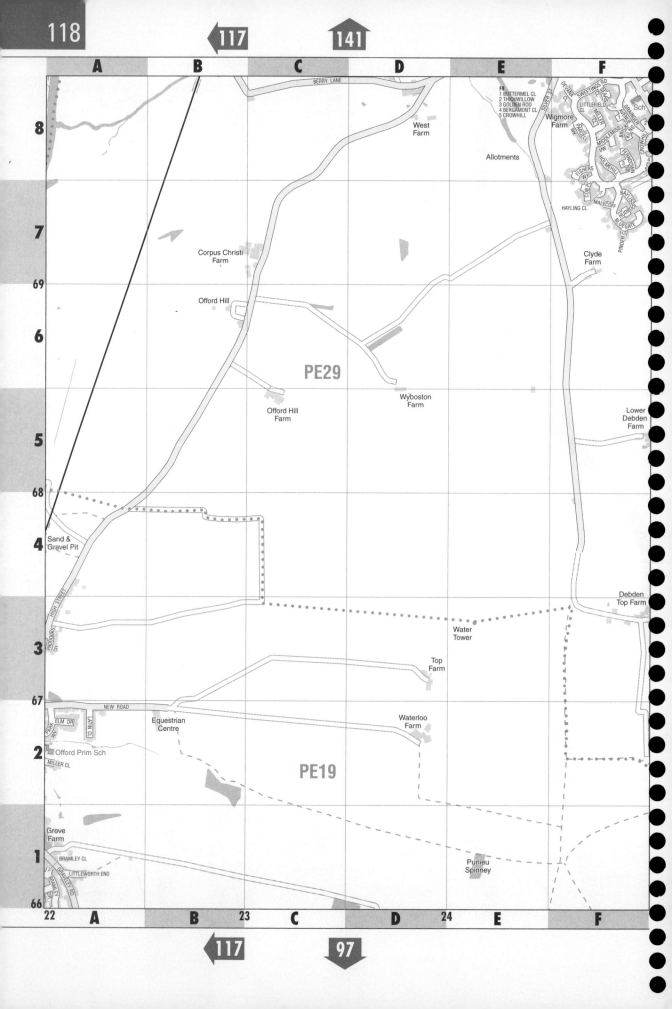

8

BERRY LANE

West
Farm

Allotments

F8
1 BUTTERMEL CL
2 THICKWILLOW
3 GOLDEN ROD
4 BERGAMONT CL
5 CROWHILL

SILVER ST
DEVANA CL
SWEETINGS RD
PEARS
GRANGER
Sch
LITTLEFIELD CL
MILLER
CROWHILL

Wigmore
Farm

MIDDLEMISS
PARCEL WK
BRICKS
FERNDOWN DR
HOLMEHILL

JOB PL
FISHERS WY

MALECOFF
HUDHOOD
BALLISS
BLUEGATE
PINDER CL GATE

HAYLING CL

7

Corpus Christi
Farm

Clyde
Farm

69

Offord Hill

6

PE29

Wyboston
Farm

Lower
Debden
Farm

Offord Hill
Farm

5

68

Sand &
Gravel Pit

4

HIGH STREET

PADDOCKS CH

Debden
Top Farm

Water
Tower

3

Top
Farm

67

NEW ROAD

PRK WAY
ELM DR
LATIN CL

Equestrian
Centre

Waterloo
Farm

2

Offord Prim Sch

MILLER CL

PE19

Grove
Farm

1

BRAMLEY CL

BRAMLEY

GRAVELEY RD

LITTLEWORTH END

Purlieu
Spinney

66

22 A B 23 C D 24 E F

117
97

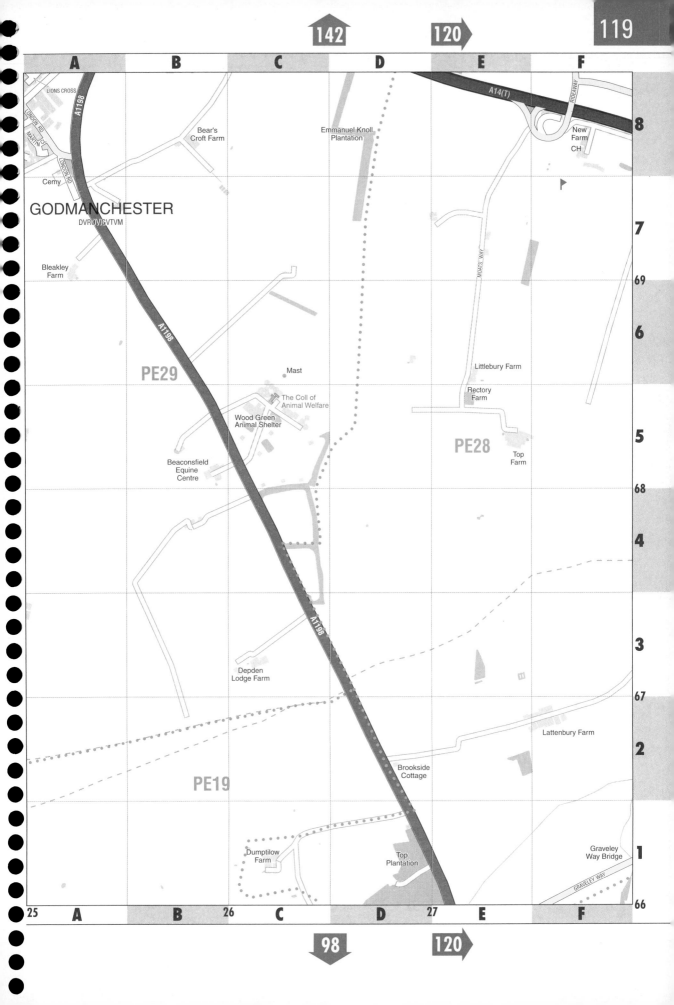

A   B   C   D   E   F

LIONS CROSS

A14(T)

RIDE WAY

A1198

LONDON RD

MARTIN

8

Bear's
Croft Farm

Emmanuel Knoll
Plantation

New
Farm
CH

Cemy

LONDON RD

GODMANCHESTER

DVROVIGVTVM

7

Bleakley
Farm

MOATS WAY

69

A1198

6

PE29

Mast

Littlebury Farm

The Coll of
Animal Welfare

Rectory
Farm

Wood Green
Animal Shelter

PE28

5

Beaconsfield
Equine
Centre

Top
Farm

68

4

Depden
Lodge Farm

A1198

3

67

Brookside
Cottage

Lattenbury Farm

2

PE19

Dumptilow
Farm

Top
Plantation

Graveley
Way Bridge

1

GRAVELEY WAY

66

25 A   B 26 C   D 27 E   F

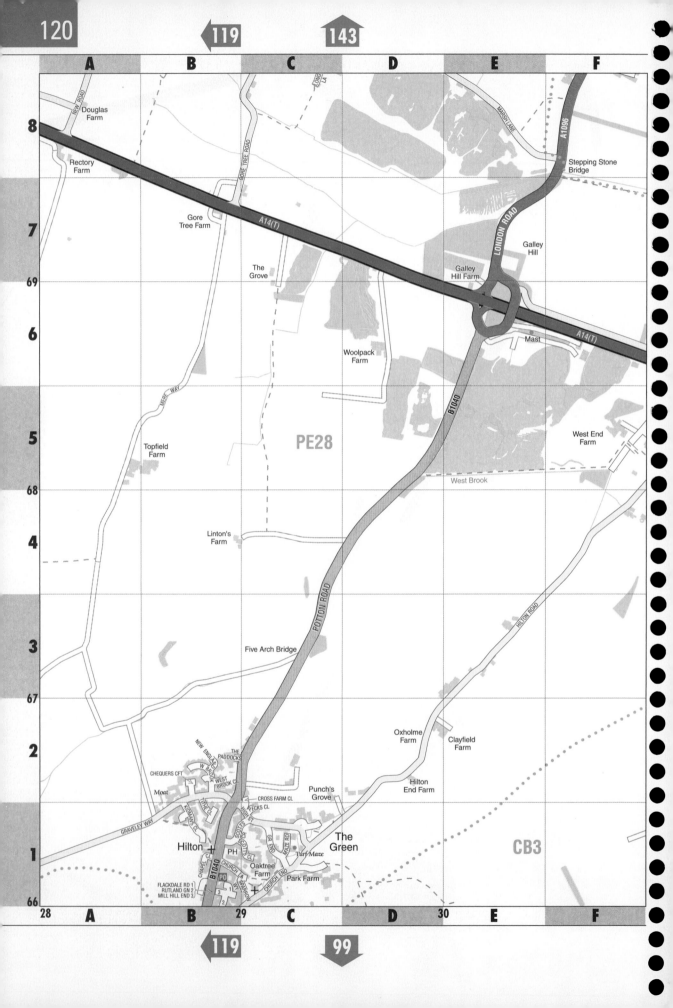

119
143

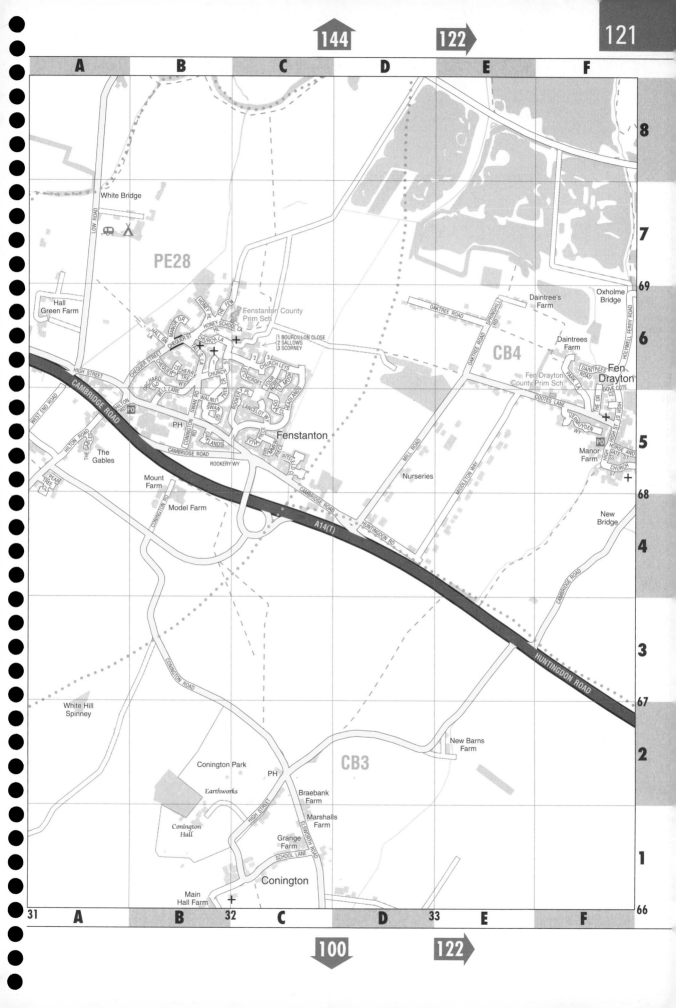

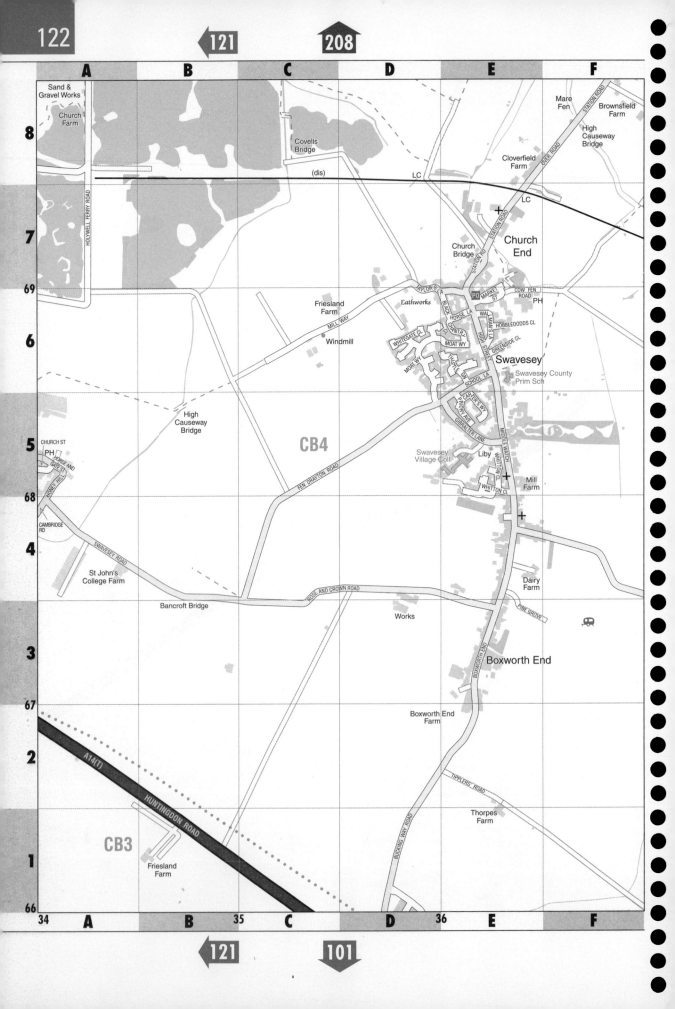

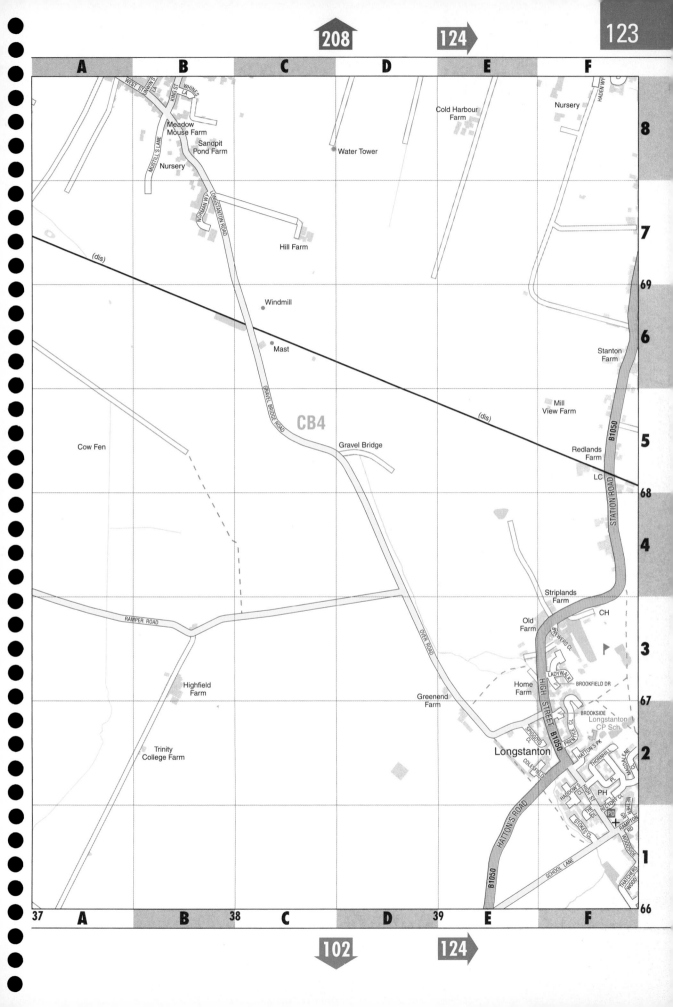

A B C D E F

8

7

69

6

5

68

4

3

67

2

1

66

Meadow Mouse Farm
Sandpit Pond Farm
Nursery
WEST ST
JANWIN'S LA
KING ST
WHINE'S LA
MUSTILL'S LANE
NORMAN WY
LONGSTANTON ROAD

Hill Farm

(dis)

Windmill

Mast

GRAVEL BRIDGE ROAD

CB4

Cow Fen

Gravel Bridge

(dis)

Cold Harbour Farm

Water Tower

Nursery
HADEN WY

Stanton Farm

Mill View Farm

Redlands Farm

LC

B1050

STATION ROAD

RAMPER ROAD

Highfield Farm

Trinity College Farm

OVER ROAD

Greenend Farm

Striplands Farm
Old Farm
Home Farm

CH
BREWERS CL
LADY WALK
BROOKFIELD DR

HIGH STREET
B1050

SPRIGGS CL
COLESFIELD
HADDOW'S CL
HIGH ST
RECTORY CL
THE
STOKES CL

Longstanton

BROOKSIDE
Longstanton CP Sch

THORNHILL
MAGDALEN LANE
HATTON'S PK
TO PRINK
PL
PH
NETHER GR
RAMPTON RD
WOODSIDE
THATCHERS WOOD

HATTON'S ROAD

B1050

SCHOOL LANE

PO

123 209

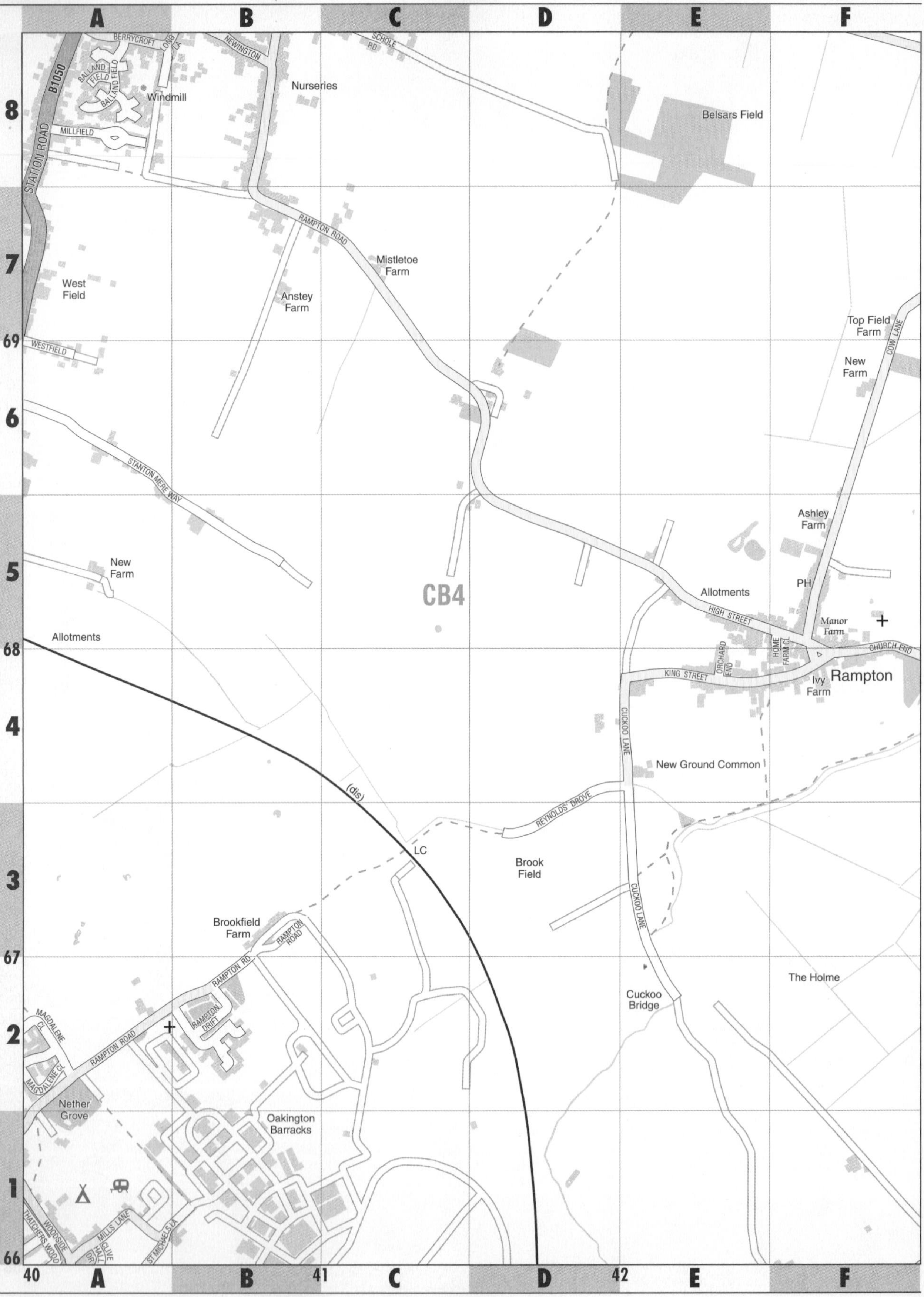

A   B   C   D   E   F

8

BERRYCROFT
LONG
NEWINGTON
SCHOLE RD
B1050
Nurseries
BALLAND FIELD
Windmill
BALLAND FIELD
Belsars Field
MILLFIELD
STATION ROAD

7

West Field
RAMPTON ROAD
Mistletoe Farm
Anstey Farm

69

WESTFIELD
Top Field Farm
New Farm
COW LANE

6

STANTON MERE WAY
Ashley Farm

5

New Farm
CB4
Allotments
PH
Manor Farm
HIGH STREET

68

Allotments
CHURCH END
ORCHARD END
HOME FARM CL
Rampton
KING STREET
Ivy Farm

4

CUCKOO LANE
New Ground Common

(dis)
REYNOLDS GROVE

3

LC
Brook Field
CUCKOO LANE

67

Brookfield Farm
RAMPTON RD
RAMPTON ROAD
The Holme

2

MAGDALENE CL
RAMPTON DRIFT
RAMPTON ROAD
MAGDALENE CL
Cuckoo Bridge

Nether Grove
Oakington Barracks

1

THATCHERS WOOD
MILLS LANE
CLIVE HALL DR
WOODSIDE
ST MICHAELS LA

66

40   A   B   41   C   D   42   E   F

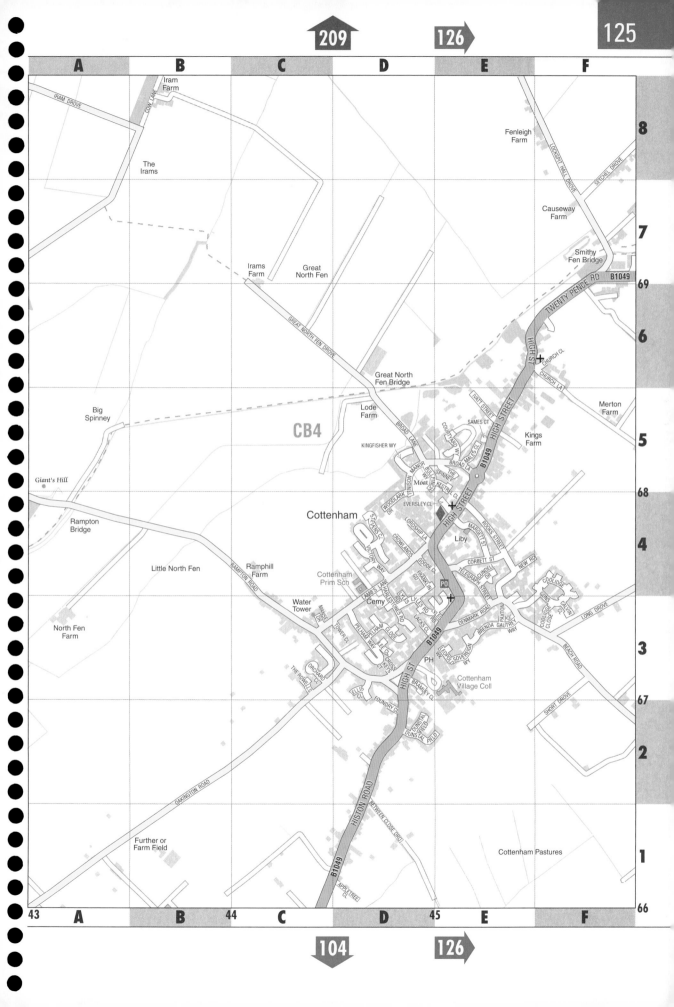

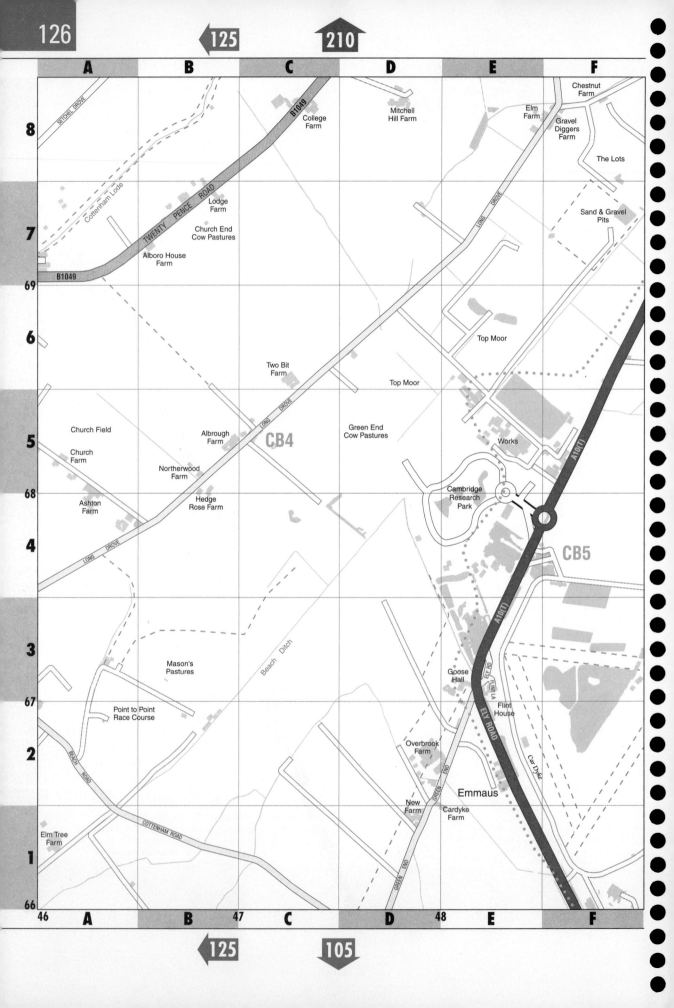

125
210

A   B   C   D   E   F

8

SETCHEL DROVE

B1049

College Farm

Mitchell Hill Farm

Chestnut Farm

Elm Farm

Gravel Diggers Farm

The Lots

Cottenham Lode

TWENTY PENCE ROAD

Lodge Farm

7

Church End Cow Pastures

Alboro House Farm

LONG DROVE

Sand & Gravel Pits

69

B1049

6

Top Moor

Two Bit Farm

LONG DROVE

Top Moor

Green End Cow Pastures

A10(T)

5

Church Field

Albrough Farm

CB4

Works

Church Farm

Northerwood Farm

Cambridge Research Park

68

Ashton Farm

Hedge Rose Farm

LONG DROVE

4

A10(T)

CB5

3

Mason's Pastures

Beach Ditch

Goose Hall

ELY RD

FLINT LA

Flint House

67

Point to Point Race Course

ELY ROAD

Car Dyke

2

Overbrook Farm

BEACH ROAD

GREEN END

Emmaus

New Farm

Cardyke Farm

1

Elm Tree Farm

COTTENHAM ROAD

GREEN END

66

46   A   B   47   C   D   48   E   F

125
105

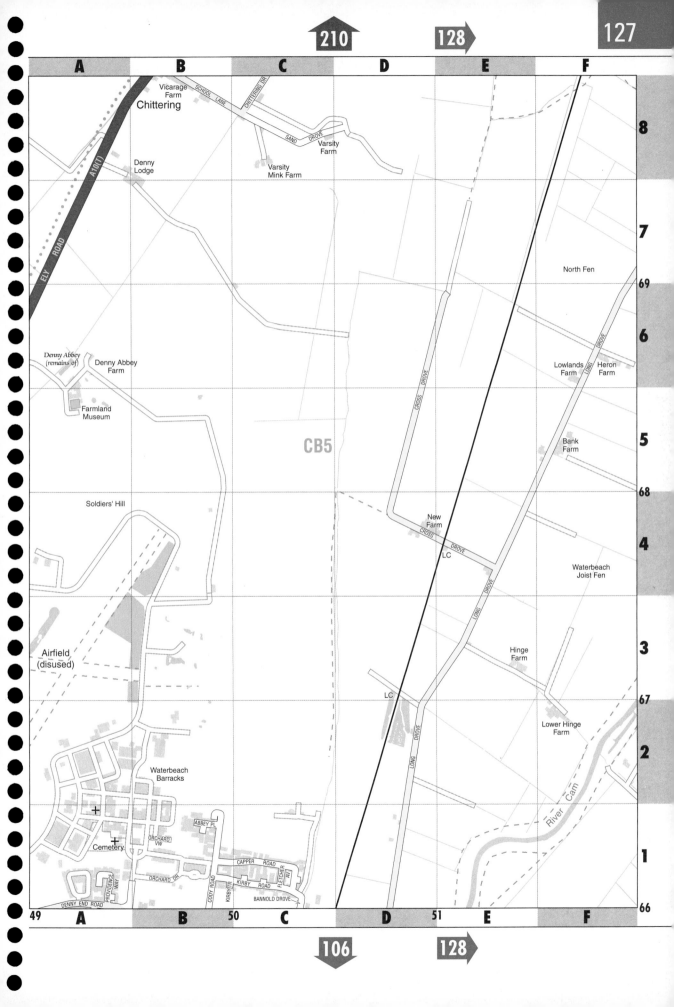

A B C D E F

8 7 69 6 5 68 4 67 3 2 1 66

Chittering

Vicarage Farm

SCHOOL LANE

CHITTERING DR

SAND DROVE

Varsity Farm

Denny Lodge

Varsity Mink Farm

ELY ROAD

A10(T)

North Fen

Denny Abbey (remains of)

Denny Abbey Farm

Farmland Museum

CROSS DROVE

LONG DROVE

Lowlands Farm

Heron Farm

CB5

Bank Farm

Soldiers' Hill

New Farm

CROSS DROVE

LC

Waterbeach Joist Fen

LONG DROVE

Airfield (disused)

Hinge Farm

LC

Lower Hinge Farm

Waterbeach Barracks

LONG DROVE

River Cam

ABBEY PL

Cemetery

ORCHARD VW

CAPPER ROAD

FLETCHER AV

ORCHARD DR

CODY ROAD

KIRBY ROAD

KIRBY TER

PROVIDENCE WAY

DENNY END ROAD

BANNOLD DROVE

49 50 51

A B C D E F

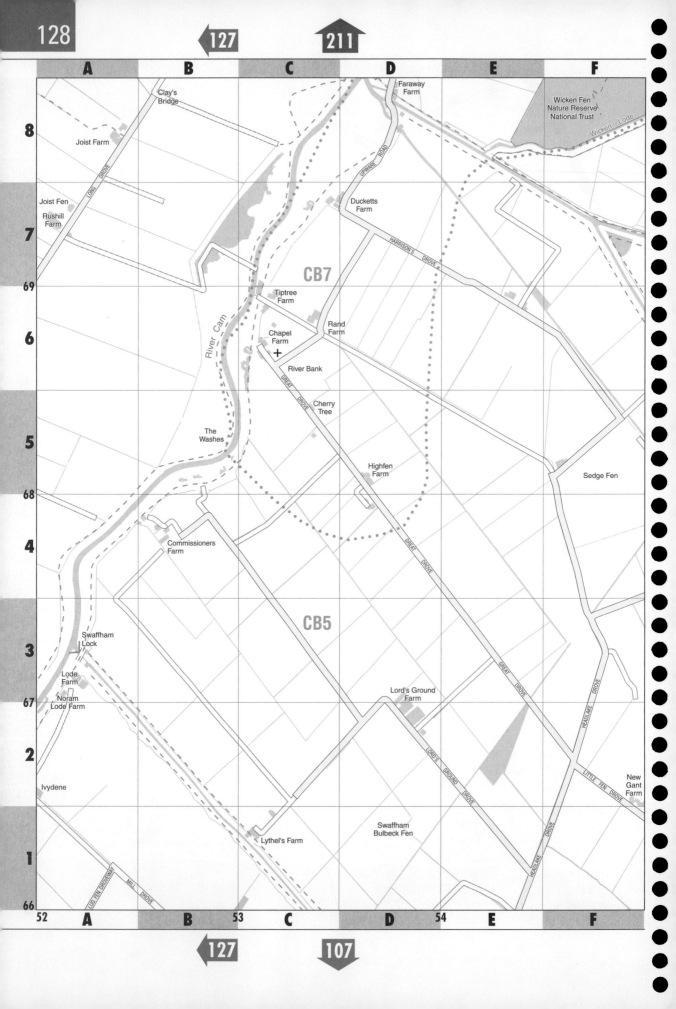

← 127

↑ 211

A B C D E F

8

7

69

6

5

68

4

3

67

2

1

66

52 A B 53 C D 54 E F

Clay's Bridge

Joist Farm

Joist Fen

Rushill Farm

LONG DROVE

River Cam

Faraway Farm

Wicken Fen Nature Reserve National Trust

Wicken Lode

UPWARE ROAD

Ducketts Farm

HARRISON'S DROVE

CB7

Tiptree Farm

Rand Farm

Chapel Farm
+

River Bank

GREAT DROVE

Cherry Tree

The Washes

Highfen Farm

Sedge Fen

Commissioners Farm

GREAT DROVE

CB5

Swaffham Lock

Lode Farm

Noram Lode Farm

GREAT DROVE

Lord's Ground Farm

HEADLAKE DROVE

Ivydene

LORD'S GROUND DROVE

LITTLE FEN DROVE

New Gant Farm

LUG FEN DROVEWAY

MILL DROVE

Lythel's Farm

Swaffham Bulbeck Fen

HEADLAKE DROVE

← 127

↓ 107

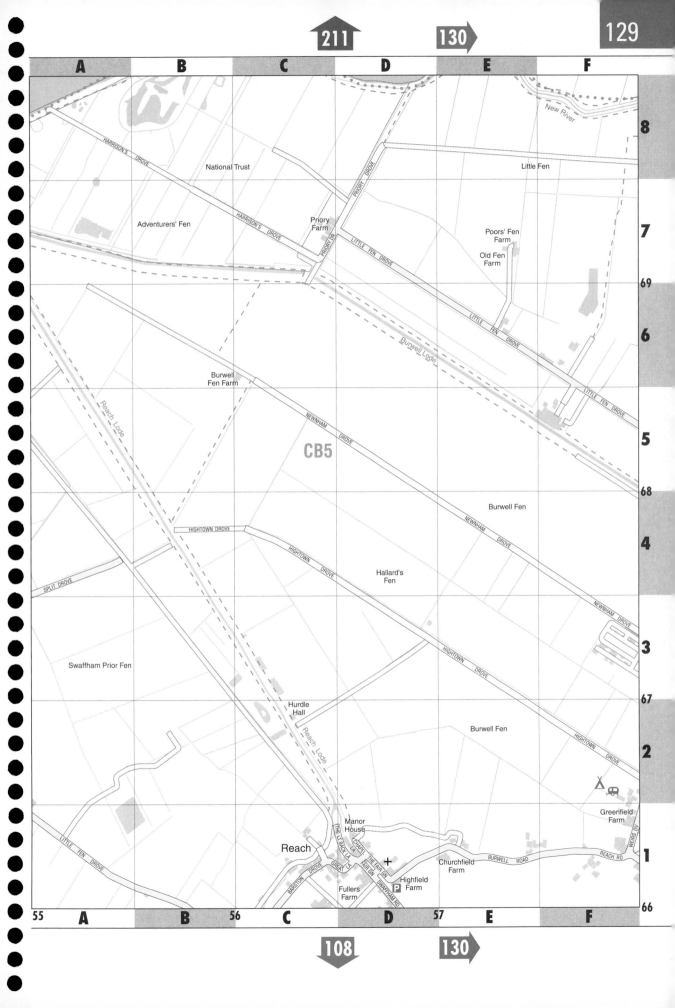

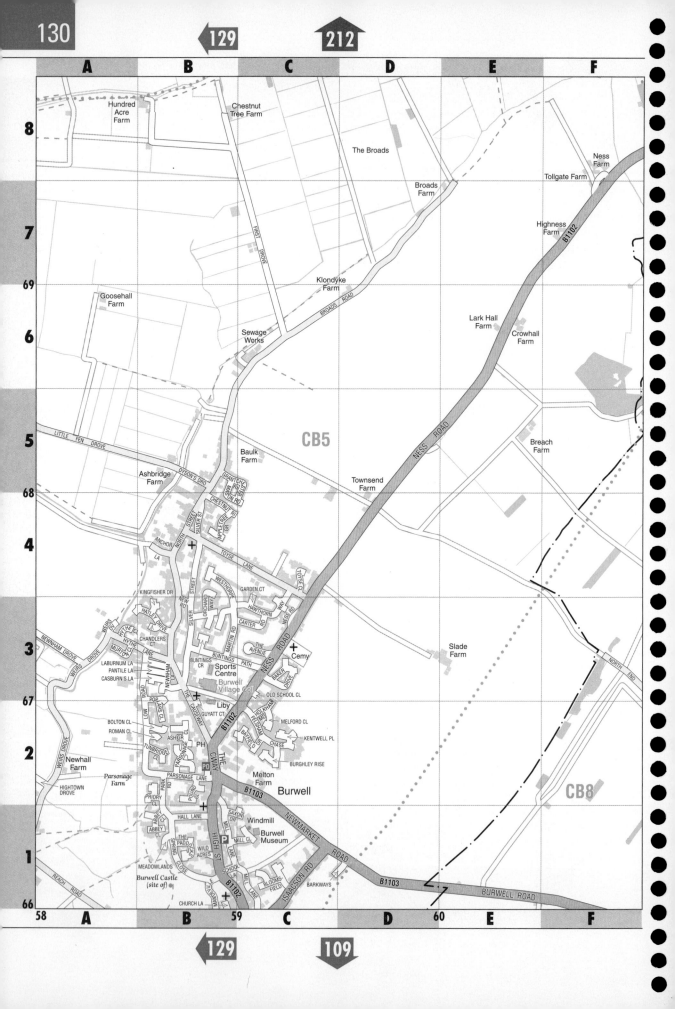

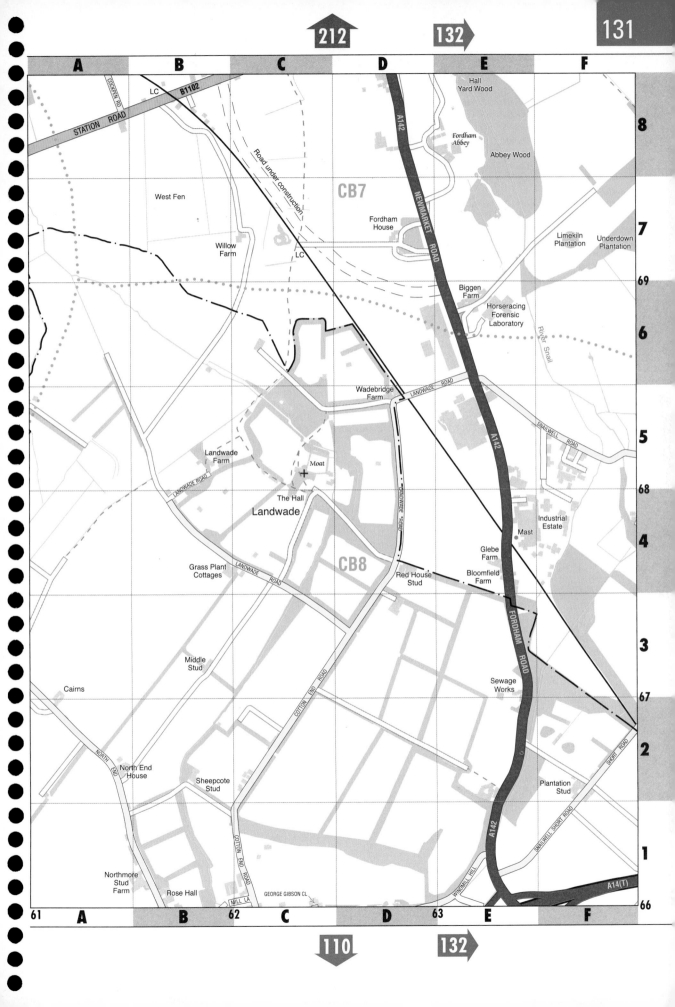

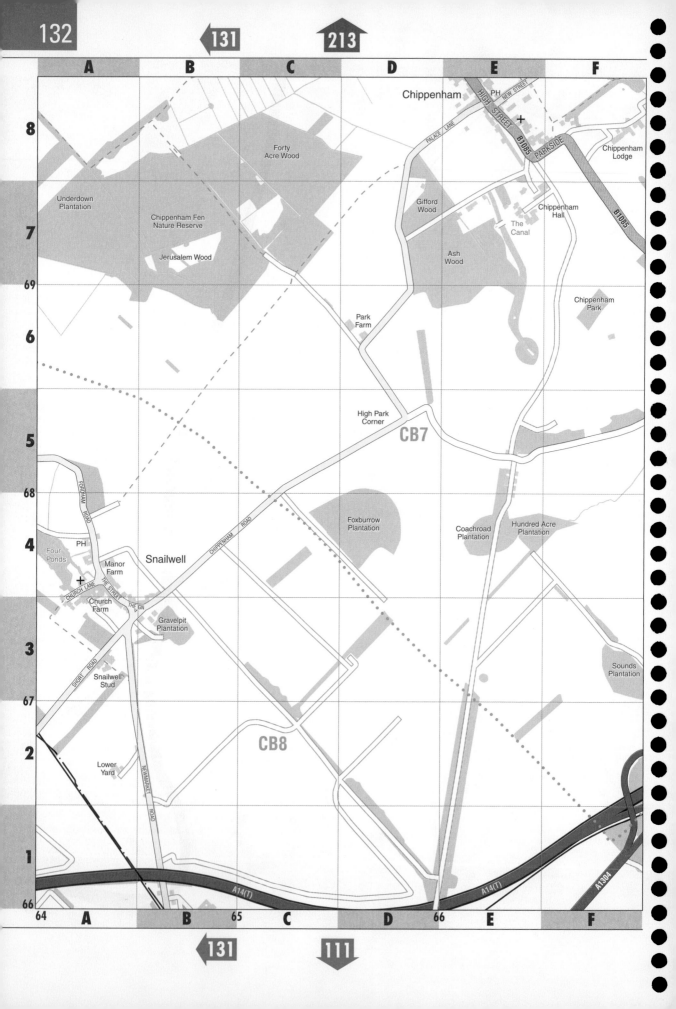

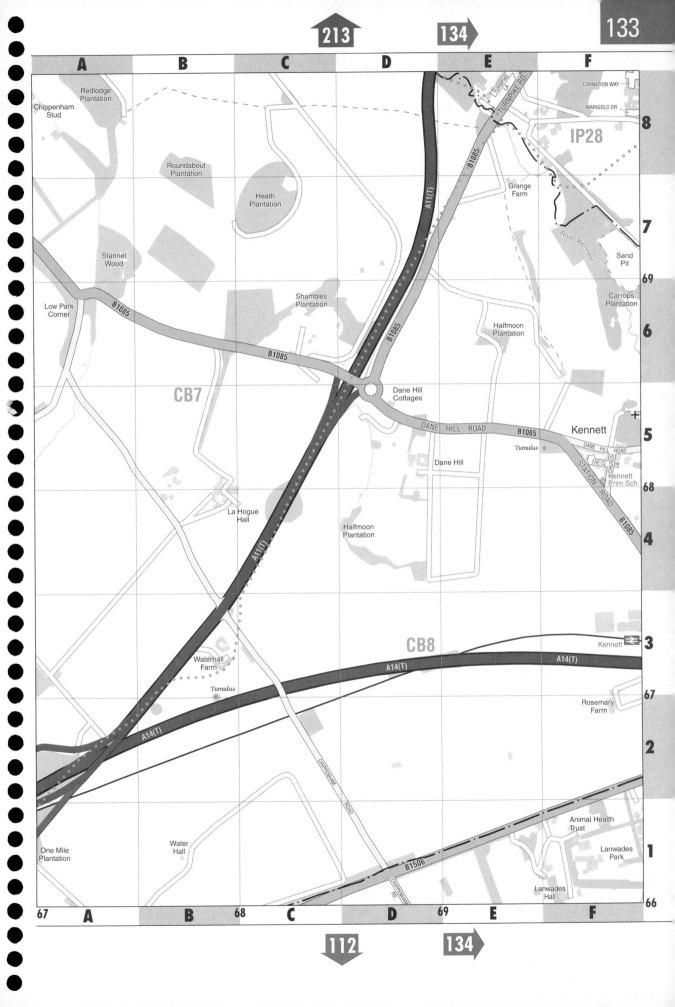

133
214

133

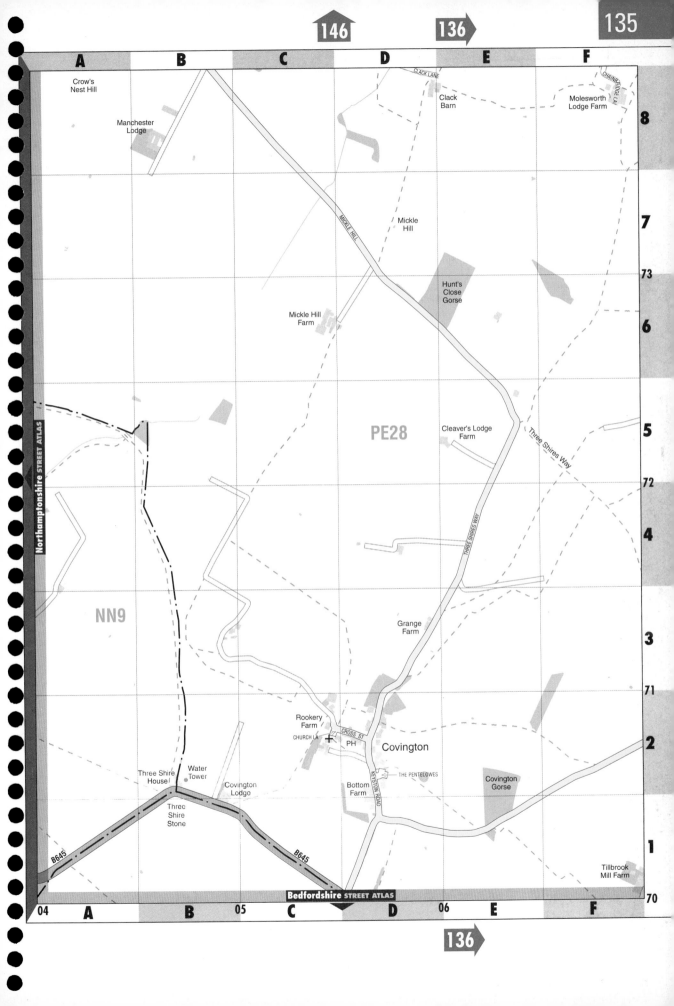

A B C D E F

8

Crow's Nest Hill

Manchester Lodge

CLACK LANE

Clack Barn

CHAINBRIDGE LA

Molesworth Lodge Farm

7

MICKLE HILL

Mickle Hill

73

Hunt's Close Gorse

6

Mickle Hill Farm

Northamptonshire STREET ATLAS

5

PE28

Cleaver's Lodge Farm

Three Shires Way

72

THREE SHIRES WAY

4

NN9

Grange Farm

3

71

Rookery Farm

CROSS ST

CHURCH LA

PH

Covington

2

Three Shire House

Water Tower

Covington Lodge

KEYSTON ROAD

THE PENTELOWES

Covington Gorse

Three Shire Stone

Bottom Farm

B645

B645

1

Tillbrook Mill Farm

70

04 A B 05 C D 06 E F

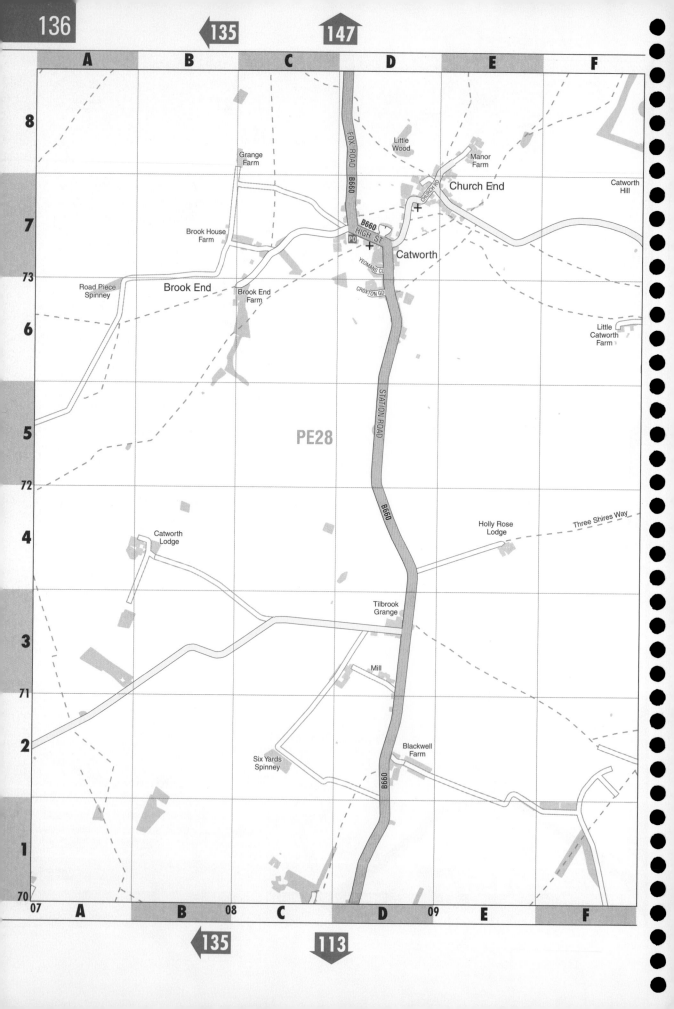

A   B   C   D   E   F

8

Little
Wood

Grange
Farm

Manor
Farm

Church End

7

B660

Catworth
Hill

Church Rd

Brook House
Farm

HIGH ST

B660

PO

Catworth

YEOMANS CL

73

Road Piece
Spinney

Brook End

Brook End
Farm

CROXTON GD

6

Little
Catworth
Farm

FOX ROAD

PE28

5

STATION ROAD

72

Three Shires Way

4

Catworth
Lodge

B660

Holly Rose
Lodge

Tilbrook
Grange

3

Mill

71

Six Yards
Spinney

Blackwell
Farm

2

B660

1

70

07   A   B   08   C   D   09   E   F

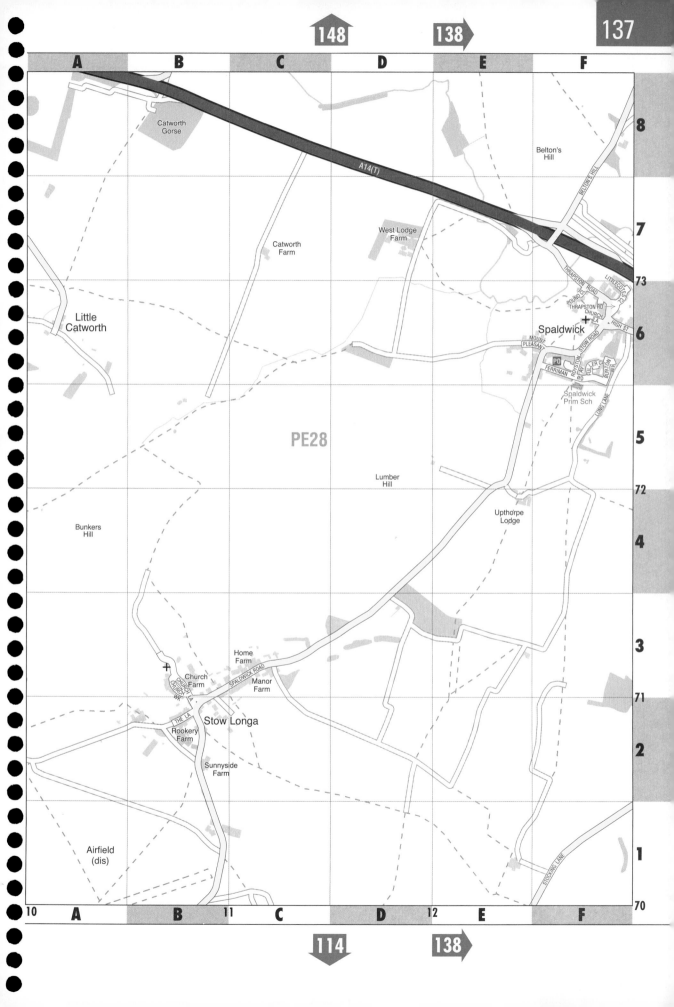

A   B   C   D   E   F

8

Catworth
Gorse

Belton's
Hill

A14(T)

7

West Lodge
Farm

73

Spaldwick

Catworth
Farm

THRAPSTON ROAD

LITTLECOTES

POUND CL

THRAPSTON RD
CHURCH LA

HIGH ST

6

Little
Catworth

MOUNT
PLEASANT

STOW ROAD

FERRIMAN
RD

ROYSTON AV

FULLER CL

BURTON
WY

PO

Spaldwick
Prim Sch

LONG LANE

PE28

5

Lumber
Hill

72

Upthorpe
Lodge

Bunkers
Hill

4

3

Home
Farm

SPALDWICK ROAD

71

Church
Farm

CHURCH LA

CHURCH WK

Manor
Farm

THE LA

Stow Longa

Rookery
Farm

2

Sunnyside
Farm

STOCKING LANE

1

Airfield
(dis)

70

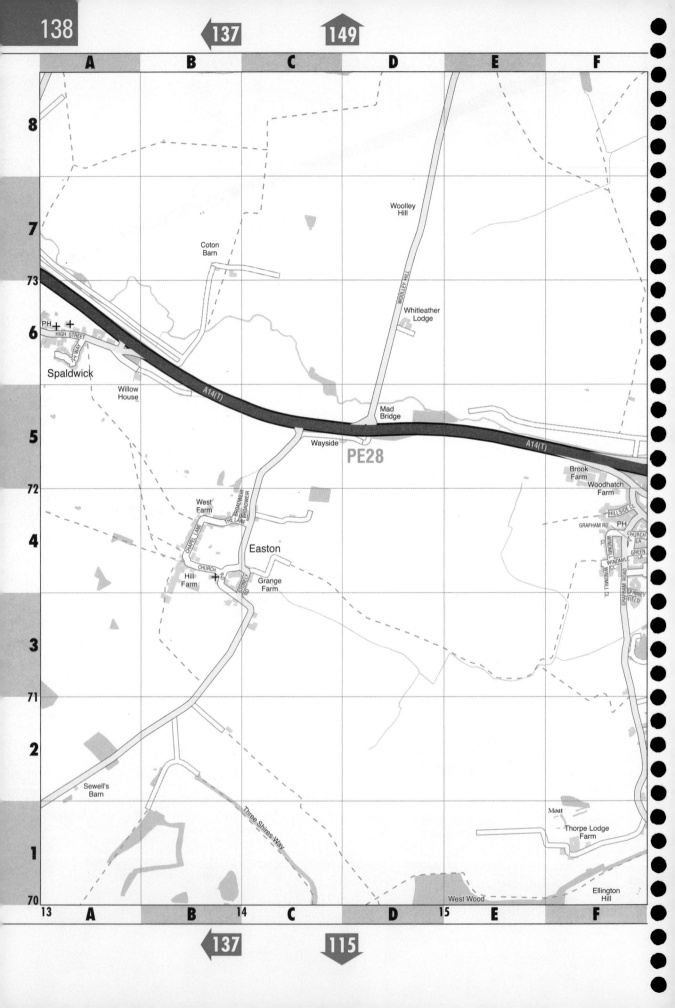

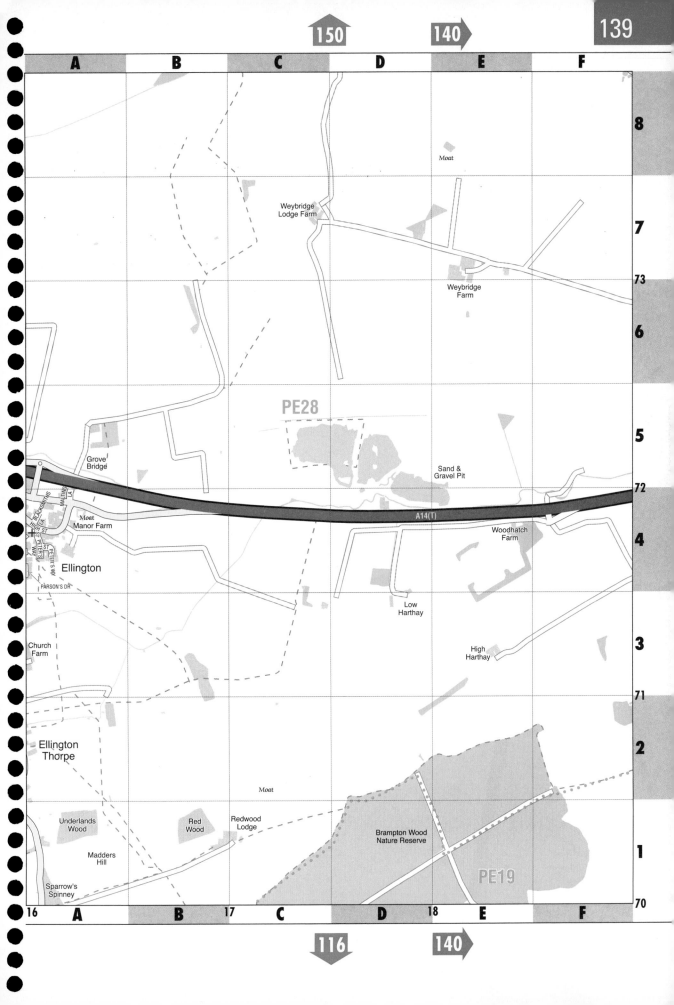

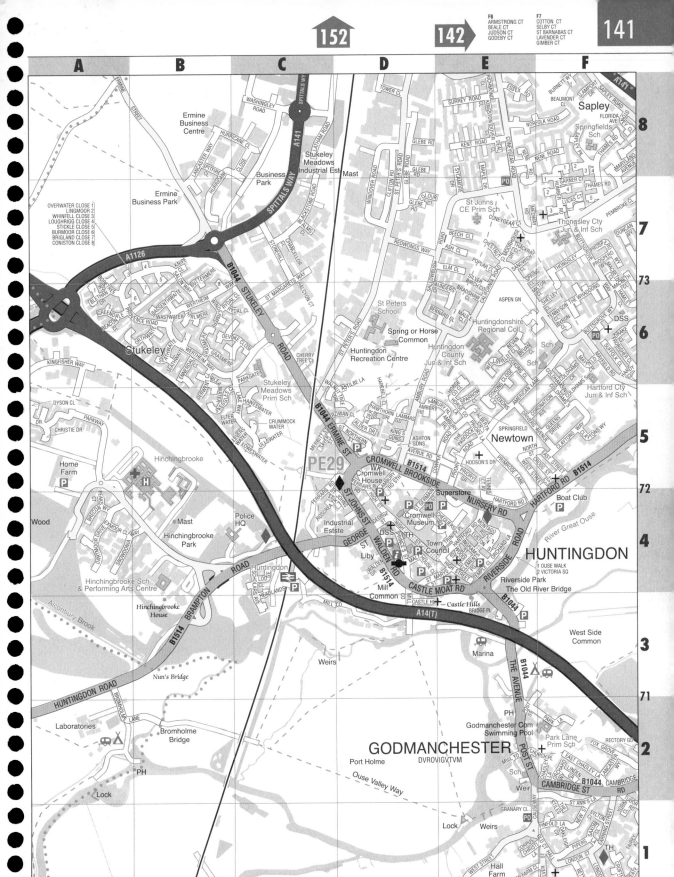

141
153

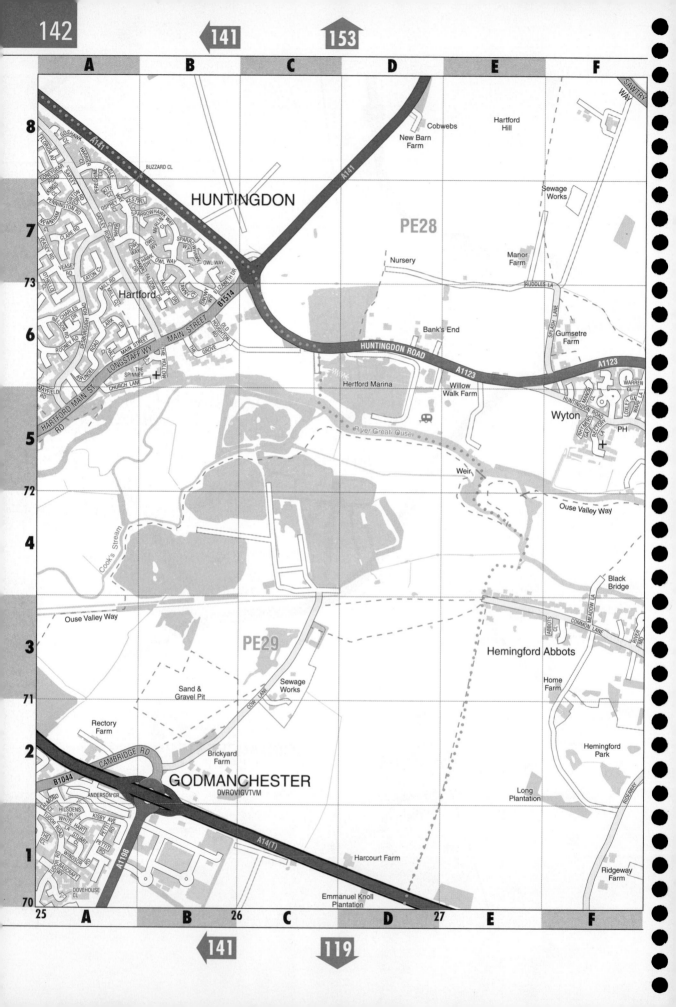

141
119

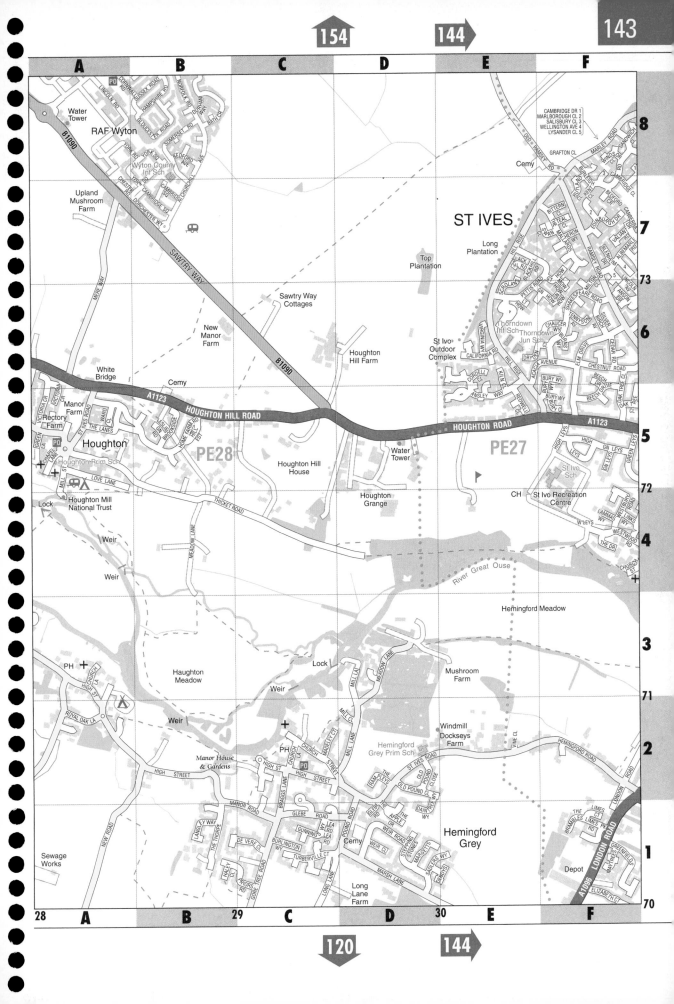

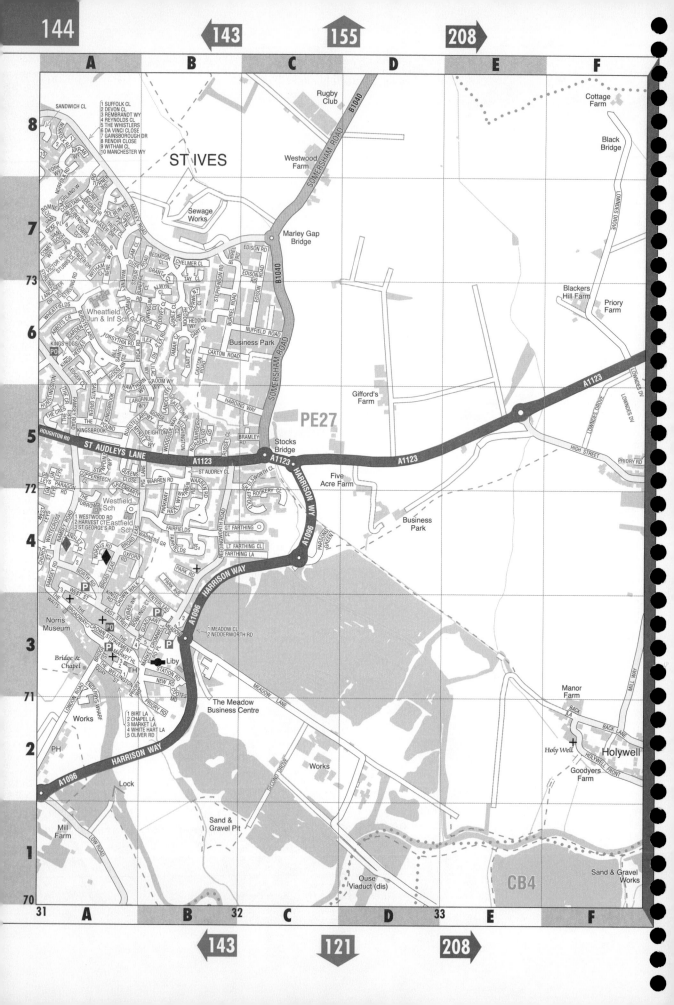

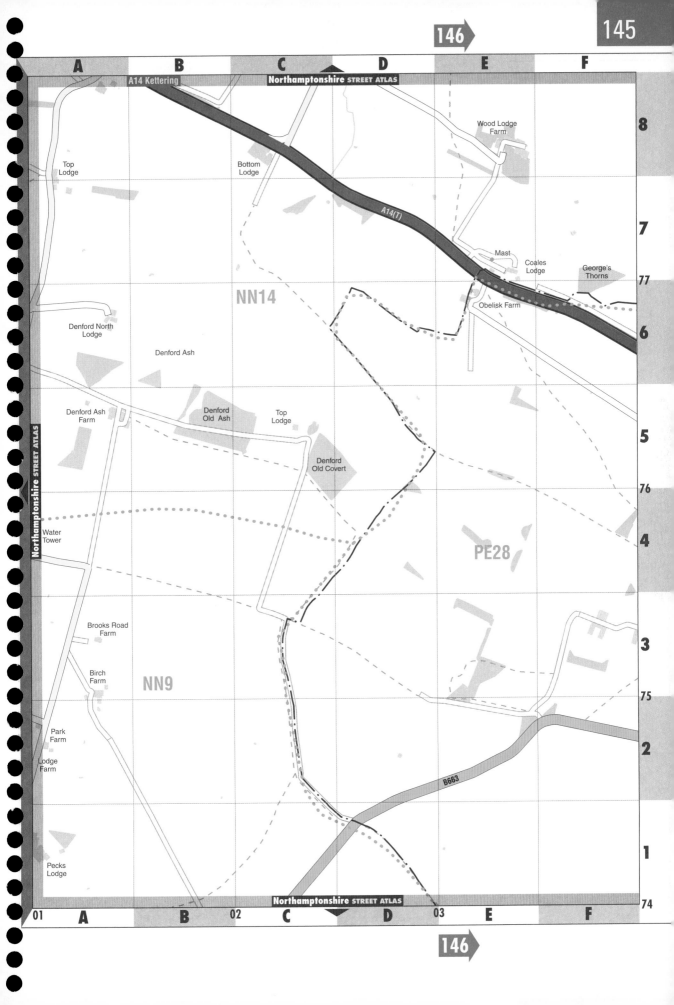

A B C D E F

Northamptonshire STREET ATLAS

A14 Kettering

8
7
77
6
5
76
4
3
75
2
1
74

Wood Lodge Farm

Top Lodge

Bottom Lodge

A14(T)

Mast

Coales Lodge

George's Thorns

Obelisk Farm

NN14

Denford North Lodge

Denford Ash

Denford Ash Farm

Denford Old Ash

Top Lodge

Denford Old Covert

PE28

Water Tower

Brooks Road Farm

Birch Farm

NN9

Park Farm

Lodge Farm

B663

Pecks Lodge

Northamptonshire STREET ATLAS

01 A B 02 C D 03 E F

Northamptonshire STREET ATLAS

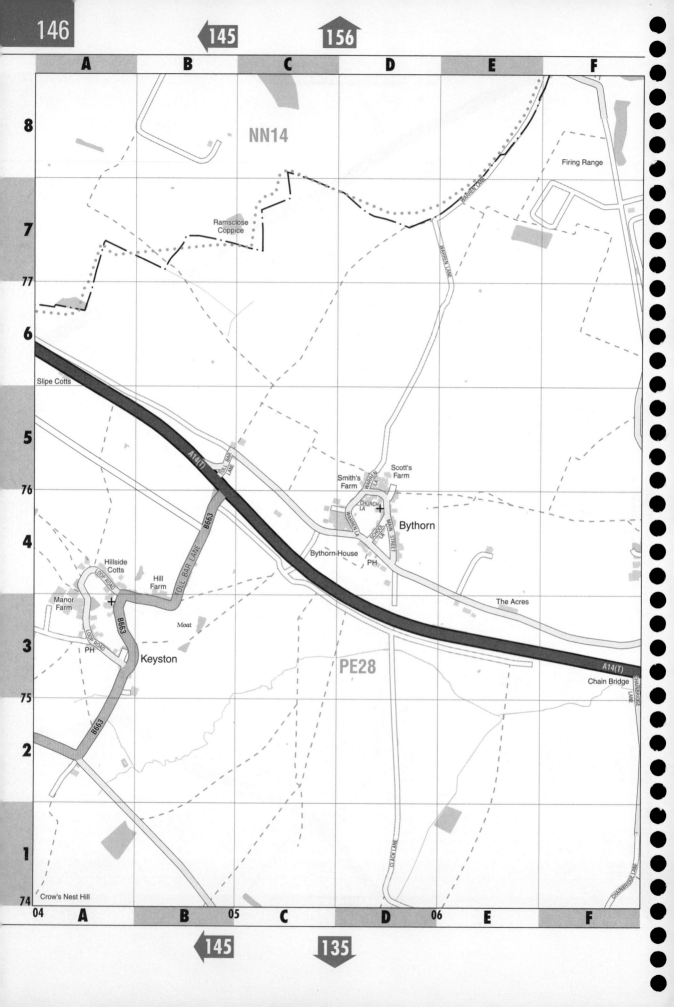

A   B   C   D   E   F

8

NN14

7

Ramsclose
Coppice

77

WARREN LANE

Firing Range

6

Slip Cotts

A14(T)

TOLL BAR LANE

5

Smith's
Farm

Scott's
Farm

WARREN LA

76

CHURCH LA

Bythorn

B663

WARREN LA

SCHOOL LA

MAIN STREET

4

Bythorn House

PH

Hillside
Cotts

LOOP ROAD

Hill
Farm

The Acres

Manor
Farm

TOLL BAR LANE

Moat

B663

PE28

3

PH

LOOP ROAD

Keyston

75

Chain Bridge

CHAINBRIDGE LANE

B663

CLACK LANE

2

1

Crow's Nest Hill

74

04   A   B   05   C   06   D   E   F

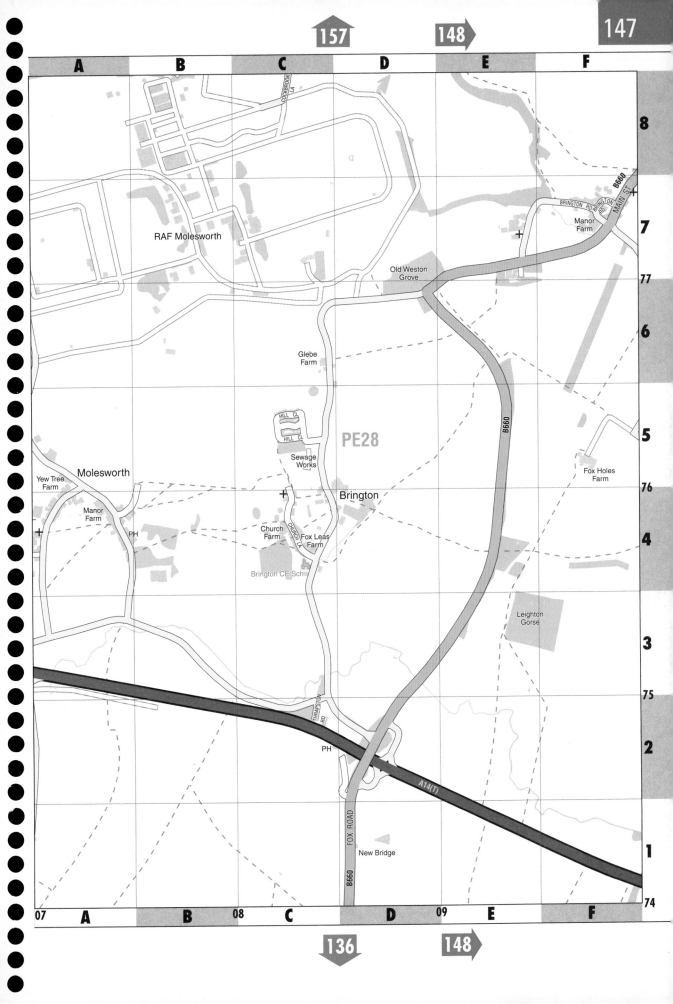

157
148

A B C D E F

8
7
77
6
5
76
4
3
75
2
1
74

COCKBROOK LA

RAF Molesworth

Old Weston Grove

Glebe Farm

HILL CL
HILL CL

PE28

Sewage Works

Molesworth

Yew Tree Farm

Manor Farm

PH

Brington

Church Farm

CHURCH LA

Fox Leas Farm

Brington CE Sch

B660

BRINGTON RD
BRINGTON RD
MAIN ST

B660

Manor Farm

Fox Holes Farm

Leighton Gorse

THRAPSTON RD

PH

A14(T)

FOX ROAD

B660

New Bridge

07 A B 08 C D 09 E F

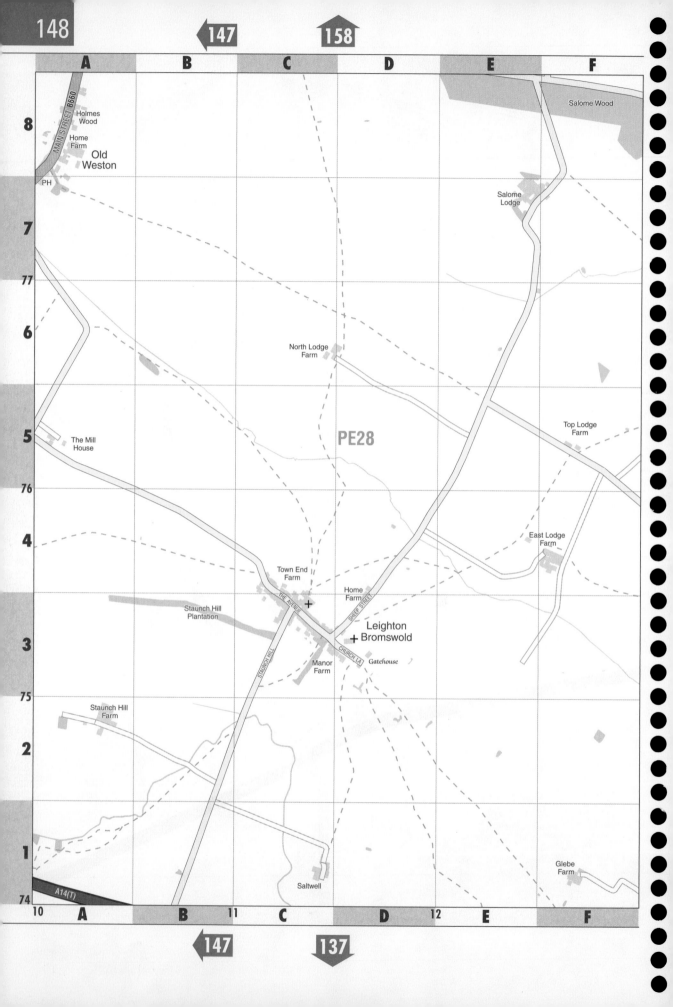

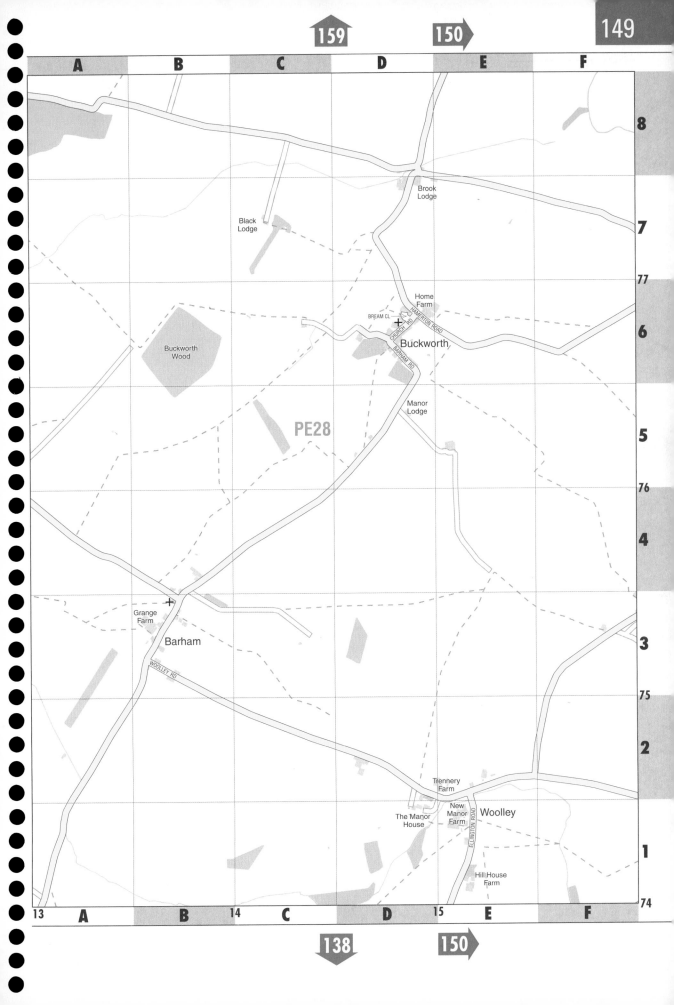

A B C D E F

8

Brook
Lodge

7

Black
Lodge

77

Home
Farm

BREAM CL

CHURCH RD

HAMERTON ROAD

6

Buckworth
Wood

Buckworth

BARHAM RD

Manor
Lodge

PE28

5

76

4

Grange
Farm

Barham

3

WOOLLEY RD

75

2

Trennery
Farm

ELLINGTON ROAD

The Manor
House

New
Manor
Farm

Woolley

1

Hill House
Farm

74

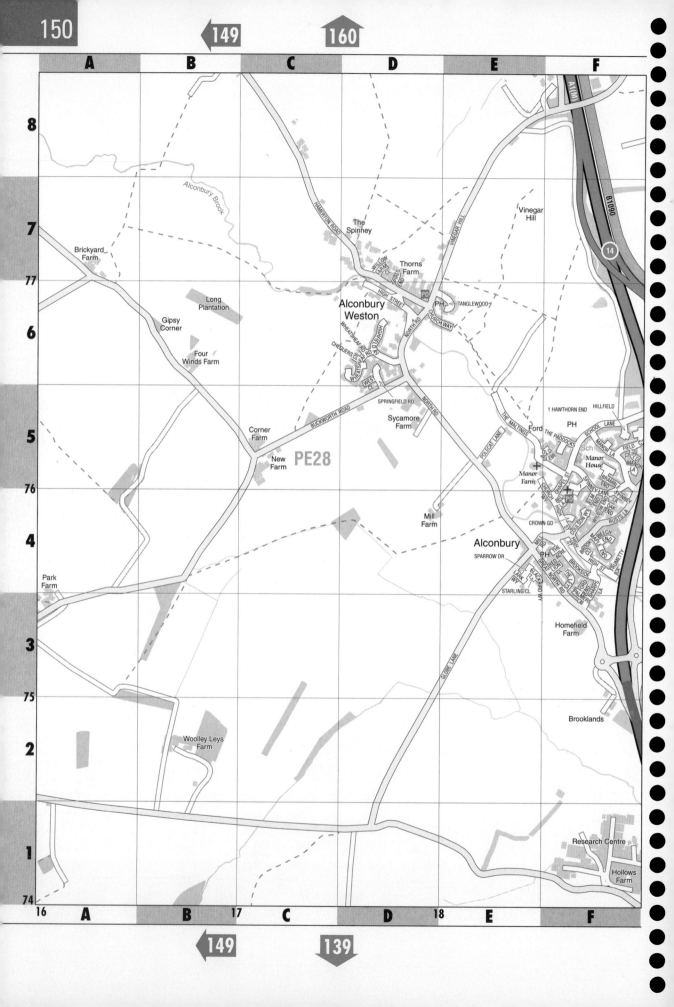

A B C D E F

8

7

77

6

5

76

4

3

75

2

1

74

16 A B 17 C D 18 E F

Brickyard Farm

Alconbury Brook

Long Plantation

Gipsy Corner

Four Winds Farm

HAMERTON ROAD

The Spinney

WILLOW FARM CL

SPIRES END

Thorns Farm

HIGH STREET

Alconbury Weston

WHEATSHEAF RD

HIGHFIELD

CHEQUERS CL

WEST CL

NORTH RD

PO

PH

TANGLEWOOD

CHURCH WAY

VINEGAR HILL

Vinegar Hill

A1(M)

B1090

14

BUCKWORTH ROAD

Corner Farm

New Farm

PE28

SPRINGFIELD RD

NORTH RD

Sycamore Farm

POLECAT LANE

THE MALTINGS

Ford

1 HAWTHORN END

HILLFIELD

PH

THE PADDOCKS

SCHOOL LANE

MANOR LA

FIELD

FIELD END

MANOR LA

Sch

Manor House

BRAMBLE END

Manor Farm

GLEBE

CHAPEL ST

PO

SPINNEY LANE

SPINNEY

ELM END

OAK

WILLOW END

RUSTS LA

CROWN GD

HIGH ST

BEECH END

MASON END

Mill Farm

Alconbury

SPARROW DR

PH

THE GREAT NORTH RD

BLACKBIRD WY

STARLING CL

LARK WY

THE REDACRE

THE LEYS

BROOKSIDE

SHARPS LA

CALLENDERS CL

HIGH ST

PRUNETTY

Park Farm

GLOBE LANE

Homefield Farm

Brooklands

Woolley Leys Farm

Research Centre

Hollows Farm

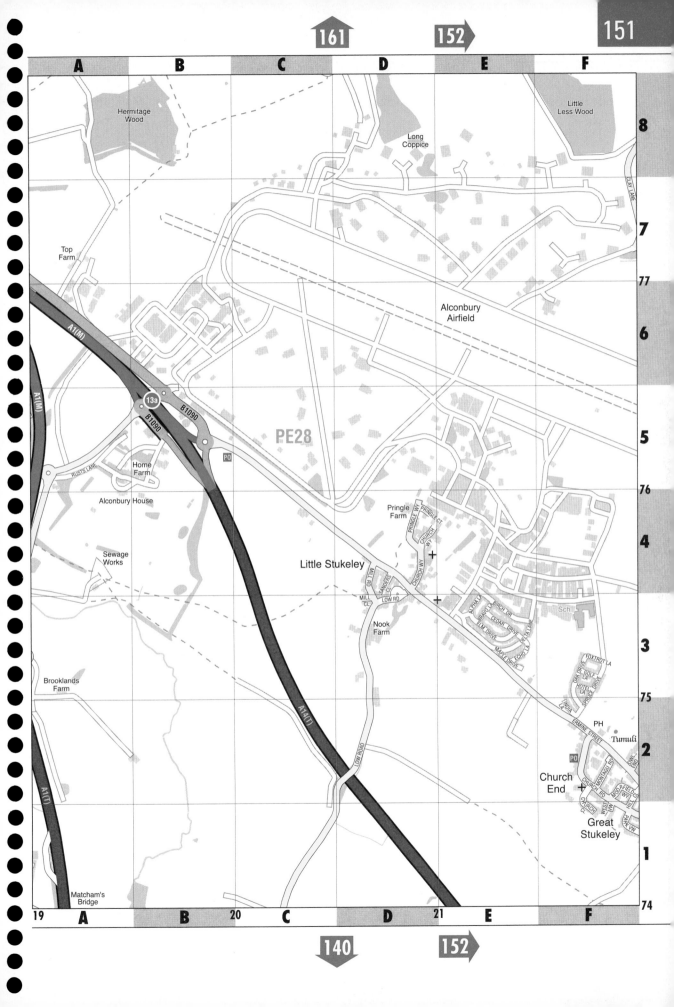

Hermitage Wood

Little Less Wood

Long Coppice

CLAY LANE

Top Farm

Alconbury Airfield

A1(M)

A1(M)

13a

B1090

B1090

PO

PE28

Home Farm

RUSTS LANE

Alconbury House

Sewage Works

Pringle Farm

PRINGLE WY
PRINGLE CT
CHURCH WY

Little Stukeley

MILL RD
SANDERS CL
MILL CL
LOW RD
CHURCH WY

Nook Farm

ALPHA LA
BIRCH DR
BRAVO LA
CEDAR DRIVE
ELM DRIVE
DELTA LANE
MAPLE DRIVE
ECHO LA

Sch

FOXTROT LA
OAK DRIVE
GOLF LA
HOTEL LA
SPRUCE DRIVE
INDIA LA

A14(T)

Brooklands Farm

A1(T)

LOW ROAD

ERMINE STREET

PH

Tumuli

PO

Church End

Great Stukeley

MONTAGU RD
CHURCH RD
WEST WY
MEADFIELD RD
ELM WY
PARK WY
OLD ONES
CHURCH CL

Matcham's Bridge

19   20   21

74   75   76   77

1 2 3 4 5 6 7 8

A B C D E F

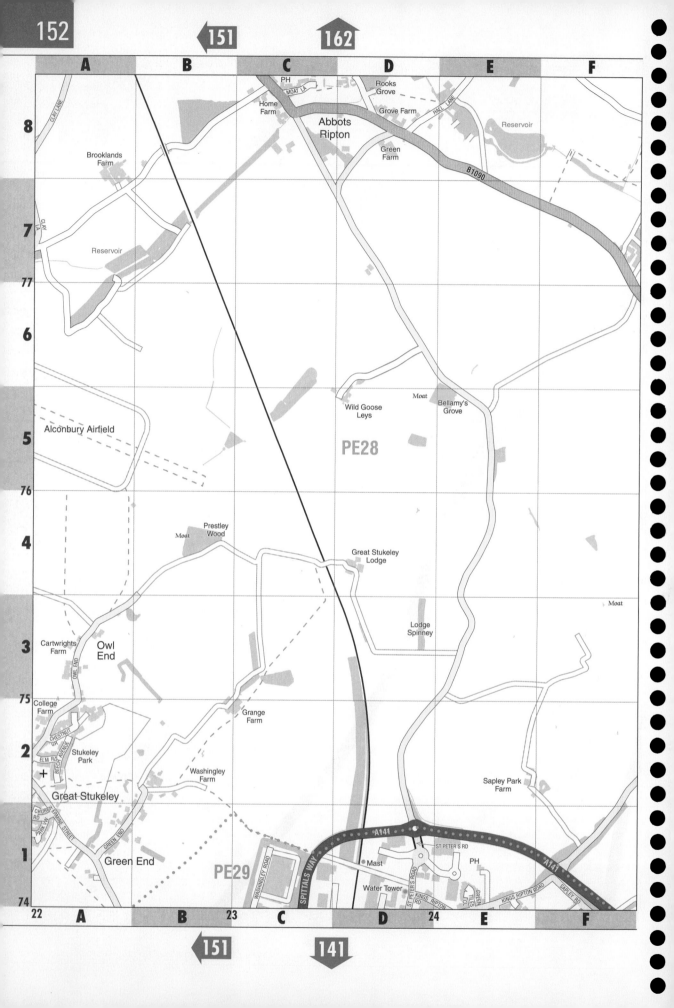

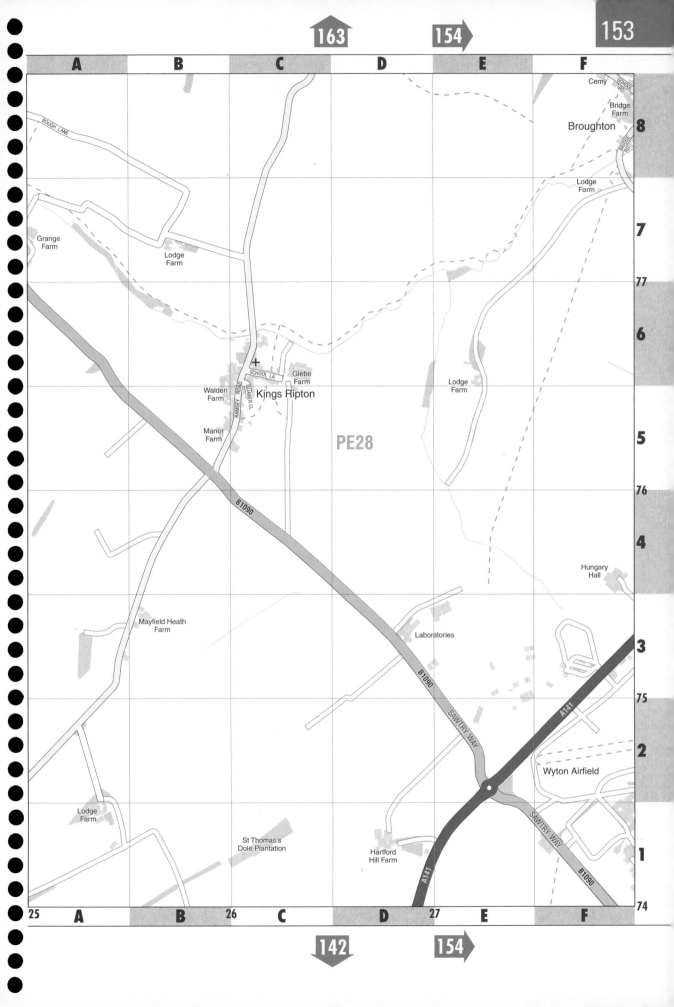

A   B   C   D   E   F

Cemy
Bridge
Farm
Broughton   8
Lodge
Farm

BOUGH LANE   7

Grange
Farm   77

Lodge
Farm   6

SCHOOL LA
Glebe
Farm
Walden   Kings Ripton   Lodge   5
Farm   Farm
Manor
Farm   PE28

B1090   76

                                                           4
                                            Hungary
                                             Hall

Mayfield Heath
Farm   Laboratories   3

                            B1090   75
                                   SAWTRY WAY
                                                      A141
                                                           2
                                            Wyton Airfield
Lodge
Farm   SAWTRY WAY   1
St Thomas's
Dole Plantation
            Hartford   B1090
            Hill Farm
                                                          74

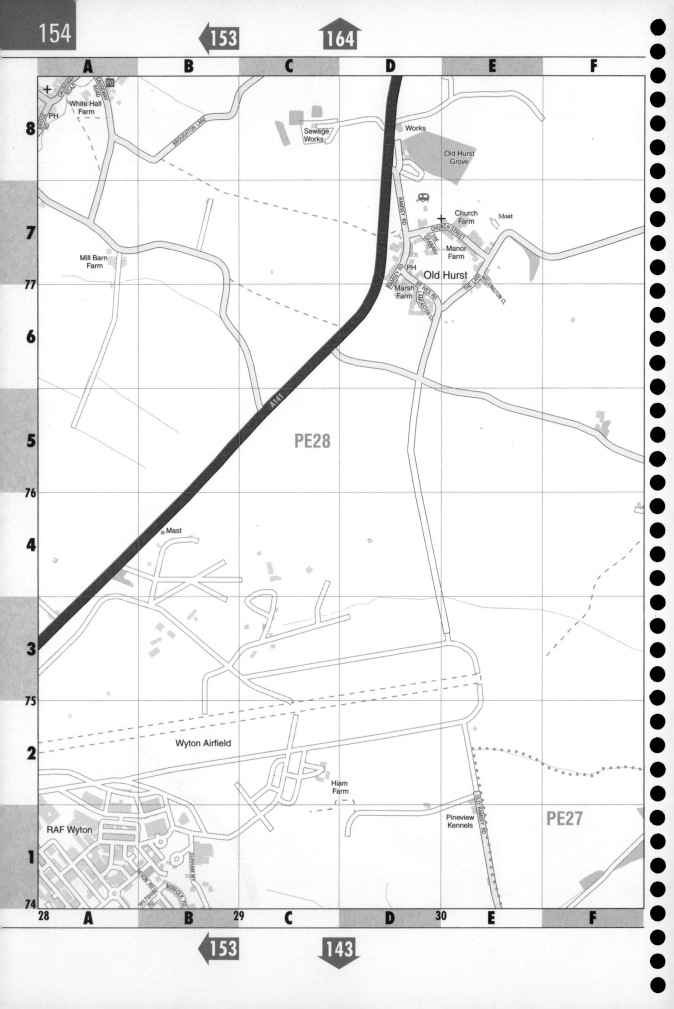

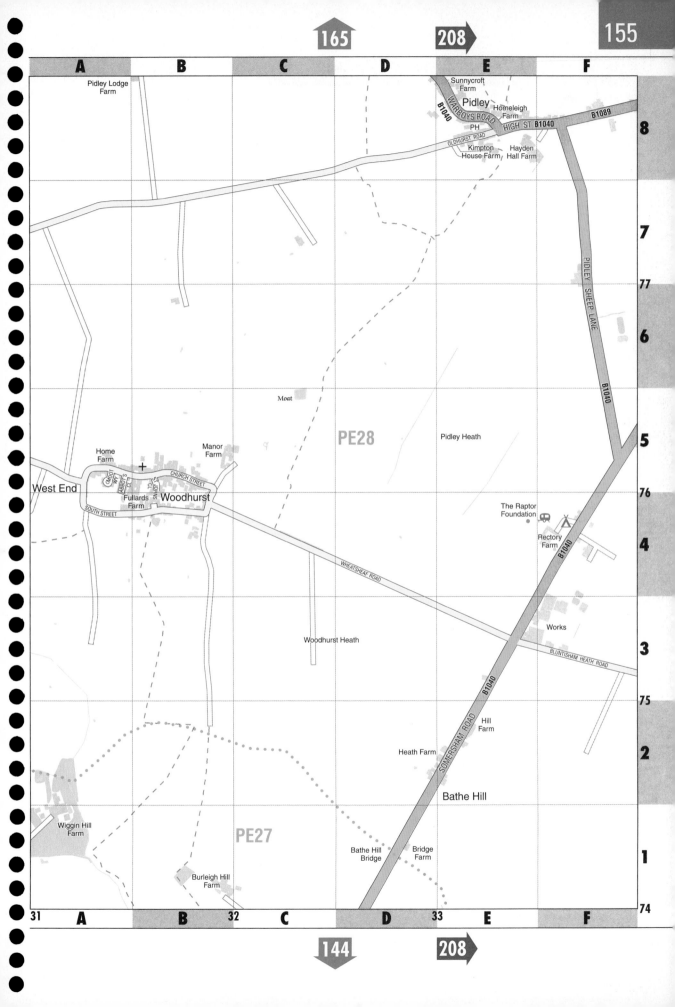

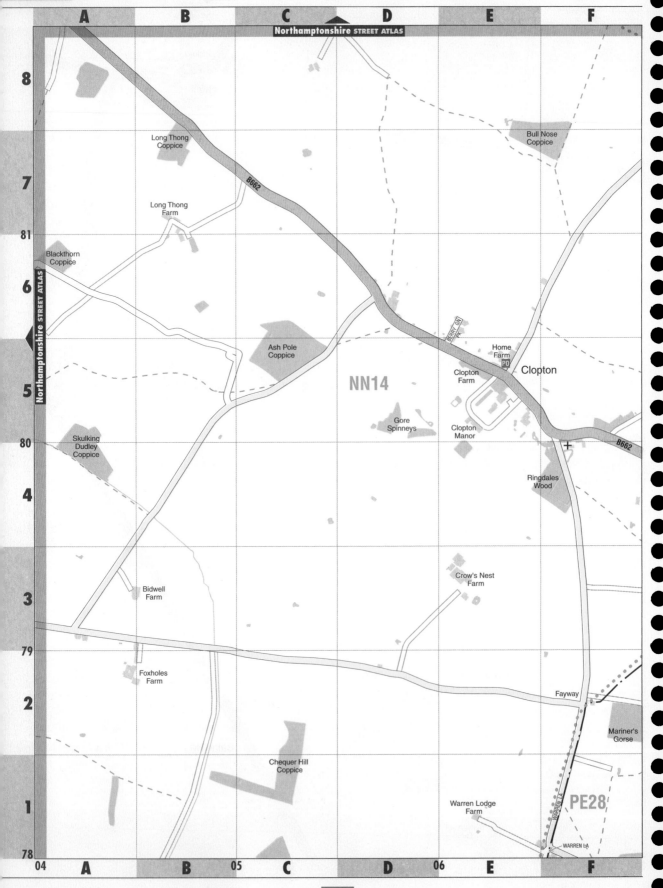

Bull Nose
Coppice

Long Thong
Coppice

B662

Long Thong
Farm

Blackthorn
Coppice

Ash Pole
Coppice

Home
Farm

Clopton

Clopton
Farm

NN14

Gore
Spinneys

Clopton
Manor

B662

Skulking
Dudley
Coppice

Ringdales
Wood

Bidwell
Farm

Crow's Nest
Farm

Foxholes
Farm

Fayway

Mariner's
Gorse

Chequer Hill
Coppice

PE28

Warren Lodge
Farm

WARREN LA

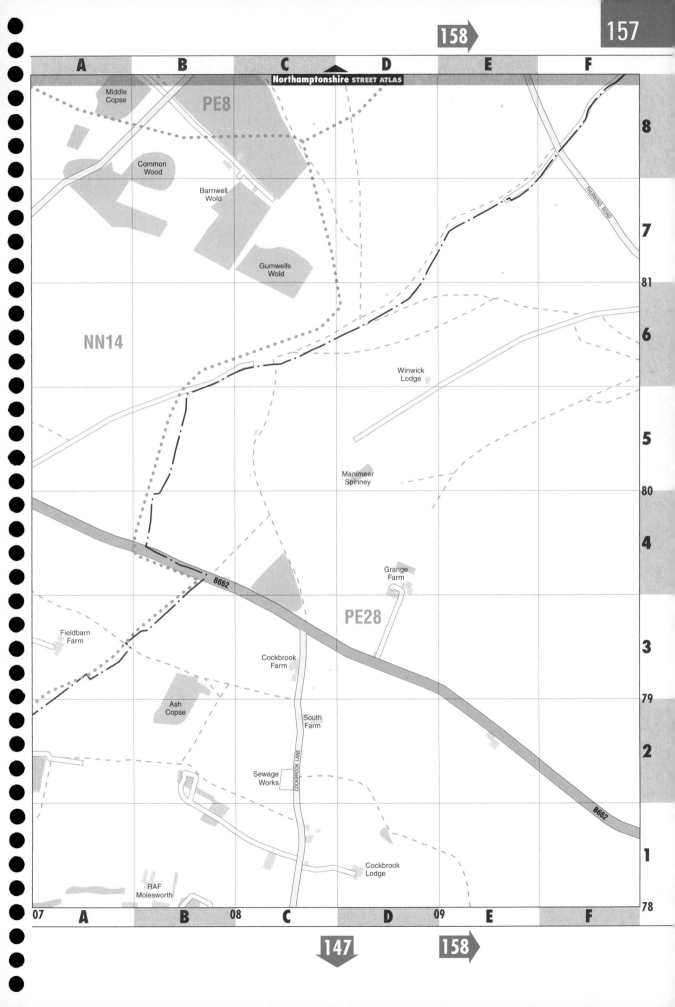

Northamptonshire STREET ATLAS

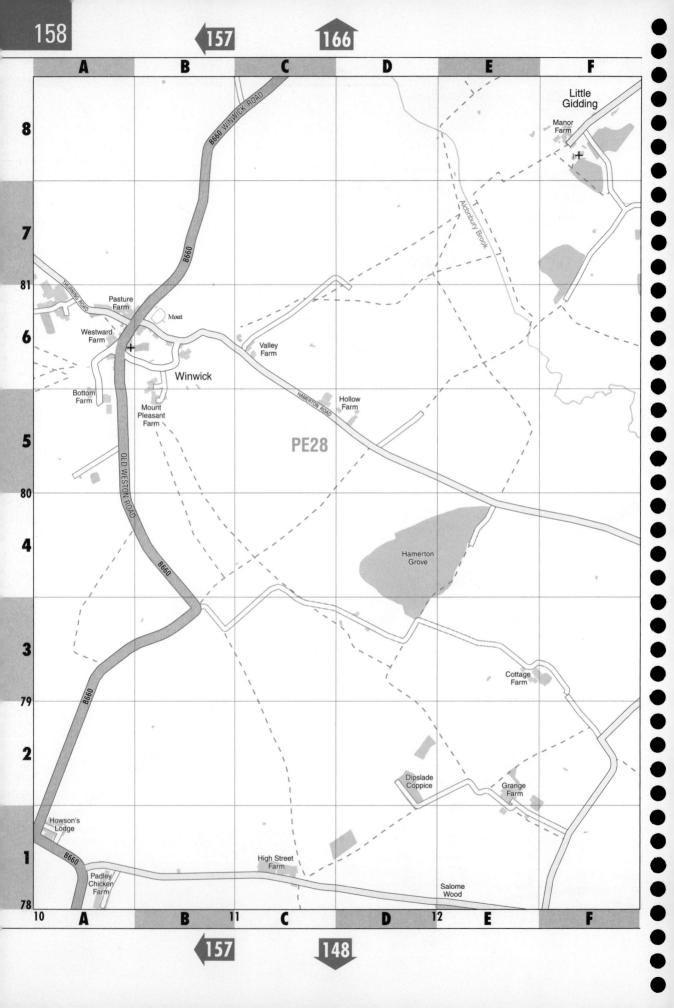

Little Gidding

Manor Farm

B660 WINWICK ROAD

Alconbury Brook

THIRNING ROAD

B660

Pasture Farm

Moat

Westward Farm

Winwick

Valley Farm

HAMERTON ROAD

Hollow Farm

PE28

Bottom Farm

Mount Pleasant Farm

OLD WESTON ROAD

B660

Hamerton Grove

Cottage Farm

Dipslade Coppice

Grange Farm

Howson's Lodge

B660

High Street Farm

Padley Chicken Farm

Salome Wood

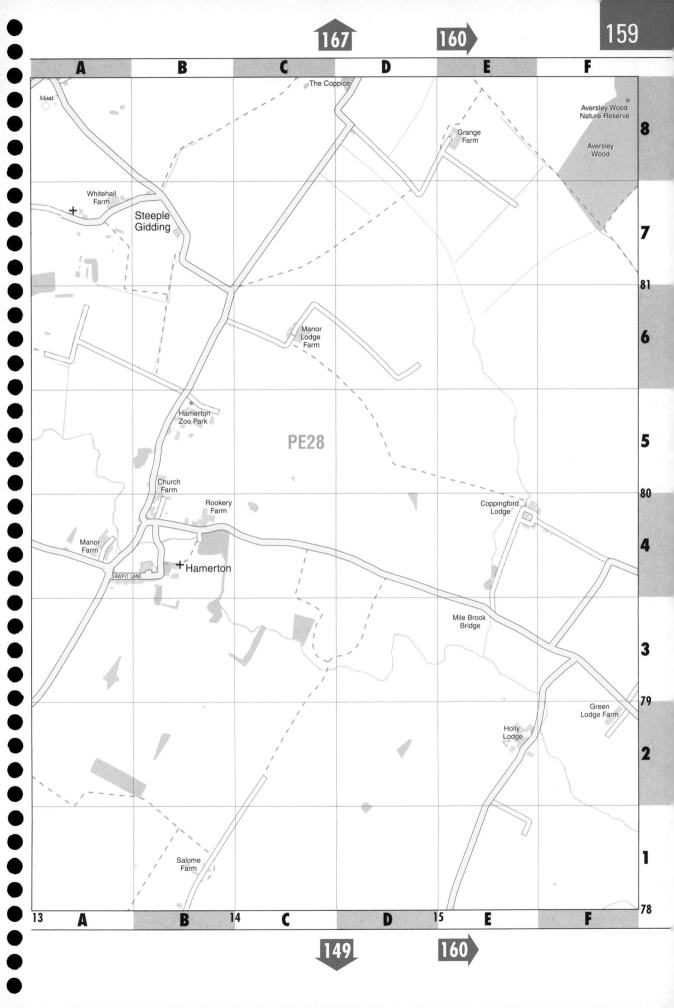

A B C D E F

8

Aversley Wood
Nature Reserve

Aversley
Wood

The Coppice

Grange
Farm

7

Moat

Whitehall
Farm

Steeple
Gidding

81

6

Manor
Lodge
Farm

Hamerton
Zoo Park

PE28

5

80

Church
Farm

Coppingford
Lodge

Rookery
Farm

4

Manor
Farm

SAWPIT LANE

Hamerton

Mile Brook
Bridge

3

79

Green
Lodge Farm

Holly
Lodge

2

1

Salome
Farm

78

13 A B 14 C D 15 E F

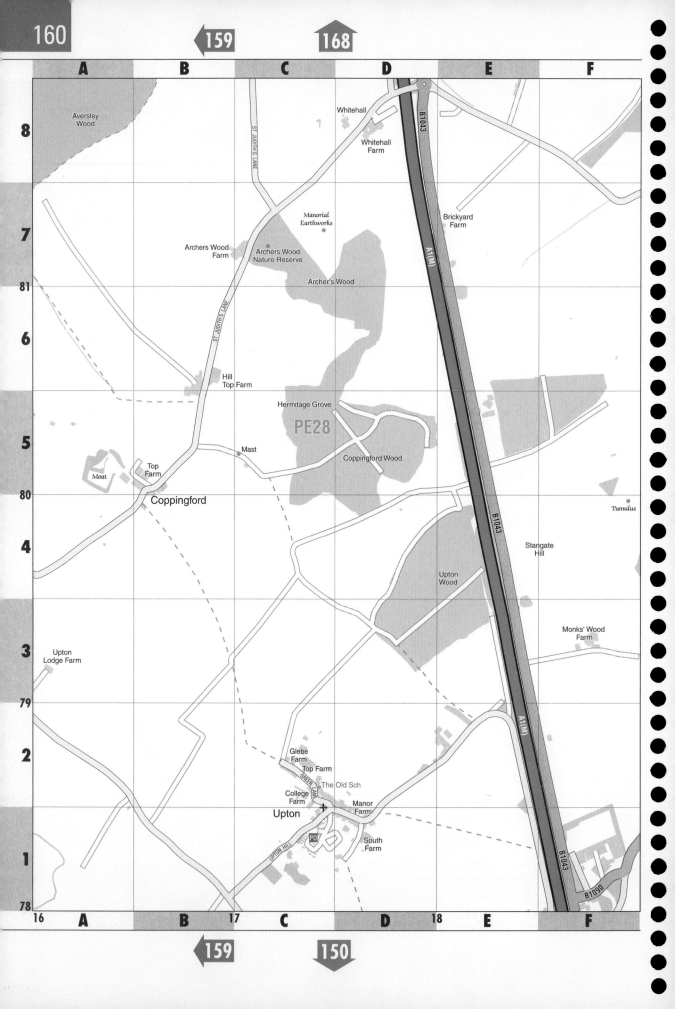

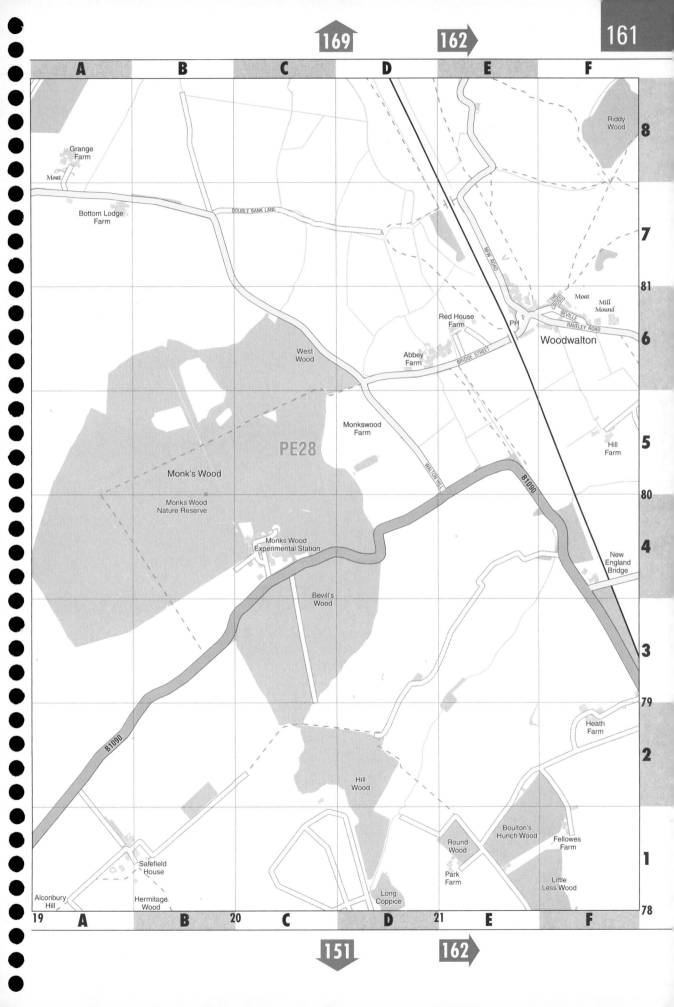

A B C D E F

Grange Farm
Moat
Bottom Lodge Farm
DOUBLE BANK LANE
Riddy Wood
NEW ROAD
THE CROSS
Moat
Mill Mound
BEVILLE
Red House Farm
PH
RAVELEY ROAD
Woodwalton
West Wood
Abbey Farm
BRIDGE STREET
Monkswood Farm
PE28
Hill Farm
Monk's Wood
WALTON HILL
B1090
Monks Wood Nature Reserve
Monks Wood Experimental Station
New England Bridge
Bevill's Wood
B1090
Heath Farm
Hill Wood
Boulton's Hunch Wood
Fellowes Farm
Round Wood
B1090
Safefield House
Park Farm
Little Less Wood
Alconbury Hill
Hermitage Wood
Long Coppice

19 A B 20 C D 21 E F

8 7 81 6 5 80 4 3 79 2 1 78

A   B   C   D   E   F

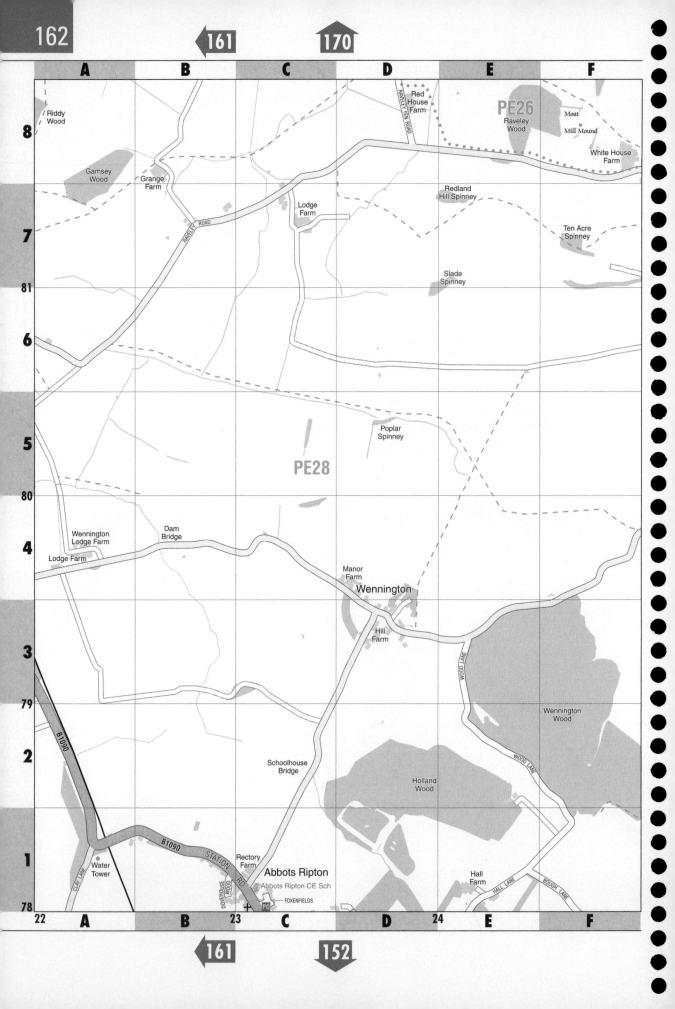

Riddy
Wood

8

Gamsey
Wood

Grange
Farm

Red
House
Farm

PE26

Moat

Raveley
Wood

Mill Mound

White House
Farm

Redland
Hill Spinney

Ten Acre
Spinney

RAVELEY ROAD

Lodge
Farm

7

Slade
Spinney

81

6

Poplar
Spinney

5

PE28

80

Wennington
Lodge Farm

Dam
Bridge

4

Lodge Farm

Manor
Farm

Wennington

3

Hill
Farm

WOOD LANE

79

Wennington
Wood

2

Schoolhouse
Bridge

WOOD LANE

Holland
Wood

B1090

1

CLAY LANE

Water
Tower

B1090

STATION RD

DOVEHOUSE WOOD

Rectory
Farm

Abbots Ripton

Abbots Ripton CE Sch

Hall
Farm

HALL LANE

BOUGH LANE

PO

FOXENFIELDS

78

22   A   B   23   C   D   24   E   F

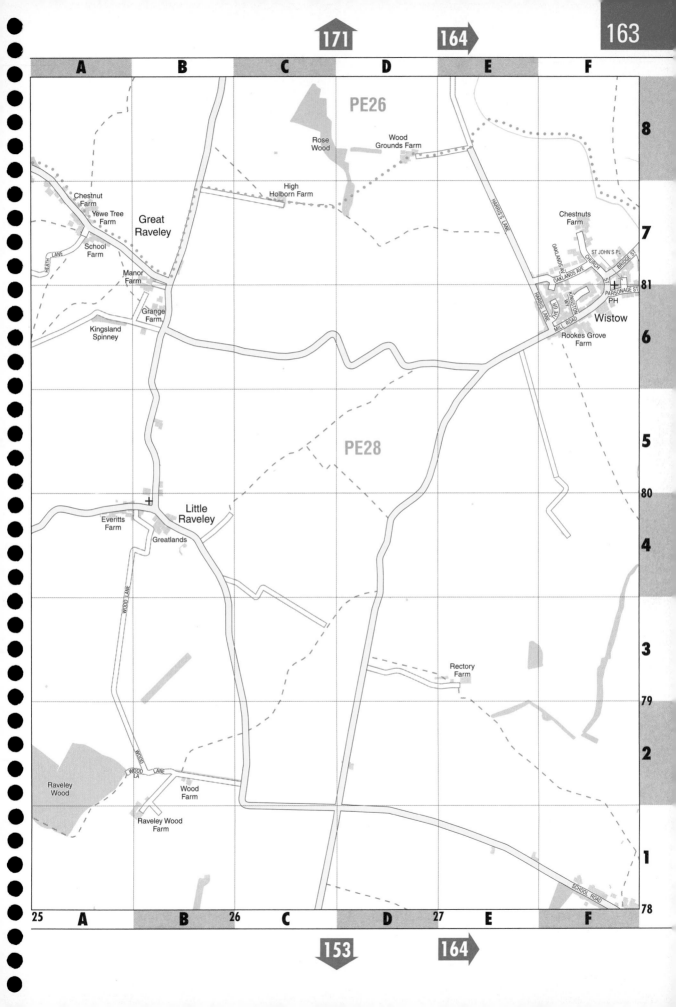

171
164

163

PE26

Rose
Wood

Wood
Grounds Farm

High
Holborn Farm

Chestnut
Farm

Yewe Tree
Farm

Great
Raveley

HEATH LANE

School
Farm

Manor
Farm

Grange
Farm

Kingsland
Spinney

HARRIS'S LANE

Chestnuts
Farm

St John's Pl

OAKLANDS AV

CHURCH

St John's Pl

OAKLANDS AVE

BRIDGE ST

PARSONAGE ST

KINGSTON

HARRIS LANE

LIME TREE GR

MILL ROAD

Wistow

PH

Rookes Grove
Farm

PE28

Little
Raveley

Everitts
Farm

Greatlands

WOOD LANE

Rectory
Farm

Raveley
Wood

WOOD LA

WOOD LANE

Wood
Farm

Raveley Wood
Farm

SCHOOL ROAD

163
172

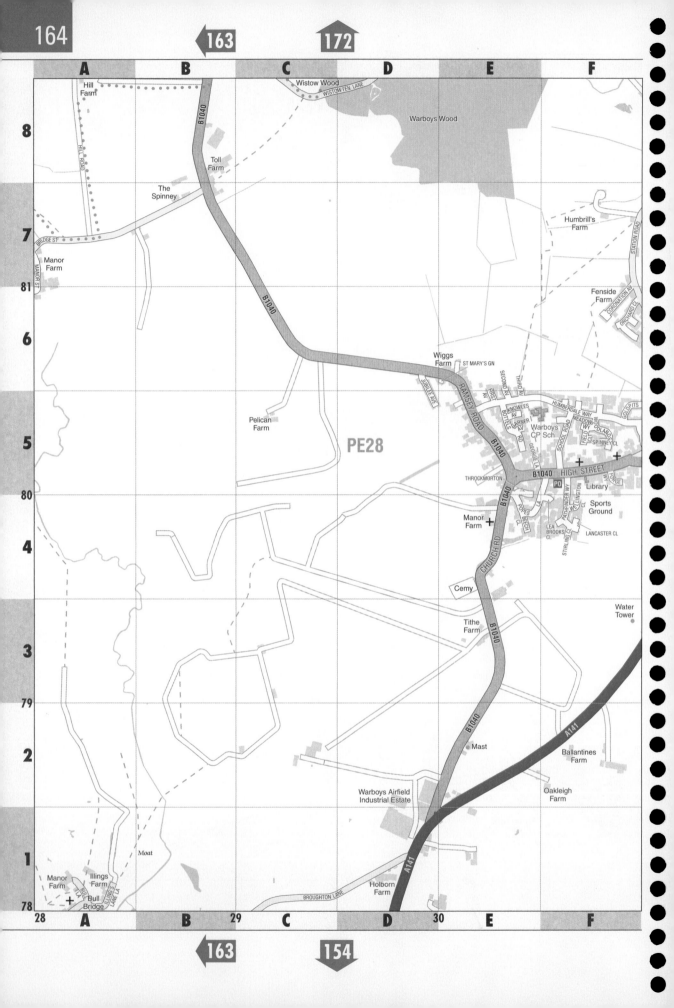

163
154

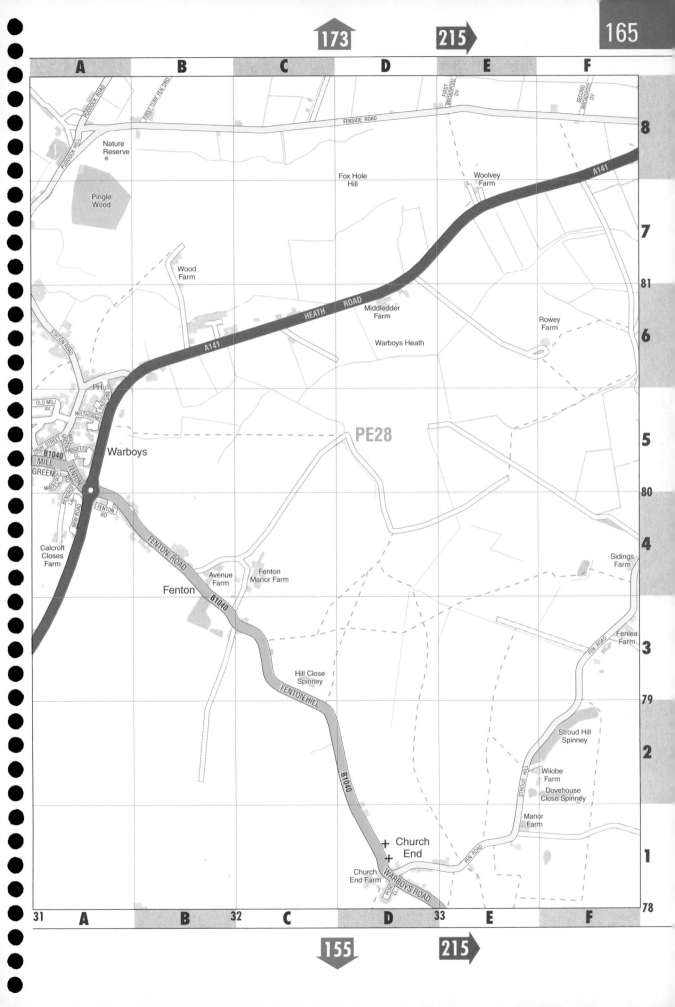

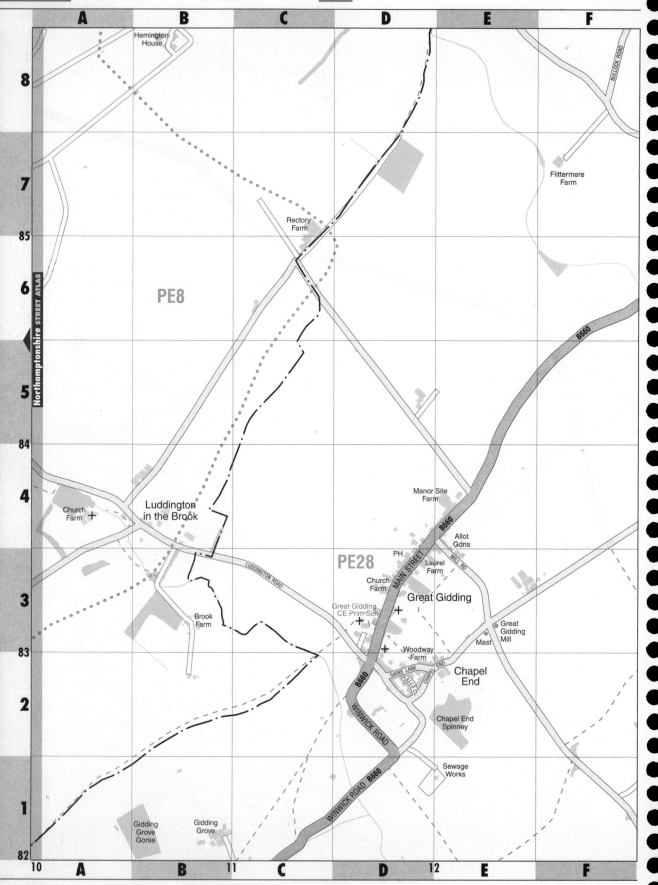

8

7

85

6

Northamptonshire STREET ATLAS

PE8

5

84

4

Church Farm

Luddington in the Brook

Brook Farm

PE28

Hemington House

Rectory Farm

Flittermere Farm

B660

Manor Site Farm

B660

Allot Gdns

PH

MAIN STREET

Laurel Farm

MILL RD

Church Farm

Great Gidding

Great Gidding CE Prim Sch

Great Gidding Mill

Mast

LUDDINGTON ROAD

3

83

Woodway Farm

GAINS LANE

DELLS CL

CHAPEL END

Chapel End

2

B660

WINWICK ROAD

Chapel End Spinney

Sewage Works

1

WINWICK ROAD

B660

Gidding Grove Gorse

Gidding Grove

82

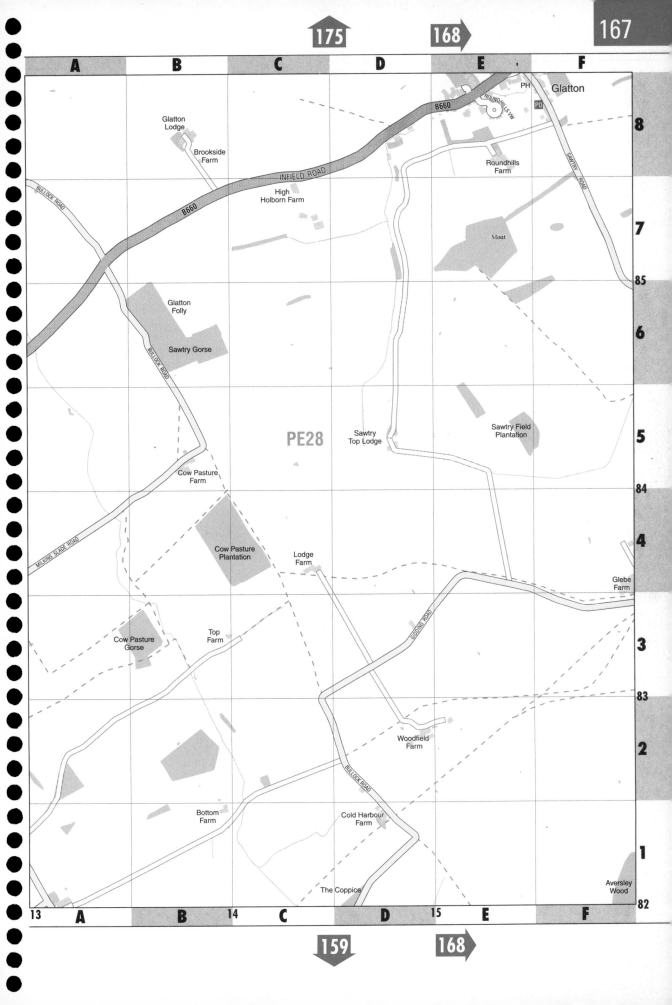

A B C D E F

8

7

85

6

5

84

4

3

83

2

1

82

Conington
Yew Tree Farm
CONINGTON LANE
COTTON CL
BRUCES CL
CHURCH ROAD
CHURCH LA
Palmer's Grove
PE7
Spot's Grove
High Fen
Middlemarsh Farm
B1043
Duckpit Fen
SAWTRY RD
GLATTON ROAD
15
Bruce's Castle Farm
Castle Grove
Moat
COOKS LANE
CREASE ROAD
Little Common Farm
Little Common

1 BLOOMFIELD WY
2 THE GRANARY
3 ALL SAINTS WY
4 ST DAVID'S WY
5 HUNTINGS DR

B1043
BROOKSIDE
WESTERMAN CL
WARREN CT
SALTERS
FAIRFIELD
RECTORY CL
CHURCH STREET
TOFT HL
CHURCH CW
Manor Farm
WHITEHOUSE RD
HIGH ST
GREEN LANE
NEWTON RD
CHAPEL END
ST ANDREW'S WAY
OLD NORTH ROAD
Glebe Farm
GIDDING ROAD
PH
THE MALTINGS
FEN LANE
Black Horse Farm
Great Common
Liby
Sawtry Com Coll
CAVENDISH RD
MOYNE RD
THE LEYS
ERNIE WY
PE28
Sawtry Sports Centre
COLLEGE CL
LONGTHE
BLINDLY
A1(M)
Stanch-hill Bridge
STRAIGHT DROVE
ASHDALE CL 1
OAKLEY DR 2
HUNTERS WY 3
HAWTHORN WY 4
WINDSOR RD 5
DEVONSHIRE CL 6
Sawtry
LAUREL CL
MAPLE CL
THE BRIARS
CRABAPPLE
MIDDLEFIELD ROAD
GREEN END ROAD
BEAUMARIS RD
BROUGHTON RD
STANCH HL
BEDFORD CL
SAXON CL
Common Barn Farm
Sawtry Roughs
Wood End Farm
MONKS END
ELM PK
BRAMBLE
CROMWELL WY
ALWIN RD
HOLBURN
SOTHEY WY
PO
CHESHAM RD
DURHAM RD
BUCKINGHAM WY
P
CANNON CL
AVERSLEY RD
GRANGE
15
Green End
High Holborn Hill
Manor House Farm
ST JUDITH'S LANE
C2
1 EWINGSWOOD
2 WHEATSHEAVES
3 STANEGATE
4 STUMPCROSS
5 COTTON CL
A1(M)
B1043
Aversley Wood

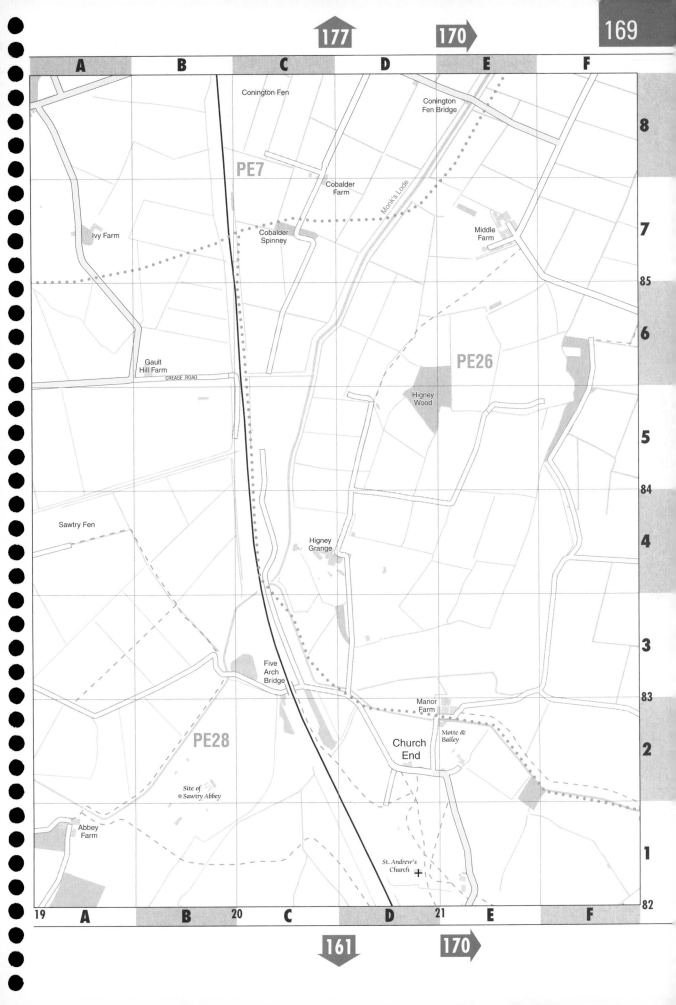

177
170

A   B   C   D   E   F

8

7

85

6

PE7

Conington Fen

Conington
Fen Bridge

Cobalder
Farm

Monk's Lode

Middle
Farm

Ivy Farm

Cobalder
Spinney

PE26

Gault
Hill Farm

CREASE ROAD

Higney
Wood

5

84

Sawtry Fen

Higney
Grange

4

Five
Arch
Bridge

3

83

Manor
Farm

PE28

Church
End

Motte &
Bailey

2

Site of
Sawtry Abbey

Abbey
Farm

St. Andrew's
Church +

1

82

19   A   B   20   C   D   21   E   F

161
170

8

7

85

6

Woodwalton Fen
Nature Reserve

Woodwalton Fen

5

PE26

84

4

Great
Raveley Fen

Wheatley's Drain

3

Great Raveley Drain

83

2

1

PE28   Moat
Farm

82

RAY'S DROVE

Lotting
Fen

HARPER'S DROVE

HEIGHTS DROVE ROAD

HEIGHTS DROVE ROAD

Common
Farm

Turf
Fen

TURF FEN ROAD

RAVELEY FEN ROAD

Lady's
Wood

RAVELEY
FEN RD

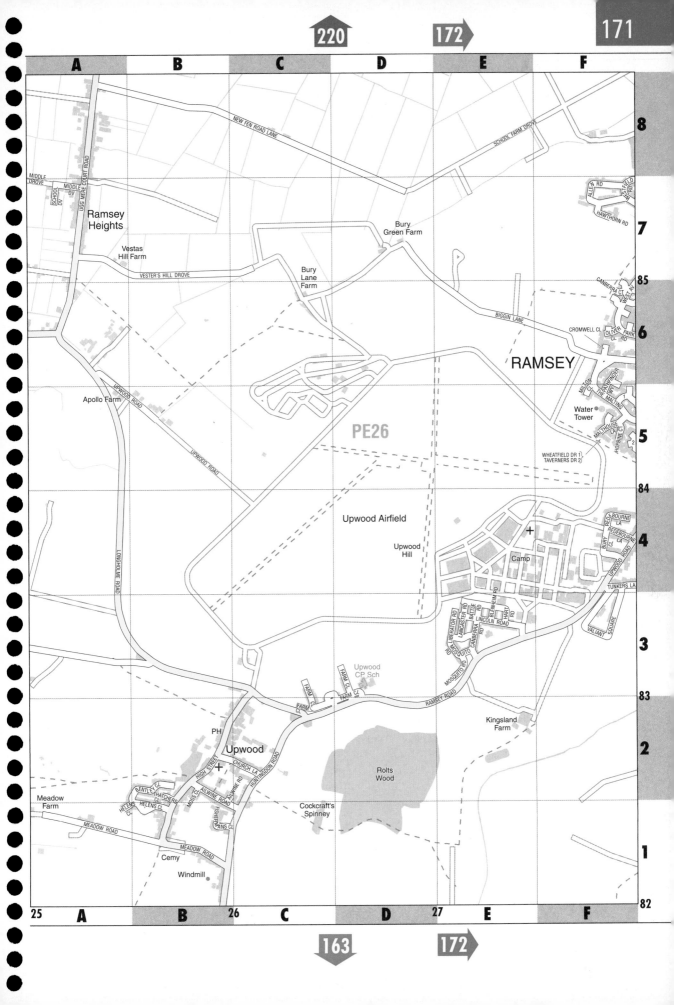

A B C D E F

8

MIDDLE DROVE

SCHOOL DV

MIDDLE DV

UGG MERE COURT ROAD

Ramsey Heights

Vestas Hill Farm

VESTER'S HILL DROVE

NEW FEN ROAD LANE

SCHOOL FARM DROVE

Bury Green Farm

Bury Lane Farm

ALLEN RD

WESTFIELD RD

HAWTHORN RD

7

CANBERRA CL

WEST LA

85

BIGGIN LANE

CROMWELL CL

OLIVER RD

PARK

6

RAMSEY

Apollo Farm

UPWOOD ROAD

MILTON

THE PATHFINDER

THE MALTING

WY

PE26

UPWOOD ROAD

Water Tower

MALTHOUSE LA

HOPBINE CT

5

2

1

WHEATFIELD DR 1
TAVERNERS DR 2

84

Upwood Airfield

Upwood Hill

Camp

REDBOURNE LA

REDBOURNE LA

BURY RD

UPWOOD ROAD

4

LONGHOLME ROAD

TUNKERS LA

LIBERATOR RD

LANCASTER RD

MOSQUITO RD

CANBERRA RD

BATTLE RD

BLENHEIM RD

LINCOLN ROAD

HART RD

VALIANT SQUARE

3

FARM CL

FARM CL

FARM CL

Upwood CP Sch

RAMSEY ROAD

83

Kingsland Farm

PH

Upwood

CHURCH LA

HIGH STREET

MOSS LA

AILWINE RD

AILWINE ROAD

HUNTINGDON ROAD

Rolts Wood

2

Meadow Farm

BENTLEY CL

THATCHERS CL

HELENS CL

HELENS CL

FISHERMANS CL

Cockcraft's Spinney

MEADOW ROAD

MEADOW ROAD

Cemy

Windmill

1

82

25 A 26 B C 27 D E F

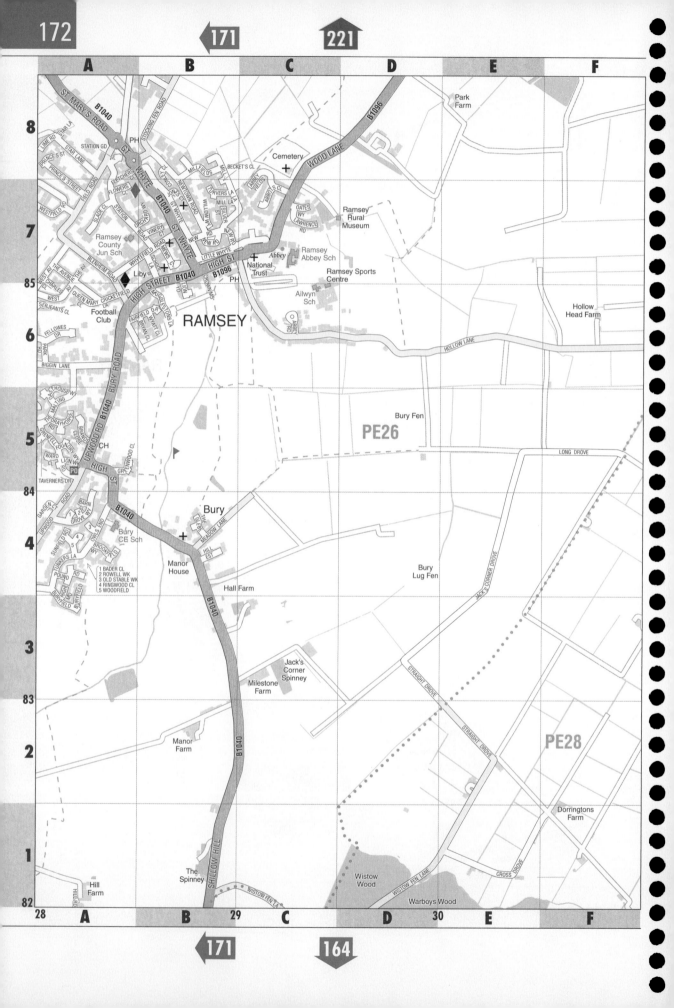

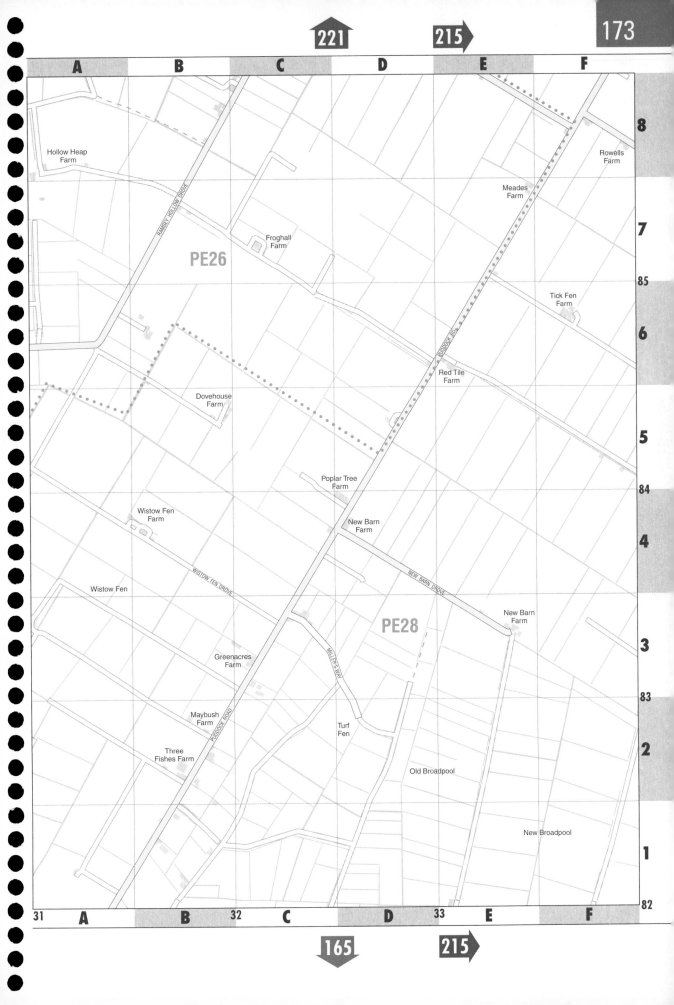

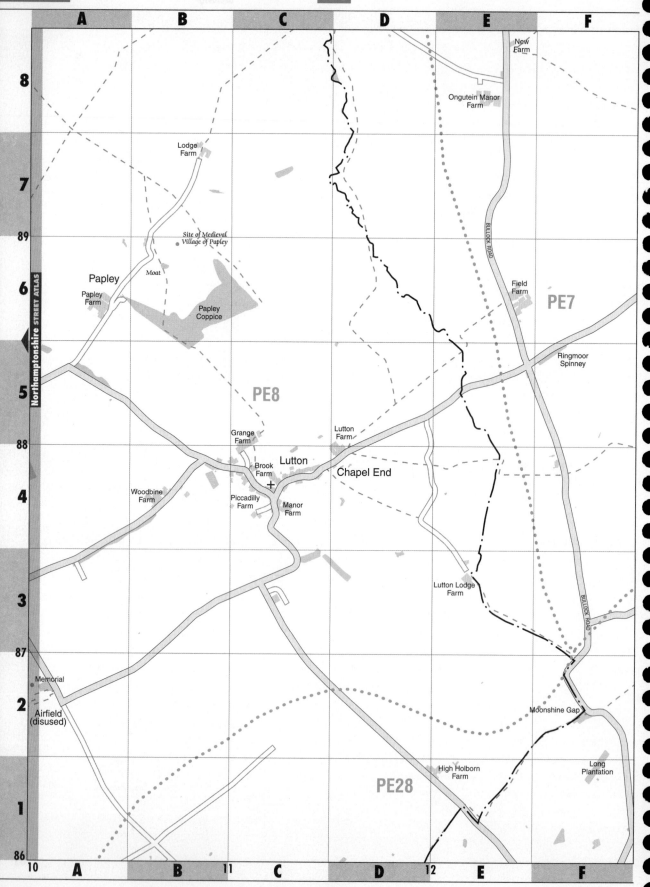

Northamptonshire STREET ATLAS

8

New Farm

Ongutein Manor Farm

Lodge Farm

7

89

Site of Medieval Village of Papley

Field Farm

PE7

Papley

Moat

6

Papley Farm

Papley Coppice

Ringmoor Spinney

BULLOCK ROAD

PE8

5

Grange Farm

Lutton Farm

88

Brook Farm

Lutton

Chapel End

4

Woodbine Farm

Piccadilly Farm

Manor Farm

Lutton Lodge Farm

3

BULLOCK ROAD

87

Memorial

Moonshine Gap

2

Airfield (disused)

High Holborn Farm

Long Plantation

PE28

1

86

10   A   B   11   C   D   12   E   F

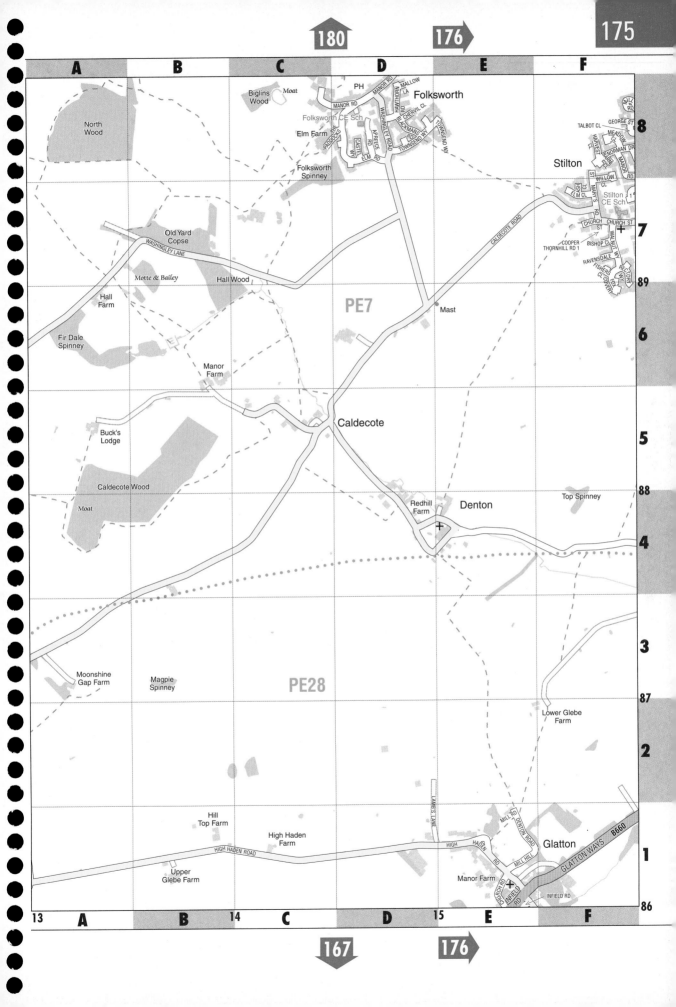

A   B   C   D   E   F

North Wood

Biglins Wood   Moat

PH   Folksworth

MANOR RD   MANOR RD   MALLOW LA   CHERVIL CL

8

Folksworth CE Sch   BLACKMANS RD

Elm Farm   THE PADDOCKS   WASHINGLEY ROAD   TOWNSEND WY   TOWNSEND WY

TALBOT CL   GEORGE ST

MEADOW   HARVEST CL   NORMAN DR

Stilton

Folksworth Spinney   APREECE RD   CASTLE WY   ELM RD

WILLOW CL   MANOR RD

MARY'S ST   ELM CL   Stilton CE Sch

Old Yard Copse   CHURCH ST   WALNUT WY   CHURCH ST   **7**

WASHINGLEY LANE   BISHOP CL   COOPER   THORNHILL RD 1

Motte & Bailey   Hall Wood   RAVENSDALE   FISHERS   RECTORY WY   CLOVERS   **89**

Hall Farm   PE7   Mast

Fir Dale Spinney   **6**

Manor Farm

Buck's Lodge   Caldecote

Caldecote Wood   **5**

Moat   Redhill Farm   Denton   Top Spinney   **88**

CALDECOTE ROAD   ✝   **4**

Moonshine Gap Farm   Magpie Spinney   PE28   **3**

Lower Glebe Farm   **87**

2

Hill Top Farm   LAMB'S LANE   MILL RD   DENTON ROAD

High Haden Farm   MILL HILL   Glatton   GLATTON WAYS   B660

HIGH HADEN ROAD   HIGH HADEN RD   **1**

Upper Glebe Farm   Manor Farm   CHURCH RD   ANFIELD RD   INFIELD RD   **86**

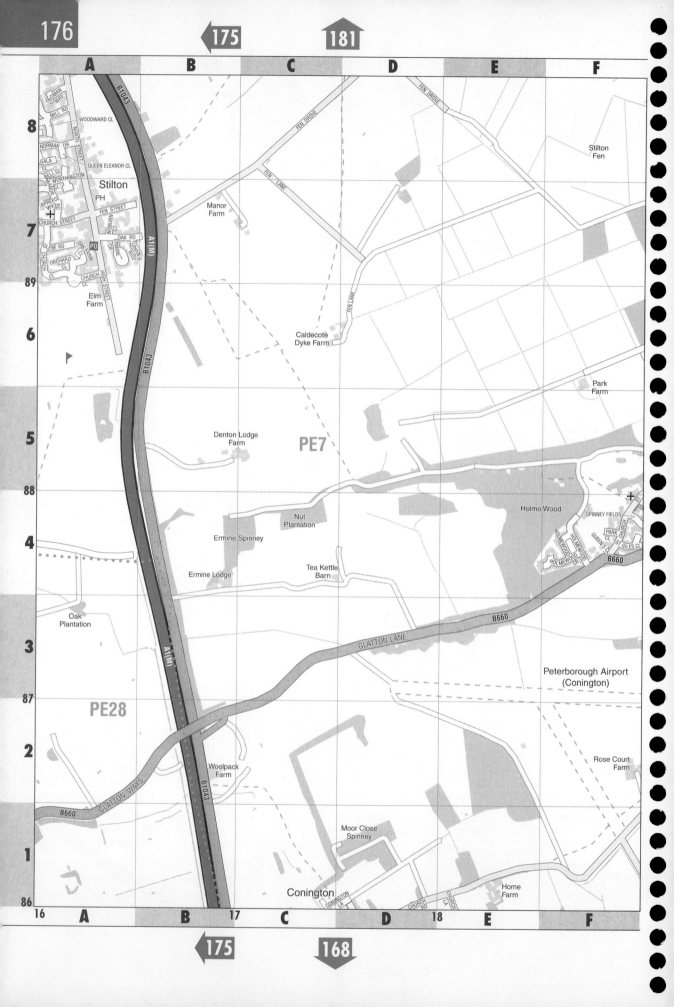

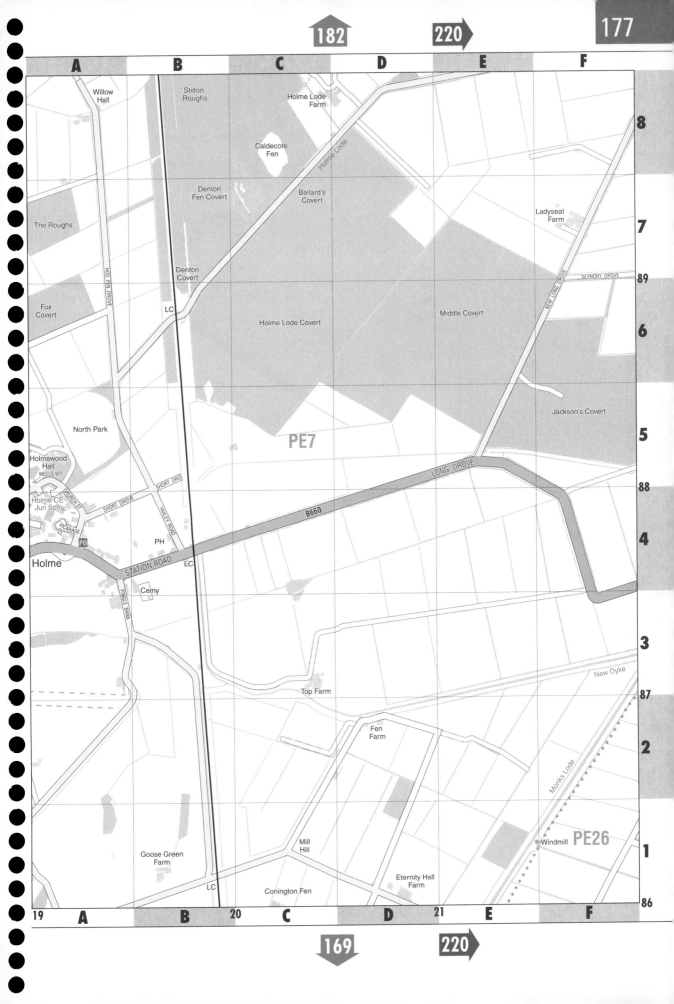

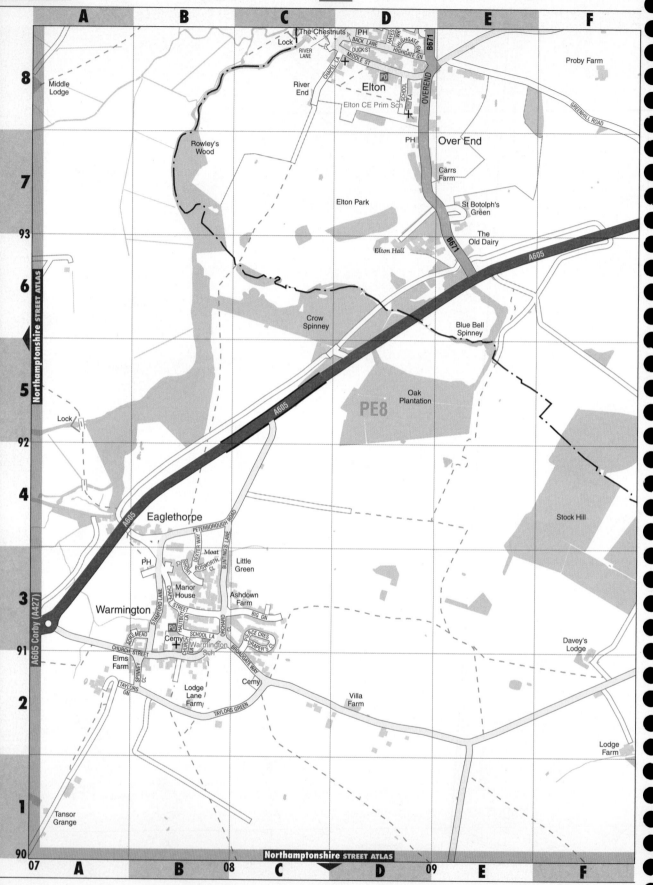

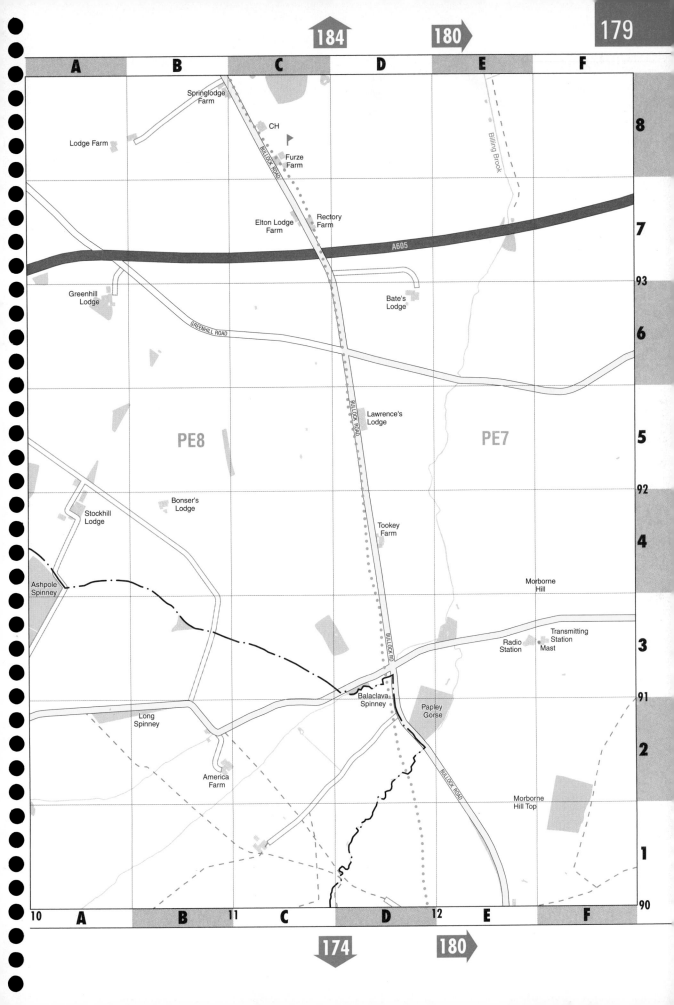

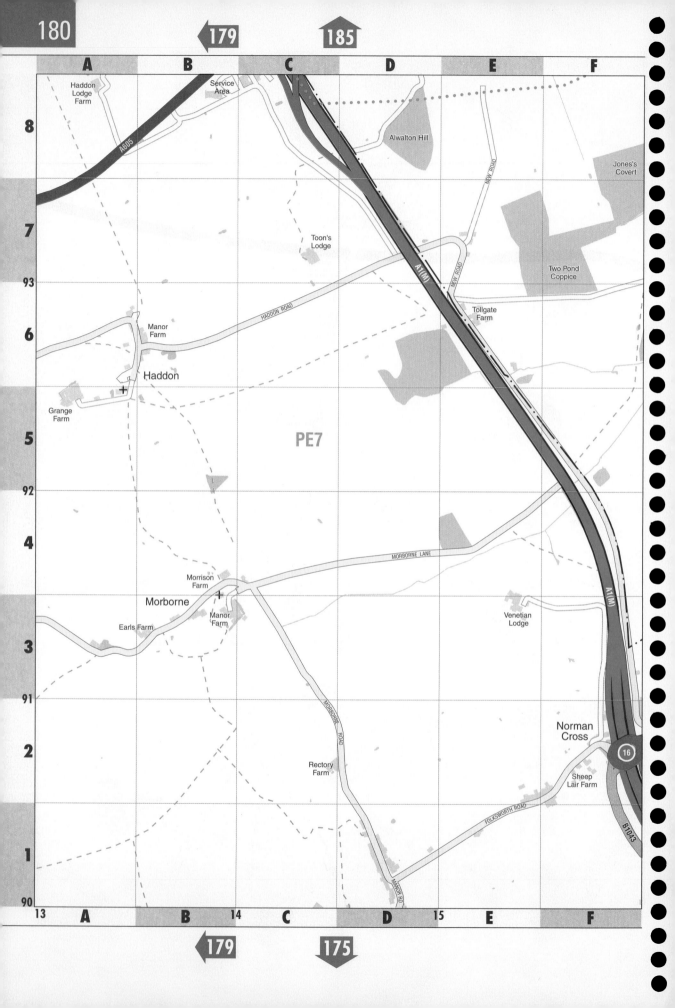

A B C D E F

8

7

93

6

Haddon Lodge Farm

Service Area

Alwalton Hill

Jones's Covert

Toon's Lodge

Two Pond Coppice

HADDON ROAD

A1(M)

NEW ROAD

Tollgate Farm

Manor Farm

Haddon

Grange Farm

PE7

5

92

4

MORBORNE LANE

A1(M)

Morrison Farm

Morborne

Manor Farm

Earls Farm

Venetian Lodge

3

91

MORBORNE ROAD

2

Rectory Farm

Norman Cross

16

Sheep Lair Farm

1

FOLKSWORTH ROAD

MANOR RD

B1043

90

13 A B 14 C D 15 E F

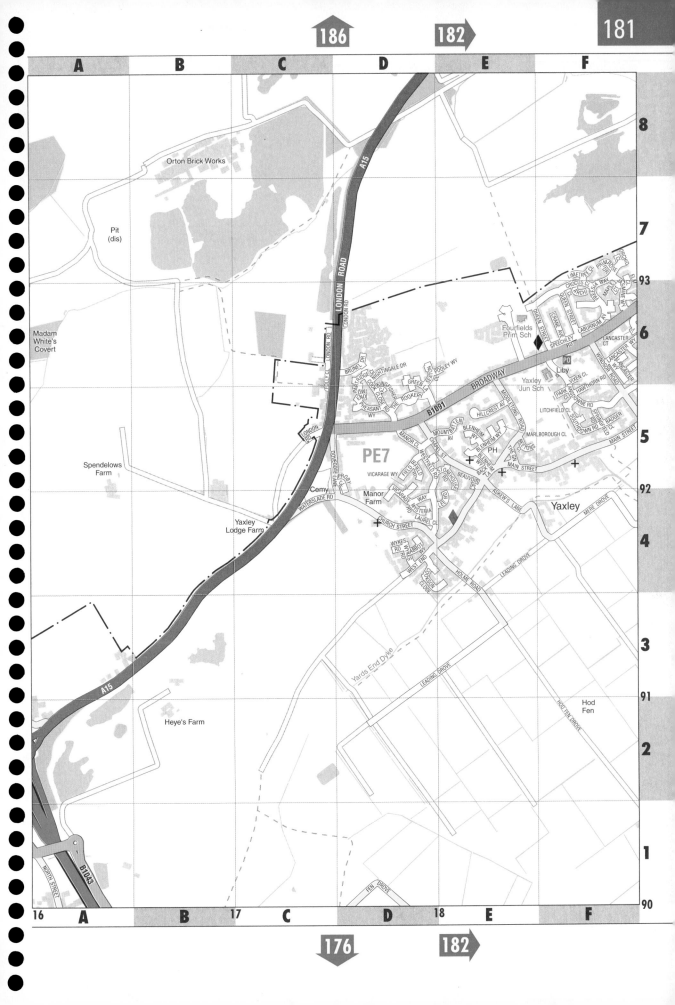

A B C D E F

8
7
93
6
92
5
4
3
91
2
1
90

Orton Brick Works

Pit
(dis)

Madam
White's
Covert

A15

LONDON ROAD

LONDON RD

FOLLY CL

Spendelows
Farm

Cemy

WATERSLADE RD

LONDON RD

DOVEDOTE LANE

PROBY

Yaxley
Lodge Farm

Manor
Farm

CHURCH STREET

VICARAGE WY
WISTERIA
LAUREL CL

WYKES
RD
TWYKES
ROW WY
WEST END
COXSON
CLOSE

Heye's Farm

A15

B1043

NORTH STREET

FEN DROVE

Yards End Dyke

LEADING DROVE

LEADING DROVE

HOD FEN DROVE

Hod
Fen

HOLME ROAD

PE7

VICARAGE WY

BRUNEL DR
PARTRIDGE DR
KINGFISHER CL
OWL
END
PHEASANT
WY
THE ROOKERY
GREEN
NIGHTINGALE DR
POOLEY WY

B1091

BROADWAY

Fourfields
Prim Sch

QUEEN STREET
CRANE AVE
SPEECHLEY RD
QUEEN STREET
LABURNUM AV
WINDSOR ROAD
HAWTHORN RD

LIMETREE CL
CROCUS CL
ORCHID CL
LARCH
MAPLE CL
ELM
PRIM ROSE
LA WY
ASH WY

LANCASTER
CT
LANCASTER
WY
PO
Liby
VIXEN CL
PARK AVE
TOWNE RD
SPRING RD
SOUTHDOWN RD
BADGER
CL
RED CL

Yaxley
Jun Sch

LITCHFIELD CL

MANOR CL
CHAPEL ST
WESTFIELD
FIELD
MAIN STREET
STONEHOUSE
RD
BEAUVOIR
PL
LEE CL
HILLCREST AV
MOUNTBATTEN
AV
BLENHEIM
WY
BLENHEIM WY
PH
THE GR
BARLEY
MIDDLETONS ROAD
BRETONS
MARLBOROUGH CL

MAIN STREET

MAIN STREET

ASKEW'S LANE

Yaxley

MERE DROVE

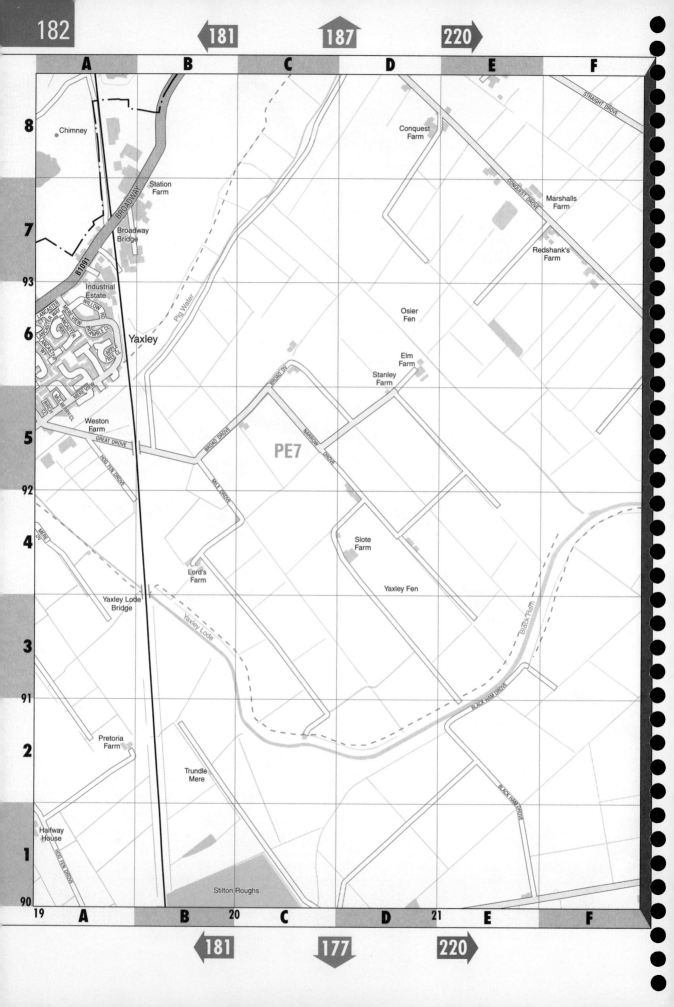

A B C D E F

Chimney

Station Farm

BROADWAY

Broadway Bridge

B1091

Industrial Estate

LANCASTER WAY
MERE VIEW
WILLOW RD
LANCASTER WAY
LANCASTER WAY
BRAMBLE CL
APPLE TREE CL

Yaxley

Pig Water

BIRCH CL
MILL CLEAM CL
MERE VIEW

Weston Farm

GREAT DROVE

HOG FEN DROVE

MERE DV

BROAD DROVE

MILE DROVE

BROAD DV

NARROW DROVE

PE7

Conquest Farm

CONQUEST DROVE

STRAIGHT DROVE

Marshalls Farm

Redshank's Farm

Osier Fen

Elm Farm

Stanley Farm

Slote Farm

Yaxley Fen

Black Ham

Lord's Farm

Yaxley Lode Bridge

Yaxley Lode

BLACK HAM DROVE

Pretoria Farm

Trundle Mere

BLACK HAM DROVE

Halfway House

HOLT FEN DROVE

Stilton Roughs

8 7 93 6 5 92 4 3 91 2 1 90

19 20 21

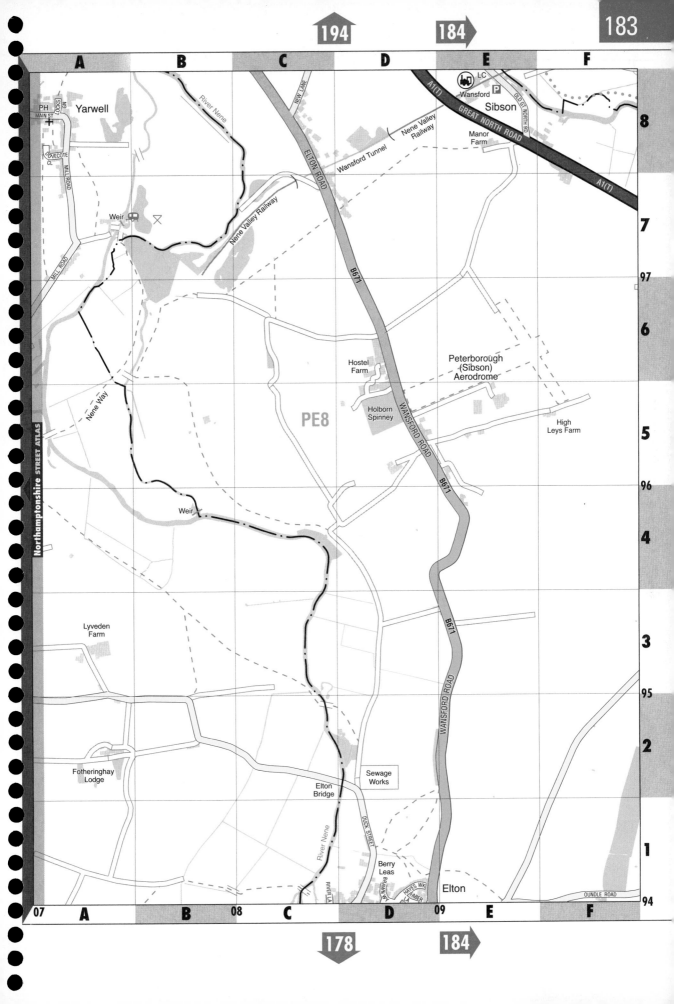

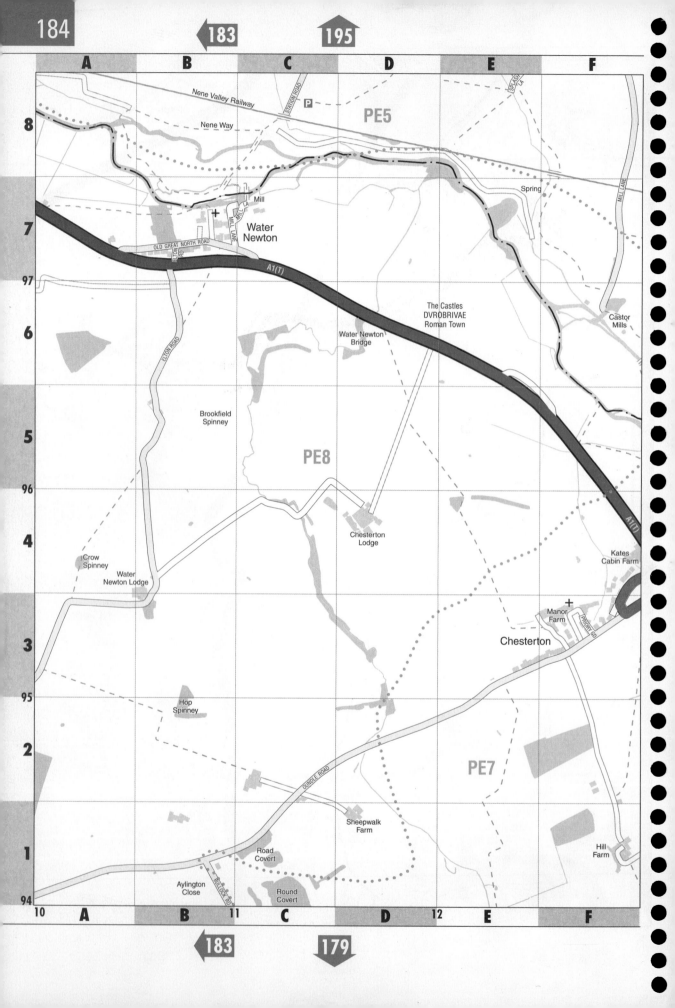

A B C D E F

8

Nene Valley Railway

Nene Way

STATION ROAD

P

PE5

SPLASH LA

Spring

MILL LANE

Mill

MILL LA

Water
Newton

OLD GREAT NORTH ROAD

ELTON RD

7

A1(T)

97

The Castles
DVROBRIVAE
Roman Town

Castor
Mills

6

ELTON ROAD

Water Newton
Bridge

Brookfield
Spinney

5

PE8

96

Chesterton
Lodge

4

Crow
Spinney

Water
Newton Lodge

Kates
Cabin Farm

Manor
Farm

PRIORY RD

Chesterton

3

95

Hop
Spinney

OUNDLE ROAD

2

PE7

A1(T)

Sheepwalk
Farm

Hill
Farm

1

Road
Covert

BULLOCK RD

Aylington
Close

Round
Covert

94

10 A B 11 C D 12 E F

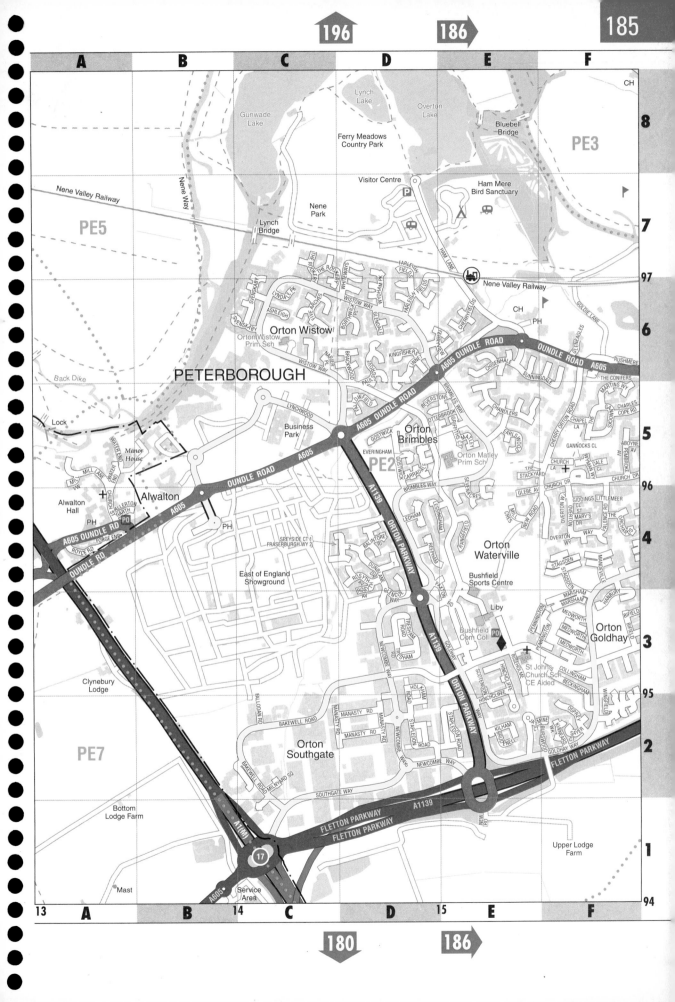

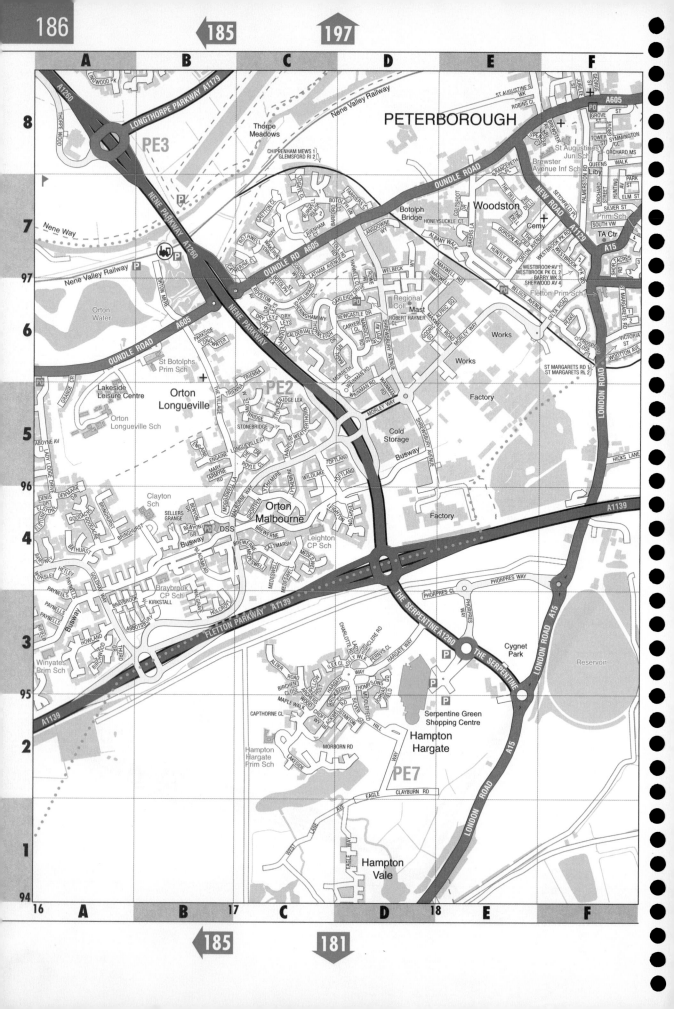

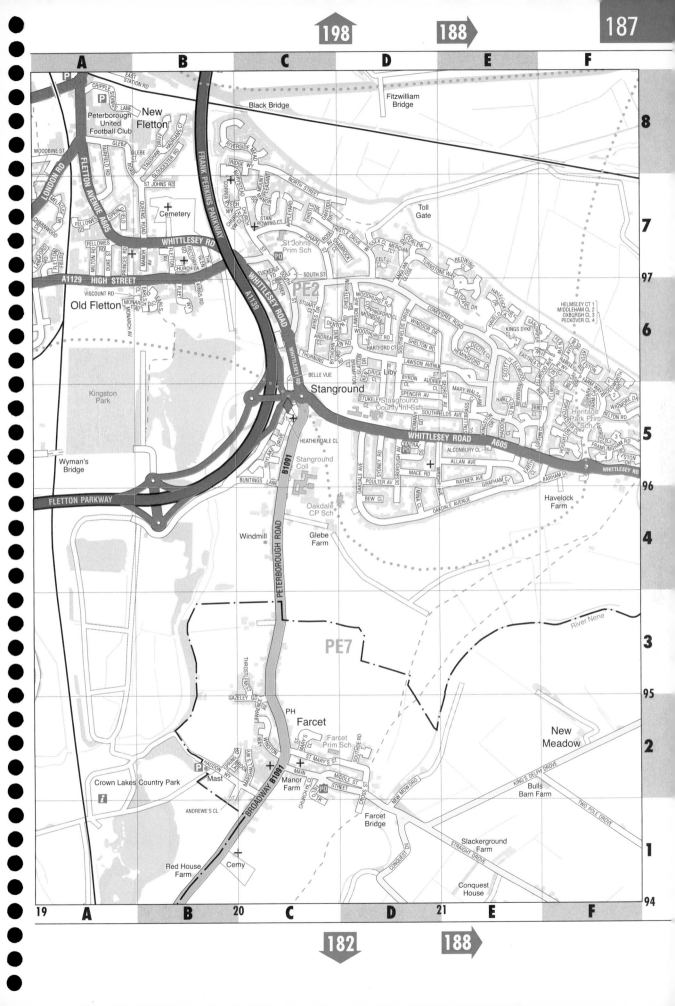

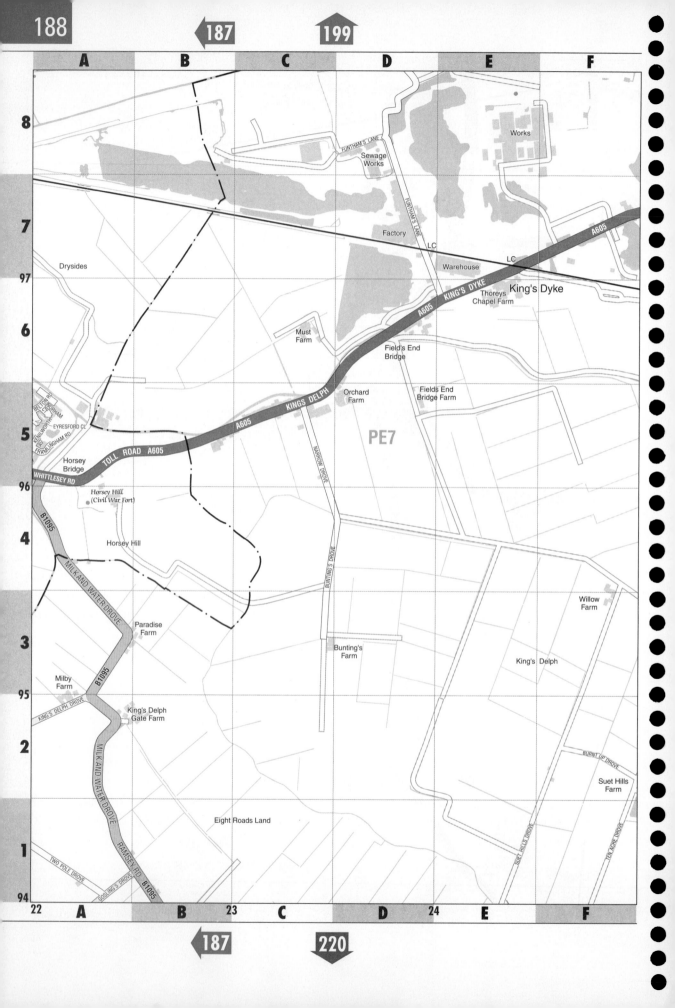

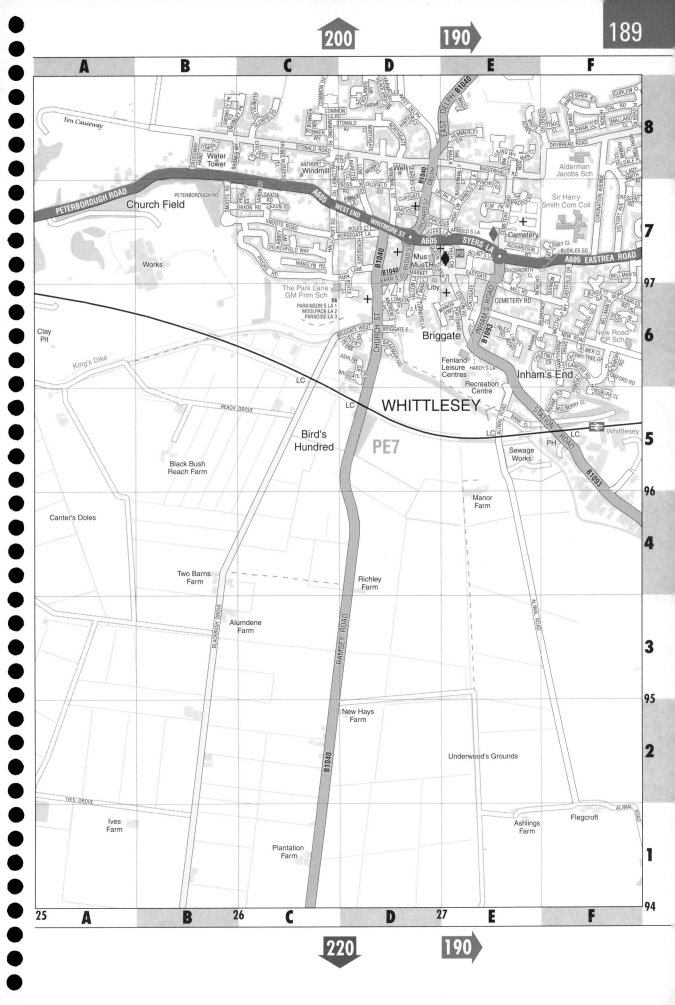

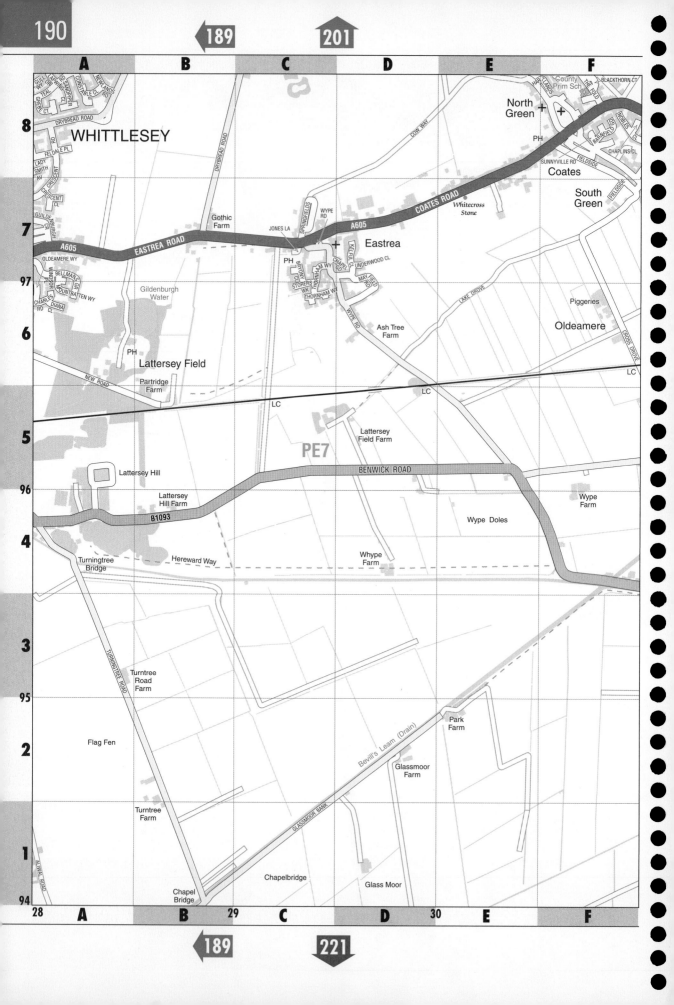

189
201

WHITTLESEY

North Green

County Prim Sch

Blackthorn Ct

THE FOLD

Coates

South Green

Gothic Farm

Jones La

WYPE RD

COATES ROAD

A605

Whitecross Stone

SPRINGFIELDS

EASTREA ROAD

A605

Eastrea

PH

Oldeamere Wy

Windsor Cl

Bellmans Gr

Mountbatten Wy

Charles Rd

Diana Cl

Gildenburgh Water

STORERS WK

BRYONY

THORNHAM WY

CHAPEL GO

UNDERWOOD CL

KELFIELD CL

MAYFIELD RD

THORNHAM WY

WYPE RD

PH

Ash Tree Farm

LAKE DROVE

Piggeries

Oldeamere

CROSS DROVE

PH

Lattersey Field

New Road

Partridge Farm

LC

LC

LC

Lattersey Field Farm

PE7

Lattersey Hill

Lattersey Hill Farm

B1093

Hereward Way

BENWICK ROAD

Wype Doles

Wype Farm

Whype Farm

Turningtree Bridge

TURNINGTREE ROAD

Turntree Road Farm

Flag Fen

Turntree Farm

Bevill's Leam (Drain)

GLASSMOOR BANK

Park Farm

Glassmoor Farm

Chapelbridge

Glass Moor

Chapel Bridge

ALWALT ROAD

189
221

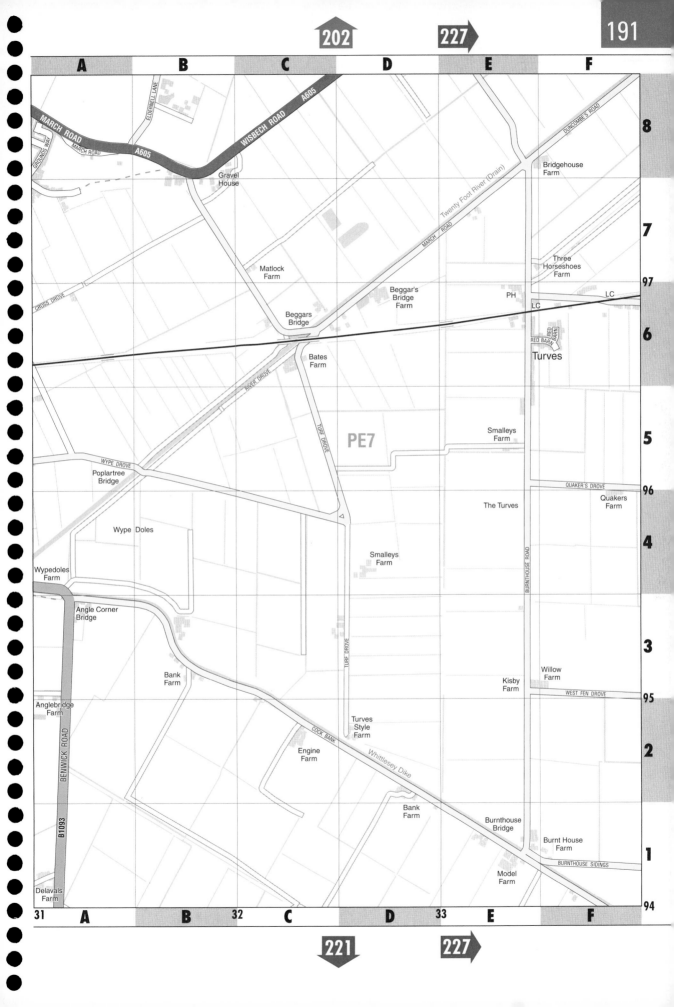

PE9

A47 Leicester

COLLYWESTON
CROSS ROADS

A47(T)

A47(T)

Wittering
Lodge

Collyweston
Great Wood

Easton
Hornstocks

Wittering
Coppice

Cross
Leys Farm

Westhay
Farm

Leicestershire STREET ATLAS

Westhay
Lodge

Windpump

St John's
Wood Farm

PE8

Law's
Lawn

Vigo
Wood

Memorial

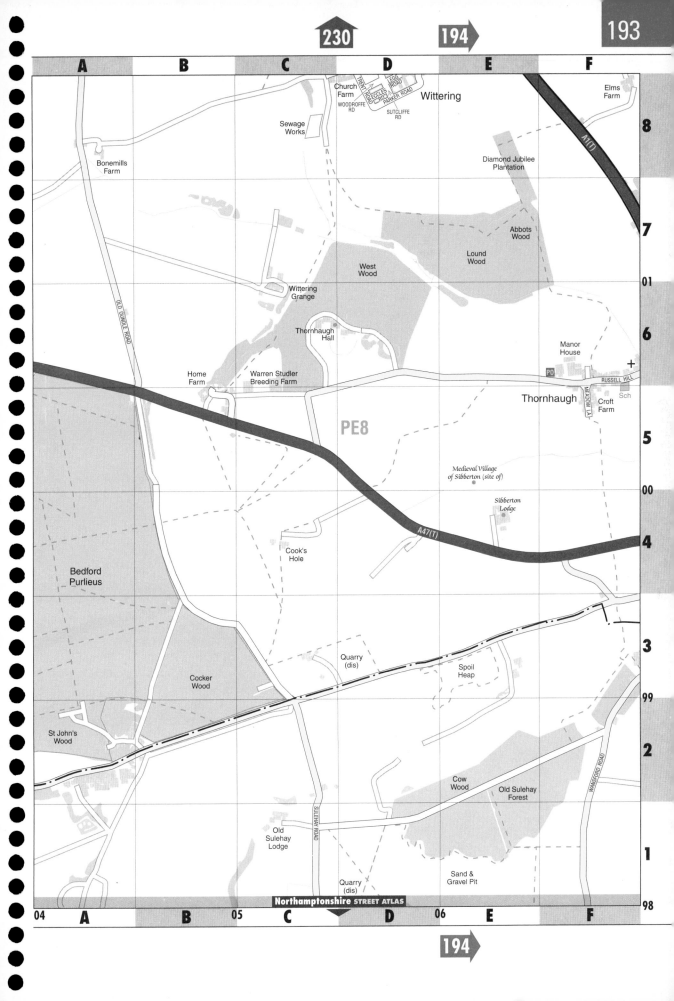

A   B   C   D   E   F

8

Elms
Farm

Church
Farm
Wittering
WOODROFFE
RD
TRENT ROAD
ECCLES
RDS
LEGGE
ROAD
PARKER ROAD
SUTCLIFFE
RD

Sewage
Works

Diamond Jubilee
Plantation

Bonemills
Farm

Abbots
Wood

7

01

Lound
Wood

West
Wood

Wittering
Grange

Manor
House

6

Thornhaugh
Hall

OLD OUNDLE ROAD

PO

RUSSELL HILL

Home
Farm

Warren Studler
Breeding Farm

Thornhaugh

Sch

MEADOW LA

Croft
Farm

PE8

5

Medieval Village
of Sibberton (site of)

Sibberton
Lodge

00

A47(T)

4

Cook's
Hole

Bedford
Purlieus

Quarry
(dis)

Spoil
Heap

3

Cocker
Wood

99

St John's
Wood

2

Cow
Wood

Old Sulehay
Forest

WANSFORD ROAD

SULEHAY ROAD

Old
Sulehay
Lodge

1

Quarry
(dis)

Sand &
Gravel Pit

98

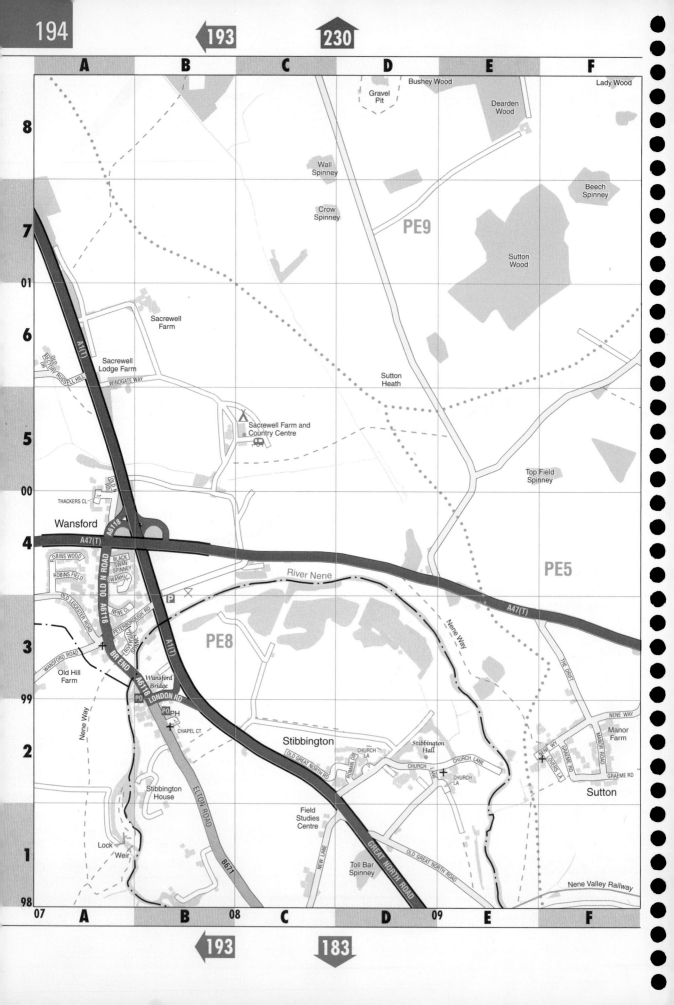

193
230

A B C D E F

8

7

01

6

Sacrewell
Farm

Sacrewell
Lodge Farm

WINDGATE WAY

THACKERS CL

Wansford

ROBINS WOOD

ROBINS FIELD

OLD LEICESTER ROAD

Wansford Road

Old Hill
Farm

Nene Way

Lock
Weir

Stibbington
House

ELTON ROAD

B671

5

00

4

3

99

2

1

98

Bushey Wood

Gravel
Pit

Dearden
Wood

Lady Wood

Wall
Spinney

Crow
Spinney

PE9

Beech
Spinney

Sutton
Wood

Sutton
Heath

Top Field
Spinney

River Nene

PE5

A47(T)

Nene Way

THE DRIFT

BLACK
SWAN
SPINNEY

SWAN HL

NENE CL

PETERBOROUGH RD

OLD N ROAD

A6118

A1(T)

A6118

BR END

Wansford
Bridge

LONDON RD

PO

PO PH

CHAPEL CT

PE8

Stibbington

OLD GREAT NORTH RD

ROMAN DR

CHURCH LA

CHURCH
LA

CHURCH LANE

CHURCH
LA

Stibbington
Hall

Field
Studies
Centre

NEW LANE

GREAT NORTH ROAD

OLD GREAT NORTH ROAD

Toll Bar
Spinney

NENE WY

NENE WY

GRAEME RD

MANOR ROAD

LOVERS LN

Manor
Farm

GRAEME RD

Sutton

NENE WAY

Nene Valley Railway

Sacrewell Farm and
Country Centre

A47(T)

A1(T)

OLD N ROAD

OLD RECTORY DR

RUSSELL HILL

07 A B 08 C D 09 E F

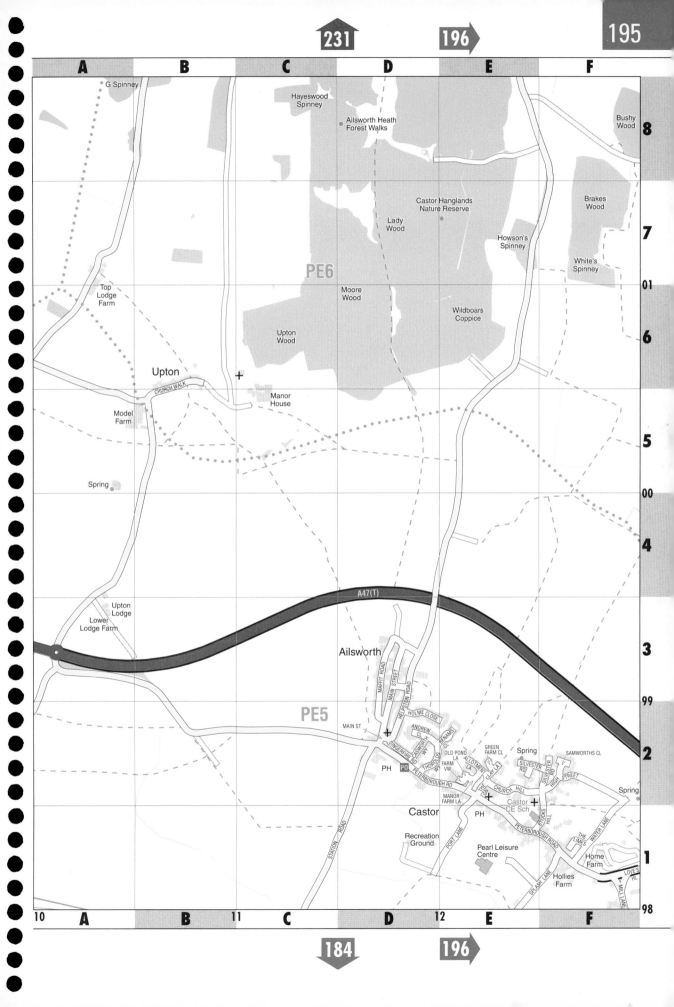

A B C D E F

G Spinney

Hayeswood Spinney

Ailsworth Heath Forest Walks

Bushy Wood

8

Castor Hanglands Nature Reserve

Brakes Wood

Lady Wood

Howson's Spinney

7

White's Spinney

PE6

01

Moore Wood

Top Lodge Farm

Wildboars Coppice

6

Upton Wood

Upton

CHURCH WALK

Manor House

Model Farm

5

Spring

00

4

Upton Lodge

A47(T)

Lower Lodge Farm

3

Ailsworth

MAFFIT ROAD
MAIN STREET
HELPSTON ROAD

99

PE5

HOLME CLOSE

MAIN ST

2

ANDREW CL
BENAMS
SINGERFIRE RD
ASHWORTH WY
THOROLDS
OLD POND
FARM VW
GREEN FARM CL
Spring
SAMWORTHS CL
ALLOTMENT LA
SILVESTER RD
SILVESTER RD
HIGH STREET
CLAY LA
PH
PO
PETERBOROUGH RD
THE
CHURCH HILL
Spring

MANOR FARM LA
Castor CE Sch
STOCKS HILL

Castor
PH
PETERBOROUGH ROAD
THE LIMES
WATER LANE

Recreation Ground
PORT LANE
Home Farm

Pearl Leisure Centre
LOVE'S HL

STATION ROAD
SPLASH LANE
Hollies Farm
MILL LANE

1

98

10 A B 11 C D 12 E F

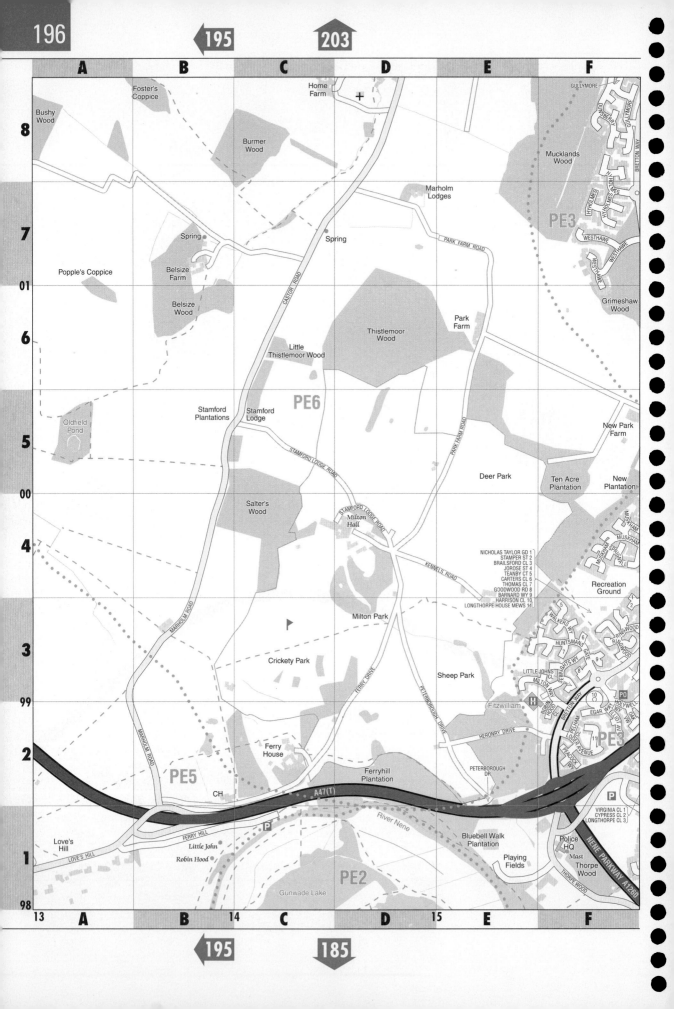

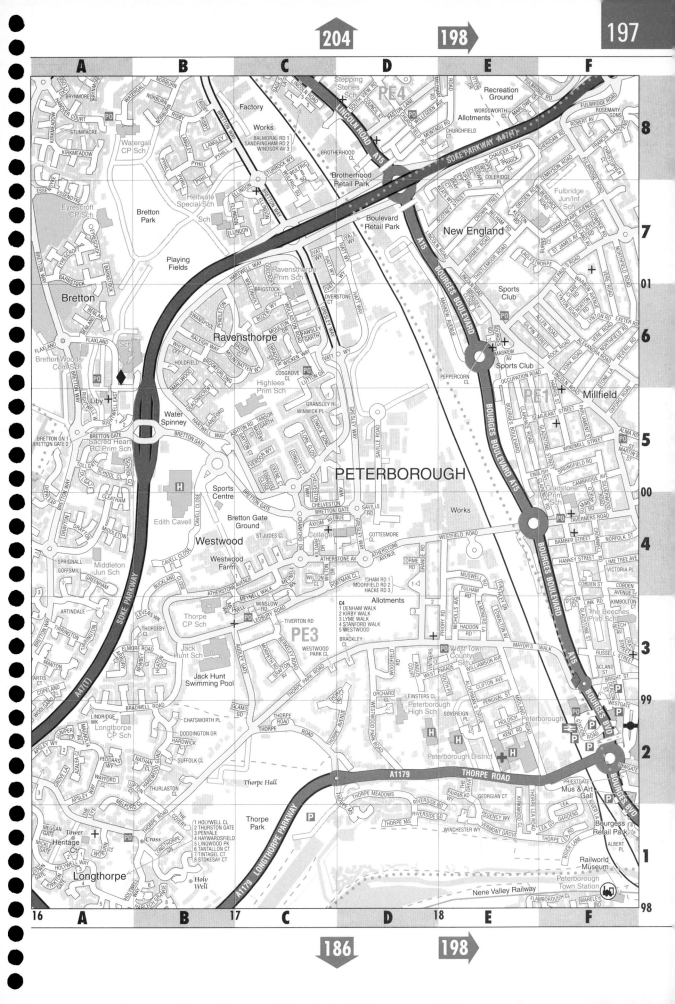

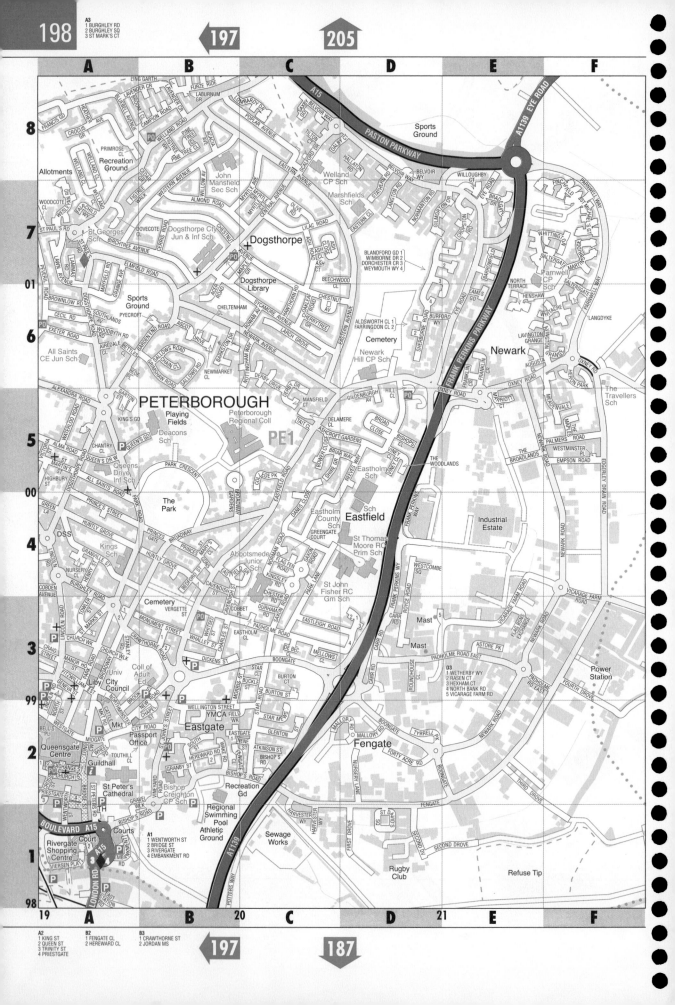

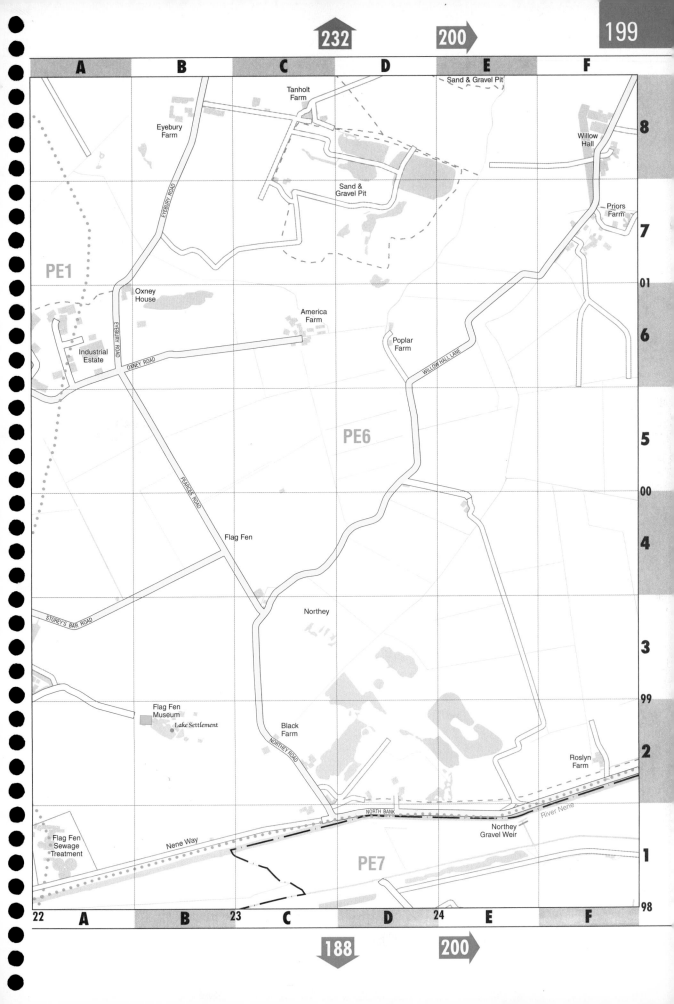

8

7

01

6

5

00

4

3

99

2

PE1

Eyebury Farm

Tanholt Farm

Sand & Gravel Pit

Sand & Gravel Pit

Willow Hall

Priors Farm

EYEBURY ROAD

Oxney House

America Farm

Poplar Farm

WILLOW HALL LANE

Industrial Estate

OXNEY ROAD

EYEBURY ROAD

PE6

PEARCES ROAD

Flag Fen

STOREY'S BAR ROAD

Northey

Flag Fen Museum

Lake Settlement

Black Farm

NORTHEY ROAD

Roslyn Farm

Flag Fen Sewage Treatment

Nene Way

NORTH BANK

River Nene

Northey Gravel Weir

PE7

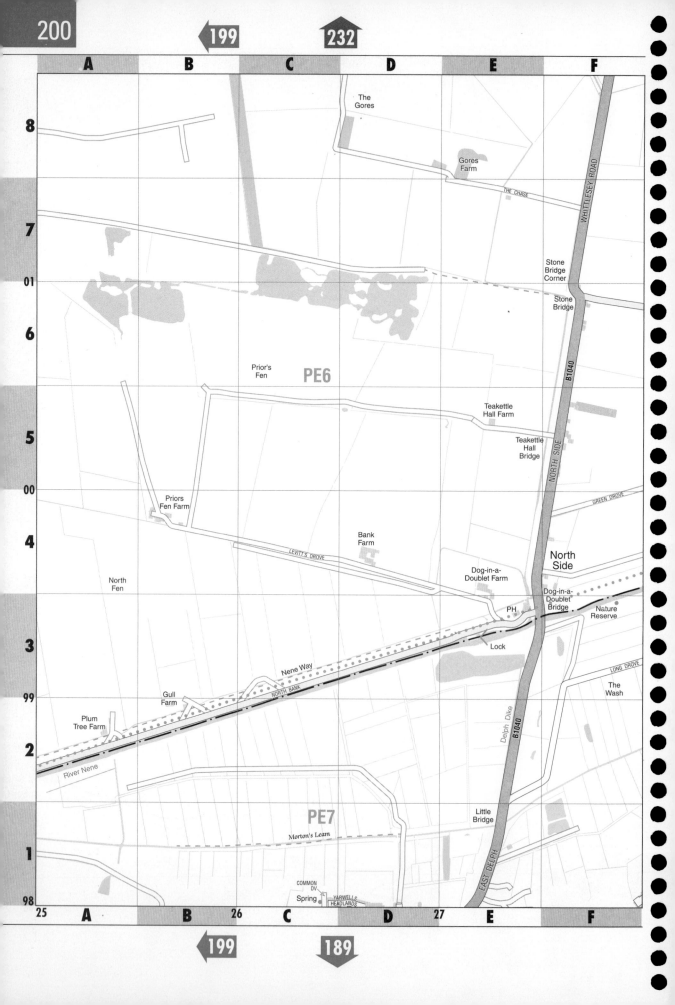

A   B   C   D   E   F

8

7

01

6

PE6

Prior's
Fen

The
Gores

Gores
Farm

THE CHASE

WHITTLESEY ROAD

Stone
Bridge
Corner

Stone
Bridge

B1040

Teakettle
Hall Farm

NORTH SIDE

Teakettle
Hall
Bridge

5

00

Priors
Fen Farm

GREEN DROVE

4

North
Fen

LEVITT'S DROVE

Bank
Farm

Dog-in-a-
Doublet Farm

North
Side

Dog-in-a-
Doublet
Bridge

Nature
Reserve

PH

Lock

LONG DROVE

The
Wash

3

Nene Way

NORTH BANK

99

Gull
Farm

Plum
Tree Farm

Delph Dike

B1040

2

River Nene

PE7

Morton's Leam

Little
Bridge

EAST DELPH

1

98

COMMON DV

Spring

YARWELL'S
HEADLANDS

25   A   B   26   C   D   27   E   F

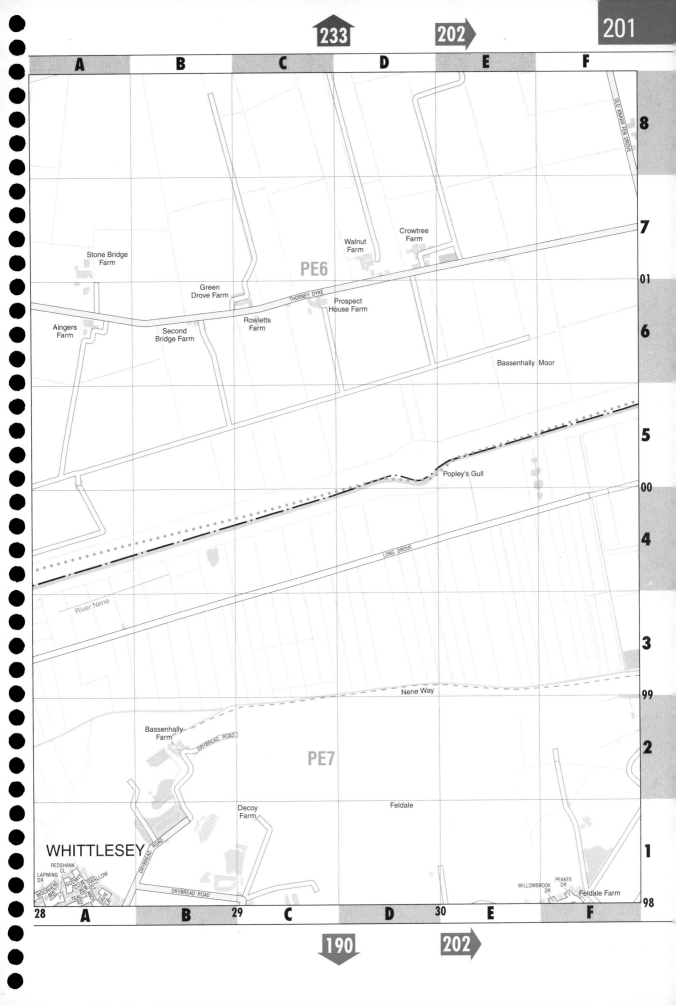

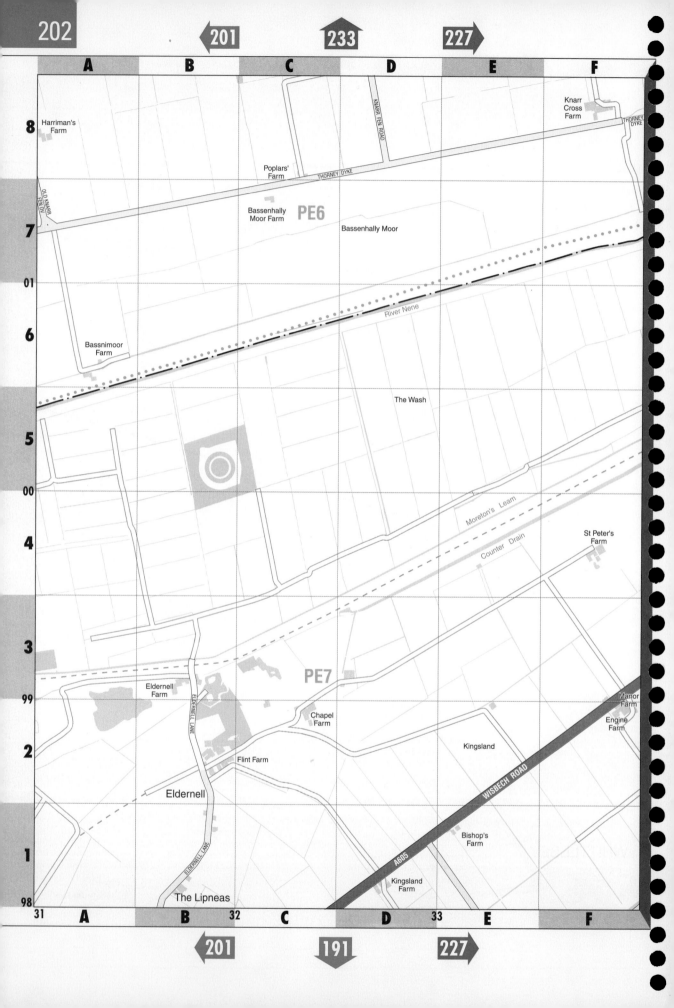

201
233
227

A B C D E F

8 Harriman's Farm

Knarr Cross Farm

KNARR FEN ROAD

THORNEY DYKE

Poplars' Farm

THORNEY DYKE

OLD KNARR FEN DY

Bassenhally Moor Farm

PE6

Bassenhally Moor

7

01

River Nene

6 Bassnimoor Farm

The Wash

5

00

Moreton's Leam

4 Counter Drain

St Peter's Farm

3 PE7

Eldernell Farm

ELDERNELL LANE

99 Manor Farm

Engine Farm

Chapel Farm

Kingsland

2 Flint Farm

Eldernell

WISBECH ROAD

1 A605

Bishop's Farm

ELDERNELL LANE

Kingsland Farm

98 The Lipneas

31 A B 32 C D 33 E F

201
191
227

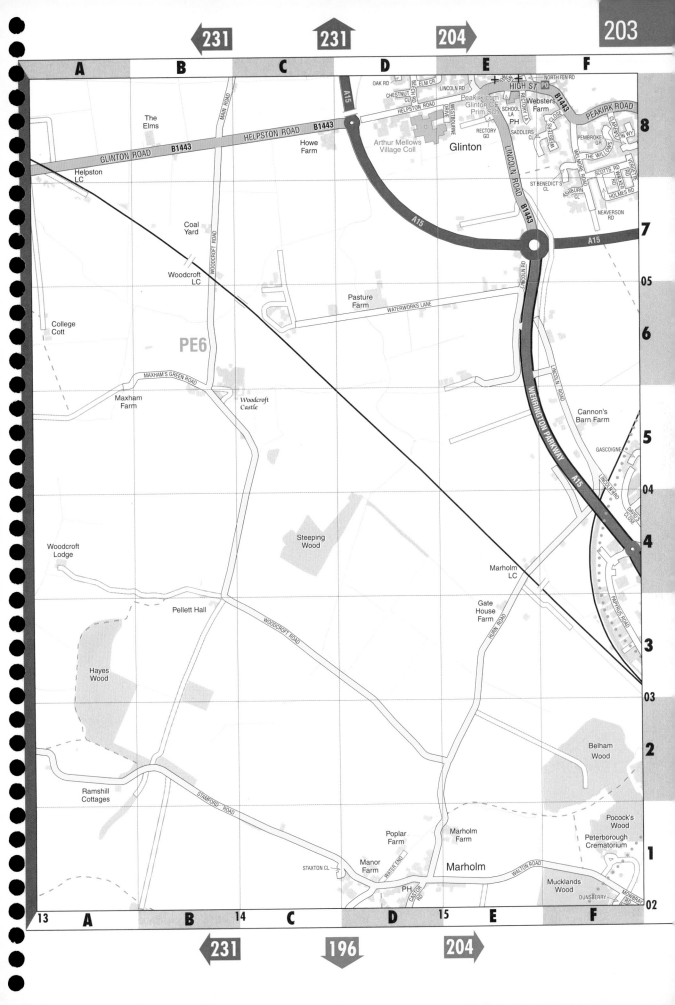

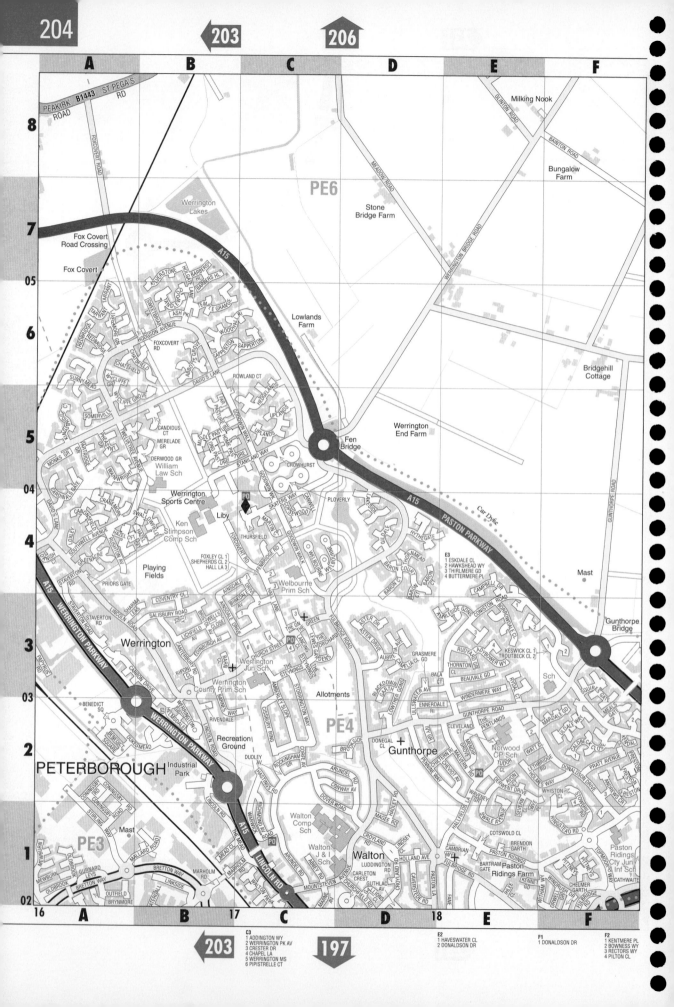

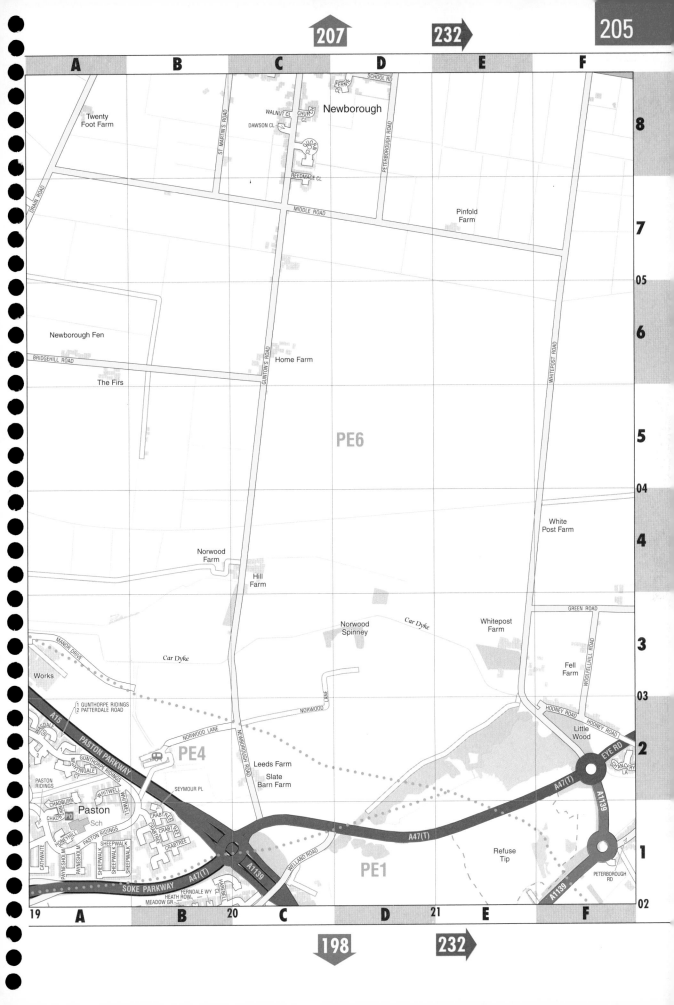

231

A B C D E F

8

Cranmore
Farm

CRANMORE DROVE

Refuse
Tip

Cranmore
Farm

STOWGATE ROAD

Cranmore
Barn Farm

Deeping
St James

B1166

B1166

Cranmore
Lodge

7

EASTGATE

B1166

LOCKS CL

WHICHCOTE ROAD

River Welland

09

Deeping
Common

Grasmere
Farm

LC

STATION ROAD

6

Cranmore
Farm

EASTGATE

Sewage
Works

STATION ROAD

PE6

5

08

PEAKIRK ROAD

CHURCH STREET

4

River Welland

Maxey Cut

3

Moorfield

MILE DROVE

Sissons
Farm

MOOR ROAD

Peakirk Moor

07

PO

Peakirk
Wildfowl Trust

2

CHESTNUT CL

RECTORY LA

FIRSDALE CL

Folly Bank
LC

B1443

THORNEY ROAD

BULL LA

PH

ST PEGA'S ROAD

Peakirk

MEADOW ROAD

GLINTON ROAD

Long
Meadow
Farm

MILKINGNOOK CL

WERRINGTON BRIDGE ROAD

PH

1

THE
MALLARDS

Folly River (drain)

LAW'S CL

06

16

A

B

17

C

D

18

E

F

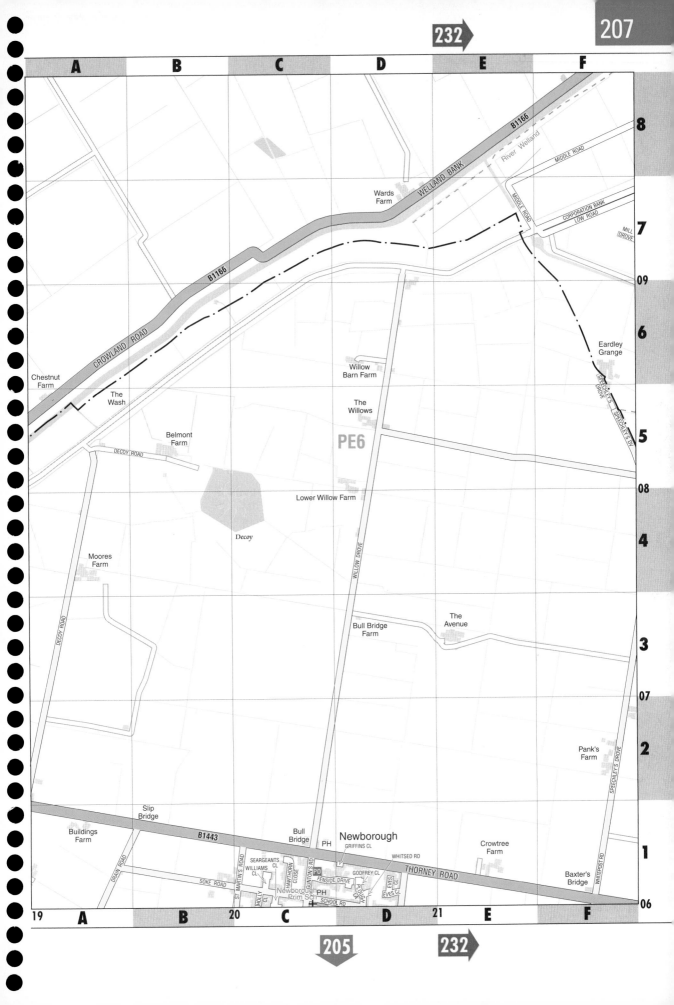

A B C D E F

8
B1166
09
7
6
5
08
4
3
07
2
1
06

Welland Bank
River Welland
MIDDLE ROAD
CORPORATION BANK
LOW ROAD
MILL DROVE
MIDDLE ROAD

Wards Farm

B1166

CROWLAND ROAD

Chestnut Farm

The Wash

Willow Barn Farm

The Willows

PE6

Eardley Grange

SPEECHLEY'S DROVE

SPEECHLEY'S DV

Belmont Farm

DECOY ROAD

Lower Willow Farm

Decoy

Moores Farm

WILLOW DROVE

Bull Bridge Farm

The Avenue

DECOY ROAD

Pank's Farm

SPEECHLEY'S DROVE

Slip Bridge

Buildings Farm

DRAIN ROAD

B1443

SOKE ROAD

ST MARTIN'S ROAD

SEARGEANTS CL

WILLIAMS CL

HAWTHORN CLOSE

HOLLY CL

GUNTON'S RD

PO

FENSIDE DRIVE

Newborough Prim Sch

SCHOOL RD

PH

Bull Bridge

PH

Newborough

GRIFFINS CL

GODFREY CL

PLOUGH

EVES CL

EVES CL

WHITSED RD

THORNEY ROAD

Crowtree Farm

WHITEPOST RD

Baxter's Bridge

19 A B 20 C D 21 E F

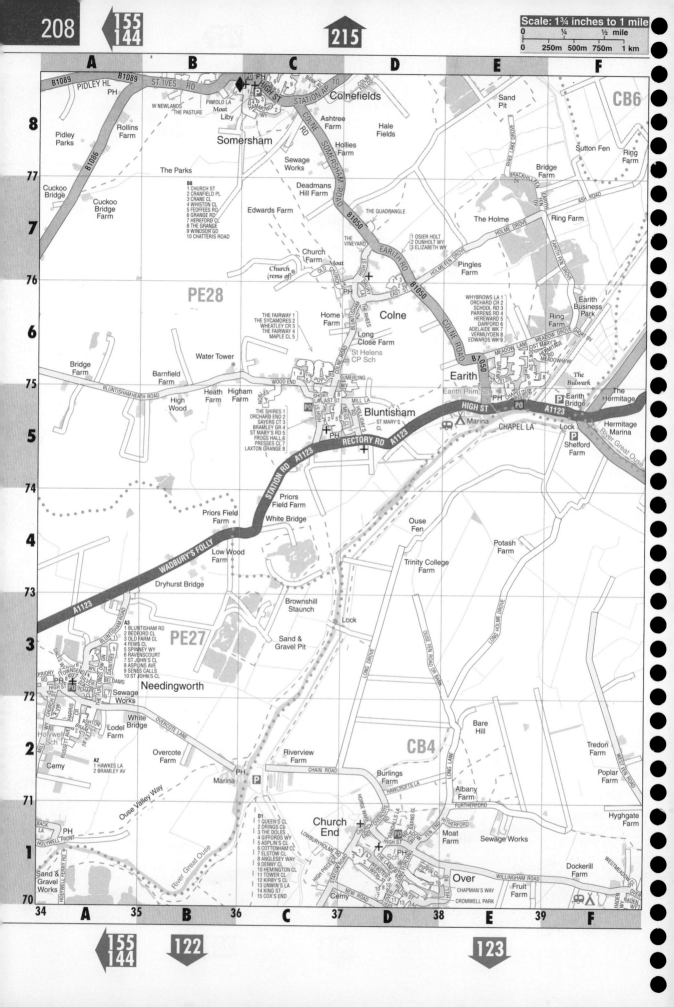

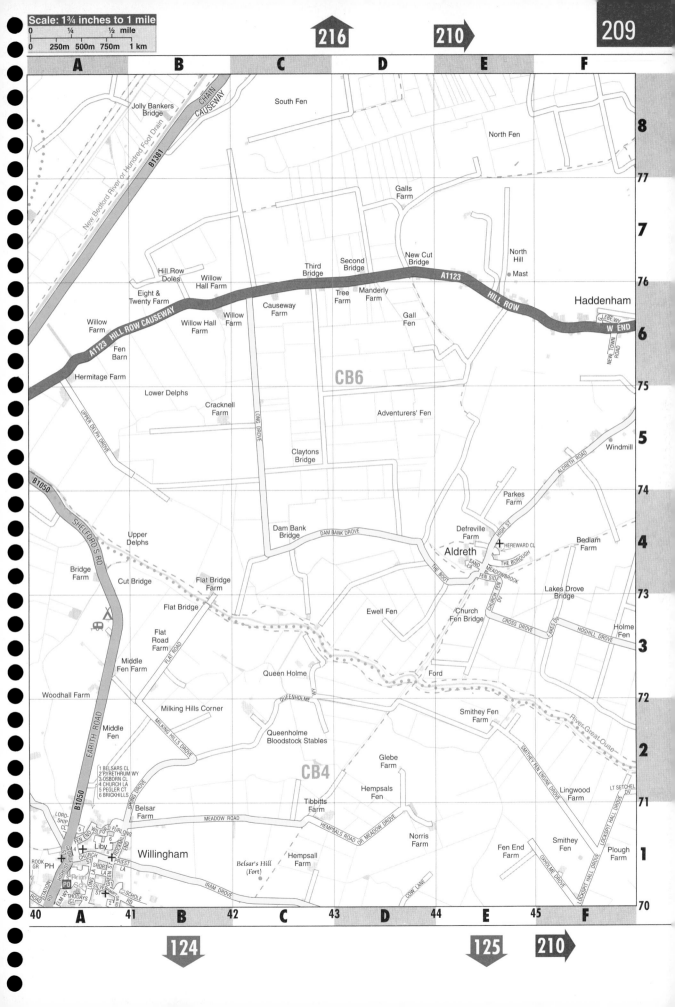

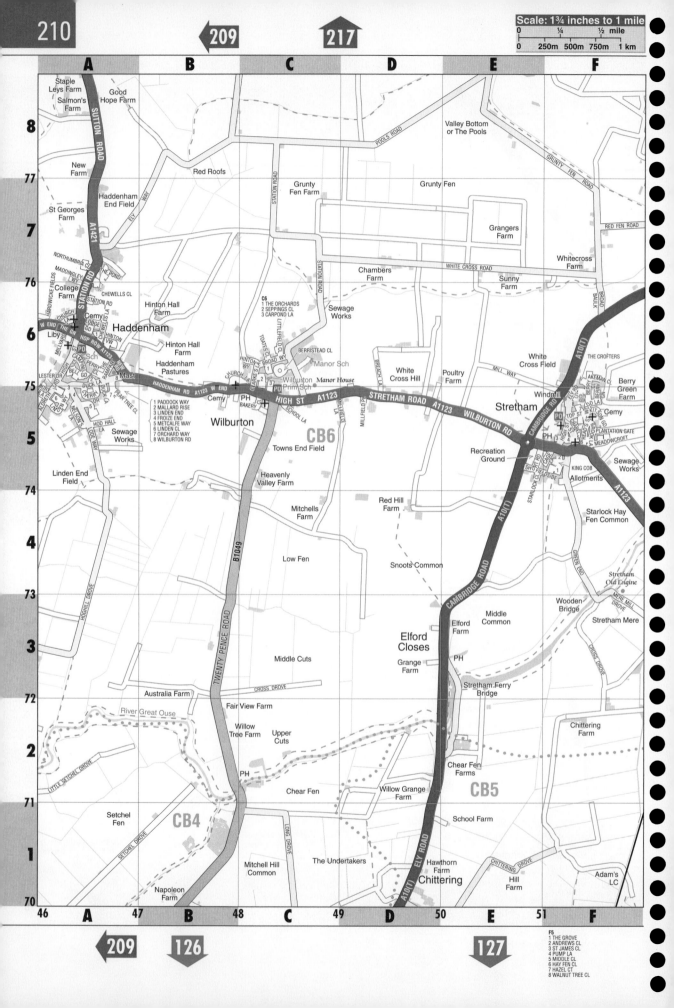

209
217

Scale: 1¾ inches to 1 mile

0   ¼   ½ mile
0 250m 500m 750m 1 km

A   B   C   D   E   F

8

Staple
Leys Farm
Salmon's
Farm

Good
Hope Farm

Valley Bottom
or The Pools

77

New
Farm

Red Roofs

Grunty
Fen Farm

Grunty Fen

GRUNTY FEN ROAD

RED FEN ROAD

St Georges
Farm

Haddenham
End Field

ELY WAY

STATION ROAD

Grangers
Farm

7

A1421

Northumbria Cl

Maddingley Wy

POOLS ROAD

WHITE CROSS ROAD

Whitecross
Farm

BROAD BAULK

76

Hardwicke Fields

College
Farm

STATION RD

STATION RD

Chewells Cl

Hinton Hall
Farm

C6
1 THE ORCHARDS
2 SEPPINGS CL
3 CARPOND LA

LITTLEFIELD DRO

Chambers
Farm

Sewage
Works

Sunny
Farm

A10(T)

THE CROFTERS

6

Church Wy

Cemy

HOP ROW A1123

HINTON
VW

Haddenham

Hinton Hall
Farm

TOATES CL

BROAD WY

Berristead CL

Manor Sch

White
Cross Hill

Poultry
Farm

MILL WAY

White
Cross Field

AKEMAN CL

BERRY

Berry
Green
Farm

Liby

THE GN

W END

PO

Hinton Hall
Pastures

CHURCH

HINTON
WY

CLARKE S L

BROAD WY

Wilburton
PO Prim Sch

Manor House

BREACH LA

Windmill

Cemy

75

Lester Dr

GD

PERRY

RAILWAY

PEAR TREE CL

HADDENHAM RD   A1123   W END

Cemy
PH BAKERY

HIGH ST   A1123

STRETHAM ROAD   A1123

WILBURTON RD

CAMBRIDGE RD

Stretham

PO

PH

MEADOWCROFT

A1123

DUCK LA

HOD HALL
LA

CODE WAY

Sewage
Works

1 PADDOCK WAY
2 MALLARD RISE
3 LINDEN END
4 FROIZE END
5 METCALFE WAY
6 LINDEN CL
7 ORCHARD WAY
8 WILBURTON RD

SCHOOL LA

MILLFIELD

MILLFIELD PL

Wilburton

CB6

Towns End Field

Recreation
Ground

SHORT ST

FIELDSIDE

KING COB

Allotments

Sewage
Works

5

Linden End
Field

Heavenly
Valley Farm

STARLOCK CL

A10(T)

GREEN END

Starlock Hay
Fen Common

74

HIGHHILL DROVE

B1049

Mitchells
Farm

Red Hill
Farm

4

Low Fen

Snoots Common

CAMBRIDGE ROAD

Stretham
Old Engine

MERE MILL
DROVE

73

TWENTY PENCE ROAD

Wooden
Bridge

Stretham Mere

CROSS DROVE

Middle Cuts

Elford
Closes

Middle
Common

Elford
Farm

3

Australia Farm

CROSS DROVE

PH

Grange
Farm

Stretham Ferry
Bridge

Chittering
Farm

72

Fair View Farm

River Great Ouse

Willow
Tree Farm

Upper
Cuts

2

LITTLE SETCHEL DROVE

PH

Chear Fen

Willow Grange
Farm

Chear Fen
Farms

CB5

71

Setchel
Fen

SETCHEL DROVE

CB4

LONG DROVE

School Farm

1

Mitchell Hill
Common

The Undertakers

ELY ROAD

A10(T)

Hawthorn
Farm

CHITTERING DROVE

Hill
Farm

Adam's
LC

Napoleon
Farm

Chittering

70

46   A   47   B   48   C   49   D   50   E   51   F

209
126
127

F5
1 THE GROVE
2 ANDREWS CL
3 ST JAMES CL
4 PUMP LA
5 MIDDLE CL
6 HAY FEN CL
7 HAZEL CT
8 WALNUT TREE CL

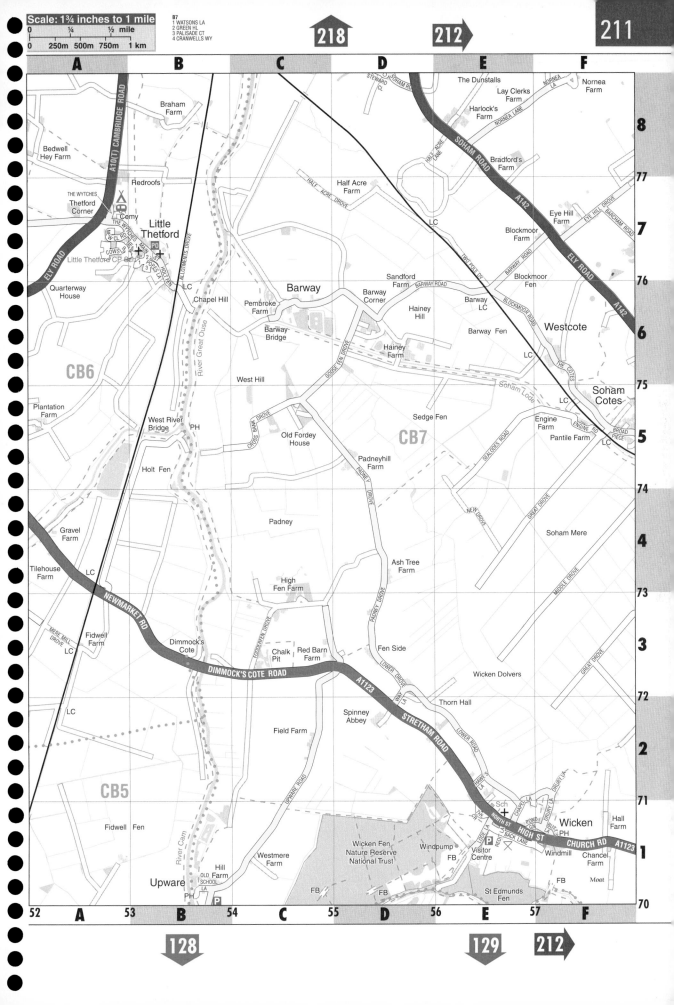

Scale: 1¾ inches to 1 mile

0   ¼   ½ mile

0   250m   500m   750m   1 km

B7
1 WATSONS LA
2 GREEN HL
3 PALISADE CT
4 CRANWELLS WY

218

212

211

A   B   C   D   E   F

The Dunstalls
Lay Clerks Farm
Nornea Farm
Harlock's Farm
Bradford's Farm

8

77

Braham Farm

A10(T) CAMBRIDGE ROAD

Bedwell Hey Farm

Redroofs

Half Acre Farm
Half Acre Drove
HALF ACRE LANE
STEWARD CL
SOHAM RD
SOHAM ROAD
A142
NORNEA LANE
NORNEA LA

Eye Hill Farm
EYE HILL DROVE
BARCHAM ROAD

7

THE WYTCHES
Thetford Corner
Cemy
Little Thetford
THE WYTCHES
NEW CL RD
MAIN ST
COWS LIP
PO
HOLT FEN
COLES LA

LC

ELY ROAD

Quarterway House

Chapel Hill

Pembroke Farm
Barway
Barway Bridge

West Hill

Barway Corner
Sandford Farm
BARWAY ROAD
Hainey Hill
Hainey Farm

Blockmoor Farm
Blockmoor Fen
BLOCKMOOR ROAD
BARWAY ROAD

Barway LC
Barway Fen
Soham Lode
LC

Westcote
A142
ELY ROAD

76

6

75

CB6

Plantation Farm

West River Bridge
PH

River Great Ouse
ALLOTMENTS DROVE

GOOSE FEN DROVE

LC

Holt Fen

CROSS BANK DROVE
Old Fordey House

Padneyhill Farm

PADNEY DROVE

Sedge Fen
CB7

SEALODES ROAD

Engine Farm
Pantile Farm
ENGINE RD
LC

Soham Cotes
THE COTES
LC
BROAD PIECE

5

74

Gravel Farm

NEWMARKET RD

Tilehouse Farm
LC

Fidwell Farm
MERE MILL DROVE
LC

Dimmock's Cote

Padney

High Fen Farm

FODDERFEN DROVE

Chalk Pit
Red Barn Farm

DIMMOCK'S COTE ROAD

UPWARE ROAD

Field Farm

Ash Tree Farm

PADNEY DROVE

Fen Side
LOWER DROVE

A1123
STRETHAM ROAD
HAWK LA
LOWER ROAD

Spinney Abbey

Thorn Hall

Wicken Dolvers

NEW DROVE
GREAT DROVE

Soham Mere

MIDDLE DROVE

GREAT DROVE

4

73

3

72

CB5

Fidwell Fen

River Cam

Hill Farm
OLD SCHOOL LA
Upware
PH
P

Westmere Farm

Wicken Fen Nature Reserve National Trust

FB

Windpump
FB

FB

Visitor Centre
P
FB

St Edmunds Fen

Sch
THE CK
NORTH ST
RED LA
BACK LANE
POND LA
CHAPEL LA
DRURY LA
HIGH ST
Wicken
PH
CHURCH RD
Windmill
Chancel Farm
A1123
Hall Farm

Moat
FB

2

71

1

70

52   A   53   B   54   C   55   D   56   E   57   F

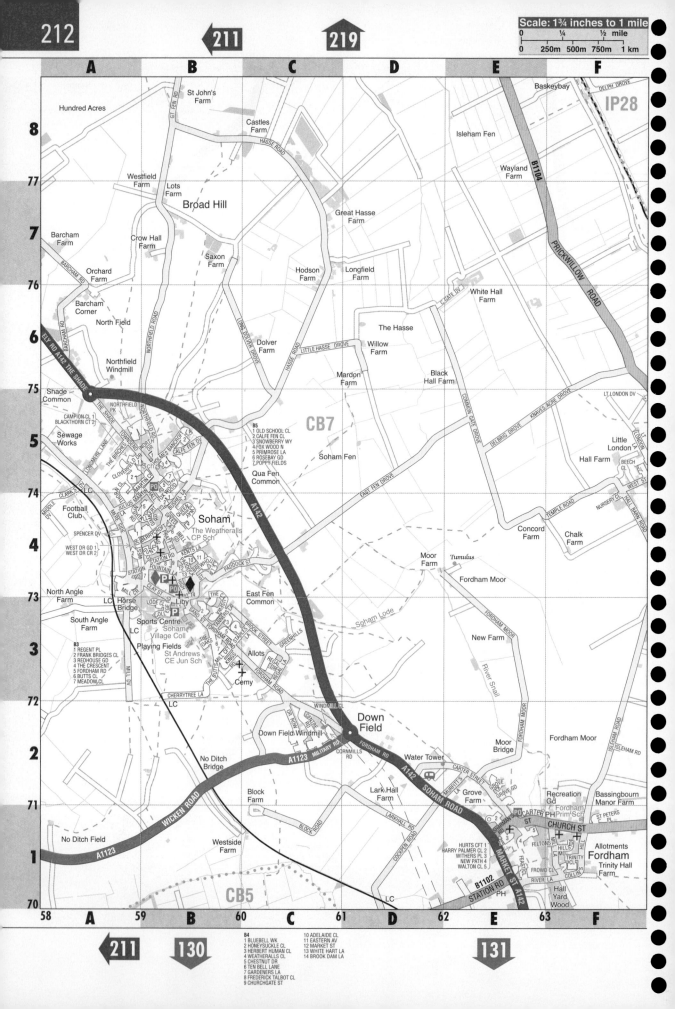

Scale: 1¾ inches to 1 mile
0   ¼   ½ mile
0   250m 500m 750m 1 km

A   B   C   D   E   F

Hundred Acres

St John's Farm

Baskeybay

DELPH DROVE

IP28

8

Castles Farm

Isleham Fen

HASSE ROAD

GT FEN RD

77

Westfield Farm

Lots Farm

Broad Hill

Wayland Farm

B1104

7

Barcham Farm

Crow Hall Farm

Saxon Farm

Great Hasse Farm

Orchard Farm

Hodson Farm

Longfield Farm

PRICKWILLOW ROAD

76

Barcham Corner

North Field

NORTHFIELD ROAD

White Hall Farm

C GATE DV

BARCHAM RD

Northfield Windmill

Dolver Farm

LONG DOLVER DROVE

The Hasse

LITTLE HASSE DROVE

HASSE ROAD

Willow Farm

6

ELY RD A142 THE SHADE

Shade Common

Mardon Farm

Black Hall Farm

LT LONDON DV

75

NORTHFIELD PK

COMMON GATE DROVE

DELBRIG DROVE

KNAVES ACRE DROVE

CB7

Campion CL 1
Blackthorn CT 2

Sewage Works

B5
1 OLD SCHOOL CL
2 CALFE FEN CL
3 SNOWBERRY WY
4 FOX WOOD N
5 PRIMROSE LA
6 ROSEBAY GD
7 POPPY FIELDS

Soham Fen

Little London

Hall Farm

BEECH CL

WEST DV

5

CALFE FEN DV

Qua Fen Common

TEMPLE ROAD

NURSERY CL

HALL BARN ROAD

LT LONDON DV

CLARK ST

LC

MIDDLE DV

Football Club

EAST FEN DROVE

A142

Concord Farm

Chalk Farm

74

SPENCER DV

Soham

The Weatheralls CP Sch

WEST DR GD 1
WEST DR CR 2

Moor Farm

Tumulus

Fordham Moor

4

STATION CROFT

KENT'S LA

PADDOCK ST

New Farm

North Angle Farm

LC Horse Bridge

MILL DV

P PO

Liby

CLAY ST

East Fen Common

Soham Lode

FORDHAM MOOR

73

South Angle Farm

Sports Centre

LODE CL

SAND ST

Soham Village Coll

BROOK STREET

GREENHILLS

River Snail

FORDHAM ROAD

B3
1 REGENT PL
2 FRANK BRIDGES CL
3 REDHOUSE GD
4 THE CRESCENT
5 FORDHAM RD
6 BUTTS CL
7 MEADOW CL

Playing Fields

St Andrews CE Jun Sch

Allots

THE OAKS

REGAL

New Farm

3

MILL DV

Cemy

THE BUTTS

MILL CFT

KINGS

REGAL LA

FORDHAM MOOR

Moor Bridge

CHERRYTREE LA

LC

WINDMILL CL

Down Field

Fordham Moor

2

No Ditch Bridge

Down Field Windmill

A1123 MILITARY RD

CORNMILLS RD

FORDHAM RD

Water Tower

A142

CARTER STREET

GROVE GD

GROVE CL

ISLEHAM RD

WICKEN ROAD

Block Farm

Lark Hall Farm

SOHAM ROAD

MURITT'S

Grove Farm

Recreation Gd

Bassingbourn Manor Farm

Fordham

1

No Ditch Field

A1123

Westside Farm

LARKHALL RD

BLOCK RD

CROCKPEN ROAD

PO CARTER ST

PH

CHURCH ST

Prim Sch

ST PETERS PL

HURTS CFT 1
HARRY PALMER CL 2
WITHERS PL 3
NEW PATH 4
WALTON CL 5

FELTONS

HILLS MDW

TRINITY CL

FROWD CL

RIVER LA

COLLINS

Allotments

Fordham

Trinity Hall Farm

CB5

B1102

STATION RD

LC

PH

MARKET ST A142

Hall Yard Wood

70

58   A   59   B   60   C   61   D   62   E   63   F

B4
1 BLUEBELL WK
2 HONEYSUCKLE CL
3 HERBERT HUMAN CL
4 WEATHERALLS CL
5 CHESTNUT DR
6 TEN BELL LANE
7 GARDENERS LA
8 FREDERICK TALBOT CL
9 CHURCHGATE ST
10 ADELAIDE CL
11 EASTERN AV
12 MARKET ST
13 WHITE HART LA
14 BROOK DAM LA

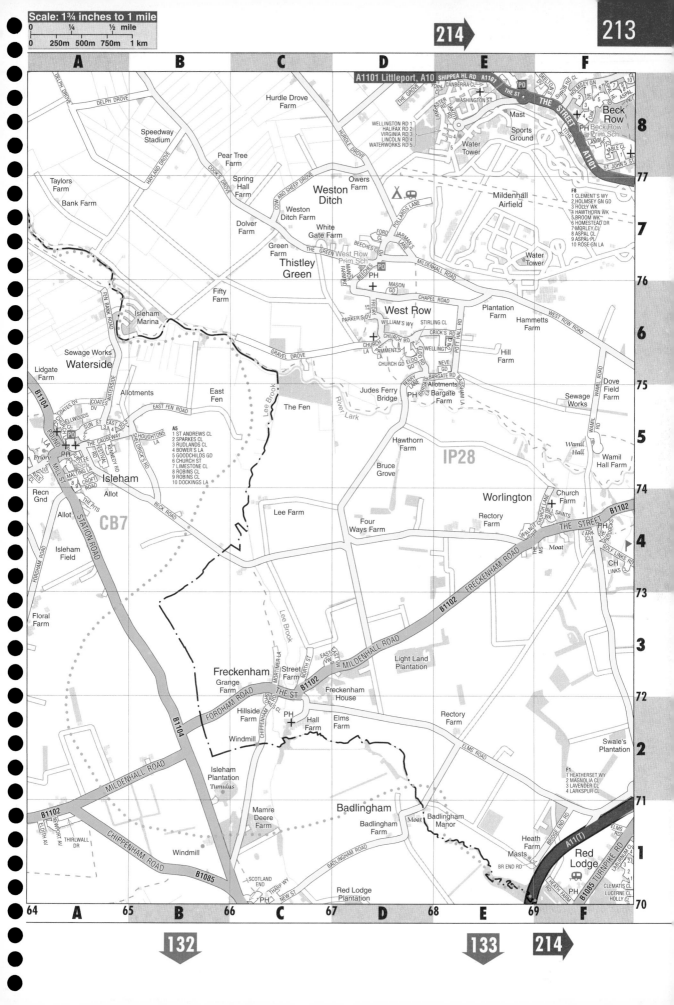

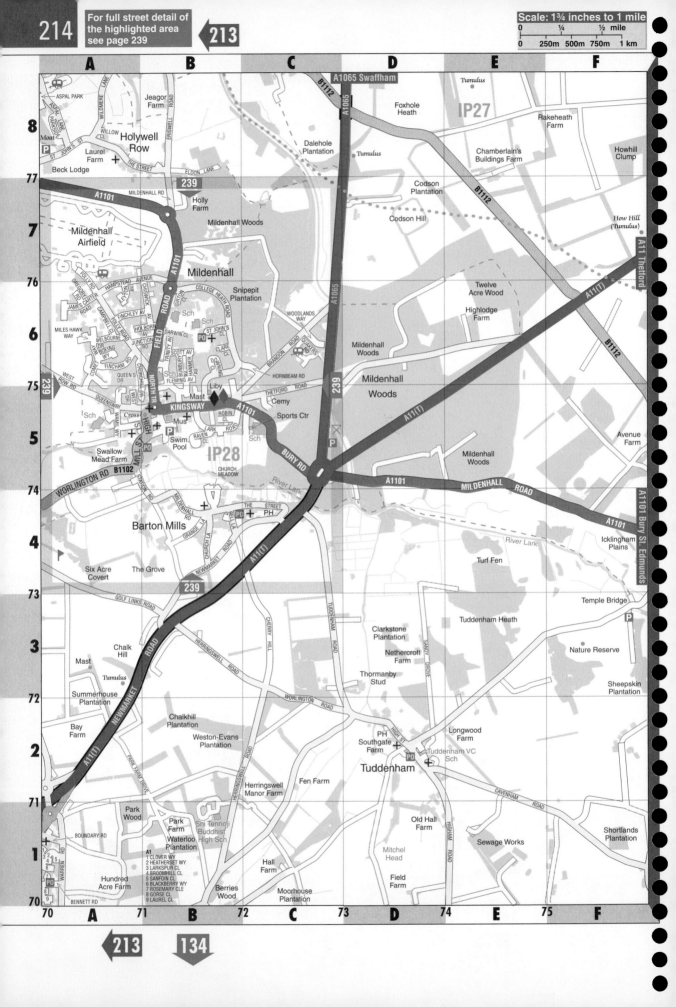

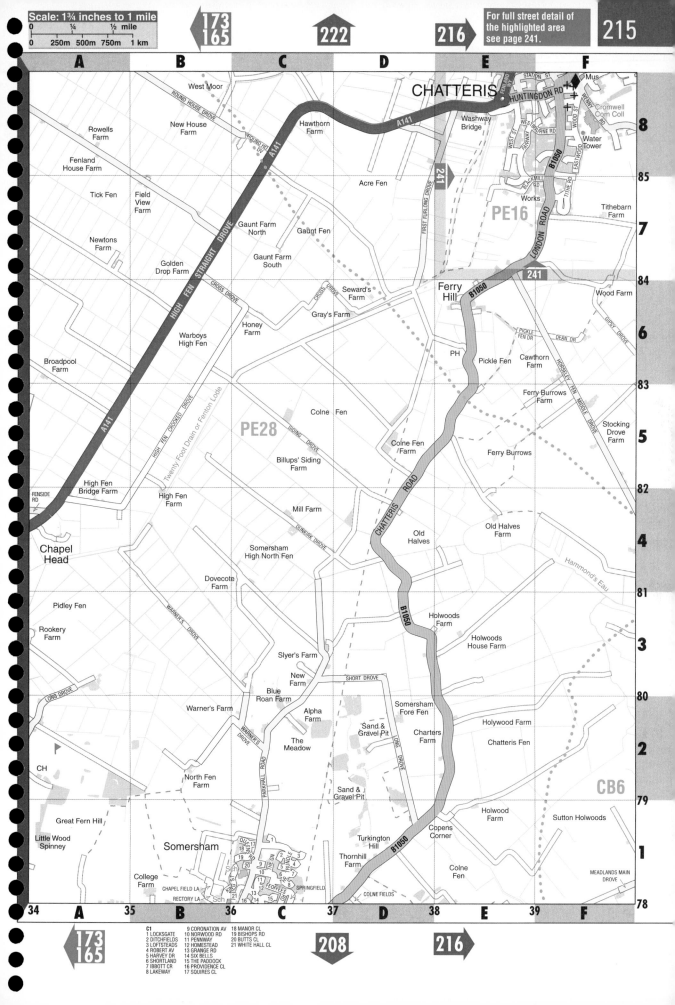

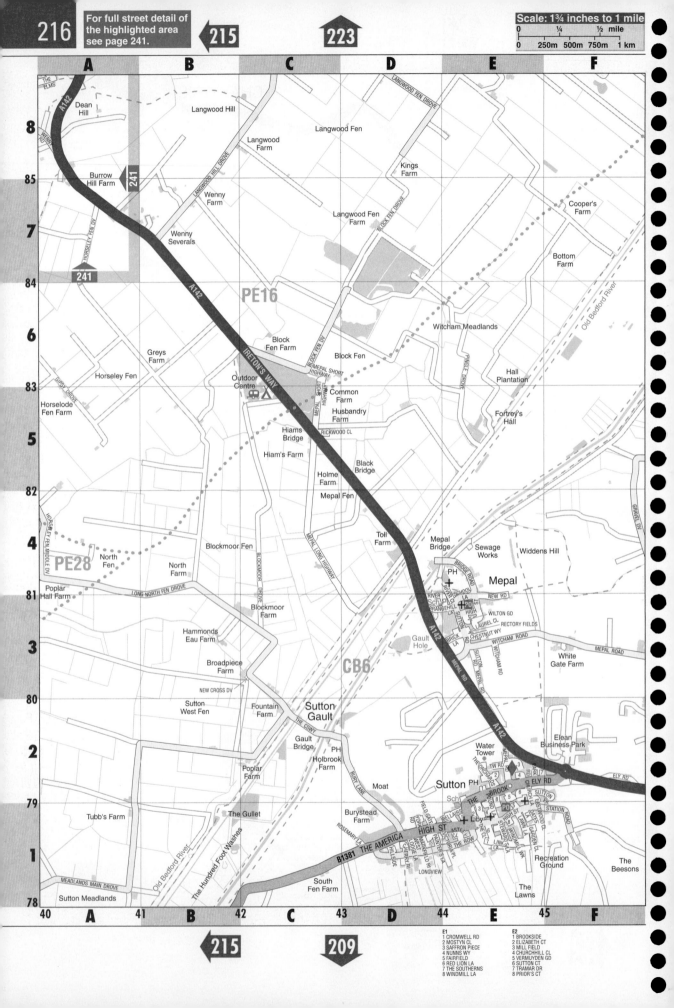

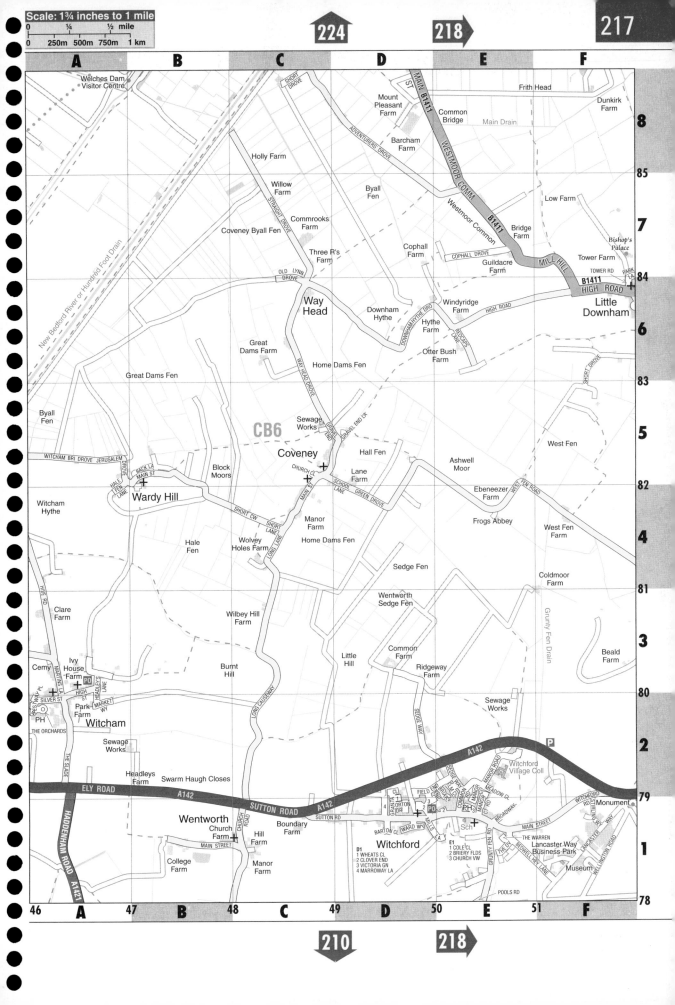

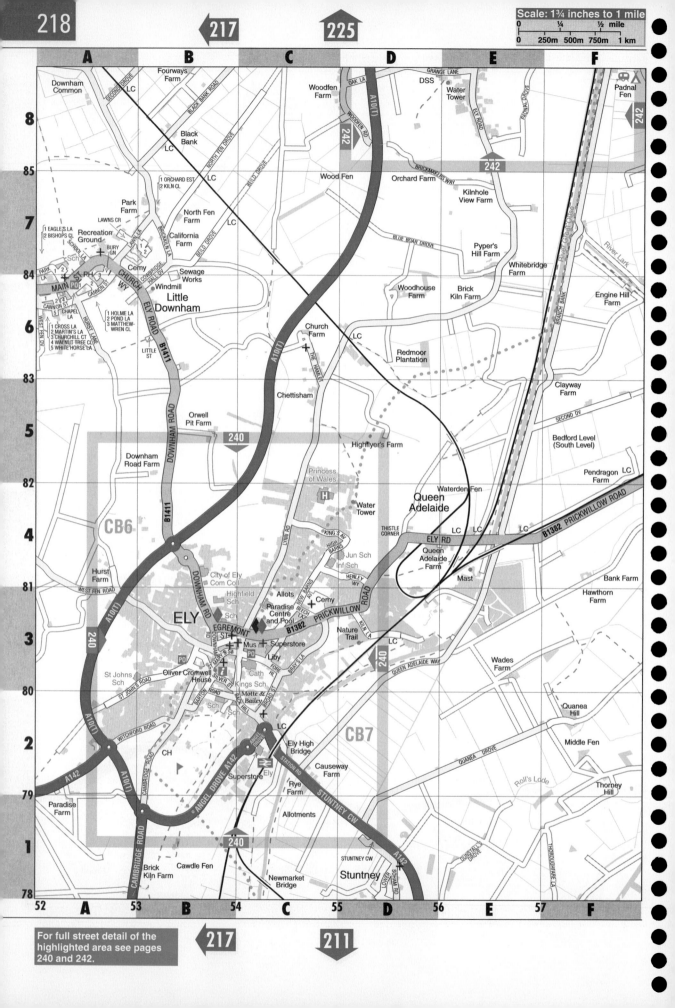

Scale: 1¾ inches to 1 mile

For full street detail of the highlighted area see pages 240 and 242.

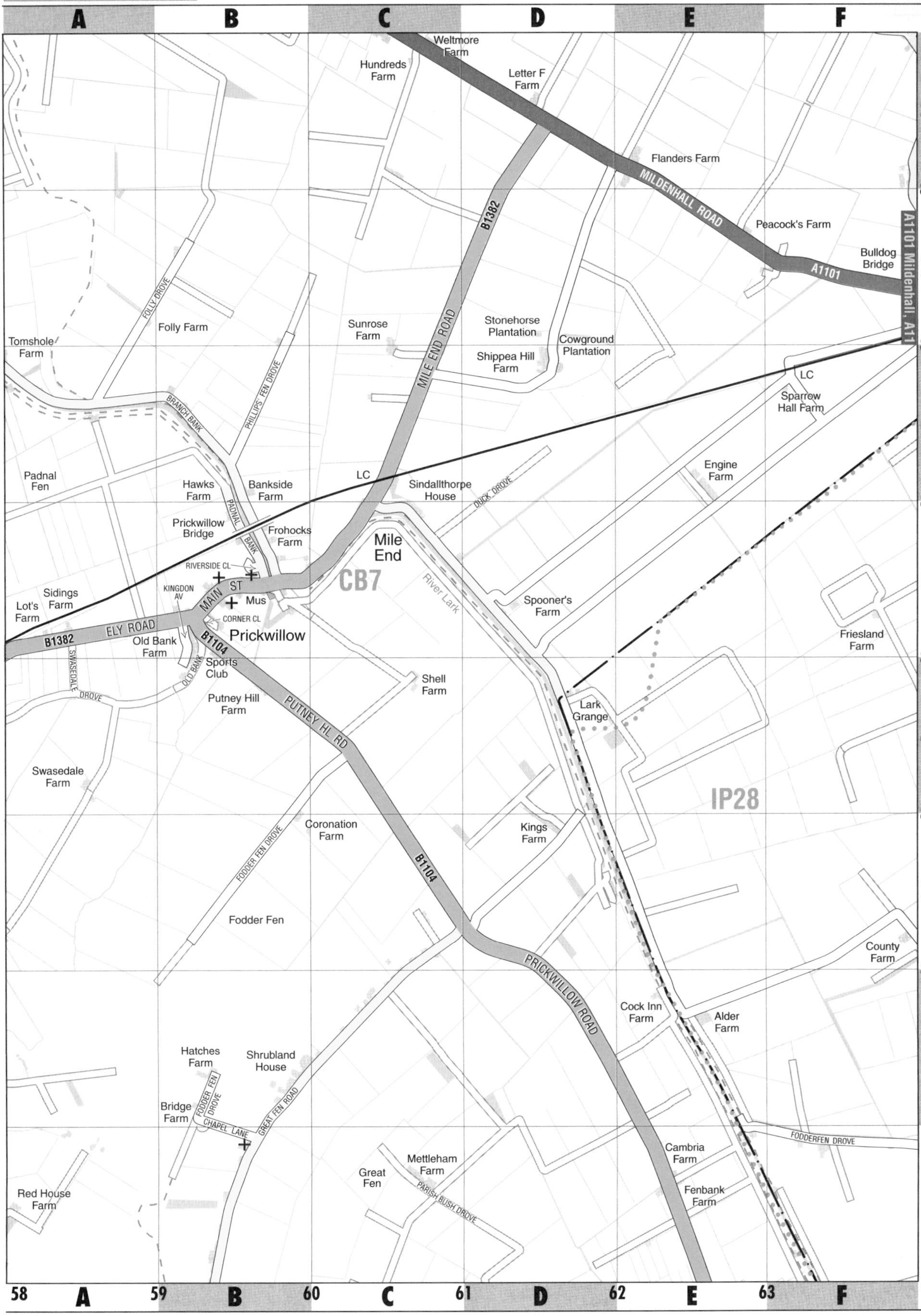
A
B
C
D
E
F
Weltmore Farm
Hundreds Farm
Letter F Farm
8
Flanders Farm
MILDENHALL ROAD
85
B1382
Peacock's Farm
Bulldog Bridge
A1101
7
A1101 Mildenhall, A11
FOLLY DROVE
Folly Farm
Sunrose Farm
MILE END ROAD
Stonehorse Plantation
Cowground Plantation
Tomshole Farm
Shippea Hill Farm
84
LC
Sparrow Hall Farm
BRANCH BANK
PHILLIPS' FEN DROVE
6
Padnal Fen
LC
Hawks Farm
Bankside Farm
Sindallthorpe House
DUCK DROVE
Engine Farm
83
PADNAL
Prickwillow Bridge
BANK
Frohocks Farm
Mile End
RIVERSIDE CL
CB7
5
KINGDON AV
MAIN ST
River Lark
Sidings Farm
Lot's Farm
Mus
Spooner's Farm
CORNER CL
B1382
ELY ROAD
Prickwillow
Friesland Farm
Old Bank Farm
B1104
SWASEDALE
OLD BANK
Sports Club
82
DROVE
Shell Farm
Putney Hill Farm
PUTNEY HL RD
Lark Grange
4
Swasedale Farm
IP28
81
Coronation Farm
Kings Farm
FODDER FEN DROVE
B1104
3
Fodder Fen
County Farm
80
PRICKWILLOW ROAD
Cock Inn Farm
Alder Farm
2
Hatches Farm
Shrubland House
FODDER FEN DROVE
Bridge Farm
CHAPEL LANE
GREAT FEN ROAD
79
FODDERFEN DROVE
Cambria Farm
Mettleham Farm
Great Fen
Red House Farm
PARISH BUSH DROVE
Fenbank Farm
1
78
58
A
59
B
60
C
61
D
62
E
63
F

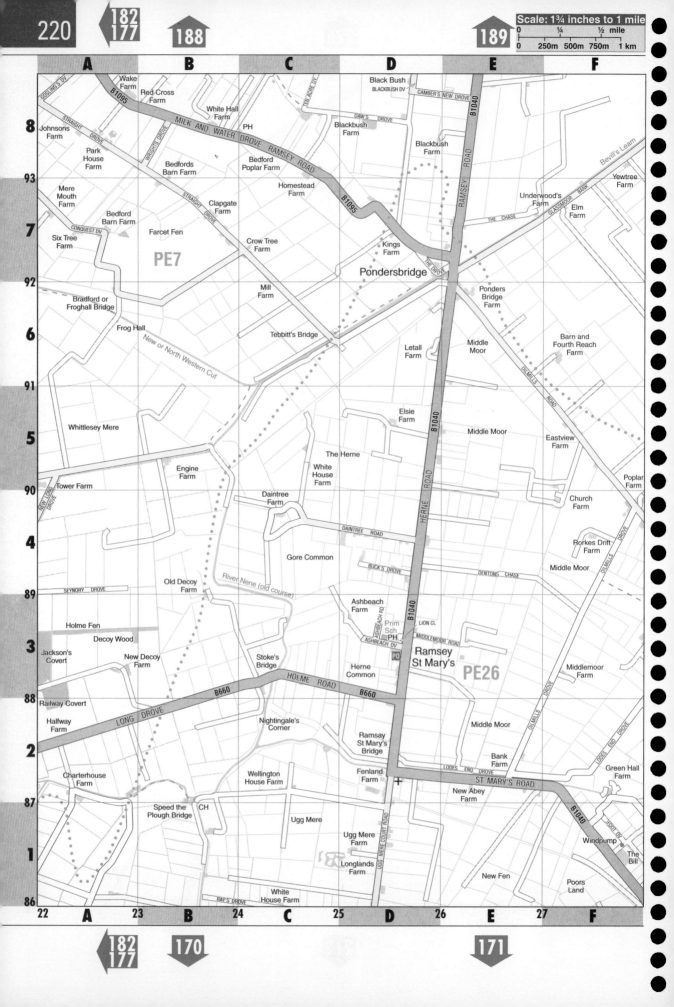

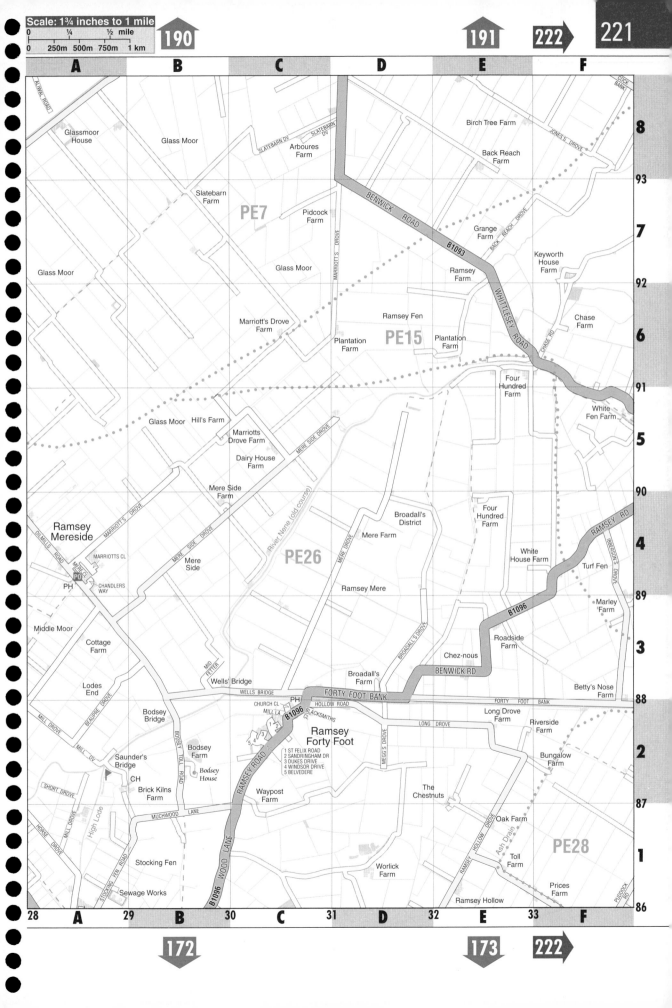

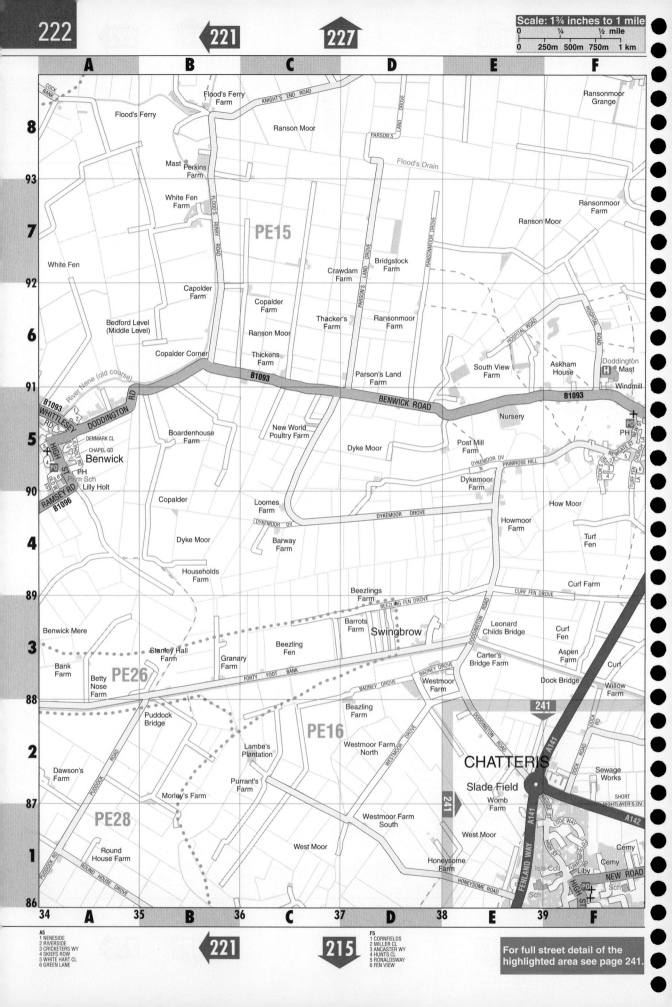

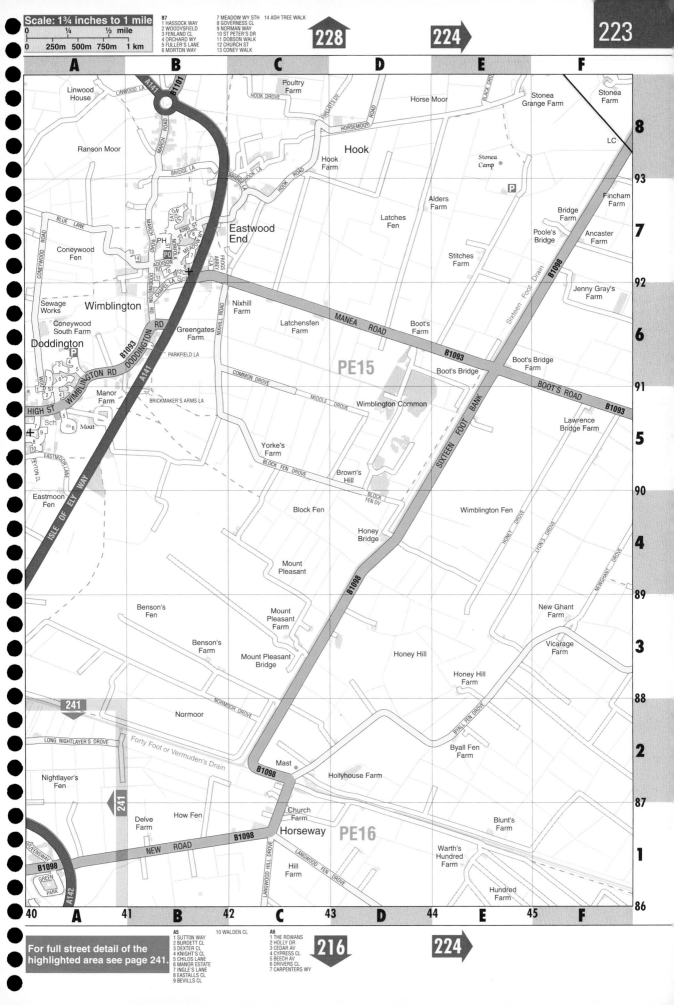

B7
1 HASSOCK WAY
2 WOODYSFIELD CL
3 FENLAND CL
4 ORCHARD WY
5 FULLER'S LANE
6 MORTON WAY
7 MEADOW WY STH
8 GOVERNESS CL
9 NORMAN WAY
10 ST PETER'S DR
11 DOBSON WALK
12 CHURCH ST
13 CONEY WALK
14 ASH TREE WALK

228   224

A   B   C   D   E   F

Linwood House
Ranson Moor
A141
LINWOOD LA
B1101
Poultry Farm
HOOK DROVE
Hook Farm
Horse Moor
Stonea Grange Farm
Stonea Farm
8
MARCH ROAD
BRIDGE LA
HOOK ROAD
Hook
LC
93
BRIDGE LA
PRIOTS DV
HORSEMOOR ROAD
Stonea Camp
P
BLACK DRO
Fincham Farm
Blue Lane
BLUE LANE
Eaton
KING ST
Eastwood End
Latches Fen
Alders Farm
Bridge Farm
7
Coneywood Fen
MARCH ROAD
MEADOW LA
PH
PO
Poole's Bridge
Ancaster Farm
CONEYWOOD ROAD
ADDISON RD
FROGS ABBEY
Stitches Farm
SIXTEEN FOOT DRAIN
B1098
92
DODDINGTON ROAD
CHAPEL LA
Nixhill Farm
Jenny Gray's Farm
Sewage Works
Wimblington
Greengates Farm
RD
Latchensfen Farm
MANEA ROAD
Boot's Farm
6
Coneywood South Farm
B1093
DODDINGTON RD
PARKFIELD LA
B1093
Boot's Bridge Farm
91
Doddington
P
WIMBLINGTON RD
COMMON DROVE
PE15
Boot's Bridge
BOOT'S ROAD
B1093
A141
Manor Farm
MIDDLE DROVE
Wimblington Common
SIXTEEN FOOT BANK
Lawrence Bridge Farm
5
HIGH ST
Sch
BRICKMAKER'S ARMS LA
Moat
Yorke's Farm
90
EASTMOOR LANE
BLOCK FEN DROVE
Brown's Hill
BLOCK FEN DV
Eastmoon Fen
PEYTON CL
Block Fen
Wimblington Fen
ISLE OF ELY WAY
Honey Bridge
HONEY DROVE
LYON'S DROVE
4
NEWGHANT DRIVE
89
Benson's Fen
Mount Pleasant
B1098
New Ghant Farm
Benson's Farm
Mount Pleasant Farm
Honey Hill
Vicarage Farm
3
Mount Pleasant Bridge
Honey Hill Farm
88
NORMOOR DROVE
BYALL FEN DRIVE
241
Normoor
Byall Fen Farm
2
LONG NIGHTLAYER'S DROVE
Forty Foot or Vermuden's Drain
241
B1098
Mast
87
Nightlayer's Fen
Delve Farm
How Fen
Hollyhouse Farm
Church Farm
Blunt's Farm
A142
QUEENSWAY
NEW ROAD
B1098
Horseway
PE16
Warth's Hundred Farm
1
B1098
GREEN PARK
Hill Farm
LANGWOOD HILL DROVE
LANGWOOD FEN DROVE
Hundred Farm
86

40   A   41   B   42   C   43   D   44   E   45   F   86

For full street detail of the highlighted area see page 241.

A5
1 SUTTON WAY
2 BURDETT CL
3 DEXTER CL
4 KNIGHTS CL
5 CHILDS LANE
6 MANOR ESTATE
7 INGLE'S LANE
8 EASTALLS CL
9 BEVILLS CL

10 WALDEN CL

A6
1 THE ROWANS
2 HOLLY DR
3 CEDAR AV
4 CYPRESS CL
5 BEECH AV
6 DRIVERS CL
7 CARPENTERS WY

216   224

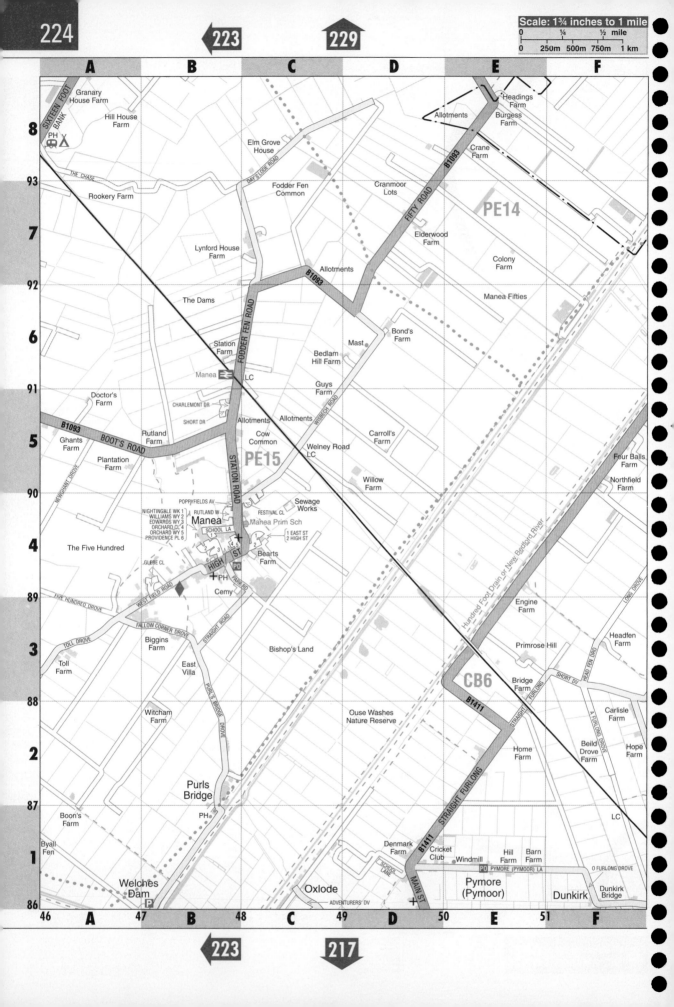

224

223

229

Scale: 1¾ inches to 1 mile
0   ¼   ½   mile
0   250m 500m 750m 1 km

A   B   C   D   E   F

8

93

7

92

6

91

5

4

90

89

3

88

2

87

1

86

46   47   48   49   50   51

SIXTEEN FOOT BANK
Granary House Farm
Hill House Farm
PH
THE CHASE
Rookery Farm
Elm Grove House
DAY'S SLOE ROAD
Fodder Fen Common
Allotments
Headings Farm
Burgess Farm
B1093
Crane Farm
FIFTY ROAD
Cranmoor Lots
PE14
Lynford House Farm
Elderwood Farm
Colony Farm
The Dams
FODDER FEN ROAD
B1093
Allotments
Manea Fifties
Station Farm
Mast
Bond's Farm
Bedlam Hill Farm
Manea
LC
Guys Farm
Doctor's Farm
CHARLEMONT DR
SHORT DR
Allotments
Allotments
WISBECH ROAD
Welney Road LC
Carroll's Farm
B1093
BOOT'S ROAD
Ghants Farm
Rutland Farm
Cow Common
PE15
Plantation Farm
NEWGHANT DRIVE
STATION ROAD
POPPYFIELDS AV
Sewage Works
Willow Farm
Four Balls Farm
Northfield Farm
NIGHTINGALE WK 1
WILLIAMS WY 2
EDWARDS WY 3
ORCHARD CL 4
ORCHARD WY 5
PROVIDENCE PL 6
RUTLAND W
FESTIVAL CL
Manea Prim Sch
Manea
SCHOOL LA
1 EAST ST
2 HIGH ST
The Five Hundred
GLEBE CL
HIGH ST
PO
Bearts Farm
PH
Cemy
PARK RD
Hundred Foot Drain or New Bedford River
LONG DROVE
Engine Farm
Headfen Farm
FIVE HUNDRED DROVE
WEST FIELD ROAD
FALLOW CORNER DROVE
STRAIGHT ROAD
Biggins Farm
Bishop's Land
Primrose Hill
SHORT DV
HEAD FEN DRO
Toll Farm
TOLL DROVE
East Villa
CB6
Bridge Farm
FURLONG
Carlisle Farm
A FURLONG DROVE
Witcham Farm
PURL'S BRIDGE DROVE
Ouse Washes Nature Reserve
B1411
STRAIGHT
Home Farm
Beild Drove Farm
Hope Farm
Purls Bridge
PH
STRAIGHT FURLONG
Boon's Farm
LC
Byall Fen
Denmark Farm
B1411
Cricket Club
Windmill
Hill Farm
Barn Farm
PO
PYMORE (PYMOOR) LA
O FURLONG DROVE
Welches Dam
P
Oxlode
SCHOOL LANE
ADVENTURERS' DV
MAIN ST
Pymore (Pymoor)
Dunkirk
Dunkirk Bridge

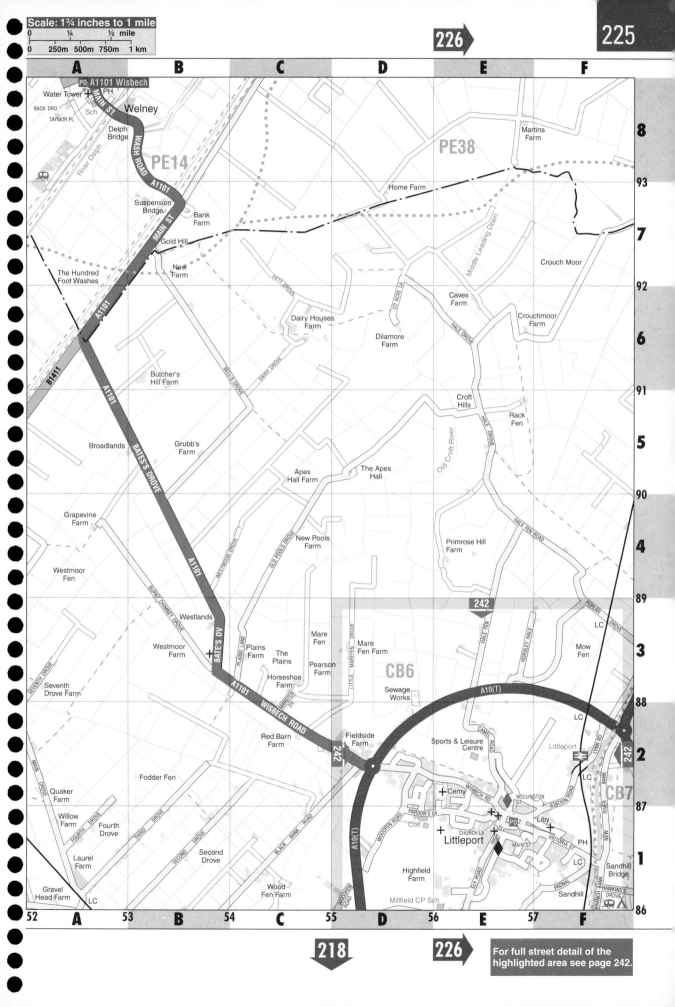

A **B** **C** **D** **E** **F**

A1101 Wisbech
PO
Water Tower
BACK DRO
TAYMOR PL
Sch
Welney
Delph Bridge
MAIN ST
WASH ROAD
River Delph
PE14
A1101
Suspension Bridge
Bank Farm
Gold Hill
MAIN ST
New Farm
The Hundred Foot Washes
A1101
B1411
Butcher's Hill Farm
BELL'S DROVE
BATES'S DROVE
Broadlands
Grubb's Farm
TIFTY DROVE
Dairy Houses Farm
DAIRY DROVE
Dilamore Farm
CO ACRE LA
HALE DROVE
Caves Farm
Middle Leading Drain
PE38
Home Farm
Martins Farm
Crouch Moor
Crouchmoor Farm
Croft Hills
Rack Fen
Old Croft River
Apes Hall Farm
The Apes Hall
Grapevine Farm
Westmoor Fen
A1101
WESTMOOR DROVE
OLD POOLS DROVE
New Pools Farm
Primrose Hill Farm
HALE FEN ROAD
POPLAR DROVE
LC
SEVENTH DROVE
BURNT CHIMNEY DROVE
Westlands
BATE'S DV
PLAINS LANE
Westmoor Farm
A1101
Plains Farm
The Plains
Horseshoe Farm
Pearson Farm
Mare Fen
MAREEN DROVE
LITTLE MAREEN DROVE
Mare Fen Farm
Sewage Works
CB6
242
A10(T)
HALE FEN
CAMEL ROAD
HORSLEY HALE
Mow Fen
LC
LC
Seventh Drove Farm
WISBECH ROAD
242
Red Barn Farm
Fieldside Farm
Sports & Leisure Centre
Littleport
STATION ROAD
LYNN RD
RIVER BANK
242
CB7
LC
MAIN DROVE
Quaker Farm
Willow Farm
FOURTH DROVE
Fourth Drove
THIRD DROVE
Fodder Fen
SECOND DROVE
Second Drove
BLACK BANK ROAD
A10(T)
WOODPEN ROAD
Cemy
WISBECH RD
PARSON'S LA
Coll
PO
WELLINGTON ST
Liby
Littleport
CHURCH LA
MAIN ST
VICTORIA ST
PH
NEW
LC
CB7
Laurel Farm
ELY ROAD
Highfield Farm
Sandhill
PADNAL
BRANCH BANK
HAWKINS'S DROVE
Sandhill Bridge
Gravel Head Farm
LC
Wood Fen Farm
WOODEN FEN
Millfield CP Sch

8
93
7
92
6
91
5
90
4
89
3
88
2
87
1
86

52 **A** 53 **B** 54 **C** 55 **D** 56 **E** 57 **F**

218

226 →

For full street detail of the highlighted area see page 242.

225

A   B   C   D   E   F

A10 Downham Market

8

Ferry
Farm

Southery Fens

Bakers
Farm

Turf Fen
Farm

93

Cross
Drains
Farm

PE38

Mill
House
Farm

CROSS DROVE

Ferry
Farm

MILL DV

COMMON DROVE

Sedge Fen
Farm

7

Crouch
Moor Drain

Scotland
Farm

LC

River Great Ouse

River
Farm

SEDGE FEN RD

92

Cold
Harbour
Farm

Wools
Farm

Horse
Fen
Farm

Willow Row Drain

BLACK HORSE DROVE

FESTIVAL WY

Sch

Sewage
Works

Chain
Farm

PH

Wannage
Farm

6

PO

Brandon
Creek

Creek Farm

Little
Ouse
Farm

FARTHING DROVE

LONG DROVE

**Black Horse
Drove**

Four Scores Farm

91

CB6

LC

Willow
Row
Farms

Bank Farm

Creeks End Mill Drain

5

LC

Plantation
House

Stokes
Farm

90

ANCHOR DROVE

Six Acre
Plantation

4

TEN MILE BANK

Little
Ouse

School
Farm

SMITH'S DROVE

Sch

89

Denver
Farm

Church
Farm

Brandon
Bank

A10(T)

White
Hall Farm

Anchor
End
Farm

3

POPLAR DV

LYNN RD

Woolpit
Farm

Orchard
House

88

SHEPHERD'S DROVE

WHITE HORSE ROAD

Little Ouse River

CB7

2

Bridge
Farm

May
Farm

Temple
Farm

White
House

87

Glover
Farm

MILDENHALL   ROAD

CROSS DROVE

1

Old Bank
Farm

Hill
Farm

A1101

Burnt Fen

HAWKINS'S DV

86

Wesleyan
Farm

58   A   59   B   60   C   61   D   62   E   63   F

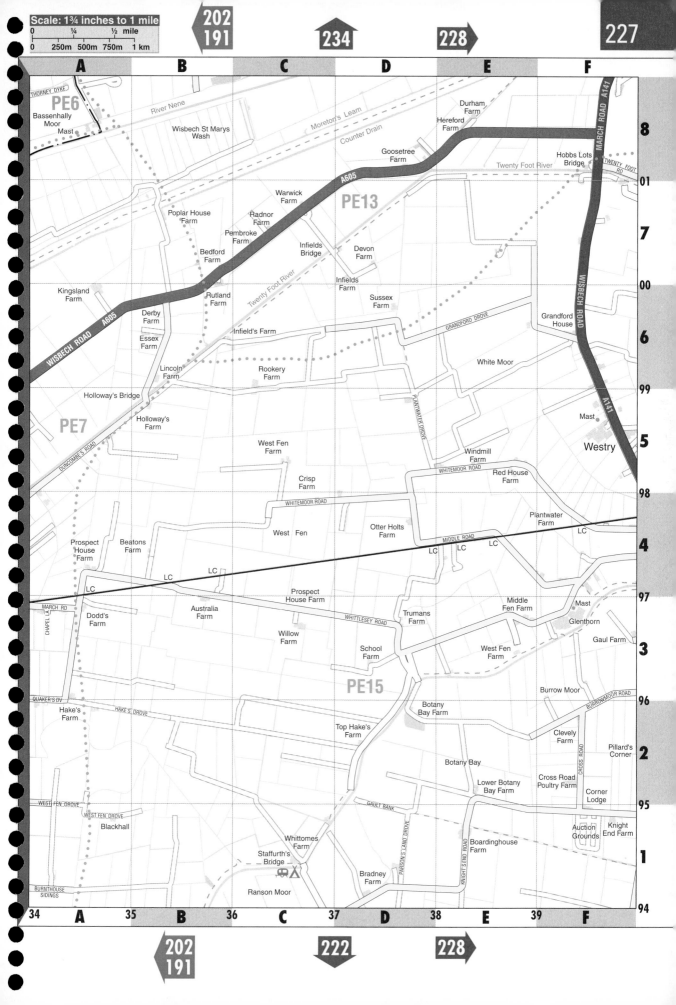

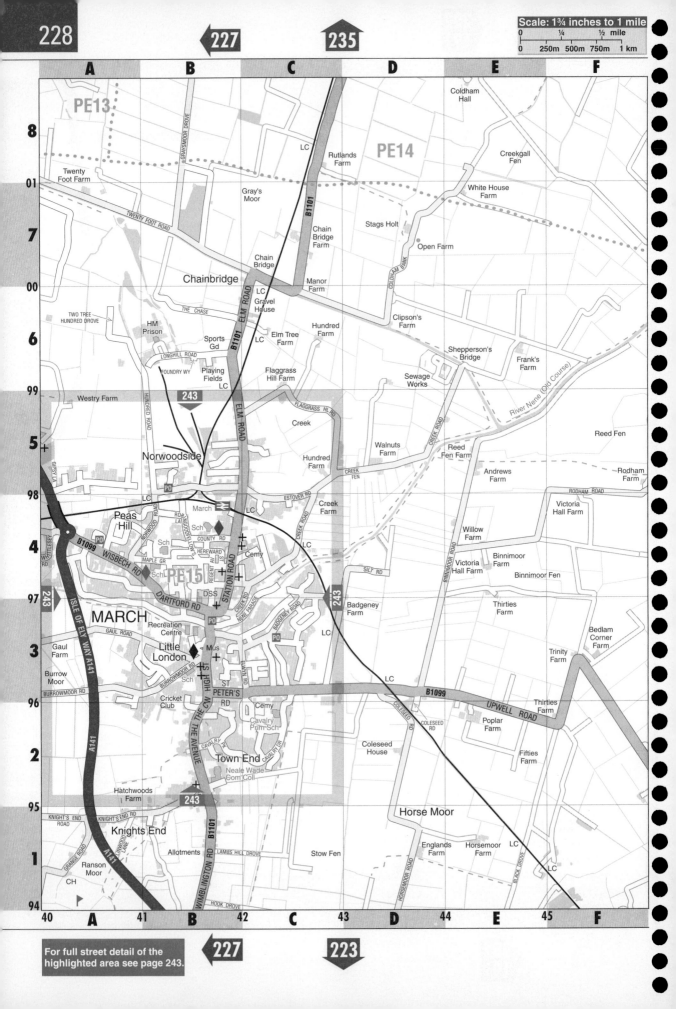

228

227

235

Scale: 1¾ inches to 1 mile
0   ¼   ½ mile
0   250m 500m 750m 1 km

A   B   C   D   E   F

8

01

7

00

6

99

5

98

4

97

3

96

2

95

1

94

40   A   41   B   42   C   43   D   44   E   45   F

PE13

PE14

PE15

Twenty Foot Farm

Gray's Moor

Coldham Hall

Creekgall Fen

White House Farm

Rutlands Farm

Stags Holt

Open Farm

Chain Bridge Farm

Chain Bridge

Chainbridge

Manor Farm

Clipson's Farm

Shepperson's Bridge

Frank's Farm

LC Gravel House

HM Prison

Sports Gd

Elm Tree Farm

Hundred Farm

Sewage Works

River Nene (Old Course)

TWENTY FOOT ROAD

GRAYSMOOR DROVE

B1101

THE CHASE

TWO TREE HUNDRED DROVE

LONGHILL ROAD

FOUNDRY WY

Playing Fields

Flaggrass Hill Farm

243

Westry Farm

Norwoodside

Creek

FLAGGRASS HL RD

Hundred Farm

Walnuts Farm

Reed Fen Farm

Reed Fen

Rodham Farm

PO

March

Peas Hill

Creek Farm

CREEK ROAD

CREEK FEN

Andrews Farm

RODHAM ROAD

ESTOVER RD

Victoria Hall Farm

Sch

COUNTY RD

HEREWARD

Cemy

Willow Farm

Victoria Hall Farm

Binnimoor Farm

Binnimoor Fen

MAPLE GR

Sch

DSS

STATION ROAD

SILT RD

BINNIMOOR ROAD

MARCH

Recreation Centre

Little London

Mus

Badgeney Farm

243

Thirties Farm

Bedlam Corner Farm

Gaul Farm

GAUL ROAD

PO

ST PETER'S RD

Trinity Farm

Burrow Moor

BURROWMOOR RD

Cricket Club

Cemy

Cavalry Prim Sch

B1099

UPWELL ROAD

Thirties Farm

A141

ISLE OF ELY WAY A141

WISBECH RD

DARTFORD RD

THE AVENUE

THE CW HIGH ST

CAVALRY LA

Town End

Neale Wade Com Coll

Coleseed House

COLESEED RD

Poplar Farm

Fifties Farm

Hatchwoods Farm

243

Horse Moor

Knights End

KNIGHT'S END ROAD

KNIGHT'S END RD

DIMMOCK LANE

Allotments

LAMBS HILL DROVE

Stow Fen

Englands Farm

Horsemoor Farm

Ranson Moor

CH

GRANGE ROAD

A141

WIMBLINGTON RD

B1101

HOOK DROVE

HORSEMOOR ROAD

BLACK DROVE

227

223

For full street detail of the highlighted area see page 243.

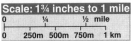

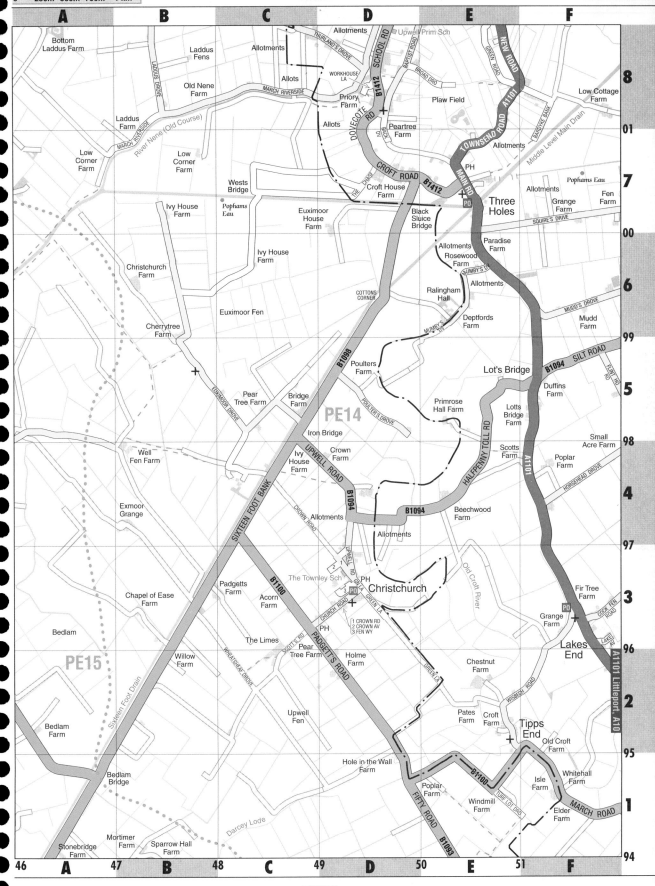

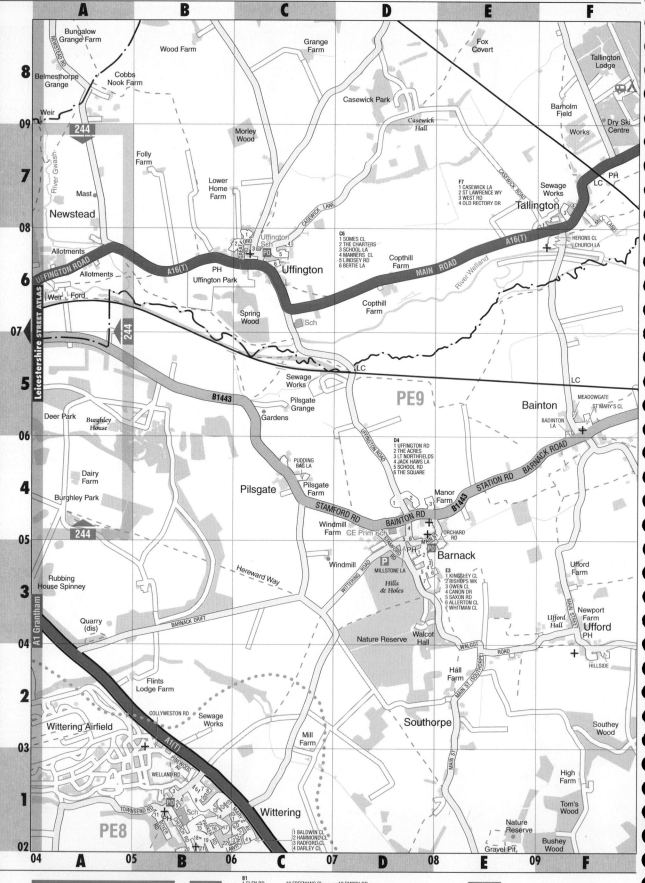

Scale: 1¾ inches to 1 mile

0   ¼   ½ mile

0   250m 500m 750m 1 km

Leicestershire STREET ATLAS

8

Bungalow
Grange Farm

Wood Farm

Grange
Farm

Fox
Covert

Tallington
Lodge

Belmesthorpe
Grange

Cobbs
Nook Farm

Casewick Park

Barholm
Field

Dry Ski
Centre

Weir

09

244

Morley
Wood

Casewick
Hall

Works

7

River Gwash

Folly
Farm

Lower
Home
Farm

Casewick Lane

F7
1 CASEWICK LA
2 ST LAWRENCE WY
3 WEST RD
4 OLD RECTORY DR

Sewage
Works

PH
LC

Mast

Tallington

08

Newstead

Uffington
Sch

A16(T)

HERONS CL
CHURCH LA

Allotments

GREAT FORD

PO

C6
1 SOMES CL
2 THE CHARTERS
3 SCHOOL LA
4 MANNERS CL
5 LINDSEY RD
6 BERTIE LA

6

Uffington Road

Allotments

PH

Uffington Park

A16(T)

Uffington

Copthill
Farm

Main Road

River Welland

Weir   Ford

Copthill
Farm

07

244

Spring
Wood

Sch

LC

LC

Sewage
Works

PE9

Bainton

MEADOWGATE
ST MARY'S CL

5

B1443

Pilsgate
Grange

Gardens

BADINTON
LA

Deer Park

Burghley
House

06

UFFINGTON ROAD

D4
1 UFFINGTON RD
2 THE ACRES
3 LT NORTHFIELDS
4 JACK HAWS LA
5 SCHOOL RD
6 THE SQUARE

BARNACK ROAD

Dairy
Farm

PUDDING
BAG LA

Pilsgate
Farm

STATION RD

4

Burghley Park

Pilsgate

Manor
Farm

B1443

Ufford
Farm

244

STAMFORD RD

Windmill
Farm

BAINTON RD

ORCHARD
RD

05

Rubbing
House Spinney

CE Prim Sch

PH

PO

Barnack

Ufford
Hall

Ufford

3

A1 Grantham

Hereward Way

Windmill

WITTERING ROAD

Hills
& Holes

E3
1 KINGSLEY CL
2 BISHOPS WK
3 OWEN CL
4 CANON DR
5 SAXON RD
6 ALLERTON CL
7 WHITMAN CL

Newport
Farm

PH

Quarry
(dis)

BARNACK DRIFT

MILLSTONE LA

HILLSIDE

04

Nature Reserve

Walcot
Hall

WALCOT   ROAD

2

Flints
Lodge Farm

Háll
Farm

MAIN ST (SOUTHORPE)

Southey
Wood

COLLYWESTON RD

Sewage
Works

03

Wittering Airfield

A1(T)

Mill
Farm

Southorpe

MAIN ST

High
Farm

PINEWOOD AV

1

WELLAND RD

PO

PH

Sch

CHURCH RD

Wittering

1 BALDWIN CL
2 HAMMOND CL
3 RADFORD CL
4 DARLEY CL

Nature
Reserve

Tom's
Wood

TOWNSEND RD

PARKER RD

LAWRENCE

02

PE8

Gravel Pit

Bushey
Wood

For full street detail of the
highlighted area see page 244.

193

194

B1
1 GLEN RD
2 NENE CL
3 CHATER RD
4 HARVEY CL
5 THE LIMES
6 BROWNES RD
7 EXETER RD
8 THE HOLT
9 BURGHLEY AV
10 FREEMANS CL
11 MANOR CL
12 ST MICHAEL'S RD
13 ST JOHN'S RD
14 ST GEORGE'S RD
15 BROADHURST RD
16 NEWMAN CL
17 MALTBY CL
18 CARNEGIE RD
19 EMBRY RD
20 HALL LA
21 LEGG RD
22 JEFFERSON CL

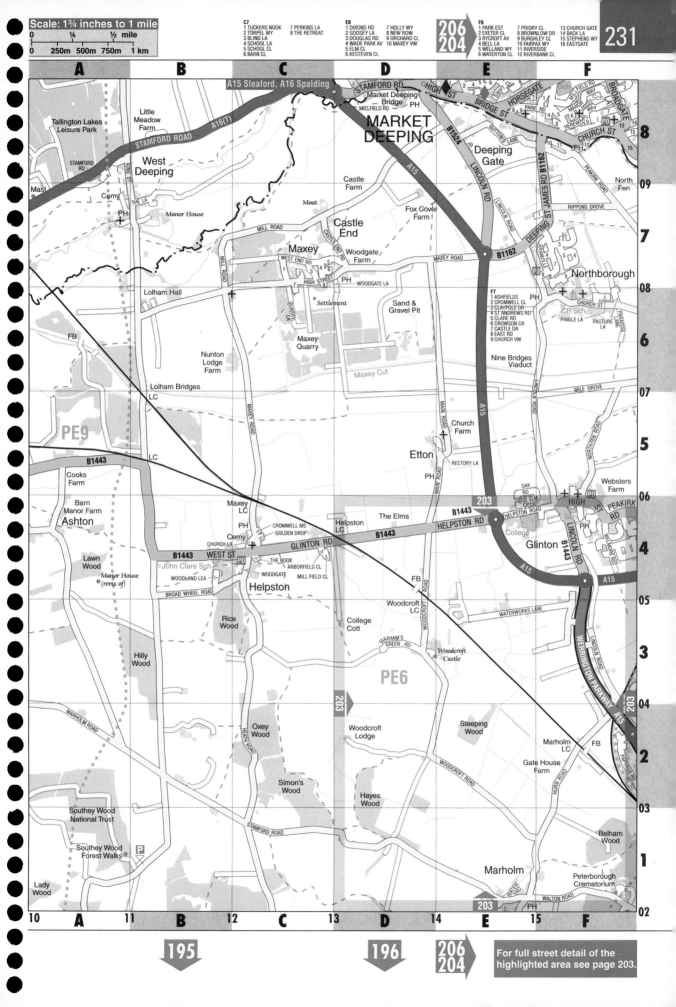

B8
1 ABBOTS DR
2 GLEBE GD
3 CORONATION AV
4 CHAPEL ST
5 STRICKLANDS DR
6 ALDERLANDS CL
7 PENWALD CL
8 TATWIN DR
9 BECCELM DR

207
205

A   B   C   D   E   F

C8
1 SNOWDON CL
2 CRAWFORD GD
3 KENNULPHS CL

Middle Rd
Crowland High Wash
Corporation Bank
Low Rd
Broadway
Monks Rd
A1073 Spalding
Crowland
Sch
Alderlands
Ashley's Barn
Harvester Way
Crease Drove
Plank Drove
Peterborough Road
A1073
Barbers Drove
Harrington Dr
Tarrington's Drove
Greenbank Farm
B1040
Green Drove
Sheppard's Drove
Empsons Farm
Old South Eau
Falls Bridge
Empsons Farm
South Eau Farm
Blue Bell Farm
Kennulph's Farm
Poplar Farm
Eardley Grange Farm
Wright's Drove
Toll House Farm
Old Farm
Hundreds Farm
Hundreds Road
Vine House Farm
Nene Terrace
St Vincent's Cross
St Vincent's Cross Farm
French Drove
Blue Bell Bridge
Old Hall Farm
Falls Drove
Speechley's Drove
Pepper Lake Farm
Horseshoe Bridge
Moor's Farm
Gray's Farm
Olympia Farm
A1073
Singlesole Farm
Cross
Bennett's Pieces
Hangman's Corner
Bell Drove
PE6
Steam House Farm
Hill Farm
Flood Farm
B1443 Thorney Road
Hill Farm
Fletchers Farm
Mason's Bridge
Thorney Road
Powder Blue Farm
B1443
Cat's Water Plantation
Little Tower's Fen
Singlecote Farm
Crowland Road
Lodge Farm
Hurn Farm
Turves Farm
Crowland Rd
Elm Tree Farm
Oakhurst Farm
Northolm Farm
Cat's Water Plantation
Cat's Water
The Reaches
Bedford Level (North Level)
Middle West Farm
Rose Farm
Buke Horn Plantation
Great Towers Fen
Buke Horn Farm
Bukehorn Road
B1443
ASH CL 1
LAUREL DR 2
BERBERIS CL 3
ORCHARD CT 4
Windmill
A1073
Northolme Coppice
Catwater Farm
Northam Cl
Eye Green
Newstead Cl
PH
Green Rd
Hightrees Farm
A47(T)
Abbey House
The Causeway
Pode Hole Farm
Guys Fen
Toneham Farm
Eye Green Industries
Crowland Rd
Turves Road
Thorney Road
A47(T)
Pasture House Farm
Causeway Toll Farm
Willow Hall Lane
Toneham Lane
A47(T) Eye Road
Cem'y Lib'y
PO
GLEBE
HIGH ST
BACK LANE
Fountains Pl
Hayne's Farm
Chicell's Hurst
Thorney River
Hill Farm
PH
Peterborough Rd
Little CL
Eye CE Sch
Eye
Bar Pastures
Bar Pasture Farm
Barlees Fen
Whittlesey Rd
Eyebury Rd
Lindisfarne Rd
Sand & Gravel Pit
Nipcot Road

207
205
199
200

A1
1 BEAULIEU CT
2 HODNEY RD
3 TINTERN RI
4 MOORE'S LA
5 ST BENET'S GD
6 CHANCERY LA
7 BEECH LA
8 IXWORTH CL
9 DELAPRE CT
10 WALSINGHAM WY
11 GLASTONBURY CL
12 CARTMEL WY
13 DEERHURST WY
14 BOXGROVE CL
15 NEW RD
16 WESTMINSTER GD
17 MONKS DR
18 ST BEE'S DR
19 ST OLAVE'S DR
20 ST ALBAN'S DR

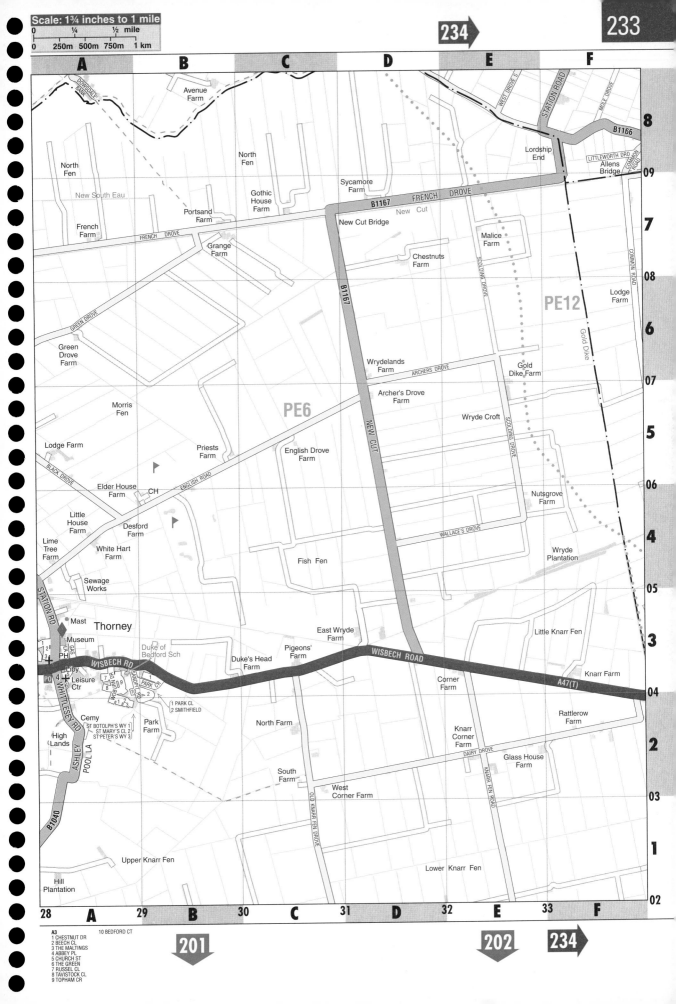

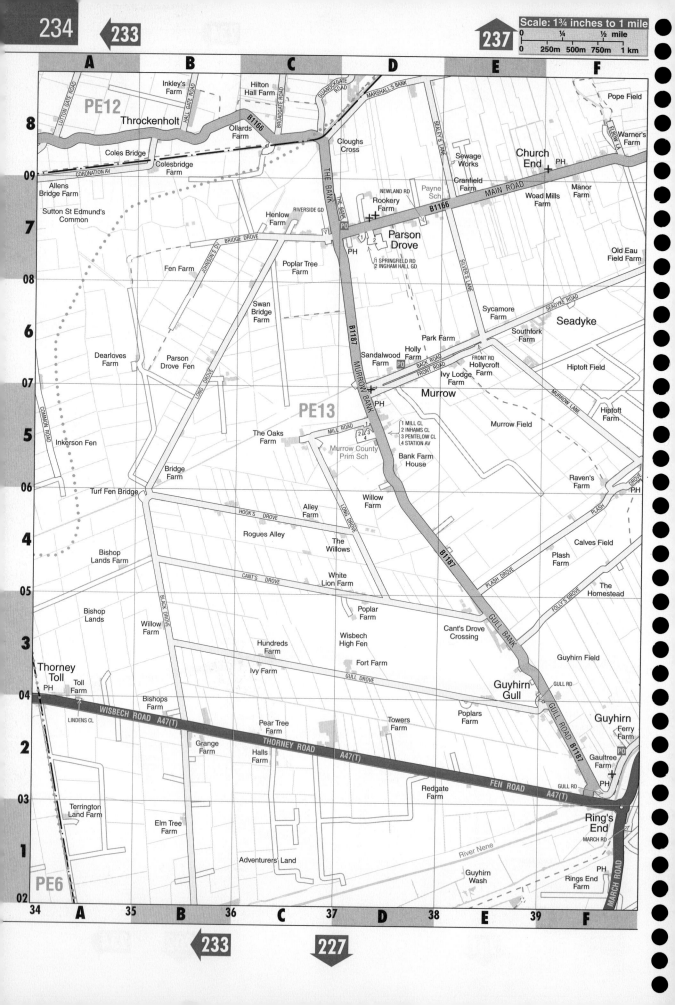

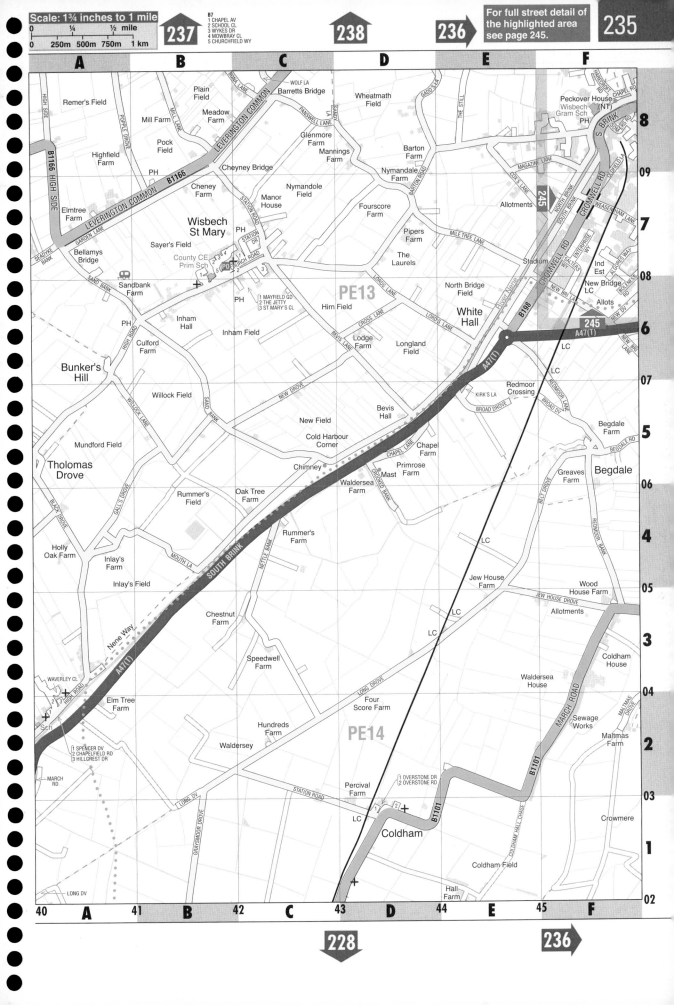

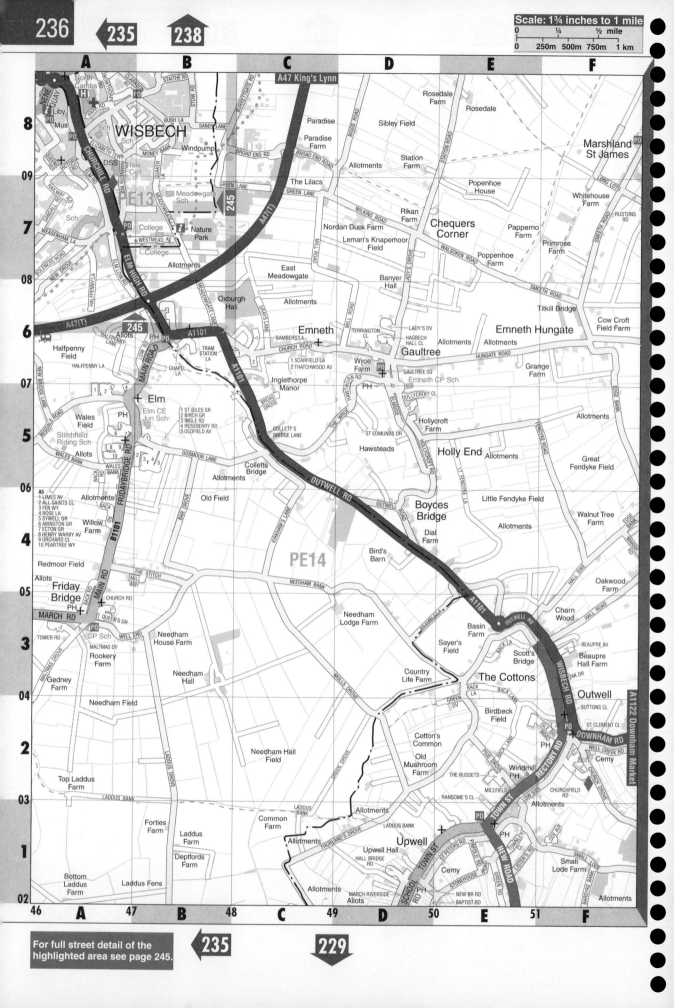

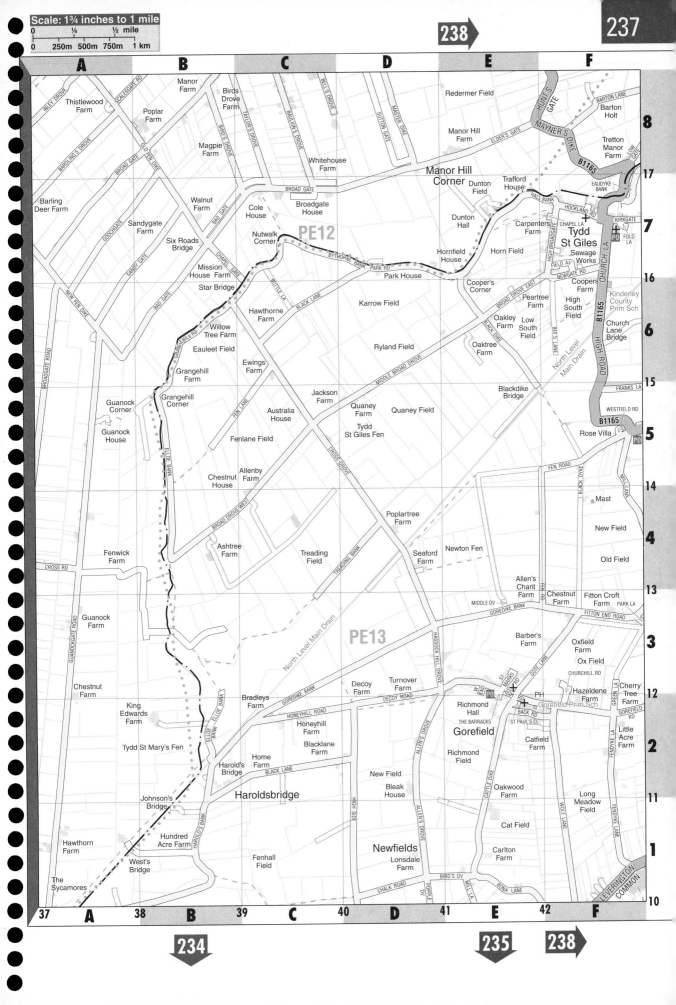

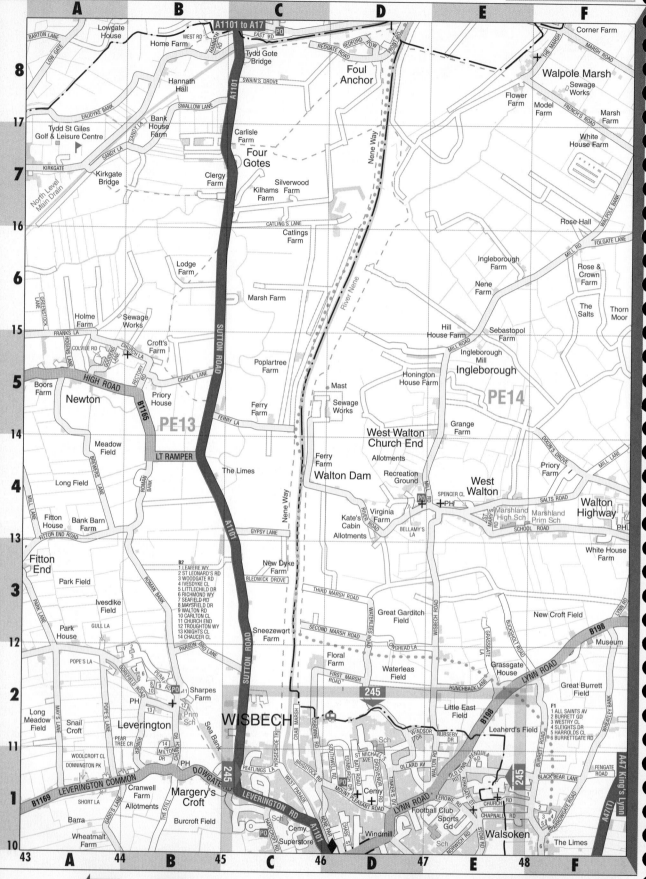

Scale: 1¾ inches to 1 mile

0   ¼   ½   mile

0   250m 500m 750m 1 km

A **B** **C** **D** **E** **F**

A1101 to A17

Corner Farm

Lowgate House

BARTON LANE

LOW GATE

WEST RD

HANNATH RD

EAST RD

PO

REDGATE ROAD

BEDFORD ROW

FRONT RD

THE MARSH

MARSH ROAD

Home Farm

Tydd Gote Bridge

Foul Anchor

Walpole Marsh

Sewage Works

8

Hannath Hall

SWAIN'S DROVE

Flower Farm

Model Farm

TRENCH'S ROAD

Marsh Farm

EAUDYKE BANK

SWALLOW LANE

Nene Way

White House Farm

17

Tydd St Giles Golf & Leisure Centre

SANDY LA

Bank House Farm

A1101

Carlisle Farm

WALPOLE BANK

FOLGATE LANE

7

KIRKGATE

Kirkgate Bridge

CLERGY Farm

Four Gotes

Kilhams Farm

Silverwood Farm

Rose Hall

Rose & Crown Farm

16

North Level Main Drain

CATLING'S LANE

Catlings Farm

Ingleborough Farm

MILL RD

The Salts

Thorn Moor

6

GREENSTOCK LANE

Lodge Farm

River Nene

Marsh Farm

Nene Farm

Sebastopol Farm

15

Holme Farm

FRANKS LA

Sewage Works

Croft's Farm

Hill House Farm

Ingleborough Mill

Ingleborough

PE14

ROGERS LANE

GOODS LANE

CHURCH LA

COLVILE RD

RECTORY RD

CHAPEL LANE

Poplartree Farm

Honington House Farm

DIXON'S DROVE

5

Boors Farm

HIGH ROAD

Newton

Priory House

B1165

SUTTON ROAD

Mast

Sewage Works

West Walton Church End

Grange Farm

Priory Farm

MILL LANE

14

Meadow Field

PE13

FERRY LA

Ferry Farm

LT RAMPER

The Limes

Allotments

West Walton

SALTS ROAD

Walton Highway

PH

4

Long Field

BREWERS LANE

ROMAN BANK

Ferry Farm

Walton Dam

Recreation Ground

PO

MILL RD

PH

Marshland High Sch

Marshland Prim Sch

SCHOOL ROAD

13

Fitton House

Bank Barn Farm

FITTON END ROAD

GYPSY LANE

Kate's Cabin

Virginia Farm

RIVER ROAD

BELLAMY'S LA

ST MARY'S RD

White House Farm

Fitton End

Park Field

Allotments

B2

New Dyke Farm

BLEDWICK DROVE

3

PARK LANE

Ivesdike Field

ROMAN BANK

1. LEAFERE WY
2. ST LEONARD'S RD
3. WOODGATE RD
4. IVESDYKE CL
5. LITTLECHILD DR
6. RICHMOND WY
7. SEAFIELD RD
8. MAYSFIELD DR
9. WALTON RD
10. CARLTON CL
11. CHURCH END
12. TROUGHTON WY
13. KNIGHTS CL
14. CHAUCER CL

Third Marsh Road

WATERLESS ROAD

WISBECH ROAD

Great Garditch Field

New Croft Field

B198

Museum

12

Park House

GULL LA

PARSON DRO LANE

SUTTON ROAD

Sneezewort Farm

Floral Farm

Second Marsh Road

HYGHEAD LA

Waterleas Field

BUCKSHOLT ROAD

GRASSGATE

Grassgate House

LYNN RD

B198

Great Burrett Field

2

Long Meadow Field

MAY'S LANE

POPE'S LA

BOREFIELD ROAD

PERRY RD

PH

PO

Sharpes Farm

First Marsh Road

Floral Farm

245

HUNCHBACK LANE

LYNN ROAD

Little East Field

Leaherd's Field

WHEATLEY BANK

F1

1. ALL SAINTS AV
2. BURRETT GD
3. WESTRY CL
4. SLEIGHTS DR
5. HARROLDS CL
6. BURRETTGATE RD

Snail Croft

Leverington

PEAR TREE CR

Prim Sch

WISBECH

CRAB MARSH

OSBORNE RD

Sch

WINDSOR DR

NURSERY DR

OLD LYNN

KIRKGATE

PENDULA

B198

245

BLACK BEAR LANE

FENGATE ROAD

A47 King's Lynn

11

WOOLCROFT CL

DONNINGTON PK

MILTON DR

PH

SEA BANK

PEATLINGS LA

HORSESHOE TER

WEST PARADE

BRIGSTOCK RD

SOUTHWELL RD

EDINBURGH RD

BATH RD

GROSVENOR

ST MICHAEL'S AVE

OLLARD AV

WALTON RD

LEROWE RD

BARRETT ROAD

A47(T)

1

B1169

LEVERINGTON COMMON

Cranwell Farm

THE STILL

SHORT LA

GARD'S LANE

DOWGATE ROAD

Margery's Croft

245

LEVERINGTON RD

A1101

NENE PAR

CHASE ST

MOUNT PLEASANT ROAD

Cemy

TINKER'S DV

Football Club Sports Gd

CHURCH

CHAPNALL RD

STOW RD

Walsoken

SPARROWGATE ROAD

The Limes

Barra

Wheatmalt Farm

Burcroft Field

Sch

PO

Cemy Superstore

Windmill

NORWICH RD

10

43 **A** **44** **B** **45** **C** **46** **D** **47** **E** **48** **F**

For full street detail of the highlighted area see page 245.

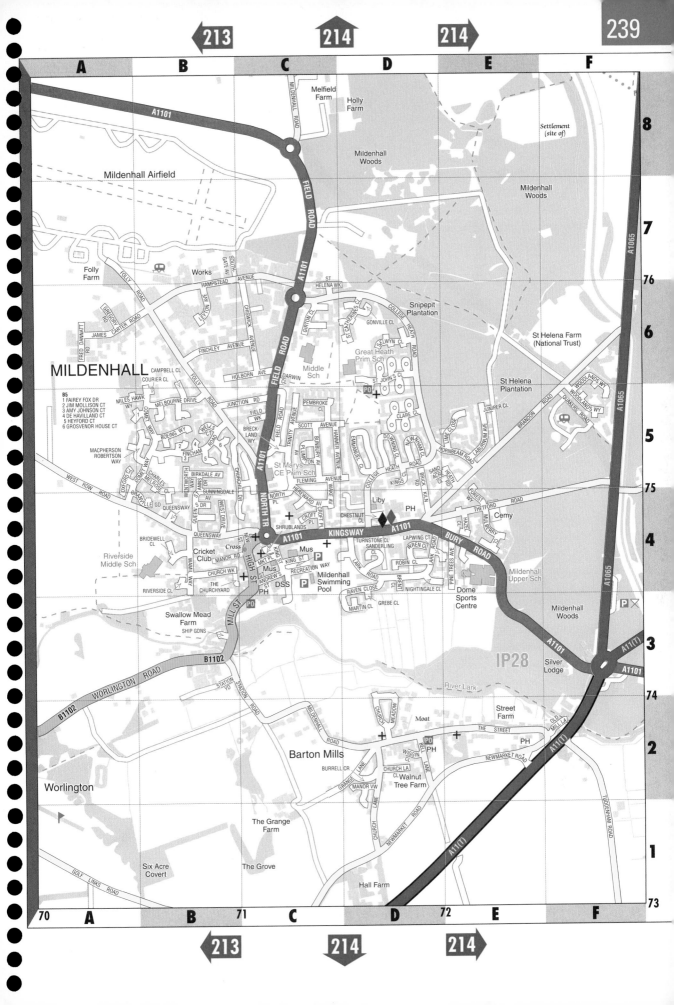

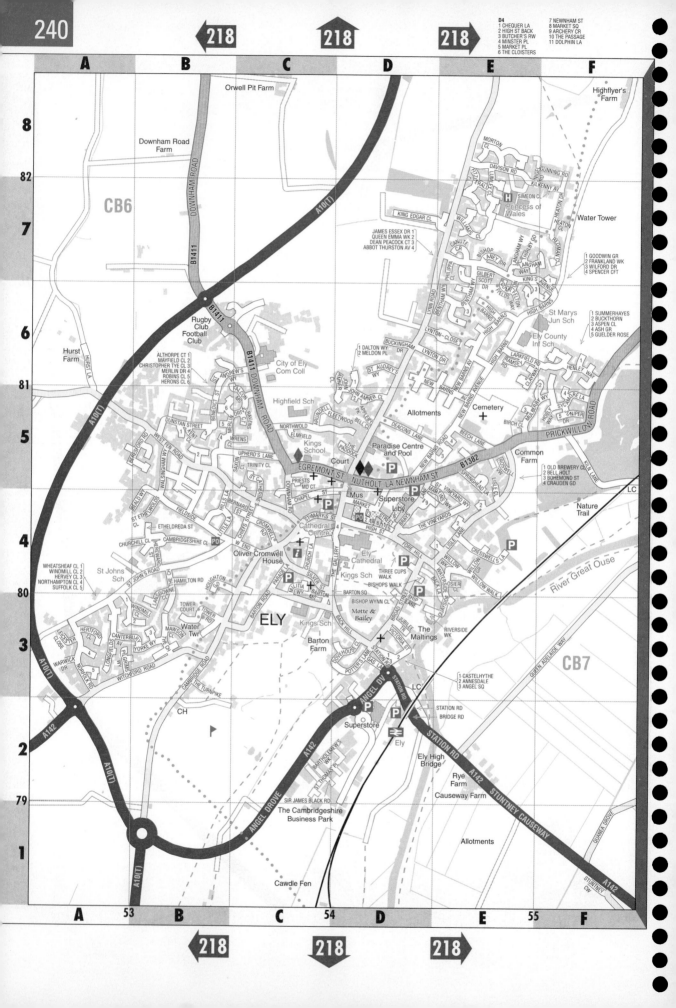

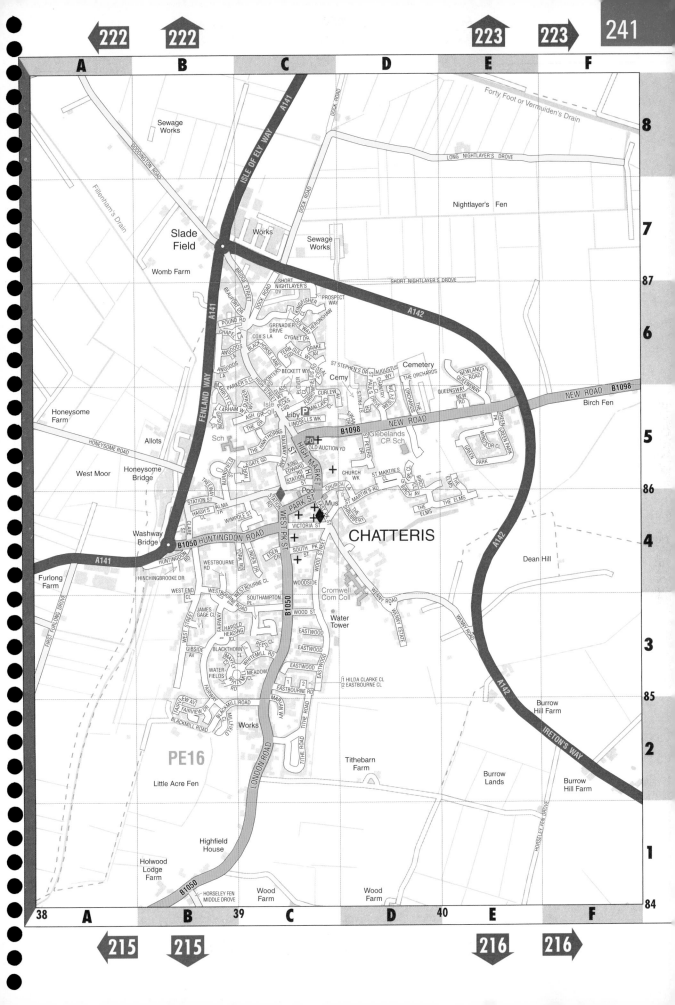

← 222   222 ↑   223 ↑   223 →

A   B   C   D   E   F

8

Forty Foot or Vermuiden's Drain

LONG NIGHTLAYER'S DROVE

Nightlayer's Fen

7

Sewage Works

Slade Field

Works

Sewage Works

SHORT NIGHTLAYER'S DROVE

87

Womb Farm

SHORT NIGHTLAYER'S DV

PROSPECT WAY

A142

6

Honeysome Farm

Cemetery

Cemy

NEW ROAD   B1098

Birch Fen

5

Allots

Isle

Liby P

B1098

NEW ROAD

Glebelands C.P. Sch

Sch

PO

OLD AUCTION YD

West Moor

Honeysome Bridge

86

Honeysome Road

Pool

Mus

CHATTERIS

Washway Bridge

Station St

4

A141

B1050   HUNTINGDON ROAD

Victoria St

Dean Hill

Furlong Farm

HINCHINGBROOKE DR

Westbourne Rd

WOODSIDE

Cromwell Com Coll

WENNY ROAD

A142

West End Cl

Water Tower

3

James Gage Cl

Wood St

85

Blackthorn

EASTWOOD

EASTWOOD

Burrow Hill Farm

Water-Fields

EASTWOOD

1 Hilda Clarke Cl
2 Eastbourne Cl

PE16

Works

TITHE ROAD

IRETON'S WAY

2

Little Acre Fen

Tithebarn Farm

Burrow Lands

Burrow Hill Farm

Highfield House

1

Holwood Lodge Farm

B1050

HORSELEY FEN MIDDLE DROVE

Wood Farm

Wood Farm

84

38   A   B   39   C   D   40   E   F

← 215   215 ↑   216 ↑   216 →

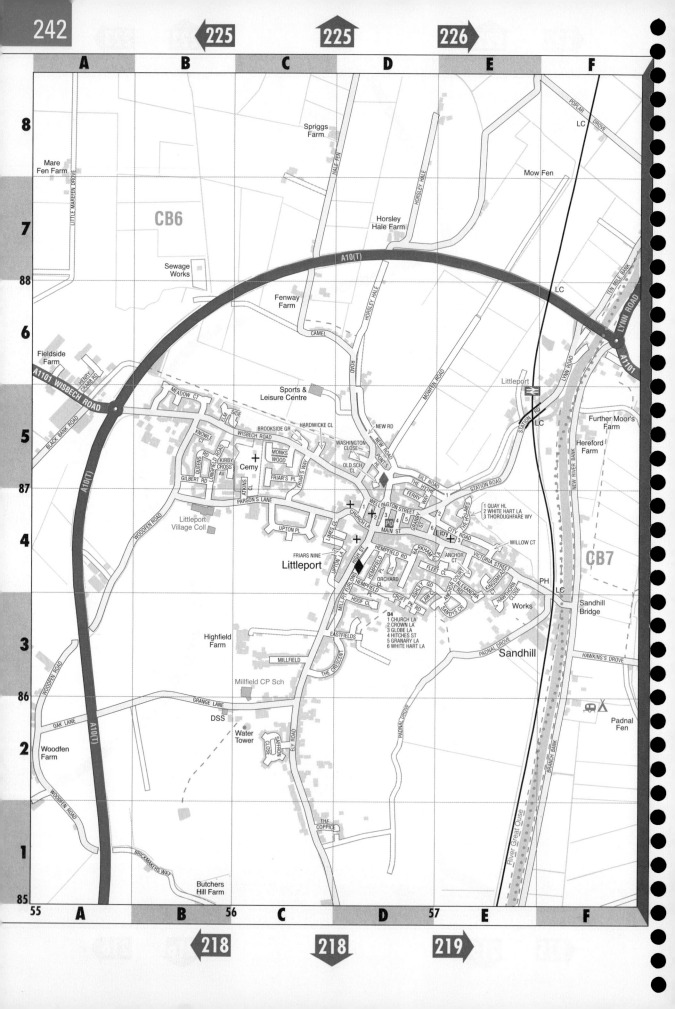

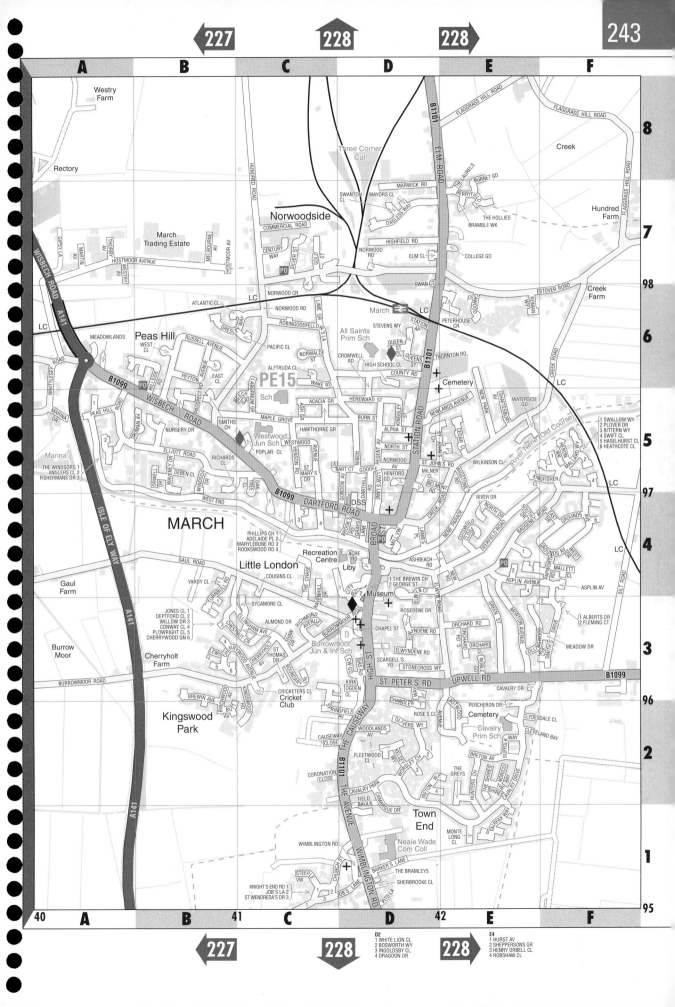

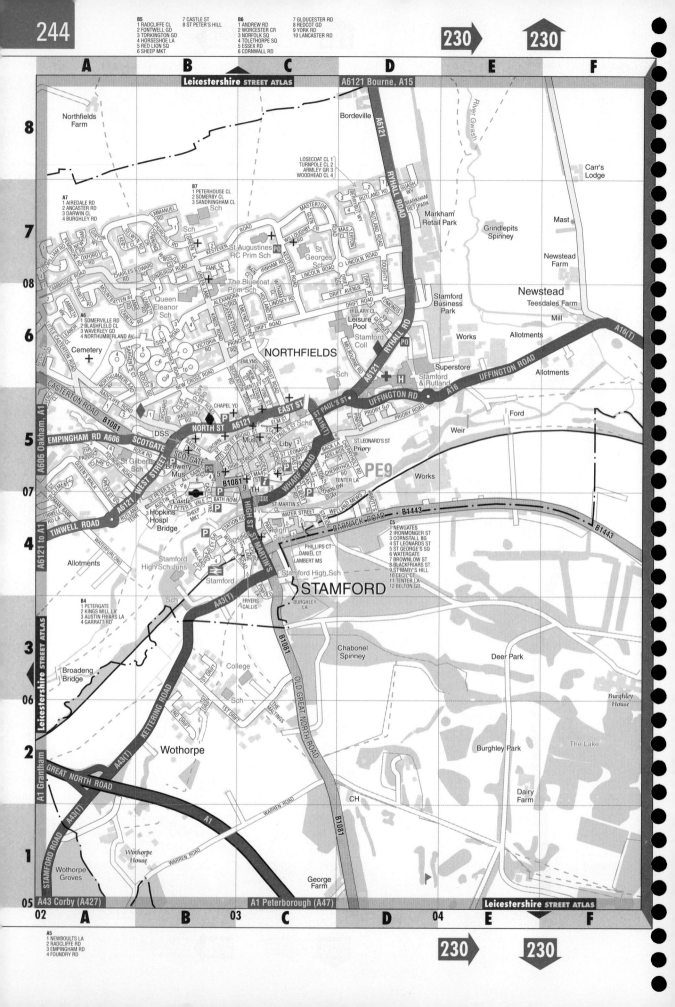

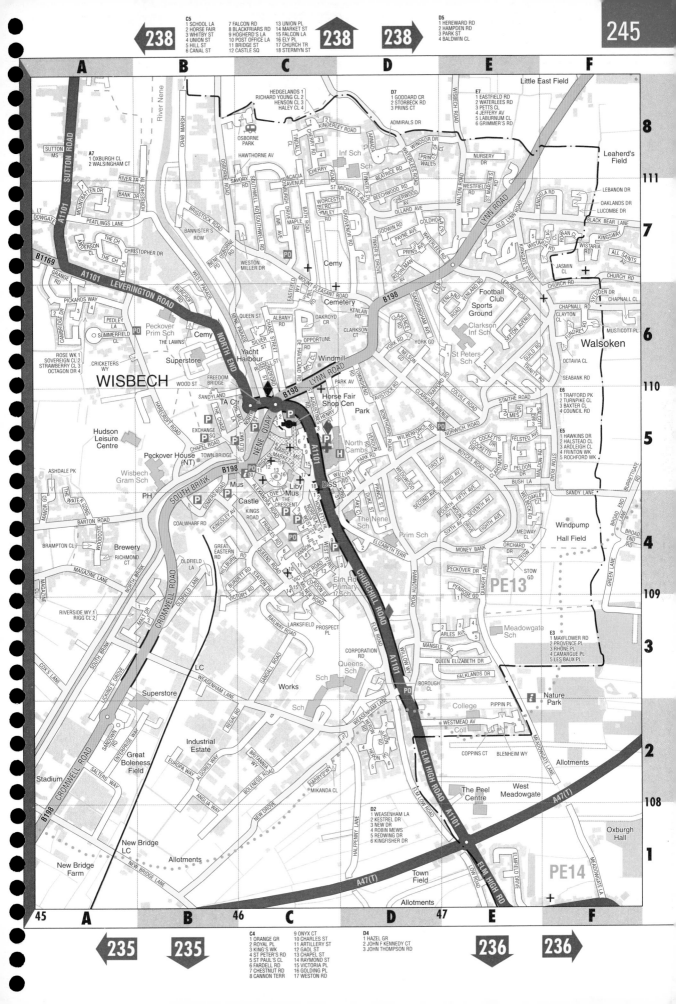

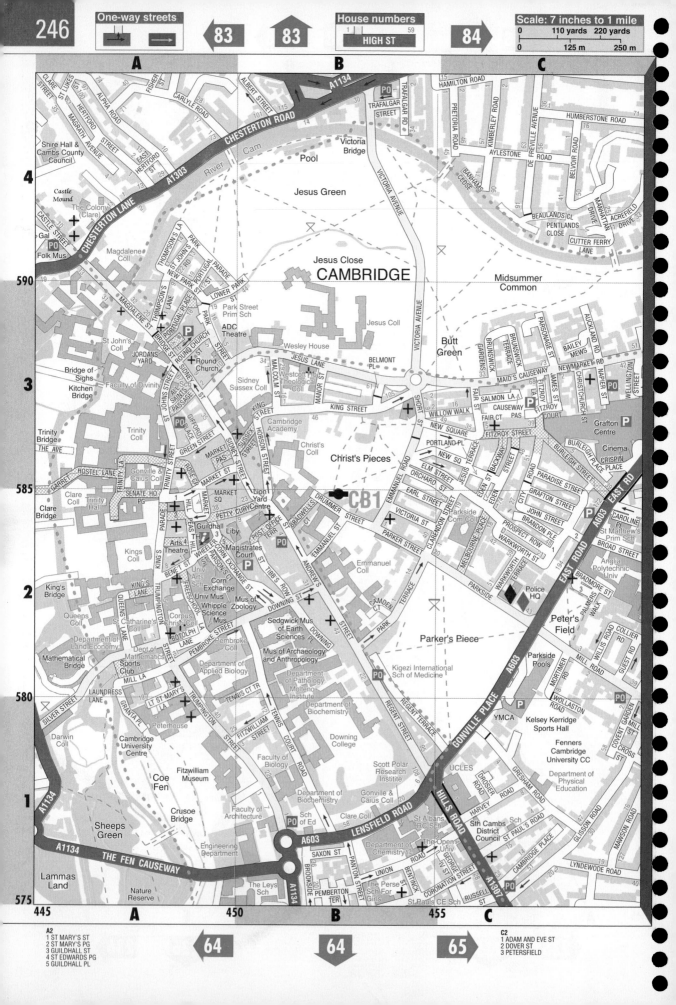

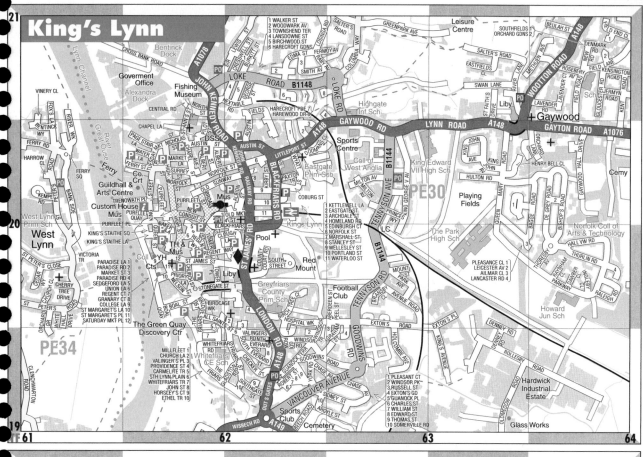

King's Lynn

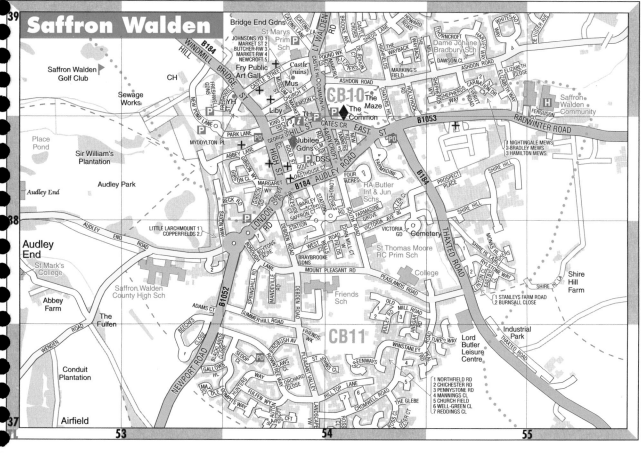

Saffron Walden

Index

Church Rd 6 Beckenham BR2..........**53** C6

Place name	Location number	Locality, town or village	Postcode district	Page and grid square
May be abbreviated on the map	Present when a number indicates the place's position in a crowded area of mapping	Shown when more than one place has the same name	District for the indexed place	Page number and grid reference for the standard mapping

Public and commercial buildings are highlighted in magenta   **Places of interest** are highlighted in blue with a star★

Abbreviations used in the index

Acad	**Academy**	Comm	**Common**	Gd	**Ground**	L	**Leisure**	Prom	**Prom**
App	**Approach**	Cott	**Cottage**	Gdn	**Garden**	La	**Lane**	Rd	**Road**
Arc	**Arcade**	Cres	**Crescent**	Gn	**Green**	Liby	**Library**	Recn	**Recreation**
Ave	**Avenue**	Cswy	**Causeway**	Gr	**Grove**	Mdw	**Meadow**	Ret	**Retail**
Bglw	**Bungalow**	Ct	**Court**	H	**Hall**	Meml	**Memorial**	Sh	**Shopping**
Bldg	**Building**	Ctr	**Centre**	Ho	**House**	Mkt	**Market**	Sq	**Square**
Bsns, Bus	**Business**	Ctry	**Country**	Hospl	**Hospital**	Mus	**Museum**	St	**Street**
Bvd	**Boulevard**	Cty	**County**	HQ	**Headquarters**	Orch	**Orchard**	Sta	**Station**
Cath	**Cathedral**	Dr	**Drive**	Hts	**Heights**	Pal	**Palace**	Terr	**Terrace**
Cir	**Circus**	Dro	**Drove**	Ind	**Industrial**	Par	**Parade**	TH	**Town Hall**
Cl	**Close**	Ed	**Education**	Inst	**Institute**	Pas	**Passage**	Univ	**University**
Cnr	**Corner**	Emb	**Embankment**	Int	**International**	Pk	**Park**	Wk, Wlk	**Walk**
Coll	**College**	Est	**Estate**	Intc	**Interchange**	Pl	**Place**	Wr	**Water**
Com	**Community**	Ex	**Exhibition**	Junc	**Junction**	Prec	**Precinct**	Yd	**Yard**

Index of localities, towns and villages

A

Abbots Ripton	162	C1
Abbotsley	57	C5
Abington Piggots	11	E5
Ailsworth	195	D3
Alconbury	150	E4
Alconbury Weston	150	D6
Aldreth	209	E4
Alwalton	185	B4
Arbury	83	D6
Arrington	44	C1
Ashdon	21	B1
Ashley	91	F7
Ashton	231	A4
Ashwell	2	E4
Ashwell End	2	A5

B

Babraham	50	E1
Badlingham	213	D1
Bainton	230	F5
Balsham	53	A2
Bar Hill	102	C3
Barham	149	B3
Barley	6	F2
Barnack	230	E3
Barrington	29	E8
Bartlow	21	A7
Barton	63	B3

Barton Mills	239	C2
Barway	211	C6
Bassingbourn	12	F4
Beck Row	213	F8
Begdale	235	F5
Benwick	222	A5
Bird's Hundred	189	C5
Black Horse Drove	226	B6
Blackhall	227	A1
Bluntisham	208	D5
Bottisham	86	F6
Bourn	60	C6
Boxworth	101	B5
Boyces Bridge	236	D4
Brampton	140	C2
Brampton Park	140	D1
Brandon Bank	226	E3
Brandon Creek	226	D6
Bretton	197	A6
Briggate	189	E6
Brington	147	D4
Brinkley	70	E2
Broad Green	8	C3
Broad Green	91	D4
Brook End	136	B6
Broughton	153	F8
Buckden	117	B3
Buckworth	149	E6
Bunker's Hill	235	A6
Burrough End	70	E4
Burrough Green	70	F3
Burton End	37	C8
Burwell	130	C2

Bury	172	B4
Bythorn	146	D4

C

Caldecote	80	B1
Caldecote	76	B1
Caldecote	175	D5
Calford Green	24	F7
Cambridge	246	B4
Camps End	22	A1
Cardinal's Green	37	B1
Carlton	55	A7
Carlton Green	55	A4
Carlton Hill	55	A8
Castle Camps	22	F4
Castle End	231	D7
Castor	195	D1
Catworth	136	D7
Caxton	78	F1
Chainbridge	228	B7
Chapel End	174	D4
Chatteris	241	D4
Cherry Hinton	65	F5
Chesterton	84	A6
Chesterton	184	E3
Cheveley	91	C6
Childerley	80	C8
Childerley Gate	80	D4
Chippenham	132	E8
Chittering	127	B8
Chrishall	8	D4

Christchurch	229	D3
Church End	77	D4
Church End	169	D2
Church End	165	D1
Church End	151	F2
Church End	136	E7
Church End	122	E7
Church End	208	C1
Church Field	189	B7
Clayhithe	106	D5
Claypit Hill	61	D2
Clopton	156	E5
Coates	190	F8
Cockayne Hatley	25	C8
Coldham	235	D1
Coldham's Common	84	D2
Colne	208	D6
Colnefields	208	D8
Comberton	62	C5
Commercial End	108	C3
Conington	168	C8
Conington	121	C1
Coton	82	B2
Cottenham	125	D4
Coveney	217	C5
Covington	135	D2
Cowlinge	73	D1
Crawley End	8	D5
Cropley Grove	92	D3
Crow End	60	D7
Crowland	232	B8
Croxton	76	F4
Croydon	27	A7

D

Dalham	92	E8
Deeping Gate	231	E8
Deeping St James	206	A7
Denny End	105	F8
Denton	175	E4
Diddington	96	A8
Dillington	94	C7
Ditton Green	90	E1
Doddington	223	A6
Dogsthorpe	198	C7
Down Field	212	D2
Dry Drayton	102	C1
Duck End	97	F5
Dullingham	70	D8
Dullingham Ley	71	A5
Duloe	74	A6
Dunkirk	224	F1
Duxford	32	C1
Dyer's Green	13	C8

E

Eaglethorpe	178	B4
Earith	208	E6
East Hatley	43	B1
East Perry	115	E3
Eastfield	198	D4
Eastgate	198	B2
Easton	138	C4

Eastrea 190 D7
Eaton Ford 74 C5
Eaton Socon 74 B3
Eldernell 202 B2
Ellington 139 A4
Ellington Thorpe 139 A2
Elm 236 B5
Elmdon 9 A4
Elsworth 100 C4
Eltisley 77 E4
Elton 178 D8
Ely 240 C3
Emmaus 126 E2
Emneth 236 C6
Emneth Hungate 236 E6
Etton 231 D5
Everton 40 C3
Exning 110 A8
Eye 232 B1
Eye Green 232 B2
Eynesbury 74 F3

F
Farcet 187 C2
Fen Ditton 84 F5
Fen Drayton 121 F6
Fen End 57 D6
Fengate 198 D2
Fenstanton 122 C5
Fenton 165 B4
Fitton End 238 A3
Flint Cross 15 B2
Folksworth 175 D8
Fordham 212 F1
Fowlmere 15 D8
Foxton 30 C5
Freckenham 213 C3
Friday Bridge 236 A4
Fulbourn 66 F4

G
Gamlingay 41 D5
Gamlingay Cinques 41 B6
Gamlinghay Great Heath 40 E3
Gaultree 236 D6
Girton 82 F8
Glatton 175 F1
Glinton 203 E8
Godmanchester 141 E2
Gorefield 237 E2
Grafham 116 A7
Grantchester 64 A4
Graveley 97 F4
Great Abington 34 C6
Great Bradley 55 F7
Great Chesterford 18 D2
Great Chishill 7 F2
Great Eversden 45 E8
Great Gidding 166 E3
Great Gransden 58 D5
Great Paxton 96 E4
Great Raveley 163 B7
Great Shelford 48 F5
Great Staughton 93 F6
Great Stukeley 152 A2
Great Wilbraham 68 A7
Great Wratting 39 D5
Green End 93 A3
Green End 62 B6
Green End 152 A1
Guilden Morden 10 E4
Gunthorpe 204 D2
Guyhirn 234 F2

H
Haddenham 210 B6
Haddon 180 B6
Hadstock 20 C6
Hail Weston 95 B1
Hamerton 159 B4
Hampton Hargate 186 D2
Hanchet End 38 C1
Hardwick 81 B3
Hardwick 117 A5
Hare Park 88 A3
Harlton 46 D5
Haroldsbridge 237 C2
Harston 48 A3
Hartford 142 A6
Haslingfield 47 B6
Hatley End 25 B5
Hatley St George 43 A3
Hauxton 48 B4

Haverhill 24 C8
Hazel Stub 23 C7
Helpston 231 C4
Hemingford Abbots 142 E3
Hemingford Grey 143 E1
Herringswell 134 E8
Heydon 8 A5
High Cross 82 E2
Highfields 80 D2
Hildersham 34 F5
Hilton 121 B1
Hinxton 18 A7
Histon 104 C4
Holly End 236 E5
Holme 177 A4
Holywell 144 F2
Holywell Row 214 A8
Hook 223 D8
Horningsea 106 A1
Horse Moor 228 D1
Horseheath 37 A3
Houghton 143 A5
Huntingdon 141 F4

I
Ickleton 18 A4
Ickleton 9 A8
Impington 104 C2
Ingleborough 238 E5
Inham's End 189 F6
Islands Common 74 E7
Isleham 213 A5

K
Kennett 133 F5
Kennett End 134 A2
Kentford 134 B2
Keyston 146 B3
Kimbolton 113 F6
King's Dyke 188 E6
Kings Hedges 83 E7
Kings Ripton 153 C5
Kingston 61 A3
Kingswood Park 243 B2
Kirtling 72 E6
Kirtling Green 72 C4
Kirtling Towers 72 D7
Knapwell 100 E2
Kneesworth 13 A6
Knights End 228 A1

L
Lakes End 229 F3
Landbeach 105 D7
Landwade 131 C4
Lark Hall Corner 69 A1
Lattersea Field 190 B6
Leighton Bromswold 148 D3
Leverington 238 B2
Lidgate 73 E8
Linton 35 E3
Litlington 12 B2
Little Abington 34 B7
Little Catworth 137 A6
Little Chishill 1 C7
Little Ditton 90 F2
Little Downham 218 B6
Little End 74 C1
Little Eversden 46 A7
Little Gidding 158 F8
Little Gransden 58 D3
Little Heath 41 C4
Little Linton 35 B3
Little London 243 C4
Little Ouse 226 D4
Little Paxton 96 B2
Little Raveley 163 B4
Little Shelford 48 E3
Little Staughton 93 B2
Little Stukeley 151 C4
Little Thetford 211 B7
Little Wilbraham 86 E1
Little Wratting 39 D3
Littlebury Green 9 F2
Littleport 242 C4
Lode 107 C2
Lolworth 101 F5
Long Meadow 107 F2
Longstanton 123 E2
Longstowe 59 F3
Longthorpe 197 A1
Luddington in
   the Brook 166 B4
Lutton 174 C4

M
Madingley 81 E5
Manea 224 B4
March 243 B4
Margery's Croft 238 B1
Marholm 203 E1
Market Deeping 231 D8
Marshland
   St James 236 F8
Maxey 231 C7
Melbourn 14 C5
Meldreth 29 A2
Mepal 216 E4
Mildenhall 239 A6
Mile End 219 C5
Mill End 72 E5
Mill Green 22 D7
Millfield 197 F5
Milton 105 E2
Molesworth 147 A5
Morborne 180 B3
Morden Green 11 C1
Moulton 112 E6
Murrow 234 D5

N
Needingworth 208 B3
Nene Terrace 232 D6
New England 197 B8
New Fletton 187 B8
New Meadow 187 F2
New Wimpole 28 B8
Newark 198 E6
Newborough 207 D1
Newfields 237 D1
Newmarket 111 B5
Newnham 64 C8
Newnham
   Croft 64 D7
Newstead 244 E6
Newton 31 C8
Newton 238 A5
Newtown 64 E2
Newtown 141 E5
Newtown 114 A5
Norman Cross 180 F2
North Green 190 B6
North Side 200 F4
Northborough 231 F7
Northfields 244 E4
Norwoodside 243 C7
Nosterfield End 22 F5

O
Oakington 103 B5
Odsey 3 C1
Offord Cluny 117 F3
Offord D'Arcy 117 F3
Old Fletton 187 A6
Old Hurst 154 E7
Old Weston 148 A8
Old Wimpole 44 F3
Orton Brimbles 185 D5
Orton Goldhay 185 F3
Orton Longueville 186 C4
Orton Malbourne 186 C4
Orton Southgate 185 D5
Orton Waterville 185 E4
Orton Wistow 185 C6
Orwell 45 E4
Outwell 236 F3
Over 208 E1
Over End 178 E7
Owl End 152 A3
Oxlode 224 C1

P
Pale Green 23 D1
Pampisford 33 B5
Papley 174 A6
Papworth Everard 99 B3
Papworth St Agnes 98 D5
Parson Drove 234 D7
Paston 205 A1
Peakirk 206 B7
Peas Hill 243 B6
Peterborough 197 D5
Pidley 155 B4
Pilsgate 230 C4
Pondersbridge 220 D7
Prickwillow 219 B5
Pymore (Pymoor) 224 E1

Q
Queen Adelaide 218 D4

R
Rampton 124 F4
Ramsey 172 B6
Ramsey Forty Foot 221 C2
Ramsey Heights 171 A7
Ramsey Mereside 221 A4
Ramsey St Mary's 220 D3
Ravensthorpe 197 C6
Reach 129 C1
Red Lodge 213 F1
Ring's End 234 F1
Romsey Town 65 B8
Royston 5 B6

S
St Ives 143 E7
St Neots 74 E4
Sandhill 242 E3
Sapley 141 F8
Sawston 33 A7
Sawtry 168 A3
Saxon Street 91 B3
Seadyke 234 F6
Shepreth 29 E4
Shingay 26 F2
Shudy Camps 22 B5
Sibson 183 E8
Six Mile Bottom 68 F7
Slade Field 241 B7
Snailwell 132 B4
Soham 212 B4
Soham Cotes 211 F5
Somersham 215 B1
South Green 190 F7
Southoe 95 E5
Southorpe 230 D2
Spaldwick 137 F6
Stamford 244 D4
Stanground 187 C5
Stapleford 49 D4
Staughton Green 94 A7
Staughton Highway 94 A5
Steeple Gidding 159 B7
Steeple Morden 11 B2
Stetchworth 90 A2
Stetchworth Ley 71 B7
Steventon End 21 C2
Stibbington 194 C2
Stilton 176 A7
Stirtloe 117 B2
Stonely 114 B3
Stourbridge Common 84 B4
Stow Cum Quy 86 A6
Stow Longa 137 C2
Streetly End 37 A5
Strethall 9 F4
Stretham 210 E5
Studlands Park 110 F8
Stukeley 141 B6
Stuntney 218 D1
Sturmer 24 F4
Sutton 216 E2
Sutton 194 F2
Sutton Gault 216 C2
Swaffham Bulbeck 108 B1
Swaffham Prior 108 E4
Swavesey 122 E6
Swingbrow 222 D3

T
Tadlow 26 A3
Tallington 230 E7
Temple End 55 D2
Tetworth 40 F7
Teversham 85 C1
The Cottons 236 E3
The Green 122 D1
The Lipneas 202 B1
Thistley Green 213 C7
Tholomas Drove 235 A5
Thorney 233 A3
Thorney Toll 234 A3
Thornhaugh 193 F5
Three Holes 229 E7
Thriplow 31 C2
Throckenholt 234 B8
Tilbrook 113 B7
Tipps End 229 F2
Toft 61 E4

Top End 93 B1
Toseland 97 E2
Town End 243 D7
Trumpington 64 E2
Tuddenham 214 D2
Turves 191 F6
Tydd St Giles 237 F7

U
Uffington 230 C6
Ufford 230 F3
Upend 92 A1
Upend Green 91 F2
Upton 160 C1
Upton 195 B6
Upware 211 B1
Upwell 236 D1
Upwood 171 C2

W
Walpole Marsh 238 F8
Walsoken 245 F6
Walton 204 D1
Walton Dam 238 D4
Walton Highway 238 F4
Wansford 194 A4
Warboys 165 A5
Wardy Hill 217 B4
Waresley 57 E2
Warmington 178 A3
Water End 25 B3
Water Newton 184 C7
Waterbeach 106 C7
Waterside 213 A6
Way Head 217 C6
Weald 76 B4
Welches Dam 224 A1
Welney 225 B8
Wendy 27 C4
Wennington 162 D4
Wentworth 217 B1
Werrington 204 B3
West Deeping 231 B8
West End 155 A5
West Perry 115 D2
West Row 213 D6
West Walton 238 E4
West Walton
   Church End 238 D5
West Wickham 37 B7
West Wratting 53 E5
Westcote 211 F6
Westley Bottom 69 C7
Westley Waterless 70 C5
Weston Colville 54 B7
Weston Ditch 213 C7
Weston Green 54 D5
Westry 227 F5
Westwick 103 E7
Westwood 197 B4
Whaddon 28 C1
White Hall 235 E6
Whittlesey 189 D5
Whittlesford 32 B5
Wicken 211 F1
Wiggens Green 23 E2
Wilburton 210 B5
Willingham 209 B1
Willingham Green 54 D8
Wimblington 223 A6
Wintringham 75 F4
Winwick 158 B6
Wisbech 245 A6
Wisbech St Mary 235 B7
Wistow 163 F6
Witcham 217 A2
Witchford 217 D1
Withersfield 38 C4
Wittering 230 C1
Woodditton 90 E3
Woodhurst 155 B4
Woodland Green 24 E7
Woodston 186 E7
Woodwalton 161 F6
Woolley 149 E1
Worlington 213 E4
Wothorpe 244 B2
Wrestlingworth 25 C4
Wyton 142 F5

Y
Yarwell 183 A8
Yaxley 181 F4
Yelling 98 C1

A

A Furlong Dro CB6 .....224 F2
Abbey Cl Burwell CB5 ...130 B1
Sawtry PE28 ....168 B4
Abbey Fields PE26 .....172 C7
Abbey La Lode CB5 .....107 C2
Swaffham Bulbeck CB5 ...108 B3
Abbey Pl 4 Thorney PE6 233 A3
Waterbeach CB5 ....127 B1
Abbey Rd Cambridge CB5 .84 A3
Peterborough PE4 ......204 C1
Ramsey PE26 ....172 C6
Abbey St Cambridge CB1 ..84 A2
Ickleton CB10 ....17 F3
Abbey Way PE7 ....189 C7
Abbey Wlk CB1 ....84 A2
Abbot Thurston Ave 4
CB6 ....240 E6
Abbot Way PE7 ....181 D4
Abbot's Cl PE28 ....155 A5
Abbots Cl Cambridge CB4 .83 E7
Hemingford Abbots PE28 .142 F3
Ramsey PE26 ....172 C7
Abbots Cres PE27 ......144 A6
Abbots Dr 1 PE6 ......232 B8
Abbots Ripton CE Sch
PE28 ....162 C1
Abbots Way CB5 ....106 A1
Abbotsbury PE2 ....186 A3
Abbotsley Rd PE19 ......57 E8
Abbotsmede Jun Sch
PE1 ....198 C4
Abbott Cl PE28 ....140 C3
Abbott's Cl PE9 ....244 D4
Abbott's Grove Cotts CB9 24 F3
Abbotts Cl SG8 ....12 A2
Abbotts Ct 2 CB9 ....24 E5
Abbotts Gr PE4 ....204 B6
Abbotts Rd CB9 ....39 A1
Abington Gr 6 PE14 ...236 A5
Abington H CB1 ....34 B6
Abington Rd SG8 ....11 F2
Aboyne Ave PE2 ....185 F5
Abrahams Cl CB4 ......105 D6
Abram's La SG8 ....8 C4
Acacia Ave
Peterborough PE1 ....198 B8
St Ives PE27 ....143 E6
Wisbech PE13 ....245 C8
Acacia Gr March PE15 ...243 C5
St Neots PE19 ....75 A6
Acer Rd PE1 ....198 B6
Acheson Rd PE28 ......117 D8
Ackerman Gdns 4 PE19 .74 C2
Ackerman St PE19 ......74 C2
Ackroyd Rd 2 SG8 ....5 E8
Acland St PE1 ....197 F3
Acorn Ave CB3 ....102 C4
Acre Rd Carlton CB8 .....55 B8
March PE15 ....243 D4
Acre The PE28 ....150 F4
Acrefield Dr CB4 ......246 C4
Acremead PE8 ....178 A3
Acres The 2 PE9 ......230 D4
Acton Way CB4 ....83 D5
Adam & Eve St 1 CB1 .246 C1
Adam's La PE19 ....96 E4
Adams Ct CB5 ....106 C7
Adams Rd Cambridge CB3 .83 B2
Swaffham Prior CB5 ....108 D5
Adastral Cl CB8 ....110 E4
Addenbrookes Hospl
CB2 ....65 A3
Addington Way 1 PE4 .204 C3
Addison Rd PE15 ......223 B7
Adelaide Cl 10 CB7 .....212 B4
Adelaide Pl 2 PE15 ....243 C4
Adelaide St PE9 ....244 C5
Adelaide Wlk 7 PE28 ..208 E6
Admirals Dr PE13 ......245 D8
Admirals Way PE19 .....74 A2
Adventurers' Dro CB6 ..224 C1
Ailwine Rd PE26 ....171 B2
Ailwyn Sch PE26 ....172 C6
Aingers Rd CB4 ....104 B4
Ainsdale CB1 ....65 F5
Ainsdale Dr PE4 ....204 B4
Ainsworth Ct 4 CB1 ....84 A1
Ainsworth Pl CB1 ....84 B1
Ainsworth St CB1 ....84 A1
Aintree Rd SG8 ....5 F6
Airedale Cl PE1 ....198 A6
Airedale Rd 1 PE9 ....244 A7
Airport Way CB1 ....85 B2
Akeman Cl CB6 ....210 F6
Akeman St Cambridge CB4 83 C5
Landbeach CB4 ....105 C6
Alamein Ct PE19 ....74 C5
Albany Rd PE13 ....245 C6
Albany Wlk PE2 ....186 D7
Albemarle Rd PE27 .....143 F7
Albemarle Way CB4 .....83 E7
Albert Pl PE3 ....197 F1
Albert Rd Stamford PE9 .244 C5
Stow cum Quy CB5 ......86 A5
Albert St CB4 ....246 B4
Alberta Cres PE29 .....141 E5
Albert's Dr 1 PE15 ....243 F3
Albion Row 6 CB3 ......83 C3
Albion Yd 5 CB3 ....83 C3
Alconbury Airfield PE28 151 E6
Alconbury CE Sch PE28 .150 F5
Alconbury Cl PE2 ......187 E5
Alde Rd CB9 ....39 A1
Aldeburgh Cl 4 CB9 .....23 E7
Alder Cl 1 PE19 ....74 B5
Alder Dr Bourn CB3 ......79 C3
Huntingdon PE29 ....141 D5
Alder Rd PE7 ....186 C3
Alderlands Cl 6 PE6 ...232 B8
Alderman Jacobs Sch
PE7 ....189 F8
Alderman's Dr PE3 .....197 E3
Aldreth Rd CB6 ....209 F5
Aldsworth Cl 1 PE1 ...198 D6
Alec Rolph Cl CB1 ......66 D5
Alex Wood Rd CB4 ......83 E6
Alexander Rd SG19 ......25 B4
Alexandra Rd
Littleport CB6 ....242 E4
Peterborough PE1 ....197 F6
Stamford PE9 ....244 B6
Wisbech PE13 ....245 C5
Alfric Sq PE2 ....186 D6
Alftruda Cl PE15 ....243 C6
Algar Dr CB8 ....70 F8
Algores Way PE13 .....245 B2
Alington Rd PE19 ....74 E1
Aliwal Rd PE7 ....189 F1
All Saints Ave
1 Leverington PE13 .....238 F1
Leverington PE13 ....245 F7
All Saints CE Jun Sch
PE1 ....198 A6
All Saints Cl
St Ives PE27 ....144 A6
2 Wisbech PE14 ....236 A5
All Saints Gn PE27 ....144 A6
All Saints Pas CB2 .....246 A3
All Saints Prim Sch
March PE15 ....243 D6
Newmarket CB8 ....111 B3
All Saints Rd Fulbourn CB1 66 F5
Newmarket CB8 ....111 A3
All Saints' Rd PE1 .....198 A5
All Saints' St PE9 ......244 B5
All Saints Way 3 PE28 .168 C4
All Saints Wlk IP28 ....213 F4
All Souls La CB3 ....83 B4
Allan Ave PE2 ....187 E5
Allen Ct CB2 ....64 D2
Allen Farm Cl PE29 ....141 E1
Allen Rd
Peterborough PE1 ....197 E6
Ramsey PE26 ....171 F7
Allen's Dro PE13 ......237 D1
Allen's Orch PE28 .....140 E1
Allens Cl CB3 ....63 B4
Allerton Cl 6 PE9 .....230 D3
Allerton Garth PE7 .....185 A4
Allington Wlk CB9 ....23 E8
Allotment La PE5 ......195 E2
Allotments Dro CB6 ....211 B7
Alma Rd PE1 ....197 F5
Alma Terr PE16 ....241 B4
Almond Cl PE29 ....142 A1
Almond Dr PE15 ....243 C3
Almond Gr CB3 ....102 C4
Almond Rd
Peterborough PE1 ....198 B7
St Neots PE19 ....74 F6
Almoners' Ave CB1 ......65 C3
Almoners La PE3 ......197 E3
Alms Cl PE29 ....141 C7
Alms Hill CB3 ....60 D7
Alms La 3 SG7 ....2 D4
Alnwick Ct 1 PE19 ....74 F2
Alpha La PE28 ....151 E3
Alpha Rd CB4 ....246 A4
Alpha St PE15 ....243 D5
Alpha Terr CB2 ....64 D3
Alstead Rd CB4 ....104 B5
Alsyke Cl PE28 ....116 A7
Althorpe Ct 1 CB6 .....240 B5
Alwin Cl PE28 ....168 B3
Alwyn Cl PE27 ....144 B6
Alwyne Rd CB1 ....65 C2
Amberley Slope PE4 ....204 C3
Ambleside Gdns PE4 ...204 D3
Ambrose Way CB4 .....104 C4
Ambury Hill PE29 ......141 E5
Ambury Rd PE29 ....141 D5
Ambury Rd S PE29 .....141 D5
America The CB6 ......216 D1
American Air Mus★ CB2 .16 F8
American La PE29 .....141 E5
Amwell Rd CB4 ....83 F8
Amy Johnson Ct 3
IP28 ....239 B5
Ancaster Rd 2 PE9 ....244 A7
Ancaster Way
Cambridge CB1 ....65 C7
3 Doddington/Wimblington
PE15 ....222 F5
Anchor Ct CB6 ....242 E3
Anchor Dro PE38 ......226 F4
Anchor La CB5 ....130 B4
Anderson Cl PE13 .....245 A7
Anderson Cres PE29 ...142 A2
Andrea Cl PE2 ....187 C6
Andrew Cl PE5 ....195 D2
Andrew Rd
1 Newmarket CB8 ......110 E5
St Neots PE19 ....74 F2
1 Stamford PE9 ....244 B6
Andrewe's Cl PE7 ......187 B1
Andrews Cl 2 CB6 .....210 F5
Andrews Cres PE4 .....204 F2
Angel Dro CB7 ....240 D2
Angel Sq 3 CB7 ....240 D3
Angell's Mdw SG7 ....2 D4
Angle End CB1 ....67 F8
Angle La SG8 ....29 E5
Anglers Cl 2 PE15 .....243 A5
Anglers Way CB4 ....84 C5
Anglesey Way 8 CB4 ..208 D1
Anglia Polytechnic Univ
CB1 ....246 C2
Anglia Way PE13 ......245 B2
Anglian Bsns Pk SG8 .....5 B7
Anglian Cl PE2 ....187 D6
Angoods La PE16 ......241 B6
Angus Cl 2 CB1 ....65 A8
Angus Ct PE3 ....197 D3
Animal Health Trust
CB8 ....133 F1
Ann Suckling Rd CB9 ...39 A2
Anne Rd PE9 ....244 A6
Anne's Cl CB8 ....110 B8
Annesdale 2 CB7 ......240 D3
Annesley Cl PE28 ......168 B4
Annington Cres SG8 ....13 A8
Ann's Rd CB5 ....84 E4
Ansley Way PE27 ......143 E5
Anson Dr PE27 ....143 F6
Anson Pl 2 PE19 ....74 A2
Anstey H★ CB2 ....64 C2
Anstey Way CB2 ....64 D2
Antelope Way 2 CB1 ....66 A7
Anthony Cl PE7 ....189 C8
Antonia Cl CB9 ....24 E7
Anvil Ave SG8 ....12 A2
Anvil Cl CB2 ....49 C4
Apollo Way CB4 ....83 E8
Apple Cl PE19 ....96 F8
Apple Gr PE19 ....74 C4
Apple Orch The PE28 ...143 D2
Apple Tree Cl PE7 .....182 A6
Appleby Pk CB6 ....240 D5
Appletree Cl CB4 ......125 D1
Appletree Gr CB5 ......130 B4
Appletrees CB3 ....102 C3
Appleyard PE2 ....187 C7
Apreece Rd PE7 ....175 D8
Apreece Way PE7 ......176 A7
Apsley Way PE3 ....197 A2
Apthorpe St CB1 ....66 F6
Apthorpe Way CB4 ......84 A7
Aragon Cl Buckden PE19 .117 B4
Cambridge CB4 ....83 E7
Aragon Pl PE28 ....113 F5
Arber Cl CB5 ....86 E6
Arborfield Cl PE6 ......231 C4
Arbury Cl PE3 ....197 A3
Arbury Prim Sch CB4 ....83 E5
Arbury Rd CB4 ....83 E6
Arcadia Gdns CB4 .....103 C5
Archers Cl CB5 ....108 B3
Archers Dro PE6 ....233 D6
Archers Wood PE7 .....186 C3
Archers Wood Nature
Reserve★ PE28 ....160 C7
Archery Cres 9 CB7 ...240 D4
Archway Ct CB3 ....64 B7
Arden Rd CB4 ....83 F8
Ardleigh Cl 3 PE13 ....245 E5
Ardross Ct CB8 ....68 F6
Argyle St CB1 ....65 B8
Arles Ave PE13 ....245 E3
Armada Cl PE13 ....245 D8
Armingford Cres SG8 ....14 E7
Armitage Way CB4 ......83 F8
Armley Gr 3 PE9 ......244 D7
Armshold La CB3 ....61 D2
Armstrong Cl
Newmarket CB8 ....111 B3
Perry PE28 ....115 D3
Armstrong Ct 1 PE29 ..141 F8
Arnhem Cl PE19 ....74 C5
Arnold's La PE7 ....189 E7
Arran Cl CB1 ....65 F6
Arran Way PE27 ....144 A8
Arrendene Rd CB9 ....38 F1
Arthur Mellows Village Coll
PE6 ....203 D8
Arthur St CB4 ....83 C4
Artillery St 11 PE13 ....245 C4
Artindale PE3 ....197 A3
Artis Ct PE3 ....197 A3
Arundel Cl CB4 ....83 C5
Arundel Cres PE19 ......74 E2
Arundel Rd
Huntingdon PE29 ....142 A6
Peterborough PE4 ....204 C1
Arundell CB6 ....240 C5
Ascham La CB2 ....32 B4
Ascham Rd CB4 ....83 E4
Ascot Dr PE1 ....198 B6
Ascot Rd SG8 ....5 F6
Ash Cl Huntingdon PE29 ..141 E7
Peterborough PE1 ....198 C7
Stilton PE7 ....175 F7
1 Thorney PE6 ....232 F3
Ash Ct Brampton PE28 ..140 C3
Peterborough PE1 ....198 C7
Ash Gn CB10 ....18 D1
Ash Gr Burwell CB5 ....130 B2
Chatteris PE16 ....241 C5
4 Ely CB7 ....240 F5
Haverhill CB9 ....38 E1
March PE15 ....243 C5
Melbourn SG8 ....14 C5
Ash Pk PE4 ....204 B6
Ash Rd Earith PE28 .....208 F7
Peterborough PE1 ....198 C7
Ash Tree Cl 14 PE15 ....223 B7
Ashbeach Dro PE26 ....220 D3
Ashbeach Prim Sch The
PE26 ....220 D3
Ashbeach Rd
March PE15 ....243 D4
Ramsey PE26 ....220 D3
Ashburn Cl PE6 ....203 F7
Ashbury Cl CB1 ....65 B6
Ashcroft PE19 ....98 B2
Ashcroft Gdns PE1 ....198 C5
Ashdale Cl 1 PE28 .....168 B3
Ashdale Pk PE13 ......245 A5
Ashdon CP Sch CB10 ....21 B1
Ashen Gn CB2 ....49 A5
Ashfield PE28 ....113 F5
Ashfield Rd CB4 ....84 B5
Ashfields 1 PE6 ....231 F7
Ashlea Cl CB9 ....24 B6
Ashlea Rd CB9 ....24 B6
Ashleigh PE2 ....185 C6
Ashley Gdns CB6 ......242 D3
Ashley Pool La PE6 ....233 A2
Ashley Rd Cheveley CB8 .112 A1
Newmarket CB8 ....111 E2
Ashley Way CB2 ....32 F8
Ashline Gr PE7 ....189 D6
Ashmead Dr CB3 ....81 A3
Ashton Cl PE27 ....208 A2
Ashton Gdns PE29 .....141 D5
Ashton Rd PE3 ....197 B5
Ashvale CB4 ....83 D7
Ashwell & Morden Sta
SG7 ....3 D2
Ashwell Rd
Guilden Morden SG8 .....10 F2
Newnham SG7 ....2 A1
Ashwell St Ashwell SG7 ....2 D3
Bassingbourn cum Kneesworth
SG8 ....13 A3
Askers Field CB3 ....78 E2
Askew's La PE7 ....181 E4
Aspal Cl 8 IP28 ....213 F8
Aspal Hall Rd IP28 .....213 F8
Aspal La IP28 ....214 A8
Aspal Pk
Beck Row, Holywell Row
& Kenny Hill IP28 ......214 A8
Mildenhall IP28 ....213 F8
Aspal Pl 9 IP28 ....213 F8
Aspen Cl 3 Ely CB7 ....240 E5
Haverhill CB9 ....38 E1
Aspen Gn PE29 ....141 E6
Asplin Ave PE15 ....243 E4
Asplin's Cl 5 CB4 .....208 D1
Asplin's La PE19 ....117 F3
Asplins Ave 8 PE27 ....208 A3
Aster Dr PE4 ....204 D3
Astilbe La PE29 ....141 D5
Astley Cl CB6 ....216 E1
Astore Pk PE1 ....198 E3
Atherstone Ave PE3 ....197 B4
Atherton Cl CB4 ....83 E5
Athlone Cl CB3 ....99 A3
Atkins Cl Cambridge CB4 ..84 A7
Littleport CB6 ....242 C5
Atkinson St PE1 ....198 C2
Atlantic Cl PE15 ....243 B6
Atterton Rd CB9 ....38 D1
Aubretia Ave PE4 ......204 D3
Auckland Rd CB5 ......246 C3
Audley Cl SG19 ....58 E4
Audley Gate PE3 ......197 C3
Audley Way CB1 ....37 A3
Augers Rd 4 CB1 ....65 F6
Augusta Cl PE1 ....198 E6
Augustus Cl
2 Cambridge CB4 ....83 E8
Haverhill CB9 ....24 D7
Augustus Way PE16 ....241 D6
Aureole Wlk CB8 ......110 E8
Austin Friars La 3 PE9 .244 B4
Austin St PE9 ....244 B4
Avenells Way 2 SG19 ...41 D5
Avenue Rd
Huntingdon PE29 ....141 D5
St Neots PE19 ....74 F6
Avenue The Burwell CB5 .130 C3
Cambridge CB3 ....246 A3
Girton CB3 ....103 B1
Godmanchester PE29 ....141 E3
Leighton PE28 ....148 C3
Madingley CB3 ....81 F7
March PE15 ....243 D2
Newmarket CB8 ....111 A3
Ramsey PE26 ....172 A7
Aversley Rd PE28 ......168 C2
Aversley Wood Nature
Reserve★ PE28 ....159 F8
Aves Cl CB7 ....213 A5
Avon Ct Eaton Socon PE19 .74 C3
Peterborough PE4 ....204 E2
Axiom Ave PE3 ....197 C4
Axis Way 6 PE19 ....74 B5
Aydon Rd PE7 ....187 F6
Aylesborough Cl 4 CB4 .83 D7
Aylesford Way CB2 ......49 B4
Aylestone Rd CB4 .....246 C4
Ayre Ct 5 PE19 ....75 A5
Ayres Dr PE2 ....187 C6
Azalea Cl PE3 ....197 A2

B

Babraham CE Prim Sch
CB2 ....50 D1
Babraham Rd
Babraham CB2 ....50 B1
Cambridge CB2 ....65 C2
Babraham Rd *continued*
Fulbourn CB1 ....50 E8
Great Shelford CB2 ....49 E8
Sawston CB2 ....32 F8
Stapleford CB2 ....50 B6
Back Dro Upwell PE14 ...229 D8
Welney PE14 ....225 A8
Back Hill Ely CB7 ....240 D3
Hadstock CB1 ....20 B6
Back La Bourn CB3 ......79 B4
Burrough Green CB8 ......70 F4
Coveney CB6 ....217 B5
14 Deeping St James PE6 .231 F8
Elton PE8 ....178 D8
Ely CB7 ....240 D4
Eye PE6 ....232 A1
Haslingfield CB3 ....47 B4
Holywell-cum-Needingworth
PE27 ....144 F2
Ickleton CB10 ....18 A3
Market Deeping PE6 ....206 A7
Melbourn SG8 ....14 C4
Outwell PE14 ....236 E3
Stamford PE9 ....244 C5
Wicken CB7 ....211 E1
Yaxley PE7 ....181 E5
Back Rd Elm PE14 ......236 A5
Gorefield PE13 ....237 E2
Linton CB1 ....35 C3
Murrow PE13 ....234 D6
Wisbech PE14 ....236 A3
Back Reach Dro PE15 ..221 E7
Back St SG7 ....2 D3
Bacon's Yd SG7 ....2 D4
Bad Gate PE12 ....237 B7
Badcock Rd CB3 ....47 B5
Bader Cl
Peterborough PE3 ....197 B6
1 Ramsey PE26 ....172 A4
Badgeney Rd PE15 .....243 E4
Badger Cl PE7 ....181 F5
Badinton La PE9 ......230 F5
Badlingham Rd CB7 ....213 C1
Badminton Cl CB4 ....83 C6
Badney Dro PE16 ......222 D3
Bagot Pl 5 CB4 ....83 F8
Bagsham La IP28 ......213 E6
Bahram Cl 1 CB8 ......110 E4
Bailey Cl CB9 ....24 D7
Bailey Mews CB5 ......246 C3
Bain Cl PE9 ....244 C7
Bainton Rd Barnack PE9 .230 D4
Newborough PE6 ....204 F8
Bakehouse Hill CB8 .....70 E8
Baker Dr CB5 ....130 C3
Bakers Cl CB3 ....62 D6
Bakers La Barley SG8 ......6 F3
Linton CB1 ....35 D2
Peterborough PE2 ....186 E7
Bakers Way PE28 ......115 E2
Bakery Cl Fen Ditton CB5 ..84 E5
Wilburton CB6 ....210 C5
Bakewell Rd PE2 ......185 C2
Bala Ct PE4 ....204 E3
Baldock Rd SG8 ....4 C4
Baldock St SG8 ....5 D6
Baldock Way CB1 ....65 B5
Baldwin Cl
1 Wisbech PE13 ....245 D5
1 Wittering PE8 ....230 C1
Baldwins Cl CB3 ....60 C5
Baldwins Manor SG19 ...58 D4
Balingdon La 1 CB1 ....35 D3
Balintore Rise PE2 .....185 D4
Balland Field CB4 ......124 A8
Ballard Cl CB4 ....105 D3
Balmoral Rd 1 PE4 ....197 C8
Balmoral Way PE19 .....74 E2
Balsham Rd Fulbourn CB1 .67 B2
Linton CB1 ....35 D3
Bamber St PE1 ....197 F4
Bambers La PE14 ......236 C6
Bancroft Cl CB1 ....65 B6
Bancroft La CB7 ....212 B5
Bandon Rd CB3 ....82 F6
Banff Cl 2 CB4 ....83 E7
Banhams Cl CB4 ......246 C4
Bank Ave PE28 ....208 C8
Bank Cl PE7 ....189 E5
Bank Dr PE13 ....245 A7
Bank The PE13 ....234 C7
Bannister's Row PE13 ..245 B7
Bannold Ct CB5 ....106 B8
Bannold Dro CB5 ......106 C8
Bannold Rd CB5 ....106 D8
Banworth La CB4 ......105 D6
Baptist Rd PE14 ....229 D8
Bar Cl CB2 ....49 C5
Bar Dro PE14 ....236 B4
Bar La Hatley SG19 ......42 E2
Stapleford CB2 ....49 C4
Tadlow SG19 ....25 E8
Barbara Stradbroke Ave
CB8 ....89 B7
Barber Cl PE2 ....187 C7
Barbers Dro PE6 ....232 C8
Barbers Hill PE4 ....204 B7
Barcham Rd CB7 ....211 F7
Bardling's Dro PE12 ....237 A8
Bardney PE2 ....186 A4
Bardyke Bank PE14 ....229 F7
Baretts Cl PE7 ....189 D8
Barford Cl PE2 ....186 C7
Barford Rd PE19 ....74 E2
Bargate La IP28 ....213 D5
Bargate Rd IP28 ....213 D6
Barham Cl PE2 ....187 F5
Barham Ct SG8 ....14 D6

Barham Rd PE28 ...149 D6
Barker Cl
 Hail Weston PE19 ...95 A1
 Waterbeach CB5 ...106 B8
Barker's La PE15 ...243 D1
Barkham's La CB6 ...242 D4
Barkston Dr PE1 ...198 B6
Barkway Rd SG8 ...5 E5
Barkway St SG8 ...5 D5
Barkways CB5 ...130 C1
Barleuy Ct 6 PE19 ...74 D5
Barley Rd
 1 Eaton Socon PE19 ...74 C3
 Great & Little Chishill SG8 ...7 A7
Barley VP Sch SG8 ...7 A2
Barley Way CB1 ...35 D2
Barlings Ct CB8 ...111 A4
Barn Cl Huntingdon PE29 .142 A7
 6 Maxey PE6 ...231 C7
 Peterborough PE4 ...204 B3
 Ramsey PE26 ...172 A4
 Stilton PE7 ...175 F8
Barn Hill PE9 ...244 B5
Barnabas Oley CE Prim Sch
 SG19 ...58 E4
Barnack CE Prim Sch
 PE9 ...230 D4
Barnack Drift PE9 ...230 B3
Barnack Rd Bainton PE9 .230 E4
 St Martin's Without PE9 ..244 C4
Barnard Cl 1 PE19 ...74 F1
Barnard Way
 1 Cambridge CB4 ...83 D5
 9 Peterborough PE3 ...196 F3
Barnes Cl Cambridge CB5 .84 D2
 St Neots PE19 ...74 E6
Barnes Way
 Peterborough PE4 ...204 B3
 Whittlesey PE7 ...189 B8
Barnfield Gdns PE7 ...190 F8
Barnfield La PE28 ...98 D7
Barns Cl CB4 ...208 D1
Barns The PE19 ...117 B4
Barnstock PE3 ...197 A7
Barnwell Dr CB1 ...84 E2
Barnwell Rd CB1 ...84 D1
Baron Ct Eaton Socon PE19 74 B4
 Peterborough PE4 ...204 D4
Baron's Way CB3 ...99 B3
Barons La CB2 ...30 C5
Baros Cl CB1 ...22 A7
Barracks The PE13 ...237 E2
Barringer Way PE19 ...74 F7
Barrington CE Sch CB2 ..46 F1
Barrington Rd Orwell SG8 45 F1
 Shepreth SG8 ...29 D6
Barron's Gn SG8 ...29 F4
Barrons Way 1 CB3 ...62 C5
Barrow Cl CB2 ...64 E5
Barrow Rd CB2 ...64 E5
Barrowcrofts CB4 ...104 B5
Barrowfield PE1 ...198 E7
Barr's St PE7 ...189 D7
Barry Lynham Dr CB8 ..111 C2
Barry Wlk 3 PE2 ...186 F7
Barsey Cl CB9 ...38 C1
Barston Dro CB5 ...108 C7
Bartholemew's Wlk CB7 240 C2
Bartholomew Cl CB10 ...18 E2
Bartlow Rd
 Castle Camps CB1 ...22 D4
 Hadstock CB1 ...20 D7
 Linton CB1 ...35 E2
Barton Cl Cambridge CB3 .64 B8
 Witchford CB6 ...217 D1
Barton La PE13 ...237 F8
Barton Mews CB7 ...240 C4
Barton Rd Cambridge CB3 .64 B8
 Comberton CB3 ...62 D5
 Ely CB7 ...240 C3
 Haslingfield CB3 ...47 A7
 Wisbech PE13 ...245 A4
Barton Sch CB3 ...63 B4
Barton Sq CB7 ...240 D4
Bartons Cl CB1 ...53 B2
Bartons Pl 2 CB8 ...110 E5
Bartram Gate PE4 ...204 E1
Barway Rd CB7 ...211 E7
Bascraft Way PE29 ...142 A1
Basil Gn PE2 ...186 D6
Bassenhally Ct PE7 ...189 E7
Bassenhally Rd PE7 ...189 E8
Bassenthwaite PE29 ...141 B6
Basset Cl 3 CB4 ...83 F8
Bassingbourn Cty Prim Sch
 SG8 ...12 D4
Bassingbourn Rd SG8 ...12 B3
Bassingbourn Village Coll
 SG8 ...12 E4
Bateman Mews CB2 ...64 E7
Bateman St CB2 ...64 E7
Bate's Dro CB6 ...225 B3
Bateson Rd CB4 ...83 D4
Bates's Dro CB6 ...225 B5
Bath Cres PE28 ...143 B8
Bath Rd PE13 ...245 C7
Bath Row PE9 ...244 B4
Bathurst PE2 ...186 A4
Battle Gate Rd CB3 ...80 A8
Battle Rd PE26 ...171 E3
Baulk La SG19 ...43 A3
Baulk The Thriplow SG8 ...31 B2
 Whittlesey PE7 ...189 E8
Baulkin's Dro PE12 ...237 C8
Baulks The CB2 ...32 E7
Bawtree Cres CB1 ...35 E3
Baxter Cl 3 PE13 ...245 E6
Baycliffe Cl 1 CB1 ...65 D5
Bayfield Dr CB5 ...130 C2
Bayford Pl 1 CB4 ...83 F8
Bayliss PE29 ...118 F7
Beach Rd CB4 ...125 F3
Beachampstead Rd 1
 PE19 ...93 F6
Beacon Cl PE29 ...141 A6
Beald Way CB6 ...240 B4
Beale Ct 2 PE29 ...141 F8
Beales Way CB4 ...84 A7
Bean Cl 2 PE19 ...75 A6
Bear La SG7 ...2 D4
Beatrice Rd PE13 ...245 D7
Beatty Rd PE19 ...74 B2
Beauchamp Cl PE19 ...74 B3
Beaufort Dr PE16 ...241 B6
Beaulands Cl CB4 ...246 C4
Beaulieu Ct 1 PE6 ...232 A1
Beaumaris Rd PE28 ...168 C3
Beaumont Cl PE29 ...141 F8
Beaumont Cres CB1 ...65 D3
Beaumont Ct CB9 ...24 B6
Beaumont Rd CB1 ...65 D3
Beaumont Vale CB9 ...24 B6
Beaupre Ave PE14 ...236 F3
Beaupre Dro PE26 ...221 A2
Beauvale Gdns PE4 ...204 E3
Beauvoir Pl PE7 ...181 E5
Beaver Cl 8 PE19 ...74 B5
Bec Rd PE19 ...74 E5
Beccelm Dr 9 PE6 ...232 B8
Beche Rd CB5 ...84 A2
Beche Way CB4 ...105 C7
Beck Rd CB7 ...213 B4
Beck Row Prim Sch
 IP28 ...213 F8
Becket's Cl PE26 ...172 B8
Beckett Way PE16 ...241 C6
Beckingham PE2 ...185 F3
Bede Pl PE1 ...198 A6
Bedford Ave PE28 ...143 B8
Bedford Cl
 2 Needingworth PE27 ...208 A3
 St Ives PE27 ...143 F7
Bedford Ct 10 PE6 ...233 A3
Bedford Row PE13 ...238 D8
Bedford St
 Peterborough PE1 ...198 B4
 St Neots PE19 ...74 E6
 Wisbech PE13 ...245 C6
Bedford Way PE28 ...168 C3
Bedwell Hey La CB6 ...217 E1
Beech Ave
 7 Doddington/Wimblington
 PE15 ...223 A6
 Little Stukeley PE28 ...152 A2
 Peterborough PE1 ...197 F3
Beech Cl
 Great Shelford CB2 ...48 E3
 Huntingdon PE29 ...141 E7
 Isleham CB7 ...212 F5
 2 Thorney PE6 ...233 A3
 Warboys PE28 ...164 E4
Beech Croft CB8 ...70 D2
Beech Dr PE27 ...143 F5
Beech End PE28 ...150 F4
Beech Gr Haverhill CB9 ...23 E8
 March PE15 ...243 C5
 St Neots PE19 ...74 F6
Beech La Ely CB7 ...240 E5
 7 Eye PE6 ...232 A1
 Pampisford CB2 ...33 B5
Beech Rd PE6 ...203 D8
Beech Way CB1 ...35 C2
Beeches Cl IP28 ...213 D7
Beeches Prim Sch The
 PE1 ...197 F3
Beeches Rd IP28 ...213 D7
Beeches The CB4 ...83 F5
Beechside SG19 ...41 C6
Beechwood Ave
 Bottisham CB5 ...86 F6
 Melbourn SG8 ...14 C5
Beechwood Cl
 Exning CB8 ...110 C8
 Peterborough PE1 ...198 C7
Beechwood Rd PE13 ...245 D7
Beehive Centre Ret Pk
 CB1 ...84 B2
Bee's La PE13 ...237 F6
Beeson Cl PE19 ...95 F2
Beeston Dr PE7 ...187 F5
Beeton Cl SG8 ...14 C6
Beetons Cl PE7 ...181 E5
Beezling Cl 9 PE19 ...74 C6
Beezling Fen Dro PE26 .222 D3
Begdale Rd PE14 ...235 F5
Begwary Cl 7 PE19 ...74 B5
Beild Dro CB6 ...218 B7
Belbin Way CB2 ...32 D8
Beldam Ave SG8 ...5 E5
Beldam's Cl CB3 ...61 D4
Beldams PE27 ...208 A3
Belgrave Rd CB1 ...65 C8
Belgrave Sq PE28 ...168 B4
Belham Rd PE1 ...197 E7
Bell Cl Ely CB6 ...240 D5
 Meldreth SG8 ...14 A8
 Stilton PE7 ...176 A7
Bell Dro PE6 ...232 F6
Bell Foundry Cl 1 SG19 .41 D5
Bell Gdns
 Haddenham CB6 ...210 A6
 Soham CB7 ...212 B4
Bell Hill CB4 ...104 B4
Bell Holt 2 CB7 ...240 E4
Bell La Alconbury PE28 ...150 F4
 Barton Mills IP28 ...239 D2
Bell La *continued*
 Fenstanton PE28 ...121 B5
 4 Market Deeping PE6 ...231 F8
 Nuthampstead SG8 ...1 A2
 Southoe & Midloe PE19 ...95 E6
Bell Rd CB5 ...86 E5
Bellairs CB6 ...216 E1
Bellamy's La PE14 ...238 D4
Belle Isle PE28 ...140 B3
Belle Isle Cres PE28 ...140 B3
Belle Vue PE2 ...187 C6
Bellman's Cl PE7 ...189 F7
Bellman's Rd PE7 ...189 F6
Bellmans Gr PE7 ...190 A7
Bell's Dro Littleport CB6 .225 B6
 Sutton St James PE12 ...237 C8
Bell's Pl PE1 ...198 A2
Bells Mdw SG8 ...11 A5
Belmont Pl CB5 ...246 B3
Belmont Rd PE15 ...243 D5
Belmore Cl 1 CB4 ...83 C5
Belsars Cl 1 CB4 ...209 A1
Belsay Dr PE2 ...187 F5
Belsize Ave PE2 ...186 E6
Belt Dro PE14 ...235 F4
Belt The CB8 ...73 D8
Belton Rd PE7 ...187 F5
Belton St PE9 ...244 C5
Belton's Hill PE28 ...137 F7
Belvedere 5 PE26 ...221 C2
Belvoir Rd CB4 ...246 C4
Belvoir Way PE1 ...198 C8
Benams Cl PE5 ...195 E2
Bencroft La PE28 ...165 A4
Bendyshe Way CB2 ...30 A8
Benedict Sq PE4 ...204 A2
Benedict St CB6 ...240 B5
Benefield Rd CB8 ...112 F6
Benet Cl CB4 ...105 C1
Bene't St CB2 ...246 A2
Benians Ct CB3 ...83 B3
Benland PE3 ...197 A6
Bennett Rd IP28 ...214 A1
Benny's Way CB3 ...82 B2
Benson Pl 5 CB4 ...83 C4
Benson St 4 CB4 ...83 C4
Benstead End CB1 ...68 A8
Bentham Way CB6 ...240 E6
Bentinck St CB2 ...246 B1
Bentley Cl PE26 ...171 B2
Bentley Rd CB2 ...64 E5
Bentley St PE9 ...244 C5
Benwick Prim Sch PE15 222 A5
Benwick Rd
 Doddington PE15 ...222 D5
 Ramsey PE26 ...221 E3
 Whittlesey PE7 ...221 D7
Benyon Gr PE2 ...186 B4
Berberis Cl 3 PE6 ...232 F3
Beresford Rd CB6 ...240 A5
Bergamont Cl 5 PE29 ..118 F8
Bergamot Rd CB9 ...23 C8
Bergholt Cl 4 CB5 ...84 E4
Berkeley Rd PE3 ...197 C3
Berkley Ct 1 PE19 ...74 E4
Berkley St PE19 ...74 E4
Bermuda Rd CB4 ...83 C4
Bermuda Terr CB4 ...83 C4
Bernard Cl PE29 ...141 D6
Bernard Rd PE28 ...140 D3
Bernard St CB6 ...240 C4
Berristead Cl CB6 ...210 C6
Berry Cl CB6 ...210 F5
Berry Gn CB6 ...210 F5
Berry Green Pk NN14 ...156 E5
Berry La PE29 ...118 C8
Berrybut Way PE9 ...244 D7
Berrycroft Soham CB7 ...212 B4
 Willingham CB4 ...124 A8
Berryfield PE15 ...243 E7
Bertie La 6 PE9 ...230 C6
Betjamin Rd SG8 ...5 D8
Betjeman Rd SG8 ...13 D1
Betony Vale SG8 ...5 E5
Bettles Cl PE1 ...198 A6
Betts Cl PE29 ...141 F1
Between Close Dro
 CB4 ...125 D2
Bevan Cl PE29 ...141 E6
Beverley Cl SG8 ...5 B8
Beverley Gdns PE9 ...244 A6
Beverley Way 4 CB2 ...64 D3
Beverstone PE2 ...185 D5
Beville PE28 ...161 F6
Bevills Cl 16 PE15 ...223 A5
Bevis La PE13 ...235 C6
Bew Cl PE2 ...187 D4
Bicton Ind Est PE28 ...114 B7
Bifield PE2 ...185 F3
Big Gn PE8 ...178 C3
Biggen The CB2 ...17 E8
Biggin Abbey★ CB5 ...84 F8
Biggin La Fen Ditton CB5 ..84 F8
 Ramsey PE26 ...171 E6
Biggs Rd PE14 ...236 D8
Bigram's La PE19 ...114 C7
Bilberry Cl 1 PE19 ...74 C5
Bilberry End CB1 ...20 C7
Bill Rickaby Dr CB8 ...111 A5
Binnimoor Rd PE15 ...228 E4
Birch Ave PE16 ...241 D5
Birch Cl Cambridge CB4 ...83 F5
 Chatteris PE16 ...241 D5
 Ely CB7 ...240 E5
 Yaxley PE7 ...182 A5
Birch Dr PE28 ...151 E3
Birch Gr 2 PE14 ...236 B5
Birch Trees Rd CB2 ...49 A6
Birchen Cl PE7 ...186 C3
Birches The CB7 ...212 A5
Birchtree Ave PE1 ...198 A7
Birchwood PE2 ...186 A3
Birchwood Ave PE15 ...243 B2
Bird Farm Rd CB1 ...66 E5
Bird La PE19 ...95 A1
Bird's Dro Gorefield PE13 237 D1
 Sutton St James PE12 ...237 B8
Birds Cl CB10 ...18 A3
Birdwood Rd CB1 ...65 D6
Birkdale Ave
 Mildenhall IP28 ...239 B5
 Peterborough PE4 ...204 B3
Birt La 1 PE27 ...144 A3
Biscay Cl CB9 ...24 C7
Bishop Cl PE7 ...175 F7
Bishop Creighton CP Sch
 PE1 ...198 B2
Bishop Laney Dr CB6 ...240 E7
Bishop Way CB4 ...104 C3
Bishop Wynn Cl CB7 ...240 D3
Bishop's Ct CB2 ...64 C1
Bishop's Pal★ CB6 ...217 F7
Bishop's Rd
 Cambridge CB2 ...64 D1
 Peterborough PE1 ...198 A1
Bishops Cl
 2 Little Downham CB6 ...218 A7
 Peterborough PE1 ...198 D5
Bishops Rd St Neots PE19 .74 F2
 19 Somersham PE28 ...215 C1
Bishops Way
 Buckden PE19 ...117 B4
 Great Paxton PE19 ...96 E4
Bishops Wlk
 2 Barnack PE9 ...230 D3
 Ely CB7 ...240 D4
Bittern Cl PE27 ...143 F7
Bittern Way 3 PE15 ...243 F5
Black Bank Rd CB6 ...218 B8
Black Bear La
 Leverington PE13 ...245 F7
 Newmarket CB8 ...110 F3
 Walsoken PE13 ...238 F1
Black Dike PE13 ...237 E6
Black Dro March PE15 ...223 E8
 Thorney PE6 ...233 A5
 Wisbech St Mary PE13 ...234 B3
Black Dyke PE13 ...237 F4
Black Ham Dro PE7 ...182 E2
Black Hill Rd PE27 ...143 E6
Black Horse Dro CB6 ...226 B6
Black Horse La
 Chatteris PE16 ...241 C6
 Swavesey CB4 ...122 E6
Black La Gorefield PE13 .237 C2
 Tydd St Giles PE13 ...237 C6
Black Swan Spinney
 PE8 ...194 A4
Blackberry Droveway
 CB5 ...108 C8
Blackberry Way 6 IP28 214 A1
Blackbird Way PE28 ...150 E4
Blackbush Dro PE7 ...220 D8
Blackdown Garth PE4 ..204 D3
Blackfriars Rd 8 PE13 .245 C5
Blackfriars St 8 PE9 ...244 C5
Blackhall Rd CB4 ...83 C7
Blackmans Rd PE7 ...175 D8
Blackmead PE2 ...186 B4
Blackmill Rd PE16 ...241 B2
Blackmore Cl 4 CB9 ...38 F1
Blacksmith Cl SG19 ...40 C3
Blacksmiths Cl
 Abbotsley PE19 ...57 B5
 Ramsey Forty Foot PE26 ..221 C2
Blacksmiths La
 Abbotsley PE19 ...57 B5
 Ellington PE28 ...139 A4
 Shudy Camps CB1 ...22 C5
Blackstone Rd PE29 ...141 C7
Blackthorn Cl
 Cambridge CB4 ...83 F6
 Chatteris PE16 ...241 C3
Blackthorn Ct
 Coates/Eastrea PE7 ...190 F8
 2 Soham CB7 ...212 A5
Blackwell Rd PE7 ...186 C2
Blackwood Rd PE19 ...74 B3
Bladon Way CB9 ...39 B1
Blair Way PE19 ...74 E2
Blake Cl SG8 ...13 D1
Blakeland Hill CB2 ...17 D8
Blakes Way PE19 ...74 B2
Blandford Gdns 1 PE1 .198 E7
Blandford Wlk 1 CB4 ...83 C6
Blashfield Cl 2 PE9 ...244 A6
Blea Wr PE29 ...141 B6
Bledwick Dro PE13 ...238 C3
Blench La CB1 ...34 F6
Blenheim Cl
 2 Cambridge CB1 ...65 E5
 3 Eaton Socon PE19 ...74 C4
 Haverhill CB9 ...39 B1
 Shepreth SG8 ...29 E4
Blenheim Dr PE27 ...143 F7
Blenheim Gr PE19 ...96 F8
Blenheim Rd PE26 ...171 E3
Blenheim Way
 Emneth PE14 ...245 E2
 1 Hardwick CB3 ...81 A4
 Yaxley PE7 ...181 E5
Blethan Dr PE29 ...141 A6
Blinco Gr CB1 ...65 B5
Blind La 3 Maxey PE6 ...231 C7
 Sawtry PE28 ...168 C3
Bliss Way CB1 ...66 A6
Block Fen Dro
 Chatteris PE16 ...216 C6
 Wimblington PE15 ...223 C5
Block Rd CB7 ...212 C1
Blockmoor Dro CB6 ...216 C4
Blockmoor Rd CB7 ...211 E6
Blois Rd CB9 ...24 F1
Bloomfield Cl PE19 ...95 E1
Bloomfield Way 1
 PE28 ...168 C4
Bloomsfield CB5 ...130 C1
Blossom St 3 CB1 ...84 A1
Blue Boar Dro CB6 ...218 D7
Blue La PE15 ...223 A7
Bluebell Ave PE1 ...198 A8
Bluebell Wlk 1 CB7 ...212 B4
Bluecoat Prim Sch The
 PE9 ...244 B6
Bluegate PE29 ...118 F7
Bluntisham Heath Rd
 PE28 ...155 F3
Bluntisham Rd
 Bluntisham/Colne PE28 ..208 D6
 1 Needingworth PE27 ...208 A3
Blunt's La PE7 ...189 E7
Blythe Gn PE28 ...115 D2
Blythe Way SG19 ...41 D5
Blyton Cl CB3 ...99 A3
Boardman Cl PE19 ...95 F2
Bodiam Way PE19 ...74 F2
Bodsey Ho★ PE26 ...221 B2
Bodsey Toll Rd PE26 ...221 B2
Boeing Way IP28 ...239 B5
Bogmoor Rd SG8 ...7 C1
Bogs Gap La SG8 ...11 B3
Bohemond St 3 CB7 ...240 E5
Boleness Rd PE13 ...245 C2
Boleyn Way CB9 ...23 D7
Boleyn Wlk 1 CB8 ...111 C3
Bolton Cl CB5 ...130 A2
Bona La PE13 ...235 B8
Boongate PE1 ...198 C3
Boot La CB2 ...29 E8
Boot The CB6 ...209 D4
Booth Way PE19 ...95 F1
Boot's Rd PE15 ...223 F6
Boretree Way PE29 ...141 A7
Borough Cl PE13 ...245 D3
Borough The CB6 ...209 E4
Borrowdale CB4 ...83 C6
Borrowdale Cl PE4 ...204 E3
Borthwick Pl PE2 ...185 D6
Bossert's Way CB3 ...80 C2
Boswell Cl PE1 ...197 E8
Bosworth Cl PE8 ...178 B3
Bosworth Rd CB1 ...65 D5
Bosworth Way 2 PE15 .243 D2
Botolph Gn PE2 ...186 C7
Botolph La CB2 ...246 A2
Bottels Rd PE28 ...164 E5
Bottisham H★ CB5 ...87 A8
Bottisham Park★ CB5 ...86 F7
Bottisham Prim Sch CB5 .86 F5
Bottisham Swimming Pool
 CB5 ...86 E6
Bottisham Village Coll
 CB5 ...86 E6
Bottle La PE13 ...237 C7
Bough La PE28 ...162 F1
Boulevard Ret Pk PE1 ..197 D7
Boundary Dr PE15 ...243 C3
Boundary Rd
 Haverhill CB9 ...24 D5
 Red Lodge IP28 ...214 A1
Bourdillon Cl 1 PE28 ...121 B6
Bourges Bvd PE1 ...197 D7
Bourgess Ret Pk PE3 ...197 F1
Bourn H★ CB3 ...60 C5
Bourn Parochial Sch
 CB3 ...60 C6
Bourn Rd CB3 ...59 F8
Bourn Windmill★ CB3 ...79 A1
Bourne Rd Cambridge CB4 84 C5
 Haverhill CB9 ...24 B8
Bower Cl PE1 ...198 C5
Bower's La 4 CB7 ...213 A5
Bowers Croft CB1 ...65 C3
Bowker Way PE7 ...189 C8
Bowlings Ct PE27 ...144 A3
Bowness Way 2 PE4 ...204 F2
Bowsers La CB10 ...20 B2
Bowthorpe Rd PE13 ...245 D5
Boxer Rd PE8 ...230 B1
Boxgrove Cl 14 PE6 ...232 A1
Boxworth End CB4 ...122 E3
Boxworth Rd CB3 ...100 C4
Boyce Cl PE7 ...189 D7
Boyces Rd PE13 ...245 E5
Boyton Cl CB9 ...39 A2
Bozeat Way PE3 ...197 C6
Brackenbury Cl 1 CB4 .104 C3
Brackhill Fen Dro PE28 .208 E8
Brackley Cl
 3 Cambridge CB4 ...83 D6
 Peterborough PE3 ...197 D3
Brackwood PE2 ...185 D6
Brackyn Rd CB1 ...65 B7
Bradden St PE3 ...197 C6
Bradegate Dr PE1 ...198 E7
Bradford's Cl CB5 ...86 E6
Bradley Rd Cowlinge CB8 ..72 F1
 Kirtling CB8 ...72 F3
Bradmore St CB1 ...246 C2
Bradshaw Cl PE29 ...141 E6
Bradwell Rd PE3 ...197 A2

Bradwells Ct CB1 ......246 B2
Braemar Gdns PE7 ....189 D6
Braggs La
  Hemingford Grey PE28 ..143 C1
  Wrestlingworth SG19 ....25 B4
Brailsford Cl **3** PE3 ..197 A4
Bramble Cl Haverhill CB9 .38 D1
  Whittlesey PE7 ....189 E6
  Yaxley PE7 ....182 A6
Bramble Ct **2** PE28 ...140 C3
Bramble End
  Alconbury PE28 ....150 F5
  Sawtry PE28 ....168 B3
Bramble La PE14 ....236 D3
Bramble Wlk PE15 .....243 E7
Brambles The
  Balsham CB1 ....53 C1
  Bar Hill CB3 ....102 D3
  Cambridge CB2 ....64 D2
  Girton SG8 ....83 A6
  Hemingford Grey PE27 ..143 F1
  3 Royston SG8 ....5 E5
Bramley Ave
  Melbourn SG8 ....14 D6
  2 Needingworth PE27 ..208 A2
Bramley Cl
  Cottenham CB4 ....125 D3
  Offord Cluny PE19 .....118 A1
Bramley Ct CB4 ....84 B6
Bramley Dr PE19 ....118 A1
Bramley Gr **4** PE28 ..208 C5
Bramley Rd Haverhill CB9 .23 C7
  St Ives PE27 ....144 B5
  Wisbech PE13 ....245 C7
Bramley Way CB3 ....81 A4
Bramleys The
  March PE15 ....243 D1
  Shepreth SG8 ....29 E4
Brampton Cl PE13 .....245 A4
Brampton Cl PE2 ......187 D6
Brampton Cty Inf Sch
  PE28 ....140 C2
Brampton Cty Jun Sch
  PE28 ....140 C2
Brampton Gdns PE19 ...75 A4
Brampton Rd
  Buckden PE19 ....117 C6
  Cambridge CB1 ....84 B1
  Grafham PE28 ....116 B7
  Huntingdon PE29 ......141 B3
  Royston SG8 ....5 F6
Brampton Wood Nature
  Reserve★ PE19 ....139 D1
Brancepeth Pl PE2 .....186 E7
Branch Bank Ely CB7 ..218 F6
  Littleport CB7 ....242 F1
Branch Rd CB3 ....62 C7
Brandon Pl CB1 ....246 C2
Brandon Rd IP28 ......239 C5
Brands Cl PE26 ....172 A5
Brangehill La CB6 .....216 D3
Brassey Cl PE1 ....197 E6
Bravo La PE28 ....151 C4
Brawn Way PE8 ....183 D1
Braybrook PE2 ....186 A3
  Braybrook CP Sch PE2 ..186 B4
Brays La PE28 ....240 D4
Breach La CB6 ....210 D6
Breach Rd PE28 ....116 A7
Bream Cl PE28 ....149 D6
Breckenwood Rd CB1 ..66 E6
Breckland Way IP28 ...239 C5
Brecon Way PE29 .....141 A4
Brenda Gautrey Way
  CB4 ....125 E3
Brendon Garth PE4 ...204 E1
Brent Cl IP28 ....239 D4
Brentwood Cl **6** CB5 ..84 E4
Breton Ave PE15 .....243 E2
Bretton Gate **2** PE3 ..197 A5
Bretton Gn **1** PE3 ..197 A5
Bretton Way Bretton PE3 197 A7
  Peterborough PE3 ......196 F2
Bretton Woods Com Sch
  PE3 ....197 A6
Brewerne PE2 ....186 A4
Brewers Cl CB4 ....123 F3
Brewers La PE13 .....238 C4
Brewers La SG8 ....29 B2
Brewery Mus★ PE9 ...244 B5
Brewery Rd CB2 ....33 A5
Brewhouse La CB7 ....212 B4
Brewin Ave PE15 .....243 B3
Brewin Chase The **1**
  PE15 ....243 D4
Brewster Avenue Inf Sch
  PE2 ....186 E8
Briar Way PE1 ....198 C5
Briars End CB6 ....217 E2
Briars The PE28 ......168 B3
Briary La SG8 ....5 C5
Brick Kiln Rd IP28 ...239 D5
Brick Kilns PE29 .....118 F8
Brick La CB6 ....216 E3
Brick Row SG8 ....8 D3
Brickberry Cl PE7 ....186 C2
Brickfields Ave CB8 ..110 D7
Brickhills **6** CB4 ...209 A1
Brickkiln La CB6 .....218 B7
Brickmaker's Arms La
  PE15 ....223 B5
Brickmakers Way CB6 .242 B1
Bridewell Cl IP28 ....239 B4
Bridewell Rd CB1 .....66 A5

Bridge Cl CB2 ....48 F6
Bridge Dro PE13 .....234 B7
Bridge End Earith PE28 208 E5
  Wansford PE8 ....194 A3
Bridge End Rd
  Freckenham IP28 ......213 E1
  Red Lodge IP28 ....213 F1
Bridge La
  Great Shelford CB2 ....48 E4
  Wimblington PE15 .....223 B8
Bridge of Sighs★ CB3 246 A3
Bridge Pl PE7 ....141 E3
Bridge Rd
  Broughton PE28 ......153 F8
  Ely CB7 ....240 E2
  Histon CB4 ....104 C2
  Impington CB4 ....83 C8
  Mepal CB6 ....216 E4
Bridge St Cambridge CB2 246 A3
  Chatteris PE16 ....241 B7
  Market Deeping PE6 ...231 E8
  Moulton CB8 ....112 F5
  2 Peterborough PE1 ..198 A1
  St Ives PE27 ....144 A3
  Whaddon SG8 ....13 B8
  11 Wisbech PE13 ...245 C5
  Wistow PE28 ....163 F7
  Wood Walton PE28 ....161 E6
Bridgehill Rd PE6 ....205 A6
Bridle End PE19 ......98 B2
Bridle Way CB3 ......63 F4
Brierley Wlk CB4 .....83 C7
Briery Fields **2** CB6 ..217 E1
Briggate Cres PE7 ...189 C6
Briggate E PE7 ....189 D6
Briggate W PE7 ......189 C6
Bright St PE1 ....197 F3
Brigland Cl **7** PE29 ..141 B6
Brigstock Ct PE3 ....197 C6
Brigstock Rd PE13 ...245 B7
Brimbles Way PE2 ....185 E5
Brimley Rd CB4 ......83 D6
Bringhurst PE2 ......186 A4
Brington CE Sch PE28 147 C4
Brinton Rd PE28 .....147 F7
Brinkley Rd Brinkley CB8 73 A4
  Carlton CB8 ....54 F8
  Westley Waterless CB8 .70 D3
  Weston Colville CB1 ...54 C8
Brinkman Rd CB1 ....35 D3
Bristol PE4 ....204 B3
Britannia Way PE13 ..245 C2
Britannic Wall CB1 ...65 F7
British Horse Racing Sch
  CB8 ....111 B8
Britten Pl CB1 ....65 D7
Broad Baulk CB6 ....210 F6
Broad Cl PE1 ....198 D5
Broad Dro Emneth PE14 236 C5
  Upwell PE14 ....229 D8
  Wisbech PE14 ....235 F5
  Yaxley PE7 ....182 B5
Broad Dro E PE13 ....237 E6
Broad Dro W PE13 ...237 B4
Broad End CB3 ....100 A4
Broad End La PE13 ...245 F4
Broad End Rd PE14 ..245 F4
Broad Gate PE12 .....237 A8
Broad La Cottenham CB4 125 E5
  Haslingfield CB3 ......47 A5
Broad Leas PE27 .....144 A4
Broad Piece CB7 .....211 F5
Broad St Bourn CB3 ..79 B4
  Cambridge CB1 ....246 C2
  Ely CB7 ....240 D3
  Haverhill CB9 ....23 F8
  March PE15 ....243 D4
  Stamford PE9 ....244 B5
  Whittlesey PE7 ....189 D7
Broad Way CB6 ......210 C6
Broad Wheel Rd PE6 .231 B4
Broadall's Dro PE26 .221 D3
Broadcroft Cres CB9 ..23 E8
Broadgate La PE6 ....231 E8
Broadgate Rd PE12 ..234 C8
Broadgate Way PE28 .178 B3
Broadhurst Rd **15** PE8 ..230 B1
Broadlands The PE1 ..198 E5
Broadmeadow CB2 ...49 F1
Broads Rd CB5 ....130 C6
Broadway Bourn CB3 ..60 D8
  Crowland PE6 ....232 B8
  Farcet PE7 ....187 C1
  Grantchester CB3 .....64 A4
  Witchford CB6 ....217 E1
  Yaxley PE7 ....181 E5
Broadway Gdns PE1 ..198 B5
Broadway The
  Oakington/Longstanton
    CB4 ....103 B5
  St Ives PE27 ....144 A3
Broadweir PE28 ......138 C4
Brockholt Rd CB3 ....78 E2
Brockley Rd CB3 .....100 B4
Brockwood Cl **2** SG19 ..41 D6
Brodsworth Rd PE7 ..187 F5
Bromholme La PE28 ..121 A6
Brook Cl Alconbury PE28 150 F4
  Histon CB4 ....104 A4
Brook Dam La **14** CB7 .212 B4
Brook End SG8 ....11 C3
Brook La Coton CB3 ..82 C7
  Farcet PE7 ....187 B2
  Stretham CB6 ....210 F5
Brook Rd
  Bassingbourn cum Kneesworth
    SG8 ....12 D4
  Eaton Socon PE19 .....74 C4

Brook Rd continued
  Kimbolton PE28 ....114 B2
  Newton CB2 ....31 B4
  Thriplow SG8 ....31 B4
Brook Service Rd CB9 ..24 A8
Brook St Elsworth CB3 ..100 B3
  Peterborough PE1 .....198 A2
  St Neots PE19 ....74 E5
  Soham CB7 ....212 C3
Brook The CB6 ....216 E1
Brookdale CB3 ....102 C3
Brooke Rd SG8 ....5 D8
Brookfield Cl CB2 ....32 F5
Brookfield Rd CB4 ....123 F3
Brookfield Rd Coton CB3 .82 B2
  Papworth Everard CB3 ..99 A4
  Sawston CB2 ....32 F5
Brookfield Way PE26 ..172 A4
Brookfields CB1 ......65 D7
Brookfields Cl CB8 ...111 B5
Brookfields Hospl CB1 .65 C8
Brookfurlong PE3 ....197 B6
Brookhampton St CB6 .18 A5
Brooklands Ave CB2 ..64 E5
Brook's Rd PE15 ......243 D4
Brooks Rd CB1 ....65 D8
Brookside
  Alconbury PE28 ....150 F4
  Cambridge CB2 ....246 B1
  Dalham CB8 ....92 E8
  Exning CB8 ....110 C3
  Great Paxton PE19 ....96 D4
  Huntingdon PE29 .....141 D5
  Moulton CB8 ....112 F5
  Oakington/Longstanton
    CB4 ....123 F2
  Orwell SG8 ....45 D1
  Peterborough PE4 ....204 D2
  St Ives PE27 ....143 B5
  Sawtry PE28 ....168 B5
  1 Sutton CB6 ......216 E2
  Toft CB3 ....61 D4
Brookside Gr CB6 ....242 C5
Brookside La **1** CB2 ..64 E7
Broom Cl PE1 ....198 A3
Broom Way PE27 .....144 B5
Broom Wlk **5** IP28 ..213 F8
Broomhill Cl **4** IP28 ..214 A1
Brotherhood Cl PE4 ..197 D8
Brotherhood Ret Pk
  PE4 ....197 D8
Broughton La PE28 ..154 B8
Brownes Rd **6** PE8 ..230 B1
Browning Dr PE19 ...74 C6
Brownlow Dr **8** PE6 ..231 F8
Brownlow Quay PE9 ..244 C5
Brownlow Rd
  Cambridge CB4 ....83 C6
  Peterborough PE1 ....198 A3
Brownlow St **7** PE9 ..244 C5
Brown's Sq **6** PE19 ..74 F5
Broxbourne Cl **4** CB1 ..66 A7
Bruces Cl PE7 ....168 D8
Brudenell PE2 ....185 E2
Brunel Dr PE7 ....181 D6
Brunswick Ct CB1 ....66 E5
Brunswick Gdns CB5 ..246 C3
Brunswick Terr CB5 ..246 C3
Bryan Cl PE26 ....172 B6
Brybank Rd CB9 .....38 C1
Brynmore PE3 ....204 A1
Bryony Cl
  Coates/Eastrea PE7 ...190 C7
  Haverhill PE28 ....38 E1
Buchan St CB4 ....83 E7
Buckden CE Prim Sch
  PE19 ....117 B4
Buckden Rd
  Brampton PE28 ....117 D7
  Grafham PE28 ....116 A6
Bucking Way Rd CB3 ..101 D8
Buckingham Dr CB6 ..240 D6
Buckingham Rd
  Cambridge CB3 ....83 C3
  Haverhill CB9 ....23 E7
Buckingham Way PE28 168 C2
Buckland Cl PE3 .....197 B4
Buckle St PE1 ....198 C3
Buckles Gdns PE7 ...189 F7
Buckley Rd PE19 .....74 E4
Buck's Dro PE26 .....220 D4
Buck's La CB3 ....45 F7
Bucksholt Rd PE14 ..238 C3
Buckthorn **2** CB7 ..240 F6
Buckworth Rd PE28 ..150 C5
Budge Cl PE28 ....140 C2
Budleigh Cl CB1 .....65 D7
Buff La SG19 ....43 A7
Buffalo Way CB1 .....66 A7
Building End Rd SG8 ..1 F7
Bukehorn Rd PE6 ....232 D4
Bull La Broughton PE28 164 A1
  Langley CB11 ....1 F2
  Peakirk PE6 ....206 B2
  West Wratting CB1 ....53 F6
Bullard Laboratories
  CB3 ....83 A4
Bullen Cl CB1 ....65 D5
Bullfinch Way CB4 ...125 D5
Bullock Rd Elton PE8 ..184 B1
  Folksworth & Washingley
    PE7 ....174 E7
  Great Gidding PE28 ...167 B6
  Little Gidding PE28 ...167 D2
Bulstrode Gdns CB3 ..83 A2
Bulteel Cl **1** CB4 ..105 C3
Bumpstead Rd
  Haverhill CB9 ....24 B5

Bumpstead Rd continued
  Helions Bumpstead CB9 .24 B4
Bunbury Ave IP28 ....239 C5
Bunting's Dro PE7 ...188 C4
Bunting's La CB5 .....178 B3
Buntings Cres CB5 ...130 B3
Buntings La PE7 .....187 B5
Buntings Path CB5 ..130 B3
Bunyan Cl **4** SG19 ..41 D5
Burberry Rd PE19 ....117 B3
Burcroft Rd CB6 .....245 B6
Burdett Cl **3** PE15 ..223 A5
Burdett Gr PE7 ......189 F6
Burdett Rd PE13 .....245 B4
Bure Cl PE27 ....144 B6
Burford Way PE1 ....198 D6
Burgess Rd CB5 .....106 B7
Burgess's Dro CB5 ...106 C7
Burghley Ave **9** PE8 ..230 B1
Burghley Cl **9** PE6 ..231 F8
Burghley Ho★ PE9 ...244 F3
Burghley La PE9 .....244 C3
Burghley Rd
  1 Peterborough PE1 ..198 A3
  4 Stamford PE9 .....244 A7
Burghley Rise CB5 ..130 C2
Burghley Sq **2** PE1 ..198 A3
Burghleys Rd CB4 ...104 D3
Burgoynes Farm Cl CB4 104 D3
Buristead Rd CB2 ....48 F5
Burkett Way CB4 ....104 B5
Burleigh Pl CB1 .....246 C3
Burleigh Rd PE27 ...143 F8
Burleigh St CB1 .....246 C3
Burling Wlk **1** CB4 ..105 D3
Burlington Way PE28 .143 C1
Burma Rd CB2 ....32 A1
Burmer Rd PE1 ......197 E7
Burmoor Cl **6** PE29 ..141 B6
Burn St PE15 ....243 D5
Burnaby Cl PE28 ....140 C3
Burnet Gdns PE15 ...243 E7
Burnett Way PE29 ..141 F8
Burnham Cl CB1 .....66 A6
Burns Cl PE1 ....197 F7
Burns Ct **3** PE19 ..74 D5
Burns Rd SG8 ....5 C8
Burns Way PE27 .....144 B6
Burnsfield Inf Sch PE16 241 B5
Burnsfield St PE16 ..241 B5
Burnside CB1 ....65 D7
Burnt Chy Dro CB6 ..225 B4
Burnt Cl Grantchester CB3 .64 A4
  St Neots PE19 ....74 E3
Burnt Up Dro PE7 ...188 F2
Burnthouse Rd PE7 ..191 E4
Burnthouse Sidings
  PE7 ....191 F1
Burrel Rd PE27 ......144 B6
Burrell Cres IP28 ...239 C2
Burrell Way CB1 .....53 B2
Burrett Gdns **2** PE13 ..238 F1
Burrett Rd PE13 .....238 F1
Burrettgate Rd
  6 Leverington PE13 ..238 F1
  Walsoken PE13 ....245 F5
Burrough Field CB4 ..104 C1
Burrough Green Endowed CE
  Prim Sch CB8 ....70 F4
Burrowmoor Jun & Inf Sch
  PE15 ....243 C3
Burrowmoor Rd PE15 .243 C2
Burstellars PE27 ....144 A6
Burswood PE2 ....185 F2
Burton Cl CB9 ....23 E7
Burton Cl PE1 ....198 C3
Burton End Haverhill CB9 .23 E7
  West Wickham CB1 ....37 C8
Burton End CP Sch CB9 .23 D7
Burton Hill CB9 .....38 D5
Burton St PE1 ....198 C3
Burton Way PE28 ....137 F6
Burwell Mus★ CB5 ..130 C1
Burwell Rd
  Eaton Socon PE19 ....74 C4
  Exning CB8 ....110 A8
  Reach CB5 ....129 E1
  Swaffham Prior CB5 ...108 E5
Burwell Reach PE2 ..186 C7
Burwell Village Coll
  CB5 ....130 B3
Bury CE Sch PE26 ...172 A4
Bury Cl Ramsey PE26 ..171 F4
  St Ives PE27 ....143 F5
Bury Gn CB6 ....218 A4
Bury La Chrishall SG8 ..8 D1
  Haddenham CB6 ......210 A5
  Lidgate CB8 ....73 F8
  Meldreth SG8 ....14 A5
  Moulton CB8 ....112 F6
  Sutton CB6 ....216 D2
Bury Rd
  Great Shelford CB2 ...49 C4
  Kentford CB8 ....134 B2
  Mildenhall IP28 ......239 C4
  Newmarket CB8 ......111 C5
  Ramsey PE26 ....172 A5
  Snailwell CB8 ....111 E8
Bury Way PE27 ......143 F5
Buryfield PE26 ......172 A4
Burystead PE2 ......187 B8
Bush Cl PE13 ....62 D5
Bush La PE13 ....245 E5
Bushel La CB7 ....212 B4
Bushfield Com Coll PE2 185 E3
Bushfield Sports Ctr
  PE2 ....185 E4
Bushmead Gdns PE19 .74 B3

Bushmead Jun Sch PE19 74 A3
Bushmead Rd PE19 ...74 A3
Bustard Hill PE28 ...113 D8
Bustler's Rise CB2 ...17 C8
Butcher Cl **2** CB4 ..105 C3
Butcher's Hill CB10 ..18 A4
Butcher's La SG19 ...25 B4
Butcher's Row **3** CB7 240 D4
Butler Way
  Cambridge CB4 ....83 D6
  1 Haslingfield CB3 ..47 A5
Butlers Way CB2 .....32 F7
Butt Ave PE15 ....243 B2
Butt La
  Great Wilbraham CB1 ..68 A7
  Milton CB4 ....105 B3
Buttermel Cl **1** PE29 ..118 F8
Buttermere PE29 ....141 B6
Buttermere Pl **4** PE4 ..204 E3
Button End CB2 ....47 D4
Butt's La CB7 ....211 F1
Butts Cl **6** Soham CB7 212 B3
  20 Somersham PE28 ..215 C1
Butts The Fowlmere SG8 ..15 D8
  Soham CB7 ....212 B3
Buttsgrove Way PE29 .141 F7
Buxtons La SG8 ....10 F3
Buzzard Cl PE28 .....142 B8
Byall Fen Dro PE15 ..223 E2
Bydand La PE15 ......95 F2
Byfield Rd CB3 ....99 B3
Byng Cl PE19 ....74 F2
Byron Cl Huntingdon PE29 141 F6
  Peterborough PE2 ....187 D6
Byron Pl **10** PE19 ..74 F4
Byron Rd **4** SG8 ....5 E8
Byron Sq CB2 ....64 D2
Bythorn Rd PE2 ....187 D6
Bythorne Bank PE13 .237 C7

C

Cabbage Moor CB2 ...48 E8
Cadenham Rd CB5 ...108 E3
Cadwin Field CB4 ....83 F7
Caernarvon Rd PE19 .74 F2
Cage Hill CB5 ....108 D5
Cage La
  Great Staughton PE19 ..94 B6
  Stretham CB6 ....210 F5
Caldbeck Cl PE4 .....204 C3
Caldecote Cl PE2 ....187 E6
Caldecote Rd
  St Neots PE19 ....74 E3
  Stilton PE7 ....175 E7
Caldervale PE2 ......186 C6
Caledon Way **1** CB4 ..83 E8
Calfe Fen Cl **2** CB7 ..212 B5
Calfe Fen Dro CB7 ...212 B5
California Rd
  Huntingdon PE29 .....141 E6
  St Ives PE27 ....143 E6
Callander Cl CB4 ....83 D7
Calvin Cl CB4 ....125 F3
Cam Cl PE27 ....144 A7
Cam Cswy CB4 ....84 B6
Camargue Dr PE15 ..243 D2
Camargue Pl **4** PE13 ..245 E3
Camber's New Dro PE7 .220 D8
Cambrian Way PE4 ..204 C1
Cambridge & Cty Folk Mus★
  CB3 ....246 A4
Cambridge Acad CB1 246 B3
Cambridge Airport CB1 .84 F2
Cambridge Ave PE1 ..197 C5
Cambridge Cl
  Haverhill CB9 ....38 E1
  St Ives PE27 ....143 F8
Cambridge Cres SG8 ..13 A8
Cambridge Ct **10** PE19 ..74 F5
Cambridge Dr
  1 St Ives PE27 ....143 F8
  Wisbech PE13 ....245 A6
Cambridge Gdns PE19 .74 F5
Cambridge Pl CB1 ...246 C1
Cambridge Rd
  Babraham CB2 ....50 D4
  Balsham CB1 ....52 F2
  Barley SG8 ....7 A3
  Barton CB3 ....62 E1
  Ely CB7 ....240 B3
  Eynesbury Hardwicke PE19 76 B4
  Fenstanton PE28 .....121 A6
  Foxton CB2 ....30 C7
  Fulbourn CB1 ....66 A5
  Girton CB3 ....82 E8
  Godmanchester PE29 ..141 F2
  Great Shelford CB2 ...48 F7
  Hardwick CB3 ....81 B3
  Hauxton CB2 ....48 A5
  Histon CB4 ....83 C8
  Madingley CB3 ....81 F5
  Melbourn SG8 ....14 E7
  Milton CB4 ....105 C1
  Newton CB2 ....31 B4
  Oakington/Longstanton
    CB4 ....103 C4
  Orwell SG8 ....45 C1
  St Neots Rural PE19 ..75 C5
  Sawston CB2 ....32 E8
  Stamford PE9 ....244 A6
  Stretham CB6 ....210 E3
  Thetford CB6 ....211 A8
  Thriplow SG8 ....30 F3
  Waterbeach CB5 ......105 F7
  Wimpole SG8 ....27 F6

Cambridge Regional Coll
　CB4 . . . . .83 F8
Cambridge Science Pk
　CB4 . . . . .84 B8
Cambridge Sq PE28 . . . .143 B7
Cambridge St
　Godmanchester PE29 . . .141 F2
　St Neots PE19 . . . . .75 A5
Cambridge Sta CB1 . . . . .65 A7
Cambridge Summer Sch of
　Tech CB3 . . . . .64 B7
Cambridge Univ Ctr
　CB2 . . . . .246 A1
Cambridge Way CB9 . . . .38 E1
Cambridgeshire Cl CB6 .240 B4
Camden Ct CB1 . . . . . . .246 B2
Camel Rd CB6 . . . . .242 C6
Camelia Cl PE4 . . . . . . .204 D3
Cameron Rd CB4 . . . . . . .83 E7
Campbell Cl IP28 . . . . .239 B6
Campbell Dr PE4 . . . . . .204 A4
Campbell La CB2 . . . . . . .64 C2
Campbell St CB1 . . . . . . .65 B8
Camping Cl CB6 . . . . . .210 A6
Campion Cl CB7 . . . . . .212 A5
Campion Pl PE1 . . . . . . .198 B8
Campion Way SG8 . . . . . . .5 E5
Campkin Rd CB4 . . . . . . .83 F7
Camps Cl CB5 . . . . .106 B7
Camps Rd Bartlow CB1 . . .21 B7
　Haverhill CB9 . . . . .23 F7
　Helions Bumpstead CB9 . . .23 B1
Camside CB4 . . . . .84 A4
Canal St CB PE13 . . . . .245 C5
Canberra Cl
　Bassingbourn SG8 . . . . . .13 B5
　Mildenhall IP28 . . . . . . .213 E8
Canberra Ct PE26 . . . . .171 F7
Canberra Dr PE27 . . . . .143 F7
Canberra Rd PE26 . . . . .171 E3
Candidus Cl PE4 . . . . . .204 B5
Canmore Cl PE28 . . . . .168 C2
Canners Cl CB3 . . . . .61 E5
Cannon St
　Little Downham CB6 . . . .218 A6
　Wisbech PE13 . . . . .245 C4
Cannon Terr PE13 . . . . .245 C4
Cannon's Cl SG8 . . . . . . .10 F5
Canon Cl CB9 . . . . .39 A1
Canon Dr PE9 . . . . .230 D3
Canonsfield PE4 . . . . . .204 A4
Cantelupe Rd CB3 . . . . . .47 C7
Canterbury Ave CB6 . . .240 A3
Canterbury Cl CB4 . . . . .83 C4
Canterbury Rd PE4 . . . .204 B3
Canterbury St CB4 . . . . .83 C4
Cant's Dro PE13 . . . . . .234 C4
Canute Cres CB6 . . . . . .240 E7
Canwell PE4 . . . . .204 A4
Capper Rd CB5 . . . . . . .127 C1
Capstan Cl CB4 . . . . .84 A3
Capthorne Cl PE7 . . . . .186 C2
Capulet Cl PE19 . . . . . . .74 C3
Car Dyke Rd
　Landbeach CB5 . . . . . . .105 F6
　Waterbeach CB5 . . . . . .106 A6
Caravere Cl CB4 . . . . . . .83 F8
Caraway Rd CB1 . . . . . . .66 E5
Cardiff Pl SG8 . . . . .13 A8
Cardigan St CB8 . . . . . .111 A3
Cardinal Way CB9 . . . . . .38 F1
Cardinals Gate PE4 . . . .204 A5
Caribou Way CB1 . . . . . .66 A7
Carisbrooke Ct CB4 . . . . .83 C5
Carisbrooke Way
　PE19 . . . . .74 F2
Carleton Crest PE4 . . . .204 A5
Carlton Cl Haverhill CB9 . . .38 F2
　Leverington PE13 . . . . .238 B2
Carlton Green Rd CB8 . . .55 A6
Carlton Rd CB8 . . . . .70 E1
Carlton Rise SG8 . . . . . . .14 D5
Carlton Way CB4 . . . . . . .83 D5
Carlyle Rd CB4 . . . . . . .246 A4
Carmel St CB10 . . . . .18 D2
Carmen St CB10 . . . . . . .18 D3
Carnation Way IP28 . . . .133 F8
Carnegie Rd PE8 . . . . . .230 B1
Caroline Pl CB1 . . . . . . .246 C2
Carpenters Way
　PE15 . . . . .223 A6
Carpond La CB6 . . . . . .210 C6
Carr Rd PE1 . . . . .198 D3
Carradale PE2 . . . . .185 D5
Carrick Cl CB1 . . . . .65 C5
Carrington's Dro PE6 . . .232 D4
Carron Dr PE4 . . . . .204 A3
Carrops The CB8 . . . . . .134 A6
Carsey Hill CB1 . . . . .65 C5
Carter Cl Brampton PE28 .140 C3
　Duxford CB2 . . . . .17 E8
Carter Rd CB5 . . . . .130 C3
Carter St CB7 . . . . .212 E1
Carter's Way CB4 . . . . .122 C5
Carters Cl PE3 . . . . .196 F3
Carters Croft CB10 . . . . .21 B1
Cartmel Way PE6 . . . . .232 A1
Cartwright Rd SG8 . . . . . . .5 D5
Caryer Cl PE2 . . . . .186 E6
Casburn's La CB5 . . . . .130 A3
Casewick H★ CB4 . . . . .230 D8
Casewick La PE9 . . . . . .230 D7
Casewick Rd PE9 . . . . . .230 E7
Castel Way PE7 . . . . . . .175 D8
Castelhythe CB7 . . . . . .240 D3
Casterton Rd PE9 . . . . .244 A6
Castle Ave CB9 . . . . .23 F7

Castle Camps Prim Sch
　CB1 . . . . .22 E5
Castle Dr PE6 . . . . .231 F7
Castle Dyke PE9 . . . . . .244 B5
Castle End Rd PE6 . . . . .231 D7
Castle Gdns CB28 . . . . .113 F4
Castle Hill PE29 . . . . . . .141 D3
Castle Hill Cl PE19 . . . . .74 C2
Castle La CB 23 E8
Castle Manor Upper Sch
　CB9 . . . . .23 E8
Castle Mid Sch CB9 . . . . .23 D7
Castle Moat Rd PE9 . . . .141 D4
Castle Mound★ CB4 . . .246 A4
Castle Row CB3 . . . . . . .83 C3
Castle Sq PE13 . . . . . . .245 C5
Castle St Cambridge CB3 .246 A4
　Stamford PE9 . . . . .244 B5
Castle Wlk CB9 . . . . .23 E8
Castor CE Sch PE5 . . . .195 E2
Castor Hanglands Nature
　Reserve★ PE6 . . . . . . .195 E7
Castor Rd Castor PE6 . . .196 C6
　Marholm PE6 . . . . .203 D3
Casworth Way PE5 . . . .195 D2
Catharine St CB1 . . . . . . .65 B8
Catherine Cl PE2 . . . . . .186 B7
Cathwaite PE4 . . . . .204 F1
Catkin Cl CB9 . . . . .38 E1
Catling's La PE13 . . . . . .238 C7
Cattell's La CB5 . . . . . . .106 B8
Cattle Dike PE13 . . . . . .237 E2
Cattle Mkt Rd PE1 . . . . .198 A2
Causeway
　Godmanchester PE29 . . .141 E1
　Great Staughton PE19 . . .93 F6
　Pampisford CB2 . . . . .33 C5
Causeway Cl
　Great Staughton PE19 . . .93 F6
　March PE15 . . . . .243 D3
Causeway Gdns PE15 . . .243 D3
Causeway Pas CB1 . . . .246 C3
Causeway Rd PE28 . . . .154 A8
Causeway The
　Bassingbourn SG8 . . . . . .13 A5
　Burwell CB5 . . . . .130 B2
　Elsworth CB3 . . . . .100 B4
　Haverhill CB9 . . . . .23 E8
　Isleham CB7 . . . . .213 A5
　March PE15 . . . . .243 D2
　Soham CB7 . . . . .212 B4
　Sutton CB6 . . . . .216 C2
　Thorney PE6 . . . . .232 E2
　West Wratting CB1 . . . . . .53 E5
Cavalry Dr PE15 . . . . . .243 E2
Cavalry Pk PE15 . . . . . .243 D3
Cavalry Prim Sch PE15 .243 E2
Cavell Cl CB3 . . . . .47 B4
Cavendish Ave CB1 . . . . .65 B5
Cavendish Cl PE28 . . . .168 C3
Cavendish Rd CB1 . . . . . .84 B1
Cavendish St PE1 . . . . .198 B4
Cavenham Rd IP28 . . . .214 E2
Caverstede Rd PE4 . . . .204 D1
Cavesson Ct CB4 . . . . . .83 C6
Caville White CB9 . . . . . .23 C8
Cawdor Pl PE19 . . . . . . .74 F2
Cawood PE15 . . . . .243 E6
Caxton End Bourn CB3 . . .60 B7
　Eltisley PE19 . . . . .77 F3
Caxton Gibbet★ CB3 . . .78 D6
Caxton H★ CB3 . . . . . . .78 E1
Caxton La CB 30 B5
Caxton Rd Bourn CB3 . . .60 C7
　Great Gransden SG19 . . . .58 E5
　St Ives PE28 . . . . .144 B6
Cecil Ct PE9 . . . . .244 C5
Cecil Lodge Cl CB8 . . . .110 F3
Cecil Rd PE1 . . . . .198 A6
Cedar Ave PE15 . . . . . . .223 A6
Cedar Cl Grafham PE28 . .115 F7
　March PE15 . . . . .243 E5
　Melbourn SG8 . . . . .14 C5
Cedar Cres SG8 . . . . .5 B6
Cedar Dr PE28 . . . . . . .151 E3
Cedar Gr PE1 . . . . .198 A8
Cedar Rd PE27 . . . . . . .143 F6
Cedar Wlk CB5 . . . . .86 F6
Celta Rd PE2 . . . . .186 F6
Celtic Cl PE2 . . . . .187 D7
Cemetery Rd
　St Neots PE19 . . . . .74 F5
　Whittlesey PE7 . . . . . . .189 F6
Cenacle The CB3 . . . . . . .64 C7
Centenary Way PE28 . . .140 C2
Central Ave
　Brampton PE28 . . . . . . .140 D1
　Peterborough PE1 . . . . .198 D4
Central Sq PE2 . . . . . . .187 D5
Centre Dr CB8 . . . . .111 D2
Centre Rd CB7 . . . . .212 C2
Cerris Rd PE1 . . . . .198 B7
Chadburn PE4 . . . . .205 A1
Chadley La PE29 . . . . . .141 F2
Chaffinch Way CB3 . . . . .79 C4
Chain Cl PE1 . . . . .198 B6
Chain Cswy CB6 . . . . . .209 B8
Chain Rd CB4 . . . . .208 C2
Chainbridge La PE28 . . .135 F8
Chalfont Cl CB1 . . . . .65 F6
Chalk Gr CB1 . . . . .65 D4
Chalk Rd PE13 . . . . . . .237 D1
Chalklands CB1 . . . . .35 C3
Chalky La SG8 . . . . .8 D2
Chalkstone Mid Sch CB9 .24 A8
Chalkstone Way CB9 . . . .39 A1
Chalky La SG8 . . . . .8 D2
Chalky Rd CB1 . . . . .34 C3

Challis Cl CB2 . . . . .29 F8
Challis Gn CB2 . . . . .29 F8
Chalmers Rd CB1 . . . . . .65 C6
Chamberlain Way PE19 . .74 F7
Chamois Cl PE2 . . . . .32 F6
Champions Cl SG8 . . . . .15 E8
Champneys Wlk CB3 . . . .64 C8
Chancellor Cl PE29 . . . .141 C7
Chancellors Wlk CB4 . . .83 C6
Chancery La PE6 . . . . . .232 A1
Chandler's Way PE15 . . .243 D2
Chandlers PE2 . . . . .185 E5
Chandlers Ct CB5 . . . . .130 B3
Chandlers Way PE26 . . .221 A4
Chantry Cl Cambridge CB4 .83 F4
　Chatteris PE28 . . . . . . .241 D6
　Peterborough PE1 . . . . .198 A5
　Swavesey SG4 . . . . . . .122 C6
Chantry The CB1 . . . . . . .67 A5
Chapel Ave PE13 . . . . . .235 B7
Chapel Cl Hilton PE28 . . .120 B1
　Litlington SG8 . . . . .12 A2
　Needingworth PE27 . . . .208 A3
　Waterbeach CB5 . . . . . .106 B7
　Wrestlingworth SG19 . . . .25 B4
Chapel Ct PE8 . . . . .194 B2
Chapel End
　Great Gidding PE28 . . . .166 D2
　Sawtry PE28 . . . . .168 C4
Chapel Field SG10 . . . . . .41 D4
Chapel Field La PE28 . . .215 D1
Chapel Gate PE12 . . . . .237 D2
Chapel Gdns
　Benwick PE15 . . . . .222 A5
　Coates/Eastrea PE7 . . . .190 C7
Chapel Hill CB2 . . . . .47 A3
Chapel La Chatteris PE16 .241 B6
　Downham CB6 . . . . . . .218 A6
　Easton PE28 . . . . .138 B4
　Elm PE14 . . . . .236 B6
　Elton PE8 . . . . .178 C8
　Fowlmere SG8 . . . . .15 E8
　Harston CB2 . . . . .47 F3
　Kirtling CB8 . . . . .72 C5
　Melbourn SG8 . . . . .14 C6
　Newton CB1 . . . . .238 B5
　Peterborough PE2 . . . . .185 F5
　Reach CB5 . . . . .129 D1
　St Ives PE28 . . . . .143 A5
　St Ives PE27 . . . . .144 A3
　Soham CB7 . . . . .219 B2
　Tydd St Giles PE13 . . . .237 F7
　Whittlesey PE7 . . . . . . .227 A3
　Wicken CB7 . . . . .211 E1
　Willingham CB4 . . . . . .208 E5
　Wimblington PE15 . . . .223 B6
　Wisbech PE13 . . . . . . .235 D5
Chapel Rd
　Beck Row, Holywell Row
　　& Kenny Hill IP28 . . . .213 D6
　Earith PE28 . . . . .208 E5
　Great Eversden CB3 . . . .45 F8
　Weston Colville CB1 . . . .54 B5
　Wisbech PE13 . . . . . . .245 B5
Chapel Row CB8 . . . . . . .91 F8
Chapel St Alconbury PE28 .150 F4
　Cambridge CB4 . . . . .84 A4
　Crowland PE6 . . . . .232 B8
　Duxford CB2 . . . . .32 D1
　Ely CB6 . . . . .240 C4
　Exning CB8 . . . . .110 B8
　March PE15 . . . . .243 D3
　Peterborough PE2 . . . . .187 C7
　Peterborough PE1 . . . . .198 B2
　Stretham CB6 . . . . .210 F5
　Warmington PE8 . . . . . .178 B3
　Waterbeach CB5 . . . . . .106 B7
　Wisbech PE13 . . . . . . .245 C4
　Yaxley PE7 . . . . .181 D5
Chapel Yd PE9 . . . . .244 C5
Chapelfield Rd PE13 . . .235 A2
Chapelfield Way PE13 . .245 F6
Chaplains Cl CB9 . . . . . . .38 F1
Chaplin's Cl CB1 . . . . . . .66 F5
Chaplins Cl PE7 . . . . . . .190 F8
Chapman's Cl SG8 . . . . . .14 C6
Chapman's Way PE28 . .208 E1
Chapmans Cl CB4 . . . . .105 C7
Chapmans Dr CB3 . . . . . .79 C3
Chapnall Cl PE13 . . . . . .245 F6
Chapnall Rd PE13 . . . . .245 F6
Chapple Dr CB9 . . . . .38 F1
Charcoal La PE28 . . . . . .140 C3
Charlemont Dr PE15 . . .224 B5
Charles Cl
　Newmarket CB8 . . . . . . .110 E3
　Ramsey PE26 . . . . .172 A7
Charles Cope Rd PE2 . . .185 F5
Charles Dr PE29 . . . . . . .142 A6
Charles Melrose Cl
　IP28 . . . . .239 B5
Charles Rd Stamford PE9 .244 A7
　Whittlesey PE7 . . . . . . .189 F6
Charles St Cambridge CB1 .65 B7
　Peterborough PE1 . . . . .198 B3
Charles' St PE19 . . . . . . .74 F5
Charles St PE13 . . . . . . .245 C4
Charnocks Cl SG19 . . . . .41 D5
Charnwood Cl PE2 . . . . .187 A7
Charrington Cl PE29 . . . .24 C6
Charters The PE9 . . . . . .230 C6
Chartfield Rd CB1 . . . . . .65 F6
Chase Cl CB9 . . . . .39 A1
Chase Rd PE15 . . . . . . .221 F6
Chase St PE13 . . . . .245 C6
Chase The Ely CB6 . . . . .240 B4
　March PE15 . . . . .243 C4

Chase The continued
　Thorney PE6 . . . . .200 E7
　Upwell PE14 . . . . .229 D7
　Whittlesey PE7 . . . . . . .220 E7
　Wimblington PE15 . . . .224 A8
　Wisbech PE13 . . . . . . .245 A7
Chaston Rd CB2 . . . . .49 A5
Chater Rd PE8 . . . . .230 B1
Chatsfield PE4 . . . . .204 A6
Chatsworth Ave CB4 . . . .83 C5
Chatsworth Pl PE3 . . . . .197 B2
Chatteris Rd
　Chatteris PE28 . . . . . . .215 D4
　Somersham PE28 . . . . .208 C8
Chaucer Cl Cambridge CB2 .64 E6
　Wisbech PE13 . . . . . . .238 B2
Chaucer Pl PE19 . . . . . . .74 D6
Chaucer Rd
　Cambridge CB2 . . . . .64 D7
　Peterborough PE1 . . . . .197 E8
　Royston SG8 . . . . .5 C8
Chaucer Way PE27 . . . .143 F6
Chauntry Rd PE9 . . . . . . .23 F7
Chawston Cl PE19 . . . . . .74 C5
Cheddars La CB5 . . . . . . .84 B3
Chedworth St CB3 . . . . . .64 C7
Chelmer Cl PE4 . . . . . . .144 B7
Chelmer Garth PE4 . . . .204 F1
Chelmer Rd CB9 . . . . . . .24 B8
Cheltenham Cl PE1 . . . .198 B6
Chelveston Way PE3 . . .197 C5
Chelwood Rd CB1 . . . . . .65 F6
Cheney Way CB4 . . . . . . .84 C5
Chequer La CB7 . . . . . .240 D4
Chequer St PE1 . . . . . . .121 B6
Chequers Cl
　Alconbury Weston PE28 .150 C6
　Cambridge CB1 . . . . .65 C5
　Fenstanton PE28 . . . . . .121 B6
Chequers Croft PE28 . . .120 B2
Chequers La CB3 . . . . . . .99 B3
Chequers Rd CB4 . . . . .104 C3
Chequers Way PE29 . . . .141 D4
Cherry Bounds Rd CB3 . .32 B8
Cherry Cl Cambridge CB1 .65 E5
　Linton CB1 . . . . .35 B3
　Milton CB4 . . . . .105 D3
Cherry Dr SG8 . . . . .5 E7
Cherry Hill IP28 . . . . . . .214 C3
Cherry Hinton Com Jun Sch
　CB1 . . . . .66 A6
Cherry Hinton Inf Sch
　CB1 . . . . .65 F6
Cherry Hinton Rd
　Cambridge CB1 . . . . .65 B6
　Great Shelford CB2 . . . . .65 D1
　Teversham CB1 . . . . .66 A8
Cherry Holt La PE9 . . . .244 D5
Cherry Orch Fulbourn CB1 .66 D5
　Haddenham CB6 . . . . . .210 A5
　Oakington/Longstanton
　　CB4 . . . . .103 C5
Cherry Orton Rd PE2 . . .185 F5
Cherry Rd PE13 . . . . . . .245 C8
Cherry Rise CB6 . . . . . .216 D1
Cherry Tree Ave CB2 . . . .49 C4
Cherry Tree Cl
　Huntingdon PE29 . . . . . .141 C6
　Litlington SG8 . . . . .12 A1
Cherry Tree Gr PE7 . . . .189 F6
Cherry Tree Way PE28 . .121 B6
Cherry Trees CB2 . . . . . .48 C2
Cherryfields PE2 . . . . . .185 E6
Cherryholt Ave PE15 . . .243 C3
Cherryholt Rd PE9 . . . . .244 D5
Cherrytree Gr PE1 . . . . .198 C6
Cherrytree La CB7 . . . . .212 B3
Cherrywood Ave PE15 . .243 B3
Cherrywood Gn PE15 . . .243 B3
Chervil Cl PE7 . . . . .175 D8
Chervil Wlk CB3 . . . . . . .79 C3
Chesham Rd PE28 . . . . .168 C2
Chesnut Gr CB4 . . . . .83 F4
Chester Rd
　Peterborough PE1 . . . . .198 C3
　Wyton Airfield PE28 . . . .143 B7
Chesterfield Rd CB4 . . . .84 A6
Chesterton Com Coll
　CB4 . . . . .83 E4
Chesterton Gr PE2 . . . . .187 D6
Chesterton Hall Cres
　CB4 . . . . .83 F4
Chesterton Hospl CB4 . . .83 F4
Chesterton La CB4 . . . . .246 A4
Chesterton Rd CB4 . . . .246 A4
Chestnut Ave PE1 . . . . .198 C6
Chestnut Cl
　Brampton PE28 . . . . . . .140 D2
　Glinton PE6 . . . . .203 D8
　Grafham PE28 . . . . . . .116 A7
　Haslingfield CB3 . . . . . . .47 B4
　Haverhill CB9 . . . . .23 F8
　Huntingdon PE29 . . . . . .141 C6
　Mildenhall IP28 . . . . . .239 D4
　Peakirk PE6 . . . . .206 B2
　Sawston CB2 . . . . .32 E7
　Sawtry PE28 . . . . .168 B4
Chestnut Cres
　March PE15 . . . . .243 B3
　Whittlesey PE7 . . . . . . .189 E6
Chestnut Dr
　Soham CB7 . . . . .212 B4
　Thorney PE6 . . . . .233 A3
Chestnut Gr
　Little Stukeley PE28 . . . .152 A2
　St Neots PE19 . . . . .74 F4
Chestnut La SG8 . . . . . . .13 B6
Chestnut Rd St Ives PE27 .143 F6

Chestnut Rd continued
　Wisbech PE13 . . . . . . .245 C4
Chestnut Rise
　Bar Hill CB3 . . . . .102 D3
　Burwell CB5 . . . . .130 B4
Chestnut Way CB6 . . . . .216 E3
Chestnut Wlk SG8 . . . . . . .5 E5
Chestnuts The CB2 . . . . .48 A4
Cheveley Prim Sch CB8 . .91 C7
Cheveley Rd
　Newmarket CB8 . . . . . . .111 C3
　Woodditton CB8 . . . . . . .91 C3
Cheviot Ave PE4 . . . . . .204 C2
Chewells Cl CB6 . . . . . .210 A6
Chewells La CB6 . . . . . .210 A6
Cheyney Cl SG8 . . . . .11 B1
Cheyney St SG8 . . . . .11 B1
Chichester Way PE28 . . .115 D2
Chiefs St CB6 . . . . .240 C4
Chigwell Ct CB5 . . . . . . .84 C4
Chilcourt SG8 . . . . .5 C6
Childerley H★ CB3 . . . . .80 D8
Childers St PE7 . . . . . . .189 C8
Child's Pond Rd PE19 . . .75 A6
Childs La PE15 . . . . . . .223 A5
Chiltern Rise PE4 . . . . .204 C4
Chimswell Way CB9 . . . .23 C8
Chippenham Mews
　PE2 . . . . .186 C7
Chippenham Rd
　Chippenham CB8 . . . . . .133 C2
　Fordham CB7 . . . . .213 A1
　Freckenham IP28 . . . . .213 C2
　Moulton CB8 . . . . .133 D1
Chisenhale PE2 . . . . . . .185 E6
Chishill Rd Barley SG8 . . . .7 A2
　Great & Little Chishill SG8 . .7 F3
　Heydon SG8 . . . . .8 A4
Chishill Windmill★ SG8 . . .7 C2
Chiswick Ave IP28 . . . . .239 C6
Chiswick End SG8 . . . . . .14 A7
Chittering Dro CB5 . . . .127 C3
Chivers Rd CB9 . . . . .23 D7
Chivers Way CB4 . . . . . .104 C2
Chrishall Rd SG8 . . . . . . .15 F6
Christchurch St CB1 . . . .246 C3
Christie Dr PE29 . . . . . .141 A5
Christopher Cl PE1 . . . .197 F8
Christopher Dr PE13 . . .245 C4
Christopher Tye Cl
　CB6 . . . . .240 B5
Christ's Coll CB1 . . . . . .246 B3
Church Cl
　Bassingbourn SG8 . . . . . .12 E5
　Cottenham CB4 . . . . . . .125 F6
　Coveney CB6 . . . . .217 C5
　Dullingham CB8 . . . . .70 E8
　Exning CB8 . . . . .110 C8
　Great & Little Abington CB1 .34 C7
　Great Wilbraham CB1 . . . .67 F7
　Newborough PE6 . . . . .205 C8
　Ramsey PE26 . . . . .221 C2
　Stilton PE7 . . . . .176 A7
　The Stukeleys PE28 . . . .151 F2
　Whittlesford CB2 . . . . . . .32 C5
Church Cswy PE28 . . . . .168 C4
Church Dr PE2 . . . . .185 F5
Church Dro PE14 . . . . . .236 F2
Church End Arrington SG8 .44 D1
　Barley SG8 . . . . .7 A1
　Cambridge CB1 . . . . .65 F8
　Coton CB3 . . . . .82 B3
　Everton SG19 . . . . .40 C3
　Gamlingay SG19 . . . . . . .41 E5
　Hilton PE28 . . . . .99 B8
　Horningsea CB5 . . . . . .106 A2
　Leverington PE13 . . . . .238 B2
　Over CB4 . . . . .208 D1
　Rampton CB4 . . . . .124 F4
　Weston Colville CB1 . . . .54 A7
　Whaddon SG8 . . . . .28 B2
Church Farm La SG8 . . . .11 B1
Church Fen Dro CB6 . . .209 B2
Church Gate PE6 . . . . . .231 F8
Church Gdns IP28 . . . . .213 D6
Church Gn CB10 . . . . . . .18 B7
Church Hill Castor PE5 . .195 E2
Church Hill Cl PE7 . . . . .187 C1
Church La
　Abington Pigotts SG8 . . . .11 F6
　Arrington SG8 . . . . .44 D1
　Ashwell SG7 . . . . .2 D4
　Ashwell SG7 . . . . .2 D4
　Balsham CB1 . . . . .53 D4
　Barton CB3 . . . . .63 B4
　Barton Mills IP28 . . . . .239 D1
　Beck Row, Holywell Row
　　& Kenny Hill IP28 . . . .213 D6
　Brington & Molesworth
　　PE28 . . . . .147 A2
　Burwell CB5 . . . . .130 B1
　Cambridge CB2 . . . . .64 C2
　Castle Camps CB1 . . . . .22 E5
　Cheveley CB8 . . . . .91 C6
　Comberton CB3 . . . . .62 C3
　Conington PE7 . . . . . . .168 E8
　Cottenham CB4 . . . . . . .125 F6
　Covington PE28 . . . . . .135 C2
　Croydon SG8 . . . . .27 C3
　Doddington/Wimblington
　　PE28 . . . . .222 F5
　Ellington PE28 . . . . . . .138 F4
　Elsworth CB3 . . . . .100 B4

Church La continued
Ely CB7 . . . .**240** C4
Exning CB8 . . . .**110** C8
Fenstanton PE28 . . . .**121** B6
Fulbourn PE1 . . . .**67** A5
Gamlingay SG19 . . . .**41** D5
Girton CB3 . . . .**82** E8
Graveley PE19 . . . .**96** F7
Great & Little Abington CB1 **34** B7
Great Paxton PE19 . . . .**96** D5
Guilden Morden SG8 . . . . . .**10** F5
Haddenham CB6 . . . .**210** A6
Helpston PE6 . . . .**231** B4
Hemingford Abbots PE28 . .**143** A3
Hemingford Grey PE28 . . . .**143** C2
Hilton PE28 . . . .**120** B1
Huntingdon PE29 . . . .**142** A5
Isleham CB7 . . . .**213** A5
Kennett CB8 . . . .**133** F5
Kingston CB3 . . . .**61** B3
Leighton PE28 . . . .**148** D3
Linton CB1 . . . .**35** C2
Little Eversden CB3 . . . .**46** A7
Little Staughton MK44 . . . . .**93** B2
1 Littleport CB6 . . . .**242** D4
Madingley CB3 . . . .**81** E4
Milton CB4 . . . .**105** D2
Newmarket CB8 . . . .**111** A3
Newton CB1 . . . .**238** A5
Pampisford CB2 . . . .**33** B5
Papworth Everard CB3 . . . . .**99** A2
Peterborough PE2 . . . .**185** F5
Peterborough PE2 . . . .**187** B7
Ramsey PE26 . . . .**171** B2
Sawston CB2 . . . .**32** F7
Sibson cum Stibbington
    PE8 . . . .**194** E2
Snailwell CB8 . . . .**132** A3
Spaldwick PE28 . . . .**137** F6
Stamford PE9 . . . .**244** C4
Stetchworth CB8 . . . .**90** A2
Stow Longa PE28 . . . .**137** B3
Sutton CB6 . . . .**216** E2
Tallington PE9 . . . .**230** F6
Tilbrook PE28 . . . .**113** B7
Tydd St Giles PE13 . . . .**237** F6
Warmington PE8 . . . .**178** B2
Westley Waterless CB8 . . . . .**70** B5
Whittlesford CB2 . . . .**32** C5
Wilburton CB6 . . . .**210** B6
4 Willingham CB4 . . . .**209** A1
Worlington IP28 . . . .**213** F4
Wrestlingworth SG19 . . . . . .**25** B3
Church Lane Cl IP28 . . . . .**239** D2
Church Leys CB6 . . . .**121** C6
Church Mdw IP28 . . . .**239** D2
Church Mdws PE19 . . . . . .**74** F5
Church Path CB1 . . . .**20** B6
Church Pl PE29 . . . .**141** E2
Church Rd
Brampton PE28 . . . .**140** E2
Buckworth PE28 . . . .**149** D6
Carlton CB8 . . . .**55** A6
Catworth PE28 . . . .**136** D7
Chrishall SG8 . . . .**8** D3
Christchurch PE14 . . . .**229** D3
Conington PE7 . . . .**168** D8
Easton PE28 . . . .**138** B4
Everton SG19 . . . .**40** C3
Glatton PE28 . . . .**175** E1
Grafham PE28 . . . .**115** E7
Great Wilbraham CB1 . . . . . .**67** F8
Hauxton CB2 . . . .**48** A5
Leverington PE13 . . . .**245** F7
Little Stukeley PE28 . . . . . .**151** F2
Little Wilbraham CB1 . . . . . .**86** F2
Moulton CB8 . . . .**112** F5
Shepreth SG8 . . . .**29** E4
Shudy Camps CB1 . . . .**22** C5
Stow cum Quy CB5 . . . .**85** F4
Teversham CB1 . . . .**85** B2
Thistley Green IP28 . . . . . .**213** D6
Toft CB3 . . . .**61** E4
Warboys PE28 . . . .**164** E4
Wentworth CB6 . . . .**217** C1
Wicken CB7 . . . .**211** F1
Wisbech PE14 . . . .**236** A3
Wisbech PE13 . . . .**238** B1
Wisbech St Mary PE13 . . . .**235** B7
Wittering PE8 . . . .**230** B1
Church St Ashley CB8 . . . . .**91** F8
Bourn CB3 . . . .**60** C5
Buckden PE19 . . . .**117** A4
Cambridge CB4 . . . .**84** A4
12 Doddington/Wimblington
    PE15 . . . .**223** B7
Exning CB8 . . . .**110** C8
Fen Ditton CB5 . . . .**84** E6
Fen Drayton CB4 . . . .**121** F5
Fenstanton PE28 . . . .**121** B6
Fordham CB7 . . . .**212** F1
Gamlingay SG19 . . . .**41** D5
Great Chesterford CB10 . . .**18** D2
Great Eversden CB3 . . . .**45** E7
Great Gransden SG19 . . . . .**58** E4
Great Shelford CB2 . . . .**48** E4
Great Shelford CB2 . . . .**49** C4
Great Wilbraham CB1 . . . . . .**67** F8
Guilden Morden SG8 . . . . . .**10** F4
Harston CB2 . . . .**47** D2
Haslingfield CB3 . . . .**47** A5
Hemingford Grey PE28 . . . .**143** C2
Histon CB4 . . . .**104** B5
Holme PE7 . . . .**176** F4
Ickleton CB10 . . . .**18** A4

Church St continued
6 Isleham CB7 . . . .**213** A5
Litlington SG8 . . . .**12** A2
Little Gransden SG19 . . . . . .**58** E3
March PE15 . . . .**243** C1
Market Deeping PE6 . . . . . .**231** F8
Needingworth PE27 . . . . . .**208** A2
Northborough PE6 . . . .**206** A4
Northborough PE6 . . . .**231** F6
Old Hurst PE28 . . . .**154** D7
Peterborough PE7 . . . .**185** A4
Peterborough PE2 . . . .**187** C7
Peterborough PE1 . . . .**198** A2
Peterborough PE4 . . . .**204** C3
St Ives PE27 . . . .**143** F4
St Ives PE27 . . . .**144** A4
St Neots PE19 . . . .**74** F5
Sawtry PE28 . . . .**168** B4
1 Somersham PE28 . . . . . .**208** C8
Stamford PE9 . . . .**244** B1
Steeple Morden SG8 . . . . . .**11** B1
Stilton PE7 . . . .**175** F7
5 Thorney PE6 . . . .**233** A3
Thriplow SG8 . . . .**31** C1
Warmington PE8 . . . .**178** A3
Whaddon SG8 . . . .**28** B2
Whittlesey PE7 . . . .**189** D6
Willingham CB4 . . . .**209** A1
Wistow PE28 . . . .**163** F7
Withersfield CB9 . . . .**38** C4
Woodhurst PE28 . . . .**155** B5
Yaxley PE7 . . . .**181** D4
Church Terr 17 PE13 . . . . .**245** C5
Church View
9 Northborough PE6 . . . .**231** F7
Oakington/Longstanton
    CB4 . . . .**103** C6
4 St Neots PE19 . . . .**74** F5
3 Witchford CB6 . . . .**217** E1
Church View Cl PE2 . . . . .**187** B7
Church Way
Alconbury PE28 . . . .**150** E5
Alconbury Weston PE28 . . .**150** D6
Downham CB6 . . . .**218** A7
3 Haslingfield CB3 . . . . . .**47** A5
Little Stukeley PE28 . . . . . .**151** D4
Church Wlk
Chatteris PE16 . . . .**241** D5
Little Gransden SG19 . . . . . .**58** E3
Mildenhall IP28 . . . .**239** B4
Peterborough PE1 . . . .**198** A3
Stow Longa PE28 . . . .**137** B3
Sturmer CB9 . . . .**24** E5
Upton PE6 . . . .**195** B5
Churchfield SG8 . . . .**7** A1
Churchfield Ave CB2 . . . . .**32** F8
Churchfield Ct PE4 . . . . . .**197** E8
Churchfield Rd
Peterborough PE4 . . . .**197** D8
Upwell PE14 . . . .**236** F2
Churchfield Way
Whittlesey PE7 . . . .**189** C7
5 Wisbech St Mary PE13 . .**235** B7
Churchgate St 9 CB7 . . . .**212** B4
Churchill Cl 4 CB6 . . . . . .**216** E2
Churchill Ave
Haverhill CB9 . . . .**39** B1
Houghton & Wyton PE28 . .**143** B7
Newmarket CB8 . . . .**110** D5
Churchill Cl CB6 . . . .**240** A4
Churchill Coll CB3 . . . .**83** B3
Churchill Ct 3 CB6 . . . . . .**218** A6
Churchill Dr IP28 . . . .**239** B5
Churchill Rd
Gorefield PE13 . . . .**237** F3
Stamford PE9 . . . .**244** B7
Wisbech PE13 . . . .**245** D4
Churchyard The IP28 . . . .**239** B4
Cinques 8 CB6 . . . .**41** C6
Cinques The SG19 . . . .**41** B6
Cissbury Ring PE4 . . . .**204** C2
City of Ely Com Coll
    CB6 . . . .**240** C6
City Rd Cambridge CB1 . . .**246** C2
Littleport CB6 . . . .**242** E4
March PE15 . . . .**243** D4
Peterborough PE1 . . . .**198** A2
Clack La PE28 . . . .**135** D8
Clare Cl Mildenhall IP28 . .**239** D5
Stamford PE9 . . . .**244** A5
Waterbeach CB5 . . . .**106** A8
Clare Coll CB2 . . . .**246** A2
Clare Coll Pavilion CB2 . . . .**64** F5
Clare Pl CB8 . . . .**111** B2
Clare Rd Cambridge CB3 . . .**64** C8
Huntingdon PE29 . . . .**142** A7
5 Northborough PE6 . . . .**231** F7
Peterborough PE1 . . . .**197** F6
Clare St Cambridge CB4 . .**246** A4
Chatteris PE16 . . . .**241** B4
Claremont 1 CB1 . . . .**64** F7
Claremont Rd PE13 . . . . . .**245** E5
Clarence Rd
Peterborough PE1 . . . .**197** E5
Wisbech PE13 . . . .**245** D6
Clarendale Est CB8 . . . . . .**55** F6
Clarendon Rd
Cambridge CB2 . . . .**64** F6
Haverhill CB9 . . . .**23** F7
Clarendon St CB1 . . . .**246** B2
Clarendon Way PE6 . . . . .**203** F8
Clark Rd SG8 . . . .**5** D7
Clarke's La CB6 . . . .**210** C5
Clarkes Way SG8 . . . .**12** F5
Clark's Dro CB7 . . . .**212** A4
Clarkson Ave PE13 . . . . . .**245** D5
Clarkson Cl CB3 . . . .**83** B2
Clarkson Ct PE13 . . . .**245** D6

Clarkson Inf Sch PE13 . .**245** E6
Clarkson Rd CB3 . . . .**83** B2
Claudian Cl CB9 . . . .**24** D7
Clay Close La CB4 . . . .**104** D3
Clay La
Abbots Ripton PE28 . . . . .**162** A1
Castor PE5 . . . .**195** E2
Little Stukeley PE28 . . . . . .**151** F2
Clay St Histon CB4 . . . . . .**104** B5
Soham CB7 . . . .**212** B4
Claybush Rd SG7 . . . .**2** D3
Claydon Cl CB1 . . . .**22** E4
Claygate PE7 . . . .**189** D7
Claygate CB1 . . . .**65** F6
Clayhithe Rd
Horningsea CB5 . . . .**106** C5
Waterbeach CB5 . . . .**106** C6
Clayhive Dr 1 CB9 . . . .**23** F7
Claypole Dr 3 PE6 . . . . . .**231** F7
Clayton Cl PE13 . . . .**245** F6
Clayton Sch PE2 . . . .**186** B4
Claytons Way PE29 . . . . . .**141** F5
Clayway SG7 . . . .**240** E6
Clear Cres SG8 . . . .**14** D5
Cleatham PE3 . . . .**197** A4
Clematis Cl IP28 . . . .**213** F1
Clement's La CB9 . . . .**23** F7
Clement's Way 1 IP28 . . . .**213** F8
Clements Cl CB9 . . . .**23** F7
Clements CP Sch CB9 . . . . .**23** F7
Clements Dr CB9 . . . .**23** F7
Clerk Maxwell Rd CB3 . . . .**83** A2
Cleve Pl PE6 . . . .**232** A1
Cleveland Bay PE15 . . . . . .**243** E2
Cleveland Ct PE4 . . . .**204** E2
Cleves Rd CB9 . . . .**23** D6
Clifden Cl SG8 . . . .**44** D1
Cliff Cres PE9 . . . .**244** B5
Cliff Rd PE9 . . . .**244** B5
Clifton Ave PE3 . . . .**197** E3
Clifton Rd Cambridge CB1 . .**65** A6
Huntingdon PE29 . . . .**141** D7
Clive Hall Dr CB4 . . . .**124** A1
Cliveden Cl CB4 . . . .**83** C5
Cloisters The 6 CB7 . . . . .**240** D4
Close The Babraham CB2 . . .**50** E2
Godmanchester PE29 . . . . .**142** A1
Kennett CB8 . . . .**133** F5
Papworth Everard CB3 . . . . .**99** B3
Royston SG8 . . . .**5** F7
Sutton CB6 . . . .**216** E1
Clover Ct Cambridge CB1 . .**66** A5
5 Linton CB1 . . . .**35** D2
Clover End 2 CB6 . . . .**217** D1
Clover Field CB6 . . . .**23** D8
Clover Rd PE19 . . . .**74** C3
Clover Way 1 IP28 . . . .**214** A1
Cloverfield Dr CB7 . . . .**212** A5
Clydesdale Cl PE15 . . . . . .**243** E2
Clydesdale Rd 6 SG8 . . . . . .**5** E6
Coach Dr CB3 . . . .**46** D5
Coach House La CB2 . . . . . .**31** B7
Coach La CB8 . . . .**91** D5
Coalwharf Rd PE13 . . . . . .**245** B4
Coates Dro CB7 . . . .**213** A5
Coates Rd PE7 . . . .**190** D7
Cob Pl PE19 . . . .**118** F7
Cobbet Pl PE1 . . . .**198** B3
Cobden Ave PE1 . . . .**197** F4
Cobden St PE1 . . . .**197** F4
Cobholm Pl 4 CB4 . . . .**83** F8
Cock Bank
Whittlesey PE7 . . . .**191** C2
Whittlesey PE7 . . . .**221** F8
Cock Fen Rd PE14 . . . .**229** F3
Cockbrook La
Brington & Molesworth
    PE28 . . . .**147** C8
Old Weston PE28 . . . .**157** C2
Cockburn St CB1 . . . .**65** B8
Cockcroft Pl CB3 . . . .**83** B2
Cockerell Rd CB4 . . . .**83** D5
Cockerton Rd CB3 . . . .**103** E1
Cocketts Dr PE13 . . . .**245** E5
Cockfen La CB4 . . . .**105** C7
Cockhall Cl SG8 . . . .**12** A1
Cockhall La SG8 . . . .**12** A1
Cockle Cl CB2 . . . .**31** C7
Cockpen Rd CB7 . . . .**131** A8
Codrington Ct 2 PE19 . . . .**74** B3
Cody Rd CB5 . . . .**127** B1
Coggeshall Cl 5 CB5 . . . . .**84** E4
Colbron Cl SG7 . . . .**2** C4
Coldham Bank PE15 . . . . .**228** D6
Coldham Hall Chase
    PE14 . . . .**235** E1
Coldham's Gr CB1 . . . .**84** C1
Coldham's La CB1 . . . .**84** C2
Coldham's Rd CB1 . . . .**84** B2
Coldhams Cres PE29 . . . . .**141** F6
Coldhams N PE29 . . . .**141** F6
Coldhams S PE29 . . . .**141** F6
Coldhorn Cres PE13 . . . . .**245** D7
Cole Cl 1 CB6 . . . .**217** D1
Coleridge Com Coll CB1 . .**65** C7
Coleridge Ct 1 PE19 . . . . . .**74** C6
Coleridge Pl PE1 . . . .**197** E8
Coleridge Rd CB1 . . . .**65** B6
Coles La Brinkley CB8 . . . . .**70** D2
Linton CB1 . . . .**35** C2
Oakington/Longstanton
    CB4 . . . .**103** C6
Coles Rd CB4 . . . .**105** D2
Coleseed Rd PE15 . . . .**228** D2
Colesfield CB4 . . . .**123** E2
Coll of Animal Welfare The
    PE29 . . . .**119** C5

Coll of West Anglia
    CB4 . . . .**105** D3
College Cl 1 CB5 . . . .**86** E6
College Cres CB3 . . . .**47** B5
College Ct PE28 . . . .**168** C3
College Fields CB4 . . . .**83** F6
College Gdns PE15 . . . . . .**243** C7
College Heath Rd IP28 . . .**239** D6
College Pk PE1 . . . .**198** C5
College Rd Histon CB4 . . . .**104** B1
Soham CB7 . . . .**212** B4
Collett's Bridge La PE14 .**236** C5
Collier Rd CB1 . . . .**246** C2
Collier Way CB2 . . . .**49** C4
Colliers La CB5 . . . .**86** A6
Collingham PE2 . . . .**185** F3
Collings Pl 3 CB8 . . . .**110** E5
Collingwood Ave PE15 . . .**243** E5
Collingwood Ct SG8 . . . .**5** E7
Collingwood Rd PE19 . . . . .**74** B2
Collin's Hill CB7 . . . .**212** F1
Collyweston Rd PE9 . . . . .**230** B2
Colmworth Gdns 5 PE19 **74** C2
Colne Fields Colne PE15 . .**215** D1
Somersham PE28 . . . .**208** D8
Colne Rd
Bluntisham PE28 . . . .**208** C6
Colne PE28 . . . .**208** C8
Earith PE28 . . . .**208** D6
Colne Valley Rd CB9 . . . . . .**24** A7
Colts Cl PE29 . . . .**141** D7
Colts Croft SG8 . . . .**7** E2
Coltsfoot Cl CB1 . . . .**66** A5
Coltsfoot Dr
Peterborough PE2 . . . .**186** E7
Royston SG8 . . . .**5** E6
Colvile Rd Newton PE13 . .**248** A5
Wisbech PE13 . . . .**245** E5
Colville Cty Prim Sch
    CB1 . . . .**65** F5
Colville Rd CB1 . . . .**65** F6
Colwyn Cl CB4 . . . .**83** D5
Comberton Rd Barton CB3 62 F5
Little Eversden CB3 . . . .**46** C8
Toft CB3 . . . .**61** E5
Comberton Village Coll
    CB3 . . . .**62** A4
Comet Way
Mildenhall IP28 . . . .**239** B5
St Ives PE27 . . . .**144** A7
Comfrey Ct CB1 . . . .**66** A5
Commercial Rd PE15 . . . . .**243** C7
Common Acre La CB6 . . . .**225** D6
Common Dro
Southery PE38 . . . .**226** E8
Whittlesey PE7 . . . .**189** C8
Wimblington PE15 . . . .**223** C6
Common Gate Dro CB7 . . .**212** E5
Common La Ashwell SG7 . . .**2** B6
Chrishall SG8 . . . .**1** F7
Hemingford Abbots PE28 . .**142** F3
Sawston CB2 . . . .**32** D7
Common Rd
Parson Drove PE12 . . . .**233** F7
Sutton St Edmund PE12 . . .**233** F8
West Wratting CB1 . . . .**54** E2
Weston Colville CB1 . . . .**54** E4
Whittlesey PE7 . . . .**189** C8
Witchford CB6 . . . .**217** E1
Common The
West Wratting CB1 . . . .**53** F4
West Wratting CB1 . . . .**54** C3
Commons Rd PE7 . . . .**189** C8
Compton Fields CB7 . . . . .**240** E7
Conder Cl 3 CB4 . . . .**105** C3
Conduit Head Rd CB3 . . . . .**82** F3
Conduit Rd PE9 . . . .**244** C4
Coneygear Ct PE29 . . . . . .**141** E7
Coneygear Rd PE29 . . . . . .**141** E8
Coneygree Rd PE2 . . . .**187** D6
Coneywood Rd PE15 . . . . .**223** A7
Conifers The PE2 . . . .**185** F6
Coningsby Rd PE3 . . . .**204** A2
Conington La PE7 . . . .**168** C8
Conington Rd CB3 . . . .**121** B3
Coniston Cl 8 PE29 . . . . . .**141** B6
Coniston Rd
Cambridge CB1 . . . .**65** B6
Peterborough PE4 . . . .**204** E3
Conley Cl PE26 . . . .**172** B7
Connaught Cl CB9 . . . .**23** E7
Conner's Cl 2 SG8 . . . .**10** F4
Conquest Dro PE7 . . . .**187** D1
Constable Ave 4 PE19 . . . .**74** D5
Constable Cl PE7 . . . .**190** A8
Constable Rd
1 Haverhill CB9 . . . .**38** D1
St Ives PE27 . . . .**144** A7
Constables Leys PE28 . . . .**113** F5
Convent Dr CB5 . . . .**105** F8
Conway Ave PE4 . . . .**204** C2
Conway Cl
3 Cambridge CB1 . . . .**65** F6
4 March PE15 . . . .**243** B3
Conway Pl 4 PE19 . . . .**74** F2
Cook Cl CB4 . . . .**84** B6
Cook Close Rd PE7 . . . . . .**181** D4
Cook's Dro
Beck Row, Holywell Row
    & Kenny Hill IP28 . . . . .**213** B8
Earith PE28 . . . .**208** E6
Cook's Gn PE15 . . . .**222** F5
Cooks La PE28 . . . .**168** D5
Cookson Cl PE7 . . . .**181** D4
Coolidge Gdns CB4 . . . . . .**125** F4
Coombe Rd SG8 . . . .**4** A1
Coombelands Rd 3 SG8 . . .**5** E8

Cooper Thornhill Rd **1**
    PE7 . . . .**175** F7
Cooper's Cl CB8 . . . .**90** A1
Cootes La CB4 . . . .**121** E5
Cootes Mdw PE27 . . . .**144** B3
Copeland PE3 . . . .**197** A3
Copellis Cl CB6 . . . .**39** A2
Copes Cl PE19 . . . .**117** B4
Cophall Dro CB6 . . . .**217** E2
Coploe Rd CB10 . . . .**17** F3
Copper Beech Way PE2 . .**187** B7
Copperbeech Cl PE27 . . . .**144** A5
Copperfields SG8 . . . .**5** B6
Coppice Ave CB2 . . . .**49** B6
Coppice The Histon CB4 . .**104** C1
Littleport CB6 . . . .**242** C1
Coppingford Cl PE2 . . . . . .**187** D6
Coppins Cl PE28 . . . .**168** A4
Coppins Ct PE14 . . . .**245** E2
Copsewood PE4 . . . .**204** C4
Copy Hill CB9 . . . .**23** E3
Coral Park Trading Est
    CB1 . . . .**84** B2
Corbett St CB4 . . . .**125** E4
Cordell Cl PE27 . . . .**143** E6
Cordon St PE13 . . . .**245** C4
Coree Cl CB4 . . . .**65** A5
Corfe Ave PE4 . . . .**204** C2
Corfe Pl 3 PE19 . . . .**74** F2
Cormas Cl 5 SG8 . . . .**5** E8
Corn Exchange St CB2 . . .**246** A2
Corner Cl CB7 . . . .**219** B5
Cornfields 1 PE15 . . . .**222** F5
Cornish Cl CB1 . . . .**37** A3
Cornmills Rd CB7 . . . .**212** D2
Cornstall Bldgs 3 PE9 . . .**244** C5
Cornwall Cl PE19 . . . .**74** B4
Cornwall Rd
6 Stamford PE9 . . . .**244** B6
Wyton Airfield PE28 . . . . . .**143** A8
Cornwallis Dr PE19 . . . .**74** A3
Cornwallis Rd CB9 . . . .**23** F6
Corona Rd CB4 . . . .**83** E4
Coronation Ave
3 Crowland PE6 . . . .**232** B8
Huntingdon PE29 . . . .**141** E5
Parson Drove PE12 . . . .**234** A7
Royston SG8 . . . .**5** C5
9 Somersham PE28 . . . . .**215** C1
Warboys PE28 . . . .**164** F6
Whittlesey PE7 . . . .**189** F7
Coronation Cl
March PE15 . . . .**243** C2
Waterbeach CB5 . . . .**106** A7
Coronation Mews 2 CB2 **64** E7
Coronation St CB2 . . . .**246** B1
Corporation Bank PE6 . . .**207** F7
Corporation Rd PE13 . . . . .**245** C5
Corpus Christi Coll CB2 . . .**246** A2
Corpus Christi La PE29 . . . .**141** E1
Corrie Rd CB1 . . . .**65** B7
Corsican Pine CB8 . . . .**110** F5
Corunna Cl 7 PE19 . . . .**74** C5
Cosgrove Cl PE3 . . . .**197** C6
Cotes The CB7 . . . .**212** D2
Coton C of E Com Prim Sch
    CB3 . . . .**82** B2
Coton Rd CB3 . . . .**63** E5
Cotswold Cl March PE15 . .**243** E4
Peterborough PE4 . . . .**204** E1
Cottenham Cl 6 CB4 . . . .**208** D1
Cottenham Prim Sch
    CB4 . . . .**125** D4
Cottenham Rd
Histon CB4 . . . .**104** B5
Landbeach CB4 . . . .**126** B1
Cottenham Village Coll
    CB4 . . . .**125** E3
Cottesmore Cl PE3 . . . . . .**197** D4
Cotton Cl Conington PE7 . .**168** C8
5 Sawtry PE28 . . . .**168** C2
Cotton Ct 1 PE29 . . . .**141** F7
Cotton End Rd CB8 . . . . . .**110** C8
Cotton La PE19 . . . .**97** C7
Cotton's Field CB3 . . . .**102** B1
Cottrell's La CB3 . . . .**100** B4
Coulson Cl CB4 . . . .**105** C2
Coulson Way PE28 . . . .**150** F4
Council Rd 4 PE13 . . . . . .**245** E6
Council St PE4 . . . .**197** D8
Countess Cl PE19 . . . .**74** B3
County Rd PE15 . . . .**243** D6
Coupals Cl CB9 . . . .**24** C6
Coupals CP Sch CB9 . . . . . .**24** D7
Coupals Rd CB9 . . . .**24** C6
Courier Cl IP28 . . . .**239** B6
Courtland Ave CB1 . . . .**65** C5
Courtney Way CB4 . . . .**83** E4
Courtyard Way CB4 . . . . . .**125** E5
Courtyards CB2 . . . .**48** F3
Cousins Cl PE15 . . . .**243** C4
Covent Gdn CB1 . . . .**246** C1
Coventry Cl PE4 . . . .**204** B3
Covert Cl CB9 . . . .**39** A1
Covert The
1 Comberton CB3 . . . .**62** D4
Peterborough PE3 . . . .**197** B1
Cow & Sheep Dro IP28 . .**213** C7
Cow Fen Rd CB4 . . . .**122** E6
Cow La Fulbourn CB1 . . . . .**66** E5
Godmanchester PE29 . . . . .**142** C2
Great Chesterford CB10 . . .**19** A4
Rampton CB4 . . . .**124** F6
Cow Way PE7 . . . .**190** D8
Cowbridge Hall Dro
    CB6 . . . .**218** B6
Cowdell End CB3 . . . .**100** B4
Cowgate PE1 . . . .**197** F2

Cowley Cl PE28 . . . . .115 D3
Cowley Pk CB4 . . . . .84 B7
Cowley Rd CB4 . . . . .84 C7
Cowper Rd Cambridge CB1 .65 B6
Huntingdon PE29 . . . . . . .141 D5
Peterborough PE1 . . . . . . .197 F7
Cowpers Ct CB1 . . . . .74 D6
Cowslip Cl **1** SG8 . . . . .5 F5
Cowslip Dr CB6 . . . . .211 A7
Coxons Cl PE29 . . . . .141 B5
Cox's Cl CB2 . . . . .49 C4
Cox's Dro CB1 . . . . .66 F6
Cox's End **15** CB4 . . . . .208 D1
Cox's La Chatteris PE16 . . .241 C6
Wisbech PE13 . . . . .245 C4
Crab Apple Way SG19 . . . . .41 C5
Crab Marsh PE13 . . . . .245 B8
Crabapple Cl PE28 . . . . . . .168 B3
Crabtree PE4 . . . . .205 B1
Crabtree Croft CB1 . . . . . . .35 B3
Craft Way SG8 . . . . .11 B2
Crafts Way CB3 . . . . .102 C3
Craig St PE1 . . . . .197 F3
Crandal Way CB2 . . . . .49 A4
Crane Ave PE7 . . . . .181 F6
Crane Cl **3** PE8 . . . . .208 C8
Crane St PE28 . . . . .140 C3
Cranemore PE4 . . . . .204 A4
Crane's La CB3 . . . . .61 A2
Cranfield Pl **2** PE28 . . . . .208 C8
Cranfield Way
Brampton PE28 . . . . .140 D2
Buckden PE19 . . . . .117 A3
Cranford Dr PE3 . . . . .197 C4
Cranleigh Cl CB2 . . . . .64 D1
Cranmer Rd CB3 . . . . .83 B1
Cranmore Dro PE6 . . . . . . .206 D8
Cranny The PE19 . . . . .117 F2
Cranwells Way **4** CB6 . . .211 B7
Crathern Way CB4 . . . . .83 F7
Crauden Gdns **4** CB7 . . .240 E5
Craven Cl CB2 . . . . .64 D2
Craven Way CB8 . . . . .110 E6
Crawford Gdns **2** PE28 . .232 C8
Crawley End SG8 . . . . .8 D4
Crawthorne Rd PE1 . . . . . .198 A3
Crawthorne St **1** PE1 . . .198 A3
Crease Dro PE6 . . . . .232 B8
Crease Rd
Conington PE28 . . . . .168 F5
Sawtry PE28 . . . . .169 B6
Crecy Ct PE19 . . . . .74 C5
Creek Fen PE15 . . . . .228 D5
Creek Rd PE15 . . . . .243 D4
Crescent Cl PE7 . . . . .190 A7
Crescent Rd Histon CB4 . . .104 C1
Whittlesey PE7 . . . . .189 F7
Crescent The
Cambridge CB3 . . . . .83 B3
Dullingham CB8 . . . . .89 C1
Eaton Socon PE19 . . . . .74 C3
Eye PE6 . . . . .232 A1
Littleport CB6 . . . . .242 C3
Peterborough PE2 . . . . . . .186 E7
St Ives PE27 . . . . .144 A5
St Neots PE19 . . . . .74 F6
4 Soham CB7 . . . . .212 B3
Wicken CB7 . . . . .211 E1
Wisbech PE13 . . . . .245 C4
Cressener Terr **3** PE19 . . .74 F1
Cresswells La CB7 . . . . . . .240 E4
Crester Dr **3** PE4 . . . . . . .204 C3
Criccieth Way PE19 . . . . . . .74 F1
Cricket Field Rd CB8 . . . . .111 B2
Cricketers Ct PE15 . . . . . . .243 C3
Cricketers Way
3 Benwick PE15 . . . . . . .222 A5
Wisbech PE13 . . . . .245 A6
Cricketfield La PE26 . . . . . .172 A6
Crick's Rd IP28 . . . . .213 D6
Cripple Sidings La PE2 . . .187 A8
Crishall CE Prim Sch SG8 . .8 C3
Crispin Cl Haverhill CB9 . . . .23 D7
1 Impington CB4 . . . . . . .83 D7
Crispin Pl CB1 . . . . .246 C3
Crockfords Rd CB8 . . . . . . .111 A2
Crocus Cl PE7 . . . . .181 F6
Crocus Gr PE1 . . . . .198 A8
Croft Cl Brampton PE28 . . .140 D2
Histon CB4 . . . . .104 B5
Croft La Haverhill CB9 . . . . .24 B6
Oakington/Longstanton
CB4 . . . . .103 B6
Croft Park Rd CB6 . . . . . . .242 D3
Croft PI IP28 . . . . .239 C4
Croft Rd Isleham CB7 . . . . .213 A5
Newmarket CB8 . . . . .110 C6
Outwell PE14 . . . . .229 D7
Croft The CB1 . . . . .66 E5
Croft Way PE7 . . . . .186 C2
Crofters The CB6 . . . . .210 F6
Croftfield Rd PE29 . . . . . . .141 F1
Crofts The PE19 . . . . .95 F1
Crome Ditch CB3 . . . . .64 C4
Cromwell Cl
2 Northborough PE6 . . . .231 F7
Ramsey PE26 . . . . .171 F6
Cromwell Com Coll
PE16 . . . . .241 C6
Cromwell Ct **4** PE19 . . . . .74 F1
Cromwell Gdns **2** PE8 . . .75 A5
Cromwell Ho* PE29 . . . . . .141 D5
Cromwell Mews PE6 . . . . .231 F7
Cromwell Mus* PE29 . . . . .141 D4
Cromwell Pl PE27 . . . . .144 B4
Cromwell Rd
Cambridge CB1 . . . . .84 B1

Cromwell Rd continued
Ely CB6 . . . . .240 C4
March PE15 . . . . .243 D6
Peterborough PE1 . . . . . . .197 F4
St Neots PE19 . . . . .74 F3
1 Sutton CB6 . . . . .216 E1
Wisbech PE13 . . . . .245 B3
Cromwell Way PE28 . . . . . .168 B3
Cromwell Wlk PE29 . . . . . .141 D5
Crooked Bank PE14 . . . . . .235 D5
Croots Cl PE28 . . . . .140 B2
Cropston Rd PE1 . . . . .198 E7
Cross Bank Dro CB7 . . . . . .211 C5
Cross Cl CB9 . . . . .39 A1
Cross Dro
Haddenham CB6 . . . . .209 E3
Littleport CB7 . . . . .226 A1
Southery PE38 . . . . .226 E7
Stretham CB6 . . . . .210 F3
Tydd St Giles PE13 . . . . . .237 C5
Warboys PE28 . . . . .215 C6
Waterbeach CB5 . . . . .127 D4
Whittlesey PE7 . . . . .190 F6
Wilburton CB6 . . . . .210 C3
Wistow PE28 . . . . .172 E1
Cross Farm Cl PE28 . . . . . .120 C2
Cross Hall Rd PE19 . . . . . . .74 D6
Cross Keys Ct CB4 . . . . . . .125 D3
Cross La
1 Little Downham CB6 . . .218 A6
Melbourn SG8 . . . . .14 C4
Wisbech PE13 . . . . .235 D6
Cross Lane Cl SG8 . . . . .45 C1
Cross Rd March PE15 . . . . .227 D3
Sutton St Edmund PE12 . . .237 A4
Whittlesey 189 C7
Cross St Cambridge CB1 . . .246 C1
Covington PE28 . . . . .135 D2
Farcet PE7 . . . . .187 D1
Huntingdon PE29 . . . . . . .141 D5
Peterborough PE1 . . . . . . .198 A2
Cross The PE28 . . . . .161 F6
Crosshall Inf Sch PE19 . . . .74 C6
Crosshall Jun Sch PE19 . . . .74 C6
Crosshall Marina* PE19 . . .74 F7
Crosshall Rd PE19 . . . . .74 D6
Crossroad Cotts CB10 . . . . .17 C2
Crossway Hand PE7 . . . . . .189 B8
Crossways Barley SG8 . . . . . .6 F1
Linton 35 D2
Crow Hill La CB3 . . . . .79 B3
Crow Spinney La PE28 . . . .115 D2
Crow Tree St SG19 . . . . . . .58 D4
Crowhill **6** PE29 . . . . . . .118 F8
Crowhurst PE4 . . . . .204 C5
Crowland Rd
Deeping St James PE6 . . . .207 A6
Eye PE6 . . . . .232 A3
Haverhill CB9 . . . . .23 F8
Newborough PE6 . . . . .232 A2
Thorney PE6 . . . . .232 A1
Crowland Way CB4 . . . . . . .83 F7
Crowlands CB5 . . . . .125 D4
Crown Ave **2** PE14 . . . . .229 D3
Crown Cl PE19 . . . . .95 A1
Crown Gdns PE28 . . . . .150 E4
Crown La **2** CB4 . . . . . . .242 D4
Crown Lakes Ctry Pk*
PE7 . . . . .187 B2
Crown Mews PE26 . . . . . . .172 B7
Crown Rd **1** PE14 . . . . . .229 D3
Crown St
Peterborough PE1 . . . . . . .197 E7
St Ives PE27 . . . . .144 A4
Stamford PE9 . . . . .244 B5
Crown Wlk PE27 . . . . .144 A3
Crowson Cres **6** PE6 . . .231 F7
Crowthorne Cl CB1 . . . . . . .65 F6
Croxton Gdns PE28 . . . . . .136 D6
Croydon Hill SG8 . . . . .26 E8
Croydon Rd Arrington SG8 . .44 C1
Croydon SG8 . . . . .27 B8
Croyland Rd PE4 . . . . .204 D1
Crummock Wr PE29 . . . . . .141 D5
Crunch Croft CB9 . . . . .24 E5
Cuckoo La Lolworth CB3 . . .101 F5
Rampton CB4 . . . . .124 C3
Culloden Ct PE19 . . . . .74 C5
Cumberland Way **3**
PE19 . . . . .74 F1
Cundell Dr CB4 . . . . .125 E4
Cunningham Cl CB4 . . . . . . .83 E6
Cunningham Way PE19 . . . .74 A2
Curf Fen Dro PE16 . . . . . . .222 E4
Curlew Ave PE16 . . . . .241 C5
Curlew Ct PE7 . . . . .189 F8
Curlew Cres **6** SG8 . . . . . .5 E8
Curlew Gr PE2 . . . . .49 B8
Curlew Pl **2** PE19 . . . . . . .75 B6
Cutter Ferry Cl CB4 . . . . . . .84 A3
Cutter Ferry La CB4 . . . . . .246 C3
Cygnet Dr PE16 . . . . .241 C6
Cygnet Pk PE7 . . . . .186 E3
Cypress Cl
6 Doddington PE15 . . . . .223 A6
2 Peterborough PE3 . . . .197 A2
Cyprus Rd CB1 . . . . .65 C7

D

Da Vinci Cl **6** PE27 . . . . . .144 A7
Dacre Gn SG8 . . . . .5 D7
Daffodil Gr PE2 . . . . .187 C7
Dagless Way PE15 . . . . . . .243 D7
Daintree PE27 . . . . .208 A3
Daintree Rd PE26 . . . . .220 D4
Daintree Way PE28 . . . . . . .143 D1

Daintrees Rd CB4 . . . . .121 F6
Dairy Dro Littleport CB6 . . .225 C6
Thorney PE6 . . . . .233 E2
Daisy Cl CB4 . . . . .83 D7
Dakota Rd IP28 . . . . .213 E8
Dalby Ct PE1 . . . . .198 C8
Dale Cl PE2 . . . . .185 F5
Dale The CB4 . . . . .123 F1
Dale Way CB8 . . . . .32 F8
Dales Way PE27 . . . . .208 A3
Dalham Rd Ashley CB8 . . . .92 B7
Moulton CB8 . . . . .112 F4
Dalton Sq CB4 . . . . .84 B5
Dalton Way **1** CB6 . . . . . .240 D6
Dam Bank Dro CB6 . . . . . . .209 D4
Dane Dr CB3 . . . . .83 A1
Dane Hill Rd CB8 . . . . .133 D5
Danes Cl PE1 . . . . .198 C4
Danesbury Ct 84 C1
Daniel Ct PE9 . . . . .244 C4
Daphmoir Cl CB2 . . . . .29 F8
Darford **6** PE28 . . . . .208 E6
Darley Cl **4** PE8 . . . . .230 E1
Darrington Cl **1** PE19 . . .74 F1
Dart Cl PE27 . . . . .144 B6
Dartford Rd PE15 . . . . .243 C4
Darthill Rd PE15 . . . . .243 D5
Dartmoor Dr PE29 . . . . . . .141 A4
Darwin Cl
Mildenhall IP28 . . . . .239 C6
3 Stamford PE9 . . . . . . .244 A7
Darwin Coll CB3 . . . . .246 A1
Darwin Dr CB4 . . . . .83 D5
Darwin Pl CB4 . . . . .111 B1
Daules Rd PE28 . . . . .140 E1
Davey Cl **2** CB4 . . . . .104 C3
Davey Cres CB2 . . . . .49 A6
David Bull Way CB4 . . . . . .105 D3
David St CB1 . . . . .65 A8
David's Cl PE4 . . . . .203 F4
David's La PE4 . . . . .204 B6
Davie La PE7 . . . . .201 A1
Davis Cl PE19 . . . . .96 A2
Davison Rd CB6 . . . . .240 E8
Davy Rd CB1 . . . . .65 B7
Daw's Dro PE7 . . . . .220 D8
Daws Cl **5** CB1 . . . . .65 F6
Dawson Ct PE6 . . . . .205 C8
Day's Cl SG8 . . . . .5 C5
Day's Lode Rd PE15 . . . . . .224 C7
De Bec Cl PE1 . . . . .198 C3
De Freville Ave CB4 . . . . . . .246 C4
De Freville Rd CB2 . . . . . . .49 A6
De Havilland Ct **4** IP28 .239 B5
De Havilland Rd PE13 . . . . .245 C6
De La Haye Cl CB3 . . . . . . .99 B3
De Vere Cl PE28 . . . . .143 B1
Deacon St PE1 . . . . .197 F3
Deacons La PE27 . . . . .240 D5
Deaconscroft PE3 . . . . .197 B5
Deaconscroft Sch PE1 . . . .198 B5
Deal Cl PE19 . . . . .141 E8
Deal Gr CB2 . . . . .32 F8
Dean Cl CB9 . . . . .39 A1
Dean Dro PE16 . . . . .215 D4
Dean Peacock Ct **3**
CB6 . . . . .240 E6
Dean Rd CB1 . . . . .21 B8
Deans Cl CB9 . . . . .39 A1
Debdale Ct PE7 . . . . .189 F5
Deben Ave PE27 . . . . .144 A7
Deben Cl PE15 . . . . .243 B5
Deben Rd CB9 . . . . .24 B8
Decoy Rd
Borough Fen PE6 . . . . .207 A3
Gorefield PE13 . . . . .237 D2
Deene Ct PE3 . . . . .197 C5
Deeping St James CP Sch
PE6 . . . . .231 F8
Deeping St James Rd
. . . . .231 E7
Deepings Sch The PE6 . . . .231 F8
Deerfield Rd PE15 . . . . . . .243 E4
Deerhurst Way **13** PE6 . .232 A1
Deerleap PE3 . . . . .197 A5
Deerpark Rd PE28 . . . . . . .168 A4
Degas Dr PE27 . . . . .144 A7
Deighton Cl PE27 . . . . .144 B5
Delamere Gr
Little Wilbraham CB8 . . . . . .68 F6
Peterborough PE1 . . . . . . .198 C5
Delapre St **1** PE6 . . . . . .232 A1
Delbrig Dro PE15 . . . . .212 E5
Dell The
Peterborough PE2 . . . . . . .186 E7
Royston SG8 . . . . .5 C5
Dells Cl PE28 . . . . .166 D2
Delph PE7 . . . . .189 D7
Delph Cl PE7 . . . . .187 F6
Delph Dro IP28 . . . . .212 F8
Delph St PE7 . . . . .189 D7
Delta La PE28 . . . . .151 E3
Dendys PE28 . . . . .143 D1
Dengaine Cl CB3 . . . . .99 B2
Denham Rd CB8 . . . . .92 E8
Denham Wlk **1** PE3 . . . .197 C4
Denis Dr PE2 . . . . .186 A4
Denmark Pl PE15 . . . . .222 A5
Denmark Dr PE2 . . . . .186 A4
Denmark Rd CB4 . . . . .125 C3
Dennis Rd CB5 . . . . .84 F4
Denny Abbey* CB5 . . . . . .127 A6
Denny Cl **9** CB4 . . . . . . .208 D1
Denny End Rd CB5 . . . . . . .105 F8
Denton Rd Glatton PE28 . . .175 E1
Peterborough PE2 . . . . . . .187 C6

Dentons Chase PE26 . . . . .220 E4
Depot Rd CB8 . . . . .110 E6
Deptford Cl **2** PE15 . . . . .243 B3
Derby Dr PE1 . . . . .198 C6
Derby Rd CB1 . . . . .65 B6
Derby St CB3 . . . . .64 C7
Derby Way CB8 . . . . .110 D3
Derwent Cl
Cambridge CB1 . . . . .65 D5
Huntingdon PE29 . . . . . . .141 B5
St Ives PE27 . . . . .144 B6
Derwent Dr PE4 . . . . .204 E2
Derwood Gr PE4 . . . . .204 B5
Desborough Ave PE2 . . . . .187 D5
Desborough Rd PE29 . . . . .142 A6
Desmond Ave CB1 . . . . .65 F6
Devana Ct PE29 . . . . .118 F8
Devoke Cl PE29 . . . . .141 B6
Devon Cl **2** PE27 . . . . . . .144 A8
Devon Rd PE28 . . . . .154 A1
Devonshire Cl **2** PE28 . .168 B3
Devonshire Rd CB1 . . . . . . .65 A8
Dewpond Cl PE19 . . . . .75 A6
Dexter Cl **10** PE15 . . . . . .223 A5
Dexter Way PE8 . . . . .178 B3
Dial Cl PE19 . . . . .95 F2
Diamond Cl CB2 . . . . .64 E5
Diana Cl PE7 . . . . .190 A6
Dickasons SG8 . . . . .14 D7
Dickens St PE1 . . . . .198 B3
Dickerson Cl **1** SG19 . . . .41 D6
Digby Cl **3** PE8 . . . . .74 B3
Dimmock's Cote Rd
CB7 . . . . .211 B3
Dingley Cl PE1 . . . . .197 C5
Ditchburn Pl CB1 . . . . .84 A1
Ditchfield CB5 . . . . .108 D8
Ditchfields **2** PE28 . . . . .215 C1
Ditton Cl CB8 . . . . .111 A1
Ditton Fields CB5 . . . . .84 C3
Ditton Gn CB8 . . . . .90 D1
Ditton La CB5 . . . . .84 E4
Ditton Lodge CP Sch
CB8 . . . . .111 B2
Ditton Wlk CB5 . . . . .84 C4
Dixies Cl SG7 . . . . .2 D3
Dixon's Dro PE14 . . . . .238 C7
Dixons Rd **1** PE6 . . . . . . .231 E8
Dobson Wlk **11** PE15 . . .223 B7
Dock La CB5 . . . . .106 A2
Dock Rd PE16 . . . . .241 C6
Dockings La **10** CB7 . . . .213 A5
Doctor's Cl CB4 . . . . .104 D3
Docwra Rd CB3 . . . . .99 A3
Docwra's Cl SG8 . . . . .29 D5
Doddington Dr PE8 . . . . . . .197 B2
Doddington Hospl PE15 . . .222 F6
Doddington Rd
Benwick PE15 . . . . .222 A5
Chatteris PE16 . . . . .241 A6
Doddington/Wimblington
PE15 . . . . .223 B6
Dodds Mead CB3 . . . . .47 A5
Dodford La CB3 . . . . .103 C3
Dog Kennel La SG8 . . . . .5 D6
Dogget La CB1 . . . . .66 F4
Doggett Rd CB1 . . . . .66 F4
Dogsthorpe Cty Jun & Inf Sch
PE1 . . . . .198 B7
Dogsthorpe Rd PE1 . . . . . .198 A5
Dole The 104 C3
Doles The **3** CB4 . . . . . . .208 D1
Dolls Cl PE15 . . . . .53 C1
Dolphin Cl Cambridge CB1 .66 A7
3 Linton CB1 . . . . .35 D2
Dolphin La **11** Ely CB7 . . .240 D4
Melbourn SG8 . . . . .14 B6
Dolphin Way CB2 . . . . .49 B4
Dolphins Way SG19 . . . . . . .41 D6
Dome Sports Ctr IP28 . . . .239 E4
Donaldson Dr
2 Peterborough PE4 . . . .204 C4
1 Peterborough PE4 . . . .204 F1
Donegal Cl PE4 . . . . .204 D2
Donne Cl SG8 . . . . .5 D2
Donnington Pk PE13 . . . . . .238 A1
Dorchester Cres **3** PE1 .198 D7
Dorchester Way PE28 . . . . .143 B7
Doris St CB8 . . . . .110 F3
Dorling Way PE28 . . . . .140 B3
Dorvis La CB10 . . . . .21 B1
Double Bank La PE28 . . . . .161 B7
Doug Smith Cl **1** CB8 . . .110 F6
Doughty St PE9 . . . . .244 D7
Douglas House Hospl
CB2 . . . . .64 E5
Douglas Rd **3** PE6 . . . . . .231 E8
Douglas Way CB3 . . . . .79 B3
Dove Cl PE28 . . . . .121 C6
Dove Cote Cl CB4 . . . . .121 F5
Dove House Rd CB9 . . . . . . .24 A8
Dovecote Cl
Peterborough PE1 . . . . . . .198 A7
Yarwell PE8 . . . . .183 A4
Dovecote Rd PE7 . . . . .181 C5
Dovecote La PE7 . . . . .181 C5
Dovehouse Cl Ely CB7 . . . .240 D3
Fowlmere SG8 . . . . .15 E8
Godmanchester PE29 . . . . .142 A1
St Neots PE19 . . . . .74 F6
Dovehouse Wood PE28 . . .162 B5
Dover Cl PE29 . . . . .141 E8
Dover Rd PE4 . . . . .204 C2
Dover St **2** CB1 . . . . .246 C2
Dovey Cl PE27 . . . . .144 B6
Dowding Way CB4 . . . . .83 D6

Dowgate Rd PE13 . . . . . . .238 B1
Down Gate PE3 . . . . .197 A1
Downe Cl CB3 . . . . .99 A2
Downham Feoffees Sch
CB6 . . . . .218 A7
Downham Hythe Dro
CB6 . . . . .217 D6
Downham Rd Ely CB6 . . . .240 B3
Outwell PE14 . . . . .236 F2
Downham's La CB4 . . . . . . .84 A6
Downing Cl Bottisham CB5 .86 E6
Mildenhall IP28 . . . . .239 D5
Newmarket CB8 . . . . .111 A2
Downing Coll CB2 . . . . .246 B1
Downing Cres PE9 . . . . . . .244 B7
Downing Ct CB5 . . . . .108 A1
Downing Pl **2** 246 B2
Downing St CB2 . . . . .246 B2
Downlands SG8 . . . . .5 C6
Downs Cres PE9 . . . . .23 F8
Downton Dr CB9 . . . . .23 E8
Dowsdale Bank PE6 . . . . . .233 A8
Dragoon Dr **4** PE15 . . . . .243 D2
Drain Rd PE6 . . . . .205 A7
Drake Cl PE29 . . . . .141 F6
Drake Rd PE19 . . . . .74 B2
Drake Way CB4 . . . . .104 C5
Draper's Cl PE8 . . . . .178 C3
Drapers La CB9 . . . . .23 B2
Drapery Row **1** CB8 . . . .111 A3
Drayhorse Rd PE26 . . . . . .172 A5
Drayton PE3 . . . . .197 A5
Drayton Cl CB1 . . . . .66 A5
Drayton Rd CB1 . . . . .66 A5
Drewels La PE19 . . . . .56 D4
Drift Ave PE9 . . . . .244 D4
Drift Gdns PE9 . . . . .244 D7
Drift Rd PE9 . . . . .244 C6
Drift The Elsworth CB3 . . . .100 B4
Exning CB8 . . . . .110 A8
Oakington/Longstanton
CB4 . . . . .103 B5
Sutton PE5 . . . . .194 F3
Drings Cl **2** CB4 . . . . . . .208 D1
Drinkwater Cl PE14 . . . . . .110 E4
Drive The Perry PE28 . . . . .115 D1
Peterborough PE3 . . . . . . .197 E2
St Ives PE27 . . . . .143 F1
Drivers Ave PE29 . . . . .141 E5
Drivers Ct **8** PE15 . . . . . .223 A5
Drosier Rd CB1 . . . . .246 C1
Drove Rd SG19 . . . . .41 A6
Drove The Farcet PE26 . . . .220 D7
Witchford CB6 . . . . .217 E1
Drummer St CB1 . . . . .246 B2
Drury La
Bluntisham/Colne PE28 . . .208 D2
Melbourn SG8 . . . . .14 D6
Wicken CB7 . . . . .211 F2
Dry Drayton Prim Sch
CB3 . . . . .102 C1
Dry Drayton Rd
Madingley CB3 . . . . .81 D7
Oakington & Westwick
CB4 . . . . .103 A4
Dry Leys PE2 . . . . .186 C6
Drybread Rd PE7 . . . . .189 D4
Dryden Cl PE27 . . . . .143 E6
Dryden Ct **7** PE19 . . . . . .75 A7
Dryden Rd PE1 . . . . .197 E2
Dubbs Knoll Rd SG8 . . . . . .10 F5
Duberly Cl PE28 . . . . .115 C2
Duchess Cl PE19 . . . . .74 A3
Duchess Dr
Newmarket CB8 . . . . .111 D2
Woodditton CB8 . . . . .90 E8
Duck Dro CB7 . . . . .219 D5
Duck End Girton CB3 . . . . . .82 D3
Godmanchester PE29 . . . . .141 F1
Duck La Haddenham CB6 . .210 A6
St Neots PE19 . . . . .74 F4
Duck St PE8 . . . . .178 D8
Ducks La CB8 . . . . .110 C2
Duckworth Cl PE7 . . . . .189 E7
Duddery Hill CB9 . . . . .23 F6
Duddery Rd CB9 . . . . .24 A2
Dudley Ave PE4 . . . . .204 C2
Dudley Rd CB5 . . . . .84 E4
Duke of Bedford Sch
PE6 . . . . .233 B3
Duke St
Peterborough PE2 . . . . . . .187 A7
Wisbech PE13 . . . . .245 D4
Dukes Dr **3** PE26 . . . . . . .221 C2
Dukes Mdw CB2 . . . . .49 C5
Dukes Rd PE19 . . . . .74 B4
Dukesmead PE4 . . . . .204 A2
Dullingham Rd
Newmarket CB8 . . . . .110 F1
Stetchworth CB8 . . . . .89 D3
Woodditton CB8 . . . . .89 F7
Dullingham Sta CB8 . . . . . . .89 B2
Duloe Rd PE19 . . . . .74 B5
Dunblane Dr PE2 . . . . .185 D4
Duncan Way PE29 . . . . .141 F7
Duncock La CB3 . . . . .100 B4
Duncombe's Rd PE7 . . . . . .191 F8
Dundee Rd CB4 . . . . .84 A5
Dungate La CB1 . . . . .52 B6
Dunholt Way **2** PE8 . . . . .208 F6
Dunkirk Dro PE28 . . . . .215 C4
Dunmow Way CB4 . . . . .84 A5
Dunsberry Marholm PE3 . . .203 F1
Peterborough PE3 . . . . . . .196 F8

Dunsbridge Turnpike
SG8 . . . . .29 F2
Dunsey Wood Cl CB9 . . . .38 E1
Dunsmore Cl CB5 . . . . . .84 E4
Dunstal Field CB4 . . . . .125 D2
Dunstall's Dro CB7 . . . .218 E1
Dunstan Dr CB6 . . . . . .240 B5
Dunster Dr PE9 . . . . .23 E4
Durham Cl PE28 . . . . . . .168 C2
Durham Rd PE1 . . . . . . .198 C3
Durham Way
 4 Newmarket CB8 . . . . . .110 E5
 Wyton Airfield CB8 . . . .143 B8
Durnford Way CB4 . . . . . .83 C5
Duxford Airfield CB2 . . . .17 A8
Duxford CE Com Prim Sch
 CB2 . . . . .32 D1
Duxford Rd Hinxton CB10 . .18 A7
 Ickleton CB10 . . . . .17 F5
 Whittlesford CB2 . . . . . .32 D4
Dwyer-Joyce Cl CB4 . . . .104 B4
Dykemoor Dro PE15 . . . .222 C4
Dykemoor Dro N PE15 . . .222 C5
Dyson Cl
 Peterborough PE1 . . . . .197 F3
 The Stukeleys PE29 . . . .141 E8
Dyson's Dro CB5 . . . . . .130 B5

E

Eachard Rd CB3 . . . . .83 B5
Eagle Ct PE19 . . . . .75 B7
Eagle La CB8 . . . . .89 D1
Eagle Way PE29 . . . . . . .142 A8
Eagle's La 1 CB6 . . . . . .218 A7
Eaglesthorpe PE1 . . . . . .197 E7
Eames Gdns PE1 . . . . . . .198 E6
Earith Bsns Pk PE28 . . . .208 F6
Earith Fen Dro PE28 . . . .208 F7
Earith Prim Sch PE28 . . . .208 E5
Earith Rd
 Bluntisham/Colne PE28 . .208 D7
 Willingham CB4 . . . . . . .209 A2
Earl Cl 1 PE19 . . . . .74 B4
Earl Spencer Ct PE2 . . . .186 E8
Earl St CB1 . . . . .246 B2
Earls Cl PE2 . . . . .187 B6
Earls Hill Gdns SG8 . . . . . .5 C4
Earlswood PE2 . . . . .185 E5
Earning St PE29 . . . . . . .141 F1
Earth Cl PE2 . . . . .187 E5
East Chadley La PE29 . . . .141 F2
East Cl PE15 . . . . .243 B6
East Delph PE7 . . . . .189 E8
East Dr Caldecote CB3 . . . .80 C1
 March PE15 . . . . .243 F4
East Fen Dro CB7 . . . . . .212 D6
East Fen Rd CB7 . . . . . . .213 B5
East Hatley SG19 . . . . . . .43 A1
East Hertford St CB4 . . . .246 A4
East La SG19 . . . . .41 C6
East of England
 Showground★ PE2 . . . .185 C4
East Park St PE16 . . . . . .241 C4
East Perry PE28 . . . . . . .115 E2
East Rd Cambridge CB1 . . .246 C2
 Isleham CB7 . . . . .213 A5
 8 Northborough PE6 . . .231 F7
 Tydd St Mary PE13 . . . .238 C8
East St
 Bluntisham/Colne PE28 . .208 C5
 Great Gransden SG19 . . . .58 E4
 Huntingdon PE29 . . . . . .141 F5
 1 Kimbolton PE28 . . . . .113 F4
 1 Manea PE15 . . . . . . .224 C4
 St Ives PE27 . . . . .144 A3
 St Neots PE19 . . . . .74 F5
 Stamford PE9 . . . . .244 C5
East Sta Rd PE2 . . . . . . .187 A4
East View IP28 . . . . .213 C3
East Way CB2 . . . . .50 A1
Eastalls Cl 15 PE15 . . . . .223 A5
Eastbourne Cl 2 PE16 . . .241 C4
Eastbourne Rd PE29 . . . .141 C3
Eastern Ave Haverhill CB9 . .23 C8
 Peterborough PE1 . . . . .198 C8
 11 Soham CB7 . . . . . . .212 B4
Eastern Cl PE1 . . . . .198 C7
Eastfield CB4 . . . . .84 A5
Eastfield Dr PE7 . . . . . . .189 F6
Eastfield Gr PE1 . . . . . . .198 B4
Eastfield Rd
 Peterborough PE1 . . . . .198 C4
 Royston SG8 . . . . .5 E6
 1 Wisbech PE13 . . . . . .245 E7
Eastfield Sch PE27 . . . . .144 A4
Eastfield Way PE13 . . . . .245 C6
Eastfields CB6 . . . . .242 C3
Eastgate
 Great Chesterford CB10 . . .18 D2
 Market Deeping PE6 . . . .206 B6
 16 Market Deeping PE6 . .231 F8
 Peterborough PE1 . . . . .198 B2
 Whittlesey PE7 . . . . . . .189 E7
Eastholm PE1 . . . . .198 C3
Eastholm Cty Sch PE1 . . .198 C4
Eastholm Sch PE1 . . . . . .198 D5
Eastleigh Rd PE1 . . . . . .198 C3
Eastmoor La PE15 . . . . . .223 A5
Easton Rd PE19 . . . . . . .114 C3
Eastrea Ct PE2 . . . . .187 E6
Eastrea Rd PE7 . . . . . . .189 F7
Eastwood PE16 . . . . .241 C4
Eastwood Ave PE15 . . . . .243 E3

Eastwood Cl CB6 . . . . . .216 E2
Eaton Cl Cambridge CB4 . . .84 A6
 Huntingdon PE29 . . . . . .142 A7
Eaton Est PE15 . . . . .223 B7
Eaudyke Bank PE13 . . . . .237 F7
Eccles Rd PE8 . . . . .193 D8
Echo Hill SG8 . . . . .5 C5
Echo La PE28 . . . . .151 B3
Ecton Gr 7 PE14 . . . . . .236 A5
Eden Cres PE16 . . . . . . .241 C4
Eden Rd CB9 . . . . .24 A7
Eden St CB1 . . . . .246 C2
Eden Street Backway
 CB1 . . . . .246 C2
Edendale Cl CB1 . . . . .65 C5
Edenfield PE2 . . . . .186 C6
Edgcote Cl PE3 . . . . .197 C5
Edge Bank PE14 . . . . . . .236 F6
Edgeborough Cl CB3 . . . .134 A1
Edgerley Drain Rd PE1 . . .198 F5
Edinburgh Ave
 Peterborough PE4 . . . . .204 B3
 Sawston CB2 . . . . .32 F8
Edinburgh Dr
 Eaton Socon PE19 . . . . . .74 B4
 St Ives PE27 . . . . .143 F7
 Wisbech PE13 . . . . .245 C8
Edinburgh Rd
 Cambridge CB4 . . . . .84 A5
 Newmarket CB8 . . . . . . .110 E4
 Stamford PE9 . . . . .244 B7
Edison Rd PE27 . . . . . . .144 A4
Edith Cavell Hospl PE3 . . .197 B4
Edmonds Cl PE9 . . . . . . .244 D6
Edmund Cl Haverhill CB9 . .23 F7
 Milton CB4 . . . . .105 C2
Edwalton Ave PE1 . . . . . .197 E3
Edward Rd St Neots PE19 . .74 F7
 Stamford PE9 . . . . .244 B7
Edward St CB1 . . . . .84 A1
Edwards Way 3 PE15 . . . .224 B4
Edwards Wlk 9 PE15 . . . .208 E6
Edwinstowe Cl CB2 . . . . . .64 E6
Egar Way PE3 . . . . .196 F2
Egerton Cl CB5 . . . . .84 D4
Egerton Rd CB5 . . . . .84 E4
Egremont Rd CB3 . . . . . . .81 A3
Egremont St CB6 . . . . . .240 C5
Eighth Ave PE13 . . . . . . .245 E4
Ekin Rd CB5 . . . . .84 D4
Eland Way CB1 . . . . .66 A7
Elbourn Way SG8 . . . . . . .12 F5
Elbow La PE13 . . . . .234 F8
Elder Cl Cambridge CB4 . . .83 F6
 Sawston CB2 . . . . .32 D8
Eldernell La PE7 . . . . . . .191 B8
Elder's Gate PE12 . . . . . .237 E8
Eldith Ave CB7 . . . . .213 A1
Eldo Gdns IP28 . . . . .213 D6
Eldo Rd IP28 . . . . .213 D6
Eldon La IP28 . . . . .214 B8
Eleanor Cl PE9 . . . . .244 A6
Elecks La SG8 . . . . .11 D8
Eleftheda Rd CB5 . . . . . . .84 C3
Eliot Rd SG8 . . . . .5 D8
Elizabeth Ave CB8 . . . . . .110 E5
Elizabeth Ct
 5 Eaton Socon PE19 . . . .74 C4
 Hemingford Grey PE27 . .143 F1
 2 Sutton CB6 . . . . .216 E2
Elizabeth Dr PE29 . . . . . .142 B6
Elizabeth Rd PE29 . . . . . .244 A6
Elizabeth Terr PE13 . . . . .245 D4
Elizabeth Way
 3 Bluntisham/Colne
 PE28 . . . . .208 D7
 Burrough Green CB8 . . . . .70 F4
 Cambridge CB4 . . . . .83 F4
 Gamlingay SG19 . . . . . . .41 C6
Elizabethan Way PE4 . . . .140 B2
Ellesmere Rd CB4 . . . . . . .83 D6
Ellindon PE3 . . . . .197 B7
Ellingham Ave PE15 . . . . .243 C3
Ellington Rd PE28 . . . . . .149 E1
Elliot Ave PE3 . . . . .196 F2
Elliott Cl CB4 . . . . .111 A6
Elliott Rd PE15 . . . . .243 B5
Ellis Cl CB4 . . . . .125 D3
Ellison Cl CB4 . . . . .83 D7
Ellison La CB3 . . . . .81 A4
Elloe Bank Newton NG3 . .237 B2
 Tydd St Giles PE13 . . . . .237 B5
Ellwood Ave PE2 . . . . . . .187 C5
Ellwoods Cl CB7 . . . . . . .213 A5
Elm CE Jun Sch PE14 . . . .236 B5
Elm Cl Dullingham CB8 . . . .70 D8
 Haverhill CB9 . . . . .23 F8
 Huntingdon PE29 . . . . . .141 E7
 March PE15 . . . . .243 D7
 5 Market Deeping PE6 . .231 E8
 Stilton PE7 . . . . .175 F7
 Witchford CB6 . . . . .217 E2
 Yaxley PE7 . . . . .181 F7
Elm Cres PE6 . . . . .203 D8
Elm Croft PE19 . . . . .95 F3
Elm Ct Elmdon CB11 . . . . . .9 B4
 5 Sturmer CB9 . . . . . . .24 C5
Elm Dr
 Little Stukeley PE28 . . . .151 E3
 Offord Cluny PE19 . . . . .118 A2
 St Ives PE27 . . . . .143 F6
Elm End PE28 . . . . .150 F4
Elm High Rd PE14 . . . . . .245 E1
Elm Low Rd PE14 . . . . . .245 D2
Elm Pk PE7 . . . . .189 F7
Elm Rd Folksworth PE7 . . .175 D4

Elm Rd continued
 Little Stukeley PE28 . . . .152 A2
 March PE15 . . . . .243 D8
 Wisbech PE13 . . . . .245 D3
Elm Road Prim Sch
 PE13 . . . . .245 D4
Elm Side CB6 . . . . .242 B5
Elm St Cambridge CB1 . . .246 B3
 Peterborough PE2 . . . . .186 F7
 Stamford PE9 . . . . .244 C5
Elm Tree Cl CB3 . . . . .79 C3
Elm Tree Dr SG8 . . . . . . .12 F4
Elm Way Melbourn SG8 . . .14 C5
 Papworth Everard CB3 . . .99 A3
 Sawtry PE28 . . . . .168 B3
 Willingham CB4 . . . . . . .209 A1
Elm Wlk SG8 . . . . .5 F7
Elmfield CB6 . . . . .240 C5
Elmfield Dr PE14 . . . . . . .245 E1
Elmfield Rd
 Cambridge CB4 . . . . .84 A5
 Peterborough PE1 . . . . .198 A7
Elmhurst Cl CB9 . . . . .24 B7
Elmore Rd PE3 . . . . .197 A3
Elm's Ave CB2 . . . . .49 A5
Elms Cl CB2 . . . . .32 D1
Elms Rd
 Freckenham IP28 . . . . . .213 E2
 Red Lodge IP28 . . . . . . .213 F1
Elms The Chatteris PE16 . .241 E4
 Great Chesterford CB10 . .18 C3
 Haslingfield CB3 . . . . . . .47 C5
 Milton CB4 . . . . .105 C2
Elmside PE14 . . . . .236 D5
Elstone PE2 . . . . .186 A4
Elstow Cl 7 CB4 . . . . . . .208 D1
Elsworth Cl PE27 . . . . . . .144 C5
Elsworth Pl CB1 . . . . .65 A6
Elsworth Prim Sch CB3 . .100 A4
Elsworth Rd
 Boxworth CB3 . . . . .101 A5
 Conington CB3 . . . . .100 C8
Elter Wr PE29 . . . . .141 B5
Eltisley Ave CB3 . . . . .64 C7
Eltisley Rd SG19 . . . . .58 E6
Elton CE Prim Sch PE8 . . .178 D8
Elton H★ PE8 . . . . .178 D6
Elton Rd
 Sibson cum Stibbington
 PE8 . . . . .183 C8
 Water Newton PE8 . . . . .184 B7
Elvedon Way CB8 . . . . . . .110 E5
Elwyn Ct PE15 . . . . .243 D3
Elwyn Rd PE15 . . . . .243 D3
Elwyndene Rd PE15 . . . . .243 D3
Ely Cath CB7 . . . . .240 D4
Ely Cl PE4 . . . . .204 D3
Ely Cty Inf Sch CB7 . . . . .240 E6
Ely Mus★ CB7 . . . . .240 D4
Ely Rd Downham CB6 . . . .218 B6
 Ely CB7 . . . . .218 D4
 Landbeach CB5 . . . . . . .105 F8
 Littleport CB6 . . . . .242 C2
 Milton CB4 . . . . .105 E3
 Soham CB7 . . . . .211 F7
 Stretham CB6 . . . . .210 F5
 Sutton CB6 . . . . .216 F2
 Waterbeach CB5 . . . . . .126 E3
 Wentworth CB6 . . . . . . .217 A2
Ely Way CB6 . . . . .210 A7
Embankment Rd 4 PE1 . .198 A1
Embry Rd 19 PE8 . . . . . . .230 B1
Emery Cl PE28 . . . . .140 C3
Emery Pl PE19 . . . . .74 F7
Emery St CB1 . . . . .84 A1
Emlyns Gdns PE9 . . . . . . .244 C6
Emlyns St PE9 . . . . .244 C6
Emmanuel Cl IP28 . . . . . .239 D5
Emmanuel Coll CB1 . . . . .246 B2
Emmanuel Rd
 Cambridge CB1 . . . . . . .246 B2
 Stamford PE9 . . . . .244 B7
Emmanuel St CB1 . . . . . .246 B2
Emneth CP Sch PE14 . . . .236 D6
Empingham Rd 3 PE9 . . .244 A5
Empress Swimming Pool
 PE16 . . . . .241 C4
Empson Rd PE1 . . . . .198 F5
Emson's Cl CB1 . . . . .35 D2
Enderbys Wharf PE27 . . .144 A3
Engaine PE2 . . . . .186 B5
Engine Rd CB7 . . . . .211 F5
Engleric SG8 . . . . .8 D4
English Rd PE6 . . . . .233 B4
English St PE1 . . . . .197 E5
Ennerdale Cl PE29 . . . . . .141 B6
Ennerdale Rise PE4 . . . . .204 D2
Ennisdale Cl 4 CB4 . . . . . .83 E7
Enniskillen Rd CB5 . . . . . .84 B5
Enterprise Way PE13 . . . .245 A2
Erasmus Cl CB4 . . . . .83 C5
Erica Rd PE27 . . . . .144 A6
Eriswell Rd
 Beck Row, Holywell Row
 & Kenny Hill IP28 . . . . .214 B8
 Haverhill CB9 . . . . .24 D8
Ermine Bsns Ctr PE28 . . .141 B8
Ermine Bsns Pk PE29 . . . .141 B8
Ermine Cl SG8 . . . . .5 D8
Ermine Cres PE7 . . . . . . .176 A7
Ermine St Caxton CB3 . . . .78 E2
 Huntingdon PE29 . . . . . .141 C5
 Little Stukeley PE28 . . . .151 E2
 The Stukeleys PE28 . . . .141 A8
Ermine St N CB3 . . . . .99 C4
Ermine St S CB3 . . . . .78 C8

Ermine Way Arrington SG8 . .44 C4
 Sawtry PE28 . . . . .168 C3
Ernulf Com Sch PE19 . . . .74 E3
Erratts Hill CB8 . . . . .73 D1
Eskdale Cl 1 PE4 . . . . . .204 E3
Essendyke PE3 . . . . .197 A7
Essex Cl CB4 . . . . .83 E5
Essex Hill CB11 . . . . .9 B2
Essex Rd
 Huntingdon PE29 . . . . . .141 E8
 5 Stamford PE9 . . . . . .244 B6
Estover Rd PE15 . . . . . . .243 E6
Etheldreda St CB6 . . . . . .240 B4
Eurocentre Sch CB2 . . . . . .64 F7
Europa Way PE13 . . . . . .245 B2
Euston St PE29 . . . . .141 E4
Euximoor Dro PE14 . . . . .229 B5
Evans Cl PE28 . . . . .140 D3
Evans Way CB2 . . . . .32 E8
Evelyn Hospl The CB2 . . . .64 E6
Everdon Way PE3 . . . . . .197 C5
Evergreen La CB8 . . . . . . .55 F7
Evergreens CB4 . . . . .84 B5
Everingham PE2 . . . . . . .185 D5
Eversden Church Sch
 CB3 . . . . .46 A7
Eversden Cl CB3 . . . . .61 D5
Eversden Rd CB3 . . . . . . .46 C5
Eversley Cl CB4 . . . . .125 D4
Everton Hill SG19 . . . . . . .40 B3
Everton Rd SG19 . . . . . . .40 B1
Eves Cl PE6 . . . . .207 D1
Ewingswood 1 PE28 . . . .168 C2
Exchange Sq PE13 . . . . . .245 B5
Exchange St PE1 . . . . . . .198 A2
Exeter Cl Cambridge CB2 . .64 D1
 Peterborough PE1 . . . . .197 F6
 2 Market Deeping PE6 . .231 F8
Exeter Rd
 Newmarket CB8 . . . . . . .111 A4
 Peterborough PE1 . . . . .197 F6
 7 Wittering PE8 . . . . . .230 B1
Exmoor Cl PE29 . . . . . . .141 A4
Exning CP Sch CB8 . . . . .110 B8
Exning Rd CB8 . . . . .110 D6
Eye CE Sch PE6 . . . . . . .232 B1
Eye Hill Dro CB7 . . . . . . .211 F7
Eye Rd PE1 . . . . .198 F2
Eyebury Rd PE6 . . . . . . .199 A6
Eyeworth Rd SG19 . . . . . .25 B2
Eynesbury CE Sch PE19 . . .74 E4
Eynesbury Gn PE19 . . . . . .74 F4
Eyrescroft PE3 . . . . .197 A7
Eyrescroft CP Sch PE3 . . .197 A7
Eyresford Cl PE7 . . . . . . .188 A5

F

Faber La PE8 . . . . .183 D1
Fair Ct CB1 . . . . .246 C3
Fair Green The CB5 . . . . .129 D1
Fair St CB1 . . . . .246 C3
Fairbairn Rd CB4 . . . . . . .84 C5
Fairchild Way PE1 . . . . . .198 A7
Fairey Ave PE29 . . . . . . .141 F1
Fairey Fox Dr 1 IP28 . . . .239 B5
Fairfax Ct PE19 . . . . .74 F3
Fairfax Rd CB1 . . . . .84 B1
Fairfax Way March PE15 . .243 E1
 10 Market Deeping PE6 . .231 F8
Fairfield Gamlingay SG19 . . .41 C5
 5 Sutton CB6 . . . . .216 E1
Fairfield Dr PE26 . . . . . . .172 A6
Fairfield Rd PE2 . . . . . . .187 A8
Fairfield Way CB1 . . . . . . .35 D3
Fairfields St Ives PE27 . . .144 B4
 Sawston CB2 . . . . .50 A1
Fairfields Cres PE27 . . . . .144 B4
Fairhaven Cl CB5 . . . . . . .107 C2
Fairhaven Way CB8 . . . . .110 E5
Fairlawns Rd 1 CB8 . . . . .110 F2
Fairmead Way PE3 . . . . . .197 C5
Fairstead Ho Sch CB8 . . . .111 B4
Fairview Ave PE16 . . . . . .241 B2
Fairview Dr PE16 . . . . . . .241 B2
Fairview Gr CB5 . . . . . . .108 E5
Fairway Chatteris PE16 . . .241 B3
 Girton CB3 . . . . .84 A8
Fairway The Bar Hill CB3 . .102 D3
 1 Bluntisham/Colne
 PE28 . . . . .208 C5
Falcon Cl Haverhill CB9 . . .24 C8
 5 St Neots PE19 . . . . . .75 B7
Falcon Dr PE29 . . . . .142 B7
Falcon La Whittlesey PE7 . .189 D6
 15 Wisbech PE13 . . . . .245 C5
Falcon Mews CB6 . . . . . .240 B5
Falcon Rd 7 PE13 . . . . . .245 C5
Falcon Way PE19 . . . . . . .117 B3
Falconer Rd CB9 . . . . .24 C5
Falkirk Cl CB9 . . . . .39 A1
Falkland Dr PE13 . . . . . . .245 D3
Falklands Rd CB9 . . . . . . .39 A1
Falkner Rd CB2 . . . . .33 A8
Fallodan Rd PE2 . . . . . . .185 C3
Fallow Corner Dro
 PE15 . . . . .224 A3
Fallow Dr PE29 . . . . .74 B5
Fallowfield Cambridge CB4 .84 B5
 Peterborough PE2 . . . . .185 D5
Fall's Dro PE6 . . . . .232 F7
Falmouth Ave CB8 . . . . . .110 F3
Falmouth Gdns CB8 . . . . .110 A6
Falmouth St CB8 . . . . . . .110 F3
Falstaff Rd 2 PE19 . . . . . .74 C3
Fane Cl PE9 . . . . .244 B7
Fane Rd PE4 . . . . .197 E8

Fanshawe Rd CB1 . . . . . . .65 A6
Far Pasture PE4 . . . . .204 B5
Farcet Cl 5 PE19 . . . . . . .74 C6
Farcet Prim Sch PE7 . . . .187 C2
Fardell Rd 6 PE13 . . . . . .245 C4
Fardon Cl CB3 . . . . .100 A4
Farendon Rd PE28 . . . . . .140 E1
Farfield Cl PE28 . . . . .168 A5
Farleigh Fields PE2 . . . . .185 D7
Farm Cl Ramsey PE26 . . . .171 C3
 Sawtry PE28 . . . . .168 B4
Farm La
 Papworth Everard CB3 . . .99 C2
 Thriplow SG8 . . . . .31 B1
Farm Rise CB2 . . . . .32 C5
Farm View PE5 . . . . .195 E2
Farmer's End CB3 . . . . . . .61 E5
Farmer's Row CB1 . . . . . . .66 E4
Farmland Mus★ CB5 . . . .127 A5
Farmstead Cl CB4 . . . . . .104 B5
Farriers Ct PE2 . . . . .186 D7
Farringdon Cl 2 PE1 . . . .198 D6
Farringford Cl 4 CB8 . . . . .83 C6
Farthing Dro PE38 . . . . . .226 D6
Farthing La PE27 . . . . . . .144 B4
Fassage Cl CB5 . . . . .107 C2
Fastnet Cl CB9 . . . . .24 D8
Faulkner Cl CB4 . . . . . . .105 C2
Fawcett CP Sch CB2 . . . . .64 D3
Fawsley Garth PE3 . . . . . .197 C6
Feast Cl PE2 . . . . .212 E1
Feilden Way CB8 . . . . . . .110 E5
Feldale Pl PE7 . . . . .189 F8
Fellowes Dr PE26 . . . . . . .172 A6
Fellowes Gdns PE2 . . . . . .187 A7
Fellowes Rd PE2 . . . . . . .187 A7
Felsham Chase CB5 . . . . .130 C2
Felsted Ave PE13 . . . . . . .245 E5
Felton St CB1 . . . . .65 A8
Felton Way CB7 . . . . .240 E6
Feltons CB7 . . . . .212 E1
Fen Bank Rd CB7 . . . . . . .213 A6
Fen Causeway PE1 . . . . . .198 E2
Fen Causeway★ PE7 . . . . .189 A8
Fen Causeway The CB3 . . .246 A1
Fen Cl PE13 . . . . .245 E6
Fen Ditton Dro CB5 . . . . . .84 F5
Fen Drayton Cty Prim Sch
 CB4 . . . . .121 F6
Fen Drayton Rd CB4 . . . . .122 C5
Fen Dro PE7 . . . . .176 C8
Fen End Over CB4 . . . . . .208 D1
 Willingham CB4 . . . . . . .209 A1
Fen La Sawtry PE28 . . . . .168 C3
 Stilton PE7 . . . . .176 C8
 Swaffham Bulbeck CB5 . .108 A4
 Tydd St Giles PE13 . . . . .237 B5
Fen Rd
 Bassingbourn cum Kneesworth
 SG8 . . . . .12 B7
 Little Wilbraham CB1 . . . .86 D2
 Lode CB5 . . . . .107 B4
 Milton CB4 . . . . .84 D6
 Newton CB1 . . . . .237 E4
 Pidley cum Fenton PE28 .165 E1
 Shingay cum Wendy SG8 . .26 F1
 Wisbech St Mary PE13 . .234 E2
Fen Side CB6 . . . . .209 E4
Fen St PE7 . . . . .176 A7
Fen The PE28 . . . . .121 B6
Fen View
 3 Christchurch PE14 . . . .229 D3
 6 Doddington/Wimblington
 PE15 . . . . .222 F5
 Peterborough PE7 . . . . .187 F6
Fen Way 3 PE14 . . . . . . .236 A5
Fenbridge Rd PE4 . . . . . .204 C4
Fendon Cl CB1 . . . . .65 B3
Fendon Rd CB1 . . . . .65 B3
Fendyke La PE13 . . . . . . .237 E1
Fendyke Rd PE14 . . . . . . .236 E5
Fengate PE1 . . . . .198 D1
Fengate Cl 1 PE1 . . . . . . .198 D2
Fengate Rd PE14 . . . . . . .238 F1
Fenland Cl 3 PE15 . . . . . .223 B7
Fenland L Ctrs PE7 . . . . .189 E6
Fenland Rd PE13 . . . . . . .245 E6
Fenland Way PE16 . . . . . .241 B5
Fenleigh Cl CB5 . . . . .106 B8
Fennec Cl CB1 . . . . .66 B6
Fennells Cl CB9 . . . . .24 A7
Fenny La SG8 . . . . .29 A1
Fenside Dr PE6 . . . . .207 C1
Fenside Rd PE28 . . . . . . .168 C6
Fenstanton Cty Prim Sch
 PE28 . . . . .121 C6
Fenton Hill PE28 . . . . . . .165 C3
Fenton Rd Haverhill CB9 . . .24 B8
 Warboys PE28 . . . . .165 A4
Feoffees Rd 5 PE28 . . . . .208 C8
Fern Gr PE28 . . . . .23 E8
Ferndale CB1 . . . . .66 C8
Ferndale Cl CB8 . . . . .111 B5
Ferndale Rise CB5 . . . . . . .84 C4
Ferndale Way PE1 . . . . . .205 B1
Ferndown Dr PE29 . . . . . .118 F8
Fernie Cl PE6 . . . . .205 D8
Fernlea Cl CB1 . . . . .65 F7
Ferrars Ave PE19 . . . . .74 E4
Ferrars Rd PE29 . . . . . . .141 D5
Ferrars Way CB4 . . . . . . .83 D6
Ferriman Rd PE28 . . . . . .137 F6
Ferry Bank PE38 . . . . . . .226 D8
Ferry Cutter La CB4 . . . . .246 C4
Ferry Dr PE6 . . . . .196 D3
Ferry Hill PE5 . . . . .196 B1
Ferry La
 Beck Row, Holywell Row
 & Kenny Hill IP28 . . . . .213 D5

Ferry La continued
Cambridge CB4 ....84 B4
Newton PE13 ....238 B5
Ferry Meadows Ctry Pk★
PE2 ....185 D8
Ferry Way CB6 ....242 D4
Ferryview PE2 ....185 E6
Festival Cl PE15 ....224 C4
Festival Rd CB7 ....213 A5
Festival Way CB6 ....226 B6
Fews Cl 4 PE27 ....208 A3
Field Ave PE13 ....237 F7
Field Baulk PE15 ....243 D2
Field Bell PE28 ....140 F3
Field Cl Abbotsley PE19 ..57 A6
Alconbury PE28 ....150 F5
Buckden PE19 ....117 B4
Grafham PE28 ....116 A7
Linton CB1 ....35 A2
Little Paxton PE19 ....95 F2
Warboys PE28 ....164 F5
Field Cottage Rd PE19 ...74 C3
Field Cres SG8 ....5 F7
Field End Balsham CB1 ...53 A4
Witchford CB6 ....217 D2
Field Farm Cotts CB10 ...18 F7
Field Gate CB6 ....216 D2
Field La CB5 ....84 E6
Field Rd Kingston CB3 ...61 B3
Mildenhall IP28 ....239 C5
Ramsey PE26 ....172 A7
Field Rise PE7 ....181 D5
Field Row CB3 ....61 B3
Field Studies Ctr★ PE8 .194 C1
Field Terr PE7 ....187 C2
Field Terrace Rd CB8 ...110 F5
Field View Bar Hill CB3 .102 B2
Harston CB2 ....48 A4
Field Way CB1 ....65 C3
Field Wlk Mildenhall IP28 239 C5
Peterborough PE1 ....198 B2
Fieldfare Dr PE2 ....187 E6
Fieldfare Way 10 SG8 .....5 E8
Fielding Ct 2 PE19 .....74 C6
Fielding Pl PE19 ....97 F4
Fieldside Ely CB6 ....240 B4
Stretham CB6 ....210 E5
Whittlesey PE7 ....190 F8
Fifth Ave PE13 ....245 E4
Fifty Dro CB6 ....225 C7
Fifty Rd
Christchurch PE14 ......229 D1
Manea PE14 ....224 D7
Figtree Wlk PE1 ....198 B8
Fillance The SG8 ....12 D5
Finch Rd CB4 ....83 D5
Fincham Rd IP28 ....239 B5
Fincham's Cl CB1 ....35 D2
Finchfield PE1 ....198 F7
Finchley Ave IP28 ....239 B6
Finchley Gn PE3 ....197 E4
Finch's Cl CB2 ....49 C5
Finch's Rd CB3 ....46 A7
Finkle La PE7 ....189 D7
Firdale Cl PE6 ....206 C2
Firelots Dro PE15 ....223 C8
Firs The CB2 ....32 D2
First Ave Warboys PE28 ..164 E6
Wisbech PE13 ....245 D5
First Broadpool Dro
PE28 ....165 E8
First Drift PE28 ....244 B2
First Dro Burwell CB5 ...130 C7
Peterborough PE1 ....198 F8
First Furlong Dro PE16 ..241 A3
First Marsh Rd PE13 ....238 D2
First Turf Fen Dro PE28 .165 B8
Fish Hill SG8 ....5 D6
Fisher Cl CB9 ....24 D7
Fisher St CB4 ....246 A4
Fishermans Cl PE26 .....171 B1
Fishermans Dr 3 PE15 ..243 A5
Fisher's La Cambridge CB1 65 F6
Orwell SG8 ....45 D2
Fishers Cl PE7 ....175 F7
Fishers Way PE19 ....118 F8
Fishers Yd 4 PE19 ......74 E5
Fison Rd CB5 ....84 E4
Fitton End Rd PE13 .....237 F3
Fitzgerald Cl CB6 ....240 E8
Fitzroy Ct CB1 ....246 C3
Fitzroy La CB5 ....246 C3
Fitzroy St Cambridge CB1 246 C3
Newmarket CB8 ....111 A3
Fitzwilliam Coll CB3 ......83 B4
Fitzwilliam Hospl PE6 ...196 E2
Fitzwilliam Mus★ CB2 ...246 A1
Fitzwilliam Rd
Cambridge CB2 ....64 F6
Stamford PE9 ....244 A7
Fitzwilliam St
Cambridge CB2 ....246 B1
Peterborough PE1 ....198 A3
Five Arches PE1 ....197 C6
Five Hundred Dro PE15 .224 A4
Flackdale Rd 1 PE28 ...120 B1
Flag Fen Mus★ PE6 .....199 B2
Flag Fen Rd PE1 ....198 C4
Flaggrass Hill Rd PE15 ..224 B8
Flambards CI SG8 ....14 B8
Flamborough CI PE2 .....197 E1
Flamsteed Dr PE29 ......140 F5
Flamsteed Rd CB1 ....65 A6
Flat Rd CB4 ....209 B3
Flavian Cl CB9 ....24 D7
Flaxfields CB1 ....35 C3
Flaxland Castor PE3 .....197 A6
Peterborough PE3 ....197 A6

Fleam Dyke Cotts CB1 ...67 C2
Flecks La
Shingay cum Wendy SG8 ..26 D1
Steeple Morden SG8 ......11 D8
Fleet Cl PE28 ....242 D4
Fleet The SG8 ....5 C6
Fleet Way PE7 ....187 B6
Fleetwood CB6 ....240 C5
Fleetwood Cl PE15 ......243 D2
Fleming Ave IP28 ....239 C5
Fleming Ct 2 PE15 .....243 F3
Fletcher Ave CB5 ....127 C1
Fletcher's Terr 3 CB1 ..65 A8
Fletchers Cl PE26 ....172 A7
Fletton Ave PE2 ....187 A8
Fletton Fields PE2 ......187 A7
Fletton Parkway PE2 ....185 D2
Fletton Prim Sch PE2 ...186 F6
Flint Cl PE28 ....140 C2
Flint House Rd PE14 ....229 F5
Flint La CB5 ....126 E3
Flint Way PE19 ....74 E2
Flood's Ferry Rd PE15 ..222 B7
Flore Cl PE3 ....197 C5
Florence Cl PE7 ....189 F6
Florida Ave PE29 ....141 E6
Flower St 2 CB1 ....84 A1
Flowers Cl PE26 ....172 A7
Flowmere Rd SG8 ....8 A5
Fodder Fen Dro PE27 ....219 B3
Foddor Fen Rd PE15 ....224 C6
Fodderfen Dro
Beck Row, Holywell Row
& Kenny Hill IP28 ......219 F1
Wicken PE7 ....211 C3
Fold La PE13 ....237 F2
Fold The PE7 ....190 F8
Folgate La PE14 ....238 F6
Folksworth CE Sch PE7 .175 D8
Folksworth Rd PE7 ......180 E1
Folly Cl PE7 ....181 C5
Folly Dro CB7 ....219 A7
Folly Rd IP28 ....239 B6
Folly's Dro PE13 ....234 F3
Fontwell Ave CB4 ....83 C5
Fontwell Gdns 2 PE9 ...244 B5
Foot Dro PE26 ....220 F1
Footpath The CB3 ....82 C2
Ford Cl
Beck Row, Holywell Row
& Kenny Hill IP28 ......213 D7
Eaton Socon PE19 ....74 D5
Ford End Alconbury PE28 .150 F4
Hail Weston PE19 ....95 B1
Fordham Abbey★ CB7 ...131 E8
Fordham Cl SG7 ....2 D5
Fordham Moor CB7 ......212 E3
Fordham Prim Sch CB7 ..212 F1
Fordham Rd Exning CB8 .131 F3
Freckenham IP28 ....213 B2
Isleham CB7 ....213 A4
5 Royston SG8 ....5 E5
Snailwell CB8 ....132 A5
5 Soham CB7 ....212 B3
Fordham Way SG8 ....14 D5
Fordwich Cl 1 CB4 ......83 D6
Fore Hill CB7 ....240 D4
Foreman's Rd SG8 ....31 B2
Forest End CB8 ....134 A6
Forest Glade CB9 ....38 F2
Forest Rd CB1 ....65 C5
Forest Way IP28 ....239 C4
Forge Cl PE19 ....74 B2
Forge End
Great Shelford CB2 ......49 C4
Peterborough PE7 ....185 A4
Forge Way PE28 ....164 F5
Forster Rd PE28 ....140 E1
Forsythia Rd PE27 ......144 A6
Fortescue Rd CB4 ....83 E6
Forties Cl CB8 ....24 D8
Fortune Way SG8 ....12 E5
Forty Acre Rd PE1 ......198 D2
Forty Foot Bank
Doddington PE26 ....222 C3
Ramsey PE26 ....221 E2
Ramsey Forty Foot PE26 .221 C3
Foster Rd CB2 ....64 D2
Foundry Cl CB4 ....125 D3
Foundry Rd 4 PE9 ......244 A5
Foundry Way
Eaton Socon PE19 ....74 B1
March PE15 ....228 B6
Ramsey PE26 ....172 A5
Fountain La
Haslingfield CB3 ....47 B5
Soham CB7 ....212 B4
Fountains Pl PE6 ....232 B1
Four Acres
Fenstanton PE28 ....121 C6
Great Chesterford CB10 ..18 D3
Fourfields Prim Sch
PE7 ....181 C6
Fourth Ave PE13 ....245 E4
Fourth Dro
Downham CB6 ....225 A1
Peterborough PE1 ....198 F3
Fowlmere Cty Prim Sch
SG8 ....15 D8
Fowlmere Nature Reserve★
SG8 ....15 B8
Fowlmere Rd Foxton SG8 .30 D3
Heydon SG8 ....7 D4
Newton CB2 ....31 B6
Shepreth SG8 ....29 F4
Thriplow SG8 ....31 A2
Fox Cl PE19 ....75 A5

Fox Cnr SG8 ....10 F5
Fox Covert PE7 ....175 F7
Fox Gn CB8 ....55 F7
Fox Gr PE29 ....141 F2
Fox Hill SG8 ....11 A5
Fox Hill Rd SG8 ....10 F5
Fox Hollow CB3 ....102 C4
Fox Rd Balsham CB1 .....52 F3
Bourn CB3 ....60 D5
Catworth PE28 ....136 D8
Fox St SG19 ....58 E5
Fox Wood N 4 CB7 .....212 B5
Fox Wood S CB7 ....212 B4
Foxburrow Cl PE9 ....38 F1
Foxcovert Rd
Peakirk PE6 ....204 A8
Peterborough PE4 ....204 B4
Foxenfields PE28 ....162 C1
Foxglove Bank 2 SG8 ....5 D8
Foxglove Cl 3 PE19 .....74 C5
Foxley 1 PE4 ....204 C4
Fox's Cl CB4 ....105 D2
Fox's Way CB3 ....67 F8
Foxton Prim Sch CB2 ....30 C5
Foxton Rd Barrington CB2 .30 A7
Foxton Sta CB2 ....30 C6
Foxtrot La PE28 ....151 F3
Framlingham Rd PE7 ....187 F5
Francis CB7 ....23 F8
Francis Gdns PE1 ....197 F8
Francis Pas 3 CB2 ......64 E7
Frank Bridges Cl 2
CB7 ....212 B3
Frank Perkins Parkway
.....................187 B8
Frank Perkins Way PE1 .198 D4
Frankland Wlk 2 CB7 ...240 F6
Franklin Cres PE1 ....198 E6
Franklin Gdns CB4 ......125 D4
Frank's La CB4 ....84 B5
Franks La PE13 ....237 F5
Fraser Dr PE27 ....144 A7
Fraser Rd CB4 ....84 A6
Fraserburgh Way 2
PE2 ....186 C4
Freckenham Rd IP28 ....213 B3
Fred Archer Way CB8 ...111 A3
Fred Dannatt Rd IP28 ..239 A6
Frederick Talbot Cl 8
CB7 ....212 B4
Free Sch La CB2 ....246 A2
Freedom Bridge PE13 ...245 B4
Freeman Cl 10 PE8 .....230 B1
Freemantle Ct 5 PE19 ..74 B3
Freesia Way PE4 ....181 F6
Freewood La CB11 ....9 B3
French Dro PE6 ....232 E7
French's Rd
Cambridge CB4 ....83 D4
Walpole PE14 ....238 D4
Freshfields PE28 ....110 F4
Freston PE4 ....204 F4
Friar Cl CB9 ....38 F1
Friar's Cl CB1 ....65 F5
Friar's Pl CB6 ....242 C5
Friar's Way CB6 ....242 C5
Friars Nine CB6 ....242 C4
Friday St IP28 ....213 D6
Fridaybridge CP Sch
PE14 ....236 A3
Fridaybridge Rd PE14 ...236 A4
Friends Cl PE19 ....98 C2
Frinton Way 4 PE13 ....245 E5
Frobisher Cl PE29 ......141 F6
Frog End
Great Wilbraham CB1 ....67 F7
Shepreth SG8 ....29 F2
Frogge St CB10 ....18 B3
Frogmore CB8 ....110 B7
Frogs Abbey La PE15 ...223 B7
Frogs Hall 6 PE28 .....208 C5
Froize End 4 CB6 ......210 A5
Froment Way CB4 ......105 C3
Fromont Cl CB1 ....66 E4
Front Rd Murrow PE13 ..236 D4
Tydd St Giles PE13 ......238 D8
Frowd Cl CB7 ....212 E1
Frumetty La PE28 ......150 F4
Fryers Callis PE9 ....244 C3
Fryth Cl CB9 ....39 A1
Fulbourn CP Sch CB1 ...66 F5
Fulbourn Hospl
Cambridge CB1 ....65 B3
Fulbourn CB1 ....66 C5
Fulbourn Old Drift CB1 ..66 A6
Fulbourn Rd
Cambridge CB1 ....65 F5
Fulbourn CB1 ....66 D7
Fulbridge Jun & Inf Sch
PE1 ....197 F7
Fulbridge Rd PE1 ....197 F8
Fulbrooke Rd CB3 ....64 A7
Fulham Rd PE3 ....197 E4
Fuller Cl PE28 ....137 F6
Fuller's La 5 PE15 .....223 B7
Fundrey Rd PE13 ....245 F6
Funtham's La PE7 ......188 D7
Furlongs The PE27 ......208 A2
Furrells The CB1 ....35 C3
Furrowfields Rd PE16 ...241 A4
Furrows The PE27 ......144 A4
Furtherford CB4 ....208 E1
Furze Gr SG8 ....5 E5
Furze Ride PE1 ....198 B8
Fydell Ct PE19 ....75 B7

G

Gables Cl SG8 ....29 A1
Gables The PE28 ....121 A5
Gadd's La PE13 ....235 D2
Gage Cl SG8 ....5 D8
Gains La PE28 ....166 D2
Gainsborough Ave 6
PE19 ....74 C5
Gainsborough Cl CB4 ....84 B6
Gainsborough Dr 7
PE27 ....144 A7
Gainsborough Rd CB9 ...38 D1
Gala Cl PE7 ....176 A8
Galfrid Rd CB5 ....84 D2
Gall The CB7 ....240 D4
Gallions Cl PE4 ....204 D1
Gall's Dro PE13 ....235 A4
Gamlingay Cty Fst Sch
SG19 ....41 D8
Gamlingay Rd
Gamlingay SG19 ....41 D8
Potton SG19 ....41 C1
Waresley SG19 ....57 E1
Gannet Cl CB9 ....24 C8
Gannocks Cl PE2 ....185 F5
Gannocks The PE2 ......185 F5
Ganwick Cl 2 CB9 ......38 F2
Gaol St 12 PE11 ....245 C4
Garden Cl Burwell CB5 ..130 C4
Ramsey PE26 ....172 A4
Garden End SG8 ....14 D5
Garden End Rd PE1 .....198 B6
Garden Fields CB2 ......48 E3
Garden La Royston SG8 ...5 D5
Wisbech St Mary PE13 ..235 A7
Garden Wlk
Cambridge CB4 ....83 D4
Histon CB4 ....104 C5
Royston SG8 ....5 E7
Gardeners La 7 CB7 ....212 B4
Gardiners La SG7 ....2 A4
Garlic Row CB5 ....84 B3
Garner Ave PE28 ....164 E5
Garner Cl 4 CB4 ....105 C3
Garner Ct PE29 ....141 F7
Garratt Rd 4 CB4 ......244 B4
Garret Hostel La CB2 ...246 A2
Garry Dr CB4 ....84 A7
Garton St PE1 ....198 A5
Gas La Ely CB7 ....240 D3
Stamford PE9 ....244 C5
Thorney PE6 ....233 A3
Gas Rd PE15 ....243 D3
Gas St PE9 ....244 C5
Gascoigne PE6 ....203 F5
Gaul Rd PE13 ....243 B4
Gault Bank PE15 ....227 D1
Gaultree Sq PE14 ......236 D6
Gayton Cl 3 CB2 ....64 D3
Gayton Ct PE3 ....197 C5
Gazeley Gdns PE7 ......187 B2
Gazeley Rd Ashley CB8 ..92 A8
Cambridge CB2 ....64 C2
Kentford CB8 ....134 C1
Moulton CB8 ....112 F6
Gazelle Cl 4 PE19 ......74 B5
Gazelle Way CB1 ....66 B7
Geneva St PE1 ....198 A3
Geoffrey Bishop Ave CB1 67 A4
George Gibson Cl CB8 ...110 C8
George IV St CB2 ....246 C1
George La Buckden PE19 .117 A3
Royston SG8 ....5 D5
Warboys PE28 ....164 E5
George Lambton Ave
CB8 ....110 F6
George Nuttall Cl CB4 ...84 A6
George Pateman Ct 2
CB1 ....64 F7
George Pl 7 PE19 ....74 F2
George St Cambridge CB4 .83 F4
Huntingdon PE29 ....141 D4
2 March PE15 ....243 D4
Peterborough PE2 ....186 F8
Stilton PE7 ....175 F8
Willingham CB4 ....209 A1
Georgian Cl PE2 ....197 E2
Gerard Cl CB5 ....84 C2
Gerard Rd CB5 ....84 D3
Gery Ct PE19 ....74 C5
Gibralter La CB4 ....122 E5
Gibside Ave PE16 ......241 B3
Gibson Cl CB5 ....106 A7
Gidding Rd PE28 ....167 D3
Giddings Cl PE2 ....185 F4
Gifford Pl CB2 ....246 A3
Gifford's Cl CB3 ....82 E8
Giffords Way 4 CB4 ....208 D1
Gilbert Cl CB8 ....133 A4
Gilbert Rd Cambridge CB4 .83 D5
Littleport CB6 ....242 B5
Gilbert Scott Dr CB6 ...240 E7
Gildale PE4 ....204 D4
Gildenburgh Ave PE1 ...198 D5
Gill's Hill CB3 ....60 D5
Gilmorton Dr PE1 ......198 D7
Gilpin St PE1 ....197 E6
Gilvan Cl PE19 ....95 E1
Gimber Ct 5 PE29 .....141 F7
Gimbert Rd CB7 ....212 B4
Gipping Cl 1 CB9 ......23 E6
Gipson Cl PE16 ....241 B5
Gipsy Dro PE16 ....215 F6

Gipsy La PE15 ....243 A7
Girton Cl Mildenhall IP28 239 C6
Woodditton CB8 ....111 B1
Girton Coll Cambridge CB3 83 B2
Girton CB3 ....82 F6
Girton Cres PE3 ....142 A7
Girton Rd Girton CB3 ....82 F7
Haverhill CB9 ....24 B7
Girton Way PE9 ....244 A4
Gisborne Cl CB1 ....65 C6
Gladeside CB3 ....102 C4
Gladstone Prim Sch
PE1 ....197 F3
Gladstone St PE1 ......197 F3
Gladstone Way CB1 .....65 F5
Glamis Gdns PE3 ......197 B8
Glassmoor Bank PE7 ...220 F7
Glastonbury Cl 11 PE6 .232 A1
Glatton Dr PE2 ....187 D6
Glatton La PE7 ....176 D3
Glatton Rd PE28 ......168 A6
Glatton Ways PE28 ....175 F1
Glebe Ave CB6 ....185 E4
Glebe Cl Chatteris PE16 .241 D5
Great Paxton PE19 ......96 E4
Toft CB3 ....61 E5
Wimblington PE15 ......224 B4
Glebe Cres CB2 ....33 B4
Glebe Ct PE2 ....187 A8
Glebe Cty Prim Sch
CB3 ....103 E1
Glebe Gdns 2 PE6 .....232 B8
Glebe La PE19 ....117 A3
Glebe Rd Barrington CB2 .29 F8
Brampton PE28 ....140 E2
Cambridge CB1 ....65 B4
Hemingford Grey PE28 ..143 D1
Huntingdon PE29 ......141 D7
Perry PE28 ....115 D3
Peterborough PE2 ......187 A8
Sawtry PE28 ....168 A4
Stilton PE7 ....176 A7
Waterbeach CB5 ....106 A7
Glebe The Haverhill CB9 ..39 A1
Ramsey PE26 ....172 B4
Glebe Way
Haddenham CB6 ....209 F6
Histon CB4 ....104 C4
Glebelands CP Sch
PE16 ....241 E5
Glemsford Rise 2 PE2 ..186 C7
Glen Cres PE9 ....244 C7
Glen Rd 1 PE8 ....230 B1
Glen The PE7 ....187 B7
Glenacre Cl 3 CB1 .....65 E5
Glencoe Way PE2 ......185 D3
Glendale PE2 ....185 D6
Gleneagles PE2 ....185 F6
Glenfields PE2 ....189 C8
Glenmere Cl CB1 ....65 D5
Glenton St PE1 ....198 C2
Glinton Rd Helpston PE6 .203 A8
Newborough PE6 ....204 E8
Glisson Rd CB1 ....246 C1
Globe La Alconbury PE28 .150 E3
3 Littleport CB6 ....242 D4
Gloucester Rd
Brampton PE28 ....140 D1
Haverhill CB9 ....23 F7
Peterborough PE2 ......187 B7
Sawtry PE28 ....168 C3
7 Stamford PE9 ....244 B6
Wyton Airfield PE28 ...143 B8
Glover Cl CB2 ....32 F6
Glover St CB4 ....208 D1
Goddard Cres 1 PE13 ..245 D7
Godeby Ct 4 PE29 .....141 E4
Godesdone Rd CB5 ......84 A3
Godfrey Rd PE1 ....207 D1
Goding Way CB4 ....105 C2
Godmanchester Com
Swimming Pool PE29 ..141 E2
Godric Sq PE2 ....186 D6
Godsey La 2 PE6 ......231 E8
Godwin Cl CB1 ....65 C4
Godwin Rd PE13 ....245 D7
Godwin Way CB1 ....65 C4
Godwit Cl PE7 ....201 A1
Goffsmill PE3 ....197 A4
Gog Magog Way CB2 ....49 C5
Gold St PE15 ....243 C7
Goldcrest Ct 3 CB3 ....79 C3
Golden Drop PE6 ......231 C4
Golden Miller Cl PE28 ..110 D7
Golden Rod 3 PE29 ...118 F8
Goldhay Way PE2 ......185 F2
Goldie La PE2 ....185 F6
Golding Pl 15 PE13 ....245 C4
Golding Rd CB1 ....65 B6
Goldings Cl CB9 ....39 A2
Goldpits PE28 ....164 F5
Golf La PE28 ....151 E3
Golf Links Rd
Barton Mills IP28 ....214 A3
Worlington IP28 ....239 A1
Gonville & Caius Coll
CB2 ....246 B1
Gonville Cl PE28 ....239 D6
Gonville Pl CB1 ....246 C1
Goochgate PE12 ....237 A7
Goodacre PE2 ....186 A4
Goodchilds Gdns 5
CB7 ....213 A5
Goode Cl CB4 ....125 D4
Goodens La PE13 ......238 A5

Goodliffe Ave CB1 .....53 C2
Goodwin Gr **1** CB7 ...240 F7
Goodwin Wlk PE4 ....204 C4
Goodwood Rd
 8 Peterborough PE3 ..196 F3
 1 Royston SG8 ....5 F6
Goose Fen Dro CB7 ...211 C6
Gordon Ave March PE15 .243 D4
 Peterborough PE2 .....186 E7
Gordon Cl PE19 ....95 F1
Gordon Fendick Sch
 PE13 ....245 D8
Gordon Rd PE19 ......95 F1
Gordon Richards Cl **2**
 CB8 ....110 F6
Gordon Way PE2 .....186 C7
Gore Tree Rd PE28 ...120 C7
Goredike Bank PE13 .237 E3
Gorefield Prim Sch
 PE13 ....237 E2
Gorefield Rd PE13 ...237 F2
Gorse Cl **8** IP28 .....214 A1
Gorse Way PE27 .....144 B5
Goshawk Cl PE29 ....142 A8
Gosling Way CB2 ......33 A8
Gosling's Dro PE7 ....220 A8
Gosmoor La PE14 ....236 B5
Gosslan Cl PE27 .....144 A6
Gostwick PE2 ....185 D5
Gote La PE13 ....237 C8
Gough Way CB3 ....64 A8
Governess Cl **8** PE15 .223 B7
Gower Rd SG8 ....5 C7
Gowers The CB3 .....103 E1
Grace Sch of Medicine
 CB1 ....65 A8
Gracious St PE7 .....189 D7
Graeme Rd PE5 .....194 F2
Grafham Cl PE2 .....187 E4
Grafham Rd PE28 ....138 F4
Grafham Water Ex Ctr
 PE28 ....116 B5
Grafham Water Nature
 Reserve* PE28 ......115 A4
Grafton Ave PE3 ....197 C3
Grafton Cl PE27 .....143 F8
Grafton St CB1 ......246 C2
Grain Cl CB2 ....49 A5
Grainger Ave PE29 ...118 F8
Granary Cl CB1 ......141 E1
Granary La **5** CB6 ...242 D4
Granary The
 Old Hurst PE28 ......154 D7
 2 Sawtry PE28 .....168 B4
Granby St Littleport CB6 .242 D4
 Newmarket CB8 .....111 B3
 Peterborough PE1 ....198 B2
Grandford Dro PE15 ..227 E6
Grandridge Cl CB1 ....66 F4
Grange Ave PE1 .....198 A6
Grange Bottom SG8 ....5 E5
Grange Cl PE28 .....168 C2
Grange Cres PE2 ....186 A5
Grange Dr CB3 ....82 E7
Grange Farm Cl PE19 .57 B5
Grange La
 Barton Mills IP28 ....239 C2
 Littleport CB6 ......242 B4
 March PE15 ....228 A1
 Peterborough PE3 ....197 D4
 6 Somersham PE28 ..208 C8
 13 Somersham PE28 ..215 C1
 Wisbech PE13 ....245 A7
Grange The Meldreth SG8 .14 B8
 8 Somersham PE28 ..208 C8
Grangehill Rd PE13 ..237 B6
Granham's Rd
 Cambridge CB2 ....65 C1
 Great Shelford CB2 ...49 A7
Granhams Cl CB2 .....49 A6
Gransden Rd
 Abbotsley PE19 ......57 E6
 Caxton CB3 ....59 D8
Gransley Rise PE3 ...197 C5
Granta Cl
 Great Chesterford CB10 ..18 D1
 St Ives PE27 ....144 B7
 Witchford CB6 ......217 D1
Granta Cotts CB10 ...18 C2
Granta Leys CB1 ......35 B3
Granta Pl CB2 ....246 A1
Granta Rd CB2 ....32 E5
Granta Terr CB2 ......49 B4
Granta Vale CB1 ......35 D2
Grantchester Mdws CB3 .64 C7
Grantchester Rd
 Barton CB3 ....63 D7
 Cambridge CB2 ....64 B2
 Coton CB3 ....82 C1
 Grantchester CB3 .....64 B6
Grantchester Rise CB5 .130 B5
Grantchester St **3** CB3 .64 C7
Grantham Cl SG8 ......5 B8
Granville Ave PE6 ...231 F7
Granville Gdns IP28 ..239 A4
Granville St PE1 .....198 A4
Grasmere PE29 ......141 B6
Grasmere Gdns PE4 ..204 D3
Grass Plant Cotts CB8 .131 B4
Grassgate La PE14 ...228 E8
Gravel Bridge Rd CB4 .123 C6

Gravel Dro
 Beck Row, Holywell Row
  & Kenny Hill IP28 ...213 C6
 Witcham CB6 ....216 F4
Gravel End CB6 ......217 C5
Gravel End La CB6 ...217 D5
Gravel Pit Hill SG8 ...16 C8
Gravel Wlk PE1 .....198 A2
Graveley Rd PE19 ....97 A8
Graveley Way PE28 ...98 E8
Gray Ct PE1 ....197 E8
Gray Rd CB1 ....65 D6
Grayling Cl CB4 ......84 A4
Gray's Rd SG19 ......41 D6
Grays Cl SG8 ....5 C8
Grays Gr MK44 ....93 B2
Grays La Emneth PE14 .236 C6
 March PE15 ....243 D4
Graysmoor Dro PE14 .228 B8
Great & Little Shelford CE
 Prim Sch CB2 ....48 C4
Great Chesterford Sta
 CB10 ....18 C1
Great Dro Soham CB7 .211 F3
 Swaffham Prior CB7 ..128 C6
 Yaxley PE7 ....182 A5
Great Eastern Rd PE13 .245 B4
Great Eastern St CB1 .65 B8
Great Farthing CT PE27 .144 B4
Great Fen Rd CB7 ...212 B8
Great Gidding CE Prim Sch
 PE28 ....166 D3
Great Heath Prim Sch
 IP28 ....239 D6
Great Ho* CB3 ....47 B5
Great How PE27 .....143 F7
Great La CB5 ....129 C1
Great North Fen Dro
 CB4 ....125 C4
Great North Rd
 Alconbury PE28 .....150 E4
 Buckden PE19 ......117 A5
 Eaton Socon PE19 ....74 B2
 St Neots PE19 ....74 C7
 Sibson cum Stibbington
  PE8 ....183 E8
 Southoe & Midloe PE19 ..95 F4
 Wothorpe PE9 ......244 A2
Great Northern St PE29 141 D5
Great Paxton CE Sch
 PE19 ....96 B3
Great Staughton CP Sch
 PE19 ....93 F6
Great Whyte PE26 ...172 A8
Great Wilbraham Prim Sch
 CB1 ....67 F8
Great Wilbraham Rd CB1 86 F1
Greater Foxes CB1 ...66 F5
Greatford Rd PE9 ...230 C6
Grebe Cl IP28 ....239 D3
Grebe Ct PE7 ....190 A8
Grebe Way **3** PE19 ...75 B7
Green Acres SG19 ....41 C5
Green Bank Rd CB5 ..108 B2
Green Butts CB2 ......32 D5
Green Cl PE19 ....94 A6
Green Drift SG8 ....5 B6
Green Dro Coveney CB6 .217 D4
 Crowland PE6 ....232 D8
 Elm PE14 ....236 D2
 Outwell PE14 ....236 E2
 Thorney PE6 ....200 F4
 Thorney PE6 ....233 A6
Green End Comberton CB3 62 C6
 Fen Ditton CB5 ......84 E6
 Gamlingay SG19 .....41 C5
 Landbeach CB4 .....105 D8
 Little Staughton MK44 .93 A3
 Little Stukeley PE28 ..152 A1
 Stretham CB6 ....210 F4
Green End Rd
 Cambridge CB4 ......84 B6
 St Neots PE19 ....75 A5
 Sawtry PE28 ....168 B3
Green Farm Cl PE5 ..195 E2
Green Head Rd CB5 ..108 D4
Green Hedges Sch CB2 ..49 C4
Green Hill **3** CB6 ...211 B7
Green How PE27 .....143 E6
Green La Ashwell SG7 ...2 C5
 6 Benwick PE15 ...222 A5
 Brampton PE28 .....140 D2
 Christchurch PE14 ..229 D3
 Ellington PE28 ......138 F4
 Everton SG19 ....40 C3
 Great Staughton PE19 .93 F6
 Hail Weston PE19 ...95 A1
 Leverington PE13 ...237 F2
 Linton CB1 ....35 C2
 Peterborough PE1 ...198 A4
 St Ives PE27 ....143 A5
 Stamford PE9 ......244 B7
 Upton & Coppingford PE28 160 C2
 Walsoken PE14 .....245 E4
 Yaxley PE7 ....181 D6
Green Leys PE27 ....143 F5
Green Man La CB2 ....47 E3
Green Pk Brinkley CB8 ..70 D2
 Cambridge CB4 ......84 B6
 Chatteris PE16 .....241 E5
Green Rd
 Newborough PE6 ....205 F3
 Newmarket CB8 .....111 B2
 Upwell PE14 ....229 E8
Green Rd The CB8 ....33 A8
Green Side CB5 .....106 B7
Green St Cambridge CB2 .246 A3

Green St continued
 Duxford CB2 ....32 D1
 March PE15 ....243 D1
 Royston SG8 ....5 D8
 Willingham CB4 .....209 A1
Green The Ashley CB8 ..91 F8
 Beck Row, Holywell Row
  & Kenny Hill IP28 ...213 C7
 Brampton PE28 .....140 D2
 Castor PE5 ....195 E2
 Foxton CB2 ....30 B5
 Glinton PE6 ....203 E8
 Great Staughton PE19 .93 F7
 Haddenham CB6 ....210 A6
 Kingston CB3 ....61 B3
 Kirtling CB8 ....72 C5
 Lolworth CB3 ....101 F5
 Peterborough PE4 ...204 C3
 Royston SG8 ....5 D6
 Snailwell CB8 ......132 A3
 Somersham PE28 ...215 C1
 Steeple Morden SG8 ..11 C1
 6 Thorney PE6 ......233 A3
 Yaxley PE7 ....190 A8
Green Tiles Cl PE29 ..152 E1
Greenacres Duxford CB2 .32 D1
 Peterborough PE4 ...204 A4
Greenbanks SG8 ......14 C5
Greenbury Cl SG8 .....6 F1
Greendale PE29 .....141 A6
Greenfield Cl CB2 ....49 D4
Greenfield Cl **2** CB2 ..49 D4
Greenfields Eairth PE28 .208 E6
 Eltisley PE19 ....77 E4
 Hemingford Grey PE27 .143 F1
 Newmarket CB8 .....111 C3
Greenfields Way CB9 ..23 F6
Greenford St SG8 .....28 D8
Greengage Cl SG8 ....14 C4
Greengage Rise SG8 ..14 C5
Greengarth PE27 ....144 A5
Greengate Ct PE1 ...198 C4
Greenham PE3 ....197 A4
Greenhaze La CB3 ....79 B3
Greenhill Rd PE8 ....178 F8
Greenhills CB7 ......212 C3
Greenlands CB2 ......65 B3
Greenleas CB4 ......104 B5
Green's Rd CB4 ......83 E4
Greenside Cl CB4 ....122 E6
Greenstock La PE13 .238 A6
Greenway PE19 .....117 B4
Greenwood Cl
 1 Haverhill CB9 .....23 E7
 Ramsey PE26 ....172 A5
Gregory Rd IP28 .....239 A6
Grenadier Dr PE16 ..241 C6
Grenadier Rd CB9 ....23 C8
Greneway Sch The SG8 ..5 F7
Grenfell Rd PE26 ....172 A5
Grenville Way PE19 ...74 B2
Gresham Rd CB1 .....246 C1
Gresley Dr PE9 .....244 B4
Gresley Way March PE15 243 B6
 Peterborough PE3 ...197 C6
Gretton Cl PE2 ......186 C7
Greville Rd CB1 ......65 B7
Greville Starkey Ave **1**
 CB8 ....110 F5
Greys The PE15 .....243 E2
Greystoke Ct **1** CB1 ..65 C5
Greystoke Rd CB1 ....65 C5
Grieve Ct CB4 ....84 C5
Griffins Cl PE6 ....207 D1
Griffiths Ct PE2 .....185 E5
Grimmer's Rd **6** PE13 .245 E7
Grimshaw Rd PE1 ...198 B6
Grip The CB1 ....35 B1
Groat La SG19 ....41 D8
Grosvenor House Ct **6**
 IP28 ....239 B5
Grosvenor Rd PE13 ..245 D7
Grosvenor Yd CB8 ...111 A3
Grounds Ave PE15 ..243 F4
Grounds Way PE7 ...191 A8
Grove Ct PE19 ....95 F2
Grove End PE28 .....120 C1
Grove Gdns CB7 ....212 E2
Grove La Brampton PE28 .140 D3
 Peterborough PE3 ...197 A2
Grove Pk CB7 ....212 E2
Grove Prim Sch CB4 ..83 F6
Grove Rd
 Little Paxton PE19 ...95 F2
 Sawston CB2 ....33 A8
Grove St PE2 ....186 F8
Grove The Cambridge CB4 .84 B6
 Chatteris PE16 .....241 C5
 Huntingdon PE29 ...142 B6
 Linton CB1 ....35 B3
 Mildenhall IP28 .....213 D8
 Orwell SG8 ....28 D8
 1 Stretham CB6 .....210 F5
 Whittlesey PE7 .....189 F6
 Wistow PE28 ....163 F6
Grove Way PE26 ....172 A4
Grovemere Ct PE28 .114 B7
Grunty Fen Rd CB6 ..210 F8
Guanockgate Rd PE12 .234 C8
Guash Way PE9 .....244 D7
Guelder Rose **5** CB7 .240 F5
Guest Rd CB1 ....246 C2
Guild Rd PE1 ....246 C2
Guilden Morden Sch SG8 10 F5
Guildenburgh Cres PE7 190 A7

Guildhall Pl **5** CB1 ...246 A2
Guildhall St **3** CB1 ..246 A2
Guineas Cl CB1 ......110 E6
Guise La SG8 ....12 C6
Gull Bank PE13 .....234 E3
Gull Dro PE13 ......234 D3
Gull La PE13 ....238 A3
Gull Rd PE13 ....234 F3
Gull Way Chatteris PE16 .241 C6
 Whittlesey PE7 .....190 A8
Gullymore PE3 .....196 F8
Gunhild Cl CB1 ......65 D5
Gunhild Ct CB1 ......65 C5
Gunhild Way CB1 ....65 C5
Gunnell Cl CB4 .....105 D2
Gunning Rd CB6 ....240 E8
Gunning Way CB4 ....83 C6
Gunnings Way PE28 .143 C1
Gunthorpe Rd
 Newborough PE6 ...204 F4
 Peterborough PE4 ...204 E2
Gunthorpe Ridings **1**
 PE4 ....205 A2
Gunton's Rd PE6 ....205 C6
Guntons Cl CB7 .....212 B4
Gurlings CB9 ....39 A2
Gurnard Leys PE3 ..204 A1
Gurney Way CB4 .....83 E4
Guthlac Ave PE4 ...204 D1
Guyatt Cl CB5 ....130 B2
Guyhirn VC Sch PE13 .235 A2
Gwydir St CB1 ....65 A8
Gypsy La PE13 ......238 C4

H

Hacke Rd **3** PE3 ....197 D3
Haddenham Rd CB6 ..217 A1
Haddon Cl PE2 ......187 E5
Haddon Rd Haddon PE6 .180 C6
 Peterborough PE3 ...197 E3
Haddon Way PE7 ...187 B2
Haddow's Cl CB4 ....123 F2
Haden Way Over CB4 .208 F1
 Willingham CB4 ....123 F8
Hadley Rd PE4 .....204 D1
Hadrian Cl PE9 ......24 D7
Hadrians Ct PE2 ....187 B8
Hadstock Rd CB1 .....35 B1
Hagbech Hall Cl PE14 .236 D6
Hagger's Cl SG8 ......14 D6
Haggis Gap CB1 ......66 F5
Haigh's Cl PE16 .....241 B4
Hake's Dro PE15 ....227 A2
Halcyon Ct PE29 ....141 C6
Hale Ave CB4 ....83 D4
Hale Cl SG8 ....14 D6
Hale Dro CB6 ....225 E6
Hale Fen CB6 ....242 C8
Hale Fen La CB6 ....217 A4
Hale Fen Rd CB6 ....225 D6
Haley Cl
 Hemingford Grey PE28 .143 B1
 4 Wisbech PE13 ...245 C8
Half Acre Dro CB7 ..211 C7
Half Acre La CB7 ....211 D8
Halfpenny La PE14 ..245 D1
Halfpenny Toll Rd PE14 .229 E4
Halifax Rd Cambridge CB4 .83 B4
 2 Mildenhall IP28 ...213 E8
Halifax Way CB8 ....110 E5
Hall Bank PE13 .....237 E7
Hall Barn Rd CB7 ...212 F4
Hall Bridge Rd PE14 .236 D1
Hall Cl Bourn CB3 ....60 C5
 Foxton CB2 ....30 B6
 Huntingdon PE29 ...142 A6
 Little Paxton PE19 ...95 F2
Hall Cres CB2 ....33 A7
Hall Dike PE14 .....236 F4
Hall Dr Hardwick CB3 ..80 F3
 Highfields CB3 ......80 C2
Hall End CB4 ....105 D2
Hall Farm La SG19 ...58 D4
Hall Farm Rd **2** CB4 ..83 D5
Hall Gate Rd PE12 ..234 B8
Hall Green La PE28 ..121 B6
Hall La
 Abbots Ripton PE28 ..152 D8
 Brinkley CB8 ....70 E2
 Burwell CB5 ....130 B1
 Great & Little Chishill SG8 ..7 F2
 3 Peterborough PE4 .204 C4
 20 Wittering PE8 ....230 B1
Hall Rd Outwell PE14 .236 F3
 St Neots PE19 ....74 E3
Hall St CB7 ....212 B5
Hallards The **6** PE19 ..74 C6
Hallaton Rd PE1 ....198 D8
Hallcroft Rd PE7 ....189 C8
Hallfields La PE4 ...204 E1
Hallwyck Gdns **2** CB8 .110 F2
Halstead Cl **2** PE13 .245 E5
Ham La PE2 ....185 E7
Ham Mere Bird Sanctuary*
 PE2 ....185 E7
Hamden Way CB3 ....99 B3
Hamerton Rd
 Alconbury Weston PE28 .150 C7
 Buckworth PE28 ....149 D6
 Winwick PE28 ......158 C5
Hamerton Zoo Pk*
 PE28 ....159 B5
Hamilton Rd
 Cambridge CB4 .....246 A4
 Ely CB6 ....240 B4
 Newmarket CB8 .....110 E3

Hamiltons The CB8 ..110 E2
Hamlet Cl PE29 .....141 F6
Hamlet Rd CB9 ....24 B7
Hamlet The CB6 ....218 C6
Hammond Cl
 Newmarket CB8 .....110 E6
 Pampisford CB22 ....33 B5
 2 Wittering PE8 ....230 C1
Hammond Way PE2 ..208 C8
Hampden Rd **2** PE13 .245 D5
Hampden Way PE19 ..75 A3
Hampshire Rd PE28 .143 B8
Hampstead Ave IP28 .239 B6
Hampton Hargate Prim Sch
 PE7 ....186 C2
Hanaper Dr SG8 ......6 F1
Hanbury PE2 ....185 F3
Hankey St PE1 ......197 F4
Hanmer Ave IP28 ...239 C5
Hannath Rd PE13 ...238 B8
Hanover Cl Bar Hill CB3 .102 B3
 Eaton Socon PE19 ...74 D5
Hanover Ct
 3 Brampton PE28 ..140 D3
 Peterborough PE3 ...197 A8
Hansell Rd PE28 ....140 B3
Harbins La PE19 .....57 C6
Harbour Ave CB3 .....62 D6
Harcombe Rd CB1 ....65 E6
Harding Cl **1** CB5 ..106 A7
Harding Way
 Cambridge CB4 ......83 C5
 Histon CB4 ....104 B4
 St Ives PE27 ....144 B5
Hardwick Com Prim Sch
 CB3 ....81 A3
Hardwick Ct PE3 ....197 B2
Hardwick La
 1 Abbotsley PE19 ...57 B6
 Buckden PE19 ......117 A5
Hardwick Rd
 Haverhill CB9 ....24 B8
 St Neots PE19 ....74 E3
 Toft CB3 ....61 E6
Hardwick St CB3 .....64 C7
Hardwicke Cl CB6 ..242 C5
Hardwicke Fields CB6 .210 A6
Hardwicke Rd SG19 ..58 F6
Hardy Cl PE29 .....141 F6
Hardy Dr SG8 ....5 D8
Hardy Pl **1** PE19 ....74 D6
Hardy's La PE7 .....189 E6
Harebell Cl
 Cambridge CB1 ......66 A5
 Huntingdon PE29 ...141 D6
 Peterborough PE1 ...205 B1
Harecroft Rd PE13 ..245 B5
Harefield Rise CB1 ...35 E2
Harewood Gdns PE3 .197 B2
Hargate Way PE7 ...186 D3
Hargood Ct **4** PE19 ..74 B3
Hargreaves Rd **6** SG8 ..5 D5
Harland Rd PE19 .....74 E1
Harlech Ct **5** PE19 ...74 F2
Harlech Grange PE3 .197 B1
Harlestones Rd CB4 .125 D4
Harlton Cl PE2 .....187 E5
Harlton Rd
 Great Eversden CB23 ..45 F7
 Haslingfield CB3 .....46 F5
Harold Heading Cl PE16 241 B3
Harold's Bank PE13 .237 B1
Harper's Dro PE26 ..170 F7
Harrier Cl PE29 .....142 A8
Harrington Dr PE6 ..232 C8
Harris Cres PE27 ...208 A2
Harris La PE13 .....163 E6
Harris Rd CB4 ....83 D6
Harris St PE1 ....197 F6
Harrison Cl **10** PE3 ..196 F3
Harrison Way PE27 .144 B3
Harrison's Dro
 Burwell CB5 ....129 A8
 Swaffham Prior CB7 .128 D7
Harris's La PE28 ....163 E7
Harrolds Cl **5** PE13 .238 F1
Harrow Rd CB9 ......23 E7
Harry Palmer Cl **2** CB7 212 E1
Harrys Way PE13 ...245 C2
Harston CP Sch CB2 ..47 F2
Harston Rd
 Haslingfield CB3 .....47 C4
 Newton CB2 ....31 B8
Hart Cl CB9 ....38 F1
Hart Rd PE26 ....171 E3
Hartfield Rd CB8 .....70 E4
Hartford Ct PE2 ....187 D6
Hartford Cty Jun & Inf Sch
 PE29 ....141 E4
Hartford Rd PE29 ...141 E4
Hartington Gr CB1 ...65 A5
Hartlands PE7 ......190 E8
Hartley Cl CB5 .....106 B8
Hartwell Way **1** PE3 ..197 B5
Harvest Cl PE7 .....175 F8
Harvest Ct **2** PE27 .144 A4
Harvest Way PE14 ...84 A2
Harvester Way
 Crowland PE6 ......232 B8
 Peterborough PE1 ...198 C1
Harvey Cl **4** PE8 ...230 B1
Harvey Dr **5** PE28 ..215 C1
Harvey Goodwin Ave
 CB4 ....83 D4
Harvey Rd CB1 .....246 C1
Harvey St **3** PE19 ...74 E4
Haselhurst Cl **5** PE15 .243 F4

Haslingfield Endowed Sch CB3 47 A5
Haslingfield Rd
Barrington CB2 29 F8
Barton CB3 63 B2
Harlton CB3 46 E6
Hasse Rd CB7 212 C8
Hassock Hill Dro PE13 237 D3
Hassock Way 1 PE15 223 B7
Hastings Rd PE4 204 C2
Hatchet La PE19 114 B2
Hatfield Rd PE28 168 A4
Hathaway Cl 5 PE19 74 C3
Hatherdene Cl CB1 65 E8
Hatley Cl PE19 75 A7
Hatley Dr CB5 130 B3
Hatley Park* SG19 42 F2
Hatley Rd Gamlingay SG19 41 F4
Wrestlingworth & Cockayne Hatley SG19 25 B7
Hatton's Pk CB4 123 F2
Hatton's Rd CB4 102 D6
Hauston CP Sch CB2 48 C4
Hautboy La PE8 178 B3
Hauxton Industrial Effluent Disposal Plant CB2 47 F6
Hauxton Rd
Cambridge CB2 48 C8
Great Shelford CB2 48 D4
Havelock Cl SG19 41 C5
Havelock Dr PE2 187 E6
Haven The CB1 66 F5
Haverhill Rd
Castle Camps CB1 22 E4
Horseheath CB1 37 A3
Little Wratting CB9 39 F3
Stapleford CB2 49 E5
Steeple Bumpstead CB9 24 B1
Haverhill Sports Ctr CB9 24 B7
Haverhill TH CB9 24 A7
Haveswater Cl 1 PE4 204 E2
Haviland Way CB4 83 B6
Hawcrofts La CB4 208 D2
Hawe's La CB7 211 E2
Haweswater PE29 141 C5
Hawk Dr PE29 142 B7
Hawkes End PE28 140 E2
Hawkes La 1 PE27 208 A2
Hawkesden Rd PE19 75 B6
Hawkesford Way PE19 74 F7
Hawkins Cl PE28 115 D3
Hawkins Dr 1 PE13 245 E5
Hawkins Rd CB4 83 F7
Hawkins's Dro CB7 242 F3
Hawkshead Way 2 PE4 204 E3
Hawthorn Ave
Hauxton CB2 48 B4
Sawston CB2 32 F6
Hawthorn Cl
Little Paxton PE19 95 F2
Littleport CB6 242 E3
Newborough PE6 207 C1
Royston SG8 5 F7
Hawthorn Dr PE29 141 D5
Hawthorn End 1 PE28 150 F5
Hawthorn Rd
Emneth PE14 236 D5
Folksworth PE7 175 D8
Haverhill CB9 38 D1
Peterborough PE1 198 C6
Ramsey PE26 171 F7
St Neots PE19 74 E6
Yaxley PE7 181 F5
Hawthorn Way
Burwell CB5 130 C3
Cambridge CB4 83 F4
Royston SG8 5 F7
St Ives PE27 144 A5
4 Sawtry PE28 168 B3
Hawthorn Wlk 4 IP28 213 F8
Hawthorne Ave PE13 245 C8
Hawthorne Dr PE7 189 F6
Hawthorne Gr PE15 243 C5
Hawthorne Rd CB2 49 B4
Hawthorns The PE16 241 C5
Hay Cl CB1 53 B1
Hay Fen Cl 6 CB6 210 F5
Hay St SG8 11 B2
Haycocks Rd CB9 23 C8
Haycraft Cl PE28 116 A7
Haycroft The PE19 117 F2
Haydock Rd 2 SG8 5 F6
Hayes Wlk PE8 178 D8
Hayfield Ave CB2 32 F7
Hayland Dro IP28 213 B7
Hayling Ave PE19 96 A2
Hayling Cl 4 PE29 118 F7
Hayman's Way CB3 99 A2
Haymarket Rd 7 CB3 83 C3
Hayster Dr CB1 65 E6
Hayter Cl CB1 53 F4
Haywardsfield 4 PE3 197 A1
Haywoods La SG8 5 E7
Hayzen Cl CB2 29 F8
Hazel Cl Haverhill CB9 23 E7
Mildenhall IP28 239 E4
Hazel Croft PE4 204 A4
Hazel Ct 7 CB6 210 F5
Hazel Gdns 1 PE13 245 D4
Hazel Way PE27 144 B4
Hazelwood Cl CB4 83 D6
Head Fen Dro CB6 224 F3
Headford Cl CB5 84 D4
Headington Cl CB1 65 F5
Headington Dr CB1 65 F5
Headlake Dro CB5 128 E1
Headland Ave CB9 23 E7
Headlands
Fenstanton PE28 121 C5
Huntingdon PE29 141 C3
Headlands Way PE7 189 D8
Headley Gdns CB2 49 B4
Headley's La CB6 217 A2
Heasman Cl CB8 110 F5
Heath Ave SG8 5 C6
Heath Farm Rd IP28 213 F1
Heath Ho CB4 84 A5
Heath La PE28 163 A7
Heath Rd Bottisham CB1 87 B4
Burwell CB5 109 D5
Exning CB8 110 B6
Gamlingay SG19 41 A4
Helpston PE6 231 C2
Mildenhall IP28 239 E5
Newmarket CB8 111 C3
Swaffham Bulbeck CB5 108 B2
Swaffham Prior CB5 109 A3
Warboys PE28 165 C6
Heath Row PE1 205 B1
Heathbell Rd CB8 111 C3
Heathcote Cl 6 PE15 243 F4
Heather Ave PE1 198 A8
Heatherdale Cl PE7 187 C5
Heatherset Way
1 Red Lodge IP28 213 F1
2 Red Lodge IP28 214 A1
Heathfield SG8 5 B6
Heaton Cl Ely CB6 240 F7
Peterborough PE3 197 B3
Heaton Dr CB6 240 F7
Hectare The CB2 48 F7
Heddon Way PE27 144 B6
Hedgelands
Peterborough PE4 204 C5
1 Wisbech PE13 245 C8
Hedgerley Cl CB3 83 A2
Heffer Cl CB2 49 C4
Heights Drove Rd PE26 170 D6
Helen Cl 3 CB5 84 E4
Helens Cl PE26 171 B1
Helions Bumpstead Rd CB9 23 F5
Helions Park Ave CB9 24 A7
Helions Park Gdns CB9 24 A7
Helions Park Gr CB9 24 A7
Helions Service Rd CB9 24 A7
Helions Wlk CB9 24 A7
Helmsdale Gdns PE4 204 B2
Helmsley Ct 1 PE7 187 F5
Helpston Rd Castor PE5 195 D2
Etton PE6 203 C8
Glinton PE6 203 D8
Heltwate Specl Sch PE3 197 B7
Hemingford Cres PE2 187 E6
Hemingford Grey Prim Sch PE28 143 D2
Hemingford Rd
Cambridge CB1 65 B8
Hemingford Grey PE27 143 F2
Hemington Cl 10 CB4 208 D1
Hemlocks The 5 CB3 47 B5
Hemmerley Dr PE7 189 E8
Hempfield Pl CB6 242 D4
Hempfield Rd CB6 242 D4
Hempsals 12 PE19 74 C6
Hempsals Rd or Meadow Dro CB4 209 C1
Hempstead Rd 2 CB9 38 C1
Hen Brook PE19 74 F4
Henderson Cl CB9 38 C1
Henford Gdns PE15 243 D5
Henley Rd CB1 84 B2
Henley Way CB7 240 F6
Henry Crabb Rd CB6 242 A6
Henry Morris Rd
Histon CB4 104 C3
Sawston CB2 33 A8
Henry Orbell Cl 3 PE15 243 E4
Henry St
Peterborough PE1 198 A4
Wisbech PE13 245 C5
Henry Warby Ave 8 PE14 236 A5
Henshaw PE1 198 E6
Henson Cl 3 PE13 245 C8
Henson Rd PE15 243 C5
Herbert Human Cl 3 CB7 212 B4
Herbert St CB4 83 E4
Hercules Cl 3 CB4 83 E8
Hereford Cl 7 PE28 208 C8
Hereward 5 PE28 208 E6
Hereward Ave IP28 239 C5
Hereward Cl
Haddenham CB6 209 E4
Histon CB4 104 C3
2 Peterborough PE1 198 B2
Hereward Rd
Peterborough PE1 198 B2
1 Wisbech PE13 245 D5
Hereward St Ely CB6 240 B4
March PE15 243 D5
Hereward Way PE6 231 F8
Heritage Park Prim Sch PE7 187 F5
Hermitage Rd PE28 208 E6
Herne Rd PE26 220 D4
Heron Cl PE7 189 F8
Heron Ct 1 PE19 75 B6
Heron Pk PE1 198 F6
Heron Rd PE13 245 D2
Heron Way PE27 143 F7
Heron Wlk PE15 243 F5
Heronry Dr PE6 196 E2
Heron's Cl CB1 65 D4
Herons Cl 6 Ely CB6 240 B5
Tallington PE9 230 F6
Heronshaw PE16 241 C6
Herrick Cl PE1 197 E8
Herring's Cl CB5 85 F5
Herringswell Rd
Herringswell IP28 214 B2
Kentford CB8 134 B4
Herschel Rd CB3 83 B1
Hertford Cl CB6 240 A3
Hertford La SG8 8 E5
Hertford St CB4 246 A4
Hervey Cl 3 CB6 240 B3
Hethersett Cl CB8 110 E8
Hetley PE2 186 A4
Hexham Ct 3 PE1 198 D3
Heydon La Elmdon CB11 8 F4
Heydon SG8 8 B5
Heydon Rd SG8 7 E2
Heyford Ct 5 IP28 239 B5
Hicks La Girton CB3 82 E8
Peterborough PE7 186 F5
Hicks Way 4 CB9 24 E5
Hide Cl CB2 32 F6
High Barns CB7 240 E6
High Broadgate PE13 237 F7
High Cl SG8 8 A5
High Cswy PE7 189 E7
High Ditch Rd CB5 85 A4
High Fen Crooked Dro PE28 215 B5
High Fen Straight Dro PE28 215 B6
High Gn 2 Abbotsley PE19 57 B6
Great Shelford CB2 49 A6
High Haden Rd PE28 175 B1
High Leys PE27 143 F5
High Mdw Harston CB2 47 F3
Ramsey PE26 172 A3
High Piece Cres CB4 208 C1
High Rd Downham CB6 217 F6
Gorefield PE13 237 E3
Newton PE13 238 A5
Tydd St Giles PE13 237 F6
Wisbech St Mary PE13 235 A6
High Sch Cl PE15 243 D6
High Side PE13 235 A8
High St Abbotsley PE19 57 B6
Abington Pigotts SG8 11 F5
Alconbury PE28 150 F4
Alconbury Weston PE28 150 D6
Ashley CB8 91 F8
Ashwell SG7 2 D4
Babraham CB2 33 D8
Balsham CB1 53 A2
Barley SG8 6 F2
Barrington CB2 29 E8
Barton CB3 63 B4
Bassingbourn SG8 12 F4
Benwick PE15 222 A5
Bluntisham/Colne PE28 208 C5
Bottisham CB5 86 F5
Bourn CB3 60 C6
Bourn CB3 79 B3
Boxworth CB3 101 B5
Brampton PE28 140 E2
Brinkley CB8 70 D2
Buckden PE19 117 A4
Burwell CB5 109 B8
Cambridge CB1 65 F5
Cambridge CB1 66 A7
Cambridge CB1 66 C8
Cambridge CB4 84 A4
Castle Camps CB1 22 E3
Castor PE5 195 F2
Catworth PE28 136 D7
Chatteris PE16 241 C5
Cheveley CB8 91 C7
Chippenham CB7 132 E8
Chrishall SG8 8 D3
Conington CB3 121 C1
Coton CB3 82 B2
Cottenham CB4 125 E4
Croxton PE19 76 F4
Croydon SG8 27 A7
Doddington/Wimblington PE15 223 A5
Dry Drayton CB3 102 B1
Earith PE28 208 E5
Ellington PE28 139 A4
Ely CB7 240 D4
Eye PE6 232 A1
Eyeworth SG19 10 A8
Fen Ditton CB5 84 E5
Fen Drayton CB4 121 F5
Fenstanton PE28 121 A6
Fowlmere SG8 15 E8
Foxton CB2 30 B5
Fulbourn CB1 66 F5
Girton CB3 103 E1
Glinton PE6 203 E8
Grantchester CB3 64 A4
Graveley PE19 97 F5
Great & Little Abington CB1 34 C6
Great Chesterford CB10 18 E2
Great Eversden CB3 45 E8
Great Paxton PE19 96 D4
Great Shelford CB2 48 E3
Great Shelford CB2 49 A5
Great Wilbraham CB1 67 F7
Guilden Morden SG8 10 F4
Haddenham CB6 209 E4
Hail Weston PE19 74 B8
Harlton CB3 46 D5
Harston CB2 47 F3
Haslingfield CB3 47 B5
Hauxton CB2 48 C5
Haverhill CB9 24 A7
High St *continued*
Hemingford Abbots PE28 143 A3
Hemingford Grey PE28 143 C2
Hildersham CB1 34 E5
Hilton PE28 120 B1
Hinxton CB10 18 B7
Histon CB4 104 B4
Holywell-cum-Needingworth PE27 144 F5
Horningsea CB5 106 A1
Huntingdon PE29 141 D4
Kimbolton PE28 113 F4
Knapwell CB3 100 E3
Landbeach CB4 105 D6
Linton CB1 35 C2
Little Paxton PE19 95 F2
Little Staughton MK44 93 B1
Little Wilbraham CB1 86 E1
Littleport CB6 242 D4
Lode CB5 107 C2
Longstowe CB3 59 F2
Madingley CB3 81 F5
2 Manea PE15 224 C4
March PE15 243 D3
Market Deeping PE6 231 D8
Maxey PE6 231 C7
Melbourn SG8 14 C5
Meldreth SG8 14 B8
Mepal CB6 216 E3
Mildenhall IP28 239 C4
Milton CB4 105 D2
Needingworth PE27 208 A3
Newmarket CB8 110 F3
Oakington/Longstanton CB4 103 C6
Oakington/Longstanton CB4 123 F3
Offord Cluny PE19 96 F8
Orwell SG8 45 E1
Over CB4 208 D1
Pampisford CB2 33 B5
Peterborough PE2 187 A6
Pidley cum Fenton PE28 155 E8
Rampton CB4 124 E5
Ramsey PE26 171 B2
Ramsey PE26 172 A6
Royston SG8 5 D6
St Neots PE19 74 E5
Sawston CB2 32 F6
Sawtry PE28 168 B4
Shepreth SG8 29 E4
Soham CB7 212 B4
Somersham PE28 208 C8
Spaldwick PE28 137 F6
Stamford PE9 244 B5
Stetchworth CB8 90 A2
Stilton PE7 176 A7
Stretham CB6 210 F5
Sutton CB6 216 D1
Swaffham Bulbeck CB5 108 B1
Swaffham Prior CB5 108 D5
Swavesey CB4 122 E6
Tadlow SG8 26 A3
Tilbrook PE28 113 B6
Toft CB3 61 D4
Tuddenham IP28 214 D2
Warboys PE28 164 F5
Waterbeach CB5 106 B8
West Wickham CB1 37 A7
West Wratting CB1 53 F5
Whittlesford CB2 32 C5
Wicken CB7 211 E1
Wilburton CB6 210 C5
Willingham CB4 209 A1
Wisbech PE13 245 C5
Witcham CB6 217 A3
Wrestlingworth SG19 25 B4
Wrestlingworth & Cockayne Hatley SG19 25 B3
Yelling PE19 98 C1
High St Back 2 CB7 240 D4
High Street St Martin's PE9 244 C4
Higham Rd IP28 214 E1
Highbury St PE1 198 A5
Highclere Cl CB8 110 D8
Highclere Rd PE7 186 D3
Highdene Rd CB1 66 A6
Highfield Ave
Alconbury Weston PE28 150 D6
Cambridge CB4 83 E5
Highfield Cl CB2 17 D8
Highfield Cotts SG8 4 B7
Highfield Gate CB1 66 F6
Highfield Rd Histon CB4 104 C1
March PE15 243 D7
Highfield Sch CB6 240 C5
Highfields Rd CB3 80 C2
Highgate Gn PE8 178 D8
Highlands SG8 5 E6
Highlands The CB8 110 D8
Highlees Prim Sch PE3 197 C6
Hightown Dro
Burwell CB5 129 C4
Reach CB5 129 B4
Highway The PE19 94 A6
Highworth Ave CB4 83 F5
Hilda Clarke Cl 1 PE16 241 C3
Hilda St CB4 83 D4
Hildersham Rd CB1 34 D7
Hill Cl
Brington & Molesworth PE28 147 C5
Little Stukeley PE28 151 F1
Newmarket CB8 110 E3
Peterborough PE1 198 D5
Sawtry PE28 168 B3
Hill Cres CB9 39 A1
Hill Est Ramsey PE26 172 B4
St Ives PE28 143 B5
Hill Farm Rd CB2 32 B3
Hill La CB9 24 F3
Hill Rd Over CB4 208 E1
Wistow PE26 164 A8
Hill Rise St Ives PE27 143 E7
St Neots PE19 75 A5
Hill Row CB6 209 E6
Hill Row Cswy CB6 209 A6
Hill St 5 PE13 245 C5
Hill View
Dry Drayton CB3 102 D1
Lidgate CB8 73 F8
Hillary Cl PE9 244 D6
Hillburn Rd PE13 245 B4
Hillcrest CB3 102 C3
Hillcrest Ave PE7 181 E5
Hillcrest Dr 3 PE13 235 A2
Hillfield Alconbury PE28 150 F5
Foxton CB2 30 C5
Hillfield Rd CB3 62 D6
Hills Ave CB1 65 B5
Hills La CB6 240 B4
Hills Rd CB2 246 C1
Hills Road Sixth Form Coll CB1 65 A6
Hillside Orwell SG8 45 E2
Royston SG8 5 D5
Sawston CB2 32 F8
Sutton CB6 216 D1
Hillside Cl Ellington PE28 138 F4
Ufford PE9 230 F2
Hillside La SG8 44 C4
Hillside Mdw CB7 212 F1
Hillside Rd PE15 243 B5
Hillward Cl PE2 186 C6
Hillway CB1 35 C2
Hilsdens Dr PE29 142 A1
Hilton Rd PE28 120 E3
Hilton St CB4 208 D1
Hilton Turf Maze* PE28 120 C1
Hinchcliffe PE2 185 E2
Hinchinbrooke Rd PE28 117 D8
Hinchingbrooke Ctry Pk* PE29 140 F4
Hinchingbrooke Dr PE16 241 B4
Hinchingbrooke Ho* PE29 141 B3
Hinchingbrooke Hospl PE29 141 B5
Hinchingbrooke Pk* PE29 141 B4
Hinchingbrooke Sch PE29 141 A4
Hines Cl CB3 63 A4
Hines La CB3 62 C5
Hinkins Cl SG8 14 D6
Hinton Ave CB1 65 C5
Hinton Cl PE7 189 D8
Hinton Rd CB1 66 D5
Hinton View CB6 210 A6
Hinton Way
Great Shelford CB2 49 C6
Wilburton CB6 210 C6
Hinxton Rd CB2 17 E8
Hinxworth Rd SG7 2 B4
Histon Jun Sch CB4 104 B3
Histon Rd Cambridge CB4 83 C4
Cottenham CB4 104 C8
Histon Sch CB4 104 B4
Hitches St 4 CB6 242 D4
Hitherford CB4 208 E1
Hive Rd CB6 217 A4
Hives The PE19 74 D4
HM Prison Littlehey PE18 115 E1
HM Prison Whitemoor PE15 228 B6
Hoadly Rd CB3 83 B5
Hobart Ct PE15 243 C5
Hobart Rd CB1 65 C7
Hobbledodds Cl CB4 122 E6
Hobson St CB1 246 B3
Hockland Rd PE13 237 F7
Hod Fen Dro
Denton & Caldecote PE7 177 A7
Yaxley PE7 181 F2
Hod Hall La CB6 210 A5
Hodgson Ave PE4 204 B6
Hodney Rd 2 PE6 232 A1
Hodson's Dr PE29 141 E5
Hodwell SG7 2 D4
Hog Fen Dro PE7 182 A5
Hogarth Cl PE27 144 A7
Hogarth Pl 2 PE19 74 D5
Hogens La PE13 238 A5
Hogherd's La 9 PE13 245 C5
Hoghill Dro CB6 209 F3
Hog's La SG8 8 D3
Holbein Rd PE27 144 A7
Holben Cl CB3 63 B3
Holborn Ave IP28 239 B6
Holbrook Rd
Cambridge CB1 65 B4
Haverhill CB9 23 E6
Holburn View PE28 168 B2
Holcroft PE2 186 B3
Holdfield PE3 197 B6
Holdich St PE3 197 E2
Holdsworth Valley CP Sch CB8 110 F3
Holgate La PE4 204 B7

Holkham Mead CB5 ....130 C2
Holkham Rd PE2 ....185 D3
Holland Ave PE4 ......204 D1
Holland Pk CB8 ....91 C7
Holland Rd PE9 ....244 C6
Hollands Rd CB4 ......24 A6
Hollesley Ave CB9 ....23 C8
Holliday's Rd PE28 ...208 D5
Hollies Cl SG8 ....5 E6
Hollies The PE15 .....243 E7
Hollmans Cl CB1 ......66 F4
Hollow Hill PE26 .....38 B4
Hollow La PE26 ....172 E6
Hollow Rd Chrishall SG8 ..8 D1
  Elmdon CB11 ....9 C4
  Ramsey Forty Foot PE26 ..221 C2
Hollow The PE26 ......142 B6
Holly Cl Newborough PE6 207 C1
  Red Lodge IP28 .....213 F1
Holly Dr 4 PE15 .....223 A6
Holly Way 7 PE6 .....231 E8
Holly Wlk Ely CB6 ....240 F5
  3 Mildenhall IP28 ..213 F4
  Peterborough PE7 ...186 D3
Hollybush Way CB1 ....35 D3
Hollycroft Cl PE14 ...236 D5
Hollycroft Rd PE14 ...236 D5
Hollytrees CB3 ....102 C3
Holme CE Jun Sch PE7 .177 A4
Holme Cl Castor PE5 ..195 D2
  Oakington/Longstanton
  CB4 ....103 C5
Holme Dro PE28 ....208 E7
Holme Fen Dro PE28 ...208 D7
Holme La 1 CB6 ......218 A6
Holme Rd Ramsey PE26 .220 C3
  Yaxley PE7 ....181 E4
Holme Way CB2 ....32 F8
Holmehill PE29 ......118 F8
Holmes Dr PE15 ....245 E6
Holmes La CB7 ....212 B5
Holmes Rd PE6 ....203 F7
Holmes The CB6 ......242 E4
Holmes Way PE4 ......204 E2
Holmewood PE7 ....176 F4
Holmewood Cres PE7 ..176 F4
Holmsey Gn IP28 .....213 F8
Holmsey Green Gdns 2
  IP28 ....213 F8
Holt Cl 8 PE8 ....230 B1
Holt Fen CB6 ....211 B7
Holyrood Cl CB4 .....83 C6
Holywell Cl 1 PE3 ..197 A1
Holywell Ferry Rd CB4 121 F6
Holywell Front PE27 ..144 F2
Holywell Sch PE27 ...208 A2
Holywell Way PE3 ....196 F2
Home Cl Grafham PE28 .116 A6
  Histon CB4 ....104 B4
Home End CB1 ....67 A4
Home Farm Cl
  Abbotsley PE19 .....57 B6
  Rampton CB4 ....124 F4
Home Farm Rd PE28 ...143 B6
Home Pasture PE4 ....204 B5
Homefield Cl CB4 ....104 C3
Homefield Rd CB9 ....23 F5
Homerton Coll CB2 ...65 A5
Homerton St CB2 .....65 A6
Homestall Cres CB9 ..38 B4
Homestead 12 PE28 ...215 C1
Homestead Dr 6 IP28 .213 F8
Homing The CB5 ......84 E3
Honey Dro PE15 ......223 E4
Honey Hill
  9 Cambridge CB3 ...83 C3
  Fen Drayton PE28 ..122 A4
  Fenstanton PE28 ...121 B6
  Gamlingay SG19 ....41 D4
  West Wratting CB3 ..53 E5
Honeydon Ave PE19 ..74 B5
Honeyhill PE4 ....205 A1
Honeyhill Rd PE13 ...237 C2
Honeysome Rd PE16 ..241 A5
Honeysuckle Cl
  Haverhill CB9 ......38 E1
  Red Lodge IP28 ....134 A8
  2 Soham CB7 ....212 B4
Honeysuckle Ct PE2 ..186 D7
Honeyway SG8 ....5 E6
Hoo Cl PE19 ....117 B4
Hoof Cl CB6 ....242 D3
Hook Dro PE15 ......228 B1
Hook La PE15 ....223 C7
Hook Rd PE15 ....223 C7
Hook's Dro PE13 ....234 C4
Hooper St CB1 ......84 A1
Hop Row CB6 ....210 A6
Hopbine Ct PE26 ....171 F5
Hope St CB1 ....65 B8
Hopkins Cl CB4 .....84 A6
Hopkins Hospl* PE9 ..244 B4
Hopton Rise CB9 ....38 B1
Horn La Kirtling CB8 .72 B5
  Linton CB1 ....35 B2
Hornbeam Rd IP28 ...239 D5
Horningsea Rd
  Fen Ditton CB5 ....84 F6
  Horningsea CB5 ....85 A8
Horse & Gate St CB8 .121 F5
Horse Common Cl PE29 141 E5
Horse Common La PE29 141 E5
Horse Dro PE26 .....221 A1
Horse Fair 2 PE13 ..245 C5
Horse Ware CB4 .....208 D2

Horsegate
  Market Deeping PE6 ..231 E8
  Whittlesey PE7 .....189 D7
Horsegate Gdns PE16 .241 C5
Horsegate La PE7 ....189 C7
Horsehead Dro PE14 ..229 F4
Horseheath Gn CB1 ..37 C1
Horseheath Rd
  Linton CB1 ....35 D2
  Withersfield CB9 ...38 A4
Horseley Fen Dro PE28 241 E1
Horseley Fen Mid Dro
  PE16 ....241 B1
Horsemoor Rd PE15 ..223 D8
Horseracing Forensic
  Laboratory CB7 .....131 E6
Horseshoe Cl
  Balsham CB1 ....53 C2
  Elmdon CB11 ....9 B4
Horseshoe La
  2 Haverhill CB9 ...23 E7
  4 Stamford PE9 ....244 B5
Horseshoe Terr PE13 .245 B7
Horseshoes La CB1 ..54 D5
Horseshoes Way PE28 .140 D2
Horsey Hill (Civil War Fort)★
  PE7 ....188 A4
Horsham Cl 3 CB9 ..38 C1
Horsley Hale CB6 ...242 D6
Hospital Rd PE15 ...222 E6
Hostmoor Ave PE15 ..243 A7
Hotel La PE28 ......151 F3
Houghton Ave PE2 ...187 E5
Houghton Gdns CB4 ..83 C5
Houghton Hill Rd PE28 143 B5
Houghton Mill National
  Trust★ PE28 ....143 A4
Houghton Prim Sch
  PE28 ....143 A5
Houghton Rd PE27 ...143 E5
Houghtons La CB7 ...213 B5
Housman Ave SG8 ...5 C8
Howard Cl CB5 .....84 D4
Howard De Walden Way
  CB8 ....111 A4
Howard Rd Cambridge CB5 84 E4
  Eaton Socon PE19 ..74 C1
  Meldreth SG8 ......14 A8
Howard's La CB1 ....37 A2
Howe Rd CB9 ....38 F1
Howes Pl CB3 ......83 A5
Howitt's Gdns PE19 ..75 A5
Howitt's La 5 PE19 .74 F3
Howitts La PE19 ....74 F4
Howland PE2 ....186 A3
Howlett Way CB5 ...86 E6
Howletts Hill PE13 ..245 C4
Hoylake Dr PE7 .....187 C5
Huddleston Way CB2 .33 A7
Hudpool PE29 ......118 F7
Hudson Cl 1 CB9 ...24 C6
Hudson L Ctr PE13 ..245 A5
Hulatt Cl CB1 ......65 C4
Humber Rd PE29 ...141 F7
Humberdale Way PE28 164 F5
Humberley Cl 1 PE19 74 F3
Humberstone Rd CB4 .246 C4
Humphreys Rd CB4 ..83 E6
Humphries Way CB4 ..105 D3
Hunchback La PE13 ..238 E2
Hundred Rd PE15 ...243 C8
Hundreds Rd PE6 ...232 C6
Hungate Rd PE14 ...236 E6
Hunsbury Cl PE7 ...189 F6
Hunters Chase PE15 .243 E2
Hunters Way
  Kimbolton PE28 ....113 F5
  Royston SG8 ....5 E6
  3 Sawtry PE28 ....168 B3
Hunting Ave PE2 ....186 F7
Hunting Gr CB3 ....101 B5
Huntingdon Boat Club
  PE29 ....141 F4
Huntingdon Cty Jun & Inf Sch
  PE29 ....141 E6
Huntingdon Rd
  Boxworth CB3 ....101 E7
  Brampton PE28 .....141 A2
  Cambridge CB3 .....83 A5
  Chatteris PE16 .....241 B4
  Fen Drayton CB4 ...121 D4
  Houghton & Wyton PE28 142 F5
  Lolworth CB3 ......102 B5
  Ramsey PE26 ......171 C2
  St Neots PE19 .....75 A8
  Sawston CB2 ......33 A8
Huntingdon Recn Ctr
  PE29 ....141 E6
Huntingdon St PE19 ..74 F6
Huntingdon Sta PE29 .141 E4
Huntingdonshire Regional
  Coll
  Huntingdon PE29 ...141 E6
  St Neots PE19 .....74 F6
Huntings Dr 5 PE28 ..168 B4
Huntley Cl CB5 ....84 E4
Huntly Gr PE1 .....198 B4
Huntly Rd PE2 .....186 F7
Hunt's Gate PE12 ...237 F8
Hunts Cl 4 PE15 ...222 F5
Hunts End PE19 ....117 B4
Hunts La CB10 .....18 A5
Hunts Rd CB2 ......17 D8
Huntsmans Gate PE3 .196 F5
Huntsmill CB1 .....66 E4
Hurdle Dro IP28 ...213 D8
Hurdleditch Rd SG8 ..28 D8
Hurn Rd PE6 ....203 E3

Hurrell Rd CB4 .....83 C6
Hurrell's Row CB2 ..47 E2
Hurricane Cl PE29 ..141 B8
Hurrys Cl PE2 .....32 E7
Hurst Ave 1 PE15 ..243 E4
Hurst La CB6 ......240 A6
Hurst Park Ave CB4 ..83 E5
Hurstingstone PE27 ..144 A5
Hurts Croft 1 CB7 ..212 E1
Hut Field La CB3 ...99 A3
Huttles Gn SG8 ....29 E4
Hyholmes PE3 .....196 F5
Hyll Cl CB7 ....18 D3
Hyperion Way CB4 ..110 D8
Hythe Cl CB5 ......130 A3
Hythe La CB5 ......130 A3
Hythe The CB6 .....242 D5
Hythegate PE4 .....204 D4

I

Ibberson's Dro PE15 .221 F4
Ibbott Cl PE2 .....187 E5
Ibbott Cres 7 PE28 ..215 C1
Iceni Way CB8 .....110 B8
Icewell Hill CB8 ...111 A4
Ickleton Rd Duxford CB2 17 E7
  Elmdon CB11 ....9 A4
  Great Chesterford CB10 18 C2
  Hinxton CB10 ......18 B6
Icknield Cl Cheveley CB8 91 C5
  Ickleton CB10 .....18 A3
Icknield CP Sch CB2 ..33 A8
Icknield Walk Fst Sch SG8 5 F7
Icknield Wlk SG8 ...5 F6
Ida Darwin Hospl CB1 .66 D5
Ihlee Cl PE4 ......204 E1
Ilex Cl PE7 ....186 C3
Ilex Rd PE27 ......144 B6
Illing's Lane La PE28 .164 A1
Illingworth Way CB2 ..30 A5
Impala Dr CB1 .....66 A7
Imperial War Mus★ CB2 31 F1
Impett's La CB1 ....67 A4
Impington La CB4 ..104 C3
Impington Village Coll
  CB4 ....104 D3
India La PE28 ......151 E1
Infield Rd PE28 ....167 C7
Ingham Hall Gdns 2
  PE13 ....234 D7
Ingham Rd CB4 .....24 A8
Ingle Rd 3 PE14 ...236 B5
Ingle's La 1 PE15 ..223 A5
Ingoldsby Cl 3 PE15 .243 D2
Ingram St PE29 ....141 E4
Inham's Rd PE7 ....189 E6
Inhams Cl 2 PE13 ..234 D5
Inhams Way PE28 ...116 A4
Inkerman Rise PE19 ..74 C5
Inley Dro PE12 ....237 A8
Institute of Astronomy
  CB3 ....83 A3
Institute of Criminology
  CB3 ....83 C1
Institute of Public Health
  CB2 ....65 B2
International Extension Coll
  CB1 ....65 A8
Inverness Cl CB4 ...84 A5
Iram Dro CB4 ......209 B1
Ireton Cl PE19 ....74 F3
Ireton Way PE15 ...243 D2
Ireton's Way
  Chatteris PE16 ....241 F2
  Mepal PE16 ....216 C3
Irnham Rd PE29 ....244 C7
Ironmonger St 2 PE9 244 C4
Irving Burgess Cl PE7 189 C8
Isaacson Rd CB5 ...109 C8
Isham Rd 1 PE3 ...197 D4
Isherwood Cl 3 SG8 .5 C8
Isinglass Cl CB1 ...111 E2
Isle Bridge Rd PE14 .236 F2
Isle Coll PE16 .....241 C5
Isle of Ely Way
  Chatteris PE16 ....241 C7
  March PE15 ....243 A4
Isleham CE Sch CB7 .213 A5
Isleham Rd CB7 ...212 F2
Isons Cl SG8 ......15 E8
Itter Cres PE4 .....197 E8
Ivan Clark's Cnr CB1 .34 C7
Ivatt St CB4 ......125 E5
Ivatt Way PE3 .....197 C4
Ivel Cl PE19 ......74 C4
Ivelbury Cl PE19 ..117 A3
Iver Cl CB1 ....65 F7
Ives Dro PE7 ......189 A2
Ivesdyke Cl 4 PE13 .238 B2
Ivett's Cl PE13 ...45 C7
Ivy Field CB3 .....63 B4
Ivy Gr PE4 ....204 D2
Ivy Way PE28 .....138 A6
Ixworth Cl 8 PE6 ..232 A1
Ixworth Rd 2 PE6 ..23 E6
Izaak Walton Way CB4 84 C5
Izzard Rise PE19 ..96 E4

J

Jack Haws La 4 PE9 .230 D4
Jack Hunt Sch PE3 ..197 B3
Jack Hunt Swimming Pool
  PE3 ....197 B3
Jack Jarvis Cl 5 CB8 111 A3

Jack Warren Gn CB5 ..84 F3
Jack's Corner Dro PE26 172 E3
Jackson Cl CB2 ....48 C5
Jackson's La CB10 ..18 D3
Jackson's Sq CB10 ..18 D3
Jackson's Way SG8 ..15 E8
James Carter Rd IP28 239 A6
James Ct PE19 .....74 F2
James Essex Dr 1 CB6 240 E7
James Gage Cl PE16 .241 B3
James St CB5 ......246 C3
Janus CB9 ....24 D6
Jarman Way SG8 ...5 B7
Jarman's La IP28 ...213 D7
Jarvis Way CB8 ....110 C5
Jasmin Cl PE13 ....245 F7
Jasmine Ct PE2 ...185 E2
Jasmine Way PE7 ..181 F6
Jay Cl CB9 ....24 C7
Jaywick Rd CB9 ...24 A8
Jeavons La 6 CB3 ..79 C3
Jedburgh Cl 3 CB4 .83 E7
Jefferson Cl 22 PE8 .230 B1
Jeffery Ave 4 PE13 .245 D2
Jeffrey Cl 2 SG8 ...5 C8
Jellicoe Pl 3 PE19 .74 A2
Jenkins Cl PE1 ....74 B2
Jenyns Cl CB5 ....86 E7
Jepps La SG8 .....5 D6
Jermyn Cl CB4 ....83 D6
Jerusalem Dro CB6 ..217 A5
Jesus Coll CB5 ....246 B3
Jesus La CB1 .....246 B3
Jesus Terr CB1 ....246 C3
Jetty The 2 PE13 ..235 C7
Jew House Dro PE14 .235 E3
Jim Mollison Cl 2 IP28 239 B5
Job's La 2 PE15 ...243 C1
John Amner Cl CB6 ..240 D6
John Breay Cl SG8 ..29 D4
John Clare Sch PE6 ..231 B4
John Clarke Ct CB4 ..84 A6
John F Kennedy Ct 2
  PE13 ....245 D4
John Falkner Inf Sch
  CB2 ....32 E7
John Impey Way SG8 .14 D6
John Mansfield Sec Sch
  PE1 ....198 B8
John Paxton Jun Sch
  CB2 ....32 F8
John St Cambridge CB1 246 C2
  Royston SG8 ......5 D6
John Thompson Rd 3
  PE13 ....245 D4
John's Cl 6 SG8 ...15 E8
Johnson's Dro PE13 .234 B7
Joiner's Ct CB1 ...35 B2
Joiner's Rd CB1 ...35 B2
Jolley Way CB4 ....83 F6
Jones Cl 1 PE15 ...243 B3
Jones Ct PE26 .....172 B7
Jones La PE7 ......190 C7
Jones's Dro PE7 ...221 F8
Jopling Way SG8 ..48 C4
Jordan Mews 2 PE1 ..198 B3
Jordans Yd CB1 ...246 A3
Jorose St 4 PE3 ...197 A3
Joscelynes CB2 ...49 C4
Josiah Ct CB5 .....106 C8
Joyce's Ct CB2 ....32 F6
Jubilee Ave PE28 ..164 D6
Jubilee Cl Isleham CB7 213 A5
  Little Paxton PE19 .95 F2
  Waterbeach CB5 ...106 A8
Jubilee Ct CB8 ....90 A1
Jubilee End SG8 ...11 B2
Jubilee St PE2 .....186 F8
Jubilee Terr CB7 ...240 D3
Jubilee Way SG8 ...11 B2
Judson Ct 3 PE29 ..141 F8
Julian Cl CB9 .....24 D7
Julius Martin La CB7 .212 A4
Junction Rd IP28 ..239 B5
Juniper Cl IP28 ...239 E5
Juniper Cres PE3 ..197 A2
Juniper Dr CB7 ....240 F5
Jupiter Cl 2 CB9 ..24 C6
Justinian Cl CB9 ..24 D6
Jutland Rise PE19 ..74 C5

K

Kathleen Elliot Way CB1 65 F7
Kay Hitch Way CB4 ..104 B2
Keates Rd CB1 ....66 A5
Keats Cl 1 SG8 ....5 C8
Keats Ct PE19 .....74 C6
Keats Way PE1 ....197 D7
Keble Cl PE9 ......244 A7
Kedleston Rd PE7 ..187 F6
Keeton Rd PE1 ....197 E7
Kefford Cl SG8 ....12 F5
Kelful Cl PE7 .....190 D7
Kelsey Cres CB1 ...24 D7
Kelsey Kerridge Sports H
  CB1 ....246 C1
Kelsey Way PE15 ..243 D2
Kelvin Cl CB1 .....65 D5
Kemmann La CB3 ..79 B3
Ken Stimpson Comp Sch
  PE4 ....204 B4
Kendal Cl PE4 .....204 F2
Kendal Way CB4 ..84 A6
Kendrick Cl PE2 ...197 E4
Kenilworth Ave PE7 .188 A5
Kenilworth Cl 3 PE19 74 C3

Kenlan Rd PE13 ...245 D6
Kennedy Rd CB7 ..213 A5
Kennels Rd PE6 ...196 D4
Kennet Gdns PE4 ..204 E1
Kennetside CB8 ...73 D1
Kennett Prim Sch CB8 133 F5
Kennett Rd or Moulton Rd
  CB8 ....112 F7
Kennett Sta CB8 ..133 F3
Kennulphs Cl 3 PE6 .232 E2
Kent Cl Ely CB6 ...240 B5
  St Ives PE27 ......143 F7
Kent Rd Huntingdon PE29 141 E8
  Peterborough PE3 ..197 E2
Kent Way CB4 .....83 F7
Kentings CB3 .....62 B5
Kentmere Pl 1 PE4 .204 F2
Kents La CB7 ......212 B4
Kentwell Pl CB5 ...130 C2
Kenwood Gdns CB1 .35 E2
Kerridge Cl CB3 ...81 B2
Kesters CB3 ......81 B2
Kesteven Cl 6 PE6 .231 E8
Kesteven Rd PE9 ..244 B7
Kestrel Cl Cottenham CB4 125 C5
  Huntingdon PE29 ..142 A7
Kestrel Dr 2 PE14 .245 D2
Kestrel Pl 4 PE19 .75 B7
Kestrel Rd CB9 ....24 C7
Kestrel Way 7 SG8 .5 E8
Keswick Cl 1 PE4 ..204 F3
Kettering Rd PE9 ..244 B2
Kettlefields CB8 ...89 F1
Kettles Cl CB4 ....103 C5
Keynes Rd CB5 ....84 D4
Keyston Rd PE28 ..135 D2
Kidmans Cl Hilton PE28 120 B1
  Newton CB2 ....31 B7
Kigezi Int Sch of Medicine
  CB1 ....246 B2
Kildare Dr PE3 ....197 C4
Kilham PE2 ....185 E2
Kilkenny Ave CB6 ..240 E7
Kilmaine Cl CB4 ...83 F8
Kiln Cl
  2 Little Downham CB6 218 B7
  St Ives PE27 ......143 E6
Kiln House Yd SG8 ..5 C6
Kiln La CB7 ....240 F5
Kilverstone PE4 ...204 B6
Kim Rd PE28 ......114 A7
Kimberley Rd CB4 ..246 C4
Kimbolton Ct PE1 ..197 F3
Kimbolton Rd
  Hail Weston PE19 ..74 A8
  Pertenhall MK44 ..113 D1
Kimbolton Sch PE28 .113 F4
Kinderley Cty Prim Sch
  PE13 ....237 F6
Kinderley Rd PE13 ..245 C8
King Cob CB6 .....210 F5
King Edgar Cl CB6 ..240 D7
King Edward Rd PE16 241 D5
King Edward VII Rd CB8 110 E5
King George Ave CB8 .110 B8
King Hedges Prim Sch
  CB4 ....83 F7
King James Way SG8 .5 D6
King St Cambridge CB1 .246 C2
  Doddington/Wimblington
  PE15 ....223 B7
  Mildenhall IP28 ...239 C4
  14 Over CB4 ......208 D1
  1 Peterborough PE1 198 A2
  Rampton CB4 ......124 E4
  Somersham SE28 ..215 B1
  West Deeping PE6 ..231 A8
  Wisbech PE13 .....245 A5
Kingdon Ave CB7 ..219 B5
Kingfisher Cl Bourn CB3 60 C6
  Chatteris PE16 ....241 C6
  Haverhill CB9 .....24 C8
  March PE15 ....243 E5
  Sawston CB2 ......32 E6
  Yaxley PE7 ....181 D5
Kingfisher Dr
  Burwell CB5 ....130 B4
  6 Wisbech PE14 ..245 D2
Kingfisher Rd PE7 ..189 F8
Kingfisher Way
  Cottenham CB4 ....125 D5
  The Stukeleys PE29 141 A6
Kingfishers PE2 ...185 D6
King's Ave CB7 ....240 E7
King's Delph Dro PE7 187 E2
King's Dyke PE7 ...188 E6
King's Gate CB3 ...78 C6
King's Gdns
  Huntingdon PE29 ..141 D5
  Peterborough PE1 .198 A5
King's Hedges Rd CB4 83 D7
King's La Cambridge CB1 246 A2
  Elmdon CB11 ......9 A3
  St Neots PE19 .....75 A5
King's Par CB2 ....246 A2
King's Rd CB3 .....64 B7
King's Wk 3 PE13 ..245 C4
Kings Cl Huntingdon PE29 142 A7
  Mildenhall IP28 ...239 D5
Kings Coll CB2 ....246 A2
Kings Coll Sch CB3 ..83 C1
Kings Delph PE7 ..188 C5
Kings Dr CB8 ......111 B3
Kings Dyke Cl PE7 ..187 E6
Kings Gr CB3 .....63 B4
Kings Hedges PE27 ..144 A6
Kings Mill La
  Great Shelford CB2 ..48 F4

Kings Mill La *continued*
2 Stamford PE9 ... 244 B4
Kings Par CB7 ... 212 B3
Kings Rd Eaton Socon PE19 74 B3
Hardwick CB3 ... 81 A2
Peterborough PE2 ... 187 B6
St Ives PE27 ... 144 A4
St Neots PE19 ... 74 F6
Stamford PE9 ... 244 B6
Wisbech PE13 ... 245 C4
Kings Ripton Rd PE29 ... 152 D1
Kings Sch Ely CB6 ... 240 C5
Peterborough PE1 ... 198 A4
Kingsbridge Ct PE4 ... 204 A5
Kingsbrook PE27 ... 144 A5
Kingsland Way SG7 ... 2 D4
Kingsley Ave PE13 ... 245 B4
Kingsley Cl 1 PE9 ... 230 D3
Kingsley Rd PE1 ... 198 C4
Kingsley St PE15 ... 243 D5
Kingsmead Ct CB6 ... 242 E4
Kingston Cl PE29 ... 141 E8
Kingston Dr PE2 ... 187 E5
Kingston Pas 2 CB8 ... 111 A3
Kingston Rd CB3 ... 61 D1
Kingston St CB1 ... 65 A8
Kingston Vale SG8 ... 5 E5
Kingston Way PE28 ... 163 F6
Kingsway
Duxford Airfield CB2 ... 31 F1
Leverington PE13 ... 245 F7
Mildenhall IP28 ... 239 C4
Newmarket CB8 ... 110 F4
Royston SG8 ... 5 D8
Kingswood Rd PE15 ... 243 C3
Kinnaird Way CB1 ... 65 C4
Kinnears Wlk PE2 ... 185 F2
Kinross Rd CB4 ... 84 A5
Kintbury CB2 ... 17 D8
Kipling Ct PE1 ... 197 E8
Kipling Pl 1 PE19 ... 74 D5
Kipling Rd 1 SG8 ... 5 E8
Kirby Cl CB4 ... 83 F5
Kirby Cross Ave CB6 ... 242 B5
Kirby Rd CB5 ... 127 C1
Kirby Terr CB5 ... 127 B1
Kirby Wlk 2 PE3 ... 197 C5
Kirby's Cl 12 CB4 ... 208 D1
Kirk Ogden Cl PE15 ... 243 D3
Kirkgate PE13 ... 237 F7
Kirkgate St PE13 ... 245 E7
Kirkham's La PE14 ... 236 C4
Kirkmeadow PE3 ... 197 A8
Kirk's La PE14 ... 235 E5
Kirkstall PE2 ... 186 B3
Kirkton Gate PE3 ... 197 A1
Kirkwood Cl PE3 ... 197 E2
Kirkwood Rd CB4 ... 83 F7
Kirtling Rd Kirtling CB8 ... 72 D7
Woodditton CB8 ... 71 F8
Woodditton CB8 ... 90 E1
Kisby Ave PE29 ... 142 A1
Kite Cl PE29 ... 142 A7
Kitson Gdns CB6 ... 210 F5
Knapp Rise CB3 ... 47 A5
Knapp The 2 CB3 ... 47 A5
Knaresborough Ct 10
PE19 ... 74 F1
Knarr Fen Rd PE6 ... 202 D8
Knaves Acre Dro CB7 ... 212 E5
Kneesworth Ho Hospl
SG8 ... 13 C5
Kneesworth Rd SG8 ... 13 F8
Kneesworth St SG8 ... 5 C7
Knight's Cl 11 PE15 ... 223 A5
Knight's End Rd
March PE15 ... 222 C8
1 March PE15 ... 243 C1
Knights Cl
Eaton Socon PE19 ... 74 B4
13 Leverington PE13 ... 238 B2
Knights Way CB4 ... 105 D3
Knipe Cl PE29 ... 141 B7
Knowle Ct CB6 ... 242 B5
Knowles Ave PE28 ... 164 E5
Knowles Cl PE28 ... 140 E2
Knutsford Rd SG8 ... 12 E4
Kooreman Ave PE13 ... 245 D7
Kyle Cres PE28 ... 140 D2
Kym Rd PE19 ... 74 C4

L

Laburnum Ave
Mildenhall IP28 ... 239 E5
Yaxley PE7 ... 181 F6
Laburnum Cl
Cambridge CB4 ... 83 F4
Red Lodge IP28 ... 213 F1
5 Wisbech PE13 ... 245 E7
Laburnum Gr
March PE15 ... 243 C6
Peterborough PE1 ... 198 B8
Laburnum La CB5 ... 130 A3
Laburnum Way PE27 ... 144 A5
Lacey's La CB8 ... 110 B7
Lacey's Way CB2 ... 32 D1
Lacks Cl CB4 ... 125 D3
Laddus Bank Elm PE14 ... 236 C1
Upwell PE14 ... 236 D1
Laddus Dro PE14 ... 236 B8
Lady Adrian Sch CB4 ... 83 E5
Lady Charlotte Rd PE7 ... 186 D3
Lady Lodge Dr PE2 ... 186 A5
Lady Margaret Rd 1
CB3 ... 83 C3
Lady Smith Ave PE7 ... 189 F8
Lady Way PE19 ... 74 B4
Ladybower Way PE4 ... 204 E3
Lady's Dro PE14 ... 236 D6
Ladywalk CB4 ... 123 F3
Lake Ave PE14 ... 229 F3
Lake Ct PE13 ... 245 D4
Lake Dro PE7 ... 190 E6
Lake Way PE29 ... 141 C5
Lakefield Ave PE19 ... 96 A2
Lakes Dro CB6 ... 209 F3
Lakeside
Peterborough PE7 ... 186 C2
Peterborough PE4 ... 204 D4
Lakeside Cl
Little Paxton PE19 ... 96 A2
Perry PE28 ... 115 D3
Lakeside L Ctr PE2 ... 186 A5
Lakeway 8 PE28 ... 215 C1
Lambert Mews PE9 ... 244 C4
Lambeth Wlk PE9 ... 244 A6
Lamble Cl IP28 ... 213 F8
Lambourn Cl 1 CB2 ... 64 D3
Lambourne Rd CB3 ... 81 A3
Lamb's La
Cottenham CB4 ... 125 D3
Glatton PE28 ... 175 D2
Lamb's Pl PE15 ... 243 D4
Lambs Hill Dro PE15 ... 228 B1
Lammas Field 4 CB3 ... 64 C7
Lammas Gdns PE29 ... 141 D5
Lammas Rd PE1 ... 198 A7
Lammas Way
St Ives PE27 ... 143 F4
St Neots PE19 ... 74 E6
Lamport Dr PE29 ... 141 F8
Lancaster Cl
Old Hurst PE28 ... 154 D6
Warboys PE28 ... 164 F4
Lancaster Ct PE7 ... 181 F6
Lancaster Dr PE27 ... 144 A6
Lancaster Rd
Mildenhall IP28 ... 213 E8
Ramsey PE26 ... 171 E3
10 Stamford PE9 ... 244 B6
Lancaster Way Ely CB6 ... 217 F1
Godmanchester PE29 ... 141 F2
Huntingdon PE29 ... 141 B8
Yaxley PE7 ... 181 F6
Lancaster Way Bsns Pk
CB6 ... 217 F1
Lancelot Way PE28 ... 121 C5
Lancing Cl PE4 ... 204 C3
Landbeach Rd CB4 ... 105 D3
Landcliffe Cl PE27 ... 144 B5
Lander Cl 5 CB4 ... 105 C3
Landwade Rd
Exning CB8 ... 131 B4
Fordham CB8 ... 131 D5
Lane The Easton PE28 ... 138 B4
Hauxton CB2 ... 48 B4
Old Hurst PE28 ... 154 E6
Stow Longa PE28 ... 137 B2
West Deeping PE6 ... 231 B7
Lanes The
Great Wilbraham CB1 ... 67 F8
Over CB4 ... 208 D1
St Ives PE28 ... 143 A5
Langdale Cl 5 CB1 ... 66 A7
Langdyke PE1 ... 198 F6
Langford Rd PE2 ... 187 A7
Langham Rd CB1 ... 65 C6
Langham Way Ely CB7 ... 240 E7
Haverhill CB9 ... 38 B1
Langley PE3 ... 197 B8
Langley Cl PE27 ... 144 A4
Langley Way PE28 ... 143 B1
Langton Rd PE1 ... 198 D7
Langwood Cl 7 PE19 ... 74 C6
Langwood Fen Dro
PE16 ... 216 D8
Langwood Hill Dro
PE16 ... 216 B7
Lankester Rd SG8 ... 5 C5
Lansbury Cl 4 PE19 ... 74 E4
Lansdowne Cl CB6 ... 240 B3
Lansdowne Rd
Cambridge CB3 ... 82 F3
Yaxley PE7 ... 181 F6
Lansdowne Way PE2 ... 186 D7
Lantree Cres CB2 ... 64 D1
Lapwing Ct IP28 ... 239 D4
Lapwing Dr PE7 ... 190 A8
Larch Cl PE7 ... 181 F6
Larch Gr PE1 ... 198 C6
Larham Way PE16 ... 241 B5
Lark Cl IP28 ... 213 F4
Lark Cres PE29 ... 142 A6
Lark End PE19 ... 117 B3
Lark Hill CB8 ... 112 E5
Lark Rd IP28 ... 239 D4
Lark Rise CB3 ... 80 F3
Lark Way PE28 ... 150 E4
Larkfield Rd CB7 ... 240 E6
Larkhall Rd CB7 ... 212 D1
Larkin Cl Cambridge CB4 ... 84 A6
Royston SG8 ... 13 D1
Larkins Rd SG8 ... 26 F6
Larks Cl CB9 ... 24 C7
Larksfield PE13 ... 245 C3
Larkspur Cl
4 Red Lodge IP28 ... 213 F1
3 Red Lodge IP28 ... 214 A1
Latham Ave PE2 ... 186 C6
Latham Cl CB2 ... 64 D6
Latham Rd Cambridge CB2 64 D6
Huntingdon PE29 ... 141 C8
Latimer Cl CB5 ... 84 E3
Latin Cl PE19 ... 118 A2
Lattersey Cl PE7 ... 189 F7
Laundress La CB3 ... 246 A2
Laundry La CB1 ... 65 D5
Laureate CP Sch CB8 ... 110 E6
Laureate Gdns CB8 ... 110 E6
Laureate Paddocks CB8 110 E6
Laureate Sch Rd CB8 ... 110 E6
Laurel Cl Haverhill CB9 ... 38 D2
Mepal CB6 ... 216 E3
9 Red Lodge IP28 ... 214 A1
Sawtry PE28 ... 168 A3
Yaxley PE7 ... 181 D4
Laurel Dr 2 PE6 ... 232 F3
Laurels Cl PE19 ... 74 F4
Laurels The PE15 ... 243 E7
Lavender Cl 3 IP28 ... 213 F1
Lavender Cres PE1 ... 198 B8
Lavender Ct 4 PE29 ... 141 F7
Lavender Field CB9 ... 23 D8
Lavender Rd CB4 ... 84 A7
Lavenham Ct PE2 ... 186 C7
Lavington Grange PE1 ... 198 E6
Law Cl CB6 ... 242 D3
Lawn Ave PE1 ... 198 A7
Lawn La
Little Downham CB6 ... 218 A7
Sutton CB6 ... 216 E1
Lawn The CB2 ... 32 C5
Lawns Cres CB6 ... 218 A7
Lawns The Cambridge CB3 83 A2
2 Everton SG19 ... 40 C3
Melbourn SG8 ... 14 C5
Wisbech PE13 ... 245 B6
Lawrance Lea CB2 ... 47 F2
Lawrence Ave PE7 ... 187 C2
Lawrence Cl CB3 ... 82 D8
Lawrence Rd
Eaton Socon PE19 ... 74 C5
Ramsey PE26 ... 172 C7
Wittering PE8 ... 230 B1
Lawrence Way CB4 ... 83 F7
Law's Cl PE6 ... 206 F1
Laws Cres PE28 ... 140 C4
Lawson Ave PE2 ... 187 D6
Laxton Ave CB3 ... 81 A3
Laxton Cl PE19 ... 74 C4
Laxton Grange 8 PE28 ... 208 C5
Laxton Way CB4 ... 84 C6
Layer Rd CB9 ... 23 E7
Layston Pk SG8 ... 5 D5
Layton Cres PE28 ... 140 D2
Lea Brooks Cl PE28 ... 164 F4
Lea Gdns PE3 ... 197 F1
Lea Rd PE28 ... 143 C1
Leaden Hill SG8 ... 28 D8
Leaden's La PE19 ... 117 C3
Leader's Way CB8 ... 110 E4
Leading Dro PE7 ... 181 E4
Leafere Way 1 PE13 ... 238 B2
Leather La CB9 ... 23 E7
Lebanon Dr PE13 ... 245 F7
Ledbury Rd PE3 ... 197 C3
Ledger Cl PE27 ... 144 A6
Ledham PE2 ... 185 D4
Ledo Rd CB2 ... 31 F2
Lee Cl CB4 ... 125 D3
Lee Rd PE7 ... 181 E4
Leechcroft PE28 ... 121 C6
Lees La PE19 ... 95 E5
Lees Way CB3 ... 103 E1
Leete Pl SG8 ... 5 C7
Leete Rd CB1 ... 65 F5
Leete's La CB3 ... 46 A8
Leeway Ave CB2 ... 49 B5
Legg Rd 21 PE8 ... 230 B1
Leicester Cl CB6 ... 240 A3
Leighton PE2 ... 186 C4
Leighton CP Sch PE2 ... 186 C4
Leinsters Cl PE3 ... 197 D3
Leiston Rd CB9 ... 23 E7
Lemur Dr CB1 ... 66 B7
Lensfield Rd CB2 ... 246 B1
Lenton Cl PE28 ... 140 D2
Lents Way CB4 ... 84 C5
Leonard Cl 2 CB5 ... 84 E4
Leopold Wlk CB4 ... 125 E3
Lerowe Rd PE13 ... 245 E7
Les Baux Pl 5 PE13 ... 245 E3
Leslie Green Rd PE28 ... 143 B5
Lessingham PE2 ... 185 D4
Lester Dr CB6 ... 210 A6
Lester Piggott Way 3
CB8 ... 110 F6
Lethbridge Rd PE4 ... 204 E2
Lettice Martin Croft CB2 32 D5
Levellers La PE19 ... 74 F3
Levens Wlk PE3 ... 197 B3
Leverington Comm
PE13 ... 235 B8
Leverington Cty Prim Sch
PE13 ... 238 B2
Leverington Rd PE13 ... 245 A6
Levers Wr PE29 ... 141 C5
Levitt's Dro PE6 ... 200 C4
Lewes Gdns PE4 ... 204 C3
Lewis Cl
Great & Little Abington CB1 34 C5
March PE15 ... 243 B3
Lewis Cres CB1 ... 34 C5
Lexington Cl 3 CB4 ... 83 C5
Ley Rd CB8 ... 90 A1
Leyburn Cl CB1 ... 66 A7
Leys Ave CB4 ... 83 F5
Leys Rd Cambridge CB4 ... 83 F5
St Neots PE19 ... 74 E6
Leys Rectory PE19 ... 117 F2
Leys Sch The CB2 ... 246 B1
Leys The Alconbury PE28 ... 150 F4
Leys The *continued*
Little Gransden SG19 ... 58 E3
Peterborough PE3 ... 197 A1
Sawtry PE28 ... 168 C3
Leys Wlk CB2 ... 48 C4
Leyton Ave IP28 ... 239 B6
Liberator Rd PE26 ... 171 E3
Lichfield Ave PE4 ... 204 B3
Lichfield Rd CB1 ... 65 B6
Licking's Dro PE13 ... 245 A2
Lidgate Cl PE2 ... 186 C7
Lidgate Rd CB8 ... 92 E7
Lilac Cl Haslingfield CB3 ... 47 B5
Wisbech PE13 ... 245 F7
Lilac Ct CB1 ... 65 C5
Lilac End CB3 ... 47 B4
Lilac Rd PE1 ... 198 C7
Lilac Way PE27 ... 144 B6
Lilyholt Rd PE15 ... 222 A5
Lime Ave PE13 ... 245 C7
Lime Cl IP28 ... 239 E5
Lime Gr March PE15 ... 243 C6
Royston SG8 ... 5 E8
St Neots PE19 ... 74 F6
Lime Rd PE26 ... 172 A8
Lime Tree Ave PE1 ... 197 F4
Limekiln Cl SG8 ... 5 E5
Limekiln Rd CB1 ... 65 E3
Limes Ave 1 PE14 ... 236 A5
Limes Cl Bassingbourn SG8 12 E5
Littleport CB6 ... 242 C4
Limes Ct PE27 ... 143 F1
Limes Park Rd PE27 ... 143 F1
Limes Rd CB3 ... 81 A3
Limes The
Bassingbourn SG8 ... 12 E5
Castor PE5 ... 195 F1
Harston CB2 ... 47 F2
Sawston CB2 ... 32 F8
5 Wittering PE8 ... 230 B1
Limestone Cl 7 CB7 ... 213 A5
Limetree Cl
3 Cambridge CB1 ... 65 D5
Yaxley PE7 ... 181 F7
Linclare Pl 7 PE19 ... 74 C4
Lincoln Ave PE27 ... 143 F7
Lincoln Cl PE19 ... 117 A5
Lincoln Rd
Deeping Gate PE6 ... 231 E7
4 Mildenhall IP28 ... 213 E8
Peterborough PE4 ... 197 C8
Ramsey PE26 ... 171 E3
Stamford PE9 ... 244 D7
Wyton Airfield PE28 ... 143 A8
Linden Cl Cambridge CB4 ... 83 C4
6 Haddenham CB6 ... 210 A5
Linden Dr PE16 ... 241 C4
Linden End 3 CB6 ... 210 A5
Linden Gr PE29 ... 141 F2
Linden Way CB6 ... 210 A5
Lindens Cl PE13 ... 234 A2
Lindisfarne Cl 9 PE19 ... 74 F1
Lindisfarne Rd PE6 ... 232 A1
Lindridge Wlk PE3 ... 197 A2
Lindsay Cl SG8 ... 13 C1
Lindsells Wlk PE16 ... 241 C5
Lindsey Cl PE4 ... 204 D1
Lindsey Rd Stamford PE9 244 C6
5 Uffington PE9 ... 230 C6
Ling Garth PE1 ... 198 B8
Lingfield Rd 7 SG8 ... 5 E6
Lingholme Cl 2 CB4 ... 83 C5
Lingmoor 2 PE29 ... 141 A6
Lingrey Ct CB2 ... 64 D2
Lingwood Pk 5 PE3 ... 197 A1
Link Dr PE28 ... 140 C3
Link La CB6 ... 216 E1
Link Rd Peterborough PE1 197 F3
Sawston CB2 ... 32 F8
Links Cl IP28 ... 213 F4
Links The CB8 ... 89 D8
Links Way PE27 ... 143 F4
Linkside PE3 ... 204 B1
Linley Rd St Neots PE19 ... 74 E3
Whittlesey PE7 ... 189 E6
Linlithgow Cl CB3 ... 99 A3
Linnet PE2 ... 185 D6
Linton CE Inf Sch CB1 ... 35 C2
Linton Cl CB8 ... 110 F5
Linton Heights Jun Sch
CB1 ... 35 D2
Linton Liby CB1 ... 35 C2
Linton Rd Balsham CB1 ... 52 F2
Great Abington CB1 ... 34 D6
Hadstock CB1 ... 20 B8
Horseheath CB1 ... 36 F3
Linton Village Coll CB1 ... 35 B2
Linton Zoo & Gdns* CB1 35 B1
Linwood La PE15 ... 223 A8
Lion Cl PE26 ... 220 D3
Lion Wlk PE26 ... 172 A5
Lion Yd PE26 ... 172 B6
Lionel Walden Sch
PE15 ... 223 A5
Lions Cross PE29 ... 119 A8
Lisburn Rd CB8 ... 111 B3
Lisle Cl CB7 ... 240 E5
Lisle La CB7 ... 240 E4
Lister Rd PE1 ... 197 F7
Lister's Rd PE14 ... 236 E1
Litchfield Cl PE7 ... 181 F5
Litlington Rd SG8 ... 11 E1
Little Back La The CB5 ... 129 C1
Little Casterton Rd PE9 244 A6
Little Chishill Rd SG8 ... 1 C6
Little Cl PE6 ... 232 A1
Little Dowgate PE13 ... 245 A7
Little End Rd PE19 ... 74 B1
Little Farthing Cl PE27 ... 144 B4
Little Fen Dro
Burwell CB5 ... 129 E6
Swaffham Prior CB5 ... 129 A1
Little Fendyke La PE14 ... 236 E5
Little Gn CB8 ... 91 C5
Little Gransden La SG19 ... 58 D4
Little Hasse Dro CB7 ... 212 C6
Little Heath SG19 ... 41 C4
Little How PE27 ... 143 E6
Little Johns Cl PE3 ... 196 F3
Little La Ely CB6 ... 240 B4
1 Great Gransden SG19 ... 58 E4
Melbourn SG8 ... 14 C6
Little London Dro CB7 ... 212 F5
Little London La CB7 ... 212 F5
Little Marefen Dro CB6 ... 242 A7
Little Mdw CB3 ... 102 B2
Little Moor PE28 ... 121 C5
Little Northfields 3
PE9 ... 230 D4
Little Paxton CP Sch
PE19 ... 95 F1
Little Paxton La PE19 ... 95 F2
Little Ramper PE13 ... 238 B4
Little Setchel Dro CB4 ... 209 F2
Little St CB6 ... 218 B6
Little St Mary's La CB2 ... 246 A1
Little Thetford CP Sch
CB6 ... 211 B7
Little Whyte PE26 ... 172 B7
Little Wilbraham Rd CB1 86 D4
Littlechild Dr 5 PE13 ... 238 B2
Littlecotes Cl PE28 ... 137 F7
Littlefield Cl
Godmanchester PE29 ... 118 F8
Wilburton CB6 ... 210 C6
Littlemeer PE2 ... 185 F4
Littleport Sta CB6 ... 242 E6
Littleport Village Coll
CB6 ... 242 B4
Littleworth Dro PE12 ... 233 F8
Littleworth End PE19 ... 118 A1
Livermore Gn PE4 ... 204 A6
Locks Cl PE6 ... 206 B7
Locks Gn PE8 ... 183 A8
Locksgate 1 PE28 ... 215 C1
Lockspit Hall Dro CB4 ... 125 F8
Lode Ave Outwell PE14 ... 236 F1
Waterbeach CB5 ... 106 B7
Lode Cl CB7 ... 212 B3
Lode La CB7 ... 211 E1
Lode Rd Bottisham CB5 ... 86 D7
Lode CB5 ... 107 D1
Lode Way Chatteris PE16 241 C6
Haddenham CB6 ... 210 A5
Loder Ave PE3 ... 196 F2
Lodes End Dro PE26 ... 220 F2
Lodge Cl PE29 ... 141 C4
Lodge Gdns CB6 ... 210 A6
Lodge Rd SG8 ... 31 A1
Loftsteads 3 PE28 ... 215 C1
Logan's Way CB4 ... 84 A3
Lomax Dr PE28 ... 140 C3
Lombardy Dr PE1 ... 198 B8
London La PE19 ... 96 E4
London Rd Barley SG8 ... 6 F1
Chatteris PE16 ... 241 C2
Fenstanton PE28 ... 120 E7
Fowlmere SG8 ... 15 D5
Godmanchester PE29 ... 141 F1
Great Chesterford CB10 ... 18 C2
Great Shelford CB2 ... 49 B4
Harston CB2 ... 48 B3
Hemingford Grey PE27 ... 143 F1
Kimbolton PE28 ... 114 A4
Peterborough PE7 ... 186 F3
Royston SG8 ... 5 D4
Sawston CB2 ... 32 F5
Wansford PE8 ... 194 B2
Yaxley PE7 ... 181 C5
London St
Godmanchester PE29 ... 141 F1
Whittlesey PE7 ... 189 D6
Lone Tree Ave CB4 ... 83 C8
Long Cswy
Peterborough PE1 ... 198 A2
Witcham CB6 ... 217 C2
Long Dolver Dro CB7 ... 212 B6
Long Dro Bury PE26 ... 172 F5
Cottenham CB4 ... 125 F3
Downham CB6 ... 224 F3
Elm PE14 ... 235 B1
Feltwell PE38 ... 226 F6
Haddenham CB6 ... 209 C5
Holme PE7 ... 177 D5
Over CB4 ... 208 D3
Parson Drove PE13 ... 234 B5
Ramsey PE26 ... 221 D2
Somersham PE28 ... 215 D2
Waterbeach CB5 ... 106 D8
Whittlesey PE7 ... 200 F3
Long Furlong CB4 ... 208 D1
Long Holme Dro CB4 ... 208 E3
Long La Coveney CB6 ... 217 C4
Fowlmere SG8 ... 15 D8
Gamlingay SG19 ... 41 F6
Hemingford Grey PE28 ... 120 C8
Linton CB1 ... 35 C1
Over CB4 ... 208 E2
Spaldwick PE28 ... 137 F5
Willingham CB4 ... 124 A8
Long Lots PE14 ... 236 F8
Long Meadow Rd CB5 ... 107 F2

Long Nightlayer's Dro PE16 ...241 E8
Long North Fen Dro CB6 ...216 A4
Long Pasture PE4 ...204 B5
Long Rd Cambridge CB2 ...64 F4
 Comberton CB3 ...81 D2
Long Reach Rd CB4 ...84 C6
Longfellow Ave 5 PE19 .74 D5
Longfield Rd CB6 ...242 B5
Longfields CB6 ...240 A3
Longhead La PE28 ...238 D3
Longhill Rd PE15 ...228 B6
Longholme Rd PE26 ...171 A4
Longmere La CB7 ...212 A5
Longsands Com Coll PE19 ...75 A6
Longsands Par 3 PE19 .75 A6
Longsands Rd PE19 ...75 A5
Longstaff Way PE29 ...142 A6
Longstanton CP Sch CB4 ...123 F2
Longstanton Rd Oakington/Longstanton CB4 ...103 B6
 Over CB4 ...123 B7
Longthorpe Cl 3 PE3 ...197 B1
Longthorpe CP Sch PE3 197 A1
Longthorpe Gn PE3 ...197 B1
Longthorpe House Mews 11 PE3 ...196 F2
Longthorpe Parkway PE3 ...186 A8
Longueville Ct PE2 ...186 B5
Longview CB6 ...216 D1
Longwater PE2 ...186 D1
Lonsdale CB1 ...35 E2
Loop Rd PE28 ...146 C2
Lophams Cl 1 CB9 ...38 E2
Lord's Croft La CB4 ...24 A7
Lord's Gd Dro CB5 ...128 D2
Lord's La PE13 ...235 D6
Lords La PE13 ...235 D7
Lordship Cl Orwell SG8 ...45 E1
 Willingham CB4 ...209 A1
Lordship Dr SG8 ...14 C7
Lordship La CB4 ...125 D4
Loris Ct CB1 ...66 A7
Lornas Field PE4 ...186 D2
Losecoat St 1 PE9 ...244 D7
Lotfield St SG8 ...45 E1
Lottings Way PE19 ...74 C6
Loughrigg Cl 4 PE29 ...141 B7
Louthe Way PE28 ...168 C3
Love La Ashwell SG7 ...2 A5
 Houghton & Wyton PE28 ..143 A5
 Wisbech PE13 ...245 C4
Lovell Rd CB4 ...84 A7
Lovers La PE5 ...194 F2
Love's Cl CB4 ...104 C2
Love's Hill PE5 ...195 F1
Low Cl PE7 ...189 E8
Low Cross PE7 ...189 D8
Low Fen Drove Way CB5 .85 B4
Low Gate PE13 ...237 F8
Low Rd Burwell CB5 ...130 B2
 Crowland PE6 ...207 F7
 Fenstanton PE28 ...121 A4
 Hemingford Grey PE27 ...144 A1
 Little Stukeley PE28 ...151 D3
 The Stukeleys PE28 ...140 C7
 Wisbech PE14 ...245 E1
Low Side PE14 ...236 E2
Lowbury Cres CB4 ...103 B6
Lowburyholme Rd CB4 ..208 C1
Lower Downs Slade CB9 .24 A8
Lower Dro CB7 ...211 D3
Lower End CB5 ...108 E5
Lower Gower Rd SG8 ...5 D8
Lower King St SG8 ...5 D6
Lower Park St CB5 ...246 A3
Lower Rd Croydon SG8 ...26 D5
 Ely CB7 ...218 D1
 Wicken CB7 ...211 E2
Lower St SG8 ...31 B1
Loweswater PE29 ...141 C5
Lowfields CB3 ...46 B8
Lowick Gdns PE3 ...197 C5
Lowndes Dro PE27 ...144 F7
 St Ives PE27 ...144 A7
Lowry Cl Haverhill CB9 ...38 D1
 St Ives PE27 ...144 A7
Lowry Rd PE19 ...74 C6
Lowther Gdns PE4 ...204 D2
Lowther St CB8 ...110 F3
Loxley PE4 ...204 A4
Loxley Gn PE28 ...142 F5
Luard Cl CB2 ...65 A4
Luard Rd CB2 ...65 A5
Lucas Ct PE29 ...141 F7
Lucas La SG7 ...2 E4
Lucerne Cl Cambridge CB1 66 A6
 Red Lodge IP28 ...213 F1
Lucketts Cl CB4 ...104 B5
Luck's La PE19 ...117 A4
Lucombe Dr PE13 ...245 C6
Lucy Cavendish Coll CB3 83 C3
Luddington Cl PE19 ...96 E4
Luddington Rd Great Gidding PE28 ...166 C3
 Peterborough PE4 ...204 D1
Ludlow La CB1 ...67 A5
Lug Fen Droveway PE15 .223 B7
Luke St PE14 ...74 E4
Lulworth Dr CB9 ...23 E8
Lumen Rd SG8 ...5 D7

Lumley Cl CB6 ...240 E8
Lundy Cl CB9 ...24 D7
Lutton Gate Rd PE12 ..234 A8
Lutton Gr PE12 ...197 C6
Lye Cl PE19 ...94 A6
Lyles Rd CB4 ...125 D4
Lymage Rd PE28 ...115 D3
Lyme Wlk 3 PE3 ...197 C6
Lynch La SG8 ...15 E8
Lynchwood PE2 ...185 C5
Lyndale Pk PE2 ...185 C6
Lyndewode Rd CB1 ...246 C1
Lyndhurst Cl CB4 ...105 C2
Lynfield La CB4 ...84 A4
Lynn Rd Ely CB6 ...240 D6
 Littleport CB6 ...242 F6
 Wisbech PE13 ...245 C6
Lynton Cl CB6 ...240 D6
Lynton Dr CB6 ...240 D6
Lynton Rd PE1 ...197 F6
Lynton Way PE1 ...33 A8
Lynx The CB1 ...66 A7
Lyon's Dro PE15 ...223 F4
Lysander Cl 5 PE27 ...143 F7
Lythemere PE2 ...186 C4

M

Macaulay Ave CB2 ...49 B6
Macbeth CB1 ...141 F6
McCalmont Way CB8 ...111 E2
Mace Rd PE2 ...187 D5
Macfarlane Cl CB4 ...104 C2
Mackenzie Rd 5 CB1 ...84 A1
Mackerel H SG8 ...5 B6
Macpherson Robertson Way IP28 ...239 A5
Maddingley Way CB6 ...210 A7
Madecroft PE28 ...165 A5
Madeley Ct PE28 ...143 C2
Madingley H* CB3 ...81 E5
Madingley Rd Cambridge CB3 ...83 B3
 Dry Drayton CB3 ...102 B1
Madingley Sch CB3 ...81 F5
Madras Rd CB1 ...65 C7
Maffit Rd PE5 ...195 D3
Magazine Cl PE13 ...245 A4
Magazine La PE13 ...245 A4
Magdalene Cl CB4 ...123 F2
Magdalene Coll CB4 ...246 A4
Magdalene St CB2 ...246 A3
Magee Rd PE4 ...204 D1
Magna Cl CB1 ...34 C6
Magnolia Ave PE3 ...197 A2
Magnolia Cl Cambridge CB1 ...65 B5
 2 Red Lodge IP28 ...213 F1
Magrath Ave CB4 ...246 A4
Maiden La PE9 ...244 C5
Maid's Cswy CB5 ...246 C3
Mailes Cl CB3 ...63 B4
Main Dro PE6 ...225 A2
Main Rd Etton PE6 ...203 B8
 Little Gransden SG8 ...58 D3
 Parson Drove PE13 ...234 C4
 Uffington PE9 ...230 D6
 Upwell PE14 ...229 E7
 Wisbech PE14 ...236 A3
Main St Ailsworth PE5 ...195 D2
 Barnack PE9 ...230 D3
 Bythorn & Keyston PE28 ...146 D4
 Caldecote CB3 ...61 B6
 Castor PE5 ...195 D3
 Coveney CB6 ...217 B5
 Downham CB6 ...217 D8
 Ely CB7 ...219 B5
 Farcet PE7 ...187 C2
 Great Gidding PE28 ...166 D3
 Hardwick CB3 ...81 A1
 Hatley SG19 ...43 A3
 Huntingdon PE29 ...142 A6
 Little Downham CB6 ...218 A6
 Littleport CB6 ...242 D4
 Old Weston PE28 ...147 F7
 Shudy Camps CB1 ...21 F6
 Southorpe PE9 ...230 E1
 Stow cum Quy CB5 ...85 F5
 Thetford PE28 ...211 B7
 Ufford PE9 ...230 F3
 Welney PE14 ...225 A8
 Wentworth CB6 ...217 B1
 Witchford CB6 ...217 E1
 Yarwell PE8 ...183 A4
 Yaxley PE7 ...181 E5
Maio Rd CB4 ...83 F5
Maitland Ave CB4 ...84 B6
Malborne Way PE2 ...186 B4
Malcolm St CB1 ...246 B3
Malcolm Way CB8 ...111 B5
Malden Cl CB5 ...84 D3
Maldon Rd PE13 ...245 E5
Malecoff PE29 ...118 F7
Males Cl CB4 ...125 E5
Malin Cl CB9 ...24 D7
Mallard Cl Chatteris PE16 ...241 C5
 Whittlesey PE7 ...189 F8
Mallard Ct PE9 ...244 B4
Mallard La PE19 ...75 A4
Mallard Rd Peterborough PE3 ...204 A1
 Royston SG8 ...5 C6
Mallard Rise 2 CB6 ...210 A6
Mallard Way PE15 ...243 F5
Mallards The Peakirk PE6 ...206 B1

Mallards The continued
 St Ives PE27 ...143 F7
Mallett Cl PE15 ...243 F4
Malletts Rd CB1 ...66 A5
Mallory Rd PE1 ...198 C2
Mallow La PE7 ...175 D8
Mallow Wlk 1 SG8 ...5 E5
Mallows Cl 2 CB3 ...62 D6
Malory Pl CB3 ...99 A3
Malt Dr PE13 ...245 B2
Malta Rd CB1 ...65 B7
Maltby Cl 17 PE8 ...230 B1
Malthouse Cl PE28 ...141 D4
Malthouse La PE26 ...171 C5
Malthouse Way CB2 ...29 F8
Malting End CB8 ...72 D4
Malting La Cambridge CB3 64 C8
 Ellington PE28 ...139 A4
 Foxton CB2 ...30 C5
 Isleham CB7 ...213 A5
 Litlington SG8 ...12 A2
Malting The PE26 ...171 F5
Maltings Cl Moulton CB8 .112 E5
 Royston SG8 ...5 C7
Maltings La SG8 ...7 E2
Maltings The Alconbury PE28 ...150 E5
 Eaton Socon PE19 ...74 C5
 St Martin's Without PE9 ..244 C2
 Sawtry PE28 ...168 B4
 3 Thorney PE6 ...233 A3
Maltmas Dro PE14 ...235 F2
Malton La SG8 ...29 B4
Malton Rd SG8 ...45 F1
Maltsters Way CB4 ...84 A4
Malvern Cl CB8 ...111 B2
Malvern Rd Cambridge CB1 ...65 E6
 Peterborough PE4 ...204 E2
Manasty Rd PE2 ...185 D2
Manchester PE28 ...117 D8
Manchester Way 10 PE27 ...144 A8
Mandene Gdns SG19 ...58 B4
Mander Way CB1 ...65 C5
Manderston Rd CB1 ...110 E4
Mandeville Burwell CB5 ..109 B8
Mandeville Rd PE28 ...140 C1
Mandrill Cl CB1 ...66 A7
Manea Prim Sch PE15 ..224 C4
Manea Rd PE15 ...223 D6
Manea Sta PE15 ...224 B6
Maners Way CB1 ...65 C4
Mangers La CB2 ...32 D1
Manhattan Dr CB4 ...246 C4
Manners Ct 4 PE9 ...230 C6
Manor Ave CB2 ...187 B4
Manor Cl Brampton PE28 140 E2
 Buckden PE19 ...117 A3
 Graveley PE19 ...98 A5
 Little Paxton PE19 ...95 F2
 Harston CB2 ...47 F3
 Little Wilbraham CB1 ...86 D1
 2 Somersham PE28 ...215 C1
 Witchford CB6 ...217 E1
 11 Wittering PE8 ...230 B1
 Yaxley PE7 ...181 D5
Manor Com Coll CB4 ...83 F6
Manor Court Rd CB6 ...217 E1
Manor Cres CB3 ...81 A1
Manor Dr Fenstanton PE28 ...121 B6
 Peterborough PE6 ...205 A3
 Sawtry PE28 ...168 C4
Manor Farm Ct 18 PE8 ...223 A5
Manor Farm Cl CB4 ...103 C6
Manor Farm Ct PE28 ...115 D2
Manor Farm La PE5 ...195 E2
Manor Farm Rd Beck Row, Holywell Row & Kenny Hill IP28 ...213 D7
 Girton CB3 ...103 E2
 St Neots PE19 ...75 A5
 Waresley SG19 ...57 E2
Manor Gdns Buckden PE19 ...117 A4
 Peterborough PE2 ...187 C7
 Wisbech PE13 ...245 A4
Manor Gr PE19 ...75 A5
Manor House Cl 1 PE19 .74 C2
Manor House St PE1 ...198 A3
Manor La Alconbury PE28 150 F5
 Boxworth CB3 ...101 C6
 Great Chesterford CB10 ..18 D2
 Great Gransden SG19 ...58 D4
Manor Pk CB4 ...104 A4
Manor Rd Folksworth PE7 ...180 D1
 Gamlingay SG19 ...41 D6
 Haverhill CB9 ...24 B7
 Hemingford Grey PE28 ...143 B1
 Little Shelford CB2 ...48 E4
 Meldreth SG8 ...29 A1
 Mildenhall IP28 ...239 B4
 Sutton PE5 ...194 F2
 Witchford CB6 ...217 E2
Manor Sch CB6 ...210 C6
Manor St Cambridge CB1 .246 B3
 Wistow CB6 ...164 A7
Manor View Barton Mills IP28 ...239 D2
 Whittlesey PE7 ...189 D6
Manor Way Hail Weston PE19 ...95 A1
 Market Deeping PE6 ...231 F8

Manor Wlk CB1 ...67 A5
Manse Dr CB4 ...125 C3
Mansel Way CB4 ...83 E6
Mansell Rd PE13 ...245 D3
Mansfield Cl CB4 ...105 C2
Mansfield Ct PE1 ...198 C5
Manton PE3 ...197 A3
Maple Ave Sawston CB2 ...32 F5
Maple Cl 5 Bluntisham/Colne PE28 ...208 C6
 Bottisham CB5 ...86 F5
 4 Bourn CB3 ...79 C3
 Cambridge CB4 ...83 F5
 Linton CB1 ...35 B3
 Sawtry PE28 ...168 A3
Maple Cl 3 Gamlingay SG19 .41 C5
 Yaxley PE7 ...181 F6
Maple Dr Huntingdon PE29 ...141 E8
 Little Stukeley PE28 ...151 E3
Maple End PE28 ...150 F4
Maple Gr March PE15 ...243 C5
 Peterborough PE1 ...198 F5
Maple Way Melbourn SG8 .14 C5
 Royston SG8 ...5 E8
Maple Wlk PE7 ...186 C2
Maples The Fulbourn CB1 .66 E5
 Peterborough PE1 ...198 F5
March La CB1 ...65 F8
March Rd Coates/Eastrea PE7 ...191 A8
 Elm PE13 ...227 F8
 Elm PE13 ...235 A2
 Elm PE14 ...235 F2
 Welney PE14 ...229 F1
 Whittlesey PE7 ...191 D7
 Wimblington PE15 ...223 B7
March Riverside PE14 ..229 C8
March Sta PE15 ...243 B7
March Trading Est PE15 243 B7
Marchioness Way 3 PE19 ...74 B4
March's Cl CB1 ...66 E5
Marcus Ct CB7 ...24 D7
Mardale Gdns PE4 ...204 F2
Marefen Dro CB6 ...225 C3
Marfleet Cl CB2 ...48 F7
Margett St CB5 ...125 E4
Margetts PE28 ...143 D1
Marholm Rd Castor PE6 ..196 B3
 Peterborough PE3 ...204 B1
Marian Way PE16 ...241 C2
Marigold Dr IP28 ...133 F8
Marina Dr PE15 ...243 A5
Mariner's Way CB4 ...84 A3
Marion Cl CB3 ...83 B4
Maris Gn CB2 ...49 A6
Maris La CB2 ...64 C2
Markby Cl PE2 ...17 D8
Market Hill Cambridge CB2 ...246 A2
 Chatteris PE16 ...241 C5
 Haverhill CB9 ...24 A8
 Royston SG8 ...5 D6
 St Ives PE27 ...144 A3
Market La Linton CB1 ...35 B2
Market Mews PE13 ...245 C5
Market Pas CB1 ...246 A3
Market Pl 5 Ely CB7 ...240 D4
 Mildenhall IP28 ...239 C4
 St Neots PE19 ...74 E5
 Wisbech PE13 ...245 C5
Market Rd PE27 ...144 B3
Market Sq Cambridge CB2 ...246 A2
 8 Ely CB7 ...240 D4
Market St Cambridge CB2 246 A2
 Fordham CB7 ...212 E1
 3 Newmarket CB8 ...111 A3
 12 Soham CB7 ...212 B4
 Swavesey CB4 ...122 E6
 Whittlesey PE7 ...189 D7
 14 Wisbech PE13 ...245 C5
Market Way CB6 ...217 A2
Markfield Rise CB6 ...216 D1
Markham Cl CB4 ...84 D1
Markham Ret Pk PE7 ...244 D7
Markhams Cl 3 CB9 ...38 F1
Mark's Way CB3 ...103 A3
Marlborough Cl 2 St Ives PE27 ...143 F7
 Yaxley PE7 ...181 E5
Marlborough Coll The CB2 ...64 E7
Marley Rd PE27 ...143 F8
Marlowe Ct 2 PE19 ...74 D6
Marlowe Gr PE7 ...197 E5
Marlowe Rd CB3 ...64 C7
Marmora Rd CB1 ...65 B7
Marne Ave PE4 ...204 C1
Marne Rd PE7 ...189 F5
Marquis Cl 4 PE19 ...74 B4
Marriott Ct PE1 ...198 E5
Marriott's Dro PE26 ...221 A4
Marriotts Cl PE26 ...221 A4
Marritt Cl PE16 ...241 B6
Marroway La 4 CB6 ...217 D1
Marsh La PE28 ...143 D1
Marsh Rd Outwell PE14 ...236 F4
 Walpole PE14 ...238 F8
Marsh The PE14 ...238 F8
Marshall Rd CB1 ...65 A5
Marshall's Bank PE13 ..234 D8

Marshall's Cl CB1 ...85 A1
Marshall's Way PE7 ...187 C2
Marsham PE2 ...185 F3
Marshfields Sch PE1 ...198 D7
Marshland High Sch PE14 ...238 E4
Marshland Prim Sch PE14 ...238 F4
Marston Rd PE19 ...75 A3
Martin Ave PE15 ...243 A7
Martin Ct Godmanchester PE29 ...119 A8
 Mildenhall IP28 ...239 D3
 Soham CB7 ...212 A5
Martin Rd CB5 ...130 B3
Martindale Way CB2 ...32 E8
Martingale Cl 3 CB4 ...83 C6
Martingale Rd 4 SG8 ...5 E6
Martin's La 2 CB1 ...218 A6
Martins La Linton CB1 ...35 E2
 Witcham CB6 ...217 A3
Martins Way PE1 ...185 F5
Martinsbridge PE1 ...198 F7
Marwick Rd PE15 ...243 D7
Mary Armyne Rd PE2 ...186 B5
Mary Walsham Cl PE2 ..187 B5
Maryland Ave Huntingdon PE29 ...141 F8
 Swaffham Bulbeck CB5 ...108 B2
Marylebone Rd 3 PE15 243 C4
Masefield Rd PE19 ...74 C6
Masefield Way 3 SG8 ...13 D1
Maskew Ave PE1 ...197 E6
Mason Gdns IP28 ...213 D6
Mason Rd CB5 ...130 B5
Master Dike PE12 ...237 D8
Masterton Cl PE9 ...244 D7
Masterton Rd PE29 ...244 C7
Matley PE2 ...185 E5
Matt Dawson Cl 4 CB8 ..110 F6
Matthew Parker Cl PE1 105 D7
Matthew Wren Cl 3 CB6 ...218 A6
Matthews La CB8 ...55 F6
Maule Ct PE29 ...141 F6
Maurice Cl PE28 ...113 F5
Mawson Cl CB6 ...240 B3
Mawson Rd CB1 ...246 C1
Maxey Rd Helpston PE6 ...231 C5
 Northborough PE6 ...231 D7
Maxey View 10 PE6 ...231 C5
Maxham's Green Rd PE6 ...203 B6
Maxwell Rd PE2 ...186 D6
May St SG8 ...7 E2
Mayfair Gdns 1 PE13 ...235 C7
Mayfield PE19 ...117 A3
Mayfield Cl 2 CB6 ...240 B5
Mayfield Cres PE29 ...141 F6
Mayfield Prim Sch CB4 .83 C5
Mayfield Rd Coates/Eastrea PE7 ...190 D7
 Girton CB3 ...82 F8
 Huntingdon PE29 ...141 F6
 Peterborough PE1 ...198 A6
Mayflower Rd 1 PE13 ...245 E3
Mayfly PE16 ...241 B3
Maynards CB2 ...32 C5
Mayner's Dike PE12 ...237 E8
Mayor's Wlk PE3 ...197 E3
Mayors Cl PE15 ...243 D7
Maypole Croft CB1 ...37 C8
Maypole La CB6 ...90 E3
May's Ave CB1 ...53 A2
May's La PE13 ...238 A2
Mays Way CB4 ...84 C5
Maysfield Dr 8 PE13 ...238 B2
Maytrees PE29 ...143 F1
Maze Rd PE28 ...120 C1
Mead Cl PE3 ...204 B1
Mead The PE4 ...204 B1
Mead View CB4 ...103 B5
Meadenvale PE1 ...198 F5
Meadlands Main Dro CB6 ...215 F1
Meadow Bsns Ctr The PE27 ...144 B2
Meadow Cl Chatteris PE16 ...241 C3
 Little Paxton PE19 ...95 F2
 1 St Ives PE27 ...144 B3
 7 Soham CB7 ...212 B3
 Stilton PE7 ...175 B6
 Witchford CB6 ...217 E2
Meadow Ct CB6 ...242 B5
Meadow Dr PE15 ...243 F3
Meadow Drift CB3 ...100 B5
Meadow Dro PE28 ...208 E6
Meadow Farm Cl CB4 ...103 D6
Meadow Gr PE1 ...205 B3
Meadow How PE27 ...143 F6
Meadow La Earith PE28 ...208 E6
 Hemingford Abbots PE28 .142 F3
 Hemingford Grey PE28 ...143 D3
 Houghton & Wyton PE28 ..143 B4
 Linton CB1 ...35 B2
 Newmarket CB8 ...111 D1
 Offord Darcy PE19 ...208 E1
 Over CB4 ...208 D1
 Ramsey PE26 ...172 B4
 St Ives PE27 ...144 C3
 Thornhaugh PE8 ...193 F5
Meadow Prim Sch CB1 ..53 B2
Meadow Rd Great Chesterford CB10 ..18 D3
 Great Gransden SG19 ...58 B5
 Newborough PE6 ...204 D8

Meadow Rd continued
Peakirk PE6 . . . . .206 C1
Ramsey PE26 . . . . .171 B1
Upwood & The Raveleys
PE26 . . . . .171 A1
Willingham CB4 . . . . . . .209 B1
Meadow Rise CB3 . . . . . .60 C6
Meadow View PE19 . . . . . .77 E4
Meadow Way
Doddington/Wimblington
PE15 . . . . .223 B7
Earith PE28 . . . . .208 E6
Great Paxton PE19 . . . . .96 E4
Harston CB2 . . . . .48 A3
Warboys PE28 . . . . . . .164 F5
Meadow Way S 7 PE15 223 B7
Meadow Wlk CB1 . . . . . . .34 C6
Meadowbrook CB6 . . . . .209 E4
Meadowcroft CB6 . . . . . .210 F5
Meadowcroft Way 28 E8
Meadowfield Rd CB2 . . . .32 E4
Meadowgate PE9 . . . . . .230 F5
Meadowgate La PE14 . . .245 E2
Meadowgate Sch PE13 . .245 E3
Meadowground PE28 . . .116 A4
Meadowlands
Burwell CB5 . . . . .130 B1
March PE15 . . . . .243 A6
Meadowlands Rd CB5 . . .84 E3
Meadows Cl 5 PE19 . . .74 F5
Meadows The
Haslingfield CB3 . . . . . . .47 B5
Worlington PE28 . . . . . .213 F4
Meadowsweet PE19 . . . . .74 B6
Meadowsweet Cl CB9 . . .38 E1
Meals Gate PE4 . . . . . . .204 F2
Medallion Ct 1 PE19 . . .74 F5
Medcalfe Way SG8 . . . . .14 D6
Medeswell PE2 . . . . . . .186 C4
Medland Gr 6 PE19 . . . .75 A5
Medway Cl PE13 . . . . . .245 E4
Medway Rd PE29 . . . . . .141 E7
Medworth PE2 . . . . .185 F3
Meeting La Litlington SG8 .12 A2
Melbourn SG8 . . . . .14 C6
Meggan Gate PE3 . . . . .197 A1
Megg's Dro PE26 . . . . . .221 B2
Megs Cl PE28 . . . . .208 D5
Melbourn Cty Prim Sch
SG8 . . . . .14 C6
Melbourn Rd SG8 . . . . . . .5 D7
Melbourn St SG8 . . . . . . .5 D6
Melbourn Village Coll
SG8 . . . . .14 C7
Melbourne Ave PE15 . . .243 B7
Melbourne Dr IP28 . . . . .239 B5
Melbourne Pl CB1 . . . . .246 C2
Melbourne Rd PE9 . . . . .244 D6
Meldon Pl 2 CB6 . . . . .240 D5
**Meldreth Manor Sch &
Orchard Ho** CB1 . . . . . . .29 A1
Meldreth Rd
Shepreth SG8 . . . . .29 D4
Whaddon SG8 . . . . .28 C1
Meldreth Sta SG8 . . . . . .14 B7
Meldrith Prim Sch SG8 . . .14 B8
Melford Rd Burwell CB5 .130 C2
Peterborough PE3 . . . . .197 A2
Mellis Cl CB9 . . . . .38 B1
Mellows Cl PE1 . . . . . . .198 C3
Melrose Dr PE2 . . . . . . .187 A4
Melrose Gdns CB8 . . . . .110 E4
Melton Cl 1 CB8 . . . . . .111 B2
Melvin Way CB4 . . . . . .104 A4
Mendip Gr PE4 . . . . . . .204 E2
Mepal Long Highway
CB6 . . . . .216 C4
Mepal Prim Sch CB6 . . .216 D3
Mepal Rd CB6 . . . . .216 E2
Mepal Short Highway
CB6 . . . . .216 C5
Mercers Row CB5 . . . . . .84 B4
Mercian Ct PE2 . . . . . . .187 D7
Mere Cl PE26 . . . . .221 A4
Mere Dro Ramsey PE26 .221 D4
Yaxley PE7 . . . . .181 F4
Mere Mill Dro CB6 . . . . .210 F4
Mere Side CB7 . . . . . . .212 A4
Mere Side Dro PE26 . . .221 B4
Mere View PE7 . . . . . . .182 A5
Mere Way Cambridge CB4 .83 E6
Hemingford Grey PE28 . .120 B3
Houghton & Wyton PE28 .143 A6
Merelade Gr PE4 . . . . . .204 B5
Meridian CP Sch CB2 . . .62 C5
Meridian Sch SG8 . . . . . .5 E7
Merlin Cl
Huntingdon PE29 . . . . . .142 B7
St Neots PE19 . . . . .75 B7
Merlin Dr 4 CB6 . . . . . .240 B5
Merritt St PE29 . . . . . . .141 C5
Merton Rd CB4 . . . . . . .104 B3
Merton St CB3 . . . . .64 C7
Metcalfe Rd CB4 . . . . . . .83 D5
Metcalfe Way 5 CB6 . . .210 A5
Mewburn PE3 . . . . .204 A1
Mews Cl PE26 . . . . .172 B7
Meynell Gdns CB8 . . . . .111 A5
Meynell Wlk PE3 . . . . . .197 B3
Michael's Cl CB3 . . . . . .103 E1
Mickle Gate PE2 . . . . . .197 A1
Mickle Hill PE28 . . . . . .135 D7
Mid Fetter PE4 . . . . . . .204 E3
Middle Broad Dro PE13 237 D5
Middle Cl 5 CB6 . . . . . .210 F5
Middle Drift SG8 . . . . . . .5 C6
Middle Dro Newton PE13 237 E3
Ramsey PE26 . . . . .171 A7

Middle Dro continued
Soham CB7 . . . . .211 F3
Wimblington PE15 . . . . .223 C5
Middle Pasture PE4 . . . .204 B5
Middle Rd Crowland PE6 .207 F7
March PE15 . . . . .227 E4
Newborough PE6 . . . . . .205 C7
Middle St Elton PE8 . . . .178 D8
Farcet PE7 . . . . .187 C2
Great Gransden SG19 . . .58 E4
Litlington SG8 . . . . .12 A2
Thriplow SG8 . . . . .31 B1
Middle Watch CB4 . . . . .122 E5
Middle Way CB2 . . . . . . .50 A1
Middlefield PE7 . . . . . . .186 D3
Middlefield Cty Prim Sch
PE19 . . . . .74 F2
Middlefield Rd PE28 . . . .168 B3
Middleham Cl 2 PE7 . . .187 F6
Middlemiss View PE29 . .118 F8
Middlemoor Rd
Ramsey PE26 . . . . .220 D3
Whittlesford CB2 . . . . . . .32 A5
Middleton PE3 . . . . .197 A4
Middleton Jun Sch PE3 .197 A4
Middletons Rd PE7 . . . . .181 E5
Midgate PE1 . . . . .198 A2
Midhurst Cl PE4 . . . . . . .84 A5
Midland Rd PE3 . . . . . . .197 E3
Mikanda Cl PE14 . . . . . .245 C2
Milburn Dro CB8 . . . . . .112 E5
Mildenhall Airfield IP28 239 B8
Mildenhall Rd
Barton Mills IP28 . . . . . .239 C2
Beck Row, Holywell Row
& Kenny Hill IP28 . . . . .239 C8
Ely CB7 . . . . .219 E8
Fordham IP28 . . . . .213 A2
Freckenham IP28 . . . . . .213 D3
Icklingham IP28 . . . . . . .214 E4
Littleport CB7 . . . . .242 F6
Mildenhall Swimming Pool
IP28 . . . . .239 C4
Mildenhall Upper Sch
IP28 . . . . .239 E4
Mildmay Rd PE4 . . . . . .197 D8
Mile Dro Glinton PE6 . . .231 F5
Yaxley PE7 . . . . .182 B5
Mile End Rd CB7 . . . . . .219 C6
Mile Rd CB2 . . . . .50 C4
Mile Tree La PE13 . . . . .235 E7
Miles Hawk Way IP28 . . .239 A5
Milford St CB1 . . . . .84 A1
Military Rd CB7 . . . . . . .212 C2
Militia Way CB7 . . . . . . .240 C4
Milk & Water Dro PE7 . . .188 A4
Milk & Water Dro Ramsey Rd
PE7 . . . . .188 A2
Milking Hills Dro CB4 . . .209 B4
Milking Nook Rd PE6 . . .206 E1
Milking Slade Rd PE28 . .167 A4
Mill Cl Burwell CB5 . . . . .130 B1
Exning CB8 . . . . .110 B8
Hemingford Grey PE28 . .143 D2
Huntingdon PE29 . . . . . .142 A6
1 Murrow PE13 . . . . . .234 D5
The Stukeleys PE28 . . . .151 D3
Wisbech PE13 . . . . .245 C6
Mill Cnr CB7 . . . . .212 A4
Mill Comm PE2 . . . . . . .141 C3
Mill Cres PE2 . . . . .185 E4
Mill Croft CB7 . . . . .212 B3
Mill Cswy SG8 . . . . .8 C5
Mill Ct CB2 . . . . .49 A5
Mill Dro Crowland PE6 . .207 F7
Lode CB5 . . . . .128 A1
Ramsey PE26 . . . . .221 A2
Soham CB7 . . . . .212 A4
Southery PE38 . . . . . . .226 E8
Mill End Cl CB1 . . . . .65 F5
Mill End Rd CB1 . . . . . . .65 E6
Mill Field 3 CB6 . . . . . .216 E2
Mill Field Cl PE6 . . . . . .231 C4
Mill Gn PE3 . . . . .165 A5
Mill Hill Downham CB6 . .217 F7
Glatton PE28 . . . . .175 E1
Haverhill CB9 . . . . .23 F7
Newmarket CB8 . . . . . . .111 A4
Royston SG8 . . . . .5 E4
Swaffham Prior CB5 . . . .108 E5
Weston Colville CB1 . . . . .54 C6
Mill Hill End 3 PE28 . . .120 B1
Mill Hill Rd 7 PE19 . . . .74 D5
Mill La Arrington SG8 . . . .44 C3
Barrington CB2 . . . . .29 E8
Bassingbourn SG8 . . . . . .12 C5
Bluntisham/Colne PE28 . .208 D5
Burwell CB5 . . . . .130 B1
Cambridge CB2 . . . . . . .246 A2
Castor PE5 . . . . .184 F7
Duxford CB2 . . . . .32 E1
Exning CB8 . . . . .110 B8
Fordham CB7 . . . . .212 F1
Gorefield PE13 . . . . . . .235 B8
Hauxton CB2 . . . . .48 A6
Hemingford Grey PE28 . .143 D3
Hinxton CB10 . . . . .18 A7
Histon CB4 . . . . .104 D6
Ickleton CB10 . . . . .18 B4
Impington CB4 . . . . . . .104 D5
Linton CB1 . . . . .35 C2
Little Paxton PE19 . . . . . .95 E1
Newton PE13 . . . . .237 F5
Peterborough PE7 . . . . .185 A5
Potton SG19 . . . . .40 D1
Ramsey PE26 . . . . .172 B8
St Neots PE19 . . . . .74 F1

Mill La continued
Sawston CB2 . . . . .32 E7
Shingay cum Wendy SG8 . .23 C3
Stetchworth CB8 . . . . . . .89 F1
Swaffham Bulbeck CB5 . .108 B3
Tallington PE9 . . . . .230 F7
Toft CB3 . . . . .61 D5
Water Newton PE8 . . . . .184 C7
West Walton PE14 . . . . .238 F4
Whittlesford CB2 . . . . . . .32 D5
Mill Pit Furlong CB6 . . . .242 D3
Ashley CB8 . . . . .91 F8
Buckden PE19 . . . . .117 C3
Cambridge CB1 . . . . . . .246 C2
Emneth PE14 . . . . .236 D6
Fen Drayton CB4 . . . . . .121 D5
Glatton PE28 . . . . .175 E1
Great Gidding PE28 . . . .166 E3
Great Wilbraham CB1 . . . .67 F7
Haverhill CB9 . . . . .24 A7
Histon CB4 . . . . .104 B1
Huntingdon PE29 . . . . . .142 A6
Kirtling CB8 . . . . .72 E5
Little Gransden SG19 . . . .58 E4
Little Stukeley PE28 . . . .151 D4
Little Wilbraham CB1 . . . .86 D1
Lode CB5 . . . . .107 C2
Maxey PE6 . . . . .231 C7
Nassington PE8 . . . . . . .183 A7
Oakington/Longstanton
CB4 . . . . .103 D6
Royston SG8 . . . . .5 D7
Stilton PE7 . . . . .175 F8
Walpole PE14 . . . . .238 F6
Waterbeach CB5 . . . . . .106 A7
West Walton PE14 . . . . .238 D4
West Wickham CB1 . . . . .36 E8
West Wratting CB1 . . . . . .53 F7
Whittlesey PE7 . . . . . . .189 E6
Wisbech St Mary PE13 . .234 C5
Wistow PE28 . . . . .163 F6
Mill Reef Cl CB8 . . . . . .110 D7
Mill St Ashwell SG7 . . . . .2 D4
Cambridge CB1 . . . . . . .246 C1
Gamlingay SG19 . . . . . . .41 D5
Isleham CB7 . . . . .213 A5
Mildenhall IP28 . . . . . . .239 B3
St Ives PE28 . . . . .143 A5
Mill View March PE15 . . .243 D4
Peterborough PE7 . . . . .185 A5
Sawtry PE28 . . . . .152 B6
Mill Way Grantchester CB3 64 A3
Holywell-cum-Needingworth
PE27 . . . . .144 F3
Stretham CB6 . . . . .210 E6
Swavesey CB4 . . . . .122 C6
Wisbech PE14 . . . . .236 A4
Mill Yd PE7 . . . . .141 E2
Millards La CB5 . . . . . . .107 D2
Millbank CB8 . . . . .110 F4
Miller Cl
2 Doddington/Wimblington
PE15 . . . . .222 F5
Godmanchester PE29 . . .118 F8
Offord Cluny PE19 . . . . .118 A2
Miller Way PE28 . . . . . . .140 C3
Miller's Rd CB3 . . . . .61 D5
Millers Cl 4 CB1 . . . . . . .35 D3
Millfield Littleport CB6 . . .242 C3
Upwell PE14 . . . . .236 E2
Willingham CB4 . . . . . . .124 A8
Millfield Cl PE16 . . . . . .241 B2
Millfield CP Sch CB6 . . .242 C3
Millfield Pl CB6 . . . . . . .210 C5
Millfield Rd
Market Deeping PE6 . . . .231 F8
Maxey PE6 . . . . .231 D8
Millfields Way PE7 . . . . .189 F6
Millfields PE26 . . . . .172 B8
Millfields Way CB9 . . . . . .24 B8
Millington Rd CB3 . . . . . .64 C7
Mills La Longstanton CB4 .124 A1
Witchford CB6 . . . . .217 D1
Millstone La PE9 . . . . . .230 D3
Millyard CB6 . . . . .210 A6
Milner Cl March PE15 . . .243 D5
Sawston CB2 . . . . .32 E7
Milner Rd Comberton CB3 .62 D6
Wisbech PE13 . . . . .245 C4
Milnyard Sq PE2 . . . . . .185 C2
Milton Ave PE19 . . . . . . .74 C6
Milton Cl
Huntingdon PE29 . . . . . .141 E6
Ramsey PE26 . . . . .171 C5
Royston SG8 . . . . .13 C1
St Ives PE27 . . . . .143 F6
Milton Ctry Pk CB4 . . . .105 D1
Milton Dr PE13 . . . . . . .238 B1
Milton H PE6 . . . . .196 D4
Milton Rd Cambridge CB4 246 B4
Impington CB4 . . . . .104 F4
Peterborough PE2 . . . . .187 A7
Milton Road CP Sch CB4 .83 E4
Milton Sch CB4 . . . . . . .105 C2
Milton Way PE3 . . . . . . .196 E3
Mina Cl PE2 . . . . .187 D4
Minden Ct 8 PE19 . . . . .74 C5
Minerva Cl CB9 . . . . .24 C6
Minerva Way CB4 . . . . . .83 C8
Mingle La CB2 . . . . .49 B5
Minster Pl 4 CB7 . . . . .240 D4
Minster Rd Haverhill CB9 .39 A1
Royston SG8 . . . . .5 C5
Mint La PE19 . . . . .96 E4
Minter Cl CB5 . . . . .86 A5

Missleton Ct CB1 . . . . . . .65 C5
Misty Mdws CB5 . . . . . . .84 D4
Mitchells Cotts CB10 . . . .20 A5
Moat La
Abbots Ripton PE28 . . . .152 C8
Melbourn SG8 . . . . .14 C7
Perry PE28 . . . . .115 D1
Moat Way CB4 . . . . .122 E6
Moats' Way PE28 . . . . . .119 E7
Moggswell La PE28 . . . . .186 B4
Mole Dro PE12 . . . . .233 F8
Molewood Cl CB4 . . . . . . .83 C6
Molls Dro PE13 . . . . . . .236 C3
Moltens Inst CB2 . . . . . .246 B2
Monarch Ave PE2 . . . . . .187 A6
Monarch Rd PE19 . . . . . .74 B4
Moncrieff Cl 1 CB4 . . . .83 E7
Monet Ct PE27 . . . . .144 A7
Money Bank PE13 . . . . .245 E4
Moneypiece Cl
1 Haverhill CB9 . . . . . . .38 F1
3 Haverhill CB9 . . . . . . .38 F2
Monkfield La CB3 . . . . . . .79 C3
Monkfield Park Prim Sch
CB3 . . . . .79 B4
Monks Cl PE7 . . . . .189 D8
Monks Dr 17 PE6 . . . . .232 A1
Monks Gr PE4 . . . . .204 A5
Monks Mdw PE6 . . . . . .232 B8
Monks Way PE28 . . . . . .168 B2
**Monks Wood Nature
Reserve** PE28 . . . . . . .161 B4
Monkswell CB2 . . . . .64 D3
Monkswood CB6 . . . . . . .242 C5
Montagu Ct 2 PE19 . . . .74 E4
Montagu Gdns PE28 . . . .113 E5
Montagu Rd
Huntingdon PE29 . . . . . .141 E4
Little Stukeley PE28 . . . .151 F2
Peterborough PE4 . . . . .197 D8
Montagu St PE19 . . . . . .74 E4
Montague Rd PE28 . . . . .117 D8
Monte Long Cl PE15 . . . .243 E1
Montgomery Rd CB4 . . . .83 E6
Montreal Rd CB1 . . . . . . .65 C7
Montrose Ct CB4 . . . . . . .83 C7
Monument St PE1 . . . . . .198 A3
Moon Hall La CB9 . . . . . . .24 A6
Moor Pasture Way CB9 . .39 B4
Moor Rd
Great Staughton MK44 . . .93 B1
Newborough PE6 . . . . . .206 E2
Moor The SG8 . . . . .14 C7
Moore Cl CB4 . . . . .84 A6
Moore's La 4 PE6 . . . . .232 A1
Moorfield Rd Duxford CB2 32 E3
2 Peterborough PE3 . . . .197 D3
Moorfield Way PE28 . . . .151 F2
Moorhen Rd PE2 . . . . . .201 A1
Moorhouse Dr PE29 . . . .141 E7
Moory Croft Cl PE19 . . . .94 A6
Moot Way PE28 . . . . . . .155 A5
Morborne Cl PE2 . . . . . .187 D6
Morborne La PE7 . . . . . .180 D4
Morborne Rd PE7 . . . . . .180 C2
Morden Rd CB3 . . . . .99 B3
More's Mdw CB2 . . . . . . .48 F6
Moreton Ct PE7 . . . . . . .189 F8
Morland Way PE27 . . . . .144 A7
Morley Cl 7 IP28 . . . . . .213 F8
Morley Meml Prim Sch
CB1 . . . . .65 B5
Morley Way PE2 . . . . . . .186 D5
Morpeth Cl PE2 . . . . . . .186 C6
Morpeth Rd PE3 . . . . . . .197 C3
Morris Cl PE19 . . . . .117 A3
Morris St PE1 . . . . .198 B3
Mortimer La IP28 . . . . . .213 C3
Mortimer Rd
Cambridge CB1 . . . . . . .246 C2
Royston SG8 . . . . .5 E6
Mortimers La CB2 . . . . . .30 C5
Mortlock Ave CB4 . . . . . .84 B6
Mortlock Cl SG8 . . . . . . .14 C6
Mortlock Gdns CB1 . . . . .34 C5
Mortlock St SG8 . . . . . . .14 C6
Morton Ave PE15 . . . . . .243 E3
Morton Cl CB6 . . . . .240 E8
Morton St SG8 . . . . .5 D7
Morton Way 6 PE15 . . . .223 B7
Mosquito Rd PE26 . . . . .171 C3
Moss Bank CB4 . . . . .84 C5
Moss Cl PE26 . . . . .171 B1
Moss Dr CB5 . . . . .47 C5
Mostyn Cl 2 CB6 . . . . . .216 E1
Moules La CB1 . . . . .20 C6
Moulton Ave CB8 . . . . . .134 A2
Moulton CE VC Fst Sch
CB8 . . . . .112 E6
Moulton Gr PE3 . . . . . . .197 C6
Moulton Rd Ashley CB8 . .112 D2
Cheveley CB8 . . . . .91 D8
Cheveley CB8 . . . . .111 D4
Mount Dr PE13 . . . . . . .245 E4
Mount Pleasant
3 Cambridge CB3 . . . . .83 C3
Great Paxton PE19 . . . . .96 E4
Peterborough PE2 . . . . .187 C7
Spaldwick PE28 . . . . . . .137 E6
Mount Pleasant Rd
PE13 . . . . .245 C7
Mount Pleasant Wlk 2
CB3 . . . . .83 C3
Mount Rd CB9 . . . . .24 A7
Mount The Barley SG8 . . . .8 B1
Toft CB3 . . . . .61 D5
Mountbatten Ave
Stamford PE9 . . . . .244 A6

Mountbatten Ave continued
Yaxley PE7 . . . . .181 D5
Mountbatten Ct 6 PE19 .74 C4
Mountbatten Dr PE13 . . .245 A7
Mountbatten Way
Peterborough PE3 . . . . .197 B6
Whittlesey PE7 . . . . . . .190 A6
Mounteagle 2 SG8 . . . . . .5 D5
Mountford Cl CB2 . . . . . . .48 C4
Mountfort Cl 3 PE19 . . .74 E7
Mounth La PE13 . . . . . . .235 B4
Mountsteven Ave PE4 . . .204 C1
Mowbray Cl 4 PE13 . . . .235 F2
Mowbray Rd Bretton PE3 203 F1
Cambridge CB1 . . . . . . .65 C4
Mowfen Rd CB6 . . . . . . .242 D5
Mowlam Cl CB4 . . . . . . .104 C2
Moyne Cl CB4 . . . . .83 D7
Moyne Rd PE28 . . . . . . .168 C3
Muchwood La PE26 . . . . .221 B1
Mudd's Dro PE14 . . . . . .229 F6
Mugglestons La PE26 . . .172 B6
Mulberry Cl Bottisham CB5 86 F6
Cambridge CB4 . . . . .83 F5
Mildenhall IP28 . . . . . . .239 E4
Whittlesey PE7 . . . . . . .189 F5
Yaxley PE7 . . . . .182 A5
Mulberry Way PE7 . . . . .240 E5
Mullein Cl 4 PE19 . . . . .74 C5
Mumby's Dro PE14 . . . . .229 E6
Munnings Cl CB9 . . . . . . .38 D1
Muntjac Cl 5 PE19 . . . . .74 B5
Murfitt Way SG19 . . . . . .41 D6
Murfitt's La CB7 . . . . . . .212 E2
Muriel Cl CB3 . . . . .99 B2
Murrell Cl PE19 . . . . .74 F7
Murrow Bank PE13 . . . . .234 D6
Murrow Cty Prim Sch
PE13 . . . . .234 D5
Murrow La PE13 . . . . . . .234 F5
Murton Cl CB5 . . . . .130 A3
**Museum of Archaeology &
Anthropology** CB2 . . . .246 B2
**Museum of Classical
Archaeology** CB3 . . . . .64 C8
Museum of Technology
CB5 . . . . .84 B3
Museum of Zoology
CB2 . . . . .246 B2
Musgrave Way
Fen Ditton CB5 . . . . .84 F6
9 St Neots PE19 . . . . . . .74 F5
Muskham PE3 . . . . .196 F4
Musticott Pl PE13 . . . . . .245 F6
Mustill's La CB4 . . . . . . .123 B8
Muswell Rd PE3 . . . . . . .197 E4
Myrtle Ave PE1 . . . . . . .198 C7
Myrtle Ct PE1 . . . . .198 C7
Myrtle Gr PE1 . . . . .198 C7
Myrtle Way PE27 . . . . . .144 A5

N

Nansicles Rd PE2 . . . . . .186 D6
Napier Pl PE2 . . . . .185 C6
Napier St CB1 . . . . .246 C3
Narrow Dro
Whittlesey PE7 . . . . . . .188 C5
Yaxley PE7 . . . . .182 C5
Narrow La CB4 . . . . .104 B4
Naseby Cl PE3 . . . . .197 C5
Nash Rd 7 SG8 . . . . .5 D5
Nat Flatman St CB8 . . . .111 B3
Natal Rd CB1 . . . . .65 C7
Nathan Cl PE3 . . . . .197 B2
National Extension Coll
CB2 . . . . .64 F7
National Horse Racing Mus
CB8 . . . . .111 A4
Navigation Wharf 6
PE19 . . . . .74 E5
Nayland Rd CB9 . . . . . . .23 E6
Neale Cl CB1 . . . . .65 C7
Neale Wade Com Coll
PE15 . . . . .243 D1
Neaverson Rd PE6 . . . . .203 F7
Nedderworth Rd 2
PE27 . . . . .144 B3
Needham Bank PE14 . . . .236 C4
Needingworth Rd PE27 . .144 B4
Nelson Gdns PE13 . . . . .245 D6
Nelson Rd
Eaton Socon PE19 . . . . . .74 B3
Huntingdon PE29 . . . . . .142 A6
Nelson's La CB6 . . . . . . .210 A5
Nene Cl Wansford PE8 . . .194 A3
2 Wittering PE8 . . . . . .230 B1
Nene Par March PE15 . . .243 E4
Wisbech PE13 . . . . .245 B7
Nene Parkway PE3 . . . . .196 F1
Nene Pk PE2 . . . . .185 C7
Nene Quay PE13 . . . . . .245 C5
Nene Rd Eaton Socon PE19 74 C4
Huntingdon PE29 . . . . . .141 E8
Kimbolton PE28 . . . . . . .114 A7
Whittlesey PE7 . . . . . . .189 E6
Nene Sch The PE13 . . . .245 D4
Nene St PE1 . . . . .198 B2
Nene Way St Ives PE27 . .144 A7
Sutton PE5 . . . . .194 F2
Neneside 1 PE15 . . . . . .222 F2
Neptune Cl CB4 . . . . .83 C7
Ness Rd CB5 . . . . .130 C3
Nether Gr CB4 . . . . .123 F2

Netherhall Sch The CB1 .65 E4
Netherhall Way CB1 ....65 D4
Nettle Bank PE14 .....235 C4
Neve Gdns IP28 ....213 E6
Neville Rd CB1 ....65 C6
New Barn Dro PE28 ...173 D4
New Barns Ave CB7 ....240 D6
New Barns Rd CB7 ....240 D5
New Bridge La Elm PE14 235 F6
Wisbech PE14 ....245 A4
New Bridge Rd PE14 ..236 E1
New Cangle Sch CB9 ...38 F1
New Cheveley Rd CB8 ..111 C2
New Cl SG8 ....12 B2
New Close Rd CB6 ....211 A7
New Cross Dro CB6 ...216 B3
New Cross Rd PE9 ....244 B5
New Cut PE6 ....233 D5
New Dro Soham CB7 ...211 E4
3 Wisbech PE13 .....245 D2
Wisbech St Mary PE13 .235 C5
New England PE28 ....120 B2
New Farm Cl **2** SG8 ..15 E8
New Farm Cotts CB1 ...20 E7
New Fen Dike PE12 ...237 A6
New Fen Road La PE26 .171 C8
New H CB3 ....83 C3
New La PE8 ....183 C8
New Long Dro PE7 ....177 F6
New Meadow Dro PE7 .187 D1
New Park St CB5 .....246 A4
New Path **4** CB7 ....212 E1
New Pk PE15 ....243 E5
New Rd Barton CB3 ....63 B4
Burwell CB5 ....130 B3
Chatteris PE16 ......241 E5
Cottenham CB4 .....125 E4
Exning CB8 ....110 B8
15 Eye PE6 ....232 A1
Great & Little Chishill SG8 .15 B1
Guilden Morden SG8 ...11 A5
Haddenham CB6 .....210 A6
Harston CB2 ....47 F3
Haslingfield CB3 ......47 B5
Hemingford Abbots PE28 .143 A1
Hinxton CB10 ....18 B6
Histon CB4 ....104 C3
Impington CB4 ......104 C2
Littleport CB6 ....242 D5
March PE15 ....243 E4
Melbourn SG8 ....14 E4
Mepal CB6 ....216 E3
Offord Cluny PE19 ...118 A2
Outwell PE14 ....236 E1
Over CB4 ....208 D1
Peterborough PE2 ....185 E4
Peterborough PE2 ....186 E7
Ramsey PE26 ....172 B7
St Ives PE27 ....144 B3
Sawston CB2 ....32 E8
Shudy Camps CB1 .....22 C7
Upwell PE14 ....229 E8
Warboys PE28 ......165 A4
Whittlesey PE7 ......189 F6
Wood Walton PE28 ...161 E7
New River Bank CB7 ..242 F5
New River Gn CB8 ....110 B8
New Road CP Sch PE7 .189 F6
New Row **8** PE6 .....231 E8
New Sch Rd CB4 .....104 B3
New Sq CB1 ....246 B3
New St Cambridge CB1 ..84 A2
Chippenham CB7 .....132 E8
Doddington/Wimblington
PE15 ....222 F5
Godmanchester PE29 .141 F1
Mildenhall IP28 ......239 C4
St Neots PE19 ....74 E5
Stamford PE9 ....244 C6
New Town Rd CB6 ....209 F6
Newark Ave PE1 .....198 C6
Newark Cl SG8 ....5 C8
Newark Hill CP Sch
PE1 ....198 D6
Newark Rd PE1 ......198 F4
Newbey Cl PE3 ......197 B3
Newborn Cl PE2 .....187 E5
Newborough Prim Sch
PE6 ....207 C1
Newborough Rd PE4 ..205 C2
Newboults La **1** PE7 .244 A5
Newcastle Dr PE2 ....186 D6
Newcombe Way PE2 ..185 D2
Newell Cl SG8 ....44 D1
Newgate Rd PE13 ....237 F6
Newgate St PE15 ....222 F5
Newgates **1** PE9 ....244 C5
Newghant Dro PE15 ..223 F4
Newham Rd PE9 .....244 A7
Newington CB4 ......124 B8
Newlands Ave PE15 ..243 D5
Newlands Rd
Chatteris PE16 ......241 E6
Parson Drove PE13 ...234 D7
Whittlesey PE7 ......190 A8
Newman Ave SG8 ......5 F6
Newman Cl **16** PE6 ...230 B1
Newmarket Cl PE1 ...198 B6
Newmarket Com Hospl
CB8 ....111 A5
Newmarket Rd
Ashley CB8 ....91 E8
Barton Mills IP28 ....239 D1
Burwell CB5 ....130 C1
Cambridge CB5 .....246 C3

Newmarket Rd continued
Cheveley CB8 ....91 C8
Cowling CB8 ....73 D3
Fen Ditton CB5 ......85 D3
Fordham CB7 ....131 D7
Great Chesterford CB10 ..18 C3
Lidgate CB8 ....73 C6
Moulton CB8 ....112 E5
Royston SG8 ....5 F6
Snailwell CB8 ....132 B2
Stow cum Quy CB5 ...85 F4
Stretham CB6 ....211 A3
Newmarket Sports Ctr
CB8 ....110 F4
Newmarket Sta CB8 ..111 A2
Newmarket Swimming Pool
CB8 ....110 F3
Newmarket Upper Sch
CB8 ....110 F4
Newnham Cl
Huntingdon PE29 ....142 A7
Mildenhall IP28 ......239 D5
Newnham Coll CB3 ....64 C8
Newnham Croft Prim Sch
CB3 ....64 C7
Newnham Croft St **2**
CB3 ....64 C7
Newnham Dro CB5 ...129 C5
Newnham La CB5 ....130 B3
Newnham Rd CB3 .....64 C7
Newnham St **7** CB7 ..240 D4
Newnham Way SG7 ....2 B1
Newnham Wlk CB3 ....64 C8
Newport Ave PE7 ....213 A1
Newstead Cl PE6 ....232 A2
Newstead Rd PE6 ....230 A8
Newton Cty Prim Sch
PE19 ....77 E3
Newton Rd Cambridge CB2 64 E5
Great Shelford CB2 ...48 D3
Harston CB2 ....47 F1
Newton CB2 ....31 A8
Sawtry PE28 ....168 C4
Newtown
Hail Weston PE19 ....74 B8
Kimbolton PE28 .....113 F5
Newtown La PE28 ...113 F5
Newtown Rd PE26 ...172 B7
Nicholas Taylor Gdns **1**
PE3 ....196 F3
Nicholls Ave PE3 ....197 E3
Nigel Rd CB1 ....240 E8
Nightall Rd CB7 .....212 A4
Nightingale Ave
Bassingbourn SG8 ....13 A5
Cambridge CB1 ......65 C8
Nightingale Cl IP28 ..239 D4
Nightingale Ct PE4 ..205 A2
Nightingale Dr PE7 ..181 D6
Nightingale Way **1** PE19 75 B7
Nightingale Wlk **1**
PE15 ....224 B4
Nimbus Way CB8 ....110 B8
Nine Chimneys La CB1 .53 B2
Nipcut Rd PE6 ......232 C2
Nixhill Rd PE15 .....223 B6
Noble Gdns PE15 ....243 B4
Nobles Cl PE7 ......190 F8
Nobles La PE28 .....208 C5
Noel Murless Dr CB8 .110 F5
Nook The PE6 ......231 C4
Norburn PE3 ....197 B8
Norfolk Ave CB8 ....110 C5
Norfolk Rd Ely CB6 ..240 A3
Huntingdon PE29 ....141 E8
St Ives PE27 ....144 A8
Wyton Airfield PE28 ..143 B8
Norfolk Sq **3** PE7 ..244 B6
Norfolk St Cambridge CB1 .84 A1
Doddington/Wimblington
PE15 ....223 B7
Peterborough PE1 ...197 F4
Wisbech PE13 ......245 C4
Norfolk Terr CB1 .....84 A1
Norgett's La SG8 .....14 C6
Norham Ct PE7 .....188 A5
Norico Bay PE15 ....243 E2
Norman Cl PE7 .....189 E8
Norman Dr PE7 .....175 F8
Norman Pk CB3 .....102 C4
Norman Rd PE1 .....198 C4
Norman Way
9 Doddington/Wimblington
PE15 ....223 B7
Over CB4 ....123 B7
Norman's La **8** SG8 ...5 D5
Normanton Rd PE1 ..198 D4
Normanton Way CB4 .104 B5
Normoor Dro PE16 ..223 B2
Nornea La CB7 .....211 F8
Norris Mus★ PE27 ...144 A3
Norris Rd PE27 .....144 A4
North Ave CB9 ....23 E8
North Bank PE6 ....199 D4
North Bank Rd **4** PE1 .198 D3
North Brink PE13 ....245 A5
North Cambridgeshire Hospl
PE13 ....245 D5
North Cl SG8 ....5 C8
North Cotts CB2 .....64 D4
North Dr March PE15 .243 E4
Newmarket CB8 ....110 F5
Soham CB7 ....212 B5
North End
Bassingbourn cum Kneesworth
SG8 ....12 B6
Exning CB8 ....130 F3
Meldreth SG8 ....29 B2

North End continued
Wisbech PE13 ......245 B6
North End Rd CB10 ...18 A8
North Fen Dro CB6 ...218 B8
North Fen Rd PE6 ...231 F6
North La SG19 ....41 B7
North Pl IP28 ....239 C4
North Rd
Alconbury Weston PE28 .150 D5
Brampton PE28 .....140 D1
Great Abington CB1 ...33 F5
St Ives PE27 ....144 A4
Whittlesford CB2 .....32 B6
North Side PE6 .....200 F5
North St Burwell CB5 .130 B4
Cambridge CB4 ......83 C4
Folksworth & Washingley
PE7 ....181 A1
Freckenham IP28 ....213 C3
Huntingdon PE29 ....141 E5
March PE15 ....243 E6
Peterborough PE1 ...198 A2
Stamford PE9 ....244 B5
Stilton PE7 ....176 A8
Wicken CB7 ....211 E1
Wisbech PE13 ......245 C5
North Terr
Mildenhall IP28 ......239 C4
Peterborough PE1 ...198 E2
Sawston CB2 ....32 F5
Northam CI PE6 .....232 A2
Northampton Cl **4** CB6 240 A3
Northampton St CB3 ..83 C2
Northborough CP Sch
PE6 ....231 F6
Northey Rd PE6 .....199 C2
Northfield Fulbourn CB1 .67 A5
Girton CB3 ....103 E2
Northfield Cl SG19 ...41 C6
Northfield Pk CB7 ...212 A5
Northfield Rd Ashwell SG7 .2 C7
Peterborough PE1 ...197 F7
Soham CB7 ....212 A5
Wyboston PE19 ......74 A1
Northfields Ave CB4 ...83 E7
Northfields Rd CB5 ..107 D2
Northgate PE7 ......189 D8
Northgate PE7 ......189 D8
Northminster PE1 ...198 A3
Northumberland Ave **4**
PE9 ....244 A6
Northumberland Cl **2**
CB4 ....83 C4
Northumbria Cl CB6 .210 A7
Northwold CB6 .....240 C5
Norton Cl Cambridge CB5 .84 D3
Papworth Everard CB3 ..99 A2
Norton Rd Haverhill CB9 ..23 E4
Peterborough PE1 ...197 F6
Norwalde St PE15 ...243 C4
Norwich Rd PE13 ...245 E5
Norwich St CB2 ....64 E7
Norwood Ave PE15 ..243 D5
Norwood CP Sch PE4 .204 E2
Norwood Cres PE15 .243 B3
Norwood La PE4 ....205 B2
Norwood Rd March PE15 243 C6
Notley Dr CB9 ....38 C1
Nottingham Way PE1 .198 C6
Nuffield Cl CB4 ......84 B7
Nuffield Rd
Cambridge CB4 ......84 B6
St Ives PE27 ....144 C6
Nunns Way **4** CB6 ..216 E1
Nun's Orch CB4 .....104 B4
Nuns Way CB4 ....83 F7
Nursery Cl Isleham CB7 .212 F4
Peterborough PE1 ...198 A4
Nursery Dr March PE15 .243 B5
Wisbech PE13 ......245 E8
Nursery Gdns
Little Paxton PE19 ....96 A2
St Ives PE27 ....144 B5
Whittlesey PE7 .....189 F6
Nursery La PE1 .....198 D2
Nursery Rd
Huntingdon PE29 ....141 E4
St Neots PE19 ....74 F4
Nursery Way **2** CB3 ..62 C5
Nursery Wlk
Brampton PE28 .....140 C3
Cambridge CB4 ......83 C5
Nutholt La CB6 .....240 D5
Nutters Cl CB3 ......64 A4
Nuttings Rd CB1 .....84 D1

O

O Furlong Dro CB6 ...224 F1
Oak Cl PE19 ....75 A5
Oak Dr Brampton PE28 .140 C4
Little Stukeley PE28 ..151 F3
Mildenhall IP28 ......213 F8
Outwell PE14 ....236 F3
Oak End PE28 ......150 F4
Oak Farm Cl PE7 ....176 A7
Oak La Cheveley CB8 ..91 C4
Littleport CB6 ......242 A2
Oak Rd Glinton PE6 ..231 E5
Stilton PE7 ....176 A7
Oak Tree Ave CB4 ....80 B3
Oak Tree Cl March PE15 .243 C5
St Ives PE27 ....143 F5
Oak Tree Way CB4 ..104 B3
Oak View PE3 ......196 F2
Oakdale Ave PE2 ...187 D4

Oakdale CP Sch PE7 .187 C4
Oakington CE Prim Sch
CB4 ....103 C5
Oakington Rd
Cottenham CB4 .....125 B1
Dry Drayton CB3 ....102 D2
Girton CB3 ....103 E3
Oakington & Westwick
CB4 ....103 E7
Oaklands PE28 .....121 B5
Oaklands Ave PE28 .163 F7
Oaklands Dr PE13 ..245 F7
Oakleaf Rd PE1 ....198 C6
Oakleigh Cres PE29 .141 F1
Oakleigh Dr PE2 ....186 C6
Oakley Cl PE13 .....245 C4
Oakley Dr **2** PE28 ..168 B3
Oakrits SG8 ....14 B8
Oakroyd Cres PE13 .245 C6
Oaks Dr CB8 ....110 F7
Oaks The Milton CB4 .105 C2
Soham CB7 ....212 B3
Oaktree Rd CB4 ....121 D6
Oasthouse Way PE26 .172 A5
Oates' La CB6 ......216 E1
Oates Way PE26 ....172 C7
Oatlands Ave CB4 ..102 B4
Occupation Rd
Cambridge CB1 ......84 A2
Peterborough PE1 ...197 E6
Ockendon Cl PE19 ...74 B3
Octagon Dr **4** PE13 .245 A6
Octavia Cl PE13 ....245 F6
Octavia Hill Birthplace Mus★
PE13 ....245 C5
Odecroft PE3 ....197 C7
Offa Lea CB2 ....31 B7
Offord Prim Sch PE19 .118 A2
Offord Rd PE19 .....97 F6
Ogden Cl SG8 ....14 D6
Oil Mill La PE13 ....245 B5
Oilmills Dro PE26 ...220 F4
Oilmills Rd PE26 ...220 F4
Old Auction Yd PE16 .241 C5
Old Bank CB7 ......229 B4
Old Brewery Cl **1** CB7 .240 E4
Old Church La PE28 .208 C7
Old Clements La **2** CB9 .23 F7
Old Court H PE29 ...141 E1
Old Farm Cl Histon CB4 .104 B5
3 Needingworth PE27 .208 A3
Old Fen Dike PE12 ...237 B8
Old Ford La PE19 ...114 B2
Old Forge Way CB2 ..32 E8
Old Glebe PE28 ....150 C5
Old Great North Rd
St Martin's Without PE9 ..244 C3
Sibson cum Stibbington
PE8 ....194 C2
Old Haverhill Rd CB9 ..39 E4
Old Houghton Rd PE29 .142 B6
Old House Rd CB1 ...53 C2
Old Knarr Fen Dro PE6 .233 C4
Old Leicester Rd PE8 .194 A3
Old Lynn Dro CB6 ...217 C7
Old Lynn Rd PE13 ..245 E7
Old Mill Ave PE28 ..165 A5
Old Mill Cl CB2 ......29 D7
Old Mill La IP28 ....239 F2
Old Mkt PE13 ......245 C5
Old North Rd
Bassingbourn cum Kneesworth
SG8 ....13 B4
Longstowe CB3 ......60 A3
Royston SG8 ....5 C7
Sawtry PE28 ....168 D4
Wansford PE8 ......194 A3
Old Oundle Rd PE8 ..193 A6
Old Pinewood Way CB3 ..99 B4
Old Pond La PE5 ....195 E2
Old Pools Dro CB6 ..225 C4
Old Pound Cl PE28 ..143 D2
Old Ramsey Rd
St Ives PE27 ....143 E8
Woodhurst PE28 ....154 F7
Old Rectory Dr
Dry Drayton CB3 ....102 B1
4 Tallington PE9 ...230 F7
Thornhaugh PE8 ....194 A6
Old Rope Wlk CB9 ...23 E7
Old Sch The PE28 ..160 C2
Old School Cl
Burwell CB5 ....130 C3
Littleport CB6 ......242 D5
1 Soham CB7 ......212 B5
Old School Gdns **3** PE19 74 C2
Old School La
Brinkley CB8 ....70 E1
Milton CB4 ....105 D2
Wicken CB7 ....211 B1
Old Stable Wlk **3** CB6 .172 A4
Old Station Rd CB8 ..111 B4
Old Sunday Sch CB5 .106 B7
Old West Est PE15 ..222 A5
Old Weston Rd PE28 .158 A5
Oldbrook PE3 ....204 A1
Oldeamere Way PE7 .190 A4
Oldfield Ave **5** PE14 .236 B5
Oldfield Gdns PE7 ..189 D7
Oldfield La PE13 ....245 E5
Oldhurst Rd PE28 ..155 E8
Olive Rd PE1 ....198 C7
Oliver Cl PE6 ....171 F6
Oliver Cromwell Ho★
CB7 ....240 C4
Oliver Rd **5** PE27 ..144 B4
Olivers Way PE15 ...243 D4
Olivia Rd PE28 .....140 C3

Ollard Ave PE13 ....245 D7
Onyx Ct **9** PE13 ...245 C4
Open Univ The CB2 ..246 C1
Opportune Rd PE13 .245 C6
Orange Gr **1** PE13 .245 C4
Orchard Ave CB4 .....83 E5
Orchard Cl Balsham CB1 ..52 F3
Bassingbourn SG8 ....13 A5
Cottenham CB4 .....125 C3
Eaton Socon PE19 ...74 C4
Elsworth CB3 ....100 B4
Girton CB3 ....103 E1
Hail Weston PE19 ....95 A1
Haverhill CB9 ....23 F7
Lidgate CB8 ....73 E8
Little Wilbraham CB1 ..86 E2
Littleport CB6 ......242 D4
4 Manea PE15 ....224 B4
March PE15 ....243 E3
9 Market Deeping PE6 .231 E8
Peterborough PE3 ...197 D3
Stilton PE7 ....176 A7
Warboys PE28 .....164 F6
Warmington PE8 ....178 B3
9 Wisbech PE14 ...236 A5
Orchard Cres **2** PE28 .208 E6
Orchard Ct **4** PE6 ..232 F3
Orchard Dr Girton CB3 ..82 E7
Waterbeach CB5 ....127 B1
Wisbech PE13 ......245 C4
Orchard End
2 Bluntisham/Colne
PE28 ....208 C5
Rampton CB4 ......124 C4
Orchard Est
Cambridge CB1 ......65 F7
1 Little Downham CB6 .218 B7
Orchard Gate SG8 ...14 C6
Orchard Gdns PE28 .121 B5
Orchard La
Brampton PE28 .....140 E3
Huntingdon PE29 ....141 E4
Orchard Mews PE2 ..186 F8
Orchard Pightle CB1 ..20 B6
Orchard Rd Barnack PE9 .230 E4
Eaton Socon PE19 ...74 C4
Great Shelford CB2 ...49 B6
6 Haslingfield CB3 ...47 B5
Histon CB4 ....104 C5
March PE15 ....243 E3
Melbourn SG8 ....14 C5
Royston SG8 ....5 B7
Sawston CB2 ....32 F7
Stamford PE9 ....244 B5
Orchard Rd S PE15 ..243 E3
Orchard Row CB7 ...212 C2
Orchard St
Cambridge CB1 .....246 B3
Peterborough PE2 ...186 F7
Stow cum Quy CB5 ...85 F5
Whittlesey PE7 .....189 D7
Orchard Terr CB2 .....32 C4
Orchard The Ashley CB8 ..91 F7
Fen Drayton CB4 ....121 F5
Little Paxton PE19 ...95 F2
Peterborough PE4 ...204 C3
Orchard View CB5 ..127 B1
Orchard Way
Burwell CB5 ....130 B3
4 Doddington/Wimblington
PE15 ....223 B7
Godmanchester PE29 .141 F2
7 Haddenham CB6 ..210 A5
5 Manea PE15 ....224 B4
Melbourn SG8 ....14 D6
Oakington/Longstanton
CB4 ....103 C5
Offord Cluny PE19 ...97 A8
Ramsey PE26 ....172 A7
Royston SG8 ....5 C8
Orchard Way Cl CB2 ..47 F2
Orchards The
Chatteris PE16 ......241 D5
Great Shelford CB2 ...49 B6
Peterborough PE2 ...185 F4
Sutton CB6 ....216 E2
1 Wilburton CB6 ...210 C6
Witcham CB6 ....217 A2
Orchid Cl
13 Eaton Socon PE19 .74 C6
Yaxley PE7 ....181 F7
Orford Rd CB9 ....23 F6
Orkney Cl CB9 ....24 D7
Orme Rd PE3 ....197 D4
Orthwaite PE29 ....141 B6
Orton Ave PE2 .....186 E7
Orton Dr CB6 ......217 D1
Orton Longueville Sch
PE2 ....186 A6
Orton Matley Prim Sch
PE2 ....185 E5
Orton Mere PE2 ....186 B7
Orton Parkway PE2 .185 D4
Orton Wistow Prim Sch
PE2 ....185 C6
Orwell Cl PE27 .....144 A6
Orwell Dr PE15 ....243 D5
Orwell Furlong CB4 ..84 C7
Orwell Gr PE4 .....204 F1
Orwell Rd CB2 ....29 C8
Osborn Cl **3** CB4 ..209 A1
Osborne Pk PE13 ...245 C6
Osborne Rd PE13 ..245 B7
Osier Cl CB7 ....219 C6
Osier Holt **1** PE28 .208 D6
Osiers The PE19 ...117 A3
Oslar's Way CB1 ....66 E5

Osprey PE2 . . . . .185 F2
Osprey CI PE29 . . . . .142 A7
Osprey Rd CB9 . . . . .24 C7
Otago CI PE7 . . . . .189 F8
Otago Rd PE7 . . . . .189 E8
Othello CI PE29 . . . . .142 A7
Otter CI CB3 . . . . .102 B4
Otter Way 9 PE19 . . . . . . .74 B5
Otterbrook PE2 . . . . .185 D5
Oundle Rd Elton PE8 . . . . .183 F1
  Peterborough PE2 . . . . . .185 E6
Ouse Fen Rd or Bank
CB4 . . . . .208 D3
Ouse Rd Eaton Socon PE19 74 C4
  Kimbolton PE28 . . . . . . .114 B7
  St Ives PE27 . . . . .144 A7
Ouse Washes Nature
Reserve★ PE29 . . . . . . .224 D2
Ouse Wlk 1 PE29 . . . . . .141 E4
Outfield PE3 . . . . .204 A1
Outwell Rd Elm PE14 . . . .236 C5
  Emneth PE14 . . . . .236 D4
  Outwell PE14 . . . . .236 E3
Over CP Sch CB4 . . . . . . .208 D1
Over Hall La CB4 . . . . .21 D2
Over Rd Swavesey CB4 . . .122 F8
  Willingham CB4 . . . . . . .208 F1
Overchurch CI CB9 . . . . . . .23 F7
Overcote La PE27 . . . . . . .208 B2
Overcote Rd CB4 . . . . . . .208 D1
Overend PE8 . . . . .178 D8
Overhills CP Sch PE8 . . . .113 F5
Overstone Ct PE3 . . . . . . .197 C6
Overstone Dr 1 PE14 . . . .235 D1
Overstone Rd 2 PE14 . . . .235 D1
Overton Way PE2 . . . . . . .185 F4
Overwater CI 1 PE29 . . . .141 A6
Owall Wlk 8 SG8 . . . . .5 E8
Owen CI 3 PE9 . . . . .230 D3
Owen Dr SG8 . . . . .13 D1
Owl End
  The Stukeleys PE28 . . . . .151 D5
  Yaxley PE7 . . . . .181 D5
Owl Way PE29 . . . . .142 B7
Owls End PE26 . . . . .172 A4
Owlstone Rd CB3 . . . . .64 C7
Oxburgh CI
  3 Peterborough PE7 . . . .187 F5
  1 Wisbech PE13 . . . . . . .245 A7
Oxclose PE3 . . . . .197 A8
Oxford CI
  Bassingbourn SG8 . . . . . . .12 F7
  Mildenhall IP28 . . . . . . .239 A5
Oxford Rd Cambridge CB4 . .83 B4
  Peterborough PE1 . . . . . .197 F5
  St Ives PE27 . . . . .144 A4
  Stamford PE9 . . . . .244 A7
Oxford St CB8 . . . . .110 B8
Oxholme Dro CB4 . . . . . . .209 F1
Oxney Rd PE1 . . . . .198 D5
Oyster Row CB5 . . . . .84 B3

P

Pacific CI PE15 . . . . .243 C6
Paddock CI CB4 . . . . .104 C4
Paddock Row CB3 . . . . . . .100 B4
Paddock St CB7 . . . . .212 B4
Paddock The
  Eaton Socon PE19 . . . . . . .74 A4
  Ely CB6 . . . . .240 D5
  Harston CB2 . . . . .47 F2
  Huntingdon PE29 . . . . . . .141 E5
  15 Somersham PE28 . . . .215 C1
  Stamford PE9 . . . . .244 A5
Paddock Way
  1 Haddenham CB6 . . . . .210 A6
  Sawston CB2 . . . . .32 A7
Paddocks Chase PE19 . . . .118 A3
Paddocks CP Sch CB8 . . . .110 E4
Paddocks Dr CB8 . . . . . . .111 A1
Paddocks The
  Alconbury PE28 . . . . . . .150 F4
  Burwell CB5 . . . . .130 B1
  Cambridge CB1 . . . . .84 C1
  Folksworth PE7 . . . . .175 D8
  Hilton PE28 . . . . .120 B2
  Little Wilbraham CB8 . . . . .68 F6
  Whittlesey PE7 . . . . .189 E7
  Worlington IP28 . . . . . . .213 F4
Padgett's Rd PE14 . . . . . .229 C3
Padgetts CI PE28 . . . . . . .165 A5
Padholme Rd PE1 . . . . . . .198 C3
Padholme Rd E PE1 . . . . .198 E3
Padlock Rd CB1 . . . . .53 C7
Padnal Bank CB7 . . . . . . .219 B6
Padnal Dro CB6 . . . . .242 E3
Padney Dro PE28 . . . . . . .211 D5
Pages Way 3 PE28 . . . . . .140 C3
Paget CI CB2 . . . . .64 E3
Paget PI CB8 . . . . .111 A6
Paget Rd CB2 . . . . .64 D2
Painter's La CB6 . . . . .216 D1
Pakenham CI CB4 . . . . .84 A5
Palace Gdns SG8 . . . . .5 C4
Palace La CB7 . . . . .132 D8
Palisade Ct 3 CB6 . . . . . .211 B7
Palmer CI PE1 . . . . .189 F6
Palmers La
  Alconbury PE28 . . . . . . .150 F4
  Chrishall SG8 . . . . .8 C4
Palmers Rd PE1 . . . . .198 F5
Palmers SG8 . . . . .14 D6
Palmers Wlk CB1 . . . . . . .246 C2
Palmerston Rd PE2 . . . . . .186 F7
Pamment's La IP28 . . . . . .213 D6

Pampisford Rd CB1 . . . . . .34 C5
Pamplin Ct 1 CB1 . . . . . . .65 F6
Panswell La PE13 . . . . . . .235 C8
Panther Way 1 CB1 . . . . . .66 A7
Pantile La CB5 . . . . .130 A3
Panton St CB2 . . . . .246 B1
Papley Grove Farm Cotts
PE19 . . . . .77 E7
Papworth Hospl CB3 . . . . .99 C2
Papworth Rd
  Graveley PE19 . . . . .98 A5
  March PE15 . . . . .243 F4
Papyrus Rd PE4 . . . . .203 F3
Papyrus Way PE28 . . . . . .168 A4
Parade La CB4 . . . . .240 C4
Paradise Ctr & Pool
CB7 . . . . .240 D5
Paradise La
  Northborough PE6 . . . . . .231 F6
  3 Whittlesey PE7 . . . . . .189 D6
Paradise St CB1 . . . . .246 C3
Paragon Rd PE27 . . . . . . .144 A5
Parcell Wlk PE29 . . . . . . .118 A3
Parish Bush Dro CB7 . . . . .219 C1
Park Ave Histon CB4 . . . . .104 A4
  Newmarket CB8 . . . . . . .111 B3
  St Ives PE27 . . . . .144 B4
  Wisbech PE13 . . . . .245 C6
Park CI Bassingbourn SG8 . .12 E5
  Holme PE7 . . . . .176 F4
  Little Paxton PE19 . . . . . . .95 E1
  Moulton CB8 . . . . .112 F5
  1 Thorney PE6 . . . . .233 B3
  Yaxley PE7 . . . . .181 F5
Park Cotts CB8 . . . . .111 B3
Park Cres
  Little Paxton PE19 . . . . . . .95 F2
  Peterborough PE1 . . . . . .198 B5
  Thorney PE6 . . . . .233 B3
  Waterbeach CB5 . . . . . . .106 C8
Park Dr Histon CB4 . . . . . .104 C3
  Little Paxton PE19 . . . . . . .95 F1
Park Est 1 PE6 . . . . .231 F8
Park Farm Cotts CB10 . . . . .18 E5
Park Farm Cres PE7 . . . . .187 F5
Park Farm Dr IP28 . . . . . .214 A2
Park Farm La SG8 . . . . .1 A2
Park Farm Rd PE6 . . . . . .196 E5
Park Farm Way PE7 . . . . .187 F6
Park Hill CB1 . . . . .37 C2
Park La Brampton PE28 . . .117 D8
  Castle Camps CB1 . . . . . . .22 F3
  Dry Drayton CB3 . . . . .81 C8
  Fen Drayton CB4 . . . . . . .121 F6
  Godmanchester PE29 . . . .141 F2
  Histon CB4 . . . . .103 F4
  Kimbolton PE19 . . . . . . .113 F2
  Langley CB11 . . . . .1 F2
  Leverington PE13 . . . . . .238 A3
  Little Downham CB6 . . . . .217 F6
  Longstowe CB3 . . . . .59 F3
  Madingley CB3 . . . . .81 F6
  Newmarket CB8 . . . . . . .111 B3
  Newton PE13 . . . . .237 F3
  Peterborough PE1 . . . . . .198 C4
  Stamford PE9 . . . . .244 C4
  Whittlesey PE7 . . . . .189 C7
Park Lane GM Prim Sch The
PE7 . . . . .189 D6
Park Lane Prim Sch
PE29 . . . . .141 F2
Park Par CB5 . . . . .246 A4
Park Rd Brampton PE28 . . .140 C2
  Buckden PE19 . . . . .117 B4
  Burwell CB5 . . . . .130 B2
  Cheveley CB8 . . . . .91 C6
  Great Chesterford CB10 . . .18 E5
  Haverhill CB9 . . . . .23 D8
  Manea PE15 . . . . .224 B4
  Market Deeping PE6 . . . .231 E8
  Peterborough PE1 . . . . . .198 A3
  Ramsey PE26 . . . . .171 F6
  St Ives PE27 . . . . .144 B4
  St Neots PE19 . . . . .74 F6
  Sawston CB2 . . . . .32 F5
  Sawtry PE28 . . . . .168 B5
  Sutton CB6 . . . . .216 E2
  Tydd St Giles PE13 . . . . .237 D7
  Wisbech PE13 . . . . .245 D5
Park Side PE19 . . . . .95 E1
Park St Cambridge CB5 . . .246 A3
  Chatteris PE16 . . . . .241 B5
  Dry Drayton CB3 . . . . . . .102 C1
  Peterborough PE2 . . . . . .186 F4
  2 Wisbech PE13 . . . . . .245 D5
Park Street Prim & Jun Sch
CB5 . . . . .246 A3
Park Terr CB1 . . . . .246 B2
Park View
  Bassingbourn SG8 . . . . . .12 E5
  Little Stukeley PE28 . . . . .151 F1
  Needingworth PE27 . . . . .208 A2
Park Way
  Little Paxton PE19 . . . . . .95 F1
  Offord Cluny PE19 . . . . . .118 A2
  St Neots PE19 . . . . .74 F1
Parker Rd PE8 . . . . .230 B1
Parker St CB1 . . . . .246 B2
Parker's CI PE16 . . . . .241 B5
Parker's Dro IP28 . . . . . . .213 D6
Parker's Terr 2 CB1 . . . . . .84 A2
Parkers Wlk CB8 . . . . . . .110 E8
Parkfield La PE15 . . . . . . .223 B6
Parkgate PE29 . . . . .141 C6
Parkhall Rd PE28 . . . . . . .215 C2
Parkinson's La 1 PE7 . . . .189 D6
Parklands SG8 . . . . .5 E6

Parkside Cambridge CB1 . .246 C2
  Chippenham CB7 . . . . . .132 E8
  Mildenhall IP28 . . . . . . .214 A8
  Peterborough PE7 . . . . . .186 B6
Parkside Com Coll CB1 . . .246 C2
Parkside Pools CB1 . . . . . .246 C2
Parkway St Ives PE27 . . . .144 B4
  Shudy Camps CB1 . . . . . . .22 C6
  The Stukeleys PE29 . . . . .141 A5
Parkway Mid Sch CB9 . . . .23 D8
Parliament St PE1 . . . . . . .197 F5
Parlour CI CB4 . . . . .104 B5
Parnwell CP Sch PE1 . . . . .198 E7
Parnwell Way PE1 . . . . . . .198 F6
Parr CI 3 CB4 . . . . .104 C3
Parrens Rd 4 PE28 . . . . . .208 E6
Parson Drove La PE13 . . . .238 B2
Parsonage Barns CB5 . . . . .86 F5
Parsonage CI CB5 . . . . . . .130 B2
Parsonage Farm La CB8 . . .90 F2
Parsonage Rd CB5 . . . . . .130 B2
Parsonage St
  Cambridge CB5 . . . . .246 C3
  Wistow PE28 . . . . .163 F6
Parsonage Way CB1 . . . . . .35 D2
Parson's CI CB2 . . . . .246 A2
Parson's Dr PE28 . . . . . . .139 A4
Parson's La CB6 . . . . .242 C4
Parson's Land Dro PE15 222 D6
Parsons Gn PE27 . . . . . . .144 C4
Parthia CI SG8 . . . . .5 E3
Partridge CI PE7 . . . . .181 D5
Partridge Dr CB4 . . . . . . .102 B3
Partridge Dr PE4 . . . . .204 A5
Partridge Hill SG7 . . . . .2 C3
Paske Ave CB1 . . . . .23 F7
Passage The 10 CB7 . . . . .240 D4
Paston La PE4 . . . . .197 D8
Paston Parkway PE4 . . . . .204 E4
Paston Ridings PE4 . . . . . .204 E1
Paston Ridings Cty Jun & Inf
Sch PE4 . . . . .204 F1
Pasture CI PE28 . . . . .165 A5
Pasture La PE6 . . . . .231 F6
Pasture The PE28 . . . . . . .208 B8
Pastures The CB3 . . . . .81 A1
Pates CI CB3 . . . . .47 A6
Pathfinder Way
  Ramsey PE26 . . . . .171 F5
  Warboys PE28 . . . . .164 F4
Patterdale Rd 2 PE4 . . . . .205 A2
Paulsgrove PE2 . . . . .185 D5
Pavement The PE27 . . . . .144 A3
Pavilion Ct CB9 . . . . .24 B7
Paxton CI CB4 . . . . .125 E3
Paxton Hill PE19 . . . . .96 D2
Paxton Rd
  Offord Darcy PE19 . . . . . .96 F7
  Peterborough PE2 . . . . . .185 D4
Payne Ave PE15 . . . . .245 D7
Payne Sch PE13 . . . . .234 D7
Paynells PE2 . . . . .186 A3
Paynesholm PE4 . . . . .205 A1
Payton Way CB5 . . . . .106 B7
Peacock Dr CB5 . . . . .86 B7
Peacock Way PE3 . . . . . . .196 F2
Peacocks CB2 . . . . .49 A4
Peake CI PE2 . . . . .186 F6
Peakes Dr PE7 . . . . .201 F1
Peakirk cum Glinton CE Prim
Sch PE6 . . . . .203 E8
Peakirk Rd
  Deeping Gate PE6 . . . . . .231 F8
  Glinton PE6 . . . . .203 F8
  Northborough PE6 . . . . . .206 A4
Peakirk Wildfowl Trust★
PE6 . . . . .206 B2
Peaks Ct PE29 . . . . .141 A5
Pear Tree CI
  Fenstanton PE28 . . . . . . .121 A5
  Haddenham CB6 . . . . . . .210 A5
Pear Tree Cres PE13 . . . . .238 A2
Pearce CI CB6 . . . . .64 B8
Pearces Rd PE6 . . . . .199 B5
Pearl L Ctr PE5 . . . . .195 E1
Pearmain Ct CB4 . . . . .84 C5
Pearmains CI SG8 . . . . . . .45 E1
Pearson CI CB4 . . . . .105 D1
Peartree Way 10 PE14 . . .236 A5
Peas Hill CB2 . . . . .246 A2
Peas Hill Rd PE15 . . . . . . .243 A5
Pease Way CB4 . . . . .103 F4
Peate CI PE29 . . . . .141 F1
Peatlings La PE15 . . . . . . .245 A7
Peckover CI 4 PE7 . . . . . .187 F5
Peckover Dr PE13 . . . . . . .245 E4
Peckover Ho★ PE13 . . . . .245 B5
Peckover Prim Sch
PE13 . . . . .245 B6
Pecks CI PE28 . . . . .120 C1
Pecks Yd PE16 . . . . .241 C5
Peddars Way PE3 . . . . . . .197 A2
Pedley La PE13 . . . . .245 A6
Peer Rd PE9 . . . . .74 B4
Pegler Ct 5 CB4 . . . . . . .209 A1
Peldon Dr PE13 . . . . .245 E5
Pelham CI
  Cottenham CB4 . . . . .125 D3
  Peterborough PE3 . . . . . .196 F4
Pelham Ct CB4 . . . . .83 C6
Pelham Way CB4 . . . . . . .125 D3
Pelican Prep Sch CB1 . . . . .65 B4
Pemberton Terr CB2 . . . . .246 B1
Pembroke Ave
  Peterborough PE2 . . . . . .185 F5
  9 St Neots PE19 . . . . .74 F2
  Waterbeach CB5 . . . . . . .105 F8

Pembroke CI
  Huntingdon PE29 . . . . . . .141 F7
  Mildenhall IP28 . . . . . . .239 C5
  2 Newmarket CB8 . . . . .111 A7
Pembroke Coll CB2 . . . . . .246 A2
Pembroke Gr PE6 . . . . . . .203 F8
Pembroke La 2 CB1 . . . . . .35 C2
Pembroke Rd PE9 . . . . . . .244 A7
Pembroke St CB2 . . . . . . .246 A2
Pembroke Way CB1 . . . . . .85 B1
Pen CI CB1 . . . . .66 A6
Pen Hills Nature Reserve★
SG8 . . . . .4 E3
Penarth PI CB3 . . . . .64 A8
Pendleton PE3 . . . . .197 B6
Pendragon Com Prim Sch
CB3 . . . . .99 A3
Pendragon Hill CB3 . . . . . .99 A4
Pendula Rd PE13 . . . . . . .245 E7
Pennine Way PE4 . . . . . . .204 D2
Pennington PE2 . . . . .185 E3
Pennington Rd PE29 . . . . .142 A7
Pennway 11 PE28 . . . . . . .215 C1
Penrose Gdns PE15 . . . . . .243 E4
Penrwyn Ct 5 PE19 . . . . . .74 F1
Pentelowes The PE28 . . . .135 D2
Pentlands CI CB4 . . . . . . .246 C4
Pentlands The PE4 . . . . . .204 E2
Pentlow Hawke CI CB9 . . . .24 B7
Penwald CI 7 PE6 . . . . . .232 B8
Penyale 3 PE3 . . . . .197 A1
Pepper CI SG8 . . . . .12 E3
Peppercorn CI PE1 . . . . . .197 E6
Peppercorns La 2 PE19 . . .74 C2
Pepperslade CB2 . . . . .31 C1
Pepys Ho★ PE28 . . . . . . .140 F2
Pepys Rd Brampton PE28 .140 F2
  St Neots PE19 . . . . .75 A4
Pepys Road Sch PE19 . . . . .75 A4
Pepys Terr CB4 . . . . .104 C1
Pepys Way CB3 . . . . .82 E8
Percheron CI CB4 . . . . . . .104 D3
Percheron PE15 . . . . .243 E2
Percival St PE3 . . . . .197 E2
Peregrine CI PE29 . . . . . . .142 A7
Perkins La 7 PE6 . . . . . . .231 C7
Perne Ave CB1 . . . . .65 C6
Perne Rd CB1 . . . . .65 C6
Pernys CI PE7 . . . . .186 D3
Perowne St CB1 . . . . .84 A1
Perry CI CB6 . . . . .210 A6
Perry Ct CB3 . . . . .83 A2
Perry Dr SG8 . . . . .5 E7
Perry Rd Buckden PE19 . .116 F3
  Leverington PE13 . . . . . .238 B2
Perse Boys Sch The 2 . . . .65 A4
Perse Prep Sch The CB2 . . .64 E4
Perse Sch for Girls The
CB2 . . . . .246 B1
Perse Way CB4 . . . . .83 D5
Pershore Rd CB3 . . . . .81 A3
Persimmon Wlk CB8 . . . . .110 E8
Peterborough Airport
(Conington) PE7 . . . . . . .176 F3
Peterborough Coll of Adult
Ed PE1 . . . . .198 B3
Peterborough District Hospl
PE3 . . . . .197 E2
Peterborough Dr
  Bretton PE6 . . . . .196 E2
  Castor PE6 . . . . .196 D3
Peterborough High Sch
PE3 . . . . .197 D2
Peterborough Rd
  Castor PE5 . . . . .195 E1
  Crowland PE6 . . . . .232 B8
  Eye PE6 . . . . .205 F1
  Newborough PE6 . . . . . .205 D8
  Peterborough PE7 . . . . . .187 C3
  Wansford PE8 . . . . .194 A3
  Warmington PE8 . . . . . . .178 A4
  Whittlesey PE7 . . . . .189 B7
Peterborough Regional Coll
PE1 . . . . .198 B5
Peterborough Sta PE3 . . . .197 F2
Petergate 1 PE1 . . . . . . .244 B4
Peterhouse CB2 . . . . .246 A1
Peterhouse CI 1 PE9 . . . .244 B4
Peterhouse Cres PE15 . . . .243 E6
Peterhouse Dr CB8 . . . . . .111 A2
Petersfield 3 CB1 . . . . . . .246 C1
Petersfield Rd CB2 . . . . . . .17 C8
Petersfield Sch SG8 . . . . . .28 C8
Petingo CI CB8 . . . . .110 D7
Pettis Rd PE27 . . . . .143 C6
Pettit Rd PE29 . . . . .142 A1
Pettits CI CB1 . . . . .66 F4
Pettitt's CI CB3 . . . . .102 C2
Pettitt's La CB3 . . . . .102 C1
Petts CI 3 PE13 . . . . .245 E7
Petts La CB10 . . . . .19 E1
Petty Cury CB2 . . . . .246 A2
Petworth St CB1 . . . . .84 A2
Peverel CI CB5 . . . . .84 D3
Peverel Rd CB5 . . . . .84 D3
Peveril Rd PE1 . . . . .197 F6
Peyton Ave PE15 . . . . . . .243 B6
Peyton Ct PE15 . . . . .223 A5
Pheasant Gr PE4 . . . . .204 A5
Pheasant Rise CB3 . . . . . .102 A3
Pheasant Way PE7 . . . . . .181 D5
Philip Gdns PE19 . . . . .74 F2
Philippa CI CB6 . . . . .240 E7
Philipps CI CB8 . . . . .110 D4
Phillips Ave SG8 . . . . .5 E7
Phillips Chase 1 PE15 . . . .243 C4
Phillips Ct PE9 . . . . .244 C4
Phillips' Fen Dro CB7 . . . .219 B6

Phoenix Sq PE19 . . . . .74 E6
Phorpres CI PE7 . . . . .186 D3
Phorpres Way PE7 . . . . . . .186 E4
Pickards Way PE13 . . . . . .245 A6
Pickle Fen Dro PE16 . . . . .215 E6
Picknage Rd SG8 . . . . .7 A2
Pidley Hill PE28 . . . . .208 A8
Pidley Sheep La PE7 . . . . .155 D5
Pieces La CB5 . . . . .106 B8
Pieces Terr CB5 . . . . .106 B7
Pierce Cres PE8 . . . . .178 C3
Pierce La CB1 . . . . .66 F5
Pig La PE27 . . . . .144 B5
Pigeons CI SG8 . . . . .31 C2
Pightle CI Harston CB2 . . . .47 D2
  Royston SG8 . . . . .5 C7
Pightle The
  2 Bottisham CB5 . . . . . .86 E6
  Grafham PE28 . . . . .116 A7
  Haverhill CB9 . . . . .24 A8
Pilgrims CI CB10 . . . . .18 D2
Pilgrims Way CB6 . . . . . . .240 A3
Pilton CI 4 PE4 . . . . .204 F2
Pinder CI PE29 . . . . .118 F7
Pine Gr CB4 . . . . .122 E3
Pine Tree CI PE1 . . . . .198 B8
Pine Trees Ave IP28 . . . . .239 E4
Pinewood Ave
  Whittlesey PE7 . . . . .189 E7
  Wittering PE8 . . . . .230 B1
Pinfold La
  Godmanchester PE29 . . . .141 F1
  Stamford PE9 . . . . .244 D5
Pinfold Rd PE14 . . . . .236 E6
Pingle Bank PE7 . . . . .177 A4
Pingle Dro PE6 . . . . .216 E6
Pingle La PE6 . . . . .231 F6
Pinkeneys SG8 . . . . .8 D5
Pinza CI CB8 . . . . .110 E4
Piperell Way CB9 . . . . .24 A5
Pipers CI CB9 . . . . .24 C7
Pipers La PE29 . . . . .141 F1
Pipistrelle Ct 6 PE4 . . . . .204 C3
Pippin CI
  Offord Darcy PE19 . . . . . .117 F1
  Over CB4 . . . . .208 D1
Pippin Dr CB4 . . . . .84 C6
Pippin PI PE13 . . . . .245 E2
Pippin Wlk CB3 . . . . .81 A3
Pitfield CI PE28 . . . . .121 C5
Pits La PE15 . . . . .243 D1
Pits The CB7 . . . . .213 A4
Pitsdean Rd PE19 . . . . . . .57 A4
Pittneys PE4 . . . . .204 F1
Pius Dro PE14 . . . . .236 E2
Place Farm Sch CB9 . . . . . .23 F8
Plains La CB6 . . . . .225 C3
Plaistow Way SG8 . . . . .7 E2
Plane Tree CI SG19 . . . . . .41 C6
Plank Dro PE6 . . . . .232 B8
Plantation Gate CB6 . . . . .210 F5
Plantation Rd CB2 . . . . . . .33 A7
Plantwater Dro PE15 . . . .227 D5
Plash Dro PE13 . . . . .234 F4
Playles Yd SG8 . . . . .12 E5
Plough Cres PE7 . . . . .189 C8
Plough La PE6 . . . . .207 D1
Plover CI PE6 . . . . .241 C5
Plover Dr 2 PE15 . . . . . . .243 C5
Plover Rd PE7 . . . . .189 F8
Ploverly PE4 . . . . .204 C4
Plowright CI 5 PE15 . . . . .243 B3
Plum Tree CI 3 CB4 . . . . .83 D7
Plumian Way CB1 . . . . . . .53 C2
Plumpton Ave 2 PE28 . . . .239 C5
Polecat La PE28 . . . . .150 C5
Poles Ct PE7 . . . . .189 D7
Police HQ
  Cambridge CB1 . . . . .246 C2
  Peterborough PE3 . . . . . .196 F1
Pollards La IP28 . . . . .213 D7
Pond CI
  Pidley cum Fenton PE28 . .165 D1
  The Stukeleys PE29 . . . . .140 F5
Pond Gn CB7 . . . . .211 E1
Pond La 2 CB6 . . . . .218 A6
Pond The CB6 . . . . .210 A7
Pont's Hill CB6 . . . . .242 D5
Pooley Way PE7 . . . . .181 D6
Pools Rd CB6 . . . . .210 D8
Poorsfield Rd 2 CB5 . . . . .106 A7
Pope Rd PE19 . . . . .74 E4
Pope Way PE1 . . . . .197 E8
Pope's La PE13 . . . . .238 C2
Popes Ct 3 CB9 . . . . .24 E5
Popes La Thetford CB6 . . . .211 B7
  Warboys PE28 . . . . .164 C4
Popham CI PE19 . . . . .74 A3
Poplar Ave PE1 . . . . .198 C8
Poplar CI
  Great Gransden SG19 . . . .58 D4
  Great Shelford CB2 . . . . . .49 A5
  Haverhill CB9 . . . . .38 D1
  Huntingdon PE29 . . . . . . .141 D5
  March PE15 . . . . .243 C6
  Royston SG8 . . . . .5 E7
Poplar Dr SG8 . . . . .5 E7
Poplar Dro CB6 . . . . .242 D4
Poplar Farm CI SG8 . . . . . .12 D4
Poplar Rd CB4 . . . . .104 B3
Poplar Way CB2 . . . . .49 C4
Poplars CI CB5 . . . . .130 B2
Poplars The PE28 . . . . . . .208 C6
Popple Dro PE13 . . . . .235 A8
Poppy Fields 7 CB7 . . . . .212 B5

Poppyfields Ave PE15 ...224 B4
Porch Cl PE29 ....141 F1
Porson Rd CB2 ....64 D5
Port La PE5 ....195 E1
Portchester Cl PE2 ...187 F5
Porters Yd PE16 ....241 C4
Portland Ave PE1 .....197 F7
Portland Pl
  Cambridge CB1 ....246 C3
  Whittlesey PE7 ....189 E6
Portland Rd CB8 ....110 E3
Portman Cl PE3 ....197 C4
Portobello La CB2 ......32 E7
Portugal Pl CB2 ....246 A3
Portugal St CB5 ....246 A3
Portway SG8 ....14 E7
Portway Rd CB3 ....81 A1
Post Office La 10 PE13 .245 C6
Post Office Terr CB1 ..246 B2
Post St PE29 ....141 E2
Pott Hall Rd IP28 ......213 E6
Potter's La CB7 ....240 D3
Potters Way PE1 ....198 B1
Potton End PE19 ....77 E3
Potton Rd Everton SG19 ..40 D2
  Fenstanton PE28 ....120 C3
  Gamlingay SG19 ......40 F3
  Gamlingay SG19 ......41 D3
  Guilden Morden SG8 ....10 E5
  Hilton PE28 ....99 B8
  St Neots PE19 ....74 F2
  Wrestlingworth SG19 ...25 B4
Potton Wood (National
  Trust)* SG19 ....25 A8
Poulter Ave PE2 ....187 D5
Poulter's Dro PE14 .....229 D5
Pound Cl Bottisham CB5 .86 E7
  Burwell CB5 ....130 B2
  Hail Weston PE19 .....95 B1
  Spaldwick PE28 ....137 F6
Pound Gn SG8 ....10 F5
Pound Hill CB3 ....83 C3
Pound La Isleham CB7 ...213 A5
  Kimbolton PE28 ....113 F4
  Sutton CB6 ....216 E2
Pound Rd Chatteris PE16 .241 B6
  Hemingford Grey PE28 ..143 D1
  Ramsey PE26 ....172 A4
Pound The PE27 ....144 A5
Pound Way CB5 ....108 B2
Powell Cl CB3 ....61 D5
Powis Pl 3 PE19 ....74 F1
Pratt Ave PE4 ....204 F2
Pratt St CB7 ....212 B4
Prentice Cl CB4 ....123 F2
Presses Cl 7 PE28 .....208 C5
Preston Cl CB3 ....61 D5
Pretoria Rd CB4 ....246 C4
Priam's Way CB2 ....49 B4
Prickwillow Rd Ely CB7 .240 F5
  Isleham CB7 ....212 F7
  Soham CB7 ....219 D3
Priest La CB4 ....209 A1
Priestgate 4 PE1 .....198 A2
Priests Meadow Ct CB6 240 C5
Primary Ct CB4 ....84 B5
Prime Cl SG8 ....14 C6
Primrose Cl
  Cambridge CB1 ....66 A5
  Peterborough PE1 .....198 A8
Primrose Dr PE7 ....181 F7
Primrose Farm Rd CB1 ..86 E2
Primrose Hill
  Doddington PE15 .....222 E5
  Haverhill CB9 ....23 F7
  Little Gransden SG19 ...58 E3
Primrose La
  Huntingdon PE29 .....141 E5
  Soham 5 CB7 ....212 B5
  Waterbeach CB5 ....106 A8
Primrose St CB4 ....83 D4
Primrose View 3 SG8 ...5 F5
Prince Andrew's Cl 1
  SG8 ....5 D5
Prince Cl PE19 ....74 B5
Prince of Wales Cl
  PE13 ....245 D8
Prince St PE13 ....245 D5
Prince William St 6 CB4 83 C4
Prince William Way CB2 .32 F6
Prince's St
  Huntingdon PE29 .....141 D4
  Peterborough PE1 .....198 A4
  Ramsey PE26 ....172 A8
Princes Cl CB1 ....53 C1
Princes Dr PE19 ....75 A6
Princes Gate PE1 .....198 B4
Princes Gdns PE1 .....198 B4
Princes Mews SG8 ....5 C6
Princes Rd
  Peterborough PE2 .....187 A7
  Stamford PE9 ....244 B6
  Wisbech PE13 ....245 C4
Princess Dr CB2 ....49 F1
Princess of Wales Hospl
  CB6 ....240 E7
Princess Way
  Haverhill CB9 ....23 E8
  Newmarket CB8 ....110 E4
Pringle Cl PE7 ....189 C7
Pringle Ct PE28 ....151 D4
Pringle Way PE28 .....151 D4
Prins Ave PE13 ....245 D7
Prins Ct 3 PE13 ....245 D7
Prior's Cl CB4 ....104 B4

Prior's Ct 8 CB6 ....216 E2
Priors Gate PE4 ....204 A4
Priors Rd
  Hemingford Grey PE28 ..143 C1
  Whittlesey PE7 ....189 C7
Priory Ave Haverhill CB9 .23 F7
  Swavesey CB4 ....122 E5
Priory Cl Burwell CB5 ..130 B2
  Ickleton CB10 ....18 A3
  7 Market Deeping PE6 ..231 F8
  Royston SG8 ....5 E6
Priory Dro CB5 ....129 D7
Priory Gdns
  Peterborough PE7 .....184 F3
  Stamford PE9 ....244 D5
Priory Gr PE29 ....141 E5
Priory Hill PE19 ....75 B7
Priory Hill Rd PE19 ....75 A7
Priory Jun & Inf Sch CB5 84 D2
Priory Jun Sch PE19 ...75 A6
Priory La
  Huntingdon PE29 .....141 E5
  Royston SG8 ....5 D5
  St Neots PE19 ....74 E5
Priory Mews PE19 ....74 E6
Priory Park Inf Sch PE19 74 F6
Priory Rd Cambridge CB5 .84 A3
  Holywell-cum-Needingworth
  PE27 ....208 A3
  Horningsea CB5 ....106 A1
  Huntingdon PE29 .....141 E6
  Needingworth PE27 ....144 F5
  Peterborough PE3 .....197 E3
  St Ives PE27 ....144 A2
  St Neots PE19 ....74 E6
  Stamford PE9 ....244 D5
Priory St 3 CB4 ....83 C4
Priory The PE19 ....74 E5
Proby Cl PE7 ....181 D5
Prospect Pl PE13 .....245 C4
Prospect Rd PE15 .....243 B5
Prospect Row
  Cambridge CB1 ....246 C2
  9 St Neots PE19 ....74 F5
Prospect Way PE16 .....241 C6
Prospero Cl PE2 ....186 F6
Prospero Way PE29 ...141 A6
Provence Pl 2 PE13 ...245 E3
Provence Rd PE29 .....141 A6
Providence Ct 16 PE28 .215 C1
Providence Pl 6 PE15 ..224 B4
Providence Way CB5 ...127 A1
Pryor Cl CB4 ....105 D2
Pudding Bag La PE9 ...230 C4
Pudding La SG8 ....7 A1
Puddock Hill PE28 ....165 A8
Puddock Rd
  Ramsey PE28 ....221 F1
  Warboys PE28 ....165 A8
Pudgell The SG8 ....7 E2
Pump La 2 Hardwick CB3 .81 A3
  4 Stretham CB6 ....210 F5
Purbeck Rd CB2 ....65 A5
Purl's Bridge Dro PE15 .224 B3
Putney Hill Rd CB7 ....219 B4
Pyecroft PE1 ....198 B6
Pyhill PE3 ....197 B8
Pymore (Pymoor) La
  CB6 ....224 E1
Pyrethrum Way 2 CB4 ..209 A1

Q

Quadrangle The PE28 ..208 D7
Quadrant The
  4 Royston SG8 ....5 C8
  St Ives PE27 ....144 B3
Quainton Cl CB5 ....84 D3
Quaker Cl PE28 ....153 C6
Quaker La PE13 ....245 B3
Quaker Way PE16 .....241 C5
Quaker's Dro PE7 .....191 F5
Quaker's La CB9 ....24 A7
Quakers' Rd IP28 .....239 F5
Quanea Dro CB7 ....240 F1
Quarry La Haslingfield CB3 47 B4
  Maxey PE6 ....231 C6
  Swaffham Bulbeck CB5 ..108 B1
Quay Hill 1 CB6 ....242 E4
Quay The PE27 ....144 A3
Quayside CB7 ....240 A4
Queen Adelaide Way
  CB7 ....240 E3
Queen Edith Cty Prim Sch
  CB1 ....65 C4
Queen Edith's Way CB1 .65 D4
Queen Eleanor Cl PE7 .176 A8
Queen Eleanor Sch PE7 244 B6
Queen Elizabeth Dr
  PE13 ....245 D3
Queen Emma Wlk 2
  CB6 ....240 E6
Queen Mary Cl PE26 ..172 A6
Queen St Cowlinge CB8 .73 C1
  Haverhill CB9 ....24 A8
  Newmarket CB8 ....111 B3
  2 Peterborough PE1 ..198 A2
  Whittlesey PE7 ....189 D7
  Wisbech PE13 ....245 C6
  Yaxley PE7 ....181 F6
Queen Street Cl PE15 .243 C6
Queenholme Way CB4 ..209 C2
Queen's Cl Holme PE7 ..176 F4
  1 Over CB4 ....208 D1
Queen's Dr
  Mildenhall IP28 ....239 B4
  Wisbech PE14 ....236 A3

Queen's Dr W PE1 .....198 A5
Queen's Gdns PE1 .....198 A5
Queen's Mdw CB1 ....65 F7
Queen's Rd CB3 ....64 C8
Queen's Wlk PE9 .....244 A5
Queens Cl Balsham CB1 ..52 F2
  Harston CB2 ....48 A3
  St Ives PE27 ....144 A5
Queens Coll CB3 ....246 A2
Queens Ct PE19 ....74 B3
Queens Dr PE27 ....141 F5
Queens Gdns PE19 .....74 B4
Queens' La CB2 ....246 A2
Queens Rd Littleport CB6 242 E5
  Peterborough PE2 .....187 B7
  Royston SG8 ....5 D7
  Somersham PE28 ....215 C1
  Wisbech PE13 ....245 C4
Queens Sch PE13 .....245 D5
Queens St March PE15 .243 D6
  Stamford PE9 ....244 B6
  Withersfield CB9 ....38 C4
Queens View 110 A8
Queens Way CB4 ....103 D6
Queens Wlk PE6 ....186 F8
Queensberry Rd CB8 ...111 A3
Queensgate Ctr PE1 ...198 A2
Queensway
  Cambridge CB2 ....64 E6
  Chatteris PE16 ....241 D5
  Exning CB8 ....110 B8
  Haverhill CB9 ....23 E8
  Mildenhall IP28 ....239 B4
  Royston SG8 ....5 D7
  St Neots PE19 ....74 F7
  Sawston CB2 ....32 F4
  Soham CB7 ....212 B4
Quickset Rd CB11 ....9 B5
Quince Rd CB3 ....81 A3
Quinion Cl PE7 ....189 F6
Quorn Cl PE6 ....205 C8
Quy Rd CB5 ....86 B8

R

Rachel Cl 1 CB5 ....84 E4
Rackham Cl CB4 ....83 C4
Radcliffe Cl 1 PE9 ....244 B5
Radcliffe Rd 2 PE9 ....244 A5
Radegund Rd CB1 ....65 B7
Radegunds CB2 ....32 C5
Radford Cl 3 PE8 .....230 C1
Radwinter Rd CB10 .....21 B1
RAF Molesworth PE28 ..147 C8
RAF Wyton PE28 ....143 A8
Railway La PE16 ....241 C5
Railway Rd PE13 .....245 C3
Railway St CB1 ....65 F7
Railworld Mus* PE2 ...197 F1
Raine Ave CB9 ....23 D8
Raleigh Cl 3 PE19 ....74 A2
Raleigh Way PE3 .....197 B6
Ramnoth Rd PE13 .....245 D4
Ramnoth Road Prim Sch
  PE13 ....245 D4
Rampart The CB6 ....210 A6
Ramper Rd CB4 ....123 A3
Rampley La PE19 ....95 F2
Rampleys The PE28 ...143 D2
Ramply Cl PE19 ....95 F1
Rampton Drift CB4 .....124 B2
Rampton End CB4 .....209 A1
Rampton Rd
  Cottenham CB4 ....125 B4
  Longstanton CB4 .....124 A2
  Oakington/Longstanton
  CB4 ....123 F1
  Willingham CB4 ....124 B7
Ramsden Sq CB4 ....84 A7
Ramsey Abbey Sch
  PE26 ....172 C7
Ramsey Cty Jun Sch
  PE26 ....172 A7
Ramsey Hollow Dro
  PE26 ....173 B7
Ramsey Rd Benwick PE15 221 F4
  Ely PE28 ....240 E6
  Kings Ripton PE28 ....153 C5
  Old Hurst PE28 ....154 D6
  Ramsey PE26 ....221 C2
  St Ives PE27 ....143 F7
  Upwood & The Raveleys
  PE26 ....171 D2
  Warboys PE28 ....164 E6
  Whittlesey PE7 ....220 E7
Ramsey Rural Mus*
  PE26 ....172 D7
Ramsey Sports Ctr
  PE26 ....172 C7
Ramsey Way PE2 ....187 F6
Ramshill Cotts PE6 ....203 A2
Randalls La CB4 ....208 D1
Rangefield PE2 ....185 E4
Ransome's Cl PE14 ....236 E2
Ransonmoor Dro PE15 .222 D7
Raptor Foundation The*
  PE28 ....155 E4
Rasen Ct 2 PE1 ....198 D3
Ratfords Yd CB1 ....68 A8
Rathmore Cl CB1 ....65 A6
Rathmore Rd CB1 ....65 A6
Raveley Fen Rd PE15 ..162 D8
Raveley Rd PE28 ....161 F6
Raven Cl Mildenhall IP28 .239 D4
  St Neots PE19 ....75 B7

Ravenhill Dr PE15 .....243 C3
Ravens Ct CB6 ....240 C5
Ravenscourt 6 PE27 ...208 A3
Ravensdale PE7 ....175 F7
Ravensthorpe Prim Sch
  PE3 ....197 C2
Ravensworth Gdns CB1 .65 A7
Rawlyn Cl CB5 ....84 D3
Rawlyn Rd CB5 ....84 D3
Rayes La CB8 ....111 A4
Rayleigh Cl CB2 ....64 E5
Raymond St 14 PE13 ..245 C4
Rayner Ave PE2 ....187 E5
Rayner's Cl SG8 ....30 D1
Ray's Dro PE26 ....220 B1
Rayson Way CB5 ....84 D3
Reach Dro PE7 ....189 D5
Reach Rd Burwell CB5 .109 B8
  Reach CB5 ....129 C1
Reaches The PE6 ....232 C3
Read's St CB6 ....210 F5
Recreation Cl CB4 ....105 D1
Recreation Ground Rd
  PE9 ....244 B6
Recreation Rd CB9 .....23 F7
Recreation Way IP28 ..239 C4
Rectors Way 3 PE4 ...204 F2
Rectory Cl
  Brampton PE28 ....140 E2
  Great Paxton PE19 ....96 E4
  Oakington/Longstanton
  CB4 ....123 F1
  Sawtry PE28 ....168 C5
Rectory Farm Rd CB1 ..86 F2
Rectory Fields CB6 ....216 E3
Rectory Gdns
  Glinton PE6 ....203 E8
  Godmanchester PE29 ..141 F2
  Peterborough PE7 .....184 F3
Rectory La Ashdon CB10 .21 A1
  Etton PE6 ....231 E5
  1 Fowlmere SG8 ....15 E8
  Glinton PE6 ....203 E8
  Kingston CB3 ....61 B3
  Peakirk PE6 ....206 B2
  St Ives PE28 ....142 F5
  Somersham PE28 ....215 B1
  Southoe & Midloe PE19 ..95 D6
Rectory Rd
  Bluntisham/Colne PE28 ..208 D5
  Duxford CB2 ....17 D1
  Newton PE13 ....238 B5
  Outwell PE14 ....236 F2
Rectory Way PE7 .....175 F7
Red Barn PE7 ....191 E6
Red Cross La CB2 ....65 B3
Red Dock La CB8 ....73 F1
Red Fen Rd CB6 ....210 F7
Red Hill Cl CB2 ....48 E8
Red Hill La CB2 ....48 E8
Red Lion Cl PE28 .....216 E1
Red Lion Sq 5 PE9 ....244 B5
Red Well The* CB3 ....100 F2
Redbridge PE4 ....204 A6
Redcaps La CB6 ....217 E6
Redcot Gdns 8 PE9 ....244 B6
Redebourne La PE26 ...171 F4
Redfern Cl CB4 ....83 E6
Redgate Rd Girton CB3 ..82 E8
  Tydd St Giles PE13 ....238 C4
Redhouse Gdns 3 CB7 .212 B3
Redit La CB7 ....211 E1
Redlands Rd CB3 .....101 E5
Redman Cl PE7 ....240 F7
Redmoor Bank PE14 ...235 F4
Redmoor Cl PE27 .....144 B7
Redmoor La PE14 .....235 F5
Redshank Cl Haverhill CB9 24 C7
  Whittlesey PE7 ....201 A1
Redwell Cl PE27 ....143 E5
Redwing Cl PE2 ....187 E7
Redwing 5 Wisbech PE14 .245 D2
Redwing Pl 2 PE19 ...75 B7
Redwongs Way PE29 ..141 F4
Reed Cl Cambridge CB2 ..64 E1
  Chatteris PE16 ....241 C3
Reedmace Cl PE6 .....205 C8
Reeds La CB9 ....24 A8
Reepham PE2 ....185 D4
Rees Thomas Sch CB4 ..83 F6
Reeves Pightle SG8 .....7 F3
Reeves Way PE1 .....198 D5
Regal Dr CB7 ....212 C3
Regal La CB7 ....212 C3
Regal Rd PE13 ....245 B2
Regatta Cl CB5 ....84 B4
Regency Way PE3 .....197 E1
Regent Ave PE15 .....243 D5
Regent Cl PE19 ....74 B4
Regent Pl 1 CB7 .....212 B3
Regent St CB2 ....246 B1
Regent Terr CB2 ....246 B1
Rembrandt Way 3
  PE27 ....144 A7
Renoir Cl 8 PE27 .....144 A7
Resbury Cl CB2 ....50 A1
Retreat The 8 PE6 ....231 C7
Reubens Rd CB4 ....105 C7
Reynold's Cl CB9 ....38 D1
Reynolds Cl 4 PE27 ..144 A7
Reynolds Cl 6 PE19 ...74 D6
Reynolds Pl PE19 ....95 F1
Reynolds' Dro CB4 ....124 D3
Rhee Lake Dro PE28 ...208 E8
Rhees The PE28 ....208 D6

Rhone Pl 3 PE13 .....245 E3
Rhugarve Gdns 6 CB1 ..35 D2
Rhymers Gate PE28 ...142 F5
Ribble Cl PE27 ....144 B6
Ribston Way CB4 ....84 C6
Richard Young Cl 2
  PE13 ....245 C8
Richards Cl PE15 .....243 B5
Richardson Way PE7 ..189 E7
Richmond Ave
  March CB1 ....243 C3
  Peterborough PE4 .....204 C2
Richmond Cl
  Huntingdon PE29 .....141 E8
  7 St Neots PE19 ....74 F1
Richmond Ct PE13 .....245 A4
Richmond Rd CB4 ....83 B4
Richmond Way 6 PE13 .238 B2
Rickard Cl CB1 ....65 E6
Rickwood Cl CB6 ....216 C5
Rickyard The SG7 ....2 D3
Riddiford Cres PE28 ..140 C2
Riddy Cl CB2 ....48 B5
Riddy La CB3 ....60 C5
Rideaway PE28 ....119 F8
Ridge Way PE2 ....187 B8
Ridgeway
  Papworth Everard CB3 ..99 A4
  Perry PE28 ....115 D2
  St Neots PE19 ....74 F2
Ridgeway The CB1 .....35 E2
Ridley Hall Rd CB3 ....64 C8
Rigg Cl 2 PE13 ....245 B3
Rightwell E PE3 ....197 A5
Rightwell W PE3 ....197 A5
Ringers La PE13 ....238 B2
Ringstead Rd PE4 .....204 F1
Ringwood PE3 ....196 F3
Ringwood Cl 4 PE26 ..172 A4
Ripon Cl PE4 ....204 B3
Rippons Dro PE6 ....231 F7
Risby PE3 ....197 B8
Riseholme PE2 ....185 E3
Rivar Pl CB1 ....84 A1
Rivendale PE4 ....204 B2
River Cl Little Paxton PE19 .95 F1
  Mepal CB6 ....216 E4
River Dr PE15 ....243 E4
River Dro PE7 ....191 C5
River La Brampton PE28 .140 E1
  Cambridge CB5 ....84 A3
  Elton PE8 ....178 C8
  Fordham CB7 ....212 E1
  Great Paxton PE19 ....96 D3
  Haslingfield CB3 ....47 C5
  Peterborough PE3 .....197 F2
River Mdw PE7 ....142 F3
River Rd Eaton Socon PE19 74 C4
  Kimbolton PE28 ....114 B7
  West Walton PE14 ....238 D4
River Terr
  3 St Neots PE19 ....74 E5
  Wisbech PE13 ....245 A8
Riverbank Cl 12 PE6 ..231 F8
Rivergate 3 PE1 .....198 A1
Rivergate Sh Ctr PE1 ..198 A1
Riverside
  2 Benwick PE15 ....222 A5
  Cambridge CB5 ....84 B3
  11 Market Deeping PE6 .231 F8
Riverside Cl Ely CB7 ..219 B5
  Mildenhall IP28 ....239 B4
  Whittlesey PE7 ....189 D6
Riverside Gdns
  Parson Drove PE13 ....234 C7
  Peterborough PE3 .....197 D1
Riverside Mead PE2 ...187 B8
Riverside Mid Sch IP28 239 A4
Riverside Park* PE29 .141 E4
Riverside Rd PE29 .....141 E4
Riverside Spinney PE19 .194 A3
Riverside Way 1 PE13 .245 B3
Riverside Wlk CB7 ....240 E3
Riversmead PE19 ....74 E6
Rivey Cl CB1 ....35 D3
Rivey Way CB1 ....35 D2
Roan Wlk 8 SG8 ....5 E6
Robbs Wlk PE27 ....144 B8
Robert Arkenstall Prim Sch
  CB6 ....210 A6
Robert Ave
  Peterborough PE1 .....197 F8
  4 Somersham PE28 ...215 C1
Robert Jennings Cl 2 CB4 84 A6
Robert May Cl CB1 .....65 D7
Robert Rayner Cl PE2 .186 D6
Robin Cl Bar Hill CB3 ..102 C4
  Haverhill CB9 ....24 C7
  Mildenhall IP28 ....239 D4
Robin Goodfellow's La
  PE15 ....243 D5
Robin Hood Cl PE3 ....196 F3
Robin Mews 4 PE14 ...245 D2
Robingoodfellow's La
  PE15 ....243 C6
Robins Cl 5 Ely CB6 ..240 B5
  8 Isleham CB7 ....213 A5
  Peterborough PE28 ...186 E8
Robins Field PE8 .....194 A4
Robins' La CB3 ....101 F5
Robins Wood PE28 ....194 A4
Robinson Coll CB3 .....83 B1
Robinson Way CB2 .....65 A3
Robshaw Cl 4 PE15 ...243 E4
Rocester Way SG8 ....5 D8
Rochford Wlk 5 PE13 .245 C6
Rochfort Ave CB8 .....110 E5
Rock Rd Cambridge CB1 .65 A6

Rock Rd continued
Peterborough PE1 . . . . . . .197 F6
Royston SG8 . . . . .5 C8
Stamford PE9 . . . . .244 B5
Rockall Cl CB9 . . . . .24 D7
Rockingham Gr PE4 . . . .204 C2
Rockingham Rd PE28 . . .168 B3
Rockmill End CB4 . . . . .209 A1
Rodham Rd PE15 . . . . . .228 F5
Rodings The CB5 . . . . . . .84 E4
Rodney Rd PE29 . . . . . .142 A6
Roe Gn PE19 . . . . .74 B5
Roedeer Cl CB1 . . . . .66 A7
Roe's Cl CB2 . . . . .32 F8
Roger's Cl CB3 . . . . .100 B4
Rogers Rd CB5 . . . . .108 E6
Rogues La CB3 . . . . .99 D5
Roland Cl CB4 . . . . .83 E5
Rollys La SG7 . . . . .2 D4
Roman Bank
Newton PE13 . . . . .238 B4
Stamford PE9 . . . . .244 A4
Roman Cl Burwell CB5 . . .130 A2
Whittlesey PE7 . . . . . . .189 F8
Roman Dr PE8 . . . . .194 D2
Roman Hill CB3 . . . . .63 C4
Roman Way Haverhill CB9 .24 D7
March PE15 . . . . .243 E6
Perry PE28 . . . . .115 D2
Stilton PE7 . . . . .176 A8
Roman Way Fst Sch SG8 . .5 D8
Romany Gdns PE2 . . . . .187 D5
Romney Cl PE27 . . . . . . .144 A7
Romney Ct 2 PE19 . . . . .74 C5
Romsey Jun Sch CB1 . . . .65 B8
Romsey Rd CB1 . . . . .65 C8
Romsey Terr CB1 . . . . . . .65 B7
Ronaldsway 5 PE15 . . . .222 F1
Rook Gr CB4 . . . . .209 A1
Rookery Cl
Great Chesterford CB10 . .18 D3
St Ives PE27 . . . . .144 C4
Waterbeach CB5 . . . . . .106 A8
Rookery Pl PE28 . . . . . .121 C5
Rookery The Balsham CB1 53 A2
Little Paxton PE19 . . . . . .95 F2
Peterborough PE2 . . . . .185 C7
Yaxley PE7 . . . . .181 D5
Rookery Way PE28 . . . . .121 B5
Rooks St CB4 . . . . .125 E4
Rookswood Rd 4 PE15 .243 C4
Rookwood Way CB9 . . . . .24 A6
Roscrea Terr PE29 . . . . .141 D4
Rose & Crown Rd CB4 . . .122 C3
Rose Ave PE2 . . . . .187 C7
Rose Cres CB2 . . . . .246 A3
Rose Croft PE28 . . . . . . .115 E2
Rose Ct 8 PE19 . . . . .74 C4
Rose Green La 10 IP28 . .213 F8
Rose Hill CB9 . . . . .38 D5
Rose La 4 Elm PE14 . . . .236 A5
Great Chesterford CB10 . .18 E2
Melbourn SG8 . . . . .14 C6
Rose Wlk Royston SG8 . . . .5 C7
1 Wisbech PE13 . . . . . .245 A6
Rosebay Gdns 6 CB7 . . .212 B5
Roseberry Rd 4 PE14 . . .236 B5
Rosebery Way CB8 . . . . .110 C5
Rosedene Dr PE15 . . . . .243 D3
Rosefinch Cl CB9 . . . . . . .24 C7
Roseford Rd CB4 . . . . . . .83 D6
Roselea CB4 . . . . .104 C3
Rosemary Cl 7 IP28 . . . .214 A1
Rosemary Gdns PE1 . . . .197 F8
Rosemary Greene Cl CB3 78 E2
Rosemary La
Cambridge CB1 . . . . .65 C1
Sutton CB6 . . . . .216 C1
Rosemary Rd CB5 . . . . . .106 B7
Rose's Cl PE15 . . . . .243 D2
Rosie Maternity Hospl
CB2 . . . . .65 A3
Ross Cl CB9 . . . . .24 C7
Ross Piers Sports Ctr The
CB7 . . . . .212 B3
Ross St CB1 . . . . .65 B8
Roswell View CB7 . . . . . .240 E5
Rosyth Ave PE2 . . . . .185 D3
Rotherwick Way CB1 . . . .65 C3
Rothleigh Rd 2 CB1 . . . . .65 D5
Rothwell Way PE2 . . . . . .186 C7
Round Church St CB2 . . .246 A3
Round Hills Way PE28 . . .168 A5
Round House Dro PE28 . .222 A1
Roundhills View PE28 . . .167 E8
Roundhouse Cl PE1 . . . . .198 D3
Roundhouse Dr PE28 . . .115 D3
Rous Rd CB8 . . . . .111 B3
Row The CB6 . . . . .216 E1
Rowan Ave
Peterborough PE1 . . . . . .198 C6
Sawston CB2 . . . . .32 F6
Rowan Cl Bottisham CB5 . .86 F6
Huntingdon PE29 . . . . . .141 C5
Wisbech PE13 . . . . .245 F6
Rowans The
2 Doddington/Wimblington
PE15 . . . . .223 A6
Milton CB4 . . . . .105 C1
Rowe Ave PE2 . . . . .186 D7
Rowell Cl CB9 . . . . .39 A2
Rowell Wlk 2 PE26 . . . .172 A4
Rowells The CB4 . . . . . . .125 C3
Rowland Ct PE4 . . . . .204 B6
Rowlands Cl CB2 . . . . .30 C5
Rowley Ct 1 CB9 . . . . . . .24 E5
Rowley Dr CB8 . . . . .110 F4
Rowley Gdns 4 CB5 . . . . .86 E6

Rowley Mile Course
CB8 . . . . .109 E2
Rowley Rd PE19 . . . . .75 B7
Rowlinson Way CB4 . . . . .84 A3
Rows The CB8 . . . . .110 F3
Roxburgh Rd CB4 . . . . . . .83 E7
Royal Anglian Regiment
Mus★ CB2 . . . . .16 F8
Royal Ct 2 PE19 . . . . .74 B4
Royal Oak La PE28 . . . . .143 A2
Royal Pal Cl CB8 . . . . . . .110 D7
Royal Pl PE13 . . . . .245 C4
Royce Rd
Peterborough PE7 . . . . .185 A4
Peterborough PE1 . . . . .198 D3
Royle Cl PE2 . . . . .186 C5
Royse Gr SG8 . . . . .5 D4
Roysia Mid Sch SG8 . . . . .5 D8
Royston & District Hospl
SG8 . . . . .5 D4
Royston Ave
Peterborough PE2 . . . . .186 C6
Spaldwick PE28 . . . . . . .137 F6
Royston La
Comberton CB23 . . . . . . .62 C3
Elmdon CB11 . . . . .9 C6
Royston Mus★ SG8 . . . . .5 C6
Royston Rd Barley SG8 . . . .6 F3
Caxton CB23 . . . . .59 F7
Duxford CB2 . . . . .32 D3
Foxton CB2 . . . . .30 A5
Harston CB2 . . . . .47 D1
Litlington SG8 . . . . .12 B1
Royston Sta SG8 . . . . .5 C7
Royston Swimming Pool
SG8 . . . . .5 D6
Rubens Way PE27 . . . . . .144 A7
Ruddles La PE28 . . . . . . .142 E6
Rudlands Cl 3 CB2 . . . . .213 A5
Rudyard Gr PE4 . . . . .204 E3
Rush Gn CB1 . . . . .66 A6
Rushbrook Cl CB3 . . . . . . .59 F3
Rushington Cl PE27 . . . . .144 B5
Rushmere PE2 . . . . .185 F6
Ruskin Cl 2 CB9 . . . . .38 D1
Russell Ave PE15 . . . . . .243 B6
Russell Cl
Cambridge CB2 . . . . . . .246 C1
7 Thorney PE6 . . . . . .233 A3
Russell Ct CB2 . . . . .64 C7
Russell Hill PE8 . . . . .193 F6
Russell St
Cambridge CB2 . . . . . . .246 C1
Peterborough PE1 . . . . .197 F3
Wisbech PE13 . . . . .245 C6
Russet Cl PE2 . . . . .144 B5
Russet Ct CB4 . . . . .84 C6
Russet Way SG8 . . . . .14 D6
Russet Wlk 3 CB3 . . . . . . .81 A3
Russets The PE14 . . . . . .236 E2
Russett Ave PE27 . . . . . .208 A2
Rustat Rd CB1 . . . . .65 A6
Rustons Rd PE14 . . . . . . .236 F1
Rustons The CB2 . . . . .32 D1
Rusts La PE28 . . . . .150 F4
Rutherford Rd CB2 . . . . . .64 E4
Rutland Cl Cambridge CB4 83 D6
St Ives PE27 . . . . .143 F7
Rutland Gn 2 PE28 . . . . .120 B1
Rutland Rd PE9 . . . . .244 D7
Rutland Terr PE9 . . . . . . .244 A4
Rutland Way PE15 . . . . . .224 B4
Rycroft Ave
3 Deeping St James PE6 .231 F8
St Neots PE19 . . . . .74 B4
Rydal Cl PE29 . . . . .141 B6
Rydal Ct PE4 . . . . .204 E3
Rye Cl 4 PE19 . . . . .74 F1
Ryecroft La SG8 . . . . .15 E8
Ryhall Rd PE9 . . . . .244 D6

S

Sable Cl CB1 . . . . .66 A7
Sackville Cl CB1 . . . . .83 E7
Sackville St CB8 . . . . .111 B4
Sacred Heart RC Prim Sch
PE3 . . . . .197 A5
Sacrewell Farm & Cntry Ctr★
PE8 . . . . .194 C5
Saddlers Cl PE6 . . . . .203 E8
Saddlers Pl SG8 . . . . .5 C7
Sadlers Cl Coton CB3 . . . .82 B2
Hardwick CB23 . . . . .81 A1
Sadlers Way PE28 . . . . . .143 D1
Saffron Cl CB8 . . . . .242 C2
Saffron Piece 3 CB6 . . . .216 E1
Saffron Rd Histon CB4 . . .104 B3
Sawston CB2 . . . . .33 A8
Saffron St SG8 . . . . .5 F5
Sage's La PE4 . . . . .197 C8
Saggers Cl SG8 . . . . .12 D6
Sainfoin Cl PE28 . . . . .33 A8
St Alban's Dr 20 PE6 . . . .232 A1
St Albans CB8 . . . . .111 A6
St Albans RC Sch CB2 . . .246 B1
St Albans Rd CB4 . . . . . . .83 D6
St Andrew's Church★
PE28 . . . . .169 D1
St Andrew's Cl CB22 . . . . .49 C4
St Andrew's Hill CB5 . . . .106 B7
St Andrew's Pk CB4 . . . . .104 B5
St Andrew's Pl PE7 . . . . .189 D6
St Andrew's Rd CB4 . . . . .84 A3

St Andrew's St
CB8 . . . . .109 E2
Mildenhall IP28 . . . . . . .239 C4
St Andrew's Way CB6 . . .240 B6
St Andrews CE Jun Sch
Cambridge CB4 . . . . .84 C6
Soham CB7 . . . . .212 B3
St Andrews Cl 1 CB2 . . .213 A5
St Andrews Hill CB5 . . . .106 B7
St Andrews La 2 PE28 . . .113 F4
St Andrews Rd 4 PE6 . . .231 F7
St Andrews Way
Histon CB4 . . . . .104 A4
Sawtry PE28 . . . . .168 C4
St Annes CE Prim Sch
PE29 . . . . .118 F8
St Ann's La CB2 . . . . .141 F1
St Anns Dr IP28 . . . . .239 B4
St Anselm Pl 1 PE19 . . . . .74 E5
St Audleys La PE27 . . . . .144 A3
St Audrey Cl
Peterborough PE2 . . . . .187 D6
St Ives PE27 . . . . .144 B5
St Audrey's Cl CB4 . . . . .104 A4
St Audrey's Way PE29 . . .141 E7
St Augustine's Wlk PE2 . .186 E8
St Augustines Inf Sch
PE13 . . . . .245 D8
St Augustines Jun Sch
PE2 . . . . .186 F8
St Augustines RC Prim Sch
PE9 . . . . .244 C7
St Augustines Rd PE13 . .245 C5
St Barnabas Ct 3 PE29 . .141 F7
St Barnabas Rd CB1 . . . . .65 A8
St Bede's Cres CB1 . . . . . .65 E6
St Bede's Gdns CB1 . . . . .65 E6
St Bedes Comp Church Sch
CB1 . . . . .65 D6
St Bee's Dr 18 PE6 . . . . .232 A1
St Benedict's Cl PE9 . . . .203 F7
St Benet's Gdns 5 PE6 . .232 A1
St Botolph La 2 PE2 . . . .186 C6
St Botolph's Way
Haverhill CB9 . . . . .23 F8
1 Thorney PE6 . . . . . .233 A2
St Botolphs Prim Sch
PE2 . . . . .186 A6
St Catharine's Coll CB2 . .246 A2
St Catharines H CB2 . . . .82 C7
St Catharines Sq CB4 . . . .83 C7
St Catherine's CB6 . . . . .240 C5
St Catherines Ct IP28 . . .239 D6
St Catherines Prep Sch
CB2 . . . . .64 D7
St Christophers Ave 2
CB4 . . . . .83 C4
St Clement Cl PE14 . . . . .236 F2
St Clement's PE9 . . . . . . .244 A5
St Clements Pas 1 CB4 . .141 E4
St Colettes Prep Sch CB1 64 F7
St David's Sq PE1 . . . . . .198 D1
St David's Way 4 PE28 . .168 C4
St Denis's Church★ SG19 43 B2
St Edmunds Coll CB3 . . . .83 C3
St Edmunds Dr PE14 . . . .236 D5
St Edmunds Fen★ CB7 . .211 E1
St Edwards Pas 4 CB1 . .246 A2
St Ethelwolds Cl CB6 . . .240 B4
St Fabians Cl CB8 . . . . . .110 F5
St Faiths Sch CB2 . . . . . . .64 E6
St Felix CE VC Mid Sch
CB8 . . . . .110 F6
St Felix RC Sch
CB9 . . . . .23 D7
St Felix Rd 1 PE26 . . . . .221 C2
St George Ave PE2 . . . . .187 E6
St George's Rd
3 St Ives PE27 . . . . . .144 A4
14 Wittering PE8 . . . . .230 B1
St George's Sq 5 PE9 . . .244 C5
St Georges Way CB4 . . . .104 E4
St Germain Cl PE29 . . . . .141 D4
St Gilberts Cl SG19 . . . . .244 B5
St Giles Cl PE7 . . . . .176 F4
St Giles Gr 1 PE14 . . . . .236 B5
St Helena Wlk IP28 . . . . .239 C7
St Helens CP Sch PE28 . .208 D6
St Hugh's Rd PE19 . . . . . .117 A4
St Ives Rd Eltisley PE19 . . .77 E6
Hemingford Grey PE28 . .143 D2
Old Hurst PE28 . . . . . . .154 D6
Papworth Everard CB3 . . .98 F2
St Ives PE28 . . . . .143 A5
Somersham PE28 . . . . .208 B8
St Ives TH PE27 . . . . .144 A3
St Ivo Recn Ctr PE27 . . .143 F4
St Ivo Sch PE27 . . . . . . .143 F5
St James Ave PE1 . . . . . .197 F7
St James Cl 3 CB6 . . . . .210 F5
St James Rd PE19 . . . . . . .95 F3
St John Fisher RC GM Sch
PE1 . . . . .198 C4
St John's Chase PE15 . . .243 D5
St John's Cl
Mildenhall IP28 . . . . . . .239 D6
10 Needingworth PE27 . .208 A2
7 Needingworth PE27 . .208 A3
Waterbeach CB5 . . . . . .106 A9
St John's Coll CB2 . . . . . .246 A3
St John's La CB5 . . . . . . .106 A2

St John's Pl
Cambridge CB4 . . . . .83 C3
Wistow PE28 . . . . .163 F7
St John's Rd
Cambridge CB5 . . . . . . .246 A4
Coton CB3 . . . . .82 B2
Ely CB6 . . . . .240 C4
March PE15 . . . . .243 D5
13 Wittering PE8 . . . . .230 B1
St John's St
Beck Row, Holywell Row
& Kenny Hill IP28 . . . .214 A8
Cambridge CB2 . . . . . . .246 A3
Duxford CB2 . . . . .32 D1
Mildenhall IP28 . . . . . . .213 F8
Peterborough PE1 . . . . .198 B2
St Johns Ave CB8 . . . . . .111 A1
St Johns CE Prim Sch
PE29 . . . . .141 E7
St Johns Church Sch CE
Aided PE2 . . . . .185 E3
St Johns Cl PE28 . . . . . . .155 B5
St Johns Coll Sch CB3 . . .83 C2
St Johns La CB3 . . . . .99 B2
St Johns Mews PE27 . . . .96 E4
St Johns Prim Sch PE2 . .187 C7
St Johns Rd PE2 . . . . . . .187 B7
St Johns St PE29 . . . . . . .141 D5
St Johns St CB6 . . . . .240 A4
St Judes Cl PE3 . . . . .197 C4
St Judith's La PE28 . . . . .160 B6
St Kilda Ave CB4 . . . . .84 A7
St Laurence Rd CB2 . . . . .30 C5
St Laurences RC Sch
CB4 . . . . .83 D7
St Lawrence Way 2
PE9 . . . . .230 F4
St Leonard's Rd 2 PE13 238 B2
St Leonard's St 3 PE9 . .244 C5
St Louis RC VA Prim Sch
CB8 . . . . .111 A4
St Lukes C of E Prim Sch
CB4 . . . . .83 C4
St Lukes St CB4 . . . . .246 A4
St Margaret's Rd CB3 . . . .82 F6
St Margaret's Sq CB1 . . . .65 B5
St Margarets Pl 2 PE2 . .186 F6
St Margarets Rd 1 PE2 . .186 F6
St Margarets Way PE29 . .141 C6
St Mark's Ct 1 PE1 . . . . .198 A3
St Marks Ct CB3 . . . . .64 C8
St Marks Rd PE13 . . . . . .237 C3
St Marks St PE1 . . . . .198 A3
St Martin's Cl
Chatteris PE16 . . . . . . .241 D5
Exning CB8 . . . . .110 C7
Stamford PE9 . . . . .244 C4
St Martin's Rd
Chatteris PE16 . . . . . . .241 D4
Newborough PE6 . . . . . .205 B8
Wisbech PE13 . . . . .245 E7
St Martin's St 1 PE9 . . . .197 F5
St Martins Wlk CB7 . . . . .240 D5
St Mary's Earith PE28 . . .208 E6
Gamlingay SG19 . . . . . . .41 E5
St Mary's Ave PE8 . . . . . .230 D7
St Mary's CE Prim Sch
PE19 . . . . .75 A5
St Mary's Cl Bainton PE9 .230 F5
Bluntisham PE28 . . . . . .208 A5
Farcet PE7 . . . . .187 C2
Peterborough PE1 . . . . .198 B4
2 Thorney PE6 . . . . . .233 A2
3 Wisbech St Mary PE13 235 C7
St Mary's Dr March PE15 243 C5
St Mary's Gn PE28 . . . . .164 B6
St Mary's Hill 9 PE9 . . . .244 C5
St Mary's Rd
5 Bluntisham/Colne
PE28 . . . . .208 C5
Ramsey PE26 . . . . .220 E2
Sawston CB2 . . . . .33 A7
Stilton PE7 . . . . .175 F8
West Walton PE14 . . . . .238 E4
St Mary's St Ely CB7 . . . .240 C4
Farcet PE7 . . . . .187 C2
St Neots PE19 . . . . .74 C4
Stamford PE9 . . . . .244 C5
Whittlesey PE7 . . . . . . .189 D6
St Mary's Wlk
1 Everton SG19 . . . . . .40 C3
3 Fowlmere SG8 . . . . .15 E8
St Marys CE Prim Sch
IP28 . . . . .239 C5
St Marys Jun Sch CB7 . . .240 F6
St Mary's Pas 2 CB2 . . . .246 A2
St Marys Pk SG8 . . . . .5 D6
St Marys RC JMI Sch SG8 .5 D7
St Marys Sch CB2 . . . . . . .64 E7
St Mary's St 1 CB1 . . . . .246 A2
St Marys St PE29 . . . . . .141 D4
St Matthew's Ct 5 CB1 . .84 A2
St Matthew's Prim Sch
CB1 . . . . .246 C2
St Matthew's St CB1 . . . . .84 A2
St Michael's Ave PE13 . . .245 C7
St Michael's Gate PE1 . . .198 F7
St Michael's Rd 12 PE8 . .230 B1
St Michaels CB4 . . . . . . .103 A4
St Michaels La
Longstanton CB4 . . . . . .124 A1
Oakington/Longstanton
CB4 . . . . .103 A4
St Neots Rd
Abbotsley PE19 . . . . .57 A7
Comberton CB3 . . . . .81 D3
Coton CB3 . . . . .82 B3

St Neots Rd continued
Eaton Socon PE19 . . . . . .74 C4
Eltisley PE19 . . . . .77 D4
Hardwick CB3 . . . . .80 C3
Knapwell CB23 . . . . .79 D5
Madingley CB3 . . . . .81 D3
St Neots Sta PE19 . . . . . .75 B6
St Olave's Dr 19 PE6 . . . .232 A1
St Paul's Cl
Gorefield PE13 . . . . .237 E2
5 Wisbech PE13 . . . . .245 C4
St Paul's Rd
Cambridge CB1 . . . . . . .246 C1
Peterborough PE1 . . . . .197 F7
St Ives PE27 . . . . .144 C5
St Pauls CE Sch CB2 . . . .246 B1
St Pauls Dr PE16 . . . . . . .241 D6
St Pega's Rd PE6 . . . . . . .204 A8
St Peter's Cath PE1 . . . . .198 A2
St Peter's Dr 10 PE15 . . .223 B7
St Peter's Hill 8 PE9 . . . .244 B5
St Peter's Rd Coton CB3 . .82 B2
Huntingdon PE29 . . . . . .141 D7
March PE15 . . . . .243 D3
4 Wisbech PE13 . . . . .245 C4
St Peter's St
Cambridge CB3 . . . . .83 C3
Caxton CB23 . . . . .59 D8
Duxford CB2 . . . . .17 D8
Stamford PE9 . . . . .244 B4
St Peter's Vale PE9 . . . . .244 B4
St Peter's Way
Ellington PE28 . . . . .139 A4
3 Thorney PE6 . . . . . .233 A2
St Peters Ave CB8 . . . . . .112 F4
St Peters Cl CB8 . . . . . . .112 F5
St Peters Dr PE16 . . . . . .241 D5
St Peters Pl CB7 . . . . . . .212 F1
St Peters Rd
Outwell PE14 . . . . .236 E1
Peterborough PE1 . . . . .198 C4
St Peters Sch
Huntingdon PE29 . . . . . .141 D6
Wisbech PE13 . . . . .245 E6
St Philip's Rd CB1 . . . . . . .65 B8
St Philips CE Prim Sch
CB1 . . . . .84 C1
St Philips Rd
Cambridge CB1 . . . . .65 C8
Newmarket CB8 . . . . . . .110 F4
St Stephen's Dr PE16 . . . .241 C6
St Stephen's Pl 1 CB4 . . . .83 C4
St Thomas PE19 . . . . .77 E4
St Thomas Cl CB3 . . . . . . .62 D6
St Thomas Dr PE15 . . . . .243 C3
St Thomas Moore RC Prim
Sch PE1 . . . . .198 D4
St Thomas' Pl CB7 . . . . . .240 C2
St Thomas's Sq CB1 . . . . .65 D6
St Tibb's Row CB2 . . . . . .246 A2
St Vigor's Rd CB1 . . . . . . .66 F4
St Vincent's Cl CB3 . . . . . .82 C3
St Vincent's Cross★
PE6 . . . . .232 D6
St Wendreda's Dr 3
PE15 . . . . .243 C1
St Wendred's Way CB8 . .110 B7
Salcott Dr PE13 . . . . .245 E5
Salisbury Cl 3 PE27 . . . . .143 F8
Salisbury Rd PE4 . . . . . . .204 B3
Sallowbush Rd PE29 . . . .141 C6
Sallows 2 PE28 . . . . .121 C6
Sallows Rd PE1 . . . . .198 B6
Salmon La CB1 . . . . .246 C3
Salon Way PE29 . . . . . . .141 B7
Saltergate PE1 . . . . .198 C7
Salters Way Sawtry PE28 168 B5
Wisbech PE13 . . . . .245 A4
Saltersgate PE1 . . . . .198 F7
Saltmarsh PE2 . . . . .186 C4
Salts Rd PE14 . . . . .238 D4
Sambar Ct 3 PE19 . . . . . .74 B5
Sames Ct CB4 . . . . .125 C4
Samuel Ward Upper Sch
CB9 . . . . .39 B1
Samworths Cl PE5 . . . . . .195 F2
Sancton Wood Sch CB1 . .246 C1
Sand Acre Cl IP28 . . . . . .239 D5
Sand Bank PE13 . . . . . . .235 A7
Sand Dro CB5 . . . . .127 C6
Sand La CB6 . . . . .209 E4
Sand Rd SG19 . . . . .58 F5
Sand St CB7 . . . . .212 B3
Sandall Rd PE13 . . . . . . .245 C3
Sanderling Cl IP28 . . . . . .239 C4
Sanders Cl PE28 . . . . . . .151 D3
Sandfields Rd PE19 . . . . . .74 F4
Sandford PE3 . . . . .197 B5
Sandown Rd PE13 . . . . . .245 C4
Sandpiper Cl
Haverhill CB9 . . . . .24 B7
Whittlesey PE7 . . . . . . .190 A8
Sandpiper Dr PE2 . . . . . .187 C6
Sandpit Rd PE6 . . . . .233 A3
Sandringham Ave PE13 . .245 D6
Sandringham Cl 3 PE9 . .244 D6
Sandringham Dr 2
PE26 . . . . .221 C2
Sandringham Rd 2
PE4 . . . . .197 C8
Sandwich Cl
Huntingdon PE29 . . . . . .141 E7
St Ives PE27 . . . . .143 F8
Sandwich Rd
Brampton PE28 . . . . . . .140 D1

Sandwich Rd continued
St Neots PE19 ....75 A5
Sandy Dro IP28 ....214 D3
Sandy Gate PE12 ....237 A7
Sandy La Cambridge CB4 ..83 F4
Kimbolton PE28 ....113 C6
Tydd St Giles PE13 ....238 B7
Wisbech PE13 ....245 F4
Sandy Rd Everton SG19 ..40 B2
Lode CB5 ....107 C6
Sandyland PE13 ....245 B5
Sandys Cres CB6 ....242 E3
Sanfoin Cl 5 IP28 .....214 A1
Sapcote Way PE28 .....168 B3
Sapley Pk PE29 ....141 F8
Sapley Rd PE29 ....152 F1
Sapperton PE4 ....204 B6
Sargent's Ct PE9 ......244 A6
Sascombe Vineyard★
CB8 ....72 F3
Saunders Cl PE29 ......141 D6
Saunders Ct CB3 ....79 B3
Savile Way SG8 ....15 E8
Savile's Cl PE19 ....74 D7
Saville Rd PE3 ....197 D5
Savory Rd PE13 ....245 B7
Sawpit La PE28 ....159 A4
Sawston H★ CB2 ....32 F7
Sawston Rd CB2 ....33 D8
Sawston Village Coll CB2 32 E8
Sawtry Com Coll PE28 ..168 C4
Sawtry Rd
Conington PE28 ....167 F8
Sawtry PE28 ....168 A6
Sawtry Sports Ctr PE28 168 B3
Sawtry Way PE28 ......153 E2
Sawtry Way Cotts PE28 143 C6
Saxby Gdns PE1 ....198 C8
Saxon Cl Ely CB6 .....240 C5
Exning CB8 ....110 D8
Godmanchester PE29 ...141 F1
Sawtry PE28 ....168 C3
Saxon Dr CB5 ....130 B1
Saxon Pl PE19 ....74 F4
Saxon Rd
5 Barnack PE9 ....230 D3
Cambridge CB5 ....84 A3
Peterborough PE1 ......198 C4
Whittlesey PE7 ....189 C7
Saxon St CB2 ....246 B1
Saxon Street Rd CB8 ...91 D4
Saxon Way Bar Hill CB3 .102 B2
Melbourn SG8 ....14 C4
3 Waterbeach CB5 ......106 A7
Sayer Ct PE2 ....185 F2
Sayer St PE29 ....141 C5
Sayers Ct 3 PE28 ......208 C5
Scaldgate PE7 ....189 E6
Scales Park★ SG9 ....1 C1
Scalesgate Rd PE12 ....237 C8
Scalford Dr PE2 ....198 C8
Scaltback Mid Sch CB8 .110 B4
Scarfield La 1 PE14 ...236 C6
Scargell's Yd PE15 ....243 D3
Scarlett's La CB1 ......53 C1
Scarsdale Cl CB4 ....84 B6
Scholars Ave PE29 ....141 C4
Schole Rd CB4 ....209 A1
School Cl Cheveley CB8 ..91 C6
Gamlingay SG19 ....41 D5
5 Maxey PE6 ....231 C7
Peterborough PE3 .....197 A5
2 Wisbech St Mary PE13 .235 B7
School Dro PE26 ....171 A6
School Farm Dro PE26 .171 L8
School Hill CB4 ....104 B4
School La Alconbury PE28 150 F5
Barley SG8 ....7 A1
Barton CB3 ....63 B4
Bourn CB3 ....79 B3
Boxworth CB3 ....101 B5
Buckden PE19 ....117 B4
Burwell CB5 ....130 B1
Bythorn & Keyston PE28 .146 D4
Conington CB3 ....121 C1
Coveney CB6 ....217 D5
Downham CB6 ....218 A7
Downham CB6 ....224 D1
Eaton Socon PE19 ....74 C2
Elton PE8 ....178 D8
Fenstanton PE28 ....121 B6
Fulbourn CB1 ....66 F4
Glinton PE6 ....203 E8
Haslingfield CB3 ....47 B5
Haverhill CB9 ....23 D8
4 Histon CB4 ....104 C3
Kings Ripton PE28 .....153 C6
Little Paxton PE19 .....96 A2
Longstanton CB4 ....123 F1
Longstowe CB3 ....60 A3
Manea PE15 ....224 B4
4 Maxey PE6 ....231 C7
Mepal CB6 ....216 E3
Ramsey PE26 ....172 B7
St Neots PE19 ....74 E4
Swavesey CB4 ....122 E6
Thriplow SG8 ....31 B2
Toft CB3 ....61 D4
3 Uffington PE9 ....230 C6
Warmington PE8 ....178 B3
Waterbeach CB5 ....127 B8
Wilburton CB6 ....210 C5
1 Wisbech PE13 ......245 C5
School Rd
5 Barnack PE9 ....230 D4

School Rd continued
Broughton PE28 ....153 F8
3 Earith PE28 ....208 E6
Great Wratting CB9 .....39 E5
Newborough PE6 ....205 D8
Outwell PE14 ....229 D8
Warboys PE28 ....164 F5
West Walton PE14 .....238 E4
Woodditton CB8 ....91 A3
School St CB10 ....18 D2
Scolding Dro PE6 ......233 E5
Scorney 3 PE28 ....121 C6
Scotenoon PE2 ....185 E3
Scotgate PE9 ....244 A5
Scotland Cl CB4 ....84 B5
Scotland End CB7 .....213 C1
Scotland Rd
Cambridge CB4 ....84 A5
Dry Drayton CB3 ....81 A6
Scotney St PE1 ....197 E7
Scotney Way PE28 .....168 C3
Scotred Cl CB5 ....109 B8
Scotsdowne Rd CB2 ....64 D3
Scott Ave IP28 ....239 C5
Scott Cl
Peterborough PE2 .....187 E6
4 Royston SG8 ....13 D1
Scott Polar Research Inst
CB2 ....246 B1
Scott's Rd PE14 ....229 C2
Scotts Cl PE28 ....120 B1
Scotts Cres PE28 .....120 B1
Scotts Gdns CB2 ....32 C5
Scotts Rd PE6 ....203 F8
Scotts Yd 7 CB3 ....47 B5
Scrolans PE27 ....143 E6
Seabank Rd PE13 ......245 F6
Seadyke Bank PE13 ....235 A7
Seafield Rd 7 PE13 ...238 B2
Sealey's La PE13 ......234 D8
Sealodes Rd CB7 ......211 E5
Seargeants Cl PE6 ....207 C1
Searjeant St PE1 .....197 E5
Searle St CB4 ....83 D4
Searles Ct PE7 ....189 D8
Searles Mdw CB3 ......102 B1
Sears Cl PE29 ....118 F8
Seathwaite PE29 ......141 B6
Seaton Cl PE7 ....181 D6
Sebrights Way PE3 ....196 F3
Second Ave
Warboys PE28 ....164 E6
Wisbech PE13 ....245 D4
Second Broadpool Dro
PE28 ....165 F8
Second Drift PE9 .....244 B2
Second Dro
Downham CB6 ....218 A8
Ely CB7 ....218 F5
Peterborough PE1 .....198 D1
St Ives PE27 ....144 C2
Second Marsh Rd PE14 238 C4
Sedge Fen Rd PE38 ....226 E7
Sedge Way CB6 ....217 D2
Sedgwick Mus of Earth
Sciences★ CB2 ....246 B2
Sedgwick Cl CB1 ....65 B8
Sedley Inf Sch CB1 ....65 C7
Sedley Taylor Rd CB2 ..64 F4
Sefton Ave PE13 ......245 E6
Sefton Cl CB2 ....64 D3
Sefton Way CB8 ....110 D5
Selby Ct 2 PE29 ......141 F7
Sellers Grange PE2 ...186 B4
Selsingen Way CB2 .....32 F7
Selwyn Cl
Great Shelford CB2 .....49 A5
Mildenhall IP28 ......239 D6
Newmarket CB8 ....111 A1
Selwyn Coll CB3 ....64 B8
Selwyn Gdns CB3 ......64 B8
Selwyn Rd Cambridge CB3 .64 B7
Stamford PE9 ....244 A7
Senate House Pas CB2 .246 B2
Senes Calls 9 PE27 ...208 A3
Seppings Cl 2 CB6 ....210 C6
Serby Ave SG8 ....5 C8
Serjeants Cl PE26 ....172 A6
Serpentine The PE7 ...186 D3
Setchel 11 PE19 ....74 C6
Setchel Dro CB4 ......125 F7
Setchell Cl PE19 ......97 F5
Setchfield Pl PE2 .....186 F7
Sevenacres PE2 ....185 E5
Seventh Ave PE13 .....245 E4
Seventh Dro CB6 ......225 A3
Severn Cl PE4 ....204 E1
Severn Pl CB1 ....84 A2
Seymore Dr CB9 ....23 D7
Seymour Cl 2 CB8 ....111 C3
Seymour Pl PE4 ....205 B2
Seymour St CB1 ....65 C8
Seynory Dro PE7 ......177 F7
Shade The CB7 ....212 A5
Shadowbush Cl 2 CB9 ..38 F1
Shady Wlk 2 PE19 .....74 F5
Shaftenhoe End Rd SG8 ..7 A1
Shaftesbury Ave
March PE15 ....243 E5
St Neots PE19 ....74 F6
Shaftesbury Rd CB2 ....64 F6
Shaftesbury Way SG8 ...5 E5
Shakespeare SG8 ....5 D8
Shakespeare Ave PE1 .197 D4
Shakespeare Rd
Eaton Socon PE19 ......74 C3
St Ives PE27 ....143 F6

Shamrock Cl PE2 ......187 C7
Shannon Cl CB7 ....24 D7
Shardlow Cl 1 CB9 .....38 C1
Sharma Leas PE4 ......204 A3
Sharman's Rd CB7 ....212 E1
Sharps La PE28 ....150 F3
Shaw Dr PE15 ....243 C3
Shawley Rd PE28 ......168 A4
Sheep Mkt 6 PE9 ......244 B5
Sheep St PE28 ....148 D3
Sheepfold PE27 ....144 C5
Sheepwalk PE4 ....205 A1
Sheldrick's Rd CB7 ...213 B5
Shelford Park Ave CB2 ..49 A5
Shelford Rd
Cambridge CB2 ....48 E8
Fulbourn CB1 ....66 C3
Harston CB2 ....48 C3
Whittlesford CB2 ......32 A6
Shelford Sta CB2 ......49 B5
Shelford's Rd CB4 ....209 A4
Shelley Cl
Huntingdon PE29 ......141 F6
Royston SG8 ....13 D1
Shelley Pl 5 PE19 .....74 D6
Shelly Row 4 CB3 ......83 C3
Shelton Rd PE7 ....187 D6
Shepherd Cl SG8 ....5 E5
Shepherd's Cl
Cambridge CB1 ....66 A6
Fen Ditton CB5 ....84 F5
Shepherd's Dro CB7 ...226 B2
Shepherds Cl 2 PE4 ..204 C4
Sheppard Way PE28 ....85 B1
Sheppard's Dro PE6 ..232 D8
Sheppersons Gr 2
PE15 ....243 E4
Shepreth Rd
Barrington CB2 ....29 D7
Foxton CB2 ....30 A4
Shepreth SG8 ....30 B3
Shepreth Sta CB8 ......29 E5
Sheralds Croft La CB2 ..31 A2
Sherborne Rd PE1 ....198 D6
Sherbourne Cl CB4 .....84 B6
Sherbrooke Cl PE15 ..243 D1
Sheridan Rd PE1 .....197 F8
Sheriffs Ct CB8 ....70 F3
Sheringham Way PE2 ..186 C6
Sherlock Cl CB3 ....83 B4
Sherlock Rd CB3 ....83 B5
Sherwood Ave
4 Peterborough PE2 ..186 F7
Wisbech PE13 ....245 D7
Shetland Rd CB9 ....24 D8
Shi Tennoji Buddhist High
Sch IP28 ....214 B1
Shillow Hill PE26 .....172 B1
Shingay La CB2 ....32 F7
Ship Gdns IP28 ....239 B3
Ship La CB7 ....240 D3
Shippea Hill Rd IP28 .213 E8
Shirdley Rd PE19 ......74 F4
Shire Gr PE1 ....198 C5
Shires The
1 Bluntisham/Colne
PE28 ....208 C5
March PE15 ....243 E2
Royston SG8 ....5 E6
Shirley Cl CB4 ....105 E2
Shirley CP Sch CB4 ....84 B5
Shirley Gr CB4 ....84 B5
Shirley Rd CB4 ....104 B3
Shores Cl IP28 ....213 C3
Short Cl PE8 ....178 B3
Short Cswy CB6 ....217 C4
Short Dr PE15 ....224 B5
Short Dro Cottenham CB4 125 F2
Downham CB6 ....217 C8
Downham CB6 ....217 F5
Downham CB6 ....224 F3
Earith PE28 ....208 F6
Holme PE7 ....177 A4
Ramsey PE26 ....221 A2
Somersham PE28 ....215 D3
Short La
Bluntisham/Colne PE28 .208 C5
Coveney CB6 ....217 C4
Willingham CB4 ....209 A1
Wisbech PE13 ....238 A1
Short Nightlayer's Dro
PE16 ....241 C6
Short Rd Exning CB8 ..131 F2
Snailwell CB8 ....132 A3
Stretham CB6 ....210 E5
Short St Bourn CB3 ....60 C5
Cambridge CB1 ....246 B3
Shortacres Rd PE2 ...186 F7
Shortfen PE2 ....186 C4
Shortland 6 PE28 ....215 C1
Shortsands Yd 3 PE19 .75 A5
Shrewsbury Ave PE2 ..186 D5
Shrub House Cl IP28 .213 F8
Shrubberies The CB8 ..111 D1
Shrubbery Gr SG8 ......5 D4
Shrubbery The PE16 ..241 D4
Shrublands IP28 .....239 C4
Sibberton Lodge★ PE8 193 E4
Sibson Aerodrome PE8 183 E6
Sidgwick Ave CB3 .....64 C8
Siding Dro PE28 .....215 C5
Sidney Farm Rd CB1 ...65 E6
Sidney Gdns CB3 ......47 B6
Sidney St CB2 ....246 A3
Sidney Sussex Coll CB2 246 B3
Siggin's La CB1 ....20 D6
Silhalls Cl CB8 ....91 F7

Silt Rd Littleport CB6 .242 D5
March PE15 ....243 F4
Upwell PE14 ....229 F5
Silver Birch Ave PE7 ..143 F6
Silver Birch Cl PE29 ..141 E7
Silver Hill PE7 ....186 D3
Silver La PE27 ....208 A3
Silver St Ashwell SG7 ..2 D4
Buckden PE19 ....117 B4
Burwell CB5 ....130 B4
Cambridge CB3 ....246 A1
Ely CB7 ....240 C4
Godmanchester PE29 ..118 E8
Guilden Morden SG8 ...10 E4
Litlington SG8 ....12 A2
March PE15 ....243 C7
Peterborough PE2 ....186 F7
Ramsey PE26 ....172 B7
St Neots PE19 ....74 E4
Willingham CB4 ......209 A1
Wisbech PE13 ....245 C6
Witcham CB6 ....217 A2
Withersfield CB9 ......38 A4
Silverdale Ave CB3 ....82 B2
Silverdale Cl CB3 .....82 A2
Silverley Way CB8 .....91 F7
Silver's La PE13 .....234 E7
Silverweed PE19 ......74 C5
Silverwood Cl CB1 ....84 B2
Silverwood Rd PE1 ...197 F5
Silvester Rd PE5 ....195 E2
Simeon Cl CB6 ....240 F7
Simmer Piece PE28 ...121 C5
Simpkin Cl PE19 ......74 B2
Singerfire Rd PE5 ...195 D2
Sir Harry Smith Com Coll
PE7 ....189 F7
Sir James Black Rd
CB7 ....240 C2
Six Bells 14 PE28 ....215 C1
Six Mile Bottom Rd CB1 .69 A1
Sixteen Foot Bank
Christchurch PE14 ...229 C4
Wimblington PE15 ....223 E5
Sixth Ave PE13 ......245 E4
Skaters Way PE4 .....204 C4
Skeggles Cl PE29 ....141 B8
Skeifs Row 4 PE15 ...222 A5
Skelton Pl PE27 .....144 C5
Skelton's Dro IP28 ..213 F8
Skipper's La
West Wickham CB1 .....37 E5
West Wratting CB1 ....54 E1
Withersfield CB9 ......38 A5
Skiver Cl CB2 ....32 F6
Skylark Pl 9 SG8 ......5 E8
Slade Cl PE26 ....172 A7
Slade The Witcham CB6 .217 A2
Wrestlingworth & Cockayne
Hatley SG19 ....25 B3
Slade Way PE16 ......241 C5
Slatebarn Dro PE7 ...221 C8
Sleaford St CB1 ....84 A1
Sleford Cl CB1 ....53 B2
Sleights Dr 4 PE14 ..238 F1
Slid La CB2 ....29 F8
Slipe Cotts PE28 ....146 A6
Small Lode PE14 .....236 F1
Smallwood PE3 ....197 B5
Smeefield PE28 ....99 B8
Smeeth Rd Emneth PE14 236 E6
Marshland St James PE14 236 F7
Smith Dr PE19 ....117 B3
Smith St CB3 ....100 A4
Smithey Fen Engine Dro
CB4 ....209 E2
Smithfield 2 PE6 ....233 B3
Smith's Dr PE15 .....243 F3
Smith's Dro PE38 ....226 F4
Smith's End La SG8 ....6 F1
Smiths Chase PE15 ...243 B5
Smiths Yd PE19 ....94 A1
Snailwell Rd
Fordham CB8 ....131 F5
Newmarket CB8 ......111 B6
Snailwell Short Rd CB8 .131 E1
Snoots Rd PE7 ....189 B7
Snowberry Way 3 CB7 212 B5
Snowden Cl 1 PE6 ...232 C4
Snowdonia Way PE29 .141 A4
Snowley Pk PE7 ......189 B8
Snowy Way PE7 ......142 B6
Soham Rd Ely CB7 ....211 B8
Fordham CB7 ....212 D2
Soham Village Coll CB7 212 B3
Soke Parkway PE3 ....197 A3
Soke Rd PE6 ....207 B1
Sokemans Way PE28 ..117 D8
Somerby Cl 2 PE9 ...244 B7
Somers Cl CB4 ....83 D7
Somerset Cl CB4 ......83 D7
Somerset Rd Histon CB4 104 A3
Wyton Airfield PE28 ..143 B8
Somersham Rd
Bluntisham PE28 .....155 E2
Colne PE28 ....208 C8
Holywell-cum-Needingworth
PE27 ....144 C7
Somerville PE4 ......204 A5
Somerville Rd 1 PE9 .244 B5
Somes Cl 1 SG8 .....230 C6
Sorrel Cl 4 SG8 ....5 F5
South Brink Elm PE14 .235 B4
Wisbech PE13 ....245 A3
South Cl SG8 ....5 B7
South Dr March PE15 .243 E4
Newmarket CB8 ....110 F4
South End SG8 ....12 E3

South Green Rd CB3 ...64 C7
South La 3 CB3 ....62 C5
South Par PE3 ....197 E3
South Park St PE1 ...241 C4
South Rd Brampton PE28 117 D8
Great Abington CB1 ...33 F4
Histon CB4 ....104 B1
South St Comberton CB3 .62 C4
Great Chesterford CB10 .18 D2
Huntingdon PE29 .....141 F5
Litlington SG8 ....12 A2
Peterborough PE1 ....198 A2
Woodhurst PE28 ......155 A4
South Terr CB2 ....32 F5
South View PE2 ......186 F7
South View Rd PE4 ...197 D8
Southacre Cl CB2 ......64 E6
Southacre Dr CB2 .....64 E6
Southampton Pl PE16 .241 C5
Southbrook Field CB3 ..99 A2
Southbrooke Cl 2 CB2 .64 D3
Southdown Rd PE7 ...181 D5
Southey The 7 CB6 ..216 E1
Southey Wood Forest
Walks★ PE6 ....231 A1
Southey Wood (National
Trust)★ PE9 ....231 A1
Southfield CB10 ....18 A3
Southfields Ave PE2 .187 D5
Southfields Cl 2 CB8 .110 E4
Southfields Dr PE2 ..187 D6
Southgate Ave IP28 ..239 B7
Southgate Way PE2 ..185 C2
Southlands Ave PE1 ..198 A6
Southoe Rd PE7 ......187 D2
Southside Ct CB4 .....84 A5
Southwell Ave PE4 ...204 A4
Southwell Rd PE13 ...245 C8
Sovereign Cl 2 PE13 .245 A6
Sovereign Pl PE3 ....197 C2
Sovereign Way CB4 ...125 E3
Spalding Way CB1 .....65 D3
Spaldings La CB4 ....105 D7
Spaldwick Prim Sch
PE28 ....137 F5
Spaldwick Rd PE28 ..137 C3
Sparkes Cl 2 CB7 ....213 A5
Sparrow Cl PE29 .....141 E5
Sparrow Dr PE28 .....150 E4
Sparrow Way PE28 ...120 B1
Sparrowgate Rd PE14 238 F1
Sparrowhawk Way
PE29 ....142 B7
Sparrows Cl PE28 ...117 B8
Speechley Rd PE7 ...181 F6
Speechley's Dro PE6 .207 F2
Speed La CB7 ....212 B4
Speedwell Cl CB1 .....66 A6
Spencer Ave PE2 ....187 D5
Spencer Cl
3 Eaton Socon PE19 ..74 D6
West Walton PE14 ...238 E4
Spencer Croft 4 CB7 240 E6
Spencer Dr Melbourn SG8 14 D6
St Ives PE27 ....144 A7
Spencer Dro
1 Guyhirn PE13 .....235 A2
Soham CB7 ....212 A4
Spencer Rd CB10 ......18 D3
Spens Ave CB3 ....64 B8
Spenser Cl SG8 ....13 D1
Speyside Ct 1 PE2 ..185 D4
Spiggots Cl CB9 .....123 E2
Spindle Rd CB9 ....38 D1
Spinney Cl
2 Brampton PE28 ...140 D3
Warboys PE28 ....164 F5
Warmington PE8 .....178 B2
Spinney Dr CB2 ....49 A4
Spinney Field PE28 .138 F3
Spinney Fields PE7 ..176 F4
Spinney La PE28 .....150 F5
Spinney Prim Sch CB1 .65 E6
Spinney The Bar Hill CB3 102 B3
Cottenham CB4 ....125 E5
Huntingdon PE29 ....142 B6
Spinney Way 5 PE27 .208 A3
Spires End PE28 .....150 D6
Spitfire Cl PE29 .....141 B8
Spittals Way
Huntingdon PE29 ....141 C7
The Stukeleys PE29 .152 C1
Splash La Castor PE5 ..184 E8
St Ives PE28 ....142 F6
Split Dro CB5 ....129 A4
Spong Dro CB4 ......209 B1
Spooners Cl CB8 ......70 F8
Spratnall PE3 ....196 F4
Spring Cl Burwell CB5 .130 B1
Histon CB4 ....104 C4
Huntingdon PE29 ....141 E6
Spring Dr PE7 ....187 B2
Spring Hill MK44 .....93 A3
Spring La
Bassingbourn SG8 .....12 F3
Bottisham CB5 ....86 F6
Spring Pl PE19 ....95 A1
Springbrook PE19 ....74 F4
Springfield
Huntingdon PE29 ....141 E5
Peterborough PE2 ...187 A7
Somersham PE28 ....215 C1
Springfield Ave PE15 243 C2
Springfield Cl
Buckden PE19 ....117 A3
2 St Neots PE19 .....75 A5
Springfield Rd
Alconbury Weston PE28 .150 D5

Springfield Rd continued
Cambridge CB4 . . . . .83 E4
1 Parson Drove PE13 . . . .234 D7
Peterborough PE1 . . . . . . .197 F5
Sawston CB2 . . . . .32 F5
Yaxley PE7 . . . . .181 F5
Springfield Terr **1** CB4 . . . .83 E4
Springfields PE7 . . . . .190 C7
Springfields Sch PE29 . . . .141 F8
Springhead SG7 . . . . .2 D4
Springhead La PE7 . . . . . . .240 E5
Springhill Rd CB4 . . . . .121 E6
Spruce Dr PE28 . . . . .151 F2
Spurgeon's Cl CB1 . . . . .85 B1
Spurgeons Ave CB5 . . . . . .106 B8
Spurling Cl CB8 . . . . .91 C5
Square The
 6 Barnack PE9 . . . . .230 D4
 Stow cum Quy CB5 . . . . . . .86 A6
Squire's Dr PE14 . . . . .229 F7
Squire's Field The CB1 . . . . .67 F7
Squires Cl **17** PE28 . . . . .215 C1
Squires Ct **5** PE19 . . . . . .74 B4
Squires Gate PE4 . . . . .204 F3
Stackyard The
 Ickleton CB10 . . . . .18 A3
 Peterborough PE2 . . . . . . .185 C5
Stafford Rd PE7 . . . . .189 F6
Staffordshire St CB1 . . . . . .84 A2
Stagsden PE2 . . . . .185 F4
Stagshaw Dr PE2 . . . . .187 B8
Staithe Rd PE13 . . . . .245 E5
Stake Piece Rd SG8 . . . . .5 C5
Stakings The CB2 . . . . .32 D7
Stallebrass Cl **2** PE7 . . . .187 C5
Stamford & Rutland Hospl
 PE9 . . . . .244 D6
Stamford Ave SG8 . . . . .5 D7
Stamford Coll PE9 . . . . . . .244 D6
Stamford Endowed Sch
 PE9 . . . . .244 D6
Stamford High Sch PE9 . . .244 C4
Stamford High Sch Juns
 PE9 . . . . .244 B4
Stamford L Ctr PE9 . . . . . .244 D6
Stamford La PE8 . . . . .178 B3
Stamford Lodge★ PE6 . . . .196 C5
Stamford Lodge Rd
 PE6 . . . . .196 D4
Stamford Mus★ PE9 . . . . .244 C5
Stamford Rd
 Barnack PE9 . . . . .230 C4
 Easton on the Hill PE9 . . . .244 A1
 Helpston PE6 . . . . .231 C1
 Marholm PE6 . . . . .203 B2
 Market Deeping PE6 . . . . .231 D8
 Tallington PE9 . . . . .231 A8
 West Deeping PE6 . . . . . . .231 B8
Stamford St **3** CB8 . . . . .111 B2
Stamford Sta PE9 . . . . . . .244 B4
Stamford Yd SG8 . . . . .5 C6
Stamper St **2** PE3 . . . . . .196 F3
Stan Rowing Ct PE2 . . . . . .187 C7
Stanbury Cl CB5 . . . . .84 E6
Stanch Hill Rd PE28 . . . . . .168 C3
Stanegate **3** PE28 . . . . . .168 C2
Stanesfield Rd CB5 . . . . . . .84 D3
Stanford Bus Pk PE9 . . . . .244 D7
Stanford Wlk **2** PE3 . . . .197 C7
Stanground Coll PE7 . . . . . .187 C5
Stanground Cty Inf Sch
 PE2 . . . . .187 D5
Staniland Way PE4 . . . . . . .204 B5
Stanley Ct CB5 . . . . .84 B3
Stanley Rd Cambridge CB5 . .84 B3
 Great Chesterford CB10 . . . .18 E3
 Newmarket CB8 . . . . .111 C3
 Peterborough PE1 . . . . . . .198 A3
Stanley St **2** PE9 . . . . . .244 C5
Stanpoint Way PE27 . . . . . .144 A5
Stansfield Gdns CB5 . . . . . .66 F5
Stansgate Ave CB2 . . . . . . .65 B3
Stanton Mere Way CB4 . . . .124 A6
Stanton Sq PE7 . . . . .186 D2
Stapledon Rd PE2 . . . . .185 D2
Stapleford Com Prim Sch
 CB2 . . . . .49 C4
Staples La CB7 . . . . .212 B3
Star Cl PE1 . . . . .198 C3
Star La Ramsey PE26 . . . . .172 A8
 Stamford PE9 . . . . .244 C5
Star Mews PE1 . . . . .198 C2
Star Rd PE1 . . . . .198 C2
Starling Cl
 Alconbury PE28 . . . . .150 E4
 2 Milton CB4 . . . . .105 D3
Starlock Cl CB6 . . . . .210 E4
Stathern Rd PE1 . . . . .198 D7
Station App March PE15 . . .243 D6
 Newmarket CB8 . . . . .111 A4
 Somersham PE28 . . . . . . .208 C8
Station Ave CB4 . . . . .234 D5
Station Dr Wisbech PE13 . .245 D4
 Wisbech St Mary PE13 . . . .235 C7
Station Gdns PE26 . . . . . . .172 A8
Station La PE19 . . . . .117 F3
Station Rd
 Abbots Ripton PE28 . . . . .162 B1
 Ailsworth PE5 . . . . .184 C8
 Ashwell SG7 . . . . .3 A3
 Barnack PE9 . . . . .230 E4
 Bluntisham PE28 . . . . .208 C4
 Cambridge CB1 . . . . .64 F7
 Catworth PE28 . . . . .136 D5
 Chatteris PE16 . . . . .241 C4
 Deeping St James PE6 . . . .206 E6
 Dullingham CB8 . . . . .70 D8
 Dullingham CB8 . . . . .89 C2

Station Rd continued
Elm PE14 . . . . .235 C2
Ely CB7 . . . . .240 D3
Fordham CB7 . . . . .131 A8
Foxton CB2 . . . . .30 B6
Fulbourn CB1 . . . . .67 A5
Gamlingay SG19 . . . . .41 E5
Gedney Hill PE12 . . . . .233 F8
Great Shelford CB2 . . . . . . .49 A5
Haddenham CB6 . . . . .210 A6
Harston CB2 . . . . .47 F2
Haverhill CB9 . . . . .24 A8
Histon CB4 . . . . .104 C3
Holme PE7 . . . . .177 A4
Isleham CB7 . . . . .213 A4
Kennett CB8 . . . . .133 F5
Linton CB1 . . . . .35 B2
Littleport CB6 . . . . .242 E4
Lode CB5 . . . . .107 C2
Longstanton CB4 . . . . .123 F4
Manea PE15 . . . . .224 B5
March PE15 . . . . .243 D5
Meldreth SG8 . . . . .14 B6
Mildenhall IP28 . . . . .239 B3
Oakington & Westwick
 CB4 . . . . .103 D7
Over CB4 . . . . .122 F8
Pampisford CB2 . . . . .33 F4
Peterborough PE3 . . . . . . .197 F2
Ramsey PE26 . . . . .172 A7
St Ives PE27 . . . . .144 B3
St Neots PE19 . . . . .75 B5
Shepreth SG8 . . . . .29 C5
Soham CB7 . . . . .212 B4
Stamford PE9 . . . . .244 B4
Stow cum Quy CB5 . . . . . .106 A1
Sutton CB6 . . . . .216 F1
Swaffham Bulbeck CB5 . . .108 A2
Swaffham Prior CB5 . . . . . .108 C5
Swavesey CB4 . . . . .122 E7
Thorney PE6 . . . . .233 A4
Tilbrook PE28 . . . . .113 B7
Walsoken PE14 . . . . .236 E8
Warboys PE28 . . . . .164 F3
Waterbeach CB5 . . . . .106 B7
Whittlesey PE7 . . . . .189 E6
Wilburton CB6 . . . . .210 C7
Willingham CB4 . . . . .124 A7
Wisbech St Mary PE13 . . . .235 C7
Station Rd E CB2 . . . . .32 E3
Station Rd W CB2 . . . . .32 E3
Station St PE16 . . . . .241 B4
Station Yd IP28 . . . . .239 B3
Staughton Pl **2** PE19 . . . .74 C4
Staunch Hill PE28 . . . . .148 C3
Staverton Rd PE4 . . . . .204 A3
Staxton Cl PE6 . . . . .203 C1
Stearne's Yd **4** CB3 . . . . .47 B5
Steeple Morden Sch SG8 **11** B2
Steeple View PE15 . . . . . . .243 C1
Stephen Cl CB9 . . . . .23 F8
Stephens Way **15** PE6 . . .231 F8
Stephenson Cl SG8 . . . . .5 B7
Stephenson Rd PE27 . . . . .144 B6
Stepping Stones PE28 . . . .143 D1
Stepping Stones Sch
 PE4 . . . . .197 D8
Stermyn St **18** PE13 . . . .245 C5
Sterndale Cl CB3 . . . . .82 E8
Sterne Cl CB1 . . . . .65 B6
Sternes Way CB2 . . . . .49 C4
Stetchworth Rd
 Dullingham CB8 . . . . .70 F8
 Stetchworth CB8 . . . . .71 C8
Stevens Cl CB4 . . . . .125 D4
Stevens Way PE15 . . . . . . .243 D6
Stevenson Ct
 Cambridge CB5 . . . . .84 A3
 Eaton Socon PE19 . . . . . . .74 D6
Steward Cl **7** PE28 . . . . .211 D8
Steward's La CB6 . . . . .216 E1
Stewart Cl **2** PE28 . . . . . .140 C2
Steynings The PE4 . . . . . . .204 C3
Stibbington H★ PE8 . . . . . .194 D2
Stickle Cl **5** PE29 . . . . . .141 B7
Stiles The PE29 . . . . .141 F1
Still The Wisbech PE13 . . . .235 E8
 Wisbech PE13 . . . . .238 B1
Stilton CE Sch PE7 . . . . . . .175 F7
Stirling Cl
 Beck Row, Holywell Row
  & Kenny Hill IP28 . . . . . .213 D6
 Cambridge CB4 . . . . .84 A5
 Warboys PE28 . . . . .164 F4
Stirling Dr CB9 . . . . .23 B8
Stirling Gdns CB8 . . . . .110 E4
Stirling Rd PE27 . . . . .144 A7
Stirling Way
 Peterborough PE3 . . . . . . .204 A1
 Witchford CB6 . . . . .217 F1
Stirtloe La PE19 . . . . .117 A2
Stitch The PE14 . . . . .236 B4
Stitchfield Riding Sch
 PE14 . . . . .236 A3
Stocking Fen Rd PE26 . . . .221 A1
Stocking La
 Nuthampstead SG8 . . . . . . .1 A2
 Spaldwick PE28 . . . . .114 D8
Stockley Cl CB9 . . . . .24 C7
Stocks Cl CB5 . . . . .86 E5
Stocks Hill PE5 . . . . .195 F1
Stocks La Gamlingay SG19 . .41 D4
 Orwell SG8 . . . . .45 E1
Stockwell St CB1 . . . . .65 B8
Stokes Cl CB4 . . . . .123 F1
Stokesay Ct **8** PE3 . . . . .197 B1
Stonald Ave PE7 . . . . .189 D8

Stonald Rd PE7 . . . . .189 C8
Stone Field CB3 . . . . .102 A3
Stone La Meldreth SG8 . . . . .29 C3
 Peterborough PE1 . . . . . . .197 F5
Stone St CB1 . . . . .84 B1
Stonea Camp★ PE15 . . . . .223 E8
Stonebridge La CB1 . . . . . . .67 A4
Stonebridge Lea PE2 . . . . .186 C5
Stonecross Way PE15 . . . .243 D3
Stonehill PE28 . . . . .141 C7
Stonehill Rd CB2 . . . . .48 E7
Stonehouse Rd
 Upwell PE14 . . . . .236 E1
 Yaxley PE7 . . . . .181 E5
Stonely Rd PE28 . . . . .138 B3
Stoney Cl PE29 . . . . .141 F8
Storbeck Rd **2** PE13 . . . .245 D7
Storers Wlk PE7 . . . . .190 C6
Stores Hill CB8 . . . . .92 E8
Storey's Bar Rd PE6 . . . . . .199 A3
Storey's Way CB3 . . . . .83 B3
Storrington Way PE4 . . . . . .204 C3
Stott Gdns CB4 . . . . .84 A6
Stour PE27 . . . . .144 A6
Stour Valley Rd CB9 . . . . . .24 B7
Stourbridge Gr CB1 . . . . . . .84 C1
Stow Gdns PE13 . . . . .245 E4
Stow La PE13 . . . . .245 E4
Stow Rd Kimbolton PE28 . .113 F5
 Spaldwick PE28 . . . . .137 F6
 Stow cum Quy CB5 . . . . . . .85 F5
 Wisbech PE13 . . . . .245 F5
Stowehill Rd PE4 . . . . .204 F2
Stowgate Rd PE6 . . . . .206 B7
Straight Dro Bury PE26 . . . .172 C7
 Coveney CB6 . . . . .217 C7
 Farcet PE7 . . . . .187 E1
 Sawtry PE28 . . . . .168 D3
 Wistow PE28 . . . . .172 E2
Straight Furlong CB6 . . . . .224 E2
Straight Rd PE15 . . . . .224 B3
Strangeways Rd CB1 . . . . . .65 D4
Stratford Cl CB4 . . . . .83 B5
Stratford Pl **4** PE19 . . . . .74 C3
Strawberry CB1 . . . . .245 A6
Strawberry Fields CB9 . . . . .23 D7
Street The
 Barton Mills IP28 . . . . .239 E2
 Beck Row, Holywell Row
  & Kenny Hill IP28 . . . . . .214 A8
 Dalham CB8 . . . . .92 E8
 Freckenham CB7 . . . . .213 C3
 Great Bradley CB8 . . . . . . .55 F7
 Great Wratting CB9 . . . . . .39 E6
 Kirtling CB8 . . . . .72 D6
 Lidgate CB8 . . . . .73 D8
 Mildenhall IP28 . . . . .213 E8
 Moulton CB8 . . . . .112 F5
 Snailwell CB8 . . . . .132 A4
 Westley Waterless CB8 . . . .70 C5
 Woodditton CB8 . . . . .91 B2
 Worlington IP28 . . . . .213 F4
Streetly End CB1 . . . . .37 B5
Stretham Old Engine★
 CB6 . . . . .210 F4
Stretham Rd Wicken CB7 . .211 D2
 Wilburton CB6 . . . . .210 D5
Stretten Ave CB4 . . . . .83 D4
Stretton Ave CB1 . . . . .111 B4
Stricklands Dr **5** PE6 . . .232 B8
Strollers Way CB4 . . . . .90 A2
Stroud Hill PE28 . . . . .165 E2
Stuart Cl
 Godmanchester PE29 . . . .142 A1
 Peterborough PE2 . . . . . . .187 C6
Stuart Dr SG8 . . . . .5 D8
Stubbs Rd **3** Haverhill CB9 38 D1
 St Ives PE27 . . . . .144 A4
Studlands Park Ave
 CB8 . . . . .110 D6
Studlands Rise SG8 . . . . .5 E6
Studlands Rise Fst Sch
 SG8 . . . . .5 E5
Stukeley Cl
 Cambridge CB3 . . . . .64 A8
 Peterborough PE2 . . . . . . .187 D5
Stukeley Meadows Ind Est
 PE29 . . . . .141 C8
Stukeley Meadows Prim Sch
 PE29 . . . . .141 C6
Stulp Field Rd CB3 . . . . . . .64 A4
Stumpacre PE3 . . . . .197 A8
Stumpcross **4** PE28 . . . .168 C2
Stuntney Cswy CB7 . . . . . .240 E2
Sturmer Rd Haverhill CB9 . .24 A7
 Kedington CB9 . . . . .24 F7
Sturrock Way PE3 . . . . .197 C8
Sturton St CB1 . . . . .84 A1
Sudbury Ct PE7 . . . . .187 F5
Sudeley Gr CB3 . . . . .81 A3
Suet Hills Dro PE7 . . . . . . .188 E1
Suez Rd CB1 . . . . .65 C7
Suffolk Cl **5** Ely CB6 . . . .240 A3
 Huntingdon PE29 . . . . . . .141 F6
 Peterborough PE3 . . . . . . .197 B2
 1 St Ives PE27 . . . . . . .144 A4
Suffolk Ho★ CB8 . . . . .73 E8
Suffolk Rd **5** SG8 . . . . .5 E6
Suffolk Way March PE15 . .243 E2
 Newmarket CB8 . . . . .110 E5
Sulehay Rd PE8 . . . . .193 C1
Sumerling Way PE28 . . . . .208 C6
Summerfield CB3 . . . . .64 C8
Summerfield Cl PE13 . . . . .245 A6
Summerfield Rd PE1 . . . . .197 F4

Summerhayes **1** CB7 . . . .240 F6
Sun Hill SG8 . . . . .5 C5
Sun La **6** CB8 . . . . .111 A3
Sun St **1** Cambridge CB1 . .84 A2
 Isleham CB7 . . . . .213 A5
Sunderland Ave CB2 . . . . . .33 A8
Sundew Cl PE19 . . . . .74 B6
Sunfield Rd PE26 . . . . .172 A4
Sunningdale PE2 . . . . .185 B6
Sunningdale Ave IP28 . . . . .239 B4
Sunnybank **1** PE19 . . . . . .75 A5
Sunnymead PE4 . . . . .204 A6
Sunnyside CB5 . . . . .84 E2
Sunnyville Rd PE7 . . . . . . .190 F8
Sunset Sq **2** CB4 . . . . . . .83 D7
Surrey Rd PE29 . . . . .141 E8
Sussex Rd Stamford PE9 . .244 B6
 Wyton Airfield PE28 . . . . .143 B8
Sussex St **2** CB1 . . . . . . .246 B3
Sutcliffe Rd PE8 . . . . .193 D8
Sutton Cl CB4 . . . . .105 D3
Sutton Ct **6** CB6 . . . . . . .216 E2
Sutton Gate PE12 . . . . . . .237 D8
Sutton Mdws PE13 . . . . . .245 A8
Sutton Pk CB6 . . . . .216 E2
Sutton Rd Eyeworth SG19 . .10 A1
 Haddenham CB6 . . . . .210 A8
 Mepal CB6 . . . . .216 E3
 Newton PE13 . . . . .238 B6
 Wentworth CB6 . . . . .217 C1
 Wisbech PE13 . . . . .245 A7
 Witchford CB6 . . . . .217 C1
Sutton Way **1** PE15 . . . . .223 A5
Sutton's La PE6 . . . . .231 E8
Suttons Cl PE14 . . . . .236 F2
Svenskaby PE2 . . . . .185 A8
Swaffham Bulbeck Prim Sch
 CB5 . . . . .108 B1
Swaffham Heath Rd
 CB5 . . . . .108 C1
Swaffham Prior CE Com Prim
 Sch CB5 . . . . .108 D5
Swaffham Rd
 Bottisham CB5 . . . . .107 E1
 Burwell CB5 . . . . .109 A7
 Reach CB5 . . . . .108 E8
Swain's Dro PE13 . . . . .238 C8
Swale Ave PE4 . . . . .204 E1
Swallow Cl PE7 . . . . .201 A1
Swallow Ct **3** PE7 . . . . . . .75 B6
Swallow La PE13 . . . . .238 B6
Swallow Way
 1 March PE15 . . . . .243 F5
 1 March PE15 . . . . .243 F5
Swallowfield PE4 . . . . .204 A4
Swan Cl St Ives PE27 . . . . .143 F7
 Whittlesey PE7 . . . . .189 F8
Swan Ct PE15 . . . . .243 D6
Swan Dr PE16 . . . . .241 D5
Swan End PE17 . . . . .117 B4
Swan Gdns PE28 . . . . .121 B5
Swan Gr CB8 . . . . .110 B8
Swan La Exning CB8 . . . . . .110 B3
 1 Guilden Morden SG8 . .10 F4
 Haverhill CB9 . . . . .24 A4
Swan Rd Fenstanton PE28 .121 B5
 Whittlesey PE7 . . . . .189 F8
Swan St **2** SG7 . . . . .2 D4
Swanhill CB8 . . . . .194 A4
Swann's Cl SG8 . . . . .26 A3
Swann's Rd CB5 . . . . .84 B4
Swann's Terr **4** CB1 . . . . .65 A8
Swanspool PE3 . . . . .197 B6
Swanton Cl PE15 . . . . .243 D7
Swasedale Dro CB7 . . . . . .219 A3
Swavesey Cty Prim Sch
 CB4 . . . . .122 E6
Swavesey Rd CB4 . . . . . . .122 A4
Swavesey Village Coll
 CB4 . . . . .122 E5
Sweetbriar La PE4 . . . . . . .204 B6
Sweeting Ave PE19 . . . . . . .95 F1
Sweetings Rd PE29 . . . . . .118 F8
Swift Cl **4** March PE15 . . .243 F5
 Market Deeping PE6 . . . . .231 E8
 Royston SG8 . . . . .13 D1
 St Neots PE19 . . . . .75 B6
Swifts Cnr CB7 . . . . .66 F5
Swinburne Cl SG8 . . . . .13 D1
Swinnell Cl SG8 . . . . .13 A5
Sybil Rd PE13 . . . . .245 C6
Sycamore Ave CB5 . . . . . .198 C6
Sycamore Cl
 4 Cambridge CB1 . . . . . .65 D5
 March PE15 . . . . .243 C5
Sycamore Dr PE29 . . . . . . .141 E8
Sycamore La CB4 . . . . .240 F5
Sycamore Rd PE7 . . . . . . .189 F6
Sycamores The
 2 Bluntisham/Colne
  PE28 . . . . .208 C6
 Little Paxton PE19 . . . . . . .95 F2
 Milton CB4 . . . . .105 C2
Sydney Rd PE2 . . . . .187 D5
Syers La PE7 . . . . .189 D7
Sylton Cl PE29 . . . . .141 F1
Sylvden Dr PE13 . . . . .245 F6
Sylvester Rd CB3 . . . . .83 B1
Symington Cl PE2 . . . . . . .186 F8
Symonds Cl CB4 . . . . .104 B4
Symonds La CB1 . . . . .35 B3
Sywell Gr **5** PE14 . . . . . .236 A4

Tait Cl PE1 . . . . .198 C5
Talbot Ave PE2 . . . . .186 D6
Talbot St PE7 . . . . .175 F8
Tall Trees **3** SG8 . . . . .5 E6
Tallington Lakes L Pk★
 PE9 . . . . .231 A8
Tall's La PE28 . . . . .121 B6
Tamar Cl PE27 . . . . .144 B6
Tamarin Gdns CB1 . . . . .66 A6
Tan House La CB5 . . . . . . .109 B8
Tan Yd PE19 . . . . .74 E5
Tanglewood
 Alconbury Weston PE28 . . .150 E6
 Peterborough PE4 . . . . . . .204 B6
Tanhouse PE2 . . . . .186 C5
Tanners La CB7 . . . . .212 B3
Tannersfield Way CB8 . . . . .110 F4
Tannery St SG8 . . . . .5 C6
Tannery Drift 5 C7
Tannery Drift Sch SG8 . . . . . .5 C6
Tannery Rd CB2 . . . . .32 F6
Tansor Garth PE3 . . . . .197 C5
Tansur Ct PE19 . . . . .74 C7
Tansy Cl **7** PE19 . . . . .74 B5
Tantallon Ct **6** PE3 . . . . .197 B1
Tanyard The SG8 . . . . .12 E4
Tarrant PE4 . . . . .204 A6
Tasman Rd CB9 . . . . .24 C7
Tatwin Dr **8** PE6 . . . . . . .232 B8
Taunton Cl **2** CB1 . . . . . . .65 D7
Taverners Dr **2** PE26 . . . .171 F5
Taverners Rd PE1 . . . . .197 F4
Tavistock Cl **8** PE6 . . . . . .233 A3
Tavistock Rd
 Cambridge CB4 . . . . .83 C6
 Wisbech PE13 . . . . .245 D5
Tawny Cres PE29 . . . . .142 E8
Tay Cl PE27 . . . . .144 B7
Taylor's Dro PE12 . . . . .237 D8
Taylor's La CB4 . . . . .122 D6
Taylors Field CB8 . . . . .70 F8
Taylors Gn PE8 . . . . .178 A2
Taylors La PE19 . . . . .116 F5
Taymor Pl PE14 . . . . .225 A8
Tea Kettle La CB8 . . . . .89 F1
Teal Cl Chatteris PE16 . . . .241 C6
 St Ives PE27 . . . . .143 F7
Teal Rd PE7 . . . . .189 F8
Teanby Ct **5** PE3 . . . . . . .196 F3
Teasdale Cl SG8 . . . . .13 D1
Teasel Cl
 15 Eaton Socon PE19 . . .74 C6
 2 Royston SG8 . . . . .5 E5
Teasel Way CB1 . . . . .66 A5
Tebbutts Rd PE19 . . . . .74 E5
Tedder Way CB4 . . . . .83 C6
Telegraph St CB1 . . . . .125 E4
Temple Cl Duxford CB2 . . . .32 C1
 Huntingdon PE29 . . . . . . .141 E4
Temple End
 Great Wilbraham CB1 . . . . .68 A8
 Little Thurlow CB9 . . . . . . .55 F2
Temple Grange PE4 . . . . . .204 B6
Temple Rd PE4 . . . . .212 F4
Tempsford Rd SG19 . . . . . . .40 A4
Ten Acre Dro PE7 . . . . .220 C8
Ten Bell La **6** CB7 . . . . . .212 B4
Ten Mile Bank CB6 . . . . . . .242 F6
Tenby Cl 66 A6
Tenby Way **6** PE19 . . . . . .74 F1
Tenison Ct CB1 . . . . .64 F7
Tenison Manor CB4 . . . . . .125 D4
Tenison Rd CB1 . . . . .65 A8
Tennis Ct Ave PE29 . . . . . .141 E6
Tennis Ct Rd CB2 . . . . .246 B1
Tennis Ct Terr CB2 . . . . . . .246 A1
Tennyson Ave PE27 . . . . . .143 F6
Tennyson Cl
 Huntingdon PE29 . . . . . . .141 F6
 Royston SG8 . . . . .13 D1
Tennyson Pl PE19 . . . . .74 D6
Tennyson Rd PE1 . . . . .197 F7
Tenter La PE9 . . . . .244 C5
Tenterleas PE27 . . . . .144 B3
Tern Cl CB9 . . . . .24 C7
Tern Gdns PE16 . . . . .241 C6
Tern Way **4** PE19 . . . . . . .75 B6
Terrace The CB8 . . . . .111 A3
Terrington Cl PE14 . . . . . . .236 D6
Tetworth Hill SG19 . . . . . . .41 A7
Teversham CE Prim Sch
 CB1 . . . . .85 B2
Teversham Drift CB1 . . . . . .66 A7
Teversham Rd CB1 . . . . . . .66 E6
Teversham Way CB2 . . . . . .50 A1
Teynham Cl **1** CB1 . . . . . .65 D7
Thackeray St SG8 . . . . .13 D1
Thackers Cl PE8 . . . . .194 A4
Thackray Cl PE29 . . . . .141 E7
Thames Rd PE29 . . . . .141 F8
Tharp Way CB7 . . . . .213 C1
Thatcher Stanfords Cl
 SG8 . . . . .14 C7
Thatchers Cl PE26 . . . . . . .171 B2
Thatchers Wood CB23 . . . .123 F1
Thatchwood Ave **2**
 PE14 . . . . .236 C6
Thetford Rd IP28 . . . . .239 E4
Thetford Terr CB5 . . . . .84 C2
Thicket Rd PE28 . . . . .143 B4
Thickwillow **2** PE29 . . . . .118 F8
Third Ave Warboys PE28 . . .164 E6
 Wisbech PE13 . . . . .245 C5
Third Dro Downham CB6 . .225 B1
 Peterborough PE1 . . . . . . .198 E2

Third Marsh Rd PE14 ..238 C3
Thirlby Gdns CB7 ......240 E7
Thirleby Cl CB4 ....83 D5
Thirlmere PE29 ....141 B6
Thirlmere Gdns **3** PE4 ..204 E3
Thirlwall Dr CB7 ....213 A1
Thistle Dr PE2 ....187 C7
Thistle Gn PE4 ....122 E6
Thistlemoor Rd PE1 ....197 C7
Thoday St CB1 ....65 B8
Thodays CB4 ....209 A1
Thomas Christian Way
  CB5 ....86 E7
Thomas Cl **7** PE3 .....196 E5
Thomas Eaton Sch
  PE15 ....223 B7
Thomas Rd CB1 ....66 D5
Thomas Way **2** SG8 ....13 D1
Thomas Wlk CB11 ....9 F1
Thompson's La CB2 .....246 A3
Thompsons Gd PE7 .....186 D3
Thompsons Mdw SG8 ....11 A4
Thongsley PE29 ....141 F7
Thongsley Cty Jun & Inf Sch
  PE29 ....141 F7
Thorby Ave PE15 ....243 A7
Thorleye Rd CB5 ....84 C2
Thorn Cl CB7 ....212 A4
Thorndown Inf Sch
  PE27 ....143 E6
Thorndown Jun Sch
  PE27 ....143 E6
Thorney Dyke PE6 ......201 C6
Thorney Rd Eye PE6 ....232 B1
  Newborough PE6 ......206 E2
  Wisbech St Mary PE13 ..234 C2
Thornham Way PE7 .....190 C6
Thornhaugh H★ PE8 ...193 C6
Thornhill Pl CB4 ....123 F2
Thornleigh Dr PE2 ....186 C6
Thornmead PE4 ....204 D4
Thornton Cl Girton CB3 ..83 A6
  Peterborough PE4 ....204 E3
Thornton Rd Girton CB3 ..82 F7
  March PE15 ....243 D6
Thornton Way CB3 ......83 A6
Thorolds Way PE5 .....195 D2
Thoroughfare La CB7 ..218 F1
Thoroughfare Way **3**
  CB6 ....242 E4
Thorpe Ave PE3 ....197 C5
Thorpe CP Sch PE3 ....197 B3
Thorpe H★ PE3 ....197 C2
Thorpe Lea Rd PE3 ....197 F1
Thorpe Mdws PE3 .....197 D1
Thorpe Park Rd PE3 ...197 C3
Thorpe Rd PE3 ....197 B1
Thorpe The PE28 ......143 E6
Thorpe Way CB5 ....84 F4
Thorpe Wood PE3 .....196 F1
Thorseby Cl PE3 ......197 B3
Thrapston Rd
  Brampton PE28 ......140 B4
  Catworth PE28 ......147 C2
  Kimbolton PE28 .....113 C5
  Spaldwick PE28 .....137 F6
Three Cups Wlk CB7 ...240 D4
Three Shire Stone★
  PE28 ....135 B1
Three Shires Way PE28 .135 E4
Thrifts Wlk CB4 ....84 A4
Thriplow CE Prim Sch
  SG8 ....31 B2
Thriplow Rd SG8 ....30 F1
Throckmorton PE28 ....164 E5
Throckmorton Rd PE28 .117 D3
Throstlenest PE7 ......187 C3
Thruffle Way CB3 ......102 C3
Thulborn Cl CB1 ....85 B1
Thurland's Dro PE14 ...229 C8
Thurlaston Cl PE3 ....197 B2
Thurley Cl PE19 ....95 E5
Thurlow Rd CB9 ....39 C6
Thurnall Ave SG8 ....5 D5
Thurning Ave PE2 .....187 C6
Thurning Rd PE28 .....157 F7
Thuro Gr PE2 ....186 A3
Thursfield PE4 ....204 C4
Thurston Gate **2** PE3 .197 A1
  Sturmer CB9 ....24 D6
Tiberius Cl Haverhill CB9 .24 D7
Tilbrook Rd PE28 ......113 D6
Tillbrooks Hill CB8 .....73 C5
Tillyard Way CB1 ....65 D4
Tilton Ct PE1 ....198 C8
Tindall Cl PE13 ....245 C8
Tinker's La CB3 ....61 C2
Tinkers La PE28 ....168 B4
Tintagel Ct
  7 Peterborough PE3 ...197 B1
  2 St Neots PE19 ......74 A2
Tintern Rise **3** PE6 ..232 A1
Tinwell Rd PE9 ....244 A4
Tinwell Road La PE9 ..244 A4
Tipplers' Rd CB4 ......122 E2
Tiptree Cl CB5 ....84 F4
Tirrington PE3 ....197 A3
Tithe Ave IP28 ....213 F8
Tithe Cl PE28 ....120 B2
Tithe Rd PE16 ....241 C2
Tithe Way CB3 ....79 C3
Tiverton Rd PE3 ......197 C3
Tiverton Way CB1 ......65 C7
Toates Cl CB6 ....210 C6

Toft La CB1 ....67 F7
Toftland PE2 ....186 D5
Tolethorpe Sq **4** PE9 .244 B6
Toll Bar La PE28 ......146 B5
Toll Dro PE15 ....224 A3
Toll House Rd PE2 ....186 C7
Toll Rd PE7 ....188 A3
Tollfield PE28 ....113 F4
Tollgate PE13 ....197 A5
Tom Jennings Cl **2**
  CB8 ....110 F5
Toneham La PE6 ......232 F1
Top La PE19 ....57 B5
Top St CB6 ....210 F5
Topcliffe Way CB1 .....65 C3
Topham Cres **9** PE6 ..233 A3
Topham Pl PE19 ....74 F7
Topham Way CB4 ....83 D6
Topmoor Way PE4 .....204 F1
Torkington Gdns **3**
  PE9 ....244 B5
Torpel Way **2** PE6 ..231 C7
Tort Hill PE28 ....168 C5
Toseland Rd PE19 ....97 E4
Tothill Rd CB5 ....108 D4
Touthill Cl PE1 ....198 A2
Tower Cl
  Bassingbourn SG8 .....12 F5
  Cottenham CB4 ......125 D3
  Huntingdon PE29 ...141 D8
  11 Over CB4 ....208 D1
  Whittlesey PE7 .....189 B8
Tower Ct CB6 ....240 B3
Tower Rd Downham CB6 .217 F7
  Elm PE14 ....236 A3
  Ely CB7 ....240 B3
  Sawston CB2 ....33 A8
  Sutton CB6 ....216 E2
Tower St PE2 ....186 F8
Tower View CB1 ....35 D3
Towgood Way PE19 .....96 D4
Towler St PE1 ....198 A3
Town Bridge PE13 ....245 B5
Town Cl CB2 ....32 E7
Town Green Rd SG8 ....28 D8
Town La CB2 ....33 B5
Town Orch PE19 ....95 E5
Town Rd St Newton CB2 ..31 B7
  Outwell PE14 ......236 E1
Town The PE19 ....93 E6
Towne Rd SG8 ....5 D5
Townley Cl PE14 .....236 E1
Townley Sch The PE14 .229 D3
Townsend Cl 212 A5
Townsend Cl **3** CB4 ..105 D3
Townsend Rd
  Needingworth PE27 ..208 A3
  Upwell PE14 ....229 E7
  Wittering PE8 ......230 A1
Townsend Way
  Folksworth PE7 .....175 D8
  Folksworth & Washingley
  PE7 ....175 E8
Townshend Rd PE13 ...245 D6
Toyse Cl CB5 ....130 C4
Toyse La CB5 ....130 B4
Trafalgar Rd
  Cambridge CB4 .....246 B4
  Eaton Socon PE19 ...74 C5
Trafalgar St CB4 .....246 B4
Trafalgar Way CB3 ....102 B5
Trafford Pk **1** PE13 .245 E6
Trafford Rd PE13 ....245 D5
Tram Sta La PE14 ....236 B6
Tramar Dr **7** CB6 ..216 E2
Trap Rd SG8 ....14 D6
Travellers Sch The PE1 .198 F5
Treading Bank PE13 ..237 C4
Tredegar Cl CB4 ....83 E6
Treeway PE16 ....241 B5
Trent Cl PE27 ....144 A7
Trent Rd PE3 ....193 D8
Tresham Rd PE2 .....185 D3
Trevone Pl CB1 ....65 D7
Trienna PE2 ....186 B5
Trigg Way SG8 ....14 D6
Trinity Ave IP28 .....239 C5
Trinity Cl Balsham CB1 ..53 B2
  Bottisham CB5 ....86 F6
  Ely CB6 ....240 C5
  Fordham CB7 ....212 F1
  1 Great Paxton PE19 ..96 E4
  Haslingfield CB3 .....47 B5
Trinity Coll CB2 .....246 A3
Trinity Conduit Head★
  CB3 ....82 F4
Trinity Dr CB8 ....111 B2
Trinity H CB3 ....246 A2
Trinity La CB2 ....246 A2
Trinity Link CB9 ....39 A1
Trinity Pl PE29 ......141 E4
Trinity Rd Stamford PE9 .244 A6
  Wisbech PE13 ......245 E6
Trinity St Cambridge CB2 .246 A2
  3 Peterborough PE1 .198 A2
Troughton Way **12** PE13 .238 B2
Troutbeck Cl **2** PE4 .204 F3
Truman Ave PE15 ....243 A5
Trumpington H★ PE7 ..64 C3
Trumpington High St
  CB2 ....64 D3
Trumpington Rd CB2 ...64 E5
Trumpington St CB2 ..246 A2
Trundle The PE28 ....215 C1
Tucker's Yd PE7 .....187 C7
Tuckers Nook **1** PE6 .231 C7
Tuddenham Rd IP28 ..239 F2

Tuddenham VC Sch
  IP28 ....214 E2
Tudor Cl PE4 ....204 E2
Tudor Ct
  Bassingbourn cum Kneesworth
  SG8 ....13 B4
  Kimbolton PE28 .....113 F5
Tudor Rd PE29 ....141 F2
Tunbridge Cl
  3 Bottisham CB5 ......86 E6
  Burwell CB5 ....130 B2
Tunbridge La CB5 ......86 E6
Tunkers La PE26 ......171 F4
Tunwells Cl CB2 ....49 A5
Tunwells La CB2 ....49 A5
Turberville Ct PE28 ..143 C1
Turf Dro PE7 ....191 C5
Turf Fen La PE15 ....222 F5
Turf Fen Rd PE26 ....170 F3
Turf Lot Dro PE14 ...229 E1
Turnbull Rd PE15 ....243 B3
Turner Cl CB9 ....38 D1
Turner Rd
  Eaton Socon PE19 ...74 C5
  St Ives PE27 ....144 A7
Turners La PE7 ......189 D6
Turningtree Rd PE7 ..190 A3
Turnpike Cl **2** PE13 .245 E6
Turnpike Hill CB9 ......38 C4
Turnpike La IP28 ....133 E8
Turnpike Rd IP28 ....133 E8
Turnpike The **2** CB1 .240 B3
Turnpole Cl **2** PE9 .244 D7
Turnstone Cl IP28 ...239 D4
Turnstone Way PE2 ..187 D7
Turpin's Ride
  4 Royston SG8 ....5 D5
  Stilton PE7 ....176 A7
Turvers La PE26 .....172 B7
Turves Rd PE6 ....232 A2
Tuyar Wlk CB8 ....110 E8
Tweed Cl CB8 ....112 F6
Tweedale CB1 ....65 F5
Twelvetree Ave PE4 ..204 A5
Twenty Foot Rd PE15 .227 F8
Twenty Pence Rd
  Cottenham CB4 .....125 F6
  Wilburton CB6 .....210 B3
Two Pole Dro Farcet PE7 .187 F1
Two Tree Hundred Dro
  PE15 ....228 A6
Tydd St Giles Golf & L Ctr
  PE13 ....238 A7
Tyrrell Pk PE1 ....198 D2
Tythe Piece PE28 ....121 C5

U

Uffen Way CB2 ....32 C4
Uffington Rd
  1 Barnack PE9 .....230 D4
  Stamford PE9 ......244 D5
Uffington Sch PE9 ...230 C6
Ufford H★ PE9 ......230 F3
Ugg Mere Ct Road
  PE26 ....220 D1
Uldale Way PE4 ......204 F2
Ullswater PE29 ......141 C5
Ullswater Ave PE4 ...204 D2
Underwood Cl PE7 ...190 D7
Union La CB4 ....83 F5
Union Pl **18** PE13 ..245 C5
Union Rd CB2 ....246 B1
Union St **4** PE13 ..245 C5
Univ Arts Sch CB2 ...246 A2
Univ Botanic Garden★
  CB2 ....64 F7
Univ Concert Hall CB3 .83 C2
Univ of Cambridge
  Cambridge CB4 ......84 A2
  Madingley CB3 ......81 E6
Univ Sch of Music CB3 .83 C1
Unwin's La **18** CB4 ..208 D1
Uphall Rd CB1 ....84 D1
Upherd's La CB6 .....240 C5
Uplands PE4 ....204 C5
Upper Delph Dro CB6 .209 A5
Upper Gwydir St **1** CB1 ..84 A1
Upper King St CB2 .....5 D6
Upton Cl
  Peterborough PE2 ..187 B5
  Peterborough PE3 ..197 A2
Upton Hill PE28 ......160 C1
Upton La CB6 ....242 D4
Upton Pl CB6 ....242 C4
Upware Rd
  Swaffham Prior CB7 ..128 D8
  Wicken CB7 ....211 C1
Upwell H★ PE14 ....236 D1
Upwell Prim Sch PE14 .229 D8
Upwell Rd
  Christchurch PE14 ..229 C4
  March PE15 ....243 D3
Upwood Airfield
  Polebrook PE8 .....174 A2
  Ramsey PE26 ....171 D4
Upwood CP Sch PE26 .171 D3
Upwood Rd
  Ramsey PE26 ....171 B5
Upwood & The Raveleys
  PE26 ....171 A5

V

Valarian Cl **14** PE19 ..74 C6
Valence Rd PE2 ......185 F4
Valerian Ct CB1 ....66 A5
Valiant Rd PE27 .....143 F7
Valiant Sq PE26 .....171 F3
Valley Rise SG8 ....5 E6
Valley The CB3 ....62 D6
Valley Way CB4 ......110 E4
Valparaiso Univ CB3 ...83 C3
Van Diemans Way PE28 .116 A7
Van Dyke Pl PE27 ...144 A7
Van Gogh Pl PE27 ...144 A7
Vanners Rd CB3 ....24 A7
Varrier Jones Dr CB3 ..99 A3
Varrier Jones Pl CB3 ..99 A3
Veasey Rd PE29 .....142 A7
Vence Cl PE9 ....244 A5
Ventress Cl CB1 ......65 D5
Verdun Rd PE13 .....245 D5
Vere Rd PE1 ....197 F7
Vergette Rd PE6 .....203 F8
Vergette St PE1 .....198 B4
Vermont Gr PE3 .....197 E1
Vermuyden **8** PE28 ..208 E6
Vermuyden Gdns **5**
  CB6 ....216 E2
Vermuyden Way CB4 ..121 F5
Verulam Way CB4 .....83 D6
Vester's Hill Dro PE26 .171 B7
Vicarage Ave CB2 .....32 F7
Vicarage Cl
  Dullingham CB8 .....89 C1
  Holme PE7 ....177 A4
  Melbourn SG8 ......14 C6
  Oakington/Longstanton
  CB4 ....103 D6
  Swaffham Bulbeck CB5 .108 A1
  Waterbeach CB5 ....106 A7
Vicarage Dr CB3 ......64 A3
Vicarage Farm Rd **5**
  PE1 ....198 D3
Vicarage Farm Yd PE19 ..57 B6
Vicarage La
  Swaffham Prior CB5 ..108 D4
  Whittlesford CB2 .....32 B5
  Woodditton CB8 .....90 D3
Vicarage Rd
  Newmarket CB8 ....111 B3
  Waresley SG19 ......58 A2
Vicarage Terr CB1 ....84 A1
Vicarage Way PE7 ...181 D5
Vicarage Wlk PE19 ...93 F6
Viceroy Cl PE19 ......74 A3
Victor Cl PE27 ......144 A7
Victoria Ave PE28 ...246 B3
Victoria Cl SG19 .....25 B4
Victoria Cres Royston SG8 ..5 D7
  St Ives PE28 ....143 C5
Victoria Gn **3** CB6 ..217 D1
Victoria Pk CB4 ....83 D4
Victoria Pl
  Peterborough PE1 ..197 F4
  Sutton CB6 ....216 D1
  16 Wisbech PE13 ...245 C4
Victoria Rd
  Cambridge CB4 ....83 D4
  Haverhill CB9 ....23 D7
  Stamford PE9 ......244 B6
  Wisbech PE13 ......245 C4
Victoria Sq **2** PE29 .141 E4
Victoria St
  Cambridge CB1 .....246 B2
  Chatteris PE16 .....241 C4
  Ely CB7 ....240 D3
  Littleport CB6 .....242 E4
  Peterborough PE2 ..186 F6
  Peterborough PE1 ..198 A5
Victoria Way CB8 ....110 E7
Victory Ave PE7 .....189 F7
Victory Rd PE13 ....245 B3
Victory Way CB4 ....125 D4
Victory Wlk **7** SG8 ..5 E5
Viersen Platz PE1 ...198 A1
Viking Cl CB1 ....53 E5
Viking Way Bar Hill CB3 .102 A4
  Whittlesey PE7 .....189 E8
Villa Pl CB4 ....104 C2
Villa Rd CB4 ....104 C2
Village Col SG19 ......41 E5
Village The PE2 .....186 B5
Vine Cl Great Shelford CB2 ..49 C4
  Hemingford Grey PE27 .143 E2
Vine St PE9 ....244 C5
Vinegar Hill PE28 ...150 E7
Vinery Ct PE26 .....172 B7
Vinery Rd CB1 ....65 C8
Vinery Way CB1 ....84 C1
Viney Cl PE1 ....198 D5
Vineyard Rd PE1 ...198 B2
Vineyard The PE28 ..208 D7
Vineyard Way
  Buckden PE19 ......117 B3
  Ely CB7 ....240 E5
Vineyard Wlk CB5 .....86 E6
Vineyards The CB7 ..240 D4
Vintner Cl CB3 ....99 A3
Vintners Cl PE3 .....197 D3
Violet Cl CB1 ....66 A5
Virginia Cl **1** PE3 ..197 A2
Virginia Rd **3** IP28 .213 E8
Virginia Way PE27 ..143 E6
Viscount Ct PE19 .....74 B3
Viscount Rd PE2 ....187 A6
Vixen Cl PE7 ....181 F6
Vulcan Way PE19 .....74 B1

W

Wadbury's Folly PE27 .208 B4
Waddelow Rd CB5 ....106 A8
Wade Park Ave **4** PE6 .231 E8
Wadloes Rd CB5 ......84 D4
Wagstaff Cl CB4 ......83 F7
Wainman Rd PE2 .....186 D5
Wainwright PE4 .....204 A5
Waits The PE27 ......144 A3
Wake Ave IP28 ......239 C6
Wake Rd March PE15 .243 C6
  Peterborough PE1 ..198 B2
Wakefield Cl CB10 ....18 D3
Wakelin Ave CB8 ......49 F1
Wakelyn Rd PE7 ....189 C7
Wakerley Dr PE2 ....186 C7
Walcot Rd PE9 ......230 E2
Walden Cl **17** PE15 ..223 A5
Walden Gr PE29 .....141 D4
Walden Rd
  Great Chesterford CB10 ..18 E3
  Hadstock CB1 ....20 B6
  Huntingdon PE29 ..141 D4
Walden Way CB2 ......48 D4
Wales Bank Elm PE14 .236 A5
  Wisbech PE14 ......236 A5
Walgrave PE2 ....186 B4
Walker Rd PE6 ......203 F7
Walkers Way PE3 ...196 F3
Walkling Way CB4 ...105 D1
Wallace's Dro PE6 ...233 D4
Waller's Cl SG8 ....7 F2
Wallman's La CB4 ...122 E6
Walnut Cl
  Newborough PE6 ...205 C8
  Royston SG8 ....5 D6
Walnut Gr IP28 .....213 E4
Walnut Tree Ave CB5 ..84 A3
Walnut Tree Cl
  Bassingbourn SG8 ...12 E5
  4 Little Downham CB6 .218 A6
  8 Stretham CB6 ...210 F5
Walnut Tree Cres PE28 .121 B5
Walnut Tree Dr PE2 ..141 C6
Walnut Tree Way CB3 ..83 C7
Walnut Way PE7 ....175 F7
Walpole Bank PE14 ..238 F7
Walpole Rd CB1 ......65 D6
Walsingham Ct **2** PE13 .245 A7
Walsingham Way
  Ely CB7 ....240 B5
  10 Eye PE6 ....232 A1
Walsoken Rd PE14 ...236 E7
Walton Cl **5** CB7 ...212 E1
Walton Comp Sch PE4 .204 C1
Walton Hill PE28 ....161 D5
Walton J & I Sch PE4 .204 C1
Walton Pk PE4 ......204 C1
Walton Rd
  9 Leverington PE13 .238 B2
  Marholm PE6 ....203 E1
  Wisbech PE13 .....245 E7
Wamil H★ IP28 .....213 F5
Wamil Rd IP28 ......213 F5
Wamil Way IP28 ....239 B4
Wandlebury Ctry Pk★
  CB2 ....50 B8
Wansford Rd Elton PE8 .183 D5
  Wansford PE8 .....194 A3
  Yarwell PE8 ....193 F2
Wantage Gdns PE19 ..96 A2
Warbon Ave PE1 ....197 F7
Warboys Airfield Ind Est
  PE28 ....164 D2
Warboys Cl CB3 ....61 D5
Warboys CP Sch PE28 .164 E5
Warboys Rd PE28 ...155 E8
Ward Cl Ramsey PE26 .172 A5
  St Ives PE28 ....143 A5
Ward Rd CB1 ....65 D6
Ward Way PE28 .....217 D1
Warden Hill SG19 .....40 C3
Ware La PE28 ....142 F5
Ware Rd PE19 ....74 E6
Wareley Rd PE2 .....197 F1
Waresley Rd
  Gamlingay SG19 .....41 D6
  Great Gransden SG19 .58 B3
Warkworth St CB1 ..246 C2
Warkworth Terr CB1 .246 C2
Warmington Sch PE8 .178 B3
Warner's Dro
  Pidley cum Fenton PE28 .215 B3
  Somersham PE28 ..215 C2
Warners Gr PE27 ...144 A4
Warren Cl PE28 ......142 F6
Warren Croft PE28 ..168 B5
Warren La
  Bythorn & Keyston PE28 .146 D4
  Titchmarsh PE28 ..156 F1
Warren Rd Cambridge CB4 .84 A6
  Herringswell CB8 ...134 A7
  Red Lodge IP28 ....214 A1
  St Ives PE27 ....144 B4
  Wothorpe PE9 .....244 B1
Warren The
  3 Royston SG8 ....5 D5
  Witchford CB6 .....217 E1
Warrington St CB8 ...111 A2
Warwick Ct **6** PE19 ..74 C3
Warwick Dr CB6 ....240 A3
Warwick Rd
  Cambridge CB4 ......83 C5
  Peterborough PE4 ..204 C1
Wasdale Gdns PE4 ..205 A2
Wash La PE7 ....189 E8

Wash Rd PE14 . . . . .225 B8
Washbank Rd PE19 . . . . .74 E4
Washingley La PE7 . . . . .175 B7
Washingley Rd
  Folksworth PE7 . . . . .175 D8
  The Stukeleys PE29 . . . . .141 C8
Washington Cl CB6 . . . . .242 D5
Washington St IP28 . . . . .213 E8
Washpit La CB3 . . . . .46 D7
Washpit Rd CB3 . . . . .82 C8
Wastwater PE7 . . . . .141 B6
Water End Alwalton PE7 . .185 A5
  Marholm PE6 . . . . .203 D1
  Wrestlingworth SG19 . . . . .25 B3
Water Gdns The PE13 . .245 A5
Water La Bourn CB3 . . . . .60 D6
  Cambridge CB4 . . . . .84 B5
  Castor PE5 . . . . .195 F1
  Great Bradley CB8 . . . . . . .55 F8
  Histon CB4 . . . . .104 C3
  Melbourn SG8 . . . . .14 C5
  Oakington/Longstanton
    CB4 . . . . .103 C3
  Sturmer CB9 . . . . .24 F5
Water St Cambridge CB4 . .84 B4
  Stamford PE9 . . . . .244 C4
Waterbeach CP Sch
  CB5 . . . . .106 B8
Waterbeach Rd CB4 . . . .105 E7
Waterbeach Sta CB5 . . . .106 C6
Watercourse The CB8 . . .111 A4
Waterfields PE13 . . . . . . .241 B3
Waterfurlong PE9 . . . . . .244 A4
Watergall PE3 . . . . .197 B8
Watergall CP Sch PE3 . .197 A8
Watergate 6 PE9 . . . . . .244 C5
Waterlees Rd 2 PE13 . .245 E7
Waterloo Cl
  1 Brampton PE28 . . . . .140 C3
  Newmarket CB8 . . . . .110 D8
Waterloo Dr 2 PE19 . . . .74 F3
Waterloo Rd PE1 . . . . . . .198 A5
Watermead CB3 . . . . .102 C3
Waterside Ely CB7 . . . . . .240 E4
  Isleham CB7 . . . . .213 A5
Waterside Gdns PE15 . .243 E5
Waterslade Rd PE13 . . . .181 C4
Waterton Cl 6 PE6 . . . . .231 F8
Waterwick Hill CB11 . . . . .1 F1
Waterworks La PE6 . . . . .203 D6
Waterworks Rd 1 IP28 . .213 E8
Watsons La 1 CB6 . . . . .211 B7
Watt Cl PE4 . . . . .204 E2
Wavell Way CB4 . . . . .83 E6
Waveney Dr PE15 . . . . . .243 B5
Waveney Gr PE4 . . . . . . .204 E2
Waveney Rd PE27 . . . . . .144 A7
Waveney Terr CB9 . . . . . . .24 B7
Waverley Cl PE13 . . . . . . .235 A3
Waverley Gdns 3 PE9 . .244 A6
Way Head Dro PE26 . . . .217 C6
Way La Waterbeach CB5 . .106 B8
  Wicken PE28 . . . . .211 D2
Wayford Cl PE3 . . . . .197 A2
Wayne's La CB3 . . . . .62 C5
Weasenham La 1 PE13 245 D2
Weatheralls Cl 4 PE28 . .212 B4
Weatheralls CP Sch The
  CB7 . . . . .212 B4
Weatherthorn PE2 . . . . . .186 C5
Weavers Field CB3 . . . . . .82 E7
Webb's Rd CB1 . . . . .36 F5
Webbs Mdw SG19 . . . . . .58 D4
Webster's Way CB4 . . . . .208 D1
Websters Cl PE6 . . . . .203 F8
Weddell Rd CB1 . . . . .24 C6
Wedgewood Dr CB1 . . . . .65 F6
Wedgwood Dr PE13 . . . . .245 D5
Weir Cl Buckden PE19 . . .117 A3
  Hemingford Grey PE28 . . .143 D1
Weir Rd PE28 . . . . .143 D1
Weirs Dro CB5 . . . . .129 F1
Welbeck Rd PE13 . . . . . .245 E4
Welbeck Way PE2 . . . . . .186 D7
Welbourne PE4 . . . . .204 C4
Welbourne Prim Sch
  PE4 . . . . .204 C4
Welby Cl PE28 . . . . .115 D3
Welches Dam Visitor Ctr★
  CB6 . . . . .217 A8
Well Bottom CB8 . . . . . . .112 B8
Well Creek Rd PE14 . . . .236 F2
Well End PE14 . . . . .236 A3
Welland Bank PE6 . . . . . .207 D7
Welland Cl PE1 . . . . .198 A4
Welland Ct 9 PE19 . . . . . .74 C4
Welland Mews PE9 . . . . .244 C4
Welland Rd
  Peterborough PE1 . . . . . .198 B8
  Wittering PE8 . . . . .230 B1
Welland Way 5 PE6 . . . .231 F8
Wellbrook Way CB3 . . . . .82 F7
Wellington Ave 4 PE27 .143 F7
Wellington Cl
  Old Hurst PE28 . . . . .154 E7
  Thistley Green IP28 . . . . .213 E8
  Warboys PE28 . . . . .164 F4
  Waterbeach PE28 . . . . . .106 B7
Wellington Ct 3 CB1 . . . .84 A2
Wellington Pl SG8 . . . . . . .13 B5
Wellington Rd Ely CB6 . .217 F1
  1 Mildenhall IP28 . . . . .213 E8
Wellington St
  4 Cambridge CB1 . . . . . .84 A2
  Littleport CB6 . . . . .242 D4
  4 Newmarket CB8 . . . . .111 A3
  Peterborough PE1 . . . . . .198 B2

Wellington St continued
  St Ives PE27 . . . . .144 A3
Wells Bridge PE26 . . . . . .221 C3
Wells Cl Haslingfield CB3 . .47 A5
  Peterborough PE4 . . . . . .204 B3
Wells Ct IP28 . . . . .239 B5
Wells Way PE7 . . . . .177 A5
Wellsfield PE29 . . . . .141 E6
Welmore Rd PE6 . . . . . . .203 F8
Welney Rd PE16 . . . . . . .241 D3
Wensum Cl PE27 . . . . . . .144 B6
Wentworth Dr PE28 . . . .239 B4
Wentworth Rd CB4 . . . . . .83 C4
Wentworth St 1 PE1 . . . .198 A1
Wenvoe Cl PE1 . . . . .65 F6
Werrington Bridge Rd
  PE6 . . . . .204 E7
Werrington Cty Prim Sch
  PE4 . . . . .204 C3
Werrington Gr PE4 . . . . .204 B2
Werrington Jun Sch
  PE4 . . . . .204 C3
Werrington Mews 5
  PE4 . . . . .204 C3
Werrington Park Ave 2
  PE4 . . . . .204 C3
Werrington Parkway
  PE4 . . . . .203 E5
Werrington Sports Ctr
  PE4 . . . . .204 B4
Wertheim Way PE29 . . . .141 B6
Wesley Dr PE16 . . . . .241 D5
Wesley Ho CB5 . . . . .246 B3
Wesleyan Rd PE1 . . . . . . .198 A7
Wessex Cl PE2 . . . . .187 D7
West Ave PE26 . . . . .171 F6
West Brook PE28 . . . . . . .120 B2
West Brook Cl PE28 . . . . .120 B2
West Cl
  Alconbury Weston PE28 . .150 D6
  March PE15 . . . . .243 B6
  Waresley SG19 . . . . .57 F2
West Delph PE7 . . . . .189 D8
West Dr Highfields CB3 . . .80 C2
  March PE15 . . . . .243 F4
  Mildenhall IP28 . . . . .239 B4
  Soham CB7 . . . . .212 B4
West Drive Cres 2 CB7 212 A4
West Drive Gdns 1
  CB7 . . . . .212 A4
West Dro S PE12 . . . . . . .233 E8
West End Ashwell SG7 . . . .2 C3
  Brampton PE28 . . . . .140 C3
  Ely CB6 . . . . .240 C4
  Gorefield PE13 . . . . .237 E3
  Haddenham CB6 . . . . . . .209 F6
  March PE15 . . . . .243 B4
  Whittlesey PE7 . . . . .189 C7
  Whittlesford CB2 . . . . .32 B4
  Wilburton CB6 . . . . .210 B5
  Woodditton CB8 . . . . .71 D8
  Yaxley PE7 . . . . .181 D4
West End Cl PE28 . . . . . .241 B4
West End La CB9 . . . . .38 E8
West End Rd
  Fenstanton PE28 . . . . . . .121 A5
  Maxey PE6 . . . . .231 C7
West Fen Dro
  Downham CB6 . . . . .218 A6
  March PE7 . . . . .227 A1
  Whittlesey PE7 . . . . .191 F3
West Fen Rd
  Coveney PE6 . . . . .217 E4
  Ely CB6 . . . . .240 B5
  Willingham CB4 . . . . .208 F2
  Witchford CB6 . . . . .218 A3
West Field La CB4 . . . . . . .34 B7
West Field Rd PE15 . . . . .224 A3
West Gn CB2 . . . . .29 D7
West Hill Rd CB2 . . . . .30 B4
West Leys PE27 . . . . .143 F4
West Lodge La CB6 . . . . .216 D1
West Moor Ave CB2 . . . . .32 E8
West Newlands PE28 . . . .208 B8
West Par
  Peterborough PE3 . . . . . .197 D3
  Wisbech PE13 . . . . .245 D4
West Park St PE16 . . . . . .241 C4
West Perry PE28 . . . . .115 D2
West Rd Cambridge CB3 . .83 C1
  Gamlingay SG19 . . . . .41 C4
  Histon CB4 . . . . .104 B3
  3 Tallington PE9 . . . . . .230 F7
  Tydd St Giles PE13 . . . . .238 B8
West Row Prim Sch
  IP28 . . . . .213 D7
West Row Rd
  Beck Row, Holywell Row
    & Kenny Hill IP28 . . . . .213 F6
  Mildenhall IP28 . . . . .239 A5
West St Chatteris PE16 . .241 B3
  Godmanchester PE29 . . . .141 E1
  Great Gransden SG19 . . . .58 D4
  Helpston PE6 . . . . .231 B4
  Huntingdon PE29 . . . . . . .141 E5
  Isleham CB7 . . . . .212 F5
  Over CB4 . . . . .123 A8
  St Ives PE27 . . . . .144 A4
  St Neots PE19 . . . . .74 E5
  Stamford PE9 . . . . .244 B4
  Toft CB3 . . . . .62 B5
  Wisbech PE13 . . . . .245 D4
West Stonebridge PE2 . .186 C5
West Street Gdns PE9 . .244 A4
West Town Cty Sch PE3 .197 B4
West View PE28 . . . . .151 F1

West Way Meldreth SG8 . .28 F1
  Sawston SG2 . . . . .50 A1
West Wickham Rd
  Balsham CB1 . . . . .53 C1
  Horseheath CB1 . . . . .37 A3
West Wlk CB5 . . . . .86 F6
West Wratting Rd CB1 . . .53 B2
Westbourne Cl PE16 . . . .241 B4
Westbourne Dr PE6 . . . . .203 E8
Westbourne Rd PE16 . . . .241 B4
Westbrook Ave 1 PE2 . .186 F7
Westbrook Cl
  1 Brampton PE28 . . . . .140 C3
  Steeple Morden SG8 . . . . .3 B8
Westbrook Park Cl 2
  PE2 . . . . .186 F7
Westbrook Park Rd PE2 186 F7
Westbury Rd PE7 . . . . . . .143 F4
Westcombe Sq PE1 . . . . .198 D4
Westcott House Theological
  Coll CB3 . . . . .246 B3
Westcroft 4 CB3 . . . . .62 B4
Westering The CB5 . . . . . .84 E2
Westerman Cl PE28 . . . . .168 B5
Western Ave Haverhill CB9 .38 E1
  Peterborough PE1 . . . . . .198 B7
Westfield CB4 . . . . .124 A6
Westfield La CB4 . . . . .83 C4
Westfield Prim Sch CB9 . .24 D7
Westfield Rd
  Fowlmere SG8 . . . . .15 D8
  Great Shelford CB2 . . . . . .48 E7
  Newton PE13 . . . . .237 F5
  Peterborough PE3 . . . . . .197 E4
  Ramsey PE26 . . . . .171 F7
  Sawtry PE28 . . . . .168 B4
  Wisbech PE13 . . . . .245 E7
  Yaxley PE7 . . . . .181 D5
Westfield Sch PE27 . . . . .144 A4
Westfields CB3 . . . . .99 A2
Westgate PE1 . . . . .197 F2
Westhawe PE3 . . . . .196 F1
Westhorpe CB5 . . . . .130 B4
Westlands CB5 . . . . .62 B4
Westley Bottom Rd CB8 . .69 B8
Westmead Ave PE13 . . . .245 E2
Westmeadow Cl CB4 . . . .208 F1
Westminster & Cheshunt
  Colls CB3 . . . . .83 C3
Westminster Gdns 16
  PE6 . . . . .232 A1
Westminster Pl PE1 . . . . .198 F5
Westmoor Comm CB6 . .217 E8
Westmoor Dro
  Chatteris PE16 . . . . .222 D2
  Littleport CB6 . . . . .225 B4
Weston Ave SG8 . . . . .5 C7
Weston Cl PE19 . . . . .95 A1
Weston Colville Rd CB8 . .70 D1
Weston Ct PE19 . . . . .74 C4
Weston Gr CB1 . . . . .66 E5
Weston Miller Dr PE13 . .245 C7
Weston Rd 17 PE13 . . . . .245 C3
Weston Way CB8 . . . . . . .110 F6
Westry Ave PE15 . . . . . . .243 A7
Westry Cl 3 PE13 . . . . . .238 F1
Westway Pl PE6 . . . . .217 A2
Westwick H★ CB4 . . . . . .103 E7
Westwood 5 PE3 . . . . . . .197 C8
Westwood Ave PE15 . . . .243 C5
Westwood Jun Sch
  PE15 . . . . .243 C5
Westwood Park Cl PE3 . .197 C3
Westwood Park Rd PE3 .197 D2
Westwood Rd 1 PE27 . . .144 C4
Wetenhall Rd CB1 . . . . . . .65 B8
Wetherby Way 1 PE1 . . .198 D3
Weymouth Way 4 PE1 . .198 D6
Whaddon Gap SG8 . . . . . .28 A1
Whaddon Rd SG8 . . . . . . .28 E2
Whaddons The PE29 . . . .141 F6
Whalley St PE1 . . . . .198 B3
Wharf Rd PE9 . . . . .244 C4
Wheat Croft CB1 . . . . .35 D3
Wheatfield Cres 2 SG8 . . .5 F6
Wheatfield Dr 1 PE26 . . .171 F5
Wheatfield Jun & Inf Sch
  PE27 . . . . .144 A6
Wheatfields PE27 . . . . . . .144 A6
Wheatley Back CB4 . . . . .238 F2
Wheatley Cres 3 PE28 . .208 C6
Wheats Cl 1 CB6 . . . . . . .217 D1
Wheatsheaf Cl 1 CB6 . .240 A3
Wheatsheaf Dro PE14 . . .229 C3
Wheatsheaf Rd
  Alconbury Weston PE28 . .150 D6
  Eaton Socon PE19 . . . . . .74 C3
  Woodhurst PE28 . . . . . . .155 D4
Wheatsheaf Way CB1 . . . .35 D3
Wheatsheaves 2 PE28 . .168 C2
Wheel Yd PE1 . . . . .198 A2
Wheeler St CB2 . . . . .246 A2
Wheeler's Cl PE28 . . . . . .46 A7
Wheelwright Way CB5 . . .86 A5
Whichcote Rd PE6 . . . . . .206 E6
Whines La CB4 . . . . .123 B8
Whinfell Cl 3 PE29 . . . . .141 A7
Whipple Science Mus★
  CB2 . . . . .246 A2
Whippletree Rd CB2 . . . . .32 A5
Whistler PE19 . . . . .74 C5
Whistler The 5 PE27 . . .144 A7
Whiston Rd
  Peterborough PE4 . . . . . .204 F2
  2 Somersham PE28 . . . .208 C4
Whitacre PE1 . . . . .198 E6
Whitby St 3 PE13 . . . . . .245 C5

White Acres PE7 . . . . . . .189 E8
White Croft PE3 . . . . .197 B6
White Cross Rd CB6 . . . .210 E4
White Droveway CB5 . . . .108 A3
White Fen Droveway
  CB5 . . . . .107 B5
White Field Way CB2 . . . .32 D8
White Hall Cl 21 PE28 . . .215 C1
White Hart Cl 5 PE15 . . .222 A5
White Hart La
  Godmanchester PE29 . . . .142 A1
  6 Littleport CB6 . . . . . .242 D4
  4 St Ives PE27 . . . . . . .144 A3
  13 Soham CB7 . . . . .212 B4
White Horse La 5 CB6 . .218 A6
White House Rd CB7 . . . .226 C2
White Lion Cl 1 PE15 . . .243 D2
Whitecroft Rd SG8 . . . . . .14 A8
Whitecross PE27 . . . . . . .144 A4
Whitecross Stone★
  PE7 . . . . .190 E7
Whitegate Cl CB4 . . . . . . .122 D6
Whitegates CB8 . . . . .111 C3
Whitehall IP28 . . . . .215 B1
Whitehall Gdns CB2 . . . . .31 E1
Whitehall Way IP28 . . . . .115 D2
Whitehill Cl CB1 . . . . .84 D2
Whitehill Rd CB5 . . . . .84 C2
Whitehouse La CB3 . . . . . .83 A5
Whitehouse Rd PE28 . . . .168 A4
Whitemill Rd PE16 . . . . . .241 C3
Whitemoor Rd PE15 . . . .227 C4
Whitepost Rd
  Borough Fen PE6 . . . . . . .207 F1
  Newborough PE6 . . . . . . .205 F6
Whiteway Dro CB5 . . . . . .107 F8
Whiteways PE2 . . . . .185 D6
Whitfield Cl CB4 . . . . .83 E4
Whitgift Rd CB1 . . . . .85 B1
Whiting Way SG8 . . . . . . .14 C4
Whitman Cl 7 PE9 . . . . . .230 D3
Whitmore St PE7 . . . . . . .189 C7
Whitmore Way CB5 . . . . .106 B6
Whitsed Rd PE6 . . . . .207 D1
Whitsed St PE1 . . . . .198 B3
Whittets Cl 2 SG19 . . . . .58 D4
Whittington Pl PE1 . . . . . .198 C1
Whittlesey Rd
  Benwick PE15 . . . . .221 E6
  March PE15 . . . . .243 A5
  Peterborough PE2 . . . . . .187 B7
  Thorney PE6 . . . . .200 F7
Whittlesey Sta PE7 . . . . .189 F5
Whittlesey TH PE7 . . . . . .189 D7
Whittlesford Rd
  Little Shelford CB2 . . . . . .48 F2
  Newton CB2 . . . . .31 D7
Whittlesford Sta CB2 . . . .32 E3
Whitton Cl CB4 . . . . .122 E5
Whitwell Rd CB1 . . . . . . .205 A2
Whitwell Way CB3 . . . . . .82 A2
Whybrows La 1 PE28 . . .208 E6
Whydale Rd 4 SG8 . . . . . .5 F5
Whytefield Rd PE26 . . . . .172 A7
Wicken Fen Nature Reserve
  (National Trust)★ CB7 211 D1
Wicken Rd CB7 . . . . .212 B1
Wicken Way PE3 . . . . . . .197 C6
Wiggin Cl IP28 . . . . .239 D2
Wigmore Cl PE29 . . . . . . .141 E1
Wigmore Dr PE7 . . . . . . .187 F5
Wigstone's Rd PE15 . . . .243 E5
Wilberforce Rd
  Cambridge CB3 . . . . .83 B2
  Peterborough PE1 . . . . . .197 F5
  Wisbech PE13 . . . . .245 D5
Wilbraham Rd
  Bottisham CB1 . . . . .86 F3
  Fulbourn CB1 . . . . .67 C7
Wilburton Prim Sch
  CB6 . . . . .210 C6
Wilburton Rd
  8 Haddenham CB6 . . . .210 A6
  Stretham CB6 . . . . .210 E5
Wild Acres CB5 . . . . .130 B1
Wildber Cl PE19 . . . . .74 F4
Wilderspin Cl CB3 . . . . . . .82 F6
Wilding Wlk CB4 . . . . .84 A5
Wildlake PE2 . . . . .186 C5
Wildmere La PE28 . . . . . .214 A8
Wiles Cl Cambridge CB4 . .84 A4
  Waterbeach CB5 . . . . . . .106 A8
Wilford Dr 3 CB7 . . . . . .240 E6
Wilford Furlong CB4 . . . .209 A1
Wilkin St 1 CB1 . . . . .65 A8
Wilkins Rd PE14 . . . . .236 D7
Wilkinson Cl
  Eaton Socon PE19 . . . . . .74 B3
  March PE15 . . . . .243 E6
Willesden Ave PE4 . . . . . .197 D8
William Dr 8 PE19 . . . . . .74 F1
William Law Sch PE4 . . . .204 B5
William Rd PE13 . . . . .245 C5
William Smith Cl CB1 . . . .65 A7
William Westley CE Prim Sch
  CB2 . . . . .32 D5
William's Way IP28 . . . . .213 D6
Williams Cl
  Brampton PE28 . . . . .140 C3
  Ely CB6 . . . . .240 E7
  Newborough PE6 . . . . . . .207 C1
Williams Way 2 PE15 . . .224 B4
Williamson Ave PE3 . . . . .197 E3
Willie Snaith Rd CB8 . . . .110 F6
Willingham Green Rd
  CB8 . . . . .54 D8
Willingham Prim Sch
  CB4 . . . . .209 A1

Willingham Rd CB4 . . . . .208 E1
Willis Rd CB1 . . . . .246 C2
Willmott Rd SG8 . . . . .12 F5
Willock La PE13 . . . . .235 A5
Willonholt PE3 . . . . .197 C6
Willoughby Ct PE1 . . . . . .198 E8
Willoughby Rd PE9 . . . . .244 C7
Willow Ave PE1 . . . . .198 B7
Willow Cl
  Beck Row, Holywell Row
    & Kenny Hill IP28 . . . . .214 A8
  Brampton PE28 . . . . .140 C2
  Haverhill CB9 . . . . .38 D1
  Little Paxton PE19 . . . . . .95 F1
  St Neots PE19 . . . . .74 F3
  Stilton PE7 . . . . .175 F7
Willow Cres Milton CB4 . .105 D2
  Newmarket CB8 . . . . .111 B2
Willow Ct 3 PE15 . . . . . .242 E4
Willow Dr 3 PE15 . . . . . .243 B3
Willow Dro PE6 . . . . .207 D4
Willow End PE28 . . . . . . .150 F4
Willow Farm Cl PE28 . . . .150 D7
Willow Gn PE27 . . . . .208 A3
Willow Gr Ely CB7 . . . . . .240 E4
  Lode CB5 . . . . .107 C2
Willow Hall La PE6 . . . . .199 D6
Willow Holt PE6 . . . . .186 C3
Willow La CB5 . . . . .79 C3
Willow Rd PE7 . . . . .182 A6
Willow Way Bottisham CB5 .86 F6
  Hauxton CB2 . . . . .48 B4
  Ramsey PE26 . . . . .172 B7
  Wisbech PE13 . . . . .245 D3
Willow Wlk
  Cambridge CB4 . . . . .246 B3
  Ely CB7 . . . . .240 E4
Willowbrook Dr PE7 . . . . .203 F1
Willows The Glinton PE6 .203 B4
  Great Chesterford CB10 . . .18 D3
Willowside Way 5 SG8 . . .5 C8
Wilson Cl CB4 . . . . .84 A7
Wilson Way
  Brampton PE28 . . . . .117 E8
  Milton CB4 . . . . .105 D2
Wilson's Rd CB4 . . . . .103 A8
Wilsons La SG7 . . . . .2 C4
Wilthorne CB6 . . . . .165 A5
Wilton Cl PE3 . . . . .197 C4
Wilton Dr PE3 . . . . .197 C4
Wilton Gdns CB6 . . . . . . .216 E3
Wiltshire Rd PE28 . . . . . .154 B1
Wimbish Rd CB3 . . . . .99 A2
Wimblington Rd
  Doddington/Wimblington
    PE15 . . . . .223 A5
  March PE15 . . . . .243 C1
Wimborne Dr 2 PE1 . . . .198 E7
Wimbridge Cl SG8 . . . . . .27 F6
Wimpole Avenue (National
  Trust)★ SG8 . . . . .27 F5
Wimpole H★ SG8 . . . . . . .44 F3
Wimpole Park (National
  Trust)★ SG8 . . . . .44 E3
Wimpole Rd Barton CB3 . .63 A2
  Great Eversden CB3 . . . . . .45 E7
Wimpole St PE16 . . . . . . .241 B4
Winchester Way PE1 . . . .197 E1
Winchfield SG19 . . . . .58 E5
Winchmore Dr CB2 . . . . . .64 C3
Windermere Cl 3 CB1 . . .66 A7
Windermere PE29 . . . . . .141 B6
Windermere Way PE4 . . .204 E3
Winders La CB4 . . . . .104 B5
Windgate Way PE4 . . . . .194 A6
Windlesham Cl CB4 . . . . . .83 E6
Windmill Cl
  Ellington PE28 . . . . .138 F4
  2 Ely CB6 . . . . .240 B3
  Sawston CB2 . . . . .32 F8
  Soham CB7 . . . . .212 C2
Windmill Hill CB8 . . . . . .110 C8
Windmill La Fulbourn CB1 .66 E4
  Histon CB4 . . . . .104 B4
  8 Sutton CB6 . . . . .216 E1
Windmill Sch CB1 . . . . . . .66 D5
Windmill St
  Peterborough PE1 . . . . . .197 F5
  Whittlesey PE7 . . . . .189 D8
Windmill Wlk CB6 . . . . . .216 E1
Windover Rd PE29 . . . . . .141 D7
Windrush Dr PE4 . . . . . . .204 F1
Windsor Ave 3 PE4 . . . . .197 C8
Windsor Cl
  Chatteris PE16 . . . . .241 E5
  10 St Neots PE19 . . . . . .74 F2
  Stamford PE9 . . . . .244 B7
Windsor Dr March CB8 . . .243 B5
  Peterborough PE2 . . . . . .187 D6
  4 Ramsey PE26 . . . . . . .221 C2
  Wisbech PE13 . . . . .245 D8
Windsor Gdns 9 PE28 . .208 C8
Windsor Pl PE7 . . . . .190 A7
Windsor Rd
  Cambridge CB4 . . . . .83 C5
  Godmanchester PE29 . . . .142 A1
  Newmarket CB8 . . . . .110 C4
  Royston SG8 . . . . .5 F6
  5 Sawtry PE28 . . . . . . .168 B3
  Yaxley PE7 . . . . .181 D4
Windsors The 1 PE15 . . .243 A5
Winfold Rd CB5 . . . . .106 A8
Wingate Cl CB2 . . . . .64 D3
Wingate Way CB2 . . . . . . .64 D3

Wingfield PE2 ....185 F3
Winhills Prim Sch PE19 ..75 A4
Winship Rd CB4 ....105 C1
Winslow Rd PE3 ....197 C3
Winston Way PE7 ....187 C2
Wintringham Rd **8** PE19 .74 F5
Winwick Pl PE3 ....197 C5
Winwick Rd PE28 ......158 B8
Winyates Prim Sch PE2 186 A3
Wisbech Castle★ PE13 .245 C4
Wisbech Gram Sch
 PE13 ....245 B5
Wisbech Rd
 Littleport CB6 ....242 A6
 Manea PE15 ....224 C5
 March PE15 ....243 A7
 Outwell PE14 ....236 F3
 Thorney PE6 ....233 A3
 Walsoken PE13 ....245 E8
 Welney PE14 ....229 E2
 Whittlesey PE7 ....191 C8
 Wisbech St Mary PE13 ..234 A2
Wistaria Rd
 Leverington PE13 .....245 F7
 Wisbech PE13 ....245 E7
Wisteria Rd PE7 ....181 D4
Wistow Ct **3** PE19 ....74 C6
Wistow Fen Dro PE28 ..173 B4
Wistow Fen La PE28 ...164 C8
Wistow Way PE2 ....185 D6
Witcham Bridge Dro
 CB6 ....217 A5
Witcham Rd CB6 ......216 E3
Witchford Rd Ely CB6 ..240 A3
 Witchford CB6 ....217 F1
Witchford Village Coll
 CB6 ....217 E2
Witham Cl
 9 St Ives PE27 ......144 A7
 Stamford PE9 ....244 C6
Witham Way PE4 ......204 F1
Withers Pl **3** CB7 ....212 E1
Withersfield Rd
 Haverhill CB9 ....38 A1
 Withersfield CB9 ......38 F7
Wittering Airfield PE8 .230 A2

Wittering Rd PE9 .....230 D3
Woburn Cl Cambridge CB4 83 E7
 Peterborough PE3 ....197 A1
Woburn Ct PE7 ....176 A7
Woburn Dr PE6 ....233 A2
Woburn Pl CB2 ....31 F1
Wolf La Gorefield PE13 ..237 F1
 Wisbech PE13 ....235 C8
Wolfson Coll CB3 ......64 B8
Wollaston Rd
 Cambridge CB1 ....246 C1
 Peterborough PE3 ....197 C6
Wolsey Way CB1 ......65 F7
Wood Green Animal
 Shelter★ PE29 ......119 C5
Wood La
 Abbots Ripton PE28 ...162 E2
 Broughton PE28 .....163 A2
 Papworth Everard CB3 ..99 A4
 Ramsey PE26 ....172 C8
 Stretham CB6 ....210 F5
Wood St Chatteris PE16 .241 C4
 Doddington/Wimblington
  PE15 ....223 A6
 Huntingdon PE29 ....141 E4
 Wisbech PE13 ....245 B6
Wood View PE28 ......140 B4
Woodbine St PE2 .....187 A8
Woodbrook Cl CB3 .....99 B2
Woodbyth Rd PE1 .....198 A6
Woodcock Cl
 Haverhill CB9 ....24 C7
 Histon CB4 ....104 D3
Woodcote Cl PE1 .....198 A7
Woodcote Pk PE13 ...245 A4
Woodcroft Castle★
 PE6 ....203 C5
Woodcroft Rd Etton PE6 .203 B7
 Glinton PE6 ....203 C3
Woodditton Rd
 Kirtling CB8 ....72 B5
 Newmarket CB8 ......111 A1
 Woodditton CB8 ......90 B8
Woodfen Rd CB6 ......242 A2
Woodfield Ave **5** PE26 .172 A4
Woodfield Dr PE28 ...168 A3
Woodfield Rd PE3 ....197 D3
Woodforde Cl SG7 ......2 E4

Woodgate PE6 ....231 C4
Woodgate La PE6 .....231 D7
Woodgate Rd **3** PE13 .238 B2
Woodhall La CB1 ....53 A1
Woodhall Rise PE4 ....204 B6
Woodhead Cl **4** PE9 ..244 D7
Woodhead Dr CB4 .....83 F6
Woodhouse Way CB4 ...84 A7
Woodhurst Rd PE2 ...187 D6
Woodland Lea PE6 ....231 B4
Woodland Rd CB2 ......32 F8
Woodland Wlk **2** CB3 ..79 C3
Woodlands **1** Royston SG8 .5 E6
 St Neots PE19 ....75 A7
 Warboys PE28 ....164 F5
Woodlands Ave PE15 ..243 D2
Woodlands Cl CB2 .....49 A4
Woodlands Dr SG8 .....14 B8
Woodlands Pk CB3 ....103 D1
Woodlands Rd CB2 ....49 A4
Woodlands The
 Linton CB1 ....35 B4
 Peterborough PE1 ....198 D5
Woodlands Way IP28 ..239 F5
Woodlark Dr CB4 .....125 D4
Woodlark Rd CB3 ......83 B5
Woodmans Way CB4 ..105 D2
Woodroffe Rd PE8 ....193 D8
Woodside Chatteris PE16 241 C4
 Oakington/Longstanton
  CB4 ....123 F1
Woodside Way PE27 ..144 B5
Woodston Cty Prim Sch
 PE2 ....186 F7
Woodwalton Fen Nature
 Reserve★ PE26 .....170 B6
Woodward Cl PE7 ....176 A8
Woodysfield **2** PE15 ..223 B7
Woolcroft Cl PE13 ....238 A1
Woolfellhill Rd PE6 ...205 F3
Woolgard PE3 ....197 A3
Woollards La CB2 ......49 A4
Woolley Cl PE28 ......140 D3
Woolley Hill PE28 ....138 D6
Woolley Rd PE28 .....149 B3
Woolpack La **2** PE7 ..189 D6
Woolpack Way SG8 .....29 B1
Wooton Field SG19 .....41 D4
Woottens Cl CB3 ....62 C5

Wootton Ave PE2 .....186 F6
Wootton Way CB3 .....64 A8
Worboys Ct SG8 ....10 F5
Worcester Ave CB3 ....81 A4
Worcester Cres **2** PE9 .244 B6
Worcester Rd PE13 ...245 C7
Worcester Way SG8 ...14 E6
Wordsworth Ave PE19 ..74 D6
Wordsworth Cl
 Peterborough PE4 ....197 E8
 1 Royston SG8 ......13 D1
Wordsworth Gr CB3 ...64 C8
Workhouse La PE14 ..229 D8
Worlington Rd
 Barton Mills IP28 .....214 C3
 Worlington IP28 .....239 A3
Worsley PE2 ....186 A4
Worsley Chase PE15 ..243 D2
Wortham Pl **2** CB9 ...24 A8
Wortham Rd SG8 ....5 E4
Worthington Cl PE7 ...176 A7
Worts' Cswy CB1 ......65 C2
Wothorpe Ho★ PE9 ..244 B1
Wothorpe Rd PE9 ....244 B4
Wragg Dr CB8 ....111 A6
Wratting Rd
 Great Thurlow CB9 ....39 B8
 Haverhill CB9 ....24 A8
Wren Cl IP28 ....239 D4
Wren Pk CB2 ....32 B4
Wrens Cl CB6 ....240 B5
Wrestlingworth Lower Sch
 SG19 ....25 B3
Wrestlingworth Plantation★
 SG19 ....25 A5
Wright Ave PE2 ......187 B2
Wright's Cl CB5 ....84 E6
Wright's Dro PE6 .....232 B7
Wrights Dro PE7 .....220 B8
Wrights Gr CB1 ....66 F4
Wroe The PE14 ....236 C5
Wulfric Sq PE3 ....197 C8
Wulfstan Way CB1 ....65 C4
Wyatt Cl PE26 ....172 B6
Wyboston Ct **1** PE19 ..74 C4
Wycliffe Gr PE4 ......204 A5
Wycliffe Rd CB1 ....65 C8
Wydham Pk PE2 ......185 D6
Wye Pl PE4 ....204 E1

Wykes Dr **3** PE13 ....235 B7
Wykes Rd PE7 ....181 D4
Wyman Way PE2 .....185 F5
Wynborne Cl CB4 .....83 E5
Wyndham Way CB8 ...111 A6
Wynford Way CB4 .....83 F7
Wype Dro PE7 ....191 A5
Wype Rd PE7 ....190 C7
Wytches The CB6 ....211 A7
Wyton Airfield PE28 ..153 F2
Wyton Cty Inf Sch PE28 143 B8

Y

Yardy Cl PE15 ....243 B4
Yarmouth Pl **1** CB9 ..24 A8
Yarrow Rd CB1 ....66 A5
Yarwell Cl PE2 ....186 D7
Yarwells Headlands
 PE7 ....189 D8
Yarwells Wlk PE7 ....189 D8
Yaxley Jun Sch PE7 ..181 E6
Yaxley Rd PE7 ....177 B4
Yeats Cl SG8 ....13 D1
Yeldham Pl CB9 ....24 A8
Yeomans Cl PE28 ....136 D7
Yerril Gdn **3** CB9 ....23 E7
York Cl
 Godmanchester PE29 .141 F1
 Mildenhall IP28 ......213 D8
York Gdns PE13 .....245 D6
York Rd Chatteris PE16 .241 C4
 Haverhill CB9 ....23 E7
 Peterborough PE1 ....197 F6
 9 Stamford PE9 .....244 B6
 Sutton CB6 ....216 D1
 Wisbech PE13 ....245 D6
 Wyton Airfield PE28 ..143 A8
York Sq PE28 ....143 B8
York St CB1 ....84 A1
York Terr CB1 ....84 A1
York Way Royston SG8 ...5 B8
 St Ives PE27 ....144 A8
Yorke Way CB6 ......240 B3
Young St CB1 ....84 A2
Youngman Ave CB4 ..104 C5
Youngman Cl CB4 ...104 C5

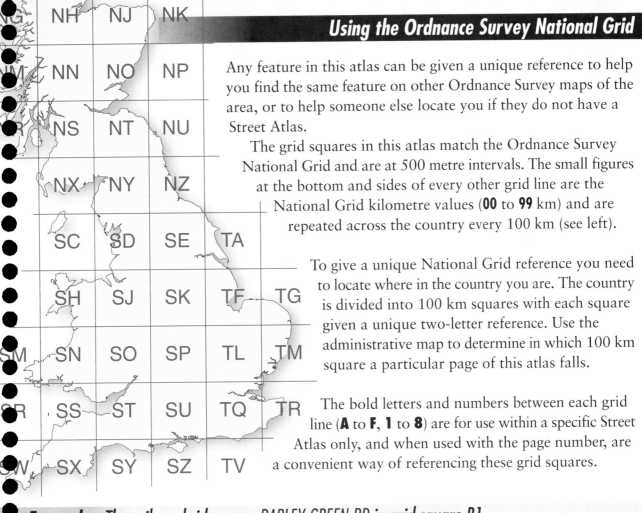

Any feature in this atlas can be given a unique reference to help you find the same feature on other Ordnance Survey maps of the area, or to help someone else locate you if they do not have a Street Atlas.

The grid squares in this atlas match the Ordnance Survey National Grid and are at 500 metre intervals. The small figures at the bottom and sides of every other grid line are the National Grid kilometre values (**00** to **99** km) and are repeated across the country every 100 km (see left).

To give a unique National Grid reference you need to locate where in the country you are. The country is divided into 100 km squares with each square given a unique two-letter reference. Use the administrative map to determine in which 100 km square a particular page of this atlas falls.

The bold letters and numbers between each grid line (**A** to **F**, **1** to **8**) are for use within a specific Street Atlas only, and when used with the page number, are a convenient way of referencing these grid squares.

Example The railway bridge over DARLEY GREEN RD in grid square B1

Step 1: Identify the two-letter reference, in this example the page is in **SP**

Step 2: Identify the 1 km square in which the railway bridge falls. Use the figures in the southwest corner of this square: Eastings **17**, Northings **74**. This gives a unique reference: **SP 17 74**, accurate to 1 km.

Step 3: To give a more precise reference accurate to 100 m you need to estimate how many tenths along and how many tenths up this 1 km square the feature is (to help with this the 1 km square is divided into four 500 m squares). This makes the bridge about **8** tenths along and about **1** tenth up from the southwest corner.

This gives a unique reference: **SP 178 741**, accurate to 100 m.

Eastings (read from left to right along the bottom) come before Northings (read from bottom to top). If you have trouble remembering say to yourself "Along the hall, THEN up the stairs"!

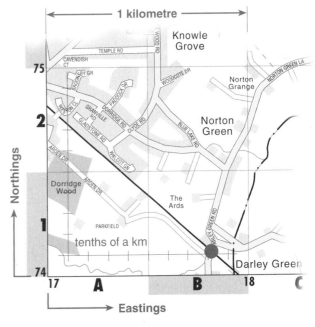

Addresses

Name and Address	Telephone	Page	Grid reference